tuck
yourself
in

Using your senses to soothe yourself,

Softening resistance to self-care

ginger clark, phd

BALBOA.
PRESS

A DIVISION OF HAY HOUSE

The information and techniques offered in this book are not intended as a substitute for medical treatment of sleep issues or for psychological or psychopharmacological treatment of anxiety, depression or trauma. Please consult a medical doctor or a psychologist or psychiatrist if you suspect you have an underlying medical or psychological condition which gives rise to difficulties with self-soothing and sleep. The suggestions offered herein may be a useful adjunct to the appropriate professional help.

Tuck Yourself In: Using Your Senses to Soothe Yourself, Softening Resistance to Self-Care by Ginger Clark, Ph.D.

Balboa Press books may be ordered through booksellers or by contacting:

A Division of Hay House
1663 Liberty Drive
Bloomington, IN 47403
www.balboapress.com
1-(877) 407-4847

Published by Balboa Press, a Division of Hay House Publishing Company

Cover art and design by Balboa Press, Liv Estrup and Phil Hinch
Interior design and typesetting by Balboa Press
Author Photo by newfacephoto.com

ISBN: 978-1-4525-6815-7 (sc)
ISBN: 978-1-4525-6816-4 (e)

Library of Congress Control Number: 2013902637

Printed in the United States of America

Balboa Press rev. date: 3/21/2013

Contents

Dedication..xiii

Introduction..xv

PART I. THE LISTENING PRACTICES...1

Chapter 1. TUCKING MYSELF IN...3

How This Book is Organized..4
Connecting with *Her*..5
Reconnecting with *Her*...7

Chapter 2. DISCOVERING *HER*...9

Sensing: A Sensory Awakening...9
Meditation 11
Listening to My Emotional Voice 13

Chapter 3. FROM LET'S GO! TO LET GO 18

Three Listening Practices..18
Listening, Asking and "Resting-into" 19
Embracing the Moment and Change 20
Noticing, Focusing and Following Through 22
"No Pain, No Gain"..22
The Shift from Let's Go! to Let Go 24
Bodyself Cycles: Completion and Interruption...............................28
How the Three Listening Practices Invite the Let Go . . Shift 30
The "Cure" in Curiosity..31
How to Begin? 31

Chapter 4. SENSING..32

What is Sensing?...32
Thinking and Sensing 32
Sensing and Shifting to Let Go 33
Heightening Sensory Awareness in Ordinary Activities.............34
Maximizing Massage Experience 35
Improving Digestive Functioning...35
Qutting Smoking...36
Sensing Experiments 38
Sitting in a Chair 38
Settling into Lying 39
Nap, Not "Cap"! 40
Sensing "Contact Points" 41
    Good for the sole! 42
    Slap happy feet!..42
    Having a foot ball! 43
    Unmasking the face..43

      "Two-lip" sensing 43

      Scalp massage 44

Neck: That Sinking Feeling... 44

Spine: "Coming to Hanging" 45

Tapping, Stretching and Dancing 46

"Every Body, Let's Get Stoned!" 46

Closing Eyes, Using Non-Dominant Hand and Reversing Order........... 46

Some Key Elements of Sensing Experiments 46

Chapter 5. MEDITATION..**49**

What is Meditation?..**50**

Why Focus on Breathing? 50

Breathing and Tension Release 52

Breath Meditation Touch Points 52

Some Benefits and Pitfalls of Meditation Practice........................**54**

Focusing to Salve and Solve 55

Focusing for Completion and Increasing Subtle Let Go . . Energy 58

Deepening Focus for Containment of Emotional Energy 60

      Focusing to release pain 61

      Focusing to ameliorate addictive behavior 63

Focusing for Discipline and Balance of Let's Go! with Let Go 64

Chapter 6. LISTENING TO YOUR EMOTIONAL VOICE..................**67**

Why Listen to Your Emotional Voice? **67**

Personalizing the Emotional Voice **69**

Experiments in Finding *Her* Voice **70**

      Ask *Her*, "What Do You Want To Do?" 70

      Ask *Her*, "What is the Matter?" 71

      Talk Out Loud... 71

      Give Voice to Emotion: *"You're Scaring Me!"* 72

      Give Voice to Sensation: *"It's Cold!" "It's Soft!"* 72

      Express! Don't Compress! 73

      Express! Don't Obsess! 73

      Talking Back to the TV... 73

      Acknowledge *Her* and Encourage Yourself 74

Listening for What Makes *Her* / You Happy **76**

      Savoring Sensory Experience 76

      Finish Tasks – Do One Thing at a Time 77

      Prepare Your Bedroom for the Day's Completion 77

      Preparation and Partaking of Food 77

      Warnings and Urgings 78

Inviting *Her* **78**

      Give Me a Break to Break You Open! 78

      Let Yourself Be Moved by Music.. 82

      Let Yourself Be Touched by Stories 83

      Invitation by Meditation 83

      Invitation by Dream 83

      Don't Make *Her* Wait Too Long! 84

      Letting *Her* Lead You 85

PART II. MEETING RESISTANCE TO SLOWING DOWN **87**

Chapter 7. MEETING YOUR RESISTANCE TO LISTENING TO YOUR BODYSELF VOICE **88**

Unresolved Trauma from Childhood or Adulthood **91**
Abandonment Trauma 91
Abuse: Intrusion Trauma 92
Ungrieved Loss 94
Inadequate Caretaker Modeling of Self-Nurturing 95
Inadequate Nurturing by Your Caretakers 95
    Waiting for repair 97
    The aim of the blame game 98
The Stance **100**
Your "Sophie's choice" and the contracted "No!" 101
The Stance Trance 102
Giving up the stance to dance! 103
Going Deeper 106

**Chapter 8. MEETING RESISTANCE TO MEETING YOUR RESISTANCE
TO YOUR BODYSELF VOICE** **108**

The Critic - Caretaker Cycle **109**
The Codependent Caretaker Stance 109
The "Critical" Caretaker 110
Meeting Your Critic 111
Checking in with Yourself 112
Asking for Help 112
    For the moment is the <u>moment</u> – the fulcrum for change 114
Going Deeper 117
The Quixotic "Fix" of Addiction **117**
Addiction: A Strategy to Avoid Unpleasant Need and Feelings 117
    How "good" and "bad" cops police the stance. 117
    The downside of "up" 119
The Rebel: "I'll Get Mine" 121
The Workaholic and the Super-achiever 121
    The experience of "enough" 122
    Deprivation-indulgence cycle 122
The Goldilocks Moment of "Just Right!" **123**
Going Deeper 125

Chapter 9. GOING FOR THE GOLDILOCKS GOLD! **126**

Gathering Gold in your Repository of Let Go . . Positivity 126
    Capacity of your positivity repository 127
    "Taking in" 127
From Break to Breakfast: Increasing your Positivity Repository Capacity 129
    Give yourself a break! 129
    Gourmet Goldilocks' recipe for "comfort" food 130
    Mastication meditation – choose 20 chews! 132
    Discovering "enough" – the Goldilocks "just right"! 133
    Conundrum of "enough" revisited 134
Goldilocks Meets Starbucks 135
    Trick or treat? 138

Double whammy of a caffeinated critic 139
The "shadow" of addiction.. 139
Blood sugar "madness" 140
Wired, tired and mired . . . and uninspired.. 141
To nap or to "cap"?.. 142
Goldilocks Rocks: An Antidote for Caffeine Withdrawal and Sugar Indulgence...... 142
Goldilocks Moments with another Person.. 144
Nap, "cap" or lap?.. 145
Going Deeper 146
Goldilocks in knead 146
Goldilocks on the couch 147
Goldilocks revisited 148
It's over! 148
Some Ways to Increase the Capacity of your Positivity Repository.................... 149
Some Suggestions for Going Deeper 149
Observation of eating and interaction with addictive behaviors 149

PART III. RECOVERING THE BODYSELF VOICE..**153**

**Chapter 10. RECLAIMING MY BODYSELF VOICE THROUGH RELATIONAL
SOMATIC PSYCHOTHERAPY**..**154**

Freeing the Bodyself Voice from the Contracted "No!" **157**
Phases of Undoing the Contraction around the "No!" 158
Yes! Taking in 158
No! The self-affirming "No!" is seen and honored 159
Yes! Sensing the Need for the "Other" and Attendant Emotions 160
No! The Commitment to the Contracted "No!" Is Fully Felt and Expressed... 160
Yes! The "Yes!" of Expansion is Possible as the Contracted "No!" is Fully Owned..162
How the Emotional Recovery Cycle Eases the Contracted "No!" to Access Her.... 164
The calm heart center... 166

**Chapter 11. WRESTING MY BODYSELF VOICE FROM THE GRIP OF CHILDHOOD
ABANDONMENT TRAUMA**..**169**

Working with a Body Memory of Abandonment 169
The trauma... 169
The work 172
Waiting for contact: the "watcher" 174
Earliest Visual Memory, a Vestige of Abandonment Trauma 174
Work on earliest visual memory... 175
The desire to crush the needy one 176
The Present of Presence 177
A snowflake moment... 177
"I want to be in your colors!" 178
"I want to be in my colors!" 179

Chapter 12. LOST AND FOUND: MY BODYSELF VOICE **180**

Preamble and Overview of Chapter **180**
One More Time with Feeling **181**
YES! Taking In Being Seen by the Attuned, Compassionate Other........................ 181
"The wound is where the light enters" 182

NO! The Self-affirming "No!" of Differentiation is Respected and Embodied...... 183
YES! Sensing the Need for the Other and the Attendant Emotions. 184
    A new neural pathway.. 184
NO! The Commitment to the Contracted "No!" is Fully Experienced. 188
    The face of the contracted "No!" 189
    I'm "not nothing"! 189
    Expressing the terror of the caretaker's "No!" to the child 191
    Rage: the other side of terror.. 192
YES! The Spontaneous Gesture of the Bodyself toward the Other is Expressed
and Acknowledged. 195
The "Ad-Vantage" of the Calm Heart Center vs. the "Disad-Vantage" of the Stance ...198
    She Who Laughs, at Last! 199
    She Who Plays, Is Amazed! 199
    Everything Changed 200
    "You Are Still Here" 202
The Precious "Soulution" of the Muzzle Puzzle: A True "Breakthrough" 202
    "Honeymoons" 203
    "Just Be with Me . . ." 204
Checking in with Yourself 206

Chapter 13. LIVING ON THE BODYSELF (*HER*) SIDE OF THE STREET 207

A Wakeup Call to the Bodyself Side of the Street **207**
Embodiment: From Bodyself Constriction to Bodyself Expansion...........................209
Embodying the Excitement and Energy of Contact.. 210
Embodying the Need for Another 212
Embodiment is Living on the "Bodyself" Side of the Street 214
Practicing the New "Pathway" with Open Eyes and an Open Heart...................216
My Posse of Positivity at My Bodyself Side 216
    Punishing myself for doing something right for myself 217
Using Listening Practices to Come Back to the Bodyself Side of the Street 218
Intoning T.S. Elliot: Nothing is Preferable to Something.................................... 218
"Filling In"... 219
Amazing – The (Almost) Unbearable Lightness of Being 220
An Invitation to Grace: Consciously Surrendering to Not-knowing 221
Living through "It's Over!" by Awakening to Signs that Life Can Begin Anew . . .222
Going Deeper 225
Listening for Sounds of Life Stirring 225
Checking in with Yourself 227

PART IV. DECOMPRESSING AND AWAKENING 229

Chapter 14. CREATING A DECOMPRESSION PERIOD 230

Why Time is Needed to Shift to Let Go 231
Importance of Taming Your Biochemical Environment 232
How Decompression Unfolds... 233
    Diving deep into a "well" of grief 234
    Not so great expectations! 235
Catching the Let Go . . Wave 237
Establishing a Decompression Period.. 239

Chapter 15. DECOMPRESSION ACTIVITIES **241**

Preparation for Decompression **241**
Organizing Activities **243**
Preparation of Sleeping Space 245
Cultivating a "Tuck Yourself In" Attitude 245
Soothing Activities **247**
Sensing: The Let Go . . Energy of Ease 248
    Coming to lying 249
    Spacious head 251
    Pelvis curling.. 251
    Abdominal massage 253
    Waving "Goodbye" to tension and stress..................... 253
    "Hang twenty" wave... 255
    Rag doll ball 255
    Make a guided tour of your contact points 255
    Eye pillows 256
    Feet first! 256
    Smallest movement 256
    Rest into it – creating sensory embeddedness 256
Meditation: Experiencing the Let Go . . Subtle Energy of Completion 258
    Completion of tasks 259
    Completion of efforting Let's Go! by resting into Let Go 259
    Completion of emotional situations................................ 261
Listening to Your Emotional Voice: Let Go . . Sweetness.................... 261
    Ask, "What is the matter?": *She* speaks through complaints.................... 264
    Sound your feelings: *She* speaks through sound and words not heard! 264
    Talk out loud: *She* may even make you laugh!.................... 264
    Acknowledgment and encouragement: *She* responds with a sweet feeling of satisfaction.................... 265
    Dance: *She* speaks through movement 266
    Ask "what would be good or fun to do now?": *She* speaks through images, urges, intuitions, inklings and that "funny feeling" 267
    Stop criticizing yourself and check in with *her*: *She* speaks through cries in the night and feelings of dread and fright 268
Customizing Your Decompression Period....................................**268**
Decompression Principles for a Shift to Let Go **269**
Tucking Yourself Back In...**269**

Chapter 16. WAKING YOURSELF UP...**271**

Dream-Catching.. 271
A Sound Awakening 272
Sleep Mask Sensing 273
Baby's "Awakening" 274
Reaching and Breathing: Experiment or Exercise?.................. 274
    A warning!... 276
Pelvic Floor Awareness 277
Child Pose 277
"Hang Ten" Wave: Standing... 278
Playing Footsies with Tootsies 278

Grand Opening: Top of the Morning to You! 279
Put Your Best Foot Forward! 281
Get off to a Rolling Good Start! 281
Having a Ball! 281
Morning "Hangover" 281
White Rabbit Wake up: I'm Late, I'm Late, I'm Late! 281
So Many Ways to Open 282
Teeth Brushing 282
Meditation 282
Soul Food 283
"Morning Pages" 283
Stop "Gab" Techniques for Emergencies 284
Live Your Own Life Each Morning 284
The Serenity Prayer 285
The Dew of Little Things 285
Bathing 285
"I Don't Want to Wake Up!" 286
Waking up Routine 286

Chapter 17. AN INVITATION TO BODYMINDFULNESS: FINDING YOUR OWN WAY 288

The Power of "Staying With" 289
Developing Your Own Bodymindfulness Practice 292
    Sweet surrender 294
The Challenge of Balance: Taking Time for Your Practice 295
    "Oldilocks" moments 296
Staying With "Staying With" 298
Finding Your Own Way 300
Finding Your Way to Connect with *Her* and Tuck Yourself In 301

ACKNOWLEDGMENTS 303

COPYRIGHT ACKNOWLEDGMENTS 304

Appendix A. The Yin and Yang of Balancing Let's Go! with Let Go 305

Appendix B. Contact Point Awareness 309

Appendix C. Adequate Caretaker Nurturing: The need for connection, repair and self-assertion 311

Appendix D. The Purgatory of Waiting in the Shadow for Repair 315

Appendix E. Using a Guide to Explore the Growing Edge of Bodyself Awareness 317

Appendix F. Healing the Shadow of Addiction 319

Appendix G. Step-wise Summary of Process of Embodying the Experience of the Therapist's Presence 322

Appendix H. Embodied Spirituality and Presence 324

Appendix I. Ode to Homecoming 328

NOTES AND SOURCES 331

INDEX 339

RECOMMENDED RESOURCES 343

ABOUT THE AUTHOR 345

DEDICATION

In memory of my mother . . .

For my clients, students, and all those who want to discover how to live in concert with their deepest desires – from sound sleeping to passionate aliveness.

INTRODUCTION

When I first sat down to write this book about my experience of tucking myself in, I was full of excitement and curiosity. I had discovered a sweet feeling which filled me upon a morning's awakening as a result of treating myself tenderly before I fell asleep the previous night. This feeling was so palpable it seemed as if it was a wordless "voice" coming from deep inside me and I came to refer to it as *"her"** (See "Notes and Sources"). I wanted more! As I continued experimenting with the listening practices described in these chapters, I made many more discoveries about the benefits and the challenges of listening to and following through on various kinds of messages from my "bodyself".

So what is this source of self-soothing wisdom I call the "bodyself"? It is a nonverbal intelligence that "speaks" through sensations, emotions, images, inklings and intuition. The listening practices offered in this book can help you slow down, tune into your bodyself "voice" and follow through on what you hear so that you can soothe yourself when you need to. A wonderful "side-effect" of these practices is that you are likely to notice an increase in energy and aliveness and perhaps even an increase in availability for contact with others. For as you are more able to nurture yourself, you may feel less deprived or depleted and discover that you have more to share with others.

As time went on I became intrigued by my periodic resistance to following through on these messages as I prepared myself for sleep. Why wouldn't I follow through by doing what I knew would help me get a good night's sleep and wake refreshed and eager to enter the new day? What could possibly be more important than treating myself tenderly and compassionately before I went to sleep so I could face the nascent day with energy and optimism?

The answers to those questions revealed themselves over a period of years as I continued working with the listening practices of sensing, meditating and "listening to my emotional voice". At one point working with a relational somatic therapist was pivotal in addressing unresolved childhood issues that interfered with optimal self-soothing. By "optimal self-soothing", I mean being able to wind down at the end of the day without engaging various addictions and activities which numb or distract from what is too uncomfortable to be felt at the moment.

If we have not developed the internal resources to deal with feelings as they come up when we slow down after a long day, we are likely to feel anxious (or depressed) and turn to less than optimal self-soothing methods such as acting out, spacing out, addictive behaviors, obsessive thinking, criticizing ourselves or others. Even if we are completely exhausted, our minds may still be spinning. If our caretakers themselves were limited in optimally self-soothing, we are likely to have missed out on having enough childhood experience of feeling calm, cared for and maybe even, valued. On the other hand, if we were adequately seen, soothed and valued for ourselves that experience, taken deeply into our bodyself and embodied likely became a self-soothing resource for the rest (no pun intended!) of our lives. The good news is that as adults we get another chance to learn to optimally self-soothe by implementing these listening practices and by working through various issues that give rise to resistance to hearing bodyself messages. In the end, listening and responding to this "voice" is all about <u>relationship</u>: embodying the experience of being faithfully listened to by another we can come to listen to ourselves with more curiosity and compassion.

Integration of feelings from past trauma and loss in the presence of another helped anchor me more deeply in my somatic experience of the present. In turn, the listening practices were central in building support for this integrative process. And with time, I found myself living more in the whole-hearted bodyself moment of the present and less through a constricted protective response from the past. When I could check in with my bodyself voice, I had more of a choice about how I treated myself. My goal is to balance the "Let's Go!"* striving, full speed ahead mode, which can numb me to its cost to my somatic awareness as well as hinder relationship intimacy, with the "Let Go . ." easing, which comes when I slow down, savor the moment, and allow the "larger picture" to emerge. When we can experience whatever feelings come up and let them go, when we can grieve our losses and treat ourselves and others with compassion, we are more likely to be living in synch with our bodyself voice.

This book can be used as a guide to living in concert with this deep source of wisdom, your bodyself voice. Thereby you can become more choiceful about the speed and sensitivity with which you live. You may discover how your resistance to slowing down is held in your body and what creative purpose that resistance originally served. Offered herein are ways to approach meeting that resistance even when it is in service of suppressing the emotional fall-out from unresolved trauma, loss or chronically strained relationships. If you do not have unresolved issues that are getting in the way of optimal self-soothing, you can fully benefit from the chapters on the listening practices. Sensing and meditation can be <u>enough</u> to optimize your capacity to listen to your bodyself voice and follow through on what you hear. To that end, my CD is available through my website, tuckyouselfin.com, to guide you in this experience. If you suspect you have some "unfinished business" from past relationships or unresolved trauma you might consider consulting a therapist to maximize the benefit of the listening practices. Perhaps the account of my work on a childhood abandonment trauma will encourage you to look at what may be unresolved for you so you too can live more bodymindfully!

I chose the term "Bodymindfulness" to describe the listening practices detailed in this book. This term speaks to the integration of the Eastern practice of mindfulness and selflessness into the more Western body/ego-oriented way of life. Bodymindfulness practice values all of human experiencing and strives toward balance – not denying the self or desires but living with them, expressing what needs to be expressed and coming back to a calm, grounded awareness I call "Let Go . ." Why not have our cake and eat it too, as long as it is the "just right" amount of cake? Sensing, meditating and listening to the emotional voice invite you to deeply experience your bodyself, yielding valuable information about your moment to moment existence. Your "bodymind" becomes "full" when you are open to receiving all these messages, including "intuition". My wish is to live the "full catastrophe" of Zorba and Kabat-Zinn**, treating everything and most everyone I meet on the way with loving kindness that flows from a deep place within. This journey began with my delight in discovering ways to tuck myself in at night and it led to discovering how to tuck myself into the bodyself moment no matter what time it is! Along the way I experience more delight, play, humor, creativity and capacity to explore the unknown.

Coming into connection with your bodyself is a gradual and continual dance of connection, disconnection and reconnection. In these chapters, you can discover many ways to connect and reconnect with your somatic experience through attentive listening for what is needed in the moment. Once you have experienced more connection, you are likely to notice more clearly when you have disconnected. Chances are you will discover your own unique indicators of disconnection but, for starters, some typical cues are holding in breathing, tension in muscles, feeling numb or spacey, thinking about or impulsively indulging in your preferred addiction. Triggers for disconnection abound – interpersonal and work stress, rushing around, working too hard, the depletion of addiction, too much of almost anything, a sudden scare, a reminder of past unresolved trauma you don't even recognize, etc.

Disconnection is inevitable – not a sign of failure, but rather an <u>opportunity</u> to practice reconnection. Sometimes the sense of reconnection is like the feeling of relief you have when a background sound suddenly ceases and with it, some tension disappears that you didn't even realize was there. As you continue your listening practice and can tolerate more somatic awareness, you are likely to surprise yourself with the discovery of new ways of staying in touch. As you connect with your sense of disconnection, your bodyself responds – all it wants is for you to turn toward it. It is here for you, you only have to listen.

As you gradually awaken to life through your bodyself, you are likely to feel more balanced and have more choices about how you live your daily life. Pacing yourself can become second nature when you sense your somatic presence as you eat, bathe, brush your teeth, prepare your food, do the dishes or drive. When you can satisfy the once frustrated need for reconnection, which underlies your habitual energy-depleting attempts at self-soothing, you can make more deeply satisfying choices. Consciously surrendering to what your bodyself wants from you, you can live an "embodied spirituality", complete with moments of grace. As you come to tuck yourself in at night, you will be also tucking yourself into the moment! For the gift of the bodyself is presence.

Part I of this book introduces you to the three listening practices and offers examples, exercises and anecdotes to illuminate their practice. If you are more interested in practice than theory, you can skip Chapter 3 and the parts of other chapters that are devoted to theory. The theoretical portions of the chapters in this book are designated as such and reading them is not necessary to benefit from the experiential processes and anecdotal examples. However, your practice may be <u>enriched</u> by a deeper intellectual understanding of how listening and being listened to can help you access your bodyself wisdom. Part II addresses sources of resistance to slowing down as well as various patterns of resistance so you can identify yours and where they came from. It also speaks to ways to meet your resistance as well as how to "meet your resistance to meeting your resistance" to listening to your bodyself voice and invites you to "Go Deeper" or "Check in with Yourself" through experiential exercises. Part III introduces the process I experienced in recovering my bodyself voice in the course of relational somatic therapy and includes an account of work on an early childhood abandonment trauma. Also included are examples of how the listening practices and my "posse of positivity" interwove to support the trauma work and the therapeutic relationship so that I could regain my full bodyself voice. Part IV offers guidelines for creating your own decompression period and for using the listening practices to tuck yourself in as well as wake yourself up! The last chapter invites you to find your own bodymindful way to practice.

Even if you don't yet readily identify with the expression "bodyself voice", I think you will gradually recognize what I am referring to as you read these chapters. You may get some clues and some encouragement for your own exploration by reading my accounts of connecting with my bodyself wisdom which unfolded using the listening practices and when needed, by working with a somatic relational therapist. Ultimately what it takes to become truly self-soothing is practice, daily practice. And in my experience, despite what the old adage says, practice does not make "perfect"; practice just makes practice more meaningful. A dear friend of mine, also a therapist and author shared a secret with me the last time we consulted about my work on this book. He said, "Most self-help books contain a 'big lie'". The "big lie" is that if you just do this and that you will heal yourself and no longer experience your conflict, negativity, "stuckness", and other issues. My truth is that while my issues remain my issues, my relationship to them is gradually changing. And sometimes I experience the magic and power of the moment where connection and change happens, creating a "heartwork" miracle. As I become more compassionate with myself, I'm more capable of self-soothing and intimacy with others as well as more open to the world at large. When you picked up this book, you may have been mostly interested in getting some help so that you could become more self-soothing and get a better night's sleep. What you discover about <u>meeting</u> your resistance to taking good care of yourself may lead you like it has me, to a life-time of discovery and awakening.

PART I

THE LISTENING PRACTICES

1

TUCKING MYSELF IN

"Sweet" is a feeling of "satisfaction . . . somewhere between peace and joy"*.

I'll never forget the sweetness of that feeling! I had just awakened from the night I had first "tucked myself in". That sweet feeling was the thank-you from what I came to call *"her"*** for attending to what *she* wanted before I drifted off to sleep. At that time I was only aware that I was following what my sensations told me I needed in order to feel less tense. I had massaged my feet, my neck, my jaw, my scalp, and my face as I lay in bed. I had tenderly attended to each place as one would to a dearly loved person and I had gratefully accepted the ministering touch.

As was my habit at that time I had already meditated to quiet my busy mind in hopes I would drift off to sleep more easily. But this night it occurred to me to give myself something more, something I had given to my massage clients for years, as well as taught to countless massage students. I am so grateful that I responded to the impulse to give to myself that night. This pivotal juncture in the long journey of discoveries led to uncovering a submerged part of myself. Connecting to this part of myself has been the key to my vitality, vulnerability, intuition, creativity, and spontaneity as well as to my ability to connect with other people. In short, *she* is the source of my life force.

For years I had trouble falling asleep and, being a light sleeper, going back to sleep once I was awakened. I used my breath as a focus for my attention to help me distance myself from my churning thoughts. These thoughts were often fueled by anxiety, especially when my internal critic questioned something I did or caused me to worry about how someone else felt about me. I realize now that using "meditation" in this way only served to deepen the split between my awareness and what was really scaring me. I was trying to get relief from my fears (not to mention some sleep) the only way I knew. I now realize that at the deepest level I was really trying to preserve a sense of self. I was choosing dissociation and constriction over annihilation and overwhelm. The price I paid for disconnecting from my fear and pain was to live in a small "safe" circle - limiting the depth of my connection with others, my potential, and my bodyself.

My sleep difficulties as well as my overbearing critic, turned out to be symptoms of an underlying terror of feeling helpless. This threatening helplessness was born from the twin childhood traumas of abandonment and intrusion as well as from inadequate caretaker nurturing. Over a period of fifty years I investigated various types of psychotherapy, meditation, and bodywork in an attempt to heal myself. This process led to many intriguing experiences – some of them delightful discoveries and others sobering disappointments. What started as an attempt at self-soothing before sleeping led to an unfolding of hidden potential and wisdom as I have learned to access and accept what *she*, this other part of me - has to offer. In the process of discovering how to connect with *her* I encountered much resistance. What unfolds here is a journey of connecting, losing connection and reconnecting.

"We" have been looking forward to sharing with you these discoveries and practices in the hopes that you, too, will uncover more of your valuable and life-affirming bodyself*. Key is the question, "How much do you want that?"

How This Book is Organized

Creating the appropriate form to tell about this unfolding has been a process of learning to listen for what <u>feels</u> right. On the one hand, the more practiced and therefore dominant part of me - the teacher and the intellect - wants to create lessons and principles and concepts. On the other, the emerging part of me that is more vulnerable and creative wants *her* story to be told *her* way. *"Tell them about us! Save the children!" she* declares.

After spending a few years writing in the more usual self-help book style of principles, techniques and examples, I felt frustrated with my results. I had created some concepts and catchy phrases but I was ignoring the <u>heart</u> of my process. I was making *her* be quiet while I was writing. Organization of the material became more and more slippery as the concepts seemed to overlap and blend. I became more and more desperate as I started over and over again. Ultimately I had to recognize I was, once again, silencing this expressive part of me out of fear. Fear of exposure, fear of being criticized, fear of failing and, ultimately, feeling overwhelmed, shamed and helpless. I had killed off this part of myself enough times already. *She* does have something to say and a unique way of saying it. And I want you to hear *her* voice. Then maybe you'll become curious about hearing your own bodyself voice.

Besides, who needs another self-help book without heart? There are enough recipe books for connecting with oneself! Or, as *she* would say, *"Another cut and dried technique book - full of tools but no heart"*. Finding my heart – my joy and pain, peace and aliveness - was what my journey has been all about. So why should my book reflect anything different? It is *she* who helped me realize that writing this book is really about wanting to be heard. Teaching is secondary. I had to be up against the writer's block wall to feel helpless enough to finally hear what *she* has been trying to tell me.

In fact I found I had to more than just <u>consider</u> *her* if I was going to be satisfied with this book, let alone to complete it. Now *she* makes the first and the last decision about how to go. When I am stuck, I ask *her* for help. When I begin, I ask *her* for inspiration. *She* embodies the energy, wit, joy, humor and creativity. Another part of me has the intellectual clarity to formulate concepts and to edit. We are learning to work as well as play together.

After all, this book is about cultivating a more intimate connection with that more sensitive and vulnerable part of you so that you can learn to soothe yourself. That part of you speaks primarily in a non-verbal language of sensations and images and emotions and impulses. You may have come to ignore that part of you in favor of your more rational, analytical abilities. You may have unwittingly thrown out the baby (your more sensitive, vulnerable side) with the bathwater (the pain, anxiety, shame, helplessness). Finding balance between the analytical, rational part of you and the intuitive, bodyself part can lead to your feeling more whole, creative and peaceful.

In order to achieve this balance you will likely need to slow down. When you slow down you can better hear the language of this other part of you. In the early chapters of this book three listening practices will be introduced to help you tune into messages from *her*, your bodyself. Very likely you will encounter resistance to hearing from the more sensitive side of you, and you may find you have trouble slowing down. For instance, you may not actually like what you begin to hear. Various sources of resistance to slowing down will be discussed along with some ways to deal with that resistance. The middle chapters address healing feelings of overwhelm and helplessness that result from childhood traumas of abandonment or intrusion or present day loss of love which challenge optimal self-soothing. To flesh out this process of bodyself recovery from trauma and loss, I will share my story of how using various listening practices interwove with being listened to by an attuned other, my therapist and helped me become truly self-soothing. The remaining chapters guide you through creating your own decompression routine and offer suggestions for beginning the day and finding your <u>own</u> way. In the process of learning how to build a foundation for connecting with and soothing yourself, you will make many discoveries, and perhaps you will sense like I did, that you have finally found what has, for years, been missing.

Connecting with *Her*

Finally Ginger let me talk for myself rather than her getting all scientific and rational and trying to impress you with her careful "thought-through-to-death" conceptualizing and organizing. I am the part of Ginger that has so much energy, emotion, creativity and good ideas. I am sweet, funny, smart, precious, and sometimes, outrageous! While I find delight in the world I also feel pain, disappointment, fear, and anger and that is the rub! To fully live and bring forth vitality, I have to be allowed to feel the pain of existence as well! Ginger has a hard time with that. She very carefully hid me for many years behind a wall of carefully-crafted thoughts and maneuvering so she would not have to realize how bad she felt. She just couldn't stand feeling out of control with pain and loneliness that she could do nothing about. She felt helpless. Unbearable helplessness!

I talk to Ginger by making her feel things in her body. Just today she was stuck on where to go next with the writing. She labored and labored. Then she really got frustrated. She had to lie down because she couldn't continue the way she was going. Her neck hurt. A big knot. Finally she focused on that knot and felt the pain of it. She started to cry. That is when she got my message: Pay attention to me! You are trying to force the issue in your writing. And, you are keeping me out. You said last week you would let me write the beginning of each chapter and now you literally deleted that promise. I will <u>knot</u> cooperate with that decision. I give you a "will knot" in your neck. I am becoming a "demanding mistress" just like your teacher said "sensing" was. You said you wanted me to help you, that you depended on me. That I was your heart. Well, you have to treat me with respect because if you don't, you will feel stuck. Now, see how your writing flows when you let me have a voice?

To get back on track you have to focus on my signals even if they are painful ones. You can't ignore me like you used to. There is no going back now. You have experienced the rewards of paying attention to me and also the pain of ignoring my cues. The stakes get higher because you are winning more and more often. You experience more and more pay-off in terms of pleasurable feelings and greater attunement when you lead a sensing class or when you work with therapy clients. You notice more the beauty in nature. The subtle hues in a rose. The distinct tastes from one strawberry to another. You delight in the delicate fragrance of purple pansies and scarlet snapdragons. The repeating patterns in someone's attire. Your nighttime dreams are clearer in meaning. You are more able to give yourself to the comfort of a nap. You are more spontaneous. You click your heels. You nip headaches in the bud. You hardly ever leave things behind when you are really <u>with</u> me. You are able to take the time you need to complete something. You notice when something is not quite right and finish it. There it is - settled.

You allow me to settle you. When you are with me, you have the sense that everything is just as it is. Complete. What happens is the only thing that could happen. Even what you cannot accept, you accept that you cannot accept it! Living in concert with me, the payoff is aliveness and peace.

I speak to you with urgings, inklings and impulses. I give you flashes, intuitions, and premonitions. I open you. I baptize you with tears. You came to have the strength to cry deeply by yourself. You found the strength to feel your pain. You let yourself come to me then. When you allow your tears to come from your heart then you touch me and I do so need to be touched. I am so grateful when you touch me that I give you a wonderful coming-home connected feeling. You can rest into me. I need to be touched. You need to be in touch with me. Beings in touch. Just now as you gave yourself to crying you heard a seagull cry, and Monhegan Island* and Charlotte came to mind. Your crying turned to sobbing, the sobs coming in rhythm with the seagull's cries. You experience, once again, that giving yourself even to pain brings a sense of harmony** It is possible for you to do that now. You can go through pain to the other side. Feeling loss, you gain. Through joining with me, you become whole.

This part of myself that I have been calling *"her"*, the part that just "spoke" above, actually expresses itself through sensations, emotions, dreams, images and urges. I have learned how to let *her* "speak" using words, but words are not how this aspect of myself usually makes itself known to me. More likely I will notice my neck is getting tense or that my mouth is dry or the music sounds sweet or I feel an urge to dance or to lie down or cry or laugh at myself. Like many people, I used to ignore these messages of sensation and emotion. When I began to experience the subtle but enormous rewards for following up on what I sensed, I made a practice of listening for these messages.

Sometimes I refer to this sense as *"her"* when there is a strong emotional component to it. At other times I just open myself to receiving what is available to my awareness at the moment. In earlier times I called the source of these sensory messages "it"**. In this book, I refer to it as *"her"* or *"she"* because the word *"she"* adds more color to what became in other drafts, quite cut and dried. When I treat this aspect of myself as a being, my story is written closer to my truth. My hope is that when *she* speaks to you in this book, you will listen and begin to hear yourself. I would like to pique your curiosity and tap into your longing for closer connection with yourself.

Perhaps you feel put off by my referring to this sensitive, vulnerable and rich part of myself as though it were an entity or a person. You may not want to personalize this aspect of your intelligence. Especially, if it sounds too much like a child, like it might when emotions speak. Using a more impersonal term like "inner consultant" or "bodyself" or "organism" or even "it" may allow you to, at least, try the experiments I propose. It doesn't matter what you call it as long as you can gradually sense of this hidden part of yourself. Likewise, it doesn't matter what gender you are or what gender you assign to it. You could call it "Bob" or your true self, your inner guide, inner voice, your heart, your treasure or "the friend". In fact, you don't have to call it anything. Sometimes it is felt as a more natural being inside you or more creature-like or just a presence. Or nothing but sensations followed by a feeling of being more connected with yourself. What does matter is that you find your own way to hear this subtle source of bodyself wisdom and its sensible, soothing, revitalizing guidance.

Reconnecting with *Her*

In the end, I know that *she* is me and I am *her*. When I notice that I am feeling harried, depressed, or out of touch I have to find *her* voice so we can connect again. We lose touch when I get too rushed and take on too many things and don't give myself time to feel what I really need at the moment. Many times a day we become disconnected, giving me a lot of practice in hooking up again. And what a relief, reconnection is! On less demanding days I find myself turning in *her* direction without making a project out of it. It just happens. Things just flow better - evidence that my daily practice of listening for *her* is paying off. Gradually I am coming into more balance.

For example, one night when I caught myself trying to get more work out of myself on this book, I stopped and checked in with *her*. Silently I asked myself "What is the matter?" I had sensed some resistance to working more. I felt *her* reply, *"I'm sick of all this work. When are we going to have fun? You always have so much to do."* The moment I got that message I remembered the sweet feeling I had had the night before as I got into bed. A rush of soothing chemicals had flowed through me that night. That feeling was the result of checking in with myself all that day. I had eaten just the right foods in the right amount and rested when I needed to. At that moment of remembering how good I had felt, I realized I had come full circle from that first "tuck myself in" sweetness one morning, many years before. Now *her* giving me that memory of how sweet I felt when I didn't push the night before made it easy to stop working and go to bed on time. I said to *her* , "You keep talking to me, honey. I love it. You are helping me so much. Thank you . . . Tha*nk you, thank you*". I'm thanking <u>her</u> and then it sounds like *she* is thanking <u>me</u>. Joined, at last. *Her* voice becomes mine and mine, *hers*.

Reconnecting with *her* is a matter of noticing *her* cues and taking time to respond to them. The cues *she* gives are sensations, images, urges, emotional feelings, surges, inklings, flashes, impulses. There are many roads to roam and they all lead home! It takes time to become familiar with them. It takes not being too tired or too much in a hurry to notice the signposts.

It takes trust to allow the time. Trusting *her* comes by finding out what happens when you take the time needed to respond. Trust comes out of repeatedly experiencing how much better you feel in terms of increased energy, ease, pleasure and inspiration when you give your attention to this part of you. With trust comes a willingness to let go of the "Let's Go!"* attitude. The more you listen and follow up on what you hear, the more you will hear. The more tuned-in you become the more balance you will experience in your daily life.

Here are some examples of several ways *she* is available to communicate with me, providing I am available to *her*:

One morning as I awakened I faced the first of four days set aside to work on this book. Feeling depleted and tired from the night before, I yearned to feel *her* again. I felt for *her* with a mild sense of panic, I had four days of writing ahead of me. I needed *her*. How could I invite back this invaluable "voice"? When I get too tired, when I try to do too much and jam my schedule I lose a sense of *her*. It is as if *she* senses there is no place for *her*. *She* can't be forced, only invited. Sometimes *she* seems to be reluctant to show *herself*, perhaps because I have been ignoring *her*. I may need to make repeated invitations but eventually *she* always shows up.

7

As I started to undress my bed to wash the sheets, I felt an impulse to playfully dump the pillow out of its satiny case. Satin pillowcases and undercases by their very nature lend themselves to slippage so following an impulse to hoist the pillow into the air. Then I allowed the pillow to drop to the bed and I let out a sound. I recognized that it felt good! Who says housework can't be fun? One more pillow slips from its case with my cry of satisfaction at the sheer recklessness of the toss. I can do it any way I want to! *She's* back! Once again.

That morning *she* wanted cold water under *her* chin as well as on *her* face. I could feel that desire. My habit had become to run cool water over my wrists after I brushed my teeth. Now sensing the coolness of the water on my wrists, my face wanted some. Then under my chin became "thirsty" for refreshment. I'm glad to oblige. I was grateful *she* was making herself known to me again.

Later, *she* made herself known at the breakfast table while I was reading a newspaper article. Tears came as I read of a young Chicana farm worker who had a lot of trouble getting accepted into medical school. Tears came – then the sounds of crying. Just letting it happen as I allowed myself to be deeply touched. The young woman had made so many efforts to no avail. Then finally someone took a chance on her. Feeling my own resonant response gave me another chance with my bodyself "*her*". I came to my writing more connected, those tears having cleaned my "writer's windshield".

This book can help you find more connectedness with this deep part of yourself by suggesting various ways to listen to yourself. You will learn how to ask questions of yourself and listen for the response. Most people encounter some resistance to connecting with themselves, whether it comes in the form of difficulty in setting aside time or in slowing down or in fear of what they feel when they become more present. Illuminating the sources of resistance as well as ways to deal with them is a unique contribution this book makes. You can learn to work through your resistance to reconnect with your bodyself and find the sweetness of your hidden treasure.

This is a personal book about an intimate process. The story of the unfolding of greater intimacy with my bodyself voice has many chapters. Each chapter's suggestions are offered to you in hopes of speaking to some, once less accessible, part of you. I hope you will follow through on that stirring.

2

DISCOVERING *HER*

"The gift of the bodyself is presence."

In this chapter I share with you how each of the three listening practices led to the eventual discovery of *her*, my bodyself voice. If you would prefer to experiment on your own before you read my account, please skip to Chapters 4, 5, and 6. Each one of those chapters is devoted to a detailed description of what the listening practices entail and how to begin experimenting. While my experiences are used to illustrate specific considerations in each chapter, the main focus of those chapters is to guide you in having your <u>own</u> experience. I want you to have the choice of having your own experience first and then you can always check back with this chapter if you are curious about mine. The next chapter, Chapter 3, can deepen your <u>intellectual</u> <u>understanding</u> of how the listening practices, taken as a group or individually can enhance your ability to self-soothe and live fully in the bodyself moment.

Sensing: A Sensory Awakening

I remember my first massage like an alcoholic remembers the first drink. A whole sensory world exploded into my consciousness. As my head was lowered into the couch, it seemed like it would be going down forever. For the first time in my memory there were no thoughts, even if only for a few moments. My thoughts had vanished as sensations took their place. I was utterly fascinated by the shift in consciousness that this experience evoked. Up until that moment, my entire conscious experience had been limited to thinking. I had been living totally in "my head".* Completely intrigued by my massage experience I took a massage workshop the first chance I had, and started teaching massage soon after. This work was the first I had ever done that felt like it came right from me. Following up on my curiosity about this awakening changed the course of my life because it led to a thirty-five year career as a massage teacher, to a dissertation on the bodymind connection and finally, to a second career as a relational somatic psychotherapist.

Several years later, in 1971, I worked with Charlotte Selver, whose bodymindfulness practice is called "Sensory Awareness"**. At the time I didn't realize that her sensing work was the foundation for the massage experience I had had a few years earlier, at the hands of the Esalen masseuse. Once again I had a deep experience of a connection with my bodyself which I recognized had been lost for a very long time. Charlotte implored "Don't take my word for it, find out for yourself!" Her invitation was music to my ears. This was not a religion or a school. There was nothing to learn or believe, only something to experience as I allowed myself to open to it.

Charlotte asked questions to be answered by each student's momentary experience - questions such as "What is needed?" and "What does it want?" The "it" she referred to was the "organism". The living organism is the totality that each of us is - not just the "body".*** Such questions led to a deep experiencing of sensory process and breathing. In response to her questions I came to experience the support under me (the earth) and the "support" of my breathing. I experienced spontaneous movement – movement without a sense of effort. My organism was moving me. I came to distinguish between "doing" and "allowing". I experienced movement freer from training and habit. Sometimes I sat, stood and moved with the ease of a child. I began to sense and respond to what my organism wanted from me – to what "it" wanted from me, and I discovered that what is often referred to as a "relaxed" state is often a condition of what Charlotte called "flabbiness" – an unaware, disconnection with the bodyself.

Charlotte* embodied the aliveness she both practiced and "preached". I was so surprised to feel pulsation when I allowed my hands to rest upon her head. The class experiment was to feel the life under our hands. Heads are supposed to be hard. After all, that is bone under all that hair! Yet I couldn't deny my experience of pulsation. Her head felt alive! I will never forget that experience, nor when she took the lemon drop I offered her with her lips. And then with a twinkle, she laughed. And so did I! We shared delight!

However, in sensory awareness practice emotions seemed to be considered more a by-product of experiencing. Sensations attendant on the pull of gravity and breathing were the primary focus, not emotions. As long as emotions or the "pull" of other people were not involved I was able to be present in my bodyself. Two and half decades would pass before I could truly be present in my bodyself as strong emotions came up, and that learning happened in a much different setting. Nonetheless, sensing practice literally laid the groundwork for what was to come. Through sensing I could become grounded in my experience of breathing, standing, lying, walking, and sitting. I could come home to myself in the sense of feeling my connection to the earth and breath – two of three important aliveness-sustaining forces of nature**. A third force, in my opinion, is the influence of "other humans".

"Get to the part about us!" she is saying to me. I think all this history and talking about other people is making *her* a little nervous. Like maybe I'll forget *her* again. All those years passed and we didn't connect. *She* was essentially lost to me all that time. Sensing practice didn't have enough room for all of *her. She* felt a kind of judgment about emotional expression from some students of that practice. That was painful. I was coming closer to *her* but was still too far away to feel *her* enough for *her* to have a life with me. I was only part of the way there. At least I could sense! But it was not yet safe for *her* to make *her* voice heard. Now I can reassure *her* that I understand *her* fear, as I haven't been too trustworthy in the past. I tell *her* that the whole section on "emotional voice" is devoted to the story of the recovery of *her*. But first, meditation, the second and intermediary step in my learning to listen to *her*, needs to be introduced.

Sensing practice enabled me to tune into my sensations in order to become more present for what I was doing. I was more in touch when I was working with another person in massage be it a student or a client or when I was taking in nourishment from food or nature. I could soothe myself before going to sleep and ultimately give myself to the comfort of the bed and the steadiness of my breathing. I felt the difference between doing and allowing in many daily activities. I sensed into how I was sitting while driving and discovered when I felt more supported I felt more awake! I prepared myself for meditating with sensing experiments and sitting became more natural and less effortful. The question "What is needed?" became my companion in this preparation.

In sum, sensing practice asks the question "What is needed?' and embodies the attitude of curiosity and allowing rather than doing. Sensing practice builds ground in feeling the pull of gravity and in breathing and discovering how is it now? and now? and now? I learned to be contained by resting into what was under me, into my breathing and being here now. I experienced that paying attention to sensations shifted my consciousness to a more present, alert and awake state. In a later chapter, sensing experiments will be offered for you to try out.

Meditation

The first time I meditated was in a workshop with Claudio Naranjo* at Esalen in 1970. We were instructed to simply notice what was going on in our minds. As the series of exercises progressed, I found myself sitting and watching my thoughts as if I were watching a movie played on an old fashioned projector. At the end of the film, symbols of various shapes would appear. I saw those same symbols flash before my eyes. The darkness that followed the end of the parade of symbols startled me and I started thinking again. For a few moments, though, I experienced not thinking! Amazing! Beginner's luck? More likely it was "beginner's mind!"** Since then, of course, meditation practice has not been so easy!

That same year a few months after I met Charlotte I was instructed in Zen meditation at Tassajara Zen Mountain Center. The two mindfulness practices, Zen and sensing, worked very well together. Indeed, Alan Watts, the Zen meditation teacher, said of Sensory Awareness, "It is the living Zen." The permissiveness of sensing helps balance the formality of Zen. Both are demanding practices. Both ask for attention to exactly what is experienced in the moment. What I took from this teaching was the practice of paying attention to breathing, both in sitting and walking meditation.

Mornings and evenings I prepared myself for "sitting" using a few sensing experiments. As I settled into sitting I brought my attention to breathing, over and over again. I came to define meditation as the process of <u>returning</u> my attention to breathing. The more often my attention left its focus the more practice I had at returning to my breath. Needless to say, I got a <u>lot</u> of practice. I discovered how important it was to just let my attention rest on my breathing and not to try too hard or chastise myself for not being able to stay with breathing more than a second or two. The sense of abidingness with myself grew. The gentle, allowing attitude I practiced in sensing class helped me to focus in sitting.

I used meditating as a way to calm myself down at the end of the day. It helped me turn down the volume on my anxiety and put my thoughts in the background. After meditating in the morning I felt more stabilized as I started my day. During this time in my life, I rarely used meditation to penetrate how I felt. I just became more able to distance myself from the din of thinking - enough distance to often feel more calmed and soothed. Unfortunately I didn't find a meditation teacher that I could have faith in for very long, so I practiced in my own way***.

Only recently have I experienced the power of focusing on emotional states and the resultant breakthroughs. I needed first to connect with my frightened, overwhelmed, helpless self with the support of an attuned therapist before I could touch those feelings when I was alone. I did not have the inner support to go through the emotional spaces I needed to by myself. That support was formed and embodied gradually through my connection with a psychotherapist. Work with a therapist can be a useful adjunct to meditation practice as well as to penetration of your resistance to taking care of yourself.

11

However, I did allow myself to feel some degree of helplessness at the end of a meditation one night some years ago. I was going through a particularly challenging situation in my professional life, and I was uncertain about which way to turn. Rational thought and analysis were not getting me anywhere. I only became more tense and frustrated. In previous years I would have asked a dream for guidance in much the same way someone else might throw the I Ching or consult Tarot cards. For me, the images produced by my own psyche are an even more direct route for guidance. I found when asking my dream life for guidance that it was important to be open and just sit deeply with the situation. For instance, I might ask my "dreamer" "What am I not seeing here?" I had found that turning toward something other than my controlling, analytical ego-dominated mind could be very helpful.

This night I tried something different. I opened my arms and hands and simply and wholeheartedly asked for guidance. I had a sense that within me was some kind of knowing that embraced way more than what I usually experience. During an intensive meditation retreat some twenty years before, I had felt a direct sense of that knowing. Even though I never again had such a profound experience of being "guided", I figured it was still part of me and could be entreated. As I sat I allowed myself to feel that I wanted help, that I needed guidance. I was not sure where this help would come from, as I did not believe in God – at least not the God from my childhood. During an evening prayer when I was 13, it suddenly had come to me that prayers were answered not by God but by my own mind dwelling on the problem until a solution was worked out. That realized I was on my own. This night however, I noticed that I began to feel somehow comforted just by the gesture of asking. It was as if something greater than myself, but paradoxically still within me, was listening to me and aware of my need.

Some months later I turned to "emptiness" for solace. If emptiness was the ultimate reality for students of Zen, then it might make sense for me, too. I again discovered that the attitude of "turning toward" opened me. I had only to ask and to be willing to accept whatever came. In fact, I've found that the more intensely I feel this need, the more soothed I feel by asking and opening. In a certain sense, this attitude of asking answers itself. This experience has deepened since I have been able to feel the depths of helplessness with my psychotherapist. Now when I meditate I can "feel through" whatever comes up and accept it. With that, the feeling of helplessness gradually dissolves into feeling soothed.

I began to understand that the value of prayer for me is in opening to feeling my vulnerability, followed by asking and then imagining being heard by something larger than myself - even if that something larger is paradoxically inside me. Whole-hearted asking seems to be healing in itself, even if it is only some part of me who is listening.

Like many of you who read "self-help" books, I grew up feeling like I had to "do it all myself". Especially the really big things. I had to protect myself. No one protected me from what was hurting me. I had to be cautious and carefully figure things out myself. I was afraid to feel how helpless and alone I was, so I buried those feelings. I had myself convinced on some level that I could and had do it myself. I gave up asking for help, even from God.

However, the solace I felt with opening and asking encouraged me to continue to experiment. Toward the end of my evening meditation, I might ask for help in teaching a sensing class, working with a client or even with writing, by "leaning" with my attention slightly to my left. It was as if I was asking my left side for help. Again I felt comfort in recognizing this was a very real part of me that was capable of helping me. I had had the experience during the daytime of cues or intuitions coming from the left side of me*. I came to regard this aspect of myself as my intuitive or wise, resourceful part that grasps more than I can. I discovered that literally turning toward this side of me seemed to help me find answers that my rational mind could not fathom.

The messages from this part of me are very subtle but if I am open to them and looking for them, they are there. They are so easily overridden, especially when I am afraid or tired or "on" caffeine. At such times I reach for something solid, something known. A technique, a principle. I think, instead of feel. I take control instead of allow. But one half of my brain can't do it alone and neither can I.

Sometimes I refer to this bodyself part of me as "my left side" and sometimes with the appellation *"her"*. What term fits for me is fluid and changes depending on the mood I am in and the kind of help I need. What is always true is that help is available if I only ask, and especially if I ask with feeling. The more I ask and the more I notice, the more help I receive. When I am open to this part of me, I am more likely to experience that everything - as it is - is "just right".**

At other times, the only solace available in meditating was reminding myself that my sole task was just to focus on breathing. I didn't have to think of anything else or work anything out or do anything but let my attention rest on breathing. Facing emptiness in this way was almost comforting. What is the purpose of my living? Just breathing and noticing. Straying from and coming back to breathing. Afterward I would feel eased. This practice of focusing on breathing guided me back to sleep when I awoke in the early morning and anxious thoughts invaded my sanctuary. I could follow my out-breath into the nether land. Thus, daily meditation practice helped me contain my anxiety at night as I passed through less-defended states on my way to sleeping and then back to waking.

Meditating helped distance me from my anxious thoughts and rest-into breathing and the experience of just being. I was the listener and also what was being listened to. I became aware that giving myself to asking, especially asking with feeling, brought some relief from the helplessness I felt. Just as with sensing, I experienced that change happens simply by paying attention to what I experienced in the moment.

In sum, meditation involves the gentle returning of attention to a focus, again and again. The question asked is "What is it?" Resting-into breathing is like being held. Returning the attention to breath is stabilizing and develops the observing self. I rest-into something larger than myself and I feel more peaceful.

Listening to My Emotional Voice

It is *her* turn to talk:

My voice was too scary for you to hear. My desperation and helplessness made you anxious, and you tried to quiet me by paying attention to your breathing. That worked for a while. At least you got stronger and calmer, but you were not very spontaneous. So serious and earnest. You worked and studied and thought and sensed and wrote and prepared lessons and did pretty well at all that. But you lacked confidence and spontaneity and didn't dare to say how you felt, especially to those you loved

13

and were afraid of losing. And all the while you were losing me. You were still doing to me what you did to survive as we were growing up. That is when you learned you couldn't say how you felt if you were sad or scared, and especially not if you were angry. They would either get mad or ignore you. It hurt you to speak and not be sensitively responded to more than it hurt to be silent. So you eventually stopped listening to me.

Yet you kept trying to find your way. You didn't even know it was me you were looking for. You discovered, quite by accident, that by following and responding to your sensations you could quit smoking. Well, that was me, guiding you. Each time you picked up a cigarette, you were killing me off. You also discovered that getting up on impulse and running to the beach, opened you to just being with all that you saw and experienced. That impulse was me, trying to awaken you to my gifts. Then you found Charlotte, who told you to trust your own experience (me!) and find out for yourself (let me show you!).

You tasted the sweet power of contacting me the day you silently asked "What is the matter, honey?" when you noticed you were anxiously looking for a place to leave your car so you could run in to get your favorite chocolate dessert. With that heartfelt question came an easing of your anxiety and you no longer needed the dessert. Now you know that easing was the relief of connecting with me. I am the source of your well-being as well as the one who feels your helplessness. All I wanted was for you to pay attention to me, to hear me and in that sense, hold me. See the fear in my eyes. See my longing. Help me! The urgency to eat that special chocolate withdrew. You could turn around and go home without the chocolate. You had me at least for the moment, and then you lost me again.

While you recognized that something special had happened, you didn't yet have the strength to really embrace me. You needed more support to feel the feelings you would have to feel to stay close to me. Sensing practice directed you to hearing some of what I had to tell you. For instance, that was me trying to get your attention when you felt various sensations – pain, pleasure, constriction or elation. As you listened for and came to trust these messages more and more, you became gradually more connected to your bodyself, to the earth and, ultimately, to me.

Then you got into meditating and found yet another way to quiet me. (I know, you were only trying to find your way, but you did keep avoiding feeling and recognizing me.) You were so serious. So, of course, Zen meditation was the only choice for you. You were exposed to the more permissive and exciting Tibetan Buddhist meditation practice as well as the rather chaotic practice of the Indian guru, Rajneesh. However you had enough of chaos growing up and inside you. Better to sit still – sit through the pain – physical and emotional. That was more familiar. You spent your childhood sitting through pain and fear. Yet the quietness of sitting practice that gradually came to you seemed to enable you to begin to open a little. You were feeling my need during that evening's meditation when you opened yourself to the feeling of asking for help. That was me, asking for help. You couldn't allow yourself to feel you needed help from another person, but at least you felt the need to ask, and you asked. In asking, you opened yourself to tapping into some of my helplessness, desperation, and need to reach out for help. You were getting closer to connecting with me.

I have to give you credit, you tried very hard to help yourself. And you tried to do it all by yourself. You tried to find your own way. Many nights you could make your fears and your thoughts huddle in the background so sleep could find you. Through sensing and experimentation you discovered how to eat so you felt vital and alive. You quit smoking, you explored spontaneous movement and painted your dreams. You could sense what you needed when you were sitting or working so you wouldn't get too tense. You could even make yourself slow down so you could prepare yourself for sleeping. You

14

became steadier and could calm yourself, yet you had no clue how much you needed to feel the longing that sourced your helplessness. You didn't yet know that you didn't <u>have</u> to do it yourself. You didn't know how I could help you or what else you needed in order for me to help you. You were still a long way from feeling how much you had needed your mother.

OK, it's time to get to the part where you get a glimmer that it was I you were listening for all along! And now, it's your turn to talk.

After my first "tuck myself in" experience of feeling so sweet the next morning, I realized I was onto something and I wanted more. Up until then I had been paying attention to what my senses told me I needed. Then I would meditate to calm my thoughts. At that time, I had not yet a sense of calling "it" *her*. What was new for me that morning I felt the sweetness, was a nascent sense of connection with what some <u>emotional</u> part of me wanted. This wasn't just about giving to gravity, to breath, and to being mindful. This feeling seemed somehow emotionally sweet, enlivening, satisfying and comforting all at the same time. <u>As if somebody loved me.</u>

I began to ask what else would it want? What else would give a sense of comfort? Following an impulse I put a glass of water by my bedside for when I woke up in the night with a dry, funny-tasting mouth. I found a special lotion to massage my feet. The glow of a lavender candle greeted me as I entered the bedroom. I became more and more interested in discovering what would make my evening's preparation more soothing. I set aside a decompression time each evening, which was devoted to slowing down and readying myself for sleep. I experimented with sensing so that I could really rest-into lying in bed.

Then one night when I was having trouble falling asleep again, I realized I hadn't gentled myself down for while. Then I found myself promising in earnest to massage my feet, head and neck every night from now on. I even spoke my intentions out loud. As I was making this promise I realized I was sounding as if I was promising a child to tuck it in properly. How could I have begrudged *her* this simple act? I had let *her* down. Now I was reaching to *her*. The "it" was becoming a "*she*".

Like most intimate relationships, connecting with *her* turned out to be a double-edged sword. When I was able to hear *her* and follow up with what *she* needed, I was rewarded with a deep sense of well being and aliveness. When I didn't listen to *her* I experienced guilt, depression, numbness and pain. When I finally contacted *her* after a period of ignoring *her, she* would complain and express *her* disappointment, *her* anger and fear. *Her* absence deprived me of a sense of vitality and aliveness. Sometimes I felt blue and hopeless. That was *her* hopelessness about being cut off from me - my not listening to *her*. Unbeknownst to me at that time, underneath that hopelessness was an unbearable longing for our mother. *Her* feelings scared me and I was scaring *her* in return by tuning *her* out. My muscles tensed to keep from expressing the anguish underneath. Aches in my neck and head appeared.

Double-edged, but a sword nonetheless. This sword helped me cut through my resistance to taking care of myself. Ultimately, what broke the standoff was gradually being able to rest my attention on the emotional and physical pain, wherever I was beginning to feel it. My experience with sensing and meditation had guided me to connect with what I felt in my body. Connecting and working through the pain of abandonment with the support of a trusted psychotherapist, gradually gave me support to experience these feelings on my own. I can now more often connect with *her*, no matter what *she* is feeling, because I am not so afraid of feeling overwhelmed. Intense feelings of anger, sadness, helplessness, fear, love or sexual longing are no longer so threatening to me. I can more easily stay with *her* and reconnect with *her* when I lose *her*.

I had acquired another way to listen and a new question to ask. When I noticed that I was feeling down or cut off I would track back to when I first started feeling down and then ask *her*, "What is the matter?" Sometimes I ask this question out loud and sometimes *she* answers in kind. More often it is a mute, almost telepathic, exchange: a query and a reply. A "felt sense"* to which I give words in order for me to communicate to you, the reader, the awareness to which I have come.

Asking "What is the matter?" focuses attention and brings about a shift in a similar way, as does focusing attention on physical pain or some other sensation. *She* may answer: *You keep reminding me of all the things you are worried about! I need to be soothed, not scared before I go to sleep. Don't tell me that it is hopeless. You always choose work. Work and work and more work. When are we going to have fun? You are so critical. You are scaring me. You are hurting me. You are being mean.* And so on.

Just connecting with *her* this way gave me some relief. I feel sorry I have done this to *her*. *She* always forgives me. Just the act of asking and listening and sometimes crying brings relief. I am here (hear!) again and not split. Besides, *she* has good ideas, and when I follow what *she* points to I always benefit. I am hurting myself when I don't pay attention to *her*. I feel shame that I am treating myself this way. I have to take responsibility for what I do to myself. I discover how deaf, mean and relentless with myself I am, like those in my childhood who should have been more protective and nurturing. With growing awareness of how *she* feels, I have more of a choice about whether to continue mistreating myself.

In sum, learning to listen to my emotional voice (*her*) has been the key to living more fully and reclaiming my bodyself life. My emotional voice can tell me why I am experiencing pain, deadness, disconnection, or difficulty settling down. Embracing *her* pain frees me from constriction to feel joy and to have more energy. When my deepest pain was heard by a therapist, I could better support myself in listening to *her*. Meditating now has new depth for me because I can experience all the way through whatever feelings come up. Sensing can give way to emotional expression when I contact the painful tension in my bodyself. A deeper release and connection with my bodyself follows.

All three listening practices embody the same underlying principle. That is, paying attention and embracing what is available in the moment brings about a shift in bodyself experiencing. This principle is the focus of the next chapter.

By definition, your journey of coming into greater connection with your bodyself will be different from mine. For instance, you may find a good meditation teacher early on, who can help you penetrate your resistance to experiencing powerful emotion so you can move through it and dissociate. Or you may have experienced more consistent caretaker nurturing or have already worked through childhood trauma and are therefore, less likely to experience much resistance to slowing down and taking care of yourself. But no matter where you are on your journey toward optimal self-soothing, I think you will find something here for you. You may be just starting to connect with your bodyself or be already deeply involved in this process. What we do share, no matter what the particulars of our history are, is the fact that this is a process of connecting and reconnecting. We lose our bodyself connection and find it, over and over again. The more we listen, the more we hear. And as we do, our lives can change in the direction of greater vitality, balance, fulfillment, and sensitivity to others and ourselves.

3

FROM LET'S GO! TO LET GO . .

"The bodyself moment is the fulcrum for change."

Three Listening Practices

Discovering your bodyself voice is the experiential heart of this book because it is the key to overcoming your resistance to listening and following through on bodyself messages so you can take better care of yourself. On the other hand, the intellectual heart of this book is this chapter on how the three listening practices bring you into the bodyself moment of change where deeper self-soothing and increased vitality occur. If intellectually understanding more about the shift from Let's Go! to the bodyself moment of Let Go . . intrigues you, read on. This chapter illuminates the dynamics and nuances of the changes you may experience when you listen to and follow through on your bodyself messages. However, if you want to get started experimenting, turn to Chapter 4!

Learning to listen and respond to my bodyself has unfolded through the gradual development of three listening practices: sensing, meditating and listening to my emotional voice (*her*). These practices are mutually supportive. They overlap in form and function. Each asks the listener to tune into sensations and come more into the present. Each practice involves the attitude of curiosity and a gentle, nonjudgmental sensing of what becomes available in the moment. The subtle effort of sustained attention is necessary – focus, not force is key. The practice of each kind of listening builds a foundation for a deeper connection with the bodyself. These listening practices provide ground and a sense of soothing so you can approach the edge of that discomfort from which you innately pull away.

> **Sensing** invites you to pay attention to your sensations and brings you into the present. Sensing grounds you in your experience of breathing and being connected to the earth. Sensing asks the question "What is needed?"
> **Meditation** invites you to return your attention to your breath in a gentle, nonjudgmental way. Meditation grounds you in your experience of breathing and strengthens your ability to bring you back to yourself or your focus. Meditation asks the question "What is it"?
> **Listening to your emotional voice** invites you to hear what pleases, annoys, scares or delights you, what makes you sad or what soothes you. When you listen to your emotional voice, you can ground yourself by contacting your emotions and responding appropriately. To hear your emotional voice, ask the question "What is the matter?"

These practices encourage being rather than doing – spontaneity over habitual responding. These practices help you notice your habitual ways of being, thinking and moving, and they help you become present, responsive and energized - as well as soothed - through reconnecting with your bodyself. This happens when you can embrace what becomes available to you through your focused awareness. Building support for acceptance of what comes up is the challenge of reconnecting with one's bodyself. (This issue is addressed in later chapters on meeting resistance to listening to your bodyself voice.)

These practices, each in its own way, helped me find more ground for being. Sensing practice laid the foundation for being available to focus on breathing and sitting in meditation. I learned to rest into the experience of my sensations, of breathing, and of what was under me. The experience of meditating helped me develop a gentle attitude toward returning my attention to breathing and deepened my ability to focus. At first I used meditating to distance myself from uncomfortable feelings and thoughts. Years of practice of sitting and paying attention to my breath allowed me to begin to experience the emotional need to ask for help. I discovered that resting-into the experience of asking was <u>itself</u> somehow soothing. Just being able to connect with the <u>discomfort</u> of feeling my need was settling.

However, to listen deeply to my emotional voice I needed more than what the grounding of sensing and meditating offered me. To really embrace *her*, I needed to feel the fear of helplessness that I was avoiding at the core of my being. To experience how deeply I felt this helplessness and to live through it, I needed to embody the supportive connection with my therapist.

Not everyone who reads this book will need that kind of reparative experience to learn how to deeply connect with and soothe him/herself as an adult. Because I endured both abandonment and intrusion trauma as a child, I had more difficulty than some in being present with my emotions and with soothing myself. However these days I am more often able to embrace whatever my emotional voice has to tell me, even though, momentarily, I may not want to.

Being able to listen to your emotional voice is the key to penetrating resistance to soothing yourself and to taking time for yourself. Meditation offers you the experience of returning time and time again to find yourself. Sensing gives you access to the raw data to attend to so you can learn how to soothe yourself. I hope that the range of experiences shared in the next chapters will guide you in finding whatever support you need to connect with your bodyself so you can deeply self-soothe and renew your spirit.

Listening, Asking and "Resting-into"

I sat down to write this morning with a deep, warm stirring of anticipation. I sat quietly to let it grow. We had agreed *she* would have the first word here. This is, after all for *her*, our story of how we met again after half a century of being alienated from each other. This warming is a sign of our connecting. I tried to stay with that feeling and at the same time I began to think about how to tell the story. How to communicate about my experiences listening and asking and resting into? But once again I lost *her* voice and instead, became quite intellectual and wrote the following paragraphs:

"One of several paradoxes I encountered in this journey of bodyself-recovery is that the act of listening contains a question and the act of asking contains an answer. When I turn my attention to listening to what my sensations are telling me, I am expressing curiosity about what is going on inside me. It is as if I am asking myself, what is happening now? In simply asking myself this question, I am already opening myself to hear an answer. The asking itself initiates the opening. The opening brings forth the capacity to receive.

Receptiveness brings with it a sense of soothing and the possibility of "resting-into". "Resting-into" refers to the sense of allowing myself to be heard or held or contained by something greater than I at that moment. What I rest-into could be a sensation, a belief or a thought. It could be my breath, my spirit, God, the universe, my higher power, a thought, mantra, the earth, my bed or just the sense of letting go of something as in Twelve-step parlance, "turning it over". A sampling of spiritual practices express this discovery in the following ways: "Knock and it shall be answered", "Seek and ye shall receive", "Keep knocking, and the joy inside will eventually open a window and look out to see who is there."*

The sense of resting-into is soothing and sometimes, sweet. It is the "reward" for asking and listening for the answer. As I ask, listen, and rest into, an attuned dialogue with myself is likely to develop. Asking invites an answer from *her* because it indicates a willingness to listen to *her*. Receptiveness to experiencing in the moment is the common factor in listening, in asking, and in resting into. Allowing myself to be vulnerable and supporting myself to receive what begins to become available to me is the real challenge.

That's for sure! Listening to me is your challenge. You said I could start and then you put me aside. You lose me when you want to impress those imaginary readers. I am the one you should try to impress. If you doubt that just remember how dead you feel when you don't have me anymore. Just keep me in mind and how you finally found me and how happy you are to have me again. Don't lose me. I am waiting here for you. If you want me enough, you will find me. You think about those other people too much and what they think. Think about how I am going to feel. Think about how you will feel if you lose me. You live with me every day, not with those people you don't even know. You wanted me now take care of me! Stay with me. I'll give you so much pleasure your head will spin. You know your whole life changes when you follow me.

Now I am sobbing with the pain of forgetting and being found. By giving voice to *her* I find myself in a flow of connecting tears. The anguish of longing is the connecting rod. I asked for *her* and in the listening for *her* response I found myself and relief from the ache of separation. Embracing loss, I find soothing.

Embracing the Moment and Change: "The moment is a 'moment' – a fulcrum for change."

The dynamics of the transformation of the experience of separation and longing into one of connection and self-soothing by embracing the bodyself voice is explained by the Paradoxical Theory of Change. The phrase "paradoxical theory of change" was coined by Gestalt psychotherapist, Dr. Arnold Beisser** to describe how change follows awareness, that is, "Change occurs when one becomes what he is, not when he tries to become what he is not." The paradox is that change occurs by embracing what is in the moment, not by trying to change it. If I try to change how I feel I am not really accepting my feeling and I meet resistance. When I open myself to asking for help, I feel my longing and my momentary helplessness. I already begin to feel relief because I have owned what was real for me in the moment – my longing. I take the chance of feeling fear or shame and own the part of me that I was denying. The acceptance of how I feel brings a shift toward fulfillment of longing because longing for help is often an expression of wanting to be seen or heard. I embrace that need by listening and my own listening begins to fulfill it. When I own my longing I have the choice to do something more about it such as cry or call someone.

Just noticing that I am rushing around and not connected to myself is the beginning of listening to myself and of change. I may choose to slow down and tune in as I become aware that I am going too fast or thinking too much and feeling scattered. Just bringing my attention to what I am experiencing initiates a <u>shift</u>. Connecting with something I can sense in the moment, like a sensation or an emotion can bring me into the present, and that is already a change. And in the present is where change happens. By itself, without force, a shift happens by embracing or owning what is experienced in the moment. All three listening practices - sensing, meditating and listening to my emotional voice - have this principle at their core.

The following incident illustrates how all three listening practices come into play to help me connect more fully with my bodyself. As I connected repeatedly with my bodyself experience of "constriction" – the muscle tension and thinking dissipated. Focus, not force changed my condition.

Awakening one recent morning I heard the words in my head "No, I don't want that!" I said them out loud. What I didn't want was the busyness in my head and the accompanying constriction in my body that began as I became more conscious. What I wanted was to feel soft and easy, giving myself to the comfort of lying in my bed. Just to sense the stirrings of a new day and a new life.

Again and again, I felt my thoughts take over. At the same time I was aware that my closed eyes pulled to a single focus toward the middle of my forehead. As I attended to that pulling sensation in my eyes, the tension eased and the space widened between my eyebrows. Again and again, I brought my focus away from thoughts and back to how lying felt. I allowed a small movement that opened the spaces between my toes. I felt connected all the way to my feet – life stirred in me all the way down there! Then my leg found just the right place on my body pillow. Thinking surrendered to sensing - for the moment, at least.

Then I remembered how I caught myself similarly the night before as I was lying in bed, waiting for sleep to come. I had not invited sleep. I had been mulling over a big decision I had to make the next day. I had allowed my mind to be held hostage by anxious thoughts. I had noticed I was feeling tense and constricted all through me. The back of my neck was tight and my chin pointed upwards, resulting in a sense that my head felt disconnected from the rest of me. My thoughts spun out into the darkness, my body dragged behind, buffeted about by my fragmented thoughts.

There would be no falling asleep in this condition! I noticed my sorry state and took action. I brought my chin in, lengthening my neck. I found the "just right" support for my head and neck. I reminded myself to just rest-into what I was sensing at the moment and <u>trust</u> that a process was unfolding. Either way something good would come from it. And besides, more would be revealed. Being receptive and rested would be the best way to discover it. I made a small movement in my torso and focused on what followed. When I noticed how I was lying, I could feel just where my limbs "wanted" to be. As I let them take the space they needed, breathing came into my awareness. I rested into the comfort of connecting with my bodyself.

That was the last awareness I remembered until waking the next morning with the words "I don't want that!" I was pleased by the discovery of the continuity of awareness from just before sleep to just after sleep. I took this as evidence that my desire to be more present was sinking in more deeply. I was becoming more committed and faithful to what I knew was best for me. I was learning to anchor myself in the present by resting-into the ongoing sensory experience of my bodyself.

Noticing, Focusing and Following Through

The words "listening, asking, and resting-into" describe how paying attention to immediate experience can bring about a shift toward more ease and presence and away from tension and distracting thoughts and action. I have chosen the more broadly cast (or consensual) words "noticing, focusing, and following through" to denote the steps of the shift. Each step makes an important and essential contribution toward the shift, even though each step may not always be experienced as separate from the others. Distracting thoughts and actions or other forms of resistance can occur at any step. Each step is discussed individually below, followed by a consideration of how each listening practice supports the individual steps.

1. <u>Noticing/Listening</u>: First, notice you are going too fast or thinking too much rather than just remaining unaware. Already you are **slowing down** and interrupting your pace. You may notice that you are feeling harried, tense, tired, cranky, cut off or in pain. You may notice tension in your neck, or your bladder, or hunger, or an emotional state such as longing or irritation. You are beginning to **listen** to yourself. Change is being initiated!

2. <u>Focusing/Asking</u>: **Stop** and **ask** yourself the questions "What do I need?" or "What is it?" or "What is the matter?" Asking deepens focus, and something offers itself. Images, emotions, intuitions and impulses to action may arise. And that, too, is change.

3. <u>Following through/Resting-into</u>: Ask yourself "What am I willing to allow ? What am I able to do about that now?" You **feel the emotion** or **take an action** such as slowing down, changing position, crying, going to the bathroom, chewing your food, turning off the computer or TV, turning down the lights, hanging up the phone or completing the task. You follow through or you don't. You have a choice – to follow through with action or to go back into the numb, split-off state where you avoid feeling pain, fear, anger, fatigue, tension, excitement, longing or helplessness.

"No Pain, No Gain"

What is the price of ignoring these sensory cues? Both the good and the bad news is that thinking about other things rather than making the needed adjustment, cuts me off from the discomfort I am feeling. Getting used to ignoring discomfort by going "into my head" instead of doing something to help myself often leads to becoming <u>more tense</u> and <u>less aware</u> of the tension at the same time.

Indeed, the mere activity of thinking can thwart each of the steps. Thinking can keep me from noticing sensations, can interrupt my focusing on them and distract me from following through with some action that could give me relief. For instance, while I was lying on the couch taking a break after completing the previous paragraph I noticed my toes were slightly, but nonetheless unpleasantly, pressed by the throw I had pulled around myself. Ignoring the sensation I returned to thinking about what I had been writing. Then my attention was drawn back to the squeezed feeling in my feet. It was not quite painful, but clearly uncomfortable and restricting. Suddenly I realized that as long as I continued thinking I would not address giving my feet the attention they were asking for. I could not yield to a deeply resting state as long as I was thinking.

Through the years I have had many experiences of paying attention to what I was sensing as I prepared to sleep or to nap. I consistently found that I could enter the resting state more quickly and more deeply if I followed through on what was needed as I sensed it. Yet, once again, here I was noticing the cramped feeling and considering not doing anything about it!

Perhaps the shift to thinking occurred in response to the uncomfortable sensation in my toes. Thinking may be triggered as a tool to decide what to do about pain or helplessness. On the other hand, thoughts are a perfect place to escape in the presence of pain, be it emotional or physical. In my experience not only do thinking and muscular holding often occur together, but both of them diminish awareness of sensation. In particular I have noticed tension in my diaphragm and in the muscles of my face, head and neck when I am preoccupied with thoughts. In any case, thoughts go on most of the time and the shift from feeling to thinking seems automatic. Shifting in the opposite direction, from thinking to feeling takes much more focus and practice.

So, what can be gained by responding to the sensation of what is needed?

(1) If I move my toes a little and let them find the space they want, I feel relief from constriction and more at ease.

(2) Then I become aware of other places that need softening or more space - like my jaw, my neck or my pelvis - and I let the tension go.

(3) This "Let Go . ." process of sensing and responding leads to more of itself and away from "Let's Go!" thoughts, and therefore allows for a deeper resting and renewal. I can rest into the peacefulness that is created by faithfully honoring these subtle messages. In *her* words: "*You can't hear me when you think*". (See below for the importance of the difference between Let Go . . and Let's Go!)

(4) Breathing responds as I sense the holding and allow the space that is needed. More oxygen comes to the once-constricted places, and renewal can take place.

(5) I end up with more energy rather than less because I have rested when I needed to by feeling the discomfort and taking action. I don't have to spend energy blocking out discomfort by unnecessarily contracting muscles and/or "going into my head".

(6) I have more trust in myself and feel happy about this discovery every time I make it, so more soothing chemicals flow through my body.

(7) With repeated experience it gets easier and easier to access this deeply restful state by shifting attention to sensations and away from "Let's Go!" thoughts. I gain a sense of agency. I become more balanced in my functioning. I have a choice I didn't have before.

(8) The benefit of following through after noticing and focusing again and again is the experience of "flow"*. Flow happens when you are faithfully following what comes up in your immediate experience. If you stay with each impulse as it comes you are likely to experience a shift in perception. Your experience is no longer limited to a sensation that becomes clearer or a muscle that gives up some tension. You may experience a rich sensory and emotional flow as you allow yourself to be moved by your experience instead of trying to control it. Your very mode of being shifts from what I call "Let's Go!" to "Let Go . ." As your perception shifts, you have a sense of well-being: that everything is just as it is or "should" be or what some call – "the larger picture".

Here is an experiment in experiencing the perceptual nature of the Let's Go! => Let Go . . shift which you can try any night you can see the moon. Position yourself where you can look at the moon comfortably for at least three minutes, whether you are standing, sitting or lying. I like to support my head with my hands clasped behind them so that my neck muscles can relax and not strain. It also helps if there are no other competing bright lights in your view field. Let your eyes soften yet gaze steadily at the moon. Instead of thinking of the moon as a disc, allow yourself to gently consider the moon as a sphere, like the earth you are standing on. I have found on numerous occasions that after awhile the moon suddenly appears in 3-D and when that perceptual shift happens, I feel a twinge of excitement and aliveness in my body. It is as if I can feel the roundness of the moon in my body – its depth becomes palpable and so does the space between me and the moon and beyond. In a sense, I "see-feel"** the moon. The more often I experiment in this way the more often the moon "pops" like this. However when I am rushing around, stressed or have had caffeine earlier in the day, the sense of the third dimension is not available to me. My busy mind with its distracting thoughts and accompanying bodily tension hinders the perceptual shift. My Let's Go! attitude does not allow the connection between me and my bodyself nor between me and the moon. That is only available when I can take the time to allow the bodyself shift to Let Go . . then I see the moon through her eyes!

The Shift from Let's Go! to Let Go . .

Noticing, focusing and following-through results in a perceptual shift from what I call a "Let's Go!" orientation to "Let Go . ." "Let's Go!" refers to a more narrowly focused, action oriented, "Let's get it done now!" attitude while Let Go . . asks me to become more receptive and focus on and feel through what I am experiencing. The exclamation point which follows Let's Go! is intended to indicate an energetic sense of urgency and excitement while the two periods after Let Go . . suggests the temporal and spatial dimensions of slowing down and listening for what comes up. The result of paying attention to what I am immediately experiencing not only brings me into the present but also causes me to slow down. Sensations and perhaps even emotions become more available to me. While increased arousal may occasionally result when I deeply connect with my ongoing experience, I will ultimately be better able to calm down. Even if I discover I am angry about something, I at least then have a chance to feel it through and take some action to resolve the troubling situation and return to the calmer Let Go . .

Let's Go! mind is oriented toward doing, to achieving and getting things done. It can be good at planning and organizing, analyzing and rationalizing. It figures things out by thinking things through. It has a "mind of its own" and is sometimes arrogant, thinking the way it construes things to be the <u>right</u> way. Let's Go! is often convinced of its own logic. It is likely to refuse to acknowledge that something can be logical but not true at the same time.

Contrary to Descartes' view ("I think, therefore I am") thinking is not reality itself but only a tool to deal with reality. When thinking is fueled by anxiety, and particularly when egged on by the internal critic, thinking becomes a formidable force. The sense of urgency to not only figure things out but also not to make mistakes can feel almost tyrannical and overwhelming. Being too careful about not making mistakes can result in constriction in mind and body. Constricted thinking sacrifices options necessary for creativity, and concomitantly contracted muscles can lead to pain.

Thinking can be a powerful tool of Let's Go! because it can block out awareness of the "interference" caused by sensations and emotions. Emotions and sensations can then seem very distant and unimportant. In addition, thoughts are conditioned by cultural judgments about sensitivity, needs, emotion, strength and vulnerability and as such they may devalue more intuitive knowing. Because of its power to distract attention from painful sensations and emotions, thinking can become addictive. Since thinking can at least momentarily exert control over emotions as well as sensations it can block important access routes to Let Go . .

Let Go . . mind embraces the realm of sensation, emotion, intuition, imagery and dreams. It follows the way of <u>being</u> and <u>receptivity</u>. This aspect of intelligence has traditionally not been highly valued and therefore not encouraged in mainstream American culture. This listening mind takes in information I am often unaware of at the time but I find myself responding to later. To become more aware of its functioning, I need to slow down.

For example, who has not had the experience of suddenly remembering where something was left once you slowed down, perhaps closed your eyes and let an image of an action or of the object come to mind? A case in point occurred one night when I left the grocery store and I realized I was not quite sure where I had parked my car. Even though I felt a pull toward the second aisle of parked cars, I found my brain directing me to the first aisle of parked cars, trying to recall what path I had taken to park the car. I couldn't see far enough to tell whether that was the correct choice and it felt a little "off" to continue in that direction. Then I remembered that I had initially felt a pull toward the second aisle. I realized that that was *her* trying to guide me – *she* remembered but couldn't communicate to me in any other way than to direct my attention to the second aisle and leave me blindly staring down that aisle but without my seeing my actual car.

I silently said to *her*, "OK, I give up, show me." Walking down that first aisle I finally saw my car neatly parked at the end of the second aisle. *She* knew all along, I just needed to trust, to follow where my intuition led me even though I couldn't see the car. *She* had a sense – a body-based sense of having walked from the car to the store and *she* knew the way even though I couldn't remember it. When I take the time to slow down or even better close my eyes and focus on the sensations in my body and allow my muscles to relax, I find my thoughts slow down too. As the anxious thinking, fretting and unnecessary actions dissipate, the bodyself messages of sensations, emotions and images become more salient. Often this shift is signaled by a change in breathing or a change in my awareness of breathing – it often deepens, slows and/or becomes audible. This signals the shift from the Let's Go! energy of everyday activity to the renewing energy of Let Go. .

Both Let Go . . and Let's Go! have actions and thoughts associated with them. Both are energetic states and require alertness, maintaining focus and following through to build energy to sustain them. Let Go . . is not a passive state. Living in the Let Go . . realm requires a great deal of "mindfulness" as the pull of Let's Go! thoughts and other addictive behaviors is quite strong. This pull is particularly compelling when ego-threatening needs and emotions arise as they might when I slow down and move toward Let Go . . Thinking and acting in Let Go . . is fluid and spontaneous and bodyself experiencing is near. On the other hand, Let's Go! thinking often serves to avoid the bodyself awareness that presses to be immediately experienced. Indeed, unresolved trauma, loss or unrepaired relationship breach can give rise to Let's Go! obsessive thinking or worrying in an attempt to keep feelings which threaten the overwhelm of helplessness at bay. It is much more difficult to shift to Let Go . . from this kind of Let's Go! cognitive activity because it is maintained by the bodyself constriction of a survival-oriented belief system as will be discussed in a later chapter.

While both Let's Go! and Let Go . . require focus, the object of focus is very different. Let Go . . focus is on internal process and is oriented in present time, while Let's Go! focus is externally oriented and takes the future and past into consideration. In fact, the Let's Go! bodyself constricted state which is held in place by past unresolved trauma and loss distorts the perception of the present and the future and often requires therapeutic intervention to shift to Let Go . . for optimal self-soothing. Let Go . . embodies being and allowing. Let's Go! spawns doing and acting. The goal of Let Go . . (if indeed, it can be said to have a goal) is "effortless effort" while Let's Go! is all effort and goal-directed. Let Go . . unfolds while Let's Go! anticipates. My sense in Let Go . . is allowing myself to be led while in Let's Go! I am leading. I need Let's Go! to get things done and to respond to a stressor while Let Go . . is needed to recover from stress and time spent in Let's Go! These states organize on a continuum of arousal, each contributing to overall functioning and both are vital in coping with the stress of everyday living. Balance between Let's Go! and Let Go . . is key to healthy organismic functioning (See Appendix A: The Yin and Yang of Balancing Let's Go! with Let Go . .).

Compared to the self-perpetuating, enduring nature of Let's Go!, Let Go . . seems ephemeral. But however fragile Let Go . . may appear to be, its power is enormous, transformative and virtually untapped in most people's lives. The importance of Let Go . . has been getting a lot of press lately because of the overemphasis on Let's Go! in this culture. Let Go . . serves not only recovery from stress and exhaustion but supports the bodyself experience of connection with ourselves, others and nature.

Shifting to Let Go . . from Let's Go! requires the discipline of "staying with" or "conscious surrender*" which leads to "bodymindfulness" and "embodied spirituality". The perceptual shift to Let Go . . enables me to experience seeming paradoxes with ease, paradoxes that are usually confounding to the logical Let's Go! mind. One of these paradoxes is that to shift to Let Go . . I have to act immediately when I sense a bodyself message in order to initiate a shift. I have to act with a sense of Let's Go! urgency and Stop! what I am doing and shift my position or turn off the TV or let myself cry. If I don't act, the moment passes and I stay in Let's Go! busyness, not paying attention to my bodyself messages. I need Let's Go! action to access Let Go . . otherwise I miss embracing the <u>bodyself moment</u>, the <u>fulcrum</u> for <u>change</u>. Another example of the interplay of Let's Go! and Let Go . . is demonstrated by those who have great skill in sports and who can also allow themselves to relax and have fun even in competition. In fact, the ability of an athlete to maintain the Let Go . . attitude in the midst of competing can be the decisive factor in winning.* So staying with the bodyself moment demands focus and surrender at the same time! Talk about an extreme sport!

The shift to Let Go . . is accompanied by soothing chemicals that give a feeling of peaceful pleasure and well-being. Staying with this experience and continuing to follow impulses deepens Let Go . . and may be experienced as a sweetness ("sweet-ease") or what I have identified as the experience of *her* being happy with me for listening to *her* and what *she* needed. The reward of connecting to my bodyself in Let Go . . is subtle and sweet while the reward of Let's Go! is more like an exhilarating rush. Why the sweet, satisfied feeling? Perhaps so I will want to do it again and thus enhance my chances of survival by taking time to recover from stress. Caring for myself brings a sweet feeling, whether it is because I allowed myself to cry, to get a hug, to eat just the right amount of food, to nap or to tuck myself in. Once recovered, I am ready for another need to arise and another chance to enter the moment. All day long, alternate Let Go . . with Let's Go! A bodyself moment of nurturing can go a long way!

Entering the bodyself moment - the fulcrum for change - is like catching a wave: you exert some Let's Go! effort to position yourself on the wave and continue to stay there, and at the same time, to Let Go . . and let yourself be carried and enjoy the ride. This attitude of paying close attention to what is and feeling for what is needed so that just the right contact is made is a function of exquisite bodyself sensing which is available when you shift to Let Go . . You don't have to wait until you go to the beach or to the grocery store or for nightfall to try this out. This sensibility is useful in most everyday activities as you can read in the following example: One afternoon as I surrendered to the warmth of the sunshine on my legs coming through my window, to the softness of the comforter and pillows that cradled me, to the gentle background sounds of the whirring ceiling fan, the windows chattering and the leaves rustling in the wind, I caught the wave of remembrance of cleaning my lamp the night before. I re-entered the moment of contact with the glass shade and the gentleness with which I wiped away the dust of the past. I again "felt" the contact between my cloth and the glass surface and I "heard" the slightly scratchy high-pitched sound it made as I rubbed, calibrating the force I applied – just what was necessary and no more. When I then noticed how gently I had been stroking away the dust I remembered how in the past I had attacked the task of cleaning this lamp by scrubbing away at the unyielding surface with more force and tension than was necessary. At that time I was just getting a task done (Let's Go!) rather than feeling out how exactly the <u>right</u> Let Go . . effort comes from sensing the contact with what is and how satisfying that bodyself moment can be.

To become available for this exquisite contact, I must be sensitive and responsive to my own needs for eating, sleeping, playing, meditating, napping, working, exercising, expressing, for reaching out and loving, whether the object of my love is a lamp or a lover, myself or another. Let's Go! and Let Go . . is about the attitude toward the moment, toward being right here in this moment and embracing it with my bodyself awareness. If I resent a task, I tense and likely use too much or too little energy. If I welcome the task as a chance to connect with what is alive in me in the moment, I can approach it with curiosity and feel for what it needs. Harsh or tender, my bodyself attitude is a choice. How do I want to live? If I treat what is before me as a chore, I miss an opportunity to connect with myself and the other whether the other is a lamp or another's heart. Imagine the sweetness that could be available if only we took the time to enter the bodyself moment and shift to Let Go . .

27

Bodyself Cycles: Completion and Interruption

Like most feelings the sweet feeling of ease and well-being of Let Go . . is both a psychological and a biological phenomenon. The very word "bodyself" implies both a bodily and a psychological experience. Biologically, when muscular tension eases, breathing comes more easily and anxious thoughts fade and psychologically a feeling of well-being and delicious peacefulness can be experienced. Let Go . . is not only the antidote for Let's Go! but it also completes the bodyself cycle of activity and rest. Completion of a bodyself cycle gives a palpable sense of relief and a shift to Let Go . . whereas interruption of a bodyself cycle can be felt as <u>tension</u> and is marked by a failure to shift to Let Go. .

Bodyself cycles of activity (Let's Go!) and rest (Let Go . .) are experienced in different ways and on different scales in any given 24-hour period. While the sleep-wake cycle normally occurs once every 24 hours, periods of alertness alternate with drowsiness throughout the day. While some cycles are relatively short in duration like inhalation and exhalation, others last 24 hours or more (ingestion-digestion-excretion). Some cycles are very predictable and regular, while others are very idiosyncratic, like letting yourself or someone else off the hook after an upset (forgiveness). For example, in the respiration cycle, inhalation must be immediately followed by exhalation before another inhalation can occur. Whereas, the rest and recuperation phase of the stress/de-stress cycle may be delayed for many hours or even days. During that time, the "flight or fight" response may repeatedly stimulated, often with detrimental consequences for mental and physical health.

Some cycles are more biologically based like the hunger-satiation cycle while others are based more on psychological need like the contact-withdrawal cycle*. Availability for intimate contact will wax and wane throughout the day with the need for "cave time" withdrawal versus "connecting time" contact. Some cycles reflect a fine mix of biological and psychological factors such as the sexual excitation/release cycle, or the indulgence/deprivation cycle, or the "emotional recovery cycle"**. Although these bodyself cycles vary widely in duration, frequency, plasticity and function they have qualities relevant to understanding the shift to Let Go . . How the autonomic nervous system supports the shift from Let's Go! to Let Go . . is addressed in the Decompression chapter.

(1) A bodyself cycle has a period of activity (Let's Go!) followed by rest (Let Go . .) and then another need arises. Completion of cycle is accompanied by tension release, a pleasurable sense of satisfaction or savoring, ease, well-being, presence and oftentimes resting. Muscle tension lessens, breathing eases, and thinking, if present can become expansive and creative. Completion of a cycle could be finishing a task, expressing an emotion, arriving at an epiphany, repairing a relationship, taking a nap or calming down after an intense interpersonal interaction.

(2) These cycles can be interrupted by Let's Go! thoughts, actions and addictions. Consequences often include muscular holding, constricted breathing and intense Let's Go! thinking. Intense thinking or obsessing begets more muscular holding (sometimes to the point of eliciting pain), reduced sensitivity and diminished availability to be present. Interrupted bodyself needs are often at the core of resistance to optimal self-soothing.

(3) Once interrupted a bodyself need for completion of the cycle presses for expression until resting is achieved and balance is restored. For example, being sleep-deprived leads to feeling sleepy and to sleeping longer and deeper once the opportunity is available. In another example, anger aroused but not felt-through can lead to projection of anger onto others, paranoid thoughts or nightmares. Flashbacks due to non-integrated trauma are another example of an incomplete cycle.

(4) To complete the bodyself cycle, contact must be made with what was interrupted*. Discovering <u>what</u> <u>is</u> <u>needed</u> <u>for</u> <u>support</u> <u>in</u> <u>making</u> <u>contact</u> is the challenge and key to completion and the eventual shift to Let Go . . Support for this contact could be awareness of breathing, of the ground, of another's love, or just taking time out. This support aids feeling through the disowned or overwhelming feelings due to unresolved trauma, or inadequate caretaker nurturing, or loss and the bodyself constriction (trauma) or contraction (stress) gives way. Then carrying out the steps of noticing, focusing and following through is likely to be followed by a shift to Let Go . . resting.

In sum, a bodyself cycle is completed when the phase of activity (Let's Go!) shifts to the resting (Let Go . .) phase and is accompanied by reduced muscle tension, ease in breathing and thinking. Interruption of a bodyself cycle is accompanied by <u>constriction</u> in bodyself activity such as holding in muscles, breathing and increased thinking. When what was interrupted is contacted by noticing (listening), focusing (asking questions) and following through ("resting-into" or acting), completion of the cycle results. Completion of a bodyself cycle is likely to be accompanied by a feeling of satisfaction, peace, savoring of experience and perhaps, even "sweet" well-being**.

The three listening practices can help you reconnect with the interrupted bodyself moment so you can take an action which will complete the interrupted cycle and shift to Let Go . . How successfully you can use these practices to soothe yourself after an upset or a Let's Go! activity depends on such factors as the quality of soothing you experienced from your childhood caretakers, the amount of stress in your life, the soundness of your biological functioning and the kind of substances you have put in your system. What causes the interruption in the bodyself cycle could be primarily psychological or biological and is likely to be some combination of both. Specific examples of what is needed to complete the more biologically driven cycles are discussed in the Decompression chapter. Completion of the more psychologically driven cycles such as the emotional recovery cycle, indulgence-deprivation and the task initiation-completion cycle is treated in the chapters on meeting your resistance to listening to your bodyself voice, reclaiming your bodyself voice and meditation. In fact, the anxiety (or depression or numbness) that accompanies difficulty with completing the emotional recovery cycle can interfere with completion of other bodyself cycles such as sleep/wake cycle and relationship repair. Successful navigation of interruptions of the emotional recovery cycle may initially require the support of a therapist to move through threatening feelings and needs to shift to Let Go . . well-being.

Becoming sensitive to my bodyself cycles and needs helps me connect with my deeper self and gives me more Let Go . . momentum. Living in concert with my bodyself rhythms means that when I feel drowsy I take a nap instead of a "cap" (cappuccino) so that Let Go . . rather than Let Go! energy, is enhanced. Gradually you too can learn to ride the wave of your bodyself rhythms rather than ignore or distort them through addictions and other avoidant behavior.

The balanced functioning of Let's Go! and Let Go . . is essential for your health and well-being and depends on your ability to access them so you can utilize their different strengths at the appropriate time. Since you are reading this book, I can guess that you, like I, need practice in accessing and exercising the gifts of your Let Go . . mind. You may be yearning for your creative, intuitive, sensitive, vulnerable side to have more of a voice in your life and in your intimate relationships. The more you turn toward listening for this, more subtle aspect of your being, the more easily you will be able to express and soothe yourself. In *her* words: *I love it when you trust me. I have so much to offer and you know it works out well, every time you do trust me.*

How the Three Listening Practices Invite the Let Go . . Shift

Each of the listening practices contributes to my ability to move from Let's Go! to Let Go . . through noticing, focusing and following-through. While all three listening practices embody listening with curiosity and staying with my experience, each practice makes a specific contribution.

Sensing plays an important role, especially in the first step, Noticing/ Listening. Sensing practice makes me aware of the raw data of experience of how the gentle turning of attention to my sensations invites letting go of tension and opening to the flow of life forces within me. More room for circulation and breathing is created as tension melts and allows more conscious sensory experience. If I am able to honor sensory messages about what is needed I find myself experiencing a rich sensory flow.

Meditation practice primarily supports the second step, Focusing/Asking. The experience of repeatedly bringing my attention back to a predetermined focus such as breathing, strengthens my ability to notice what is happening within me and then return my attention back to what is needed. I find myself reconnecting with my bodyself, again and again, as my thoughts recede from the foreground. Meditation strengthens my ability to stay with what I am experiencing as if I was continually asking the question – what is it?

Listening to my emotional voice can help penetrate resistance to the final step of Following-through/Resting-into. My need to avoid certain emotions and needs, whether through judgment or denial, can interfere with my ability to follow through or rest into what I have sensed and focused on. This step in the Let's Go! => Let Go . . shift is the most challenging one. It asks me to act by staying with my bodyself experience and expressing an emotion, completing a task or releasing muscle tension.

Can I be moved to help myself slow down when I am tired or to comfort myself when I am in need? To find out I have to gently ask myself, "What is the matter?" and wait for the answer. If I can't allow the underlying feeling of distress to emerge, I won't be able to find out what is needed or carry it out. I am likely to avoid uncomfortable topics and stay in the vague discomfort of being emotionally shut down, rather than brave the rapids of emotional turmoil. With continued practice of these ways of listening and with enough curiosity about what you experience, you can learn how to tune into yourself emotionally and follow through on what you need and ultimately rest-into the comfort you create for yourself.

The "Cure" in Curiosity

The root of the words "cure" and "curiosity" is the same – "cur", to care. Listening with care or mindfulness brings wholeness, healing and completion. All three listening practices embody a sense of curiosity about what is experienced. Whether I am sensing, meditating or listening to my emotional voice, my curiosity will lead me to ask questions about what I notice and thus deepens my focus. The asking invites penetrating and "owning" my experience. This identification with ongoing experience leads to a shift in perception as I become more present, a change that happens through paying attention to what is immediately experienced not through trying to change what is experienced. This shift from Let's Go! to Let Go . . is invited when I am able to own my experience by following through with an expression of emotion, taking an action like completing a task or turning off the TV, getting a drink of water, giving a hug, releasing muscle tension, or simply staying with what I experience. The satisfaction from faithfully responding to my own needs leads to a soothed, restful state and sometimes an unmistakable sweet feeling.

In sum, the shift from Let's Go! to Let Go . . involves a three-step process:
1. Noticing by listening
2. Focusing through asking
3. Following-through by taking action and/or resting into.

Sensing practice hones your capacity to notice, meditation helps you maintain focus, and listening to your emotional voice help you to follow through by uncovering your resistance to taking care of yourself. Then you can tuck yourself into the bodyself moment and ride the gentle Let Go . . wave.

How to Begin?

You have already begun by opening this book, not to mention getting this far! You may recognize that you have already had some of these experiences and perhaps not realized how they are connected to bodyself soothing. In the chapters that follow, there will be many examples of how focusing on what is immediate and sensory brings about a shift in awareness toward a more receptive, easy-going connected mode of being. Sensing – that is, feeling bodily constriction and opening to it is generally less threatening to most people than feeling emotional longing, sadness, fear, anger or even excitement. However, as you slow down and feel a little less constricted you may start to feel the emotions that you've been holding against. If you are not ready to feel them you may likely become anxious and shut down again. You may need more support to experience those underlying emotions in order to become more present and truly soothe yourself. That support could come from a skilled, attuned meditation teacher, and/or working with a psychotherapist on key issues. Gradually, you are likely to discover you have a real choice between staying with your bodyself or distracting yourself. You'll experience the benefits of giving to yourself and the harm of not paying attention to what you really need. When you turn to *her* instead of relying solely on thinking as your ally, you are ultimately more likely to live your life in synch with who you really are and therefore experience a certain soothing joyfulness and peaceful aliveness.

4

SENSING

"Don't take my word for it, find out for yourself!"*

What is Sensing?

Sensing is the first step in learning how to connect with your bodyself since sensing invites you to notice what you are experiencing in the moment. The data of sensing are primarily sensations. Sensing is clearer when your thinking is less driven because thinking competes for airtime and usually wins. You may find it helpful - especially in the beginning of your practice - to set aside some time just for sensing like when you are lying in bed before you go to sleep, or just after you wake up.

Sensing asks questions like "what is needed?" or "what does it want?" Asking these questions as you are lying or sitting may lead to discovering how to give your weight to what is under you. You may find yourself sitting with more ease or lying more fully and resting more deeply. As you notice and respond to what you are sensing, your mind is likely to become quieter - the activity of thinking goes more into the background.

As you give to what is needed in your bodyself, you may become more responsive in breathing. As you follow up what you sense with allowing more room here and there, breathing responds. In sensing practice, breathing is not directed, it is allowed. Breathing changes as you notice, focus, and follow through on what is needed by your organism. For example, a few minutes ago I noticed my feet were huddled together under my desk. Upon noticing this I allowed a change so they met the floor more fully. A feeling of ease ensued and a spontaneous, deeper breath emerged and along with that, a sense of clarity.

Thinking and Sensing

The questions asked while sensing are answered by immediate experience. Thinking often answers questions based on past experience. Though thinking and sensing represent different ways of knowing, both are valid and appropriate, depending on the kinds of questions asked. And both thinking and sensing can support creativity.

The quality of thinking ranges from spontaneous and free-flowing to concentrated, driven, obsessive, or even tortured. Thoughts are meant to be tools to deal with reality, but are not reality itself. Creating a world in thoughts, while no doubt creative, can sometimes become a refuge. For some it is the only haven they have for self-soothing. For them the world of sensation and emotion may threaten uncertainty, overwhelm, and pain. A refuge created solely by thinking is a double-edged sword – a haven and a prison at the same time. A way in, but no way out – predictably safe, yet a dead-end. With reference to self-soothing, thinking, at best, merely distracts you from sensing contact with the world and at worst, thinking creates isolation and even pain.

When thinking is energized by anxiety the result is bodily tension to the point of constriction, numbness, and/or pain. Thoughts are accompanied by increased activation of those muscles associated with what the person is thinking about or how anxious they are*. Continued thinking without some kind of expression or action can result in tension in the face, neck, shoulder, back or legs. Thinking affects breathing as well - you may have noticed constriction in breathing as well as in your neck or jaw when you have been ruminating about a problem, especially an interpersonal conflict.

On the one hand, thinking that arises when discomfort is present may center around what to do about the disturbance. For instance, when your bladder is full and your mouth is dry and you are lying in bed, your internal dialogue with *her* might go something like this: *"I'm uncomfortable, get up!* No, l want to lie here, maybe I'll be OK, just a few more minutes. *But we will have to get up anyway!* I know, but I am so tired. *But I hate this feeling!* Maybe I will fall asleep again, I just don't want to get up." Tension builds. Your organism needs you to get up and you want to stay down. All the muscles associated with those conflicting thoughts are activated, though at a low level. Your level of resting muscle tonus increases along with your alertness. You become more and more tense and awake the longer you lie there.

On the other hand, thinking fueled by anxiety and tension helps distract you from experiencing the tension. In fact intense thinking can serve as a type of dissociation. You can become so involved in thinking that you no longer feel your body.** That's both the good and the bad news: when not feeling your body you don't feel the pain, but when you don't feel pain you are less likely to do something about its cause.

Sensing and Shifting to Let Go . .

Sensing practice asks you to pay attention to the sensations of breathing and of sitting, lying, standing or walking. Just attending to these sensations can bring about changes such as an easing of tension or a deepening of the breath. You wouldn't notice them if you were completely absorbed in thoughts, so being able to notice them means you have taken the first step of the Let Go . . shift.

For instance, I just noticed my lips were pressed tightly together and a split second later that they were softer. I have made it part of my sensing practice to allow my jaw and lips to soften when I notice they are held together. You might say I have acquired a new habit – releasing tension around my mouth when I feel it. However, I still have a choice about whether or not to follow through when I become aware of the tension. Many times I have sensed tension and then consciously turned my back on it. Attending to the sensation of tension does not necessarily mean that you or I will go further into the Let Go . . shift, but it is a necessary first step.

Once you have noticed tension you may focus on it and then follow through with what you sense is needed. You are likely to find that in addition to the sensation of relief in that part of your body, you feel more space in that area. Subsequently, additional areas where you are tensing may come to mind so that you have the opportunity to release them as well. You may find your breathing deepening as the tension dissolves. You may feel more spacious inside and connected. You are likely to feel more peaceful and maybe even a little pleased. *She* says, *That is me you are feeling*. And as Rumi*** says, "And the joy inside will look out to see who is there". You have shifted from the tension of Let's Go! to the flow of Let Go. .

33

Let's return to the situation of lying in bed and feeling pressure in your bladder and a dry mouth. If you don't respond immediately to the impulse to get water and relieve your bladder, you will continue to lie there and think. The thinking keeps the impulses at bay and distracts you from the pressure of the need. But the needs keep pressing and intruding. Tension in your body and mind builds. Your bladder urges you to get up and relieve it. Your throat and mouth want some soothing. It's annoying. You are tired and don't want to move. Yet these other sensations call you.

Satisfying these needs will allow you to rest back into the bed with a sweet feeling of relief. From *her* perspective, you have listened to and honored *her* - the reward is the sweet feeling of being attended to and loved. This feeling goes beyond just the relief of emptying the bladder or of moistening the mouth. There arises a sense of gratefulness that you will respond and that you care for yourself. As you feel more ease, you can go more deeply into your sensory experience and Let Go. . Your attention to constriction and then following through dissolves tension. You won't need to think about what to do about pain nor will you need to think in order to escape pain. The thinking that then arises may yield creative ideas or pleasurable fantasies. The longer you put off acting on your tension, the more tense, agitated and awake you become and the further from Let Go. . *Just how long are you going to let the baby cry?* So get up and take care of yourself! I bet you will feel so much better!

The importance of responding immediately to what you sense cannot be underestimated. The key to shifting to Let Go . . is following through on what you sense. You will find yourself more in touch with the more subtle aspects of your bodyself and not so much "in your head". Perhaps you discovered as you were growing up that being in your head was the only safe place to be. As a result, dipping your toes into the waters of your sensory experience may be as risky for you as it is potentially delightful. So try it, a little at a time. If you faithfully follow what you sense a whole new world can open in you.

When you follow up immediately on what you sense, you energize the Let Go . . state and move away from Let's Go! arousal and tension. As the energy of Let Go . . builds, a sweet feeling is experienced. This sweetness contrasts to the adrenalin rush of Let's Go! As breathing shifts, tension and thoughts ease, you may be aware of feeling softer, more spacious and at the same time more connected. You break through the sensory deadness of life in the head into "all-live-ness". You are affirming your commitment to life, to *her*. Sensing is like tucking yourself into the moment. As you follow through, moment after moment, the energy of Let Go . . builds and you experience a sense of "rightness", well-being, and flow.

Heightening Sensory Awareness in Ordinary Activities

If you want to experience sensing right now turn to the next section for sensing experiments you can try out immediately. If you would first like to get a sense of how sensing is relevant to a wide variety of everyday experiences such as touch, food intake, dream recall and addictive behavior, consider the examples below. In each case, following through on what is sensed, whether with increased focus or another kind of action, is essential for enhanced functioning and well-being. Noticing, focusing and following through during each of these activities can transform it into a vehicle for a Let Go . . shift.

34

Maximizing Massage Experience

The experience of massage offers a pleasurable, non-threatening, healing way to enter the sensory world of Let Go . . Try to stay with the experience of being touched rather than checking out and going to sleep. The best time to get a massage for this purpose may be in the morning when you are not sleepy or early evening as long as you are alert. Late afternoon is a time when humans tend to drift off anyway, so that time is to be avoided for this purpose. The hands of your massage therapist provide the changing sensory stimulation to which you attend. Allow your attention to move with her hands. When you become aware of thinking about other things, Stop! and gently bring your attention back to the feeling of lying and her hands touching you. Notice your breathing - you may periodically experience a connecting (or release) breath. The breath comes spontaneously in response to a shift to Let Go . .

But you don't have to make an appointment with a professional for an opportunity to sense. All day long you have many chances to connect with your bodyself through sensing and shift to Let Go . . Whenever you are sitting, standing or lying you can shift modes by sensing. That pretty much covers every activity from doing dishes, to brushing teeth, to driving, to bathing, to applying lotion to your body, to working out, to waiting in line, or preparing to nap. You can make periodic sensory "check-ins" while you are sitting at your desk or in your consulting chair. Whenever you have a minimal need to think and can devote your attention to sensations, you can use sensing to come into the present moment and shift to Let Go . .

Improving Digestive Functioning

All the activities around eating from meal preparation to clean up are ideal for practicing sensing. For instance, when you are eating, you could slow down and notice exactly what your food tastes like instead of thinking or reading the paper. If you notice you are gulping and not chewing, Stop! and consciously chew. Notice how the contents of your mouth changes as you continue to chew. Do you chew more on one side than the other? You are likely to find that through paying close attention to your sensory experience while eating you will know exactly when to stop. You can feel exactly when you have had enough food. That moment of recognition ("re-cognition" as in reconnecting through your cognition) may come in the middle of chewing a mouthful. That is the moment to Stop! by following through on sensory cues.

You may be surprised how satisfying it is to honor that sense of "enough" and how much more often you will detect it if you respond to it when it happens. You may discover a subtle feeling of happiness or sweet energy appears after your meal. Your organism is thanking you the only way it can – by making you feel good. Slowing down and connecting with nourishing yourself facilitates digestion in numerous ways. The preceding suggestions are just appetizers for the main on course on the "Goldilocks" menu in Chapter 9.

In a similar vein, when you feel the urge to defecate, do it. On the average the peristaltic impetus or the "urge" occurs only three times every 24 hours. One time you are likely sleeping, the next time you may be on the freeway, so the third time you must act! By following through you reinforce your body's natural cycle. It is telling you what it wants from you. Listen and respond. Immediately. Your bodyself will express its gratefulness by giving you regularity and a feeling of peaceful satisfaction. The more often you follow up, the more you become sensitized to messages from your bodyself. Gradually you come to live in concert with your natural rhythms.

Qutting Smoking

A powerful example of the benefits of acting immediately on what I was sensing occurred in the spring of 1970, fully a year before I worked with Charlotte Selver. I had been practicing Tai Chi and studying spontaneous movement. The movement work required me to stay with the inner sense of what wanted to move in me and follow it. I had already experienced the sensory awakening of my first massage. I became increasingly interested in eating more healthily and felt more energy from taking supplements like brewer's yeast, wheat germ and cod liver oils. At the same time I became increasingly aware of the lousy taste in my mouth from a 10-year-old smoking habit.

I began to notice that sometimes when I inhaled, I would cough or feel a heart palpitation. I decided to respond to those sensations by putting the cigarette out. When the cigarette tasted badly even if I had just lit up, I'd put it out. Eventually I was only smoking a few cigarettes a day! When I noticed at the end of one day that I hadn't smoked any cigarettes at all, I felt a moment of fearful recognition. The next day I smoked two (probably in reaction to the fear attendant on noticing I had not smoked at all the day before). As it turned out, those two cigarettes were the last I ever smoked. Even more amazing is the fact that I never since experienced a craving for cigarettes. In times of stress I have occasionally had a smoking dream from which I awakened greatly relieved that it was only a dream. Because I followed my body's cues about the noxiousness of smoking, I was left with a strong aversive reaction to the smell of cigarette smoke.

In retrospect, I believe this surprising outcome was due to the fact that I was not trying to quit smoking. I don't remember even once thinking that I was actually quitting. I was only responding faithfully to what my senses told me about what I was doing. I didn't override those sensations and continue to smoke nor did I tell myself smoking was bad or that I should quit. I did not make an ego issue out of smoking or not smoking. I didn't tell anyone about my experiment. Actually I didn't even think about it as an experiment. I purposely stopped myself from thinking about it or reflecting on it. I resisted the impulse to write about it in my journal. I just sensed and followed through. Some part of me knew it was important not to be too conscious of the whole process and to just stay in the moment with each sensation. It was almost as if quitting smoking happened to me.

Eventually my dear friend, who had a two pack-a-day habit, noticed that I wasn't smoking. Based on my experience she experimented with this "approach". She was successful in quitting but her craving for smoking remained for years. This difference in our experience may be explained by the likelihood that I was more organismically ready give up the habit and didn't struggle with myself in any part of the process. Whereas, my friend was trying to <u>achieve</u> a <u>result</u> rather than simply respond to the bodyself feedback signaling organismic readiness to give it up.

I believe I did not experience craving after I stopped smoking because I did not set out to quit in the first place. My intent was to put out the cigarette whenever my bodyself reacted in a negative way - in effect, saying, "I don't like that." (The concept of *her* had not yet developed in me.) I just devoted myself to faithfully acting on how my sensations informed me – it was simply a matter of noticing and responding. Stop! Instantly. No time to think about the ramifications of what I was doing or not doing. If I had set out to quit there would likely have been an ego struggle with fear of deprivation in the future. You might say my ego would interfere (enter-fear!). My focus was on the moment of sensing and not the future. This was a practice, not a technique.

I really didn't "know" what I was doing – it was another instance of "Beginner's mind, beginner's luck"! In fact, when I was tempted to "know" by keeping track in my journal or confiding in someone, I felt myself pull back. That pulling back sense was almost like shutting a book or shaking my head "No!" I was responding exactly to the need of the Let Go . . moment by putting out the cigarette and by not making an ego issue out of it. Both actions – "do it!" (put it out) and "don't do it!" (reflect on it) - kept me exactly in the moment. I was not stepping outside the moment to observe or have feelings about what was happening. In effect, I would not let my Let's Go! mind take over and make a challenge of this experiment. Acting quickly and then not reflecting, apparently gave it no chance to either intercede or any fuel to change my bodyself course.

Potential ego concerns were not fed by Let's Go! thinking. I did not celebrate my "success" of smoking fewer and fewer cigarettes nor did I worry about not ever smoking again. You might say I "died into the moment" each time I put out the cigarette and each time I didn't let myself think about my progress or the future. It is now amazing to me that the <u>reward</u> of <u>acting</u> in the <u>moment</u> was greater than the potential satisfaction of the next hit of nicotine. The reward of following where your senses lead you will be referred to many times throughout this book. In this case, it was innately rewarding to be able to take deep life-enhancing breaths and to no longer expose myself to what my organism was soundly rejecting.

This issue of <u>intentionality</u> really pinpoints the difference between Let's Go! and Let Go . . Both have intention and require alertness but in Let Go . . there is a sense of giving up control by your ego to some other part of yourself – your organism, your bodyself or *her*. You allow yourself to be guided. Your effort is to continually turn your attention to the flow of sensory experience and thus away from your monkey mind*. Ultimately your effort becomes the "effortless effort". Until then a dynamic tension exists in Let Go . . You allow yourself to be led by a deeper part of you rather than succumb to a fear of loss of ego control.

In Let's Go! you lead and you don't let up or down and certainly don't let go. Let's Go! is all about intention. But as the shift to Let Go . . occurs, the intentional part of us gradually falls away. Even the intention for the intentional part of us to fall away, falls away. An effort is made right up to the end and then something else takes over, much like the experience leading to an orgasm or falling asleep. What you <u>can</u> do is focus and act and stay with what you experience. Focus, not force. Preparation and intention is necessary to stay with what leads to Let Go . . This is a practice that requires alertness and focus – and a lot of practice.

Continued practice of sensing will restore balance in your functioning – you will be more able to choose how you experience your moments. You will be more likely to "catch" yourself going too fast and slow down. You can experience how to balance your Let's Go! moments with Let Go . . moments. Practiced all day, nurturing Let Go . . moments goes a long way to keeping Let's Go! tension at bay. Just recall the reverie and ease of movement of children. They come to this state of curiosity and ease naturally - it is their nature. The effects of training and trauma interrupt it and the effort of focused attention is required to get it back. You will come to experience the unfolding of your natural functioning as you pay more attention to your immediate experience in your daily activities and yield to what your bodyself asks of you. The gifts I have received in return for my attention include freedom from smoking, eating more mindfully and healthfully, increased energy and creativity, the ability to tuck myself in and of course, that sweet feeling.

Sensing Experiments

The sensing experiments that follow are opportunities for you to come into closer connection with the experience of being bodyself aware as you go about your everyday activities. They are called "experiments" rather than "exercises" or "techniques" because they invite you to discover what is happening in the moment. The word "exercise" has the connotation of mindless repetition rather than mindful curiosity which leads to discovery. Through sensing you discover your changing experience, moment to moment. You feel it, not just do it. For instance, you are invited to feel out your connection to what's under you through your feet rather than just putting them on the floor.

Sensing experiments are designed to bring you more in touch with your sensory experience. The simplest experiments, but in some ways the most challenging, are those which simply ask you to attend to the ongoing array of sensations that are available to you when you sit or lie quietly with your eyes closed. Closing your eyes is not mandatory but helpful because certain parts of your brain quiet down when you close your eyes so you are more available to tune into more subtle aspects of your sensory experience. The first group of sensing experiments involve activities such as lying or sitting while the second focuses on a particular area and its influence on the whole of your bodyself experience.

In yet other experiments you will be asked to make a movement, which increases sensory stimulation, and then notice what you sense during or after the contraction. Sometimes you will be invited to touch or massage yourself or to actively stretch in various ways. In still others, you have the opportunity to freshly experience routine activities such as tooth brushing or showering by closing your eyes or using your non-dominant hand. In any case, increased sensory awareness is the first step toward shifting to the Let Go . . mode.

Sitting in a Chair

For instance, right now, as you are sitting, let your attention settle into your feet. Notice how they are meeting the floor. Are your feet nestled together or pushing against one another? Can you feel the bottoms of your feet touching the floor? Do you feel your heels in contact with what is under you? Your arches? Your toes? Do you sense any temperature or texture with your feet? Does one foot feel more in contact with the floor than the other? What changes do you need to allow in order to experience your feet in more contact with what's under you. What happens in breathing as you allow these changes?

One foot at a time, raise your toes a little from the floor and then let them come back to the floor. Now raise your heels, one a time and let them sink back into the floor. What do you notice in your feet, in your legs or in breathing? Is there an influence anywhere else? If you feel a need for change in how you are sitting, allow it. If you feel a need to stretch or to loosen your clothing follow it up.

Massage your feet using your hands or roll a small, soft rubber ball under your feet, one a time.

Now notice how your feet come to the floor. Experiment with where they would like to be so that you feel more connected to the floor through your legs, hips, back and breathing. Has your experience of sitting changed?

Allow your weight to go through you into what supports you. What do you sense of your sitting bones? Place your hands under your hips and find those bones. What happens, if anything in breathing? Gently slide your hands away and feel how it is now in sitting. Is there any sense of your pelvic floor?

Turn your attention to breathing. Where do you notice the movements of breathing? Without trying to change breathing, just notice it? Where does breathing want to go? Can you allow it? If you notice any constriction here or there, allow the change that is needed. You may want to make or allow a small movement to free you in some way.

Sense the space between your two hips and then between your two shoulders. Bring your elbows, one at a time, a little away from your sides -allowing some air into your armpits - allowing more room for aliveness. Where do your arms and hands want to be? Do you feel the air on your hands, between your fingers? Is there any sense of breathing?

Do you feel the air moving in and out of your head? Do you sense the temperature of the air as it comes into you and as it leaves? As the air comes into your nose let it come up into the space between your eyes. Allow your eyes to rest into your head. With each breath, give up any efforts of seeing. Let your eyes take all the space they need for refreshment. When a deeper breath comes, allow it.

Notice how your lips come together. Do they feel pressed together or are they in gentle contact with each other? Allow your jaw muscles to soften. Perhaps you feel more space inside your mouth. Do you feel where your tongue is? Allow ease through the insides of your mouth. What is happening in breathing? What do you sense of your eyes?

Bring your hand up to rest on the top of your head. What do your sense of your aliveness between your hand and the floor? Bring your hand down and let it find a resting place. Is there anything that continues in you from this experience? In your head? In your hand? In breathing? In your feet? In your sense of yourself in sitting?

Where did you notice you had less awareness or more trouble sensing? Head, neck, back, breathing, sit bones, pelvic floor, feet? What follows are experiments focused on specific areas so that you may inhabit your bodyself more thoroughly. As you become more present in the area of your head, for instance, you are likely to feel effects of this increased awareness move all through you. Ultimately you can become more deeply connected to your bodyself in your day-to-day activities. This process can begin with becoming more aware of your bodyself while sitting, lying and standing and sensing what space breathing wants.

Settling into Lying

Lying is conducive to beginning your sensing practice because you are already slowing down when you are lying. Sensing while lying will help you shift into Let Go . . more quickly and rest more deeply. Hence you will awaken more refreshed whether from a nap or a full night's sleep. At the end of the day, you have time to notice what you are sensing. The only drawback is that you may be too sleepy to pay attention very long. In any case, drifting off to sleep while sensing makes for a wonderful night's sleep. Drifting in and out of sensing while

39

lying in the morning makes for a peaceful beginning of the day. Experiments in lying are offered here and in chapters on decompression activities and waking up. Choose according to your curiosity and what brings you more into connection with yourself.

Lie on your back and give your weight into what is under you. Notice where you feel breathing. Let your eyes rest into your head. From your toes to your head, notice where you feel constriction or tightness, without "doing" anything about it. Pay attention to what unfolds. Gradually lift one shoulder away from the floor, noticing the effort it takes and what happens, if anything, in breathing. Is there a reverberation anywhere else? Give up the lifting and settle into the bed. Is there now a little more room for life or a sense of connection to the rest of you? Breathe into any space or constriction you become aware of. Try this movement with the other shoulder, taking time to feel how it is right now and then how it is after the movement. Experiment with your elbows and knees in the same manner, allowing your arms and legs to settle into the bed after the movement.

Pay attention to the settling process each time it happens, allowing each area of yourself to find its resting place and its connection to the rest of you. Lift your head slightly and allow it to settle, noticing the effort this takes and what happens in breathing. After each movement, breathe into any space that begins to open.

Notice how far apart your legs are lying. Bring them a little further apart and feel how that is. Try a little closer together. How do your legs want to lie and where do they want to be, to feel more connected to the rest of you? Like Goldilocks took to the bed of the baby bear, find the place that is "just right"! Do you notice the effects of this movement anywhere else? In breathing?

Sense the space in your armpits, one at a time. Are you aware of any pressing between your arms and sides? Experiment with allowing a little or lot more space. How does this affect your overall sense of yourself in lying? What happens in breathing as you allow more space in your armpits? As you did with your legs, find how your arms want to lie. Now notice how your legs are lying. Maybe their needs have changed. Can you allow what is needed now?

Notice what breathing feels like. How much space does breathing want? Just notice how breathing is right now, without trying to "correct" it. Allow any changes in lying so that breathing can have its way in you. Your need for circulation here or there changes with each moment. Likewise, the space you need for living changes moment to moment with the requirements of your external and internal situation.

Nap, Not "Cap"!

Just as "lying" is giving to the pull of gravity, napping is giving to the pull of sleepiness. When you feel your brain chemicals' invitation of sleepiness, rather than pushing through or grabbing a triple "cap", lie down, pay attention to sensations and follow through. When you catch yourself thinking, "STOP!" and return your attention to how lying feels.

You are likely to notice a change in breathing when you drop into the Let Go . . place. As your breathing shifts, you may feel more spacious inside and more connected to what is under you. The richer sensory perception brings a sense of spontaneity and flow. Creative ideas may come as you gradually drift off. You awaken refreshed with a sense of ease and clarity that caffeine use can't duplicate.

Sensing "Contact Points"

One useful way of conceptualizing as well as experiencing the process of connecting to the world through your bodyself employs the idea of "contact points." Contact points are simply areas where you actually greet the "outside" world. In one sense, the entire surface of your bodyself is a contact "point" because your skin is in contact with something all of the time. In fact, becoming aware of the air touching your skin or your clothing touching you is a way to help you come more into the present by connecting with your bodyself.

However, the contact points I want to focus on are the places where you can let "in" or "out" and keep "in" or "out", in relation to your inner and outer worlds. These contact points help you cope, support you and signal to another person. They mostly come in pairs, two eyes, two lips, two hands, two feet and two sit bones. Other contact points are experienced as singular such as your face, your jaw, your pelvic floor and your spine (when you are lying on your back.)

These contact points or areas are where you are likely to "hold" tension. Constriction in these areas diminishes your sensitivity and receptiveness for contact. Indeed, the function of tension in contact points may well be to keep the world at bay because of intrusion and abandonment issues from child - or adulthood. However, tension is energy depleting and is often accompanied by constriction in breathing. Both tension and concomitant excessive thinking make it difficult to slow down and sense what is needed.

Checking in with these contact points while you are meditating, sitting at the computer, standing in line, preparing food, or lying in bed preparing to sleep, or waking up helps you become more present and connected with what you are doing. You may become more alert and have more energy to give to what you are doing. You may fall asleep more easily and wake up more refreshed. You may be less likely to have a backache or headache because you will have been tuning in and feeling out what is wanted by your bodyself. When tension dissolves and breathing responds the sweet energy of aliveness and well-being is yours.

Foot work is offered first because opening the feet for contact with the earth helps ground you and gives a place for the "energy" to go as you open to experiencing other areas like your lips, head and pelvic floor. When you sense your connection to what is under you through your feet, you are less likely to become lost in thought. Indeed, allowing what is necessary throughout you to give your weight to gravity eases muscular holding and brings you out of your head and into your bodyself.

The next group of experiments invites you to sense more deeply into your head, face and neck region. While the neck is technically not a true contact area, it does lead to your head – a major source of contact with the world. Tension in the neck can block awareness of emotion and connection to the bodyself. Other experiments that facilitate sensory awareness in your head, neck, spine, pelvis and feet will be offered in this chapter and in the chapters on decompression and waking up.

A special "contact points" sensory meditation is offered in Appendix B as a preparation for breath meditation. A rich way to discover yourself moment to moment is to choose an area to focus on during the day. It could be your neck, your lips or your pelvic floor. Heightened awareness of this area can influence your entire state by serving as a signal to you when you are moving to Let's Go! It can also help you move back to Let Go . . if you follow through with what is needed. Sometimes all it takes to put me back to sleep, early in the morning after I have been awakened momentarily, is to just let my toes part a little. That small movement is a signal which takes me back into sensing and Let Go . . and lets *her* know I am wanting to reconnect and tuck us in! I listen, I focus and follow through, I don't ignore what *she* needs from me and *she* cooperates by letting me fall asleep. I don't tell *her* to go away or to "shut up." *She* is happy that I care about how *she* feels. *Her* happiness is felt as a certain sweetness as I slip off into slumber.

Good for the sole!

The attitude with which you touch yourself is more important than the specific "technique". Bring curiosity about what you touch and a willingness to respond to what is needed. Noticing, focusing and following through with tenderness and interest. When you really come into contact with yourself you will know it. Your hand will take just the right shape for your foot. You will feel the connection. Not a perfunctory gesture – but a real connection. Your foot will feel more alive and so will you – all the way through. While perfunctory is better than nothing, you know the difference in how you feel when someone gives you a heartfelt hug or shoulder rub versus an obligatory one.

Ask yourself, "Is this all I deserve? If you feel a little sad after you ask yourself that question, you are hitting pay dirt! Stay with that feeling if you can. An emotional response, no matter what flavor it is, indicates you are coming more into connection with your bodyself voice. Some aliveness is developing. If you feel nothing when you ask yourself that question, you may get some insight by checking out the chapter on resistance to listening to your bodyself voice. What if you imagined you were touching a dear friend or a baby? What attitude would you have then?

Feel out where your foot would like some refreshment. Notice the texture and yieldingness of various parts of your foot. How does it want to be moved? Where does pressure feel good and not so good? Try using your fist on the sole. Hold each toe back and stroke the underside from toe tip to ball of the foot, one at a time, giving each toe nurturing attention. You might enjoy trying some special "sole" nourishing cream or a tingly lotion. Giving yourself a pedicure or brushing your feet with a stiff brush in the shower will also heighten awareness. Most important is noticing how you approach yourself and how your feet come to what's under them after you have treated them with such respect.

Slap happy feet!

A delightful way to awaken almost any area is to tap or slap with fingers or hands, allowing your wrists and fingers to be loose. Tapping or slapping is a staccato like movement that refreshes. You can experiment with the backs or sides of your hands. The important thing is finding the right tempo and pressure so that you can open to this stimulation. First sense into the area you want to enliven. Then slap, tap or beat with softly curled fists. After you stop the movement, give yourself time to feel what continues in you.

Having a foot ball!

Use your foot to roll a ball on the floor, using some pressure. Notice where your foot is hungry for sensation and contact. I prefer using a small rubber ball the size of a tennis ball that I found at the local drug store because they are softer than tennis balls. Use them in the car to massage away tension in your back when placed between your back and the car seat.

Unmasking the face

As you are reading these words, the muscles of your face are creating a habitual expression that you may not have ever seen. Now you have a chance to experience this mask you wear - a mask created by habitual thoughts, concerns and emotions. Close you eyes and give yourself a minute or two to experience your breathing and sense your eyelids touching each other. Sense the area around your jaw and lips, the inside of your mouth, tongue and neck. Are you holding your mouth in some way? Let your attention travel to the area around your eyes. Do you notice any tension above your eyes, in your forehead? You may discover a sense of raising your eyebrows or pressing them together. When you release this holding, whether it is raised eyebrows or pursed lips, you may notice a change in tension in other places. Eventually you will become very familiar with this daytime mask and be able to start releasing it the moment you sense it.

The following "unmasking" exercise can help you experience your "original" face! Place your palms over your eyes and allow your eyes to take whatever space they need. Allow the tissues around your eyes to soften. Allow the darkness to soothe your eyes. Place your palms over your cheeks with the heels of your hands resting on your jawbone. Allow your cheeks to soften into your hands. Let your jaw sink a little as your mouth and lips soften. Place the heel of your hand above the bridge of your nose and gently but firmly slide your hand up your forehead to your hairline. Tap your face and head lightly with your fingers. Let your fingers and wrists be loose, not stiff. After you stop tapping, take time to pay attention to whatever unfolds.

The unmasking exercise can be done while lying on your back or better yet, while sitting, leaning the weight of your head into the heel of your hand with your elbow on the desk or on your leg, if you are sitting on the floor.

"Two-lip" sensing

Discovering tension around your mouth should not be too surprising. Your mouth has so many vital functions – taking in nourishment and expressing emotion, taking in air and giving affection. Tension in your jaw could reflect holding back emotion and awareness of need, refusing nourishment, rejecting intrusion, and bearing pain. To answer the question, "What is your 'original' mouth?" recall how babies greet the world – their soft mouths, slightly open, taking in, curious, making sounds and registering reaction to what interests them.

Allow your jaw to soften and the contents of your mouth to ease into the space you sense. Explore the space between your teeth and your lips with your tongue or your finger. Go slowly. Allow your lips to part. Notice how your mouth feels now. How is your tongue lying? What is the condition of the inside tissue of your cheeks? If your eyes were closed, allow them to open. Has your perception changed? Has breathing? The gentle way your lips can meet each other embodies the attitude of Let Go . .

If you allow it, brushing your teeth can awaken the experience of your mouth. Increased awareness of this key tension area so that you can follow through and shift to Let Go . . Developing a new habit of simply holding the jaw open is not being responsive to what is needed. Being awake and available is what is important. Your lips, like your breath are always available as an object for sensing and are often held or constricted. Attending to the tension in your lips and jaw can cue you in about holding in the rest of your face as well as about an emotional state. Noticing the way your lips are coming together is something you can tune into all day long. The condition of your lips is the "lip-mus" test of whether you are in Let's Go! or Let Go . .

Scalp massage

With your fingers held a little ways apart, gently but firmly, move your scalp in tiny circles. Where is your scalp the tightest? The loosest? Where does your scalp feel most grateful for the contact with your fingertips? Pay particular attention to the back of your head. Notice the attitude with which you touch yourself. Tap your head all over and then notice what unfolds in your sensations.

Neck: That Sinking Feeling

While the neck is not a contact point per se, it is the support for many critical contact areas and the site of holding in most people. Your neck is actually just the uppermost seven vertebrae in a long chain of intricately connected bones. Holding in one segment affects tension in the others. Likewise, release in one reverberates in the others. The following experiments facilitate the release of tension in the so-called "Tension Triangle" which includes the muscle that raises the eyebrows (the last muscle to give up excess tonus during relaxation), the frowning muscle, the jaw-clenching muscle and the muscle that moves the head forward when you want to indicate interest in listening to someone.

While sitting, notice how far you extend from your sit bones to the top of your head. Allow the weight of your head to gradually pull your forehead toward the floor, so that your head is hanging and you are still sitting. Your chin sinks slowly towards your chest. Notice the sensations along the back of your neck as you allow the weight of your head to be pulled by gravity. How does breathing feel right now? Allow your jaw to soften and your eyes to ease. In your own time, gradually let your head come up to the vertical. Take your time. Is breathing part of this movement? Let your head find where it wants to be. Is there any influence along your spine? Any change in the weight distribution in your sitting bones?

Notice how sitting is now. Let the weight of your head pull your head to one side, so your ear comes closer to your shoulder. Do not push or pull your head down. Simply allow the weight of your head to sink toward one shoulder. Can you feel breathing at the same time? Take your time and feel how it comes back to the vertical. Stay for a time until you are ready to allow your head to sink toward the other shoulder. Feel how your breathing responds as you gradually give up holding in your neck. When you feel the need to return to the vertical, let your bodyself direct the movement. Once your head is again in the vertical, allow a small movement as if you were nodding "Yes!" Explore that subtle movement however it unfolds. You may feel as if your head is bobbing slightly. Is there any response anywhere else in you such as an awareness of a need for change?

Spine: "Coming to Hanging"

One of my favorite experiments in sensing is called "coming to hanging." Charlotte used the phrase "coming to" to denote a process. The uninitiated would describe this movement as "bending over", but the term "bending over" does not imply the process crucial to the unfolding that can result from sensing what is asked for by your bodyself. "Hanging" occurs as you gradually let your upper torso give to the pull of gravity while standing. Try it out and see what discoveries you make and what changes you experience from your first "standing" to the next. As you come to hanging you may experience the pull of gravity on you and how your breath responds to this activity. As you gradually give to this pull you may notice spontaneous changes throughout you.

Start with standing, your feet hip's width apart and notice how your weight is distributed in your feet. Is your weight more in one foot or the other, or more toward the front or the back of your foot? Sense your weight going down through your pelvis, legs and feet into what is under you. Allow whatever needs to change, however small, so you are freer to more fully give to the pull of gravity on you. Renew your contact with the floor by taking a little step in place. What of the movements of breathing do you sense? Can you feel the air coming into you and leaving? Allow your eyes to rest, giving up any efforts to see.

Gradually let your upper body be pulled by gravity toward the floor, starting with your head, while your legs are still standing. Sensing the weight of your head, let it pull you into hanging. Take your time. Let it unfold. Notice what happens all through you as you allow yourself to be pulled forward. Allow your arms to hang and your head. Do you have a sense of your pelvic floor? Can you sense the pull on your face, your hair? Can you feel the pull on your jaw and your lips? What is happening in breathing? Let your hands slide up and down on the back of your legs from your calves to your thighs and then come back to hanging. Is there is any more giving. If your hands are dragging on the floor, you can fold your arms to give more weight for hanging. You can tap your back, arms and head by flinging your hands across your back. Don't to forget to tap the back of your neck, your underarm area, your belly, chest and sit bones. Then feel how hanging is now. Stay as long as you like.

When you feel a readiness to come back up, follow it. Slowly, take your time. Follow it faithfully, not going faster than it guides you to go. Notice what happens all through you as you come back to standing. What does breathing say to all this? Do you sense how the relationship of your lips to each other changes as you come to hanging and then to standing? The way back to standing can be delicious. Have yourself a "Maxwell House" moment as in "Good to the last drop!" Even when you sense that you are standing, give yourself a little more time to really feel standing through. How is the weight distributed in your feet now? What does your connection to what is under you feel like now? If you feel an urge to shift your weight or for a spontaneous stretch, give into it. And what is happening in breathing? What sounds are you aware of? Do your feet need to renew their contact? Then you sense you are really standing, let your eyelids open. Take in the colors and shapes around you. Let them come to you, rather than you're trying to see them. Tap your chest and shoulders and then let your arms come to rest, hanging at your sides. Do your hands and chest still feel something or do they just disappear when you are no longer "using" them?

The hanging experiment is a great way to experience the power of sensing to bring you into the bodyself moment and can be done at any point in the day when you want feel refreshed in a Let Go . . kind of way. You might want to try coming out of the "child pose" on the floor by coming up the way you would do if you were coming to standing from "hanging". While I have designated the "spine" as an area that this experiment addresses, reverberations can be experienced in many other areas.

Tapping, Stretching and Dancing

Heightening awareness of sensations all over you by tapping yourself or dancing or stretching is a delightful sensing activity. Feel how the music moves you and give to it. Allow sounds to go with the movement. With loose wrists and fingers, tap and slap until you're happy – slap happy, that is! Then stand or lie and feel what is awakened in you.

"Every Body, Let's Get Stoned!"

The next time you go hiking along a riverbed or walking along a stone-strewn beach, find a smooth, somewhat flat, goose egg-sized stone. This stone can become your ally in inviting you to stillness. As you are lying, place the stone where you feel breathing or on your forehead. Let the weight of the stone pass through you into the floor. Allow your weight to be received by what is under you. Feel the air all around you and inside of you. Let yourself be stoned.

Closing Eyes, Using Non-Dominant Hand and Reversing Order

Heighten sensory awareness in routine self-care activities by challenging your habitual way. If you close your eyes, turn off the light, use your non-dominant hand or do the task in a different order, you will find yourself slowing down and feeling more and thinking less. *She* will be amused! These experiments can be used any time to decompress and put a smile on your face.

Some Key Elements of Sensing Experiments

You will develop your own sensing experiments as you become more interested in how you function. Curiosity is the attitude that is essential for opening to the possibility of change. Pay attention until what is needed becomes clearer and then follow through. Notice, focus and following through bring about change. Sensing is about focusing, not force. You will find it interesting to take "before" and "after" sensory impressions when you do an experiment. First, notice your bodyself condition, then do an intervention such as tapping, moving, stretching, touching or just focusing. Finally, pay attention to how you are now and compare that with what you remember of your previous condition.

I recommend beginning sensing practice with awareness of your connection to what is under you and to breathing. The earth and breathing offer support to you on a continual basis. The pivotal question is, are you available to receive it? The work of sensing is to become more available to what lives in and through you. Once you are grounded in what's under you and connected in breathing, you may notice constriction in other parts of you.

Becoming more sensitized to the area around your mouth, lips and jaw can help you stay more connected to yourself in many different kinds of activities, ranging from working out to sitting at the computer to falling asleep or coming into the new day. Allowing softening upon noticing tension in your lips and jaw can become a cue to give up useless tension and runaway thinking.

Eventually you will notice how tension in one area is connected to holding in another. For instance, tension around the jaw, eyes or lower back often occurs with neck tension and agitated thinking. Another fascinating connection can be discovered between holding in the jaw and the pelvic floor. Giving up holding in one area can lead to awareness of tension or of yielding in another.

And of course, breathing is affected by holding in any area. Contacting the tension with awareness, focusing and following through with what is needed will allow an easing of the holding and what is sometimes called a "contact" or "release" breath. Simultaneously you will notice a decrease in thinking as you shift deeper into Let Go . . You can start anywhere on your sensing journey. Whatever begs your attention is a good place to start.

Whether you are sitting, lying, standing or walking, sensing gives you the ground for being present. What follows are some basic guidelines for experimentation so that you can find yourself in the midst of any activity. With practice you will be able to come home to yourself whenever you want to.

(1) Start with where you come into contact with what supports you, whether it is through your feet, sit bones or back, head and legs (if you are lying). Let your weight down through you into what is under you. Is there any response in breathing? Sense where the air is touching you. Feeling what is touching you can give a sense of your boundary, of where you begin and end.

(2) Notice any need for change and give to that, so that you are more available to your sensory experience. Allow space for what is moving within you. Notice what happens in breathing.

(3) Heighten awareness of where you meet what is under you. Massage your feet, put your hands under your sit bones, press into or lift away from the floor or bed. Free yourself to feel how you meet what is under you. (Even if you are sitting or lying, allowing your feet to be open for contact is important.) Notice any sensations in the area between your sit bones. Allow your pelvic floor to soften. Is there any room for breathing here?

(4) Allow lips to soften as your jaw gives up some of its tension. Allow more room inside your mouth. Notice where breath comes into you.

(5) Free your neck and head and let your eyes take the space they need as they come to resting. Tap your head and face. Sense the air touching you. Notice the sounds around you.

(6) Let your elbows move a little away from your sides, freeing area of your armpits and your ribcage.

(7) Experience breathing and connection with your bodyself all through.

Respond to each and every constriction, urge or discomfort with focusing, touching, rubbing, pressing, moving, or stretching until you feel yourself connected and open all the way through. Respond as if you were tending to someone you loved. Your gentle attitude and immediate response shows the commitment and sincerity of your heart for your bodyself. You are tucking yourself into the moment as surely as you may be also tucking yourself into bed. Sensing simultaneously serves a soothing and an enlivening Let Go . . function. Through sensing comes the possibility of letting go of tense muscles, tight thoughts and creating the space for the breath that signals the shift to Let Go . .

The more often you practice sensing, the more likely you will be able to use it to shift to Let Go . . Sense into your afternoon nap or chill out when you are stressed waiting in line, sitting in a dentist chair or driving in traffic. On the other hand, if you ignore your bodyself cues, you will receive fewer and fewer messages and feel more and more, out of touch and stressed.

In sum, sensing expresses curiosity about what you are immediately experiencing. You move toward your experience not away from it. Sensing dissolves muscle tension and eases thinking. As you sense what you need, your inner space increases. You are likely to experience changes in breathing as you follow through on what you need. You are more able to let go of what you don't need. You become more attuned to your organismic needs. Through sensing you restore the connection to yourself and to the moment. You experience naturalness in being and the shift to Let Go . .

To soothe yourself with sensing, increase sensory stimulation by:
(1) focusing attention on an activity such as coming to lying or breathing
(2) focusing attention on one area such as pelvic floor or lips
(3) touching, massaging, tapping and sensing weight of a stone or hand
(4) moving and stretching, tensing and releasing muscles
(5) closing eyes, using non-dominant hand, standing on one foot.

5

MEDITATION

"There is no such thing as proper breathing!"*

So why go to the trouble of taking time to develop the listening practice of meditation? Meditation will help you track *her* by enhancing your ability to <u>focus</u> on your bodyself experience. Think of sensations, emotions, inklings and images as the footprints of your bodyself or *her*. *She* says, *I like that! I get excited when you want to find me. I am so pleased you that you would go to all this trouble to develop a discipline so we can live in harmony. Just reach for me, look for me, listen for me, I am always here. I just need to feel you wanting me, turning toward me. When you try to find me, I make it easier for you to feel me. I give you many chances. I know you will forget me sometimes - just listen for me and don't make me wait too long. I get lonely and sad when you don't pay attention to me. But when you find me, you are likely to experience blessed delight.*

Meditating can strengthen your capacity to stay with your bodyself experience, provided you can tolerate what comes up as you slow down, in other words, to <u>hear</u> what *she* is trying to tell you. Indeed, meditation practice contributes to your well-being in a number of ways, each of which facilitates listening to *her* and deserves to be discussed in its own right.

In the first place, taking time to meditate gives you an experience of the value of slowing down and taking a break from the sometimes, mindless activity and tension of Let's Go! Secondly, as you continue to return your attention to your breath, again and again, your ability to focus on the present moment deepens. Thirdly, as you are more able to stay with your ongoing bodyself experience, you become more sensitive to its emergent messages. Enhanced ability to focus and to give yourself to the bodyself moment makes it more likely you can sense when

(1) a break is needed to soothe or solve
(2) a task needs to be completed
(3) an emotion needs to be expressed or a relationship repaired
(4) focusing on pain or discomfort could dissolve it
(5) that "funny feeling" occurs

And finally, meditation practice is a subtle discipline that can lead to your balancing Let's Go! with Let Go . . As your ability to stay with bodyself messages strengthens through deepening your focus and increasing containment of emotion, you may experience "embodied spirituality". Embodied spirituality implies that you are able to feel and contain whatever emotion comes up because you have a strong bodyself connection rather than dissociating, which is sometimes referred to as a "spiritual bypass".

What is Meditation?

Meditation is offered here as the process of turning and <u>returning your attention to the focus</u> – in this case, the breath. It doesn't matter how many times your attention leaves the breath, the point is to return your attention to breathing. Meditating is like strengthening a muscle. The more repetitions you do, the stronger you get. If you stop exercising, you lose strength. The more often you have to return your attention to the focus, the stronger your mind muscle becomes.

The <u>attitude</u> with which you return your attention to your breath is critical. However, it is critical that you are not critical of your efforts! Or at least, it is important that you become aware when you are being critical of your efforts. Of course in the beginning you may be tempted to try hard and then become frustrated trying to stay with your breath. Gradually, you may become more curious about the process and less and less impatient with yourself. In fact, you may sometimes find it amusing that your attention is so fickle. Setting aside time for meditation practice helps you deepen your ability to stay with and return to yourself because you are momentarily not involved in any other overt activity. If you are a particularly active person or you find it difficult to sit still, try a moving meditation like Tai Chi or Qi Chong or meditating while walking slowly. Later when your mind becomes quieter, you might find you are more attracted to sitting meditation.

Why Focus on Breathing?

Using breath as the focus of your meditation has some advantages over a mantra or an object because the breath is always available and not something you <u>make</u> happen. It is your constant companion in any activity. Breath is there for you to return to whenever you want to. No matter how many times you go away, it is waiting for you. Meditation can give you the experience of coming home to yourself by learning to rest-into your breathing.

The life-sustaining activity of breathing goes on inside you without any conscious effort on your part. You have only the effort of noticing, and noticing again and again. The sensations of breathing are varied and can be felt in different parts of you. Breathing changes with your activities and your emotional state and reflects your attempts to deal with your emotional state as well. <u>Breathing changes as you simply pay attention to it</u>. What an intriguing entity for an object of meditation!

No wonder breathing is central to many meditation and awareness practices - from Yoga to Zen to Sensory Awareness, and more than a few body-oriented psychotherapy practices like Gestalt, Reichian and Bioenergetics. The source of the connection among the latter four practices is Elsa Gindler*, Charlotte Selver's teacher. She, in turn, was influenced by students of yoga as well as by her experiments with sensing her breathing as she slowly healed herself from tuberculosis. (Other traditions acknowledge the interface between the physical and metaphysical by using the same word for life force or spirit and breath – i.e. prana and inspire.)

For Freud, dreams were the royal road to the unconscious; for bodymindfulness students, breathing is the royal road to <u>awareness</u> of the body-mind interface**. Attention to breathing can bring you more into connection with what is going on inside you and around you. Altering how you breathe can quickly and momentarily change your experience from Let's

50

Go! to Let Go . . or vice versa. Experiment with the "breath of fire" from Kundalini Yoga: Inhale and exhale as fast as you can though your nose for 30 seconds. Lightheaded, maybe? Any white lights? Changing the ratio of carbon dioxide and oxygen does alter your experience of your bodymind! "Hyperventilation" is another name for this effect, which is also common to panic disorders. But breathing techniques can also be used to <u>calm</u> panic as the following two methods suggest:

"Calming Breath" technique: "First, just breathe naturally without counting. Just breathe as your body wants you to. Then, inhale slowly and at the top of the breath hold the breath and count to 3. Then, exhale slowly and hold the breath at the bottom of the exhalation and count to 3. Then breathe naturally again to normalize breathing and repeat two more times." Try it! What do you experience? "Not Waiting to Exhale" Technique: Rather than inhale when you feel the panicky feeling, exhale as much as you can by contracting your chest muscles. (The panicky feeling is often interpreted as not getting enough air when actually the oxygen levels are too high.) When you release the contraction air will rush into your lungs without any effort on your part. To maximize calming while sitting, this forced exhalation/reflexive inhalation technique can be combined with tensing the muscles in your thighs as you exhale, pressing your feet into the floor as if you were pushing the air out of your lungs into the floor. Hold the tension in your thighs for 30 seconds while you allow the air to come back into your lungs and then exhale and inhale normally. Very gradually release the pressing and continue to breathe naturally.

Now you may have experienced that manipulation of breathing can be calming as well as energizing. What you have discovered mirrors the changes in breathing during a shift from activation in one branch of the autonomic nervous system to another – the calming parasympathetic (slows breathing) to the stimulating sympathetic (increases rate and depth). This observation has been put to good use by Reichian, Bioenergetic and Gestalt therapists throughout the last 60 years as they helped their clients become more present to their bodyself experience by directing them to attend to their experience of breathing, sensations and emotions. Changes in breathing can facilitate deep feeling, which sometimes triggers the memory of previous trauma. At that point, overwhelm may threaten and the resultant defense diminishes bodyself experiencing. For example, Fritz Perls, one of the founders* of Gestalt Therapy described anxiety as "unsupported excitement" and recommended that anxious people support themselves through contact with the ground as well as with breathing. A third grounding source is contact with another person. Excitement can be enjoyable as long as it doesn't threaten the integrity of the self.

You probably already discovered as a child that you could keep yourself from crying if you held your breath. In this way, you even might have been able to make the sad or angry or ashamed feeling momentarily go away. Cutting yourself off from the flow of feeling that is moving in you begins to deaden you even as it might "save" your sense of self for the moment. The subtle sense of power in being able to hold back emotional vulnerability can become a source of gratification and pleasure. Unfortunately it may preempt the vulnerability and openness necessary to receive love, support of another and even the support under you. Established patterns of holding back awareness of emotion and need oftentimes become the source of difficulties with intimacy later in life. These muscular holding patterns can result in back, neck, head and stomach aches, which arise in anticipation of interpersonal conflict. While these patterns are difficult to change, adequate support and contact can make change possible.

Breathing and Tension Release

Breath comes spontaneously as a part of the tension release process. Yawning is a special case of spontaneous breathing. Have you ever experienced a yawn while you were crying? I find that sometimes a yawn comes as the sad feeling and the tears are beginning to subside. Some athletes have reported yawning "attacks" before competing and attribute them to a bodyself attempt at tension reduction. Stretching and yawning often occur together, particularly as the stretch reaches its maximum. In fact stretching and yawning as a practice is a delightful way to start or end the day.

You may have also noticed how a breath follows the release of tension during bodywork. Sometimes a "release" breath occurs just as the practitioner allows the weight of her hands to settle on the person's body at the beginning of the massage or when contacting a tension area. This spontaneously-occurring "release breath" is organismically wired and signals a shift toward Let Go . . You may notice this breath as you finally settle into bed or when you are sinking deeper into a nap. Or when you discover you have been intensely ruminating and then you remember to notice how your lips are touching each other or how your feet are meeting the ground. Intense thinking is often accompanied by holding in the diaphragm as well as in the neck and jaw. Coming into contact with your lips or feet allows you to become more present and the breath signals the shift to Let Go . . The expression "Take a breather!" connotes the general awareness of how humans tend to constrict themselves in breathing and need to take time to recover.

Breathing is a sensitive indicator of the state of your organism. As any light sleeper or someone who has trouble falling asleep can tell you, a significant audible shift in the other's breathing occurs as s/he drops down into a deeper stage of sleep. You may experience this change in breathing for yourself, as you sink deeper into your nap. Or perhaps, at the end of crying you may find yourself drawing a deep breath. The distinct sound of this deeper breath that comes from the release of the abdomen differs from the more ordinary waking-state breathing sound. This is a "recovery breath" that signals the movement through your own emotional recovery cycle. Successful negotiation of this cycle is essential for coming back to oneself with full aliveness after an emotional upset, especially when you are "triggered" into "old stuff".

In sum, how you breathe is an apt metaphor for how you live. When you control your breathing to limit your feeling, you limit your aliveness and your possibility for contact and fulfillment in the world. When you have the support of breathing and/or the presence of another to go through pain and grief and come out the other side, you can reclaim your bodyself and your vitality. You become more embodied in the sense of "living your aliveness"*. On the heels of the amniotic fluid of tears is the breath, announcing and affirming life.

Breath Meditation Touch Points

In this approach to breath meditation you are asked to not manipulate your breath but only to notice how it is at the moment. This attitude shows respect for the sensitive attunement of breathing to your organismic condition. Sensing practice already embodies the principle of noninterference with breathing. Let breathing inform you of its needs rather than you telling your breath how to be. Besides, *she* needs a time to connect with you. You likely often push your bodyself limits with your Let's Go! demands. Paying attention to breathing immediately puts you in contact with your bodyself, and meditation creates space and time for you to listen.

Before you meditate, spend some time sensing so that you come to sitting practice with as much of your sensory experience available to you as possible. Increased sensory awareness can help anchor you in the present through sensing your inner space, breathing and contact with what is under you. Work with freeing your neck, back, abdomen, pelvic floor, jaw, head and feet before you sit using the experiments offered in the preceding chapter or the Contact Point Awareness experiment in Appendix B which is specifically designed for meditation preparation. If you are short on preparation time, try the child pose for a few minutes.

Breath awareness:

As you become aware of breathing, notice where you feel the movements of breathing in you. Without trying to change your breathing, just sense its movement in you. Let it have its way in you. It will change all by itself according to your organism's need. Do you notice its temperature as it moves into your nose? As it leaves your nose? Is there a sense it moves in one nostril more than another? Allow it into the area around your eyes. Allow your eyes to take the space they need and to rest. Allow the breath to bring refreshment and resting to your eyes. As the space around your eyes softens, your eyes gradually give up their efforts to see and accept the nourishment of breathing.

Let your attention go to your exhalation. Follow the exhalation all the way to the quiet place at the end of the exhalation. Notice how the inhalation begins. Follow the inhalation to its fulfillment. Notice how the exhalation begins. Just give your attention over to the experience of breathing. It is always there to nourish you without any special effort on your part - inhalation after exhalation. Like the earth, the breath is your abiding companion.

From time to time allow your attention to go to sitting and give way to any adjustments in sitting that need to be made. Notice your habitual "mask". Softening in your jaw and the insides of your mouth. Your lips, gently touching. Allow easing through your throat and mouth with the passage of air. When you notice you are raising your eyebrows, let them "sink" – allowing space between your eyes and the passage of your breath between them. Again and again without criticizing your efforts, allow your attention to return to your breath.

Becoming more quiet will make messages more accessible from your bodyself. Spontaneously images, memories, emotions and sensations will arise along with many, many thoughts. When a thought arises, notice it (bow to it) and then return to breathing, again and again. Leave everything just as it is. Do not try to get rid of anything in your mind. As in sensing practice, the point is not "doing", but "being with". Eventually you are likely to be able to rest into the experience of letting the many thoughts, feelings and images pass through you, even when you begin to sense you are on the verge of feeling overwhelmed.

Gradually you are likely to find you are able to stay with this experience for a longer time. You allow whatever needs to come up into your consciousness to pass through. You greet it and let it go. When you feel discouraged, you may be able to use that energy for your practice. Just be with that feeling and the sense of trying to get somewhere other than where you are right now. And remember - the more often you are distracted, the more practice you get returning to focus. You will find that as your ability to return to your focus strengthens, a kind of subtle energy builds. That building energy may give rise to your wanting to interrupt or shorten your session. Don't get up until the timer goes off. Experience what it is like to sit through your impatience or through your desire to do whatever seems more important than meditating at that moment. You are likely to make an important discovery if you can stay with it.

With continued practice you may find that even when you are not meditating you are noticing and able to stay with your inner experience of sensations, emotions, and intuition. You are likely to notice increased steadiness, calm and energy, all at the same time. You may discover the kind of gentle nonjudgmental effort necessary to return to your focus with the least disturbance of your process. You may find you are able to stay with the experience of Let Go . . more frequently and for increasingly longer periods because you have greater access to and can renew your connection with yourself again and again. Let Go . . cannot be forced but only invited. Like grace, falling asleep or falling in love. You make the invitation by preparation through sensing and then by allowing your attention to return to resting on your breath, again and again.

If you find you feel too "antsy" to sit still, try the following grounding experiment after you have done sensing work with your feet and neck. Sitting in a chair, slowly press into the floor with one foot as you exhale and then let up on the pressing as you inhale. Then press into the floor with your other foot as you exhale, as if you are sending your breath into the earth and then allowing your lungs to fill naturally as you let up on the pressing. Alternate sides for about five minutes. This movement while sitting is close to the experience of walking meditation, which may bring you to quiet in a storm!

Using a timer* encourages you to surrender to the Let Go . . sensory experience of sitting without having to call on your analytical mind to keep track of time. Lighting a candle and/or incense can cue your nervous system to shift to Let Go . . and over time, reminds you of your intention to reconnect. Take precautions so you are not likely to be interrupted. This is your special time to experience your breathing, your aliveness and deepen your focus. Find a quiet corner where you can sit undisturbed for a predetermined length of time. Start with an amount of time – say 5 or 10 minutes, which you sense you can stay with. Fifteen minutes works well for me in the morning after I have stretched, sensed and done a few core-strengthening exercises. When the meditation period is over, reading a passage from an inspirational book like Mark Nepo's "Book of Awakening" can deepen my bodyself connection. At bedtime, I sit for 5 to 15 minutes or so, depending on my need. I keep a pad of paper nearby in case I am inspired or want to remember something. If I write it down, I don't have to keep thinking about it!

Some Benefits and Pitfalls of Meditation Practice

Three essential elements of meditation practice - setting aside time, returning to a focus and cultivating a gentle attitude – empower you in specific ways to connect with your bodyself experience and the shift to Let Go . . I chose the word "empower" because its root, "poeir" means "to be able". The implication is that meditation practice empowers you to be "response-able" to your bodyself. Each of these distinct, but related benefits or empowerments will be discussed in the following section along with some of the pitfalls of meditation practice.

Focusing to Salve and Solve

Taking time to meditate can give you an experience of the value of slowing down and taking a break from the sometimes, mindless activity and tension of the Let's Go! mode. You create time and space to just be with whatever comes up as you attempt to focus on breathing. The necessity and rewards of taking breaks are addressed in each of the three listening practice chapters because listening and taking breaks are mutually interdependent. Taking a break helps you listen more clearly to bodyself messages and by listening to these messages you know when to take a break and what kind of break to take. Further, listening and following through on these messages is a potent source of self-soothing. In addition, during this period of relative quiescence, you are likely to discover solutions to situations that you were not even focusing on. Thus, breaks give the expected gift of salving and the unexpected gift of solving.

Salving

The first gift I received from meditation practice was the sense that I could comfort myself by focusing on breathing and allowing my thoughts to recede to the background. I could feel calmer and, yes, the word "collected" fits here too: not so pulled here and there by thoughts and feelings, worries and concerns. Coming back to breathing was soothing in that this action was in effect saying, "All this other does not matter right now; what matters is that I am here now, breathing, sitting, listening, softening, sinking into the earth and buoyed by breathing". I could rely on sitting to begin and end my day, calmer and more collected than I otherwise might have been.

However, this calmness sometimes came at a price. At those times I would feel kind of "spacey" after meditating. Just not quite "here". True, I seemed calmer on the surface, but deeper down was some subterranean pool of agitation of which I was barely aware. It stayed buried because I did not have the proper support to experience it through. Piling "calm" on top of "agita" * was the best I could do at the time. Once, during a weeklong meditation retreat tears and snot ran down my cheeks for several hours. Distressed, but steadfast, I had no idea what those tears were about. Years later in relational somatic therapy I realized that those tears had flowed from a yet-to-be-integrated traumatic experience of abandonment in childhood. Those were "trauma tears" not the "release tears" of true grieving that accompany integration and soothing.

But at that time of intense involvement in Zen meditation, I didn't yet know that what I most needed was an experience that was not available enough in childhood. And that was being connected to by a compassionate other as I experienced traumatic depths of despair, fear, anger, disappointment and grief. So when something in my present life triggered unresolved feelings arising from caretaker misattunement and childhood trauma I would become agitated and then shut down even more. When I finally found a therapist whom I came to deeply trust, I began to experience how frightened I was and had been. A sad, but ultimately, fortunate and growth promoting revelation! Intense feelings of anger, despair and grief had to be "experienced-through" and integrated in the presence of a skilled, attuned psychotherapist over many years in order to fully recover my bodyself. As a result my sitting practice was strengthened and I could cry deeply during meditation and come through to being more present afterwards.

Until then I did what I had done all my life, and that was to push away my helpless feelings without even being aware of what I was doing. I acted as if I didn't need anyone. What was actually true was that I didn't <u>want</u> to need anyone. This attitude is a common adaptation to inadequate emotional caretaking in childhood. When I sat in meditation at home, threatening feelings usually didn't come up. If they had I would have likely felt nearly as overwhelmed as I did in childhood when I learned to tense up, shut down and space out. Traumas, in this context, can be viewed as potentially <u>unfinished</u>, nonintegrated experiences in need of processing in the context of contact with a compassionate, attuned other.

Instead of spacing out during meditation, some people traumatized as children experience "freaking out" – becoming frightened and overwhelmed by the emotions and images that come up. In fact, re-experiencing emotions resulting from unresolved trauma can be <u>retraumatizing</u> rather than healing. If you feel uneasy or spooked by your experience meditating, consulting a therapist, especially one experienced with meditation could give you the support you need to go through whatever it is that is trying to make itself known to you. Even people who experience moderate anxiety when they sit quietly and focus on sensations could benefit from resolving underlying issues and the process can be life-changing. In the meantime, limiting your practice period to five minutes* or experimenting with walking meditation or Tai Chi or another form of meditation combined with movement like Yoga may be helpful.

With continued practice you may more often notice breathing, even when you are not formally meditating. You may be more likely to find yourself experiencing more quiet, calmness, noticing your surroundings and feeling sensations more often without even looking for them. Taking time-outs and softening in response to bodyself cues may occur more readily. You may feel more stable and resilient as you "sit" through many different types of experiences and come back to your bodyself again and again. You may find more of yourself in life and more life in yourself.

Solving

A second, unexpected gift of meditation practice was discovering that my bodyself knew things that I needed to know and usually ignored. Slowing down and paying attention allowed me to become more sensitive to my bodyself cues that something was amiss. For example, recently I had an experience that made me appreciate, once again, my meditation practice. I had put my laundry in the dryer, put the quarters in and pushed the coin slot. I closed the dryer door and left. Then something told me to go back, perhaps that "something" noticed that the sound of the dryer turning on was missing. Meanwhile I was distracted by such thoughts of "Too bad, I can't dry the pillowcases on the clothesline" and "Oh, I forgot to get the fabric softener sheet for the dryer". As I walked out of the laundry room all at once I felt the ground under my feet and the warm sun on my back and then I realized I "heard" no sound from the dryer. My bodyself sensed that sound was missing. I went back and checked. Sure enough, I had failed to push the crucial "Start" button. Opening to the sensations of the sun on my back brought me into the sensory dominant world of Let Go . . Then, suddenly I became aware of the sensation I had not experienced, but previous experience had led my bodyself to expect - the sound of the dryer.

Then as I wrote the previous paragraph, I wondered if I had put the laundry key back in the key bowl with my house keys. I remembered I had put my house keys and my laundry key in different pockets of my jacket when I was walking back to the house. I checked the key bowl, but only house keys were to be found. Immediately I got up and retrieved the laundry key from the pocket of this seldom-worn jacket. I wondered how long it would have taken to find the missing laundry key, if I hadn't acted on my sense of something incomplete in that moment. I felt grateful for my practice once again – a sweet gratefulness. And I am sure my gratitude will only grow with the years, as mindfulness practice helps coping with aging. So start now and don't avoid the sweet rush! You can experience the benefits of my Zen friend's admonishment "Be there before the accident happens!"

In addition to being less likely to misplace things, you will also notice that you are more likely to <u>find</u> missing things. You may find yourself focusing on and following up on sensations that you may have previously ignored. For example, one afternoon as I was balling up some plastic bags to put in the recycle drawer, I noticed a subtle feeling in my finger. Having put the bags in the drawer, I closed it and turned away. Yet my bodyself continued to signal me through the lingering sensation in my finger. Heeding its call, I opened the drawer and checked the bags. I located a small piece of paper in the bottom of one of the bags. This paper turned out to be a much needed receipt. How much time I would I have lost looking for this receipt had I not sensed and then retrieved it!

An early insight into this subtle messaging from my bodyself involved what I came to call a "headache premonition". Some years back when I had frequent painful headaches I observed that I would often get a headache following my remarking to myself or another, "It has been a long time since I have had a headache!" Inevitably (sure as sweetness), within a few hours, a headache would appear. Now some would conclude that I "caused" the headache by thinking about it in the first place. But I feel certain that the reason "headache" even came into my thoughts was because the more subtle sensing of my bodyself picked up on the cues of increasing tension in my neck. While I was not aware of the mounting, but subliminal tension, this other part was and so communicated this "awareness" the only way it could. It made "headache" come to mind and not having one at the moment, I realized I hadn't had a headache in a while and I said so. In fact, most likely the reason I was getting a headache in the first place was because I was not able to connect with what I needed at the moment. Now when it occurs to me that I haven't a headache in a while, I can treat that thought as a warning and take care of myself. In other words, I can be there, before the headache happens!

In a similar vein, you have probably had the experience of looking through some files or a stack of papers and lo, there is something you had needed but were not looking for at the moment. If you hadn't given yourself that time to just follow where you were led, you wouldn't have recovered that thing. Something in you "knew" to look there and you benefited by allowing it and by following through. It is akin to the experience of lying down when you have lost something and retracing your steps mentally. You ease into a restful Let Go . . attitude instead of frantically searching (Let's Go!). And voila! - the image of where it must be appears. Space is needed to illuminate the search. Meditation practice nurtures the possibility of allowing this space. As Virginia Wolfe observed, "It is in our idleness, our dreams that the submerged truth (or a lost item!) sometimes comes to the top"*. So when you are feeling frustrated, take a break, create a space and let yourself be led by what unfolds.

Focusing for Completion and Increasing Subtle Let Go . . Energy

The power of deepened focus gained from continually returning your attention to your breath will enable you to finish or allow completion of many kinds of situations both outside of and during the meditation experience. You will also experience the power of focused attention to bring about change by staying with the bodyself moment rather than trying to force change. This Let Go . . dynamic is due to focus not force - for the moment is the "moment" - a fulcrum for change.

The practice of meditation affords you the opportunity to experience completion. You take time out to just experience being with whatever comes up. Often what arises are uncompleted conversations, emotional issues, plans, and tasks. Creative ideas may come to you in response to a problem that you were trying to solve. (*She* has great ideas!) Sometimes all a nagging situation needs is to be experienced thoroughly for it to be completed. The nagging could be *her* begging *"Listen to me! I have something to tell you!"* When you listen, a feeling of tension reduction and satisfaction often follows. It is as if the <u>release</u> of the <u>holding</u> <u>pattern</u> of <u>incompletion</u> <u>frees</u> a <u>subtle</u> <u>energy</u> that is experienced as satisfying relief. When tension is dispelled, the once bound energy is freed. Your bodyself enjoys completion and rewards you with that satisfied, sweet feeling, "somewhere between peace and joy." Whether completion of an unfinished situation occurs passively as in the course of the meditation period or is the result of an active effort to complete a task, completion of unfinished situations is deeply relieving and satisfying**. Rest into that feeling and savor it!

Savoring

When you complete a task, you may experience a momentary Let Go . . shift - a sort of "mini-Let Go". . However if you immediately distract yourself with another task, you will miss the mini-Let Go . . and the simultaneous savoring of the experience of completion. Slowing down and finishing things allow for recovery from your Let's Go! activity. It makes *her* happy! Thoughts about the incomplete task no longer compete for your attention, the muscular holding pattern that keeps emotions in check dissolves and breathing announces the completion of the task with a longer exhalation followed by a regular, easy respiration rhythm. Completion frees emotional and muscular energy for the next activity whether it is a task, a conversation, a walk or a nap.

Developing a habit of completing tasks can give you a realistic sense of what you can actually accomplish in an hour, in a day, etc. A realistic appraisal of your energy will help you plan your time better and set better boundaries for yourself. As you come to savor the completion of a task as well as the rest in between tasks, you may discover that you have more energy to accomplish the next task, not to mention, for enjoying your life.

To give you a sense of the kind of satisfaction that is in store for you, when you pay attention to your bodyself messages about completing an activity, consider the following: Think back (hopefully, not too far back!) to the last time you ate just enough of the right kind of food at your mealtime. Recall the satisfaction you felt upon completion of that meal. You neither under- or over- ate. Your digestion was smooth and easy. You may have even felt a subtle sweet energy at the end of the meal. Afterwards, there were no self-recriminations, complaints or pains. The meal was over, complete - what lingered was the soothing sense of a meal well eaten and savored. In fact, you may have even remarked or thought about how satisfying that experience was. Just like Goldilocks said after she ate the little bear's porridge, "It was just right!"

Take another example from your organismic functioning: your skeletal muscles know the advantage in completing one task before starting another. If they could talk they would urge you to please finish what you were doing. Then they have a chance to rest and recover in order to keep from being tense and sore. A tense muscle is a partly contracted muscle. That means there are fewer fibers available for contraction when an action is needed. Fewer available fibers mean a weaker response. When you anticipate the future by worrying, your muscles contract in response. When you block from awareness what you are feeling, your muscles tense. When you rush around you miss important but subtle cues that could have led to the discovery of what needed to be completed. Worrying, tensing and rushing about commandeer muscular energy – no wonder you feel so tired. You are tired but still have so many things to finish. Why do you try to do so many things? What is it that you are not understanding or not wanting to accept about your limits? What do you need to discover to take better care of yourself?

When you allow yourself to finish a task, complete a conversation or express a feeling, your organism can rest and you can just "be". After resting, you have more energy and clarity for perceiving and for acting. Completion allows you to be ready for the next moment because you stayed with the present moment. You may be surprised at the amount of energy available to you as you experiment with this simple practice. When starting a new task, you will be less distracted by thoughts and therefore, more likely to stay with it to completion. You may find greater satisfaction upon task completion and at the same time, feel more uncomfortable when you don't complete what you are doing.

For example, when I have left something undone, I am likely to feel as if part of me is here and part of me is "over there" with the unfinished task. A case in point: one morning in the middle of making my bed, it occurred to me to put things out for breakfast. I debated whether to stay with the bed-making task or to interrupt myself. I decided to stay with it but then suddenly I found myself in the kitchen. Yet I couldn't remember what urge brought me to the kitchen. So I went back and finished the bed-making and then, upon re-entering the kitchen, it came back to me why I had come to the kitchen earlier. Suddenly, everything was in order – all of me came into focus and was present. Then I felt an energizing sense of relief. So when you discover you have started too many things, let them all go but one and complete that. Then go to the next one and stay with it until you feel the energizing satisfaction of completion. Avoid the frenetic, scattered Let's Go! energy associated with incompletion, being tense and being late and begin savoring the completion of what you can complete!

Once you have spent some time in the subtle, completion energy of Let Go . . you will notice when what you do begins to pull you in different directions. Feeling scattered can be felt through your bodyself as if something was intruding in your bodyself and vaguely disorienting you. For instance, when the picture hanging on the wall is at an angle, my bodyself feels a sense of imbalance as if something inside of me is not quite right. When you finish the task, you can no longer be fragmented by unresolved tension tugging at you due to incompleteness. A heightened awareness of what "scattered" feels like results from having sensed more deeply and having experienced more frequently, the subtle energy of Let Go . .

59

This need for completion and the ensuing satisfaction differs from an obsessive compulsive, Let's Go! anxious feeling because it <u>arises</u> from Let Go . . bodymindfulness. Completion simply feels "right" in the Zen sense of right, which means "complete" or whole. If the situation is completed, there is no trace, no more attachment to it. There is a moment of emptiness. And that signals the shift to Let Go. . For example, as I experience each breath completing itself, I find a home in just being. Expanding and contracting, the breathing cycle completes itself. I can rest-into this cycle. The next phase of the breath cannot occur without its opposite. Keeping my attention steady, I experience change. In the midst of change, I feel steady. Completion happens if I pay attention and keep my focus. Given that space, completion simply unfolds. The stuck places loosen, the pain dissipates, and the emotions release, the muscles soften and I feel life moving through me. Oftentimes I experience a sweet "All is Well" which could be savored if I had a "bodymind to do it!"

I can use the discovery of this subtle Let Go . . energy of completion to give myself a jump-start just before I sit down to write. I allow myself to complete one short task that has been nagging me. Once energized and happy, I can face the more demanding and less likely to be finished task ahead. A word of caution: discipline is needed here! Once the small task is complete, go to your larger task. Completing one small task after another one can deplete your energy for the larger one ahead.

A similar principle applies when attempting a large or complex task. Break it down into smaller pieces that can be completed and then savor each completion. When you have to clean the whole house, doing the easiest room first, gives sense of joy and completion that is immediate. In addition every time you walk back in, you can delight in Let Go . . energy of completion which may motivate you to do one more small task.

The discovery of being more likely to complete tasks and to feel greater satisfaction with doing so is not just a result of greater ability to stay with a focus but also results from your spending more time in Let Go . . Because you are slowing down, you are more likely to notice what is not completed and be more available to feel the satisfaction of completion when you do complete something.

The tendency to not complete a task may have to do with avoiding the feeling of emptiness as in "what now?" that can result from completion. The pause in between tasks that could refresh actually might threaten because some unwanted feeling or thought might arise. Or perhaps the pleasurable savoring of Let Go . . could actually be uncomfortable for you. For whatever reason, you may be compelled to deny yourself that reward. Perhaps you feel unworthy or judge yourself as self-indulgent if you take the time to savor the bodyself moment of completion? In any case, the regular completion of tasks may escape you until you can tolerate feeling what is actually going on inside you. And you may need some help to embrace what you are beginning to feel.

Deepening Focus for Containment of Emotional Energy

The ability to maintain a focus and not be distracted for long by thoughts, activities and addictions builds with continued meditation practice. Energy builds when I don't allow myself to be distracted by doing whatever occurs to me in the middle of something else. I gain the Let Go . . energy of completion instead of the Let's Go! excitement of new stimulation attendant on distracting myself over and over again. I am rewarded with a sense of agency and heightened energy. Now the challenge becomes containing this energy. Increased energy can be threatening even if it is pleasurable. Sometimes the very fact the energy is pleasurable makes it feared. It might be helpful to entertain such questions as "How good am I allowed to feel? How much energy am I able to feel? What emotions are tolerable to me?"

The energetic issue of containment also occurs when emotions start to come up during meditation. Emotions can arise from incomplete or unfinished situations. An emotion is a signal that moves through the bodyself and presses for expression or action. If an emotion feels threatening we are likely to do something to not feel it with the result that the situation stays incomplete. We may experience tension in the form of increased thinking, muscular holding, anxiety, depression or dissociating and becoming numb or spacey. We may feel an urge toward whatever we usually do to quell this internal disturbance – food, work, sex, drugs, caffeine, etc.

If you suspect an emotion is trying to emerge during meditation, you could try asking yourself, "If I was feeling something with respect to this situation what might it be?" This is one way to get in touch with your emotional voice. If you continue to feel anxious and not able to sense or move through an emotion that starts to come up during meditation, you might find help by consulting a meditation teacher or therapist familiar with meditation.

Focusing to release pain

The ability to contain emotional energy is also at issue when I focus on physical pain. One night, I discovered that when I connected with the on and off pulsing pain of a toothache, I actually fell asleep. When I first sensed it that night as I was lying in bed, wanting to fall asleep, I was alarmed. "What can I do about this disturbing pain at this late hour? Do I have to get dressed and find an open drug store?" Then I remembered reading about the possibility of pain management by going into the pain, not away from it. I focused directly on where the pain was coming from and joined with it. In a Buddhist sense, "I died into the moment" of pain as I gave up my resistance to the pain by tensing against what I was feeling and by being anxious. The pain really wasn't so bad once I settled into it. And voila! I fell asleep. The toothache disappeared and never came back. I'm not recommending this technique as a way to avoid dental work, but as a stopgap measure which saved me from a fitful night of anxiously trying to avoid pain.

"Dying into the moment" refers to completely letting go into the experience of the moment and/or following through with some expression or action as I did when I focused on the unpleasant sensations attendant on smoking and put out the cigarette. However, containment of emotional energy was not an issue in that case because I was not trying to stop smoking. In the above example I focused on the pain in my tooth, and in the next example on pain in my neck.

During a writing period I used the power of focused attention to join with the pain I was feeling in my neck. I knew I was also feeling frustrated with writing as well as with the lack of fun in my life at the time. It is hard to say what came first, the awareness of the deprivation, the frustration, or the pain. Pressing my fingers directly on the pain site on my neck focused my attention on the pain and then I let sounds come out which expressed the pain I was feeling. As I cried, a series of visual images appeared which allowed me to understand what the tension was all about. Fortunately I previously had had enough emotional support from my therapist to be able to go into pain and feel the surfacing emotions all the way through. So joining with the pain in this way, freed the energy of my emotions bound up in the tension of resisting the pain and resulted in a shift to Let Go . . As the neck pain dissipated, I rested deeply and awakened refreshed.

Keeping your focus by staying with your bodyself can transform the experience of the tension of pain into the pleasure of release. What was once annoying, anxious-making and tension-producing is no longer, just is and then it is gone. For example, one night I experimented for the first time with taking a couple of over-the-counter sleeping pills, hoping they would enable me to fall asleep quickly. I was trying to go to sleep an hour and a half earlier than I had the night before. I knew, from previous experience (and from knowledge of the sleep-wake cycle) that I would have trouble falling asleep that much earlier than had been my recent habit. With a busy workday ahead of me, I felt desperate.

Fall asleep, I did, but three hours later I awoke with an uncomfortable frenzied, fidgetiness in my legs. They just couldn't find any way to lie peacefully. My right hip and leg was tense and achy. Half awake, I found myself thinking stress-inducing thoughts like "This must be what 'restless leg' syndrome is like. This is horrible, I'll never get back to sleep, I won't be able to be present for my clients tomorrow and then I'll feel bad about myself, etc, etc." I tried various positions, first one side then the other side. No help there. My legs grew intolerably antsy. I felt trapped and helpless. Then I decided to put my aching leg outside the covers. The cool air helped. As my eyes closed, I tried to sink deep into just being there and resting. But the struggle continued.

Finally I remembered to focus my attention exactly on the pain itself. I kept bringing my attention to the worst edgy, painful tension site. I drifted into sleep and dreamed the following dream: I was getting deep tissue bodywork from two bodyworkers. One, a woman, was working on my chest area as I lay on my left side. The other, a man, worked into my posterior right hip muscles. The tense edginess in my hip welcomed the attention. As he shifted his focus to work simultaneously into the deep anterior hip muscles, I was filled with a sense of exhilaration, gratitude and relief. His impulse was right on with laser-like intensity – the intensity of the tension was matched and melted into the ecstatic (remember I was dreaming this) sense of being met. This is the epitome of a "hurts-so-good" experience. A huge "Yes"! telegraphed through my bodyself. I felt my leg jerk spasmodically several times as the tension released. As I awakened I was aware my leg had been jerking! The pain was gone and I eased back into sleep. The next morning I eagerly wrote down this healing dream experience and threw the sleeping pills away. I vowed to stick to valerian or passion flower tea as a sleep aid from then on.

In order to focus so closely on the pain I have to be able to tolerate the helplessness I feel. Instead of trying to get away from it sometimes I enter it and then I often find myself surprisingly empowered. Certainly some would approach this situation by reaching for painkillers or by focusing on the thought "This is not my body!" or "This is only my body!" Such "rising above" thoughts are a good tool for dissociating if I was being tortured, but do not increase my capacity for compassion with myself or for intimacy with others. When I dissociate from my bodyself, I leave myself open to almost anything happening to me because I don't feel it. Just as when I tense against pain, it becomes worse, when I dissociate as a way to deal with pain, more harm can come to my bodyself. In the previous example, I was able to surrender to the sense of helplessness I felt and take action by focusing on the pain. Staying with the pain allowed a deep bodyself release and I was able to then easily fall asleep.

Using focused attention to deal with annoying sounds is another way of "dying into the moment" of irritation and letting go. I have used it when I found myself irritated by the sounds made by gardeners and construction workers while I was meditating. However, I haven't had much luck dying into the sound of a car alarm. But then, that sound is, by design, a nuisance. You can discover for yourself the power of focused attention to undo a habitual response by focusing on the tickle that usually leads to a sneeze. You have to summon great will power to suppress a sneeze because your body really likes to sneeze away obstructions. Sneezing feels so good, it wouldn't surprise me if endorphins were released. On the other hand if you want to get even more enjoyment out of your sneezes, try the suggestion of my colleague, Dr. Beverly Morse and breathe rapidly and deeply through your mouth before you release the sneeze!

Focusing to ameliorate addictive behavior

The containment of increased energy and emotion becomes an issue when focused attention is used to deal with addictions, since addictive behavior often serves the avoidance of unwanted emotion. On the one hand, simply becoming more aware of how the habit manifests begins to subtly change the behavior, even when no effort toward change is made. For instance, changes in eating and spending habits often occur in the course of keeping track of ongoing behavior in a journal. In a similar vein, many people find that writing about emotional concerns and troubling issues in a journal helps them manage their emotions and is soothing. Paying attention itself is to some extent "containing" because it is like listening to yourself and asking yourself "What is it?" as you do in meditation. Focusing without judgment on what you are doing indicates that you care, that you are interested and curious, and therein lies the "cure".

On the other hand, if the feelings that are being denied by the addictive behavior are too threatening, it is less likely that you will experience spontaneous change simply by paying "even-handed" attention to the addictive behavior. In fact, you may not be able to pay attention in an even-handed way because you fear feeling deprived and eventually want to rebel and indulge. You may find yourself forgetting to pay attention or to keep track. When my smoking addiction let loose of me, it was in the wake of my following through on the unpleasant sensations I experienced before I put out the cigarette. I did not "try" or struggle, I only noticed how my bodyself was responding and then I followed through. In any case, unless you can "die into the moment" of noticing what you are doing, you are likely to feel anxious when you try to change your addictive behavior. Support for feelings is needed so they can be <u>felt</u> <u>through;</u> then, the power of focused attention to lead to real behavioral change.

Experiencing deeply threatening emotion may be just too difficult to do alone; if so you'll need the attuned presence of another to help you ride the emotional wave underlying addictive behavior. Together, you can begin to hear the cries and the needs that once went unheeded and begin to respond to your bodyself voice with soothing embrace and acceptance. With repeated experiences of being heard by another, you can gradually come to self-soothe by compassionately listening to your bodyself and following through on what you truly need or feel, instead of engaging an addictive behavior or dissociation. Then you are more likely to find yourself experiencing that subtle, gentle Let Go . . energy as you, again and again, connect with your bodyself rather than disconnect with denial or addiction.

The result of my having experienced this "in-between" place occurred during one morning's meditation period as I followed up on a suggestion I read in Mark Nepo's "Book of Awakening"*. As I sat in meditation and allowed myself to re-experience the last words spoken to me by my leave-taking partner, ten years prior, I felt myself give into the pain of loss and of longing for something that while once very sweet could never be again. At the same time I could hear the birdsongs outside, the "tinking" sounds of the water beginning to boil in the ceramic tea kettle, the mechanical rumble of the refrigerator compressor while tears slid down my cheeks. As I gave into the sobs I found myself contained by this "ground of sound" and the "almost sound" of my breathing. Those tears had waited a very long time to be shed – they were waiting for the appropriate bodyself awareness container to be created. I suspect that had I not already worked through the pain of childhood abandonment, I could not have allowed these deep feelings to emerge without becoming overwhelmed by them.

With continued meditation practice you are likely to find yourself feeling contained or grounded by your awareness of the steady rhythm of breathing, the periodic sounds of birds, the wind in the trees, the whirring of the ceiling fan, the waves on the shore as you give yourself to experiencing through whatever comes up. Your capacity to simply be with what you experience without thoughts hijacking your focus will grow and will allow you to gaze at the moon and find it suddenly become three dimensional just as you feel a burst of peaceful, joyful excitement all through your bodyself. Gradually you develop the discipline of resting-into and being contained by an awareness larger than yourself and you shift into the Let Go . . moment.

Focusing for Discipline and Balance of Let's Go! with Let Go . .

Meditation is a subtle discipline with very practical consequences. As your mindfulness deepens, you will find yourself spontaneously slowing down, noticing sensory cues, taking breaks, finishing tasks, finding things. And since Let Go . . becomes more easily accessed, you are better able to meet the challenge of balancing Let's Go! with Let Go . .

Keeping your focus is important for deepening and perpetuating both Let Go . . and Let's Go! However, staying with Let's Go! is much easier than deepening Let Go . . because Let's Go! chemicals support heightened arousal and a sharpened, narrowed focus. Furthermore, Let's Go! easily overrides Let Go . . as it must for your immediate survival. But long-term survival requires you to learn to shift back and forth between Let's Go! and Let Go . . as it most benefits your organism. To recover from Let's Go! you need to slow down, listen to bodyself messages and take care of yourself.

With increased meditation practice you will be confronted with choosing between following messages from your bodyself and from your workaday mind. And gradually you may find that you can mindfully accommodate them both. For example, as I took a break in teaching a massage class, I could feel that my hands were slightly oily. On the way to the kitchen to wash them, my Let's Go! mind interrupted and wanted me to check my voice mail messages. The latter impulse brought a rush of anticipation - "Did anyone call, do I have to respond, what is going on in my private practice, with my family and friends?" This fine fodder for the Let's Go! mind is much more exciting than taking care of the mild annoyance of the coating of lotion on my hands. I entertained ignoring the sensation in my hands – "After all, they don't feel that oily! But what about the fact that you just touched three or four people; how about getting that feeling off your hands so you just have you there? That's what you tell your students to do!"

Then I felt the craving of the other part of me for stimulation – the stimulation of potential contact – "maybe there are calls for me – someone to respond to – something exciting." Yet I haven't completed this other task; I just came out of the classroom having worked with several students. Completing that task means washing my hands. My bodyself sensation (sticky hands) pulls me toward the kitchen and my Let's Go! driven mind pulls me toward the office to check messages. Catching myself in the midst of these competing needs allowed me to give in to my bodyself need for completion before I responded to the pull toward stimulation from others. My reward was the delicious relief of slowing down and connecting to my bodyself, not to mention the feeling of clean hands. I took a little longer to really experience the washing and rubbing. I savored that sweet satisfaction as I strolled (rather than rushed) down the corridor to the answering machine, my paws refreshed! Letting go readied me for the next Let's Go!

It is not a question of "either/or" but rather of listening and pacing so that you can connect with yourself and come into balance. In Let Go . . being, you embrace and open, in Let's Go! doing, you defend and protect. Both energies are necessary and complete each other. Let Go . . energy is sweet, soft, subtle and soothing. It builds slowly and is unmistakable in its gentleness as it gathers. It is the energy of surrendering, rather than conquering, which is the energy of Let's Go! Let's Go! energy is strong, surging, and stimulating. In a Let's Go! rush, you spend rather than build energy. Let's Go! energy depletes, while Let Go . . energy restores. See Appendix A: Yin and Yang of Balancing Let's Go! with Let Go . .

The quality of the effort you make as you continually return your attention back to your focus is key to shifting to Let Go . . You, of course, have to make some effort. But this effort has to be at once gentle and resolute. It is the effort of consciously surrendering to your immediate experience. You only have to attend to what is there in the moment, without trying to change it. As you focus on breathing, you give up efforts to judge or to change it. As you allow your eyes to soften, you give up efforts to see. Rather than holding a pose, you let sitting find you as you respond to the dynamic tension between the pull of gravity and breathing. As your thoughts and feelings pass through you, you give up efforts to control them. You allow the experience of what is, to move through you. And all the while you remember to return your attention to your breathing. And therein lies the rub.

In order to consciously surrender to the experience of "now" you will need to have the inner support to feel emotions such as fear, anger, grief and joy without dissociating. Unresolved trauma whether due to inadequate caretaker nurturing or abandonment and/ or intrusion may make it difficult for you to experience through whatever feelings come up. Threatening feelings like helplessness, rage, or terror that result from non-integrated trauma may stand in the way of your being able to deeply self-soothe or receive soothing from another. For, optimal self-soothing requires that you are able to connect to your bodyself or to allow someone to connect to you. Otherwise, you are likely to turn to addictive substances or behaviors or to dissociation when threatening feelings arise because you can't adequately self-soothe or take in soothing from others.

A later chapter is devoted to explaining how you can become optimally self-soothing by taking the risk of letting another person know who you really are and what you feel. When the other can be present with you in an attuned way, you are more likely to surrender to the experience of your feelings and not dissociate from them. Giving up your efforts to be something (ie strong, smart, successful, helpful), you are more likely to experience deep contact with yourself and another. Can you imagine that someone would want to be with you, just as you are? I can't imagine a more deeply soothing experience to embody. Embody means literally to "in-corporate" and the challenge is whether I can "take into" the core of my corporeal being the sense "I matter just as I am". As a result I can call on this now embodied experience to ground myself whether I'm alone or with another.

In sum, through meditation practice an attitude of resolute gentleness toward yourself and your efforts to practice can be cultivated. As you experience more and more the gentle attitude of returning your attention to your breath, you may become gentler toward yourself. You "show up" for yourself and at the same time refrain from being hard on yourself when you notice you are not showing up and being hard on yourself! You're more aware of your limits, of the pain of transgressing them and more likely to pull back and take care of yourself. As with sensing, you can develop the subtle discipline of paying attention and yielding to messages from your bodyself. You will find you are taking tasks to completion and not losing track of things as often. You let your bodyself "re-mind" you. You are likely to be impressed with how "right on" this part of you is as you allow it to speak to you more often.

You are likely to experience more Let Go . . energy in your life. You are more likely to let go of trying to make things happen all the time and begin to feel that what is happening is just what happens, and may even have a sense of rightness or completeness to it. The sense of rightness comes because you are less tense and in a more accepting Let Go . . frame of mind. As you invite Let Go . . you will be less likely to be anxious about the way things unfold because you can rest-into yourself and breathing. You can more easily remind yourself that things can work out just fine even if not the way you expected. You are building a home in the Let Go . . moment as you practice returning again and again to your breath.

As your focus deepens and your bodyself connection strengthens you have the opportunity to join with and dissolve tension, pain and turmoil. However, you may find, as I did, that sometimes you need help in contacting what is upsetting you whether it is pain, tension, emotion or a dream. The next chapter on listening to your emotional voice will help you understand and begin to penetrate your resistance to listening to your bodyself voice. The rewards of listening to your emotional voice are accessing greater vitality, humor, creativity and self-soothing.

6

LISTENING TO YOUR EMOTIONAL VOICE

"S/he has gifts for you."

Why Listen to Your Emotional Voice?

Of the three listening practices, listening to your emotional voice* is likely to be your greatest challenge - and will reap your greatest reward. Through sensing, you learn to rest into gravity and breathing – you find your ground in the forces of nature. Through meditating, you come to rest into the experience of returning your attention to breathing, so no matter what else is going on, you can find your ground in the experience of an abiding awareness. However, surrendering to the pull of gravity and the rhythm of breathing is one thing, but experiencing the pull of emotion and the threat of past or present pain is quite another.

In fact, sensing and meditating can be misused to foster a transcendent state that for the most part bypasses emotion – a "spiritual bypass", so to speak. When that happens you may feel a little spacey, and others may experience you as a bit distant or aloof. A price you may pay for such transcendence is less availability for intimate contact with others and your bodyself. Listening to your emotional voice, however, invites you to deeply contact yourself so that you can tap the source of your humanness and vitality and experience the expansiveness of your joy as well as the depth of your sorrow and pain. As you can allow this deep contact, you are likely to discover compassion for both yourself and for others.

Here's an example of listening to my emotional voice:

One morning while working on how to begin this chapter I found myself making false start after false start. My frustration mounted. In desperation I lay down. Sensing led me to feel how my feet were constricted by the afghan that covered them. Freeing my toes liberated my attention from obsessive thinking, and meditating helped me stay present with my experience of lying and feeling frustrated, but it wasn't until I could join with the pain and frustration of so many false starts that I began to feel movement inside me. The act of focusing on the physical and emotional pain I was experiencing embodied the question, "What is the matter?" As I let myself go into the pain the tears flowed. With the tears came images of another frustrating situation involving a family member from whom I had received a message that morning - just one more frustrating situation with no clear solution and about which I felt helpless and sad.

The crying ended in a deep breath. That breath seemed to grasp at life, having been released from the task of holding back my feelings. I witnessed how what was living in me could take care of itself, if only I would feel it and allow its expression. All it needed from me was my taking the time to ask, "What is the matter?" and to lie down, sense my bodyself and feel through what came up. With the deep, expanding breath came the experience of what it was that I had been trying to write about. Namely, entering the pain and experiencing the constriction yielded to the expansion of breath, energy flow and inspiration.

Sensing and meditating helped me notice what I was feeling. However, I was only able to embrace the emotions that came up because I was not too afraid to feel them. Were I too frightened of being overwhelmed by a sense of powerlessness, I would still be feeling frustrated and tense. Connecting with my bodyself not only involves feeling sensations but also emotions. Similarly, through sensing I can feel how my toes are constrained and allow more space. Through listening to my emotional voice I can feel <u>how</u> I hurt and in so doing allow myself to open. I may need to take a break, not just because I am experiencing tension here or there, but also because I have worked too long and need to play. My toes don't feel lonely or deprived but <u>I</u> sometimes do. The question is whether I can allow myself to feel my emotional needs? Does feeling my loneliness or deprivation threaten me with feeling helpless, worthless and overwhelmed? And if I dare not feel it, how can I do anything about it?

Emotional pain is often more difficult to connect to than bodily pain – even if the bodily pain is the result of emotional pain, as it often is. You may have noticed a certain pain in your heart when you thought of a really hurtful situation. A pained heart <u>hurts</u>. This distinction between bodily and emotional pain is subtle because you are likely to have an emotional reaction to whatever bodily pain you feel. Further, you may attempt to block whatever emotional pain might be threatening by tensing muscles and holding your breath. Pain is thus created through constriction and is identified as a bodily pain. Experiencing emotional pain, often much more so than bodily pain, may threaten your sense of self by bringing up issues of vulnerability, helplessness and humiliation.

Having had the repeated experience of a soothing connection with another person lays the foundation for feeling emotions and not being overwhelmed by them. Ideally this connection occurs in the context of adequate nurturing in childhood, and requires accurate sensing of the child's needs for emotional <u>containment</u> as well as for <u>stimulation</u>. You learn to experience emotion in tolerable amounts through the caretaker's attentive response to your momentary bodyself state. Your "good enough" caretaker does not allow your distress to become overwhelming, but rather connects with you and soothes you through eye contact, a gentle voice and physical holding. She makes repeated attempts to find out "<u>what</u> <u>is</u> <u>the</u> <u>matter?</u>" Gradually you are able to give up tension and rest-into contact with her - you are soothed and contained. In this way you learn how to experience emotions and needs and not be overwhelmed by them. This embodiment of emotional "self-regulation" allows you to shift from Let's Go! excitation to Let Go . . ease.

This principle of containment applies to the positive emotions such as joy and sensual pleasure as well as the so-called "negative" emotions of fear, shame, disgust, anger and grief. You needed your caretaker to delight in your excitement as much as you needed her to soothe your upset and to back off when you were in danger of being over-stimulated. The sensitivity of the interactions with your caretaker teaches your nervous system how to regulate your bodyself energy – how to calm down or build excitement without shutting down - not too much, not too little. Your capacity to be spontaneous, expansive, to interpret and express your emotions, to honor your needs, to encourage and soothe yourself is nurtured or hindered by early caretaking experiences. Thus, your ability to emotionally self-regulate (to go through the emotional recovery cycle) as an adult depends directly on how you were responded to as a child.

If your caretaker did not respect your needs for sensitive connection and soothing your bodyself likely responded by shutting down and tensing up and/or dissociating when strong emotions or intense stimulation threatened. That was all your nascent bodyself could manage to protect you from increasing external or internal stimulation. You may have had to make do with living in an emotionally and physically constricted inner world. To open to bodyself aliveness and the capacity for self-soothing, you may benefit from the experience of an attuned therapist being there to encourage you as you give up holding against your emotions, little by little. Your self-protective, judgmental attitude toward your vulnerability and emotions can then gradually give way to resonance with your bodyself voice and you become more self-soothing.

Listening to your emotional voice is a double-edged sword – in order to experience more vitality and joy, you must also be able to feel your pain and despair. Feeling clearly how you hold against your emotional voice will ultimately make more energy available to you. If your caretaking experience as a child was less than adequate, you will likely need the support of another to plumb the depths of this listening practice. In the next chapter, the nature of those deficits will be explored as well as how to understand and deal with the resulting resistance to taking care of yourself. In the meantime, you can experiment with the suggestions and invitations offered in the following sections.

In sum, *she* has gifts for you. Listening to *her* can bring more humor, joy, spontaneity, fun, passion, compassion, flow, rest, creativity, emotional sensitivity and responsiveness into your life. You are likely to become more able to soothe and encourage yourself. You will be less likely to get stuck in emotional tangles or experience "creative blocks". You will be more likely to penetrate your resistance to taking care of yourself and gradually give up your addictions. You may experience being in synch with life more often – the quiet joy that everything is "just right" as it is - and be more open to joining with others.

Personalizing the Emotional Voice

I like to call this other part of me, *"her"* because the term reminds me of my humanness. I am not an object even if I was sometimes treated as if my feelings didn't matter and even if I came to treat myself that way sometimes. Calling my emotional voice *"her"* reminds me that *she* is a "being" to relate to, to build trust with, to get to know. I cannot control *her*, I can only invite *her*. I can be curious about *her* and find out what *she* likes and what makes *her* happy. I know when I get it right because I feel a certain sweetness and gratefulness in response. *Her* happiness sometimes feels like the love of a child. Other times it is a feeling of excitement or a sense of grace. *Her* tears touch my heart for *she* is my heart. And being my heart, *she* resonates with the hearts of others.

I call this response *"her"* because I feel more when I imagine or sense that I am connecting to a delightful, creative, vulnerable, spirited part of myself. If I just think of connecting to the right side of my brain or my organism, I don't have the feeling of desire and compassion that I do when I call it *"her"*. Consider the difference in emotional tone between asking yourself, "What does it want?" and "What is the matter?" I am less likely to be emotionally touched when I regard this part of myself as an "organism" or an "it". When I use the word *"her'* I am more likely to appreciate *her* vulnerability and feel sorry when I ignore *her*. When I treat an urging as *her* voice, I feel closer to my humanness. Feeling distant from my feeling self is how I spent most of my life. While meditating and sensing were to some degree soothing to me, these practices did not allow me to fully embrace my emotional voice. I ultimately discovered that in order to soothe myself I needed a deeper connection to my emotional voice and that was made possible through attuned contact with a therapist. Now both sensing and meditating support my awareness of *her*. What you decide to call this part of you, if indeed you call it anything, is up to you. The point is to experiment with whatever helps you to come into better connection with <u>your</u> bodyself.

While your emotional voice is not a child or even your "inner child", it has some childlike qualities. As you nurture your connection with your emotional voice, it in turn, nurtures and helps you. It likes regularity yet is the source of spontaneity. All work and no play makes it go away. Getting in touch with your emotional voice can give you humor and heart, inspiration and innuendo, fun and fantasy, emotion and energy, spontaneity and sensual delight as well as compassion for yourself and others. In short, you become more human and more alive. Calling *her*, "*her*" (or "*him*") can make relating to your bodyself a more personal process. Over the course of this connecting and reconnecting, you can discover your deeply human nature.

Experiments in Finding *Her* Voice

What follows are some suggestions for how you can join with this oftentimes delightful energy, no matter what you choose to call it. I hope that by sharing my discoveries you will feel some resonance and experiment for yourself. So, take your time and notice, focus and follow through. If you have trouble following through, refer to the next chapter on resistance.

One sure way to invite the presence of this sweet, playful, wise part of you is to slow down and pay attention to what you are sensing and doing. Connecting with your emotional voice is really about <u>reconnecting</u> with your bodyself. You will find *her* and lose *her* countless times. At every reunion you will experience some sense of ease, sweetness, energy or joy. Your mission is to find out what pleases *her* and brings *her* back or allows *her* to stay longer. As you do you will increase your capacity to de-stress by shifting to Let Go . .

Ask *Her*, "What Do You Want To Do?"

Listen, feel, sense and go toward what *she* likes . . . One morning while still lying in bed, I checked in with *her* about how to start the chapter on listening to the emotional voice. I wanted to know how to encourage you, the reader, begin to listen for the "*her*" in you. *She* replied, *Just tell them what I like to do!* Great idea! Instead of the stretching and yawning that I have learned to do, *she* would rather undulate, wiggle and jiggle. *She* likes curvy, wavy movement. *She* likes to rock back and forth. *She* enjoys shaking and even throwing herself around. *She* likes to surrender to gravity and see where *she* ends up. *She* experiments without much thought. In short, *she* is playful. *I like to make noise, she* says, and proceeds to do just that. Amazingly enough, in that moment *her* sounds were joined by those of the construction workers across the street (who, of course, could not hear *her*!). They were howling like dogs and cats and a random parrot or two when one of them sang out "Welcome to the Jungle". Talk about synchronicity. I was astonished, not to mention, amused.

I had a brief fantasy (*her* idea!) of getting up and crossing the street to howl with them. I must admit I can do a very good cat and dog or rather, *she* can. I was elated that these grown macho men had lost it for a while. (Or maybe found it!) What better validation could I (or *she*) get? *She* is good at knowing when it is time to play. When you listen to *her*, you will feel more in tune with the world and experience a sense of flow - a sense that everything is just right, just as it is.

How about trying this? On the way home from work ask your *"her"* what would be a satisfying way to end the day. Again, notice any images, flashes, urges, sensations or emotions that come up. Notice the words of songs that may suddenly sound in your head. *She* rarely speaks in words but rather prefers a more subtle and sensual language. *She* has been trying to communicate with you throughout the day but you may have missed it. Now you have a chance to slow down and pay attention. Notice what makes *her*/you happy. You can tell when you get it right because you will feel good – at ease, relieved, maybe even lighter and sweeter.

Or, the next time you go to the beach let yourself respond to any impulse toward spontaneous actions such as falling to your knees in the sand as you sense its inviting warmth. For example *she* led me to discover the wonder of viewing the ocean upside down by bending over forward, head down so I could take in the view from between my legs! Or on another occasion while running across the sand I suddenly turned and started running backwards in wide curving arcs – fueled by the delightful exhilaration of following what *she* wanted.

Ask *Her*, "What is the Matter?"

The question, "What is the matter?" can evoke an attitude of paying attention as you would to a child - with tenderness, interest and compassion. That is, if you are not afraid or ashamed of your own vulnerability. If you notice you are feeling repelled by the idea of asking yourself "What is the matter?" it may be because of your own fear of being weak, needy or vulnerable. If you think this might be an issue for you, read on – this <u>fear</u> could be a very important source of resistance to being able to take good care of yourself.

Ask yourself "What is the matter?" when you find yourself tired, anxious, depressed or cranky. Ask yourself out loud and then wait for a feeling, an urge, an image, some tension or a sensation to appear. Ask again. In response, you may find yourself holding or touching yourself in some way. Stay with that – exaggerate it. This is a communication from your bodyself – your *"her"* – your nonverbal right-brain functioning. Or you may notice that you are staring at something or your feet have taken you to another room. Give yourself time to take that subtle indication seriously. What is it trying to tell you? Its message will be clearer if you give it your full attention. If you ignore it like a mother who ignores a plea from a child, it will eventually stop talking to you. You need this connection if you want to live with full vitality. *She* will withhold *her* treasure of pleasure, energy, health and well-being if you do not take *her* seriously. As you follow through on what *she* is trying to tell you, you will gradually shift to Let Go . . Let Go. . is where *she* thrives, so you more than just survive.

Talk Out Loud

Not only is it a good idea to ask *her* questions out loud, but also to answer in kind. This practice may seem strange to you especially if you haven't talked to yourself in a while. You may be surprised how making your self-talk audible cuts through the rumination and gets to the point. My experience is that when I speak my thoughts out loud the words convey more emotional tone than when I am just thinking. Consequently, I am more likely to take myself seriously and respond. Or maybe even laugh at myself. In any case, my bodyself condition is more likely to change for the better when I move from my head to my heart and feel what I am saying.

In my experience *her* messages are more like telepathic awareness, a "felt-sense" of my emotional response. Just making sounds to express this sense would be actually closer to my experience of my inner response, yet I find some satisfaction and clarity, not to mention delight in the words that come out. And sometimes I am deeply touched by what *she* says to me.

Give Voice to Emotion: *"You're Scaring Me!"*

For example, one evening as I was showering, I noticed I was absolutely terrorizing myself with worry about a situation which occurred earlier in the day. I was haranguing and tormenting myself about a "mistake" I had made at work. At this point, I had done all that could be done and I needed to get some sleep. As I concentrated on the feelings and tension I was experiencing, I became aware that I was doing this to myself (as opposed to not having a choice about what was happening to me). As this recognition crystallized, I felt a response in me of pain and fear. It expressed itself in the audible protest, *"You're scaring me!"* I paused. *Her* poignant, plaintive tone and *her* words riveted my attention. *"Don't tell me scary stories before I go to bed. I hate that! Stop!""*

Hearing this voice pleading and protesting all in the same breath made me feel really sorry. I stopped terrorizing myself. I recognized *her* plaintive tone and sensed the underlying anger and demand. That was what I would have liked to have expressed to my caretaker. Failing that, I had become as relentless in my torment of myself as he was in his demands. He was not moved by my cries. But now I had a chance to change this pattern. I heard *her* plea and stopped. I felt sorry I was causing *her*/me so much pain.

For the rest of the sleep preparation time that evening I focused on making my way as gentle and soothing to myself as possible. I had already endured quite enough. For this technique to work of course, you have to allow yourself to feel how vulnerable you are and feel deserving of letting yourself off the hook. In any case, you probably can imagine how surprised, touched and gratified I was that I found myself connecting with *her* and acting compassionately toward myself.

Give Voice to Sensation: *"It's Cold!" "It's Soft!"*

Contacting your emotional voice will help you pace yourself, as does paying attention to your sensations and what they tell you. In fact you can give your sensations a voice by responding to what you sense. For instance, as you get out of the shower the cold air might shock you a little. You could say, "Yikes! It's freezing", or "I'm freezing" – with some emotion in your voice. Maybe add a little movement like shaking or trembling or a little toe dance for emphasis instead of stoically standing silently while you grab a towel and dry yourself off. Why do this? In order to feel your life force, to feel energized, to have fun, to get in touch with your experience, to get out of your head and just be with what is right now – in short, to shift to Let Go . .

Another example of talking out loud in order to get more in touch with *her* is to simply speak aloud what you are sensing at the moment. You climb into bed and feel the soft sheets and say, "Mmmmmm, I like this . . . soft". Just keep it simple. Giving a voice to your experience is meant to deepen your experience of the moment by bringing your more into contact with your bodyself.

Express! Don't Compress!

An interesting but painful experiment in giving voice to what you sense can be experienced the next time you bump your head or your hip or shin or toe. Instead of sucking it up and pretending it didn't hurt, try a vocalization about the pain. "Ow! That hurts! Yikes! I'm sorry! @#&!!!" Cry, if you can. My experience is that if I allow myself to express that pain I feel and especially, if I cry, the pain goes away faster. This may be due in part to the fact that endorphins are secreted in tears of anguish. I forget about it sooner and the bump is less palpable. In any case the crying and vocalization is a kind of working through and acceptance. Then I'll be less likely to take the repressed upset out on someone else by being irritable or by making a disparaging remark to myself thus adding insult to injury. Just feel the pain as it happens, allow the needed expression and then it dissipates.

The emotional expression helps bring the incident to completion. You allow your bodyself to react and cry and that itself is soothing. Would you force a child to pretend it wasn't hurting – to deny the child the truth of that experience? Allow the truth to be expressed and it will be over sooner. If you don't, you will likely find there will be some consequence of your denial down the road, like reduced awareness, increased tension and banging your head again! Pay attention next time you bump yourself – you will see what I mean! Give yourself a chance to be a sensitive human and honor your living process.

Express! Don't Obsess!

During one morning's shower I caught myself obsessing about a recently contacted "match.comer"*. Upon noticing the increasing busyness in my head and tension in my body, I found myself asking out loud, "Is this how we want to start this new day?" The answer came quickly and was clearly expressed as "No way!" I recognized instantly that I could spend the whole morning filling my head with possibilities and that would only make me feel worse and at the same time not allow me to enjoy the day before me. My attention went quickly into the feeling of warm water on my back, the fragrance of lavender bodywash and as I contemplated what song I could sing, a playful funny froglike voice started singing! The obsessing vanished along with the tension. Perhaps that new match.comer was just one of the proverbial frogs I had to kiss!

Talking Back to the TV

Talk back to the TV whenever you feel an emotional reaction to what is being said or how you feel about being held captive or about their attempts to hold you captive! You may find yourself quite amused at what comes out of you. I find it especially satisfying to say something just before I follow up on my impulse to turn it off. How delightful to have this power to shut them down just when they ask me to stay tuned for what is coming up next! Express congratulations, joy, protest and sorrow. Let yourself laugh and/or cry and tell them where to go. Be witty and wild. Whatever strikes you. Enjoy your richness, indulge your raunchiness, your sensibility and your sense of humor. The whole point of these experiments is to practice with connecting with that alive, reactive part of you that holds the key to discovering what you need in the moment to soothe yourself or to feel more alive.

Acknowledge *Her* and Encourage Yourself

Acknowledgment and encouragement is our two-way street. I acknowledge *her* and *she* encourages me. The words are spoken so spontaneously, they even surprise <u>me</u>, "This is good! You (We) are doing great! Thank you!" They are often preceded by a happy feeling or a warm recognition. I feel so happy when I acknowledge *her*. The happiness I feel is also *her* being happy that I noticed *her*.

I am also happy that I <u>remembered</u> to recognize *her*. Instead of focusing on all that has yet to be done, I acknowledge what I have done and *her* having helped me. Now I have more energy because I can accept or "rest-into" rather than constrict at the specter of endless work to do. I experience the shift from the anxious Let's Go! orientation of "What is wrong?" to the surrendered Let Go . . orientation of "It's all right!" Even if it is not what I expected – still everything is working out and finding its place. With *her* guidance and encouragement, I am learning to just take my time and feel it through. I am learning to rest-into my experience and the rhythm that I need. Not too fast, not too slow – not too much or too little – the Goldilocks principle of "just right". When I find out what works for *her*, it <u>always</u> works better for me!

The more I acknowledge *her*, the more *she* talks to me. Without even thinking about it, I sometimes hear the words, *"I like it!"* or "We (you) did good!" or "Thank you!" Sometimes I say them out loud. This is not some superficial affirmation but the heartfelt truth spoken in the moment. It is a sweet voice that says this. It is hard to tell who is speaking, *she* or I, but we both feel delight. As we talk with each other this way, the positive "de-stressing" Let Go . . chemicals flow. We soothe each other or we congratulate each other and all is right with the world. A sense of gratitude, generosity and sweetness abounds.

On more than one occasion I have left the house on the way to my car and felt that nagging feeling of "Have I forgotten something?" Now I slow down and pay attention and when I feel that urging I go back. *She* is most often right – I have left something on the counter or on the floor by the door and I thank *her* for trying to tell me. What would I do without *her*? *She* saves me so much time, not to mention frustration by remembering what I have seemingly forgotten, as long as I pay attention and follow through on *her* urgings.

Another example of *her* guiding me is when I found myself standing in front of a display in a grocery store aisle and staring blankly at the products. *She* has led me there and is keeping me there until I remember what it was that I needed. While I didn't go to that aisle with anything special in mind, *she* knew what was needed and was trying to get me to realize it. If I have the presence of mind to recognize that *her* feet and eyes have brought me there and I have only discover the reason, I can thank *her* and be grateful that we are in this together! I tell her *she* is so smart!

The ways *she* tries to help are very subtle so I need to pay close attention to my sensory experience and listen for the little hesitations which may indicate that something is not quite right or complete and I need to slow down. Another example of the subtlety of *her* signaling occurred one day when I looked out of the window and noticed most the cars were parked on my side of the street. "It must be street cleaning day", I thought to myself. Through the living room window, I seemed to be able to make out the blue hood of my car, though a tree was blocking my view of the whole car. I found myself looking again later. This time I stood there longer. "Is that my car; is that the right blue color?" I asked myself. To each question I answered, "Yes!" but I still felt a tad uncertain. That feeling of uncertainty was my bodyself urging me to look again. Then a visual image (another of *her* attempts!) flashed of my going to the bedroom window to get a better view, but I didn't follow up on it. I talked myself out of it, not recognizing that the part of myself with the broader view still had *her* doubts. I ignored that visual suggestion and went back to my desk. Later when I left for work, I found a parking ticket on my car, which was parked on the opposite side of the street. I was taken aback and started to feel upset. Then I said aloud, acknowledging *her*, "You tried to tell me, thank you." My voice was gentle. I did not berate myself. I felt sorry that I had not given enough attention to that sensitive, quiet and very valuable part of my bodyself.

Now I am coming to rely on *her* to help me, especially when it comes to finding my parked car in a lot or a parking structure. *She* is great at sensing where it is, I have only to slow down and let *her* lead me to it. Of course it helps to get on the right floor to begin with and to make note of the surround before I leave the parking area. To paraphrase the hymn, "Amazing Grace"*:

"I once was lost and now I am found . . . . . "
When I am blind, *her* eyes can see . . .

The following examples, which I call "Amazing Graces", illustrate the sense of *her* finding me when I have lost "my place". On this day I allowed myself to meditate instead of just flying into compulsive action in anticipation of a very busy day. I was so grateful that I followed the impulse to sit even though I really didn't "have time" to do that because I made a valuable discovery. For several days I had been "background thinking" about a quote from S. Suzuki's "Zen Mind, Beginner's Mind". Over the past twenty years I have read and reread this book, opening it at random for inspiration. At the end of the meditation period I opened the book for the first time in months. With *her* guidance I resisted the temptation to thumb through the pages of the book, trying to find the passage I had been thinking about. To my astonishment, when I opened the book, there was the quote I was thinking about, marked by one of the flyleaves.

Not only was it satisfying to find it but all the more so because I had wanted it. I just trusted and let it unfold (or more precisely, open!). I could have taken away the bookmarker and plowed through the book, trying to find it. But it was already found. This passage was what I had last read, many months ago. However, I had no conscious memory of what I had last read in this book. *She* must have remembered and was waiting to show me. I had been feeling the need for a renewed commitment to finding and being led by *her*. And *she* was here (hear) all the time. The quote I had in mind was "When you have that mind, you have the joy of life. When you lose it, you lose everything"*. In other words, first do right by *her* and then all will fall into place.

Another delightful discovery happened one morning after I had lain awake during much of the first and last parts of the night. My wakefulness that night was due to having had a good writing period and being excited about getting so close to finishing a chapter. A part of a phrase from "The Illuminated Rumi"** occurred to me while still lying in bed that morning as I contemplated my wakefulness. "Awake all night as watchful as thieves" were the words. I picked up the book and turned right to that passage. The phrase had just come to mind though I hadn't read the passage in weeks. *She* knew where it was in the book, even though I was not even thinking about the passage when I opened the book. I just opened it. How could I not trust *her*? Maybe I should call *her* "Grace"***! To quote from Suzuki Roshi, "The truth is always near at hand, within your reach."**** You just have to reach!

My experience with *her* confirms this truth. A case in point: one evening as I was getting ready for bed, in acknowledgment of how good it had been to feel *her* with me I pleaded, "Please don't leave me! I feel so good being together with you." *She* answers me with an awareness that could be expressed as, *"Leave you? You are the one who leaves me! You start thinking about tomorrow or try to get more stuff done even though it is time to go to bed or you worry about other stuff and lose me. I am here. Waiting for you to join me!"* Ask *her* for help and acknowledge how *she* helps you and how well you work together. You will receive in return a sweet feeling. That is *her* thanking you.

The next morning, I felt so grateful that I could once again, feel *her.* "Thank you for coming back!" I cried. I felt *her* with me – in my falling tears followed by the subtle, shimmering energy streaming from the floor of my pelvis all through me. *She* was back. When I feel in touch with *her* like this, I feel complete. I am fully bodyself connected.

The more you listen to *her* the more you will find yourself thanking *her* for *her* insights, her cues, her feelings, her warnings, her urgings and images. You will find yourself noticing that the sweet feeling comes to you more and more often. Out of gratitude you thank *her* and then you feel the sweetness that is *her* way of thanking you back. There <u>is</u> <u>no</u> end <u>to this well of good will</u>. Talking to *her* is a way of staying connected to yourself and to the sense of the flow of Let Go . . Thanking *her* is just one of several ways that talking out loud can be helpful to you in maintaining contact with your bodyself. These are all excellent ways to decompress before bedtime. As you will hopefully discover for yourself, thanking *her* evokes the <u>same</u> feeling as encouraging yourself – a warm, happy, soothing feeling.

"Slow down, listen for clues and let yourself be drawn toward *her* . . ."

Listening for What Makes *Her* / You Happy

Savoring Sensory Experience

If you notice that the moon looks particularly bright as you step out of the car, spend a few minutes taking in this brightness. It is the least you can do to reward *her* for bringing your attention to it. And you may be rewarded in turn by what you experience! When a bird's song pierces your concentration, let it reverberate a while. Allow the sound to be a wake-up call! When your attention is beckoned by a sudden change in light as you sit at your desk look up and ask, "What is it?!" Find out what treat *she* has in store for you. When the hue of a flower attracts you, give yourself more time to be with it. When you are drawn by the scent of ripe strawberries as you prepare your cereal or you notice the yellow roses and remember how delightfully different, reminiscent of nutmeg their scent can be, Stop! Give yourself time to delight in the fragrance. *She* brings the scented memory to you, but will you give yourself the chance to follow through and revisit these yellow delights and experience them anew? Delighting in *her* delight is savoring – *her* delight in your delight feels sweet.

Savoring your sensory experience makes *her* happy and will increase the chances that *she* will contact you again soon. Being too task oriented can lead to missing out on special momentary delights of being that can restore your spirit. Maybe you'll end up doing one less thing but you may feel less tense at the end of the day. On the other hand, the energy that comes from the experience of savoring can help you to complete what you started. In any case, you will benefit by meeting *her* when you savor the bodyself moment.

Finish Tasks – Do One Thing at a Time

She loves it when I just do one thing at a time and bring it to completion before I start something else. Then *she* gets the experience of savoring – satisfaction – the pause that refreshes – exhalation - momentary emptiness. When I do too many things at that same time – *she* feels scattered and *she* hates that. *She* gets tense, tired and wired. However, if I am tired it is best to listen to *her* about whether to finish the task or not. *Her* priority is how *she* feels, not what I think. *She* says doing too much feels like being stuffed with food. *She* can help me find the Goldilocks "just right" place in many arenas if I only would listen. Often it is most satisfying to give to the feeling of tiredness and rest or sleep and resume with renewed energy at a later time. This renewed energy is *her* thanking me for paying attention to our need for self-soothing. *She* will let me know what is needed for optimal energy, if I only give *her* the chance.

Prepare Your Bedroom for the Day's Completion

As much as *she* likes savoring and finishing tasks she also likes preparation for activities, even if the activity is sleeping. Preparation for sleeping can be a ritual that acknowledges your awareness of the importance of a deep, satisfying sleep. In this ultimate Let Go . . state, your bodyself repairs itself and immune functioning is enhanced in preparation for a new round of activity.

She loves it when I mindfully prepare *her* sleeping place, turning down the covers and placing the pillows the way *she* likes them. *She* knows when I am considering how *she* feels. *She* feels happy when I enter the bedroom and everything is ready for *her* to climb into bed. *She* notices if I carelessly set down the glass of water by the bed. *She* wants it tenderly placed as if I cared how *she* felt when *she* needed water in the middle of the night. *She* needs to experience that taking care of *her* is not a chore – it serves a vital connection between us.

Preparation and Partaking of Food

She can tell when I prepare our food mindfully because the vegetables are steamed just right, the pasta is al dente and the sauce thoroughly mixed. The colors of the salad ingredients seem brighter and crisper. The milk on the cereal tastes colder, the fruit - both sweet and tangy - artfully settle into the grains. *She* feels just where each thing wants to be. *She* notices all these details - not in a compulsive way, but in a sensual, caring, spontaneous, appreciative way. When I am eating in a perfunctory way, I don't really taste, not to mention, chew. *She* knows when I am detached and distracted from these daily activities - when I am not really with *her*. *She* feels the lack of caring and pulls back. The less I give to her, the less *she* can give to me. The more attentive I am to *her* needs, the more satisfied and content I feel.

She hates that feeling of being too full and goes away because I have not listened and that depresses *her*. When I stuff myself it hurts *her*. I am not paying attention to what *she* really needs. *She* may need to cry or be angry or sexual and I am "stuffing *her* down" by stuffing myself. Another way to "stuff *her* down" i.e. to keep from feeling what *she* needs is to eat chocolate or a rich dessert. So when I find myself fantasizing about desserts or chocolate, I ask myself, "What is the matter?" Usually the answer is that I am tired or lonely or there is something coming up that I don't want to do or feel. I may be feeling forced or I may be forcing myself. Sometimes life no longer feels sweet and I want something to make me feel sweet. If I go for the sugar, I may feel happy for the moment but then I crash. Then I am even farther away from *her*. I become weak and cranky and the only recovery is found in sleep and then eating well again. It is in joining with *her* that I feel the true sweetness.

One afternoon, having taken a nap break to reconnect with *her*, I found myself eating more slowly. I was chewing and tasting instead of stuffing myself mindlessly as if I was attempting to get the meal over with. I could really see the food before me. I was present. *She* loves it when eat with *her* as if I am feeding *her*. (It had been weeks since I felt so connected in eating. I had put myself under too much pressure for all that time. No wonder I had a hard time contacting *her*. This is not just about the sensation of being too full – it is about losing *her*.)

When I don't get *her* signals and end up eating too much, *she* "pays me back" with a bellyache. *She* knows <u>exactly</u> when "enough" happens – as clearly as a child knows. In fact *her* discrimination is so finely tuned that *she* can tell when I have eaten enough protein, starch or fat. Then *she* rewards me for respecting *her* limits with a satisfied feeling and a subtle energy rush at the end of the meal. Just give yourself time and ask *her* "what do you want right now?" If you let *her* be in charge, you will eat just enough and know when to stop.

She excels at selecting the right foods in appropriate combinations and creating innovative dishes. Just take time and look and smell and taste and notice your reactions. These sensations are part of appetite and the beginning of taking in food. *She* can help you make more healthy and tasty food choices, not to mention more delightful and artful presentation!

She is indispensable when it comes to detecting when something is not right for you to eat or breathe or touch. You just have to tune into your bodyself reaction and trust it. *She* can help you remember what you may have eaten that made you sick, if you take time and travel back into your sensory experience over the past hours or days. *She* wants to be healthy and safe and will try to signal you about what might be dangerous to you. *She* wants to stay alive!

Warnings and Urgings

I hear *her* protest when I begin to talk on my cell phone without the headset. *She* "reminds"* me about the potential effect of microwaves on the brain. *She* doesn't want something bad to happen. *She* is the one who reminds me to buckle up and to double-check the front door to see if it is locked. That is *her* urging when I find myself wondering if I locked the door. *She* doesn't want to have trouble falling asleep because I didn't make sure it was locked. *She* has an inside track on what is needed to be safe and healthy. I have only to listen.

Inviting *Her* . . .

Give Me a Break to Break You Open!

All three listening practices contribute toward my taking an appropriate break. Sensing can give me the bodyself cues of tiredness and tension to let me know I need a break. Meditating gives me the experience of taking a break and strengthens my ability to notice when my attention is waning and I am becoming distractible. Listening to my emotional voice will cue me in to when I am becoming cranky about working so long or feeling frustrated. *She* can tell me what <u>kind</u> of break to take. *Her* message is serious business and may need to be followed because I just may be working too much!

When I suspect I need a break, I try lying down on my back. If my eyes are heavy I probably need a little rest. As I am lying I take all the space I need, giving myself to what supports me and to breathing. If my toes are cramped or my legs askew, I often find myself in my head, thinking and thinking. Then I notice what is needed and follow through. That helps me focus on my bodyself needs rather than my thoughts. Then I allow myself to drift away and come back and then sink deeply. I may then experience a breath that signals the shift to Let Go. . I find myself again, more spacious and gentled and perhaps inspired. Sometimes *she* needs ten minutes or maybe even 15 or 20, then I feel myself rising to the surface of consciousness. Sensing and meditation practice can take me that far. But sometimes I may need more than just a rest. Maybe I need to move or play or cry. Listening to my emotional voice can give me a clue.

She likes it when I lie down, to rest or to nap because it gives *her* a chance to appear and to talk to me. Sometimes *she* gives me a clever or amusing image or idea. *She* delights me with inspiration and renewed energy. For *her* to appear however, I must sense my lying and give to myself what is needed. More room for my toes, more support for my neck or perhaps some massage to my tense muscles. Sensing my arms and wrists I may notice my wrists are held at an angle, my hands clasped across my chest. I ask myself "What do I need to allow in order to feel more of a living connection through my wrists into my arms and hands?" Answering, my elbows move slightly away from my sides as my clasped hands slide lower on my torso. This movement allows a connection in sensation from my arms through my wrists into my hands. A deeper breath comes. As I surrender to what is under me and allow breathing as it wants to be, I deeply rest.

When I take my bodyself urgings seriously, the stage is set for *her* to appear. Sometimes I ask *her* for help. I am coming to rely on accessing *her* wisdom. *She* never disappoints me no matter how many times I have ignored *her*. *Her* spirit is strong. *Let me delight you. I have great ideas. Just let me be with you. I can help you. Be gentle with yourself. You are writing about us. You are letting others know about how to find connection with the "me" in them. This is a beautiful soulful work. Give me a chance!* I feel so vulnerable as I turn toward *her*. Can I depend on this ephemeral, spirited creature? Is *she* resilient enough? *She* was chased away for such a long time. Now I am inviting *her* back. And that is all *she* needs. Dear Reader, just give *her* more chances to be with you. You will see how dependable *she* is. And how good you will feel.

One afternoon, after struggling with a difficult section, I decided to lie down. After sensing into my lying, I drifted off and was awakened by words that went with an image of a man saying that he wanted to move (in the sense of "dance")! I instantly recognized that was *her* telling me that only way *she* could – through an image that *she* wanted a change of pace. I was making myself be too still and thereby de-pressing my energy. *She* wanted to mix it up a little.

During another nap break, I was startled and amused by an image of a smiling girl, jumping down the aisle of a big church in a gunnysack! Now there's a creative way to break up the solemnity of work! I recognized *her* right away. I was delighted – *she* made me giggle. *She* was trying to tell me to lighten up - that I would not get any further if I continued to press myself the way I had been doing. *She* needs to play, not just to rest or cry out in pain. When you give yourself the inner space to live you will begin to feel a need to expand into outer space! Your emotional voice can be an entertaining guide and take you to new heights, if you allow it. <u>Following through</u> on *her* message to "chill" was more difficult. Why am I so stingy with myself? With *her*? I never am sorry when I have followed *her*.

While *she* can help me figure out what kind of break to take and for how long, I must proceed slowly and notice *her* cues. *She* is likely to disappear if I engage in some activity that increases my tension rather than relieves it. For example, one afternoon during a nap break, I felt my inspiration return. But before I sat down to write, I let myself be distracted by an unfinished task of adding the contents of one lotion bottle to another. I stayed with it too long and in the process, I noticed my back began to hurt. I pushed through anyway, ignoring the pain for a time. Our cocoon of communication vaporized in contraction and pain. Eventually I found myself losing interest in the task (*she* wasn't totally into it) and I became aware of my deeply aching back.

How could I have fooled myself that I could get away with ignoring this pain? How do I know when to quit? *Her* answer is *"when it occurs to you to quit."* And if not quit, take a break and check out what *she* needs. When I feel an ache or when I have an image of stopping I need to take those as signs that *she* is talking to me. Sometimes I may not be able to finish what I've started. I have to choose between not having the good feeling of finishing the task, coupled with a backache or alienating *her*. *She* likes me to finish the task but not when it costs *her* tension and pain. Staying in touch with *her* necessitates fine discrimination and a delicate balance.

My self-assigned task for that afternoon was to complete some writing, not finish distributing the lotion to the sink dispenser. That could happen anytime. The writing was now. The inspiration to write a section had been given to me. But that gift of inspired, connected energy had dissipated as I kept myself to the lotion transfer task and in the muscular "efforting" in my strained back. My state of mind had shifted so I was not as available to feeling the flow inside me. Some of that precious energy was spent and the rest was bound up in muscle tension. I tried to write but was not inspired. Fortunately not all was lost, it never is. After lunch and a nap *she* returned to guide me in writing these words.

What struck me about this experience was that I didn't realize until later that I had been pushing myself and ignoring the pain in my back in order to continue the lotion bottle task. It was a task I knew I would not finish then anyway. *She* was upset that I continued even though the pain was intense. *She* was sad that pain did not stop me. I learned early on that bodily pain or for that matter any kind of pain was not necessarily a reason to stop what was happening to me. In fact I came to understand by my caretaker's actions and words that I <u>deserved</u> that pain. Previous trauma can lead to difficulty receiving and responding appropriately to bodyself cues. In fact, going on in spite of pain, pretending it didn't hurt could be a challenge and a statement of self-defeating defiance as well as a creative survival tool of childhood – the "I can take it" attitude.

However, the lotion bottle task had an appeal and was a challenge – getting it just right so the lotion would flow and not get stuck at the lip of the dispenser bottle. I felt very focused. The Let's Go! challenge was exciting! I had figured out a way to do it. But then I kept at it past where my body was able to go without contracting. That familiar pushing attitude and the muscular contraction took away the Let Go . . feeling of flow that had birthed the inspiration to write. Feisty Let's Go! had overtaken the fragile Let Go . . inspiration.

Undaunted, I tried the same activity again on the next break. This time I noticed when I was feeling energized by what I was doing but had not yet shifted to Let's Go! arousal. I took just enough of a break to renew my energy and to release the accumulating tension in my back and neck. I felt pleased as the lotion swirled into the dispenser. Then I stopped. The task was not completed, but my purpose was. I had a break and I was ready to return to writing with a kinder, gentler energy toward myself and my work. *She* was still with me. *She* was pleased and so was I – we had a mutually satisfying break – *she* had some fun and in return, gave me ease and energy.

Sensitive attunement to my sensory and emotional cues will give me an indication of when "to hold and when to fold" whether it applies to taking or ending a break. Taking too much time on a break dissipates energy and not taking enough time will not renew energy. I have to feel out when it is time to fold (take a break, shift to Let Go . .) and when to hold (stay with the task or on the break).

A sensitively attuned mother knows when her child needs to rest even when the child does not seem to want to. Mom's job is to read the cues, interpret the cry, know his rhythms and tenderly soothe the child toward rest and renewal. When the rest period is over, she returns to greet him and play. Connection is needed at both ends of the rest period. By sensitively attuning to my bodyself cues I can get it "just right".

For example, one morning before writing, I was reading the newspaper a little too long and putting off starting on my book. The first article had piqued my interest and touched me emotionally. My energy had been rising but now was in danger of being consumed by continuing to read. All of a sudden I heard a chorus of birds calling (*she* attunes to birdsong). I recognized that it was time (like right now!) to give in to returning to writing my book. On that note, I left <u>my</u> perch at the kitchen table and turned toward writing and paying attention to my experience. My step became lighter and I felt more free and ready to be led. As *her* voice came, we sang and chanted more lively than we had in some time. I became available to whatever pressed to be expressed. I had read just enough to get my energy going and quit the moment I was called, so my energy did not dissipate. Being in touch with *her* is key to energy management.

She has the best ideas for breaks and may surprise you! For example, one afternoon, I recognized I needed a break and stopped focusing on writing. I asked *her* what *she* would suggest. All of a sudden I saw an image of three of my big couch pillows on the floor in front of me. In a flash I felt in my body how it might feel to lie on them, although I had heretofore not lain on them! *She* never said a word. I tried it out – heavenly restful and sweetly pleasing it was – just right! Ask and *she* will answer with images, sensation and sweet surprises.

So when you take breaks listen for *her* and ask what does she want? Pay attention to your sensations and ask what is needed? *She* may not come right away. You may have to invite *her* again and again, by creating the space for *her* to breathe into. But as you wait and Let Go . . *she* will come. When you begin to feel softer, take that as a signal indicating *she* is there. It is as if *she* waits until *she* feels your sincerity and your willingness to give to *her* the space to tell you what *she* needs. If you have kept *her* away too long, you are likely to have to wait longer for *her*. If you don't feel *her* presence after you have slowed down and sensed, ask, "What is the matter?"

The most difficult challenge for me remains being able to respond appropriately with taking a break when I am in the middle of a demanding project. I get the messages from my bodyself that it needs a break – my neck is a little tight, the flesh around my sit bones aches,

I can't seem to get anywhere, reading the same thing over and over and still no inspiration comes. No wonder. Frustration sets in. These are cues that point to this being the perfect time to give into these messages and shift to Let Go . . and away from the goal oriented striving of Let's Go! It's time to fold, not hold, it's time to take a break. Yet I often persist in pushing myself. What is needed is a break, yet that is all too often the hardest thing to do.

If my experience of difficulty taking a break reminds you of yourself, try asking yourself the following questions: Are you entitled to take a break or must you continue to push yourself? Were you loved for who you were or did you only get approval when you produced? Do you carry around inside you a voice that continues to drive you toward doing and away from being? Answers to these questions could provide clues to why it is hard for you to listen and give yourself what you need.

Let Yourself Be Moved by Music

When you are feeling stuck, depressed or agitated turn to the radio for music. You have probably already discovered how synchronistic this experience can be – how the perfect song appears with heart searing sound and lyrics. And Voila! - What was lost is now found! *She* wants to come back – *she* just needs your invitation.

Music has the added dimension of inviting you to move. More of *her* will be available to you (and hence more energy) if you allow what you feel to bring you into movement. Give yourself a chance to embrace the movement moment fully. Try Gloria Esteban's "Turn the Beat Around" if you would like to experience being moved by rhythm and "dance like no one is watching!" If you listen with your whole bodyself, the movement will arise from impulses deep inside you. Let your sound and movement fly. Now you can return to your activity, revitalized and more present and available for what is needed.

One evening, as I resisted the impulse to distract myself with the TV while doing exercises, I realized I must have been afraid of just being with myself. Why else the near compulsion to read or watch TV while I engage in body oriented activities like eating, exercising, defecating, falling asleep, teeth flossing, you name it, etc? These are all occasions to join with *her*, yet I often choose to split off and leave *her*. I risk injuring myself in mindless exercise or the discomfort of stuffing myself by not being available to *her* messages. If I hadn't turned off the TV, I would not have made this discovery just then. What a gift! *She* was so ready to talk to me. No wonder I wasn't relating to the Rumi readings in the preceding weeks. I had not been attending to *her* and *her* voice was muted.

Energized by this recognition, I put on some music and let myself be moved. How alive, even sprightly, the core-connected movement and sound became. How surprised I was as an image of dancing with my mother emerged – along with the joyous knowing that she would understand these feelings. Indeed, this same mother from whom I had been estranged for many years but had rejoined in friendship five years before she died. Moving easily, I felt ageless – my mother and me. What a reward for listening to *her*, for not distracting myself once again. I am so grateful that *she* is so forgiving, I just needed to turn toward *her* and *she* came. Nothing is worth losing *her*. I am so sorry. This dear one is my best friend and I must treat *her* well and listen to *her* - feed *her* well and not rush *her*. Sensing and meditation have merit, but to have fun, to feel the zest for life and connection with others, I need *her*.

Let Yourself Be Touched by Stories

Reading a touching story or newspaper article can have much the same effect as listening to music, in terms of awakening me to my core feelings and hence to *her*. I sometimes find myself moving out of a morning funk when I connect emotionally with a news account. I actually search the morning's paper for such a story and almost always find something heart rending. Beginning the day with an open heart is a very good energetic start!

You can also access *her* by allowing your heart to be touched by a TV program or even a commercial. When you notice a little tug or twinge, let it develop. Tears open your connection to *her* and to renewal and to getting unstuck and alive again. *She* loves to be found!

Invitation by Meditation

One morning I was softly despairing that I had lost *her* the previous night in a series of events which included a couple of long distance phone calls and a half-hearted watching of a TV program while balancing my check book and sorting through the mail. I ignored the tug I felt while I tried to do two things at once - scanning the mail and keeping track of the TV story. I dismissed the thought that I didn't really need to leave the TV on - albeit muted - while I finished my fiduciary activity. I had even forgotten my rule about no TV while I am doing my exercises during a writing period. I had begun to treat the evening as if it were a regular evening and not a writing evening. I felt scattered as I went off to bed. I fretted, "How will I write about *her* in the morning when I have treated *her* so badly tonight? I have lost *her*. What was I thinking? I know better!" I vowed during my evening meditation to tune into what *she* would try to tell me the next day.

With renewed resolve, I awakened the next morning and followed all of the directives from *her* that I could feel. I followed my already well-established morning routine to a "T". This routine contained my energy so I could focus on being just in the moment with what was before me. Stretches, exercises, meditation, inspirational reading, checking messages, breakfast and the newspaper. As I was finishing my cereal and an article, I noticed my curiosity pique about another article on the same page. My commitment on a writing morning is to stop reading when my cereal is gone or at least, shortly thereafter. As I started to check out another article, I felt *her*. It was as if *she* made me aware that I was reading more than enough – like the sense I have when I take that one bite too many. I smiled and got up <u>immediately</u>. I could feel some excitement at just having responded in the moment to what "*she* wanted". My action was saying, "I want to be connected with you!" The excitement I felt was *her* response was the excitement I felt. Renewed energy was my reward! At least *she* was still talking to me. I felt grateful and happy that I could have another chance to join with *her* energy. I need *her* to help me write, especially this chapter which is so much about *her* and is the heart of this book.

Invitation by Dream

Asking for a dream, remembering the dream and working on it is a powerful and rewarding way to access what *she* needs to tell me. Sometimes I can connect with what *she* needs to tell me if I ask for a dream during my bedtime meditation. I like to treat dreams as visual representations of sensations and emotions – ephemeral messages from my bodyself. For example, the sensation of a full bladder often evokes an early morning dream of looking for a toilet.

These bodyself messages are often subtle, fragile and fleeting. They have a very short shelf life. You need to respond right away so that their value to you isn't lost. You know how it is with remembering dreams. Dreams are born out of the Let Go . . state of sleep and vanish when you shift to Let's Go! alertness. To remember (re – member as in make it a member of your waking consciousness) a dream you usually must write it down or speak it or at least go over it in your mind. So when you awake and you become aware of a dream image, Stop! and catch it. Then it can become an integrated part of you to which you can go back.

In addition, you have probably noticed that as you retell the dream more of it becomes available. You may begin to experience some emotions or insight that you were not aware of when you first awakened. Focusing on the dream fragment and immediately following through connects you to this communication from the more hidden part of you. As you gradually move back into Let Go . . you are able to retrieve more of your dream experience.

Sometimes dreams contain images of feelings that are unwanted or disowned – like fear, anger, shame, disgust, sadness or sexual excitement. As I connect more to the images in my dream, I connect with my feelings and reclaim the energy of the feelings. Owning these feelings I can become more whole and alive. I am in effect, completing myself by identifying and integrating these feelings. But this road to self-completion is usually open only if I catch these images immediately. A good example of the benefits of connecting to my bodyself voice via working on a dream is found in Chapter 14 on Awakening.

Don't Make *Her* Wait Too Long!

Don't make *her* wait too long after *she* suggests something or the energy which could be gained by enacting it will no longer be available. When you follow up <u>immediately</u> on what *she* suggests you will gain energy even though you are spending it by doing what *she* indicates. *Her* energy is the expansive and joyful Let Go . . energy, not the depleting or constricting energy of Let's Go! You'll have more energy by going with the flow than holding against it. It is a seeming paradox to respond with Let's Go! speed to the bodyself message toward Let Go . . but that is what is needed to feel alive and connected with *her* and to maximize Let Go . . energy.

I discovered I need to do just the right amount of pleasure giving or emotionally touching activity (like savoring a ripe plum or reading something moving) before I ask *her* to pay attention for long stretches or intense work. The resultant energy and happy feeling would then fuel my work. All the while I encourage myself as I go, taking little breaks to renew my energy. For example, one morning I found myself saying to myself aloud "You are doing well!" Then I said to *her*, "Thank you for helping me by making me get up and type instead of read over what I had already written. That was bold!" My usual way would have been to read over what I had written the night before or at least type up the new notes from the morning's awakening.

But that morning *she* had me going right to the computer to type and good stuff it was. So satisfying to just do it! Not playing it safe by reviewing and perhaps dissipating the energy for what needed to be said. I acted as if what was to come out was the next thing that needed to. That hasn't always produced good writing in the past but there was no choice here. I just found myself at the computer working. That was *her* urging. "Thank you, dear one, for sensing the right (write) time! I have to trust you and that is scary. Can I trust that you know what is best for me? I haven't trusted you in a long time. I have not tried it your way. I have been terrified that if I didn't follow my own strict rules and work hard, I would lose everything. How could you give me anything? All you seem to want to do is lighten up and play."

Yes, I know it seems that way because <u>you</u> never play. So then I need to play more. I am OK with working sometimes because you are writing good things and you are helping other people find their "Her's" or "Him's". That is a good reason for me to sit back a little and wait. But don't make me wait too long. I lose my energy and then you hardly hear me and I think you actually forget about me. Just keep checking in with me like the Zen monk* did with himself so he wouldn't lose himself. Like now, your neck is aching and you need to lie down, no matter if it is only an hour into writing and you are not tired. Just take a few minutes. Something even better may come out! Something you haven't even let me come to yet! You know I give you great ideas. I am keeping track. You just have to tune into me. So get quiet and rested enough so you can tune into me. Trust me.

Letting *Her* Lead You

When *she* feels the sun on *her* back *she* wants to lie down to let it really sink in. *She* senses the change in light before I even notice and then sends me off running to the beach, just in time for a glorious sunset. As *she* treads across the yielding warm sand, *she* suddenly drops to *her* knees. *She* acts without thinking. *She* acts as *she* feels the impulse. *She* <u>is</u> the impulse. *She* is the source of "premonitions" and that "funny feeling". *She* senses things before I do. *She* finds missing things. *She* is the "hidden observer" and the source of untapped knowledge. *She* is a conduit for the less conscious processes in my brain. *Her* knowledge gives rise to images in dreams and fantasy and incorporates stimuli into dreams upon awakening.

In the previous chapter I recounted how listening to my bodyself cues (that was *her*) made me realize I had not pressed the "Start" button on the dryer in the laundry room before I had gone all the way back to my apartment. A few moments after I gave into *her* pleasure in feeling the sun on *her* back, I realized I didn't hear the dryer turning. Not only did *she* save me the frustration of returning an hour later to find that my clothes were still wet but *she* gave me the momentary pleasure of soaking up some rays! In other examples I shared how *she* kept me from misplacing my keys as well as losing a receipt because I was able to slow down and listen to *her* silent signaling.

I have only to notice these urgings, inklings and hunches – notice, then focus and follow through. When we spend more time together, I feel more content and happy. I feel blessed. For *her*, everything has a "life". *She* has a feeling connection with everything. *She* doesn't want me to set the cup of tea on the photo of the child in the newspaper. It feels somehow disrespectful. If I leave the tea cup there, *her* presence dims. *She* will hold back from me a little by being less likely to inform me about the rightness of the next move I make. *She* feels calmer when I put things back into place and scattered when I leave them just anywhere. Putting things away is soothing because it shows I care about how *she* feels. Through contact with *her*, I discover respect for living, respect for my organism, respect for the time it takes – to exhale, to come to lying, to chew, to wake up, to reconnect and restore.

In sum, listening to your emotional voice is key to soothing yourself and thereby regulating your energy. As you listen closely and follow through on *her* subtle cues, you are likely to find that you are sleeping more soundly and having more fun, being more productive and more communicative with others. You will better sense when to take a break and when it is time to get back to work. You'll be able to free more energy and use it more wisely. Your energy will increase as you give up bodyself holding, sense your emotions and give yourself to play, music, humor and creativity. As you learn to encourage yourself you become more expansive and spontaneous. Relating to *her,* being attentive to *her* needs, encouraging, acknowledging and expressing can prepare you for the intimacy of relating to others.

When you find yourself feeling stuck, irritable, with low energy, depressed or resistant to taking care good care of yourself, you can turn to *her* for help. Listening to *her* is the key to understanding your resistance to taking care of yourself. Sensing and meditating can lead you to the door but *she* holds the key. You may find you need someone to hold your hand as you attempt to fit the key into the lock. The next chapter, Meeting Your Resistance to Listening to Your Bodyself Voice, addresses some blocks to being able to contact and soothe yourself. On the other hand, if you would like to get started creating your own decompression routine turn to chapters 14 and 15 and you can put the listening practices to work *or into play* tonight!

PART II

MEETING RESISTANCE TO SLOWING DOWN

7

MEETING YOUR RESISTANCE TO LISTENING TO YOUR BODYSELF VOICE

"Recognize your stance and come out of your trance to dance!"

If you are having trouble stopping your workaday activity so you can begin to "decompress" at the promised time, or if you try to listen for your bodyself voice but don't hear anything, or when you do hear something, you don't follow through – this is the chapter for you! Herein you will find out how to meet your resistance by <u>understanding</u> its origins and hopefully thereby have compassion rather than judgment for yourself. In a later chapter you will discover how to meet your resistance by <u>experiencing</u> it in your body when you allow another person to meet your resistance. By gradually surrendering to the feelings and needs behind that resistance, you allow <u>yourself</u> to be met, that is, you meet yourself! Now, how's that for "openers'?

She is excited that you are taking on this challenge – nothing pleases *her* more – your bodyself will be so grateful – for you, delightful surprises are in store! *She* knows this is *her* chance as well as yours to be met so you can gain the full bodyself capacity to experience aliveness, presence, love and soothing. *She* knows when you have trouble listening to *her*, it's likely because you weren't listened to as a child so you treat *her* as you were treated. *She* is forgiving and *she* understands that you can't meet *her*, if you feel threatened by your feelings and your bodyself need for connection with another. *She* will give you another chance.

As you attempt to listen to your bodyself voice for cues on how best to use your decompression period before going to sleep, you may hear yourself protesting or making excuses and pleas:

"I'm tired, I worked hard today, I want to stay up and have fun!"
"So what if I'm beat, I can take it, I don't need to be pampered."
"I don't care how late it is; I don't want to miss something."
"I'm really burned-out, but <u>they</u> need me."
"Still too much work to do and it has to be done right."
"Forget what happened today, I'm 'outta' here:
    Just one more game to play
    Just one more bill to pay
    Just one more bowl of ice cream
    Just one more chapter before I dream
    Just one more person to call
    Just one more song, that's all
    Just one more drink, so I won't think."
"You are such a loser; there you go again, wasting time!"

"Just one more" sounds a little like a child's plea who doesn't yet want to go to sleep, doesn't it? Something more <u>is</u> needed indeed but the "just one more" litany is not going to address the underlying need for soothing in an optimal way. At one level, avoidant habits like distraction, denial, dissociation, obsessive thinking and doing, as well as the various addictions <u>are</u> an attempt to take care of yourself, even though they can have unwanted, energy-depleting or self-destructive side-effects. Still, they often represent the best you can do at that moment in the face of underlying threatening needs and feelings of which you are not yet aware but could surface if you slow down and listen to your bodyself.

Where do those uncomfortable feelings and needs come from?

You might be wondering how you can figure out what is behind your resistance if you can't yet identify the feelings that you are not quite aware of. An understandable concern! I am hoping that at least you were able to identify with one or more of the excuses I just listed so that you could sense I had some idea of what goes on in you. The way you talk to yourself about your feelings and needs often echoes what you heard or saw in your childhood. How your caretakers took care of themselves and you, gave you some sense of whether or not your needs and feelings were important to them. (I use the word "caretaker" rather than "parent" because it reflects the fact that our parents are usually our first teachers of "caretaking" – we learn from them how to "take care" of ourselves and sometimes the key caretaking figures were not our parents.) Their attitude toward self-nurturing was communicated overtly through words and often covertly through behavior. And since they were so vital to you - you literally couldn't survive without them - and because you needed whatever love and attention they <u>could</u> give, you paid attention to these messages and took them in at a deep level.

But you don't have to take <u>my</u> word for it, try this experiment instead:

Take a few minutes and reflect on what you tell yourself when you catch yourself avoiding slowing down at night. Write down what you come up with. Then write about what you think your caretakers' attitude about self-care was. Do you detect any fragments of what you heard or saw in childhood in what you now say to yourself or in how you treat yourself when you try to slow down and truly nurture yourself? And while you are at it, please reflect on your caretakers' attitude toward vulnerable feelings such as love, sadness, shame and fear. Try to remember how well they played and expressed joy and pride in you. Did they take time to listen to you and find out what your interests were? Did they make an effort to understand your needs and feelings and work out conflicts and hurt feelings and say "I'm sorry" when they were wrong? Did they let you "off the hook" when you were truly sorry and said so? When something bad happened did you feel like you could go to them with the expectation of working it out? Was it possible to do a "good enough" job in their eyes? Were <u>they</u> able to enjoy "time-off" without engaging in addictions? If you or your caretakers were not "busy" or working all the time was that called being "lazy" or if tender feelings were expressed that was labeled "weak"? When you were happy about an achievement did they celebrate with you or did they call you a "show-off" or "too big for your britches"?

Considering what you feel in response to these questions will help you make better use of the material in this chapter on overcoming your resistance to self-soothing. And by the way, tracing your difficulties with self-soothing back to interactions with your caretakers in childhood is not about blaming them but rather, explaining and understanding what you "took in" so you can have compassion for yourself and maybe even, for them!

Now I will describe some scenarios and situations which are likely to result in unresolved feelings and conflicting needs that could be behind the resistance you encounter when you try to slow down at night. Before you can do something about your resistance it is important to identify its dynamics and where it comes from. Each of these unresolved situations, whether from childhood or recent times can leave in its wake, troubling feelings and the discomfort of unmet needs which press for expression. You have to deal with these feelings and needs in some way to be able to fall asleep at night, let alone have some peace during the day. Your habitual way of dealing with this discomfort is likely to be reminiscent of what you did or saw while you were growing up. You may need some help ferreting out what these situations were that once were so troubling that you may have had to deny their effects on you. Particularly challenging could be getting in touch with your need for another when that need wasn't adequately met in childhood; then threatening emotions often had to go "underground".

I know this must sound like I am trying to get you to dig up "trouble". Please let me remind you, you are <u>already</u> having trouble, every night, trying to soothe yourself so you can fall asleep and wake up refreshed, ready for the new day! And even if you don't have a problem falling asleep, as some do not, you might have trouble winding down and soothing yourself in a healthy way or you may have trouble falling back asleep once awakened in the wee hours. In any case, as you identify where your resistance comes from, you have a chance to feel more <u>compassion</u> for yourself and for your challenges and compassion is an excellent start and essential for optimal self-soothing.

All these situations that I have listed below can result in residual Let's Go! feelings like anxiety and irritability and now call for a soothing Let Go . . resolution. A Let Go . . resolution is likely to require going through the emotional recovery cycle supported by grounding in your bodyself and an attuned "other" – the shift from the upset of Let's Go! to the "All is well" of Let Go . . When you read the following list, notice what you feel in your bodyself or what thoughts come to mind. Such responses are likely clues to what might be behind your resistance to slowing down at night, even if part of you is saying to yourself, "No way!" Please take into consideration that the effects of unresolved trauma are often compounded by inadequate childhood nurturing and vice versa.

Unresolved Trauma in Childhood or Adulthood:
    Intentional/ Unintentional: Abandonment or Abuse

Ungrieved Loss in Childhood or Adulthood:
    Family, Friends, Pets, Lovers, Disabilities, Jobs

Inadequate Caretaker Modeling of Self-Nurturing

Inadequate Nurturing by Childhood Caretakers:
    Caretakers who are critical, depressed, "ragers", needy,
    narcissistic, work-alcoholics, addicts, detached
    Sense of never being "off the hook", never good enough,
    smart enough, helpful enough

Unresolved Trauma from Childhood or Adulthood

Abandonment Trauma

To help you understand how feelings from unresolved childhood trauma can creep up and interfere with your resolve to go to bed on time, I offer this example of resistance I encountered one night and what I was able to discover about it on my own by just <u>paying attention</u> to <u>how</u> I <u>felt</u>. (Several years later the needed deeper work was done on the issue of longing as connected to an unresolved childhood abandonment trauma*.) This night as I was playing yet another game on the computer, I finally noticed how late it was getting. I knew I should stop playing and get some much needed sleep. Previously I had found that if I stopped when I was first aware of the impulse to stop, I could immediately gain a sense of connection with *her* and feel a flash of joy and momentary exhilaration with having followed through on *her* urging. But I didn't always follow through on the impulse to stop and so it was on this occasion. I persisted playing, but remarked aloud "I don't <u>care</u> if I end up tired; I need to have fun <u>now</u>. I need a win! I work so much and I deserve some fun." Then I felt very sad as well as the underlying loneliness of working so late and having no one to come home to with whom I could share my day or a hug. No wonder I wanted to continue playing, ironically enough, the game of "Solitaire"! I was trying to avoid experiencing my underlying sadness by engaging in a distracting activity which might eventually give me the momentary "high" of having won at "Solitaire" even if I had lost at "Hearts"! My defiant gaming had hidden for the moment my fear of the dark quiet and the loneliness that threatened to emerge if I slowed down and asked myself what was I avoiding feeling by playing yet another game.

This incident occurred during a period of time when I was not as able as I am now to notice what I was feeling, let alone focus, follow through and shift to Let Go . . What I am more likely to do these days when I see that my decompression period cut-off point is nigh is to turn off the computer and take some time to notice what feeling or need is lurking beneath the surface. When I notice I am experiencing longing, I can now feel it deeply and let myself cry or leave a friend a voice mail which might be accompanied by a few tears. And if I feel I need a live connection, I call my sister who is nearly always up late! Just the sound of her sweet voice greeting me can bring my latent tears to the fore because I can hear in her voice her love for me. Often no more than a minute is necessary for the tears or the sadness to dissipate. For the longing I had felt before bedtime was the longing for connection with another which I sometimes can't soothe on my own. When I hear my sister's voice, my bodyself fills with that "being loved" feeling and I experience the "All is well" and shift to Let Go . .

Because of the many years of work on various issues stemming from childhood including a tragic experience of unintentional abandonment trauma I am now able to recognize my longing and feeling it, take the appropriate action to soothe myself and Let Go . . Before that work I had often remarked that it was just "too lonely to cry by myself", never knowing why I felt that way. Working through that unresolved trauma I realized that longing for a loved one to return was connected with great bodyself distress both because that person didn't come in time but also because no one was there to help me with the terror, rage and despair in the wake of that experience. Had someone, preferably my mother, been aware enough to try to connect with me at that time, my bodyself could have gone through all those feelings in the safety and love of <u>her</u> embrace. Then that traumatic experience of abandonment would have been <u>integrated</u> as something that had happened and was now <u>over</u>.

Instead I was left having to deal with the intense, overwhelming feelings and needs on my own which resulted in dissociation from the entire experience, distancing from my mother, my bodyself and from my need for a person to help me. This event was pivotal in my saying "No!" to my need for another. Sadly, this "No!" was reinforced by other disappointing or even frightening interactions in childhood. Dissociating is a common protective response to overwhelming terror or pain but these feelings are still intact and go dormant. While they are just out of reach of daily consciousness, they can be triggered by an event which is often benign but mirroring some aspect of the traumatic one. Once triggered it may feel as if the terrifying experience is happening again, complete with all the feelings and overwhelm.

Abuse: Intrusion Trauma

Intrusion trauma is a "twin" of abandonment trauma because when the child is abused, it often feels abandoned no matter whether the abuse is sexual, physical or emotional. And when a child feels abandoned it is often vulnerable to being abused in an attempt to get its needs for connection met. Anxiety that arises from unresolved intrusion trauma is often especially threatening when others did not do anything to help the child. If the caretaker treated the child as an extension of himself as narcissists often do, the child's body became "his". He could do with the child whatever he wanted; the child complied out of fear and need for contact. What the child often does in defense is deny its feelings, tense its muscles and hold its breath, becoming as numb or invisible as possible. By refusing to cry or perhaps even to eat, the child sacrifices its bodyself connection for a sense of control. Numbing and tensing is the only kind of self-soothing available to this child who, as an adult likely turns to some kind of addictive behavior. For, slowing down and listening could bring up the anxiety resulting from suppressed terror, shame, rage and helplessness of the childhood experience of abuse.

In the case of sexual abuse, if the child's body experienced "pleasure" when it was stimulated, as an adult the person may guard against experiencing the pleasure of potentially soothing contact before "s/he gets into trouble". As an adult she may feel that her sexuality is not her own. How tragic that something so precious is made toxic through the exploitation of the child's innocence and need for contact. Since sexual abuse of a child by a caretaker often occurs around bath and bed-time, setting aside time for decompression activities before bedtime may be especially challenging. Bedtime may evoke a body memory of danger or threat in the dark quiet and staying busy and distracted can keep feelings at bay. Pleasurable sensations can be an important source of "de-stressing" chemicals which support soothing and the shift to Let Go. . but when associated with violation they may elicit anxiety and avoidance. No wonder there is resistance to slowing down and listening to the bodyself voice.

Another less dramatic but more common example of the effect of a controlling or even intrusive, narcissistic caretaker on the sense of body ownership occurred when a client of mine noticed she was making herself wait for a long time when her bladder was full. She asked herself, "What could possibly be more important than giving myself relief?" In a flash she realized of course that was her caretaker's influence. She would have to go and it would be inconvenient for him. Because of her fear of him, she knew she better not come into conflict with him so she waited, like a "good girl". Underneath she was angry; it not only hurt to wait so long but also it made her anxious. But she had to withhold her "No!" to him and instead said "No!" to her bodyself. Repeated occurrences reinforced the habit of not listening to her bodyself needs. So, is it any wonder that when she still said "No!" to herself she felt a little tense and out of touch? The tenseness was telling her, her need was not getting met and was a cue to listen and follow through.

Punishment can result in traumatic feelings for the child depending on whether the caretaker-child connection was restored. Whether corporeal or emotional (such as verbal abuse or "silent treatment"), the pain of anger-fueled, intentional separation can feel life-threatening and cause unbearable anxiety for the child. The child will do nearly anything, including humiliating itself by begging and pleading to restore the connection. If the caretaker has been abused as a child he may go into a trance* during the punishment, repeating an abusive pattern from his own past. The child's pleas may only incite further withholding of contact because the child's vulnerability triggers the unconscious memory of how the caretaker's vulnerability was responded to. Whereas, in the case of a caretaker who did not experience abuse as a child, the perception of the vulnerability of the child is more likely to trigger compassion and softening. The shock and terror in the child's eyes should snap him out of his anger and distancing. The child's pleas and terror are tantamount to the wolf's submissive bearing its neck. But for a caretaker who was heartlessly or sadistically treated as a child himself, such a display of terrified helplessness may only energize his sadism. By attempting to crush the vulnerability of his offspring, he is attempting to silence the pain of his own crushed vulnerability.

When the caretaker meets the child's pleas with indifference, rage or further humiliation and does not return and reconnect, the child continues to feel abandoned and unworthy of love. Shame, anger, sadness, terror and despair continue on a deep level – a veritable stress-chemical bath. To add insult to injury, the caretaker may ridicule or threaten the child for crying or for being angry. For example, after corporeal punishment the caretaker might say, "Stop crying or I'll give you something to cry about!" So the child gets the message that his feelings count for nothing. The child's pain, sadness and terror do not touch the heart of the caretaker. There is no appeal. He has no right to feel anything. His feelings and needs do not matter. Worse, he may conclude he is a "nothing" and deserves nothing.

Sometimes the caretaker may perceive the punishment as a means of protecting the child by teaching the "right way" to do things to avoid punishment by society. In this case, the caretaker tries to deliver the preemptive strike. "Life is tough and to survive in this world I must teach my child to follow the rules or to be tough and not trust or depend on others." When the caretaker is not sorry for hurting the child, the child may assume he actually deserved to be hurt. This conclusion can fuel a relentless inner critic that forms to deliver strikes preemptive to those of the caretaker.

Further, if the child has a sense that the punitive behavior is excessive or undeserved, it becomes all the more enraging, humiliating and/or terrifying. "This person who is supposed to care for me is actually trying to hurt me. What does that mean about me and my caretaker and what can I expect from the rest of the world?" Unfortunately he may conclude on some level that the caretaker is right – he is worthless and should not expect compassion from others or from himself.

In sum, a childhood event can become traumatizing when soothing was inadequate either because no one came or the child was too upset to accept the soothing that was offered, as a later section, "Waiting for repair" will demonstrate. With adequate soothing the <u>urge</u>

93

to <u>cry</u> does not become associated with "crying forever" or "too lonely" but rather with an eventual calming down and a shift to Let Go . . When the need for the help of another evoked by a trauma can finally be embraced there is no longer a bodyself price to pay in terms of residual bodily tension, anxiety nor a resolve to never let oneself need another. Residual feelings, expectations and attitudes as a result of non-integrated childhood trauma are often a source of anxiety that can lay beneath resistance to listening to the bodyself voice and being able to shift to Let Go . .

No matter when the trauma occurred or whether it involved abandonment or abuse, the unresolved needs and feelings need to be witnessed by another so they can be integrated and a sense of safety and bodyself well-being can abide. Because feelings associated with trauma are often intense and threaten the person with a sense of overwhelm and helplessness, professional help is often necessary to integrate them successfully. The evocative term "trauma vortex" denoted by Peter Levine* dramatically depicts the pull of the unresolved feelings in the wake of trauma as a dynamic vortex. Once triggered, the vortex "sucks" the victim down into overwhelming, recycling feelings of helplessness, rage, terror, horror, dread and despair. An experience of a trauma in adulthood which is similar to a nonintegrated childhood trauma can compound the disruptive effects on the ability to self-soothe in a healthy way.

The work on residual feelings from unresolved trauma is in some ways similar to, though more complex than the usual process of how a child learns to deal with emotional upset. Namely, the child reaches out for another person and is held and listened to while the feelings move through its bodyself – fear, shame, anger, despair and sadness – until calm and contentedness are restored**. The bodyself constriction of upset Let's Go! feelings of fear and anger give way to Let Go . . tears and softening as the child opens to love and feeling connected with another person and his own bodyself. This contentedness is the Let Go . . sense that all is well and that another can be counted on to come and help when needed. The consistent experience of being embraced when the child goes through feelings of upset to being soothed gradually becomes stored as a "bodyself memory". This process is the basis for the emotional recovery cycle and when repeated again and again develops the capacity for optimal self-soothing. And, sometimes self-soothing requires being able to call for help and being met with the embrace of another. Chapter 10 addresses this process in detail for the adult.

Ungrieved Loss

Ungrieved loss or interrupted grieving of a loss whether of a pet or a person, often gives rise to anxiety which can interfere with healthy self-soothing especially in the evening. Emotions and the need for connection often come up in the hours before bedtime when the daily distractions are fewer, threatening the potential of an evening calm. Sometimes a loss in adulthood brings up unresolved feelings of loss from childhood, especially when the child was not given enough support to grieve. The good news is that now is a chance for both losses, past and present, to be grieved but the bad news is that grieving the loss as an adult is likely to become even more challenging. In addition to sadness, other potentially disturbing latent feelings are fear, guilt, shame, resentment, despair, helplessness, hopelessness and longing. If you suspect that unresolved grief contributes to your not being able to compassionately listen to your bodyself, you could get some resolution by consulting a therapist who specializes in grief work and/or join a grief group. You may be stuck in one feeling or another and need support to move through it, so you can finally deeply grieve your loss and open to loving again and truly Let Go . . Taking in the presence of the compassionate other affirms that your heart is finding a way to live through this loss – that there is yet more for you if you can feel through all your feelings, reach out to another and shift to Let Go . . Otherwise you are left with anxiety and the threatening feelings of overwhelm, shame, rage, despair and hopelessness and perhaps even denial of your need to reach out for contact because it brings up the memory of painful loss.

Inadequate Caretaker Modeling of Self-Nurturing

Perhaps your parents were not great at self-soothing in a healthy way, that is, soothing that didn't involve alcohol or "pot". Or they may have judged activities like therapy, yoga, massage, meditation, and candle-lighted baths, as self-indulgent. Further, they may have dismissed self-nurturing and emotions as unimportant. Perhaps feelings were for "sissies" so they said "tough" or told you to "buck-up" when you had a problem with the way they treated you or with their expectations of you. So you didn't get to experience how healthy self-soothing could be part of your life, nor did you get any encouragement for efforts you made in that direction. If you tried to express your feelings you may have been labeled as "too sensitive". How sad it is that bodyself wisdom could be summarily dismissed with that one ignorant phrase. Chances are your parents' parents had similar attitudes. No wonder you now have trouble taking what you hear seriously when it is time to slow down and shift into Let Go . . Parents who don't soothe themselves in healthy ways are less likely to engender healthy self-soothing in their children.

Inadequate Nurturing by Your Caretakers

To understand the effects of inadequate nurturing by caretakers it helps to appreciate what adequate nurturing would look like. It is estimated that if your caretakers were able to respond to you at least 30% of the time in a supportive, attuned manner you are very likely to have a strong sense of self and be able to self-soothe in a healthy way. (The other 70% of the time is spent making up for the "misses"!)* Ideally, and I do mean ideally, your parents were delighted by your arrival in their world and you saw "de – light" in their eyes when they looked at you. You thereby came to feeling loved just for who you were. Ideally, your parents were available to you enough of the time to listen to your feelings and respond to your needs so that you were able to calm down after being upset and they shared in your excitement when you were happy. Ideally, you experienced that reaching out to another resulted often enough in getting the help you needed without being shamed for not being able to do it all yourself. And on the other hand, you were free to enjoy the discovery of what you <u>could</u> do all on your own! Being listened to and appropriately responded to enough of the time enabled you to eventually listen to and soothe yourself because you had embodied the repeated experience of being comforted. And when you needed something more you could ask for it without fear of being shamed as 'needy'. In these many ways, the loving and protective embrace of your parents enabled you to be able to embrace yourself and experience the sweet soothing accessible through your bodyself experience and shifting to Let Go . .

Ideally again, when the child is upset, the parent responds by coming to the child and listening to what the child says is the matter. Even if the child can not yet speak, the parent listens for "what is the matter?" and stays with the child until it is clear what is needed. She then responds appropriately with some combination of touch and sound (holding, rocking, stroking, talking, singing) until the child goes through the whole range of feelings which were evoked by the situation and becomes calm. These feelings can occur in almost any order but often include fear, anger, shame, and finally, sadness. This natural "emotional recovery cycle" of the bodyself is completed when the child relaxes into the parent's arms and feels the sweet contentment of being loved. The upset is over: no residual body tension or no held-back emotions. The child's breathing is easy as it rests into the experience of being met heart to heart* and shifts to Let Go . .

If your parents did not receive this kind of nurturing in their childhood, they were more likely to have difficulty "getting it right" often enough for you as a child, even when they tried their best. Their frustration at being so helpless and even worse, their anger at not being able to understand and soothe you, was likely communicated to you through their touch, facial expressions, and the sounds they made. Even when you were too young to understand their words, your bodyself reacted to their emotional energy and tension with tension of its own. Your experience of upset becomes associated with <u>even</u> more tension because of the way they habitually responded to you. So now your <u>upset</u> <u>feelings</u> become a <u>trigger</u> for even <u>more</u> <u>distress</u> and you have insufficient bodyself resource to calm yourself down. Your urge to cry and reach out for help in distress often results in more distress – shame, anger, fear, sadness and despair – Let's Go! upset abounds. No wonder you don't want to let yourself cry when you sense some sadness as you slow down and listen to your bodyself voice. No wonder you want to avoid slowing down and discovering what your anxiety is all about!

If your parents consistently heard your voice – sad, angry, or happy – you would be more likely to value your own voice – your feelings, emotions, intuitions – and be able to access your bodyself wisdom and soothing. You would be better able to grieve the loss of love and open to loving again. You would know your truth and not have to make up stories about what has happened to you in order to protect your image of your parents or yourself; you would be able to face what happens as you grow-up because someone had been there to help you understand the feelings and events of your childhood. You would be more able to go through the emotional recovery cycle and shift to Let Go . . with a minimum of residual feelings or tension. You could come through difficult times and happy times with your bodyself intact. You could reach out to steady yourself in particularly challenging times. You could celebrate your accomplishments and take delight in daily surprises. You could hear your emotional voice albeit mad, sad, glad or bad! Because your parents expressed to you their joy, pride and enthusiasm and joined in your happiness, you would be more likely to welcome these feelings as an adult and invite others to share them with you. Embracing "positive" Let Go . . emotions is essential for the capacity to self-soothe and to have a cozy relationship with your bodyself.

Not your experience? Not even close? Don't despair. If you weren't adequately nurtured during childhood, you still have a chance to learn how to self-soothe; try out the listening practices in this book and if you need more help consider consulting a therapist. The next few chapters are likely to help you anticipate the benefits of finally admitting that sometimes we just can't do it all ourselves and that sometimes reaching out is the perfect thing to do to meet our resistance and become optimally self-soothing!

If your caretakers were burdened with depression, disability, debt, dysfunctional family members or by addiction (to substances, work, rage or sex), narcissism, immaturity, psychosis, or perfectionism, they were likely not able to adequately nurture you. Perhaps your caretaker was simply distant as "in another world" or just not home enough. When "no one is home" and something really bad happens – an accident, a death, a severe illness, a fight, a molestation, you are left to your own devices to deal with overwhelming feelings on your own. A situation can become traumatic when no one listens to your story or soothes your feelings. For instance, an attentive caretaker would likely notice your upset if you were harassed by a bully whether it was a family member or a neighbor. She would help you find a way to deal with the threat rather than just leave you feeling scared or angry or bad about yourself. You would then know that she felt you didn't deserve to be treated that way. Children take in how they are <u>responded to</u> as if that reflected their worth, no matter how often the caretaker says "I love you!" The adage "Actions speak louder than words" applies here. Usually children figure it is their own fault if they don't <u>feel</u> loved and then try to "do better" to get what attention is available. But despite their best efforts children may not experience adequate caretaker nurturing or appreciation for their intrinsic worth, both of which are so vital to a strong sense of self-esteem. And that sad state of affairs leaves the child, at best, anxious for the approval of others to continually bolster its sense of self-worth.

Waiting for repair . . .

Much of what has been described in the preceding section gives rise to anxiety due to repeated experiences of failure to repair breaches in the caretaker-child connection. "Re-pair" is an apt word for restoring the sense that "we as a <u>pair</u> are OK". A relational repair is essential after a falling out between a caretaker and child whether it was due to a misunderstanding, a criticism or a punishment. To restore the connection, the caretaker needs to create a space wherein he affirms his love for the child by talking about what happened, exchanging apologies and expressions of caring. Otherwise the child still feels "on the hook" and remains vigilant. A narcissistic or perfectionistic or even a workaholic caretaker can be particularly critical and not be especially aware of the harmful effects of frequent criticism on the child's self-esteem. The experience of the child is often that he can't ever do enough to please the caretaker. The child stays anxious until the caretaker gives the nod of approval but that does not come often enough. The expressions, "I had to 'turn myself inside out' or 'bend over backwards' to try to please you and still it was never enough to get the love I needed", aptly describe the <u>bodyself</u> experience of this futile effort. The child often has to give up on getting praise and make do with the <u>absence</u> of criticism. The child of a critical caretaker often becomes even more critical of himself in a pre-emptive maneuver of self-defense.*

For the child, sorting out where he stands with his caretaker who is <u>narcissistic</u> is often even more challenging because when praise comes, it is in service of the mother's need to feel good about <u>herself</u> and has little to do with her love for the child. But to the child the praise, at first at least, sounds like something the child wants, yet the anxiety about its own basic love-worthiness does not go away. Unawares, the child is sensing the anxious needs of the caretaker but the child's anxiety goes unsoothed by the mother. No wonder children in these situations are likely to conclude that their own needs are not very important for they may not even be noticed by their caretakers.

In addition to anxiety, the experience of lack of repair after a rebuke or a punishment can also create a mixture of mistrust of the other and pernicious self-doubt. And to add insult to injury is the effect on the child when the caretaker comes back after a breach of connection and apologizes, then begs forgiveness saying, "I'll never do that again" and then does it again. At first the child forgives because he feels sorry for the seemingly contrite and/or tearful caretaker and is seduced into making the caretaker feel better. In this way, the child's need and love for the caretaker is used against the child; now the child has to do something with the sense of betrayal by the person most loved. And that something, is likely to be self-blame and a simultaneous distancing from the need for the caretaker. Now the caretaker has become the source of pain and terror, rendering him impotent as a source of connection and comfort for the child. The anxiety due to the submerged Let's Go! emotions like fear, anger, hurt, resentment and shame is palpable in the child's experience and results in bodyself tension and vigilance. As a consequence the child is deprived of the soothing calmness of a bodyself shift to Let Go . . The child learns that the beloved caretaker is not trustworthy and so feels caught between the need for the other on the one hand and on the other hand, strong feelings of fear, anger, shame and a sense of injustice. Repeated experiences create in the child, great anxiety, insecurity, a sense of being all alone and having to "do it" herself as well as a tendency to harshly judge herself and others.

Similarly the child of a rage-aholic or substance abuser will experience nearly constant vigilance and anxiety in varying degrees because of the unpredictability of the caretaker's moods and behavior toward the child and/or other members of the family. The experience of unpredictability in a caretaker can lead to the child's feeling undeserving of love, particularly when the caretaker could be diagnosed with a personality disorder*. Also when children are exposed to caretakers with anger management issues and who are given to unfair accusations, harsh judgments or random violent outbursts, the child may become fearful of its own anger when it presses for expression. This kind of vigilance and anxious "waiting for repair" attitude** can be seen in the adult when he is continually worried about whether someone is angry with him after a disagreement or when someone doesn't call back in a certain amount of time. This reaction could be a projection of his disowned anger at not being responded to and feeling so vulnerable. And surely children in these situations do not get the sense that their need for connection nor their feelings are important to the caretaker. And even more so, when someone does not step in and stand up to the abusive parent on the child's behalf. Since the one who is supposed to love and protect them has now become the source of pain and terror, these children not only often have difficulty reaching out to others, but also recognizing their own need for nurturance and may begin to withdraw or act out and otherwise deny their need for another person.

The aim of the blame game

Unfortunately children often tend to blame themselves when bad feelings abound in the household. This self-blaming tactic is a survival technique in that it is a way to feel not so helpless in the face of overwhelming feelings and of the limited capacity of the caretaker to connect. "Maybe if I am a better boy or a good girl, maybe if I am more helpful, get better grades, rub dad's shoulders or mom's feet, maybe if I make them laugh, do more chores, take care of the baby, keep them from fighting then they will be happy and not so angry, or depressed, or distant. There must be something I can do to make this situation more bearable and hopeful, less tense or explosive." However, the reality is that over the long haul, there is little the child can do to change the character of the caretaker – to make him/her less angry, more loving and responsive and that hopeless prospect is too frightening to bear. Accepting the limitations of the caretaker's ability to love, to listen and to protect is not possible if the child is to muster the courage and hope to continue on. By blaming himself he grasps for a sense of control even if his behaviors can't change his situation very much – he can at least do <u>something</u>. He looks for a "Let's Go!" something to do and stays vigilant, on guard, and tense.

There is no one to rest into, no one safe, at least not at home. Perhaps a visit to grandma's house provides some respite and the possibility of shifting to Let Go . . even if she was not so good at comforting her own child, she may be better with her grandchild.

Sadly, this self-blame is not all the child's doing. The caretaker's behavior may have actively contributed to the child's blaming itself. If the caretaker had an anger management problem, was addicted to substances, was mentally disordered, over-burdened, narcissistic or perfectionistic, chances are good that the caretaker sometimes directly blamed the child for how s/he was feeling or when something went wrong.

Another childhood scenario which fosters self-blame, anxiety and difficulty with slowing down and listening to bodyself messages is that of the needy caretaker and her child. Here the caretaker is very needy (even worse, also narcissistic) and makes the child feel responsible for the caretaker's needs and perhaps for the care of the rest of the family as well. In this case, the child's feelings and needs are almost completely subverted by the needs of the family. The reward for this sacrificed childhood is to feel <u>very</u> <u>important</u> but alas, <u>not</u> <u>loved</u> <u>for</u> <u>oneself</u>. This scenario is a perfect training ground for learning the behaviors typical of a "codependent". A "codependent" is defined by Melody Beattie*, author of "Codependent No More", as someone who does for someone else what they should learn to do for themselves. No matter how challenging the family situation is, children adapt themselves to their environment to get whatever they can of their needs met. If your family situation had this flavor, you are likely to experience a fair amount of anxiety trying to take care of all the needy friends and family that look to you for help while at the same time you don't get your own needs for nurturance met. No wonder you have difficulty when you slow down and try to listen to what your bodyself has to say about that situation and still get a good night's sleep!

Remember, the point of the exploration in this chapter is not to blame your parents or yourself but to <u>explain</u> and <u>understand</u> how you came to have difficulties listening to your bodyself and slowing down in the interests of taking good care of yourself. Even with the best of intentions, your caretakers were not likely to be able to give you what they didn't have access to themselves. So whether they just couldn't give themselves a break and thereby didn't model healthy self-soothing or whether they had troubled relationships with their own parents so they didn't adequately attend to your needs and feelings, your ability to self-soothe was likely compromised. If you didn't get enough experience being listened to, understood, connected to, calmed down or celebrated, you are now likely to have difficulty listening to what is really going on in your bodyself. And, even when you do find out, you may have trouble dealing with the feelings that come up or expressing what you need so you can eventually calm down and shift to Let Go . . At least distracting yourself with another Let's Go! activity keeps the unwanted feelings at bay, that is, until you lie down and try to fall asleep. Then the feelings press toward awareness and you may find yourself, restless, tense and thinking, thinking, thinking . . .

And what are you telling yourself as you lie there, thinking and thinking, or wracked with worry and concern? Why can't you give yourself to the comfort of your bed, to the gentle darkness of the night and shift to Let Go . .? What you are saying to yourself could be something that has roots in your childhood experiences and, believe it or not, is likely an attempt at protecting yourself from something even more threatening. It may be quite a challenge for you to see how being preoccupied with worrying or with critical thoughts about yourself could serve a self-protective function so I ask you to stay with me as I try to explain what has become so clear and useful in helping me become more self-soothing.

The Stance

By now you may have identified at least one of the scenarios or situations described here which could give rise to some residual anxiety that you try to avoid feeling by distracting yourself when you attempt to slow down and listen to your bodyself. Perhaps you have discovered by reading the preceding section that indeed you do downplay your need to be nurtured in some important ways, including not reaching out to others. If you have great difficulty giving to yourself by implementing the listening practices as proposed in these chapters, please consider the possibility that your difficulty may arise from a coping strategy you developed most likely as a result of childhood experiences, which I am calling a "stance".

Some therapists call this creative strategy, "your story". Your "story" is an attempt to try to make some sense out of what was happening when you experienced a trauma or when you were inadequately nurtured and you had no one with whom to share your feelings. What you told yourself was in service of gaining a sense of control so you could manage feelings that were threatening to overwhelm you. Your "story" by definition functions to deny, minimize, or judge your need to reach out to another and to be loved and it achieves this end by determining beliefs about yourself and others. Another, more dynamic description of your efforts to adapt to the limitations of your caretakers is what my therapist, Bob Hilton, Ph.D. calls an "adaptive self"*. You develop an adaptive self, complete with a set of behaviors and beliefs with which you strongly identify in order to adapt to the limitations of your caretakers at the expense of some important needs, particularly to be loved for yourself. The "stance" is a core belief of the adaptive self and at the heart of the "story".

I prefer the word "stance" to the word "story" because "stance" invokes both a mind and <u>body</u> attitude and bespeaks of intention. The stance is determined by a belief about oneself in relation to others which organizes behavior and is accompanied by bodyself tension. Your stance can be identified by a succinct verbal statement which motivates certain coping (or adaptive) behaviors and can be experienced as a pattern of bodyself tension especially in the neck, jaw, forehead, and torso (abdomen, stomach, chest, back). Stances such as "I don't need anyone!" or "I can handle it" or "That's it, I'll do it myself" or "You can't get to me" is the result of a "decision" (a declaration, cry, protest, resolve) that you very likely made a long time ago. It represents a declaration which helped you survive by adapting to the conditions you found yourself in as you were growing up. You may be able to recall a pivotal incident which crystallized your decision if you think back on some of your earliest memories (the not-so-happy-ones, of course!). This resolve or conviction helped you deal with the limitations of your parents' ability to love and nurture you and still get whatever attention was available. Your stance protected you from feeling so vulnerable to their limitations (and perhaps from not even seeing them) by giving you a sense of self, of independence and control. So then you were less likely to experience being overwhelmed by uncomfortable feelings and needs which had little chance of being met. But the price you are likely to pay for maintaining the stance is diminished awareness of your bodyself due to numbness and tensing against the threatening needs and feelings, increased difficulty in reaching out to another or taking in nurturing and love, as well as in sensing what you truly need for self-soothing.

As a child you likely struggled with having to maintain a sense of control in a relational world that threatened to feel out of control at any moment because the caretaker was not available in the way you needed to feel valued. For instance, a child needs the caretaker to listen to its hurt, his anger, his grief and disappointment and needs to hear that the caretaker cares that it hurt the child. Such caretaker "attunement" could have helped you reconnect to your bodyself so that you could go through the emotional recovery cycle and shift to the well-being of Let Go . . But when your caretaker's heart was not available, you were in a real bind. Approaching your caretaker on the caretaker's terms would mean giving up some part of yourself. This created a perpetual "no-win" situation for you and forced a kind of "Sophie's choice"*. If you reached out in longing for connection, your caretaker's needs may have overwhelmed your needs, threatening yourself with annihilation once again. On the other hand, if out of self-protection you withheld reaching for your caretaker, you sacrificed your fundamental need for connection. Either way you lost. But in answering your caretaker's "No!" to your need for nurturance with a "No!" of your own, you could gain some sense of control, a sense of being able to <u>do</u> <u>something</u> to feel a little powerful. More devastating than even losing your caretaker is losing your self - the sense that you matter or even exist.

Your "Sophie's choice" and the contracted "No!"

Like Sophie, you were faced with sacrificing a valuable part of yourself no matter which choice you made. Denying your need for your caretaker is like trying to "kill the needful baby inside" you. The fear of being abandoned ("No, don't leave me!"), the fear of being abused ("No, don't hurt me!") and the fear of not being loved for who you are can result in the stance contraction of "No, I don't need/want you, you can't get to me!" Your bodyself contracts** around your "No!" as your muscles tense, your body twists, breathing restricts and your energy moves to your head. Your sense of self becomes organized around this "No, I don't need you! I don't need your love. I won't let you get to me. I will not humiliate myself by pleading! No! No! No!" You think, you judge, you criticize, you "space out". Your "No!" may be heard in your pessimism or sarcasm. The energy of this "No!" may be expressed through rebellion and acting out or suppressed through compliancy or caretaking. You may hide your need for another from yourself or make yourself, along with your needs, disappear through tensing your body and dissociation. The dilemma becomes how to feel deeply soothed without the threat of the pain of unmet needs which continually arise. No wonder you have trouble taking good care of yourself as an adult. The attempt to be nurtured has previously meant giving up some essential need or part of yourself.

Living in the contracted "No!" place means you cannot breathe deeply nor can you soften and truly Let Go . . You must stay on guard lest you re-experience the unresolved pain of abandonment or intrusion. You may heighten the contraction of your muscles in order to feel a sense of control and to deny the vulnerability of your heart by not feeling the emotional pain of feeling unloved or inadequate. This "No!" you say to your need for another is anchored by suppressed anger which maintains your stance and obscures the underlying despair. The resultant body tension and holding in breathing reduces the flow of bodyself messages and simultaneously increases the Let's Go! energy flow to your head, fueling thinking, worrying, criticizing, vigilance, and addiction.

While nearly squeezing the life out of you, the tightening of your muscles may also paradoxically serve to give you a sense of control. Holding onto "yourself" is something you <u>can</u> do, even though getting what you really need from your caretaker is hopeless. There is no one else to hold onto or to hold you, so you "self-hold" for dear life. There may even be some satisfaction, if not pleasure, in creating this kind of tension because it affirms a sense of self which does not give into the despair of helplessness. Even if this tension puts you in the hospital, makes you take pain pills, leads to addiction or your demise, you have some sense of control.

Without even your being aware of it, this bodyself sacrifice you make can become a commitment that lasts a lifetime. The word "stance" itself bespeaks a sense of rigidity and inflexibility as well as a sense of bracing for what is to come. This mind-body attitude influences many of your critical life-choices, from your occupation, to your mate and friends as well as how you self-soothe. Underlying the stance is the often subconscious devaluing of the need to be loved for yourself and settling for a sense of power or control through behaviors adapted to the environment to get recognition. The sacrifice is blaming <u>yourself</u> for not being loved just as you are. Instead, in order to be "loved", "I have to take care of you, and/or the family, be the 'best' at whatever, work my guts out, entertain you, be tough, not complain, cry or be angry."

Below are other stances (and the associated "adaptive self")* which will be further elaborated in the next chapter:

"Work is my most important need!"	(Work-aholic)
"You have needs, I don't!"	(Codependent)
"Success is my most important need"	(Super-achiever)
"I don't care (about anyone)!"	(Rebel)
"I don't need anyone"	(Loner)

The Stance Trance

By "stance trance" I mean being under the sway (trance) of the stance. Not everyone who has trouble with healthy self-soothing is in the grips of a stance-trance but unawares, many are. In the stance trance you are blind to the limitation of the loved one to meet your need to be loved for who you are. You may never have asserted your stance aloud, in fact, you quite likely didn't. You may have sensed it as a very "loud" thought as if you were talking to yourself (or screaming at someone else) inside your head. Nonetheless you became convinced of its veracity and led your life accordingly, reacting to others as though it was true, and often assuming that they believed it too. It dictated how you saw yourself in the world and how you expected to be treated and how you treated yourself and others. This stance creates a <u>vantage</u> point which was intended to give you an "<u>ad</u>-vantage" when what you really needed was in short supply or not available at all. But eventually as you will discover, the stance which enabled you to adapt to and survive a compromising situation begins to compromise your life as an adult and becomes a "<u>dys</u>ad-vantage".

However skewed, it did offer a vantage point which was preferable, at least when you were a child, to facing the painful reality that your need for love would never be met by the ones who mattered to you most. Like self-blame, the stance has a pre-emptive function – you blame yourself for what goes wrong before someone else blames you and you adapt your behavior accordingly. For instance, the stance of "I don't need you!" is an attempt to preempt the impact of the wounding by the other when you think his actions indicate he doesn't truly care about you in some fundamental ways. From your stance trance, you peer out of the "hole" in your wounded heart rather than look out from your "whole" heart. To regain your whole heart and full access to your bodyself, you may likely have to be met in your pain and in your withholding by a compassionate other, thereby releasing the "constriction" around your heart. That is, your "No!" to your need to be loved for who are can gradually give way to the mutual "Yes!" in the presence of a compassionate other. Then you will be more likely to see with open eyes and an open heart, the "whole picture" rather than the distorted view embodied in your stance. With repeated experiences of this nature, you may gradually give up your identification with past pain and how you survived it (the stance trance) and enjoy experiencing contact with your bodyself and another in the present.

Giving up the stance to dance!

Giving up the stance trance requires your creating enough support to go through the feelings which have been held back for so long and to finally grieve the limitations of your parents and have compassion for yourself. With full access to your feelings and needs you can go through the emotional recovery cycle and live in reality, rather than in a trance that blinds you to reality. Since stances often result from unresolved trauma or inadequate caretaker nurturing, work on your stance can be greatly facilitated by the assistance of an attuned other who has personally experienced this sometimes perilous emotional terrain. In short you need a well-experienced "guide"* with whom you can develop a strong and trusting relationship in addition to your developing greater bodyself awareness with the listening practices.

Up until then, the stance is all you have to hold onto because it's so threatening to allow yourself to love or be loved lest you become overwhelmed by the feelings of the childhood struggle to be loved. If you start to have loving feelings for someone, you are likely to come up against strong resistance to letting yourself experience them deeply. Admitting to wanting, not to mention taking in the love of another could open you to re-experiencing the unbearable pain around the unmet need in childhood. As your bodyself feels the impulse toward loving and connecting, you are likely in a real bind. You are probably not aware that this is why you are having trouble in your relationship or maybe not even being with someone long enough to call it a "relationship". You may choose a partner who has similar issues with vulnerability and who, in fact may be even less vulnerable than you are; so now you may not have to face your own challenge of opening your heart. Imagine how these conflicted feelings and needs could make it difficult to self-soothe in a healthy way at night or anytime for that matter!

The bodyself constriction "around the No!" you say to your need for another sets up a fierce conflict deep inside you of which you may only be vaguely aware. You are likely to experience strong ambivalence toward this other or to be set on having to have that particular unavailable person. You are likely to be blinded by your stance since the stance arises out of the difficulty with accepting the limitations of the loved one. While you may sometimes see evidence s/he is not available, you focus on the opposite indications and imagine that s/he is falling in love with you, but you tell yourself, s/he is just not aware of it! You may notice those limitations, but you don't allow yourself to feel them for very long because if you did, those long repressed feelings which your stance was developed to shield you from would begin to clamor for recognition.

If you find that you become focused on having to have that particular one person who is not so available and you experience the pain of not being met again and again yet you can't let go of wanting that person, take heart! This could be an ideal opportunity to finally work on your childhood issue of not being able to deal with the limitations of your caretaker in loving you. It takes commitment and courage to experience the pain you need to face and the feelings you will need to work through to come out of your stance trance and see the world through your whole heart and live in your full bodyself reality.

103

For me, this effort has been totally worth the time and energy. Living in my bodyself truth is a relief and a pleasure: *she* is my anchor and my treasure; *she* gives me joy and solace beyond measure. Besides, now I can be a better guide to others who want to fully experience bodyself aliveness and loving relationships with themselves and others, not to mention optimal self-soothing.

You may not yet be ready to take this journey; you may need to experience more frustration in trying to soothe yourself in an optimal way and in finding a satisfying relationship. You may need to experience the pain of another failed relationship and of being torn between your need to protect yourself from feeling the pain of the past and the desire to experience love and connection. I hope for your sake that you will get tired of repeating the same old pattern and give yourself a chance to live and love fully. Be prepared to experience deep and powerful feelings as you slowly build the capacity to be more present in your bodyself through these listening practices. Your stance is held in place by fear of feeling powerless and despairing, not to mention, angry in the face of the limitations of your parents to give you what you needed. In order to give up the stance, you need to feel through fear, anger, shame, and despair to finally grieve your caretaker's limitations. In order to truly grieve this loss you must be able to sense there is "something more" for you, more valuable than the denial of your need to be loved and your clinging to have that certain one's love. For me, the "something more" was felt in the abiding presence of my therapist which steadied me as I experienced the depths of my struggle with nearly overwhelming feelings. Then as I became deeply connected to my bodyself experience, I was more capable of optimal self-soothing.

To wit, recently in a therapy session I was working with how I felt about the prospect of seeing someone again with whom I had broken up because he was simply not emotionally available to fall in love with me. I imagined him sitting across from me and I said aloud, "I won't let you get to me!" It was a very clear and strong statement and I felt pleased how readily it was voiced. However my therapist pointed out that that statement could be coming from my stance such that I might also be saying "No!" to my organismic need for another person rather than just to the one who couldn't return my love. I looked at my therapist and as I sensed him very clearly, little tears formed. I felt immediately that I didn't want to say that "No!" to my therapist's caring. Clearly, I did not want to maintain my stance with him and keep him out. The sense of a shared presence – my letting in his presence and letting myself be seen by him - was the "something more" which made it worth giving up my stance of not "letting you get to me". What I needed was a real choice about who I opened my heart to and to do that I needed to sense the true limitation of the other which meant to had to face the pain of the limitations of my childhood caretakers. As long as I was entranced by my stance, I would not see the other clearly in terms of his limitations to be open to me. (The unfolding of this work is detailed in subsequent chapters).

As I stayed with the recognition I found myself spontaneously stretching and reaching and opening my jaw as my tensed muscles released. The blessed relief of Let Go . . I felt deeply what I would be missing if I had stayed stuck in that stance - my enjoyment of being "in relationship" with another and with my bodyself experience. I sensed I didn't need my therapist as in having to have him; I needed to have "me" – the embodied experience of me being met in my need for contact and being seen by the other. Owning my desire for contact allowed me to be present and share those moments of aliveness. My therapist was clearly not that "other one" who was so limited in his ability to love me. I felt very satisfied and "sweet" - somewhere between joy and peace – excellent preparation for a better night's sleep!

Ultimately working on these deep issues can make possible regaining your bodyself and as you do, you can actually choose whether you live in illusion or not! Until I worked through these issues and could more reliably hear my bodyself voice, I didn't have the choice "to stance or not to stance". Up until then powerful emotional forces were working inside me and the only way I knew how to sustain my sense of self was to maintain my stance. Even though my stance had painful consequences, what had seemed worse was the reality that I couldn't face as a child. As an adult I found the support I needed and I took it in; then I could finally face and grieve what had been true all along. Now I feel more free to dance, released from the anger of the contracted stance. Now I'm no longer blind to whom I choose, so surely I have nothing to lose! Coming out of your stance takes time because you have to have enough support in your bodyself as well as from a trusted other who can meet you where you may have never been met before. And my journey has been worth it as you may gather from the anecdote below.

"I know who I am!"

She is nudging me to share with you a recent triumph in breaking through my stance trance and finding my voice. Because we are both so happy about it for it demonstrates the power of being seen in the moment as well as of the embodied experience of having been seen in the past. When I am under the sway of my stance trance and I reach out to someone who then seems to be unavailable, I sometimes interpret this unavailability as saying something about my value to this person. For instance, I might see my friend across the courtyard and approach only to discover she is engaged with someone and doesn't seem to notice my existence, even though it appears she is looking in my direction. Under the sway of my stance trance I would likely conclude that she doesn't want to talk to me, doesn't like me, is mad at me, I'm not good enough, or I'm inappropriate, etc and then feel shame, sadness and turn away. Submerged anger is likely to arise and then the stance of "I don't need anyone" would assert itself. Because this cycle has been so repetitive, I feel shame, for I think I should be able to weather the occasional perceived "rejection" better.

Because this cycle was unhappily so familiar, I chose to work on it in a recent training workshop. My trainee therapist explored other possibilities with me: what else could be going on with my friend besides my dire interpretations and what other choices do I have in terms of a response. But it wasn't until she suggested I try on the phrase "I know who I am" that I felt a shift in me. Most impactful was that I felt valued by her because she thought enough of me to give me that phrase to remind myself of my value. Then I recognized that I do know who I am and I do feel I have value and can support that feeling in my bodyself as a result of all the work I had done with my own therapist. Without that previous embodied experience of his seeing me I would not have had this referent - this solid resource to draw on. We slowed down the process of what happens in me after I see signs of the other's unavailability. I imagined pressing a "Pause" button so I could put some space between what I actually saw and what I made of it which in turn would determine how I responded. I decided to make "I know who I am" my mantra for awhile, with the emphasis on the first "I". I know who I am even if the other doesn't – I have value even if it appears the other doesn't think I do. I can acknowledge I wanted the attention of the other but I am still OK even if I don't get it. I may be disappointed but I don't lose myself; I am no longer forced to make a "Sophie's Choice". I just have to remember to tell myself, "I know who I am" and reinforce the new neural pathway* in my emotional brain.

In sum, while you may not be aware of the bind you were in as a child, it is likely to persist today albeit somewhat out of your awareness. It may be sensed in your bodyself holding and the way you perceive what happens to you. You are probably still using the same coping strategies, have the same stance, and find yourself making the same choices and mistakes, over and over again. And when you do, you are likely to criticize yourself. Then to soothe your troubled feelings you may turn to one or another of the addictions – food, sex, substances, work, etc. which results in your feeling guilty and then being critical all over again. The "<u>resi - stance</u>" <u>maintaining cycle</u> involving "the critic" and addiction is discussed in the next chapter along with several other stances with which you may identify. Now you have a chance to alter this cycle by discovering what your stance is, identifying situations that have led to your dilemma and then creating the support to work through the feelings and needs that have for so long been waiting to be met. The next three chapters could be pivotal in pointing the way to overcoming your resistance listening to your bodyself voice so you can optimally self-soothe.

Identifying your stance is key to dancing through your "resi-stance"!

Going Deeper:

Identify your excuses and pleas when it is time to get ready for bed and when you know you need to slow down and shift to Let Go . .

Identify unresolved situations, past or present which could lead to uncomfortable feelings and needs which may contribute to your resistance to self-soothing in a healthy way. If you didn't try the exercise at the beginning of this chapter, check it out before you go onto the next chapter.

Can you identify your contracted "No!" in your pessimism, your bodyself tension, judgment of others or self-criticism, sarcasm, acting out, addictive behavior, etc.

Try to identify your stance from the list below and then consult the next chapter for more clues about your resi - stance and how you maintain it. Reading the next chapter may help you see yourself in one of these stances. It is possible that your stance is so unconscious that it just seems like the "truth" about the way life is as well as your place in it. However it may be at the core of your resistance to taking better care of yourself.

"Work is my most important need!"	Work is never done
"Success is my most important need"	(Super-achiever): Failure is not an option, I need to be the best
"You have needs, I don't!"	(Codependent): I know what is best for others and they need me.

"I have to do it all myself"	(Martyr): I don't need anyone but everyone depends on me
"I don't care (and don't need anyone)!"	(Rebel): I will get mine!
"I don't need anyone!"	(Loner): Don't trust anyone.

Dear Reader: Take a chance and let us show you how to dance out of the stance trance! For I can't dance when you are in your stance because you can't feel me: my need to be loved for who I am, my desire to reach out to another and my anger about not being loved for who I am. Therefore, I am not real to you. Feel me and become real. When you are so careful to not make someone mad, that makes me sad. I would so rather be glad and sometimes even "bad"! I'm waiting to dance with you as you find the support to come out of your trance. In the next chapter you can meet your inner critic and/ or addict who likely help you maintain your stance trance which keeps you from your most alive and joyous dance!

8

MEETING RESISTANCE TO MEETING YOUR
RESISTANCE TO YOUR BODYSELF VOICE

How do you meet your resistance to meeting your resistance?
By meeting your "inner critic" and your "inner addict", a little at a time!

The repetition of the phrase "meeting resistance" in this chapter title, highlights what a challenge it can be to listen to your bodyself voice as you try to take better care of yourself. Even if you are confused by this seeming "double talk" please continue. If the section on the inner critic doesn't hit home, the one on addiction will likely give you some insight into how you resist meeting your resistance. Despite your best intentions, you may find yourself stymied by your resistance but perhaps you can sense your <u>resistance</u> to <u>giving up your resistance</u>! The previous chapter may have helped you understand the conflict that could live within you as result of unresolved situations such as inadequate caretaker nurturing or trauma, which now have become a source of resistance to listening to your bodyself voice. This chapter can help you understand how <u>you maintain</u> this resistance and what you can do to get more clues as to what your bodyself needs from you, so you can meet your resistance to becoming more self-soothing. Even if you decide to see a therapist so you can get more support in experiencing and meeting your resistance, you can find out <u>right now</u> more about how your resistance operates by observing yourself more closely. Your *her/him* is waiting for you!

In the end, overcoming your resistance is an "inside job". Even though at some point you may need the attuned presence of another person – <u>you</u> still decide when to let your resistance melt away, one moment after the other. One of the key forces in maintaining the stance and keeping unresolved, threatening feelings at bay is the "inner critic". It's that voice that comments critically and often times, relentlessly when you look in the mirror or when you realize something you did hurt someone or when you drop something or forget something or make a mistake. How the critic operates in the role of an "enforcer" (critics can be very tough!) of a stance is clearly seen in the critic-caretaker cycle discussed below. The second force which plays a key role in maintaining "your resistance to your resistance" is addictive behavior. Addictive behavior is an attempt at self-soothing that doesn't require giving up your stance or your critic. In fact, it may even fuel your critic's efforts and enforce your stance. In response your addictive behavior may become more entrenched.

Your resistance to sensing bodyself messages is held in place by the muscular tension and the attitude toward yourself and others associated with your stance. So whatever supports maintaining your stance will keep you from overcoming your resistance to taking good care of yourself. Both addictions and the critic make bodyself messages less available so that you have fewer clues as to what you need for optimal self-soothing. The critic distracts you from your bodyself voice by obsessive nit-picking, haranguing, worrying and making you tense, and addictions tend to numb your bodyself voice.

Meeting your resistance to meeting your resistance sounds challenging and it is! But it's not impossible; there are success stories. I am one and you can be one, too!

The Critic - Caretaker Cycle

I want to first give you a sense of how the critic can operate in maintaining <u>denial</u> of the need for nurturance, whether by being an "enforcer" of the stance or just being critical of your needs, feelings or almost anything or anyone else. Then I will give you some suggestions for getting to know your own critic better – remember, what we are about here is meeting the resistance to meeting our resistance! The work of meeting your critic is good preparation for therapy dealing with childhood issues, unresolved grief and trauma, relationship issues and just plain old "I want to take better care of myself, but I am stuck" issues! I want you to have a sense of what you can do on your own, as well as, to encourage you to consider how reaching out to someone for help, however daunting, could be life-changing.

The Codependent Caretaker Stance

The critic-caretaker cycle is a paradoxical dynamic that can occur when your need to be connected to was not adequately met as you were growing up. In an effort to preempt the pain of not being responded to in an adequately nurturing way, your critic may harshly judge your need to be nurtured. Your caretaker may have not been in touch with her own need for nurturance and therefore, was oblivious or even contemptuous of yours. In any case, you may have become critical of your own need for nurturance in order to <u>protect yourself</u> from feeling the disappointment of those needs not having been met. Denying your nurturance need is, in fact, one way to take care of your caretaker and gives rise to the "caretaker" or "codependent" stance. Yet your nurturance need persisted and now may express itself as a projection onto others. While blinded to your own needs, you "see" your needy face in the visage of another. Since the perception of neediness is likely to bring up intolerable feelings of helplessness and shame, you may be driven to take care of the other and, at the same time, you may have subliminal feelings of <u>contempt</u> for <u>those</u> needy ones. You may not realize that you are attempting to care for yourself through caring for them, because that awareness would cause you to have contempt for yourself. Better to have contempt for <u>them</u> than yourself!

Thus your criticalness of your own need for caretaking can turn you into a caretaker for others – hence the term "critic-caretaker cycle". You may even pride yourself in how well you take care of others and/or feel superior to those other "needy" people. There is no end to the energy drain when you caretake others – there are so many of them and they are all bottomless pits (since they may have depended on you to take care of them at the expense of learning how to do it themselves.) In fact, some of them are not even <u>that</u> needy; they only appear to you to be so. This perception of neediness is likely, in itself, evidence of the strength of your projected unmet need. Better them be needy, than you! In any case, you may feel they are not appreciative enough, in fact, sometimes they seem even resentful of your efforts. And, surprise, surprise, you find yourself feeling critical and even resentful of them. Resentment feels more powerful than needy. So better you feel resentful than <u>needy!</u>

The resentfulness you may feel is likely fueled by your original resentfulness toward your caretaker for not attending to your rightful needs long ago. If you sacrificed your needs for nurturing, to take care of the one who was supposed to take care of you, that sacrifice may have been the only way you could get her to appreciate you and for you to feel important.

You may have adopted a stance which declared, "I don't have needs, I will take care of needy you" and accepted what you could get, at the expense of denying your need to be loved for yourself. And because you may still not accept that you need nurturing, you may not (until now!) have taken steps to discover your blocks to getting those needs fulfilled. So you are likely very tired, cranky and, yes, needy!

Burned-out, at the point of exhaustion and total exasperation you may cry "What about me?" to the surprise of those around you. You may even, God forbid, feel angry or resentful toward the others. But remembering what your caretaker's coldness, indifference or even meanness felt like, you are likely to quickly move away from those harsh feelings. You may not be able to bear to act toward others like your caretaker may have acted toward you. Besides, admitting to yourself you have needs puts you face to face with the limitations of your caretaker and the feelings of despair you have not enough support to feel. So better not to go there! Now your <u>critic</u> has the upper hand, admonishing you for not being giving, and for being resentful so you become the caretaker once again. The critic's messages keep you in line, further depleting your energy and at the same time distancing you from your need to be taken care of. You have no support for your "That's enough 'No!'", your "I'm-tired 'No!'", the "Now-it-is-my-turn 'No!'" This is the "No!" that was not heard and honored by your caretaker. You will likely need someone else to help you hear and embrace your "No!" In so doing you may come to say "Yes!" to your need for nurturance. Better to nurture <u>you</u> than them!

As long as you are in denial about your own needs, the other's gratitude will <u>never be enough</u> to satisfy <u>your</u> need, because you are still sacrificing yourself and not open to letting nurturing in. You are likely to continue to take care of someone else when you are in need, just as you likely had to do as a child. The shorter route of just taking care of yourself or asking someone to help you is not open to you, because it is humiliating to admit you have needs (There's the critic again!). As an adult you have a choice about who to take care of, yourself or the other, but you still choose the other. You may be too afraid to feel your own repressed, overwhelming need for love and contact and your sense of powerlessness to get it. I hope you will take a chance and get the help you need to face the deprivation and terror of your childhood, express your anger and frustration and grieve what you didn't receive. Then you can begin to truly take in nurturing contact, perhaps for the first time. That, in itself, can take you a long way toward being able to listen to your bodyself for what you need now. You may be able to do this yourself, but, more likely, you will need the help of a therapist and/or an Alanon group. And, better <u>now,</u> than never!

The "Critical" Caretaker

When you deny your own nurturance needs instead of trying to meet another's, you may also deny or judge another's needs for nurturing care. For instance, many years ago I caught myself contemptuously judging a massage client for being so "picky" about what she wanted me to do. Imagine! She seemed to think that she deserved "special treatment." At the time, I judged her as overly sensitive and self-protective. I even felt miffed at her telling me my pressure was too much when I felt like I was "barely" touching her. What I took as criticism of my work gave rise to my criticism of her. Touché! My critic was in overdrive that day, criticizing the person who was criticizing me. It was only several years later when I recognized how afraid <u>I</u> was to ask for what I wanted, lest I be judged the way I had judged my client. I was afraid of asking for "too much" or making my own massage therapist feel criticized and, perhaps, risk his withholding his caring from me. These concerns directly mirrored my experience of my caretakers' hypersensitive reactions to my complaints – one tended to withdraw or fall apart and the other was likely to criticize or shame me.

While I was overtly judgmental of people who asserted their needs, I was also secretly envious. For instance, I might comment to myself, "What chutzpah! She went for the biggest piece – just like that – the one I wanted but didn't dare reach for." Underlying my judgment of her was the "No!" that had been said to me as a child when I started to take what I wanted. Wanting my caretaker's approval, I denied myself and then turned the anger I felt – (my own "No!" to being deprived) into resentment and judgment of the other. In short, judging or disowning your needs can result in judging another's neediness, as well as, in trying to vicariously meet your own needs by taking care of the other.

Meeting Your Critic

You can begin to work with your critic on your own by following the suggestions in the proceeding paragraphs and by consulting Hal and Sidra Stone's excellent book "Embracing Your Critic"*. Your critic was likely formed to help protect you from further humiliation by your caretakers. Its preemptive tactic is to terrify and humiliate you before they get to you. Your critic often does even a better job of controlling you than your caretakers did because the critic anticipates hurtful outcomes and swiftly and surely alerts you to potential danger every chance it gets. Sometimes just labeling this critical noise in your head as a "critic" provides some distance and softens its impact.

But if your caretaker was woefully inadequate and especially if she was very critical, narcissistic or angry, you may quickly reach an impasse or feel in danger of being overwhelmed by emotion when you try to do this work on your own. Working with a therapist could give you the emotional support you need to deal with the sense of powerlessness you will likely feel in the face of a devastating and, perhaps, even sadistic critic. Without this support the terrified vulnerable child part of you is no match for the heartless critic. A heartless parent gives rise to a heartless critic. If no one interceded on your behalf and stopped the emotional or physical abuse in childhood, you may have difficulty meeting and slowing down this relentless critic on your own. If the critic discovers that it has a heart, then you can experience the true protective function of the critic. This discovery can be more easily made with the heartfelt support of an attentive, caring other, who does not shrink from the cruelty of your critic and can help you find your heart for yourself.

What follows are some examples of some ways to intervene when the critic is the only voice you hear inside your head. Your critic may make you worry whether other people are mad at you or make you agonize over what you fear is a mistake. You may have a "Why did I?" critic - one that makes you question over and over "Why did I do (or say) that?" The critic often fills the unknown with its worrisome, doomsday predictions and sometimes toxic messages. Gradually you will discover the main messages and tactics of your critic. As you begin to understand its function, the way it operates and how it feels in your bodyself, it becomes less surprising and less toxic. You will be able to anticipate its appearance by noticing what triggers it. My critic can be triggered by my making a mistake, by hurting someone, expressing anger and even by a spontaneous gesture of affection or self-assertion. In any case, it is important to find out what triggers your critic so you can anticipate it. When you notice that you feel badly, ask yourself when did you last feel good? What happened

111

to bring that good feeling to an end? It's a safe bet that your critic was involved somewhere along the line, even if someone else was too. The critic can make it very <u>difficult</u> to go through the <u>emotional</u> <u>recovery</u> <u>cycle</u> even after the small upsets that inevitably happen.

Checking in with Yourself:

The goal here is not to get rid of the critic (for that is impossible) but to discover how it can support rather than terrorize you. Make a list of the messages of the critic and then study your list for any similarities to messages you may have received from your parents or caretakers. You are likely to discover the original protective function of the critic by considering these messages as warnings or preemptive strikes. How might the messages on this list have been helpful in surviving your childhood? If you greatly feared your caretaker's anger or abandonment, your critic is likely to be relentless and not let you off the hook in an attempt to protect you from your caretaker's wrath or withdrawal. Your critic often makes it nearly impossible to hear what your <u>emotional</u> <u>voice</u> is trying to say. That takes practice and the support of your bodyself and perhaps of another.

Asking for Help

The next step is the most difficult, especially if you were cruelly or sadistically treated. The task is to find another voice to answer the critic. This voice is, at first, likely to sound like a hurt, frightened, vulnerable child. It might cry or complain about being so mistreated or even say, "Stop!" you are scaring (hurting) me!" Hopefully, you will feel touched by its pleas and the tone of its voice. But your critic may try to smash it for sounding so weak. At this point you may need the intervention of a caring, supportive other, who does not shrink from the sadistic force of the critic and can help the vulnerable part of you fight back and can help you grieve the hopelessness of your childhood situation.

If you can't hear the plea of your emotional voice, "Stop, you're hurting me!" then you are likely to continue hurting yourself. If you turn a deaf ear or a cold shoulder to your fear, sadness or helplessness, you are likely to be critical of yourself or others when helplessness is perceived. The stance of "I don't have needs" can give you a sense of control. But for that, you pay a great price. What you gain in a sense of control, you are likely to lose in empathy for another and yourself. And the energetic disturbance of the cry continues albeit "underground". Then neither you nor another can truly soothe you. Your resistance to letting another's presence deeply soothe you, gives you a sense of self at the expense of not feeling truly safe and being able to shift to Let Go . . For if you could accept your need for another and felt worthy of being loved, you could have the choice of letting another's caring "in" and be soothed or you could soothe yourself.

An even more subtle ramification of saying "No!" to your needs for nurturance is not being aware of <u>how</u> <u>angry</u> you are about having been scared, thwarted, or intimidated. Afraid to speak out – angry that you just can't be yourself and feel loved – that you feel you have to walk on eggshells to be liked. The energy of this disturbance is likely to be used against yourself in worry and self-criticism – that others don't like you, that you make too many mistakes, that you are a loser, etc. You are likely to need the support of another to feel how angry you are that you have had to be so careful, that the needs of others were always put before yours and the other was so self-absorbed. If you were sadistically treated, you are likely to be extremely hard on yourself, as well as, terrified of your own anger toward others.

Since no one intervened to help you as a child, you are likely to need someone else to help you feel you have a right to say "Stop!" and a right to be angry, not to mention being loved and soothed. When anger is pushed down out of awareness, it can show itself in unhelpful ways when you are "under the influence" of chemical addiction. I call this "the shadow of addiction" and it will be discussed in the next chapter.

Eventually you may feel "I hate you!" anger toward the critic (anger originally engendered by the caretaker's withholding love). Better to hate them (critic and caretaker) than yourself! Listening and giving voice to the vulnerable part of you gives this part more power and that process begins to equalize the energy between the two voices. The critic acts as though power, not love is the essential issue for survival. In order to protect you, the critic tries to control you rather than love you. The task now is to help the critic find its heart for the vulnerable part of you. To meet this challenge you may need the listening heart of another. Then you will be able to hear your emotional voice, for your critic's dominance over "air time" is often the cause of your not being able to find its voice. Eventually you may recognize that this critic is really trying to protect your vulnerability, however misguided its efforts may seem.

When you are able to make your critic back off and stop terrorizing or nagging you, you can fall asleep more easily. For to fall asleep, you must pass through a vulnerable in-between state where you are likely to experience feelings, images and thoughts that you may not even be aware of in your everyday waking state. Since your critic is on the alert to stifle feelings and needs that threaten the self's integrity, you need to come to terms with your critic or it will keep you awake and anxious trying to deal with what rises to consciousness. When you do, you will be better able to shift from the constriction and arousal of Let's Go! to the expansion and surrender of Let Go . .

The following two examples illustrate what might unfold when you focus and follow through on noticing you are criticizing yourself. If the self-criticism has not been going on too long, no longer than a few minutes, you can more easily interrupt it with a minimum of accompanying emotional release. Sometimes just saying out loud, "Stop!" or shaking your head will interrupt the critical thoughts. But if, as in the second example, the criticism has been going on for hours or days, you may find you have to do some serious focusing and emotional release work to really reconnect with your bodyself and move into a more expansive feeling place of soothing and well-being.

One morning, many years ago, upon awakening, I started thinking about the day of writing ahead and I felt scared. Then I reminded myself about another newly released book on learning to sleep well. *She* said, *"Stop! you are scaring me again. Don't scare me. You are scaring me first thing in the morning. That's not the way to start our day!" She* is right, I thought. I reached down and stroked my foot with both hands and discovered a whole new way to awaken my foot, leg and hip. Turning over on my belly, I worked my neck and then found a wonderful movement to enliven my torso. I moved as if I were a bear, scratching itself against a tree! *She* has such good ideas. I'd never get to them if I had not let *her* interrupt my scaring us.

Ah! If only it were always that simple to quiet the critic! The night before, I had been thinking darkly on and off for several hours, which is why I woke up in the morning with thoughts of doom and gloom. While I was able to brush the darkness away for an hour or so, the more <u>primal</u> layer that generated those thoughts emerged later as I sat down to write. I felt a sense of heaviness in anticipation of struggle. I had been feeling disconnected from *her* and "in my head" during

113

the previous two weekends of writing. I just finished an article about Thomas Wolfe's first editor slicing away a third of his book, "Look Homeward, Angel!" which was originally titled "O Lost: the tale of a buried life". As I connected with his sense of struggle I, too, felt criticized and buried. I let myself go into it. I found silent words to connect with the feelings: "It is so hard. I try so hard. This is hard!" I allowed myself to go into the bodyself contraction of the "hardness". The sense of squeezing and, at the same time, defeat became more intense. I felt like I was being crushed, and I wanted to hold out against the perpetrator by squeezing even harder so as to feel in <u>control</u> of my bodyself contraction; as in, I am doing this to myself, making myself small and hard and unfeeling. "Don't let him win again. Don't let him get to you. Don't let him humiliate you by making you feel defeated. I don't care if I needed him, I'll never let him get to me again" (my stance). And in shutting him out to protect what self I had left, I lost access to the more creative, vulnerable, expansive part of my bodyself I now call *"her"*.

For the moment is the <u>moment</u> – the fulcrum for change . . .

As I went deeply into the contraction and sense of resisting, I found anguish and then, tears. With the release, came breath and expansion. The space around me felt clearer, more permeable and three-dimensional and so did I. There was space to move and create in. I found *her* again. *Her* spirit had nearly been broken, but in this moment, *she* mends. I protect *her* by listening to *her* plea to stop criticizing *her*. Rather than shrink away, I hear *her* anguish, anger, sadness and pain. *She* can cry as much and as long as *she* wants. *She* surely <u>does</u> have something to cry about! Now *she* is free to breathe in life and to inspire me. We sit down to write, renewed. The paradoxical theory of change is in evidence here – change happens by connecting more deeply with what <u>is</u> in the moment.

Ironically, writing about connecting with *her* is a form of exposure and shame threatens when exposure is nigh. Writing is putting myself out in the world by sharing my heart. The critic challenges: "What makes you think anyone is interested in what you have to say?" My caretaker seemed to not, and he was supposed to care the most about me. Why should I put myself out there, be vulnerable and show what is really important to me, when I only got crushed? As long as such past experiences remain untouched by compassion and therefore unmet, I am condemned to live in the past, as it is held in my bodyself. When I met the contraction with squeezing of my own, I was able to touch the possibility of expansion and feel what was denied me and, in turn, what I had denied myself. I experienced how I shut down my bodyself in an attempt to avoid feeling humiliated by being so helpless and unable to stop the undeserved punishment. Humiliated, that I caused the caretaker who was supposed to love me, to hurt me. My open heart became a broken heart. My broken heart became a shutdown heart, and a shutdown heart can neither truly love nor create.

Because months earlier I had traveled the torturous path to that tiny point of contraction with my therapist, this time I was able to open my shut-down heart <u>on</u> <u>my</u> <u>own</u>. Because this pain had already been witnessed by another, it was no longer solitary and treacherous territory. As I came through the pain, I had been beheld by an attuned other. I could literally <u>live</u> my feelings, because the listening other knew for himself how this devastation felt and did not shrink from my experience. Once there was no comfort but the solace of my bed and the muffled whimpering, muffled lest I get "something to cry about". When I found someone who could "hold" me by really being with me, I was able to pass through the depths of despair. Now I am more able to navigate the sometimes treacherous terrain of the critic on my own because I am less afraid of being annihilated by shame, helplessness, fear and pain.

Critical to successfully dispelling the sway of the critic is the <u>awareness that</u> <u>the</u> <u>critic</u> <u>has</u> <u>been</u> <u>triggered</u>. The following two instances of encounters with the critic occurred on the same day, just ten minutes apart. The first I was able to deal with on my own, however, the second was so compelling that I ended up leaving a message asking for feedback from my friend. As the Beatles' song goes, "I get by with a little help from my friends!" I am so grateful that I no longer believe I have to do it all on my own.

One morning as I walked the sandy beach, I found myself ruminating about my recent dreams of taking tests for which I was not prepared. I realized that my critic had gotten a hold of my mind again and was telling me what a failure I was for not being as accomplished as one of my oldest friends - not getting my work out, finishing my book or buying a house – in other words, not utilizing my full potential. (Ironically this was the very friend who was the first person to tell me with a very concerned look that I was way too hard on myself.) In the midst of all that, I noticed how the morning sun's shadow partly filled the tracks and prints in the sand made by patrolling trucks and passersby. The subtle shift in the color of the sand in the shady and lighted parts and the varying shapes gave me such delight as well as the <u>recognition</u> that I could take this in. The thought came to me that I am okay, just as I am – I can be here now and experience this beauty – what more is there really? The burden of what I hadn't achieved fell away with this recognition. Anxiety shifted to a moment's sadness and then to a peaceful delight and knowing. Let's Go! had shifted to Let Go . . and the critical thoughts vanished. In this instance the critic was silenced by the shift in my attention to the play of colors and shapes in the sand and the appreciation of myself for seeing them.

However, ten minutes later another challenge to my peace of mind arose. I found myself wondering if something I had written in an email to a fellow I had just begun to date was off-putting to him. I was trying to grapple with the anxiety I was feeling, because he hadn't contacted me after our last date when he had promised to be better about staying in contact. Gradually I became convinced that I had revealed something about myself that he didn't like and that would explain his not contacting me. Long familiar with my obsessive ruminating about what I did wrong and yet unable to pry my mind away from focusing on it, I left a phone message for an old friend explaining what was happening in my head. Her reply came easily: "Sounds like your critic to me"!

That was just what I needed to hear – a friendly voice that doesn't buy into my critic and is familiar with how my critic can easily hold sway in matters of the heart. Immediately came tears of recognition – it <u>was</u> the critic again. Alone, I just couldn't distance myself enough to realize this was <u>only</u> the critic's voice I was hearing, not what was actually <u>true</u>. I needed to hear another voice – a voice of a trusted friend to give me perspective – to put some distance between my heart and the critic's torment. Besides, she said, if he was put off by your revealing something essential about you, he isn't the right one for you. Then I was able to again believe what I already knew but had lost sight of in my anxiety - that the real reason he hasn't called is more likely that he isn't ready yet, he hasn't sufficiently grieved the loss of his last relationship. His grieving is something I don't have control over; in fact I don't even have control over his liking me. So there is nothing I can do about his not calling me. I have to find another way to deal with the anxiety of wanting a connection and not getting it.

Calling my friend and sharing my feelings – my anxious thoughts and ultimately my sadness about feeling longing and not getting a response – is the "another way". Sometimes there is nothing to do but just feel through the feelings with a compassionate other. The external situation is still the same – he hasn't called – but I feel reconnected to my bodyself and alive and happy with the connection I <u>do</u> have with my friend. I remind myself that I have consciously made a choice to try to stay open to a potential relationship with this man because I haven't met anyone I have liked this much in many years. I know I can back out anytime, but I have so far chosen to continue work with how I shut down and not feel my longing and then how I can come back to my bodyself feelings. I can find a home in my bodyself whether I am feeling my longing for him or feeling present for what else is happening right now.

My critic gets triggered by the <u>anxiety</u> I begin to feel when I am feeling longing and not receiving. My critic tries to protect me from the shame of unfulfilled longing for another by not getting involved in the first place; I find something wrong with the other and then cut him off if he doesn't behave just right. But when its efforts fail to divert me, the critic blames me for not being loved. The critic is all about control or at least the illusion of control. The critic does not know how to <u>grieve</u> – potentially devastating feelings are to be avoided at all costs even if it means throwing the baby out with the bathwater – cutting off feeling longing and the anxiety it brings (bathwater) and staying closed to letting in love (the baby). For this I needed another to connect with so I could allow the opening of my heart for myself and for another. With the awareness that the man is not available (rather than I am undesirable), I can feel the connection with my friend and my bodyself. My tears express the sadness of longing and not yet receiving, the gratefulness of having such a dear friend and the happiness of being freed from the grips of the critic. Then I find the sweetness of loving in the bodyself moment. I want to be able to enjoy the feelings that have been stirred by contact with the man and then to weep and to regain my sense of connection with *her*. Crowding out or at least weakening the critic's influence by maintaining connection with my bodyself is my goal.

Being able to stop criticizing yourself when you catch yourself is quite an accomplishment, because often a great deal of unacknowledged emotional energy is behind the criticism. Your disowned feelings of fear or anger can be subverted by the act of self-criticism in order to protect you from the consequences of feeling overwhelmed by your helplessness to getting your deeper needs met. To stop criticizing yourself you may need, as did I, the help of an attuned other. When I was able to deeply feel through how much I was hurting myself, what purpose that served and become aware of how that torturous behavior impacted the heart of someone who cared about me, I was able to more consistently interrupt its harangue.

Coming to terms with your critic and being able to deeply soothe yourself is likely to involve learning to tolerate strong emotion. The critic's preemptive "No!" to you is a mirror of your defensive "No!" to your need for nurturance from your caretaker. When your critic is acting as an enforcer of your stance, its purpose is likely to protect you from being overwhelmed by the terror of helplessness in the face of no one's being there for you as a child. However, trying to survive while in the grips of your critic (and the contracted "No!" of your stance) eventually produces its own anxious suffering, bodily tension and threatening sense of helplessness. You may be not only terrified of your early helplessness but also, of your own shame and rage <u>in reaction</u> to this helplessness. These strong feelings may need the support of another's attuned presence so that you can truly possess your bodyself with its rich and varied emotions that can support your aliveness and are essential for communication and empathy for others and self-compassion.

Going Deeper:

Track your critic: what triggers it, when does it happen and what does it say? If you have identified your stance, what kind of comments does the critic make that reinforce your stance? Get to know your critic; it has valuable information about your resistance to optimal self-soothing. What helps you deal with a critic attack? Keep track of your discoveries, build a dossier of your "inner critic" and the critic might realize you are serious and may back off a bit!

The Quixotic "Fix" of Addiction

If you can say this section heading, fast, three times while tying your shoes, you don't need to read this section! So, you <u>are</u> still with me on the quest of finding out more about how you resist meeting your resistance to slowing down and listening to your bodyself messages. What you discover in what follows may be what finally convinces you to attempt to become more aware of when and how you pull away from paying attention to your bodyself voice. While work on your critic may require the help of a therapist, understanding more about the dynamics of whatever you may be "addicted" to is something you can do on your own. At some point, it is possible that you may want some outside help whether it takes the form of a support group or therapy, however, some of the "addictions" I will discuss, like caffeine, chocolate, and sugar don't have support groups!

If you have been trying to pay more attention to what you say to yourself and what you feel in your body, you have already prepared the way for this next exploration. After discussing the function of addictions and a few more "stances" with which you may identify, I will introduce you to Goldilocks. She has "just right" treats for you!

Addiction: A Strategy to Avoid Unpleasant Need and Feelings

Addictions, like the stance and the critic are major players in maintaining your resistance to listening to the more sensitive and vulnerable parts of your bodyself experience so that you can become self-soothing in an optimal way. The critic is the enforcer of attitudes that keep you from being compassionate with yourself and from getting your deeper needs met, while the addictions often are used to soothe yourself from the attacks of the critic. Addictions are at least superficially quick fixes for discomfort, but eventually, they create more problems than they solve and make it harder to hear your bodyself messages. Your reluctance to give up addictive behavior is likely to be the <u>main</u> way you resist meeting your resistance to hearing your bodyself messages.

Uh-oh, I can hear it now, you are saying (and maybe even out loud if you're practicing what I have been preaching!), "Now she is going to ask me to give up my favorite feeling quick-fix!" Wait, slow down, breathe, feel your feet on the floor, I am only asking you to read to the end of this chapter and see what you think then. Perhaps you'll feel tempted to try the experiment that I'll propose at that point.

How "good" and "bad" cops police the stance.

The critic and your addiction work together like the "bad" and "good" cop in policing your efforts to get in touch with yourself. The bad cop, of course, is the critic, mean and harsh and in the very least, annoying. The good cop is the addiction, nice and soothing at first, but she can't be trusted. She is actually more insidious than the bad cop because she can get a hold of you and make you feel good and bad at the same time, whereas your critic only makes you feel bad. Your addiction can really mess with your body chemistry which makes you even less capable of becoming more in touch with your bodyself, even if you wanted to be. Tangling with her can get you really confused about who you are and why you are here in the first place. But of course, you need to come to your own conclusions. All we, Goldilocks and I, want is a chance to show you another way.

To understand your resistance to listening to your bodyself voice, it is useful to consider addictive behavior as a strategy to avoid experiencing unpleasant or threatening needs and feelings. Any behavior can become addictive when you are able to avoid, even if only momentarily, a need or feeling that makes you feel too vulnerable. In this sense "vulnerable" refers to feeling longing, inadequacy, shame, guilt, sadness, fear, hopelessness, anger or sometimes even to feeling the more "positive" emotions of joy, pride, pleasure or sexuality. Instead of these discrete feelings, you may experience discomforting "free floating" anxiety or agitated depression or even numbness. Because you lack the inner (self) and outer (other people) support to experience what this disturbance is trying to tell you, you try to get rid of the discomfort. You turn to activities that are distracting (work, internet, video games) or those that give you a biochemical boost (eating, sex, raging, gambling) or directly to chemicals themselves (caffeine, drugs, alcohol). Substances and activities tend to be readily available and more subject to your control than people. Besides, people have already demonstrated how unreliable they can be as sources of support and soothing. In this sense, addictions can be used as a substitute for soothing contact with others as well as your bodyself.

Addictions develop out of a need for soothing. You may feel agitated or empty as a result of not being available to feel and express certain emotions. You try to find some balance, perhaps more aliveness or calmness. Engaging in addictions can give you a sense of control over how you feel and that sense, in itself, is soothing. If you could soothe yourself by sensing, listening to your emotional voice or by turning to another you wouldn't need to engage in addictive activity. If you were connected to your bodyself, you could listen to your emotional voice for what is needed in the moment to feel better and then follow through. But when you are cut off from your bodyself because you are afraid of what you will hear, you have to find soothing somewhere else. And there are so many "somewhere elses", so many temporary fixes. Some activities and substances that make the bad and dangerous feelings go away have consequences that bring up more unwanted feelings (like shame and fear) which fuel the cycle of addiction-denial-addiction. Each round of the cycle makes your bodyself less available to you, and so you are further from accessing the underlying need and feelings and consequently your ability to truly self-soothe.

She wants to share *her* take on my critic-addict cycle:
Stop being so hard on us, you have come so far in listening to me, remember "practice not perfection". I am not mad at you; I am your guide, not your warden. I have lots of patience for you, just keep trying, I see your good intentions, unlike the caretaker who would not let you explain or give you a second chance. Please be gentle with yourself, only then will you be able to hear me. When you use caffeine or too much chocolate, I fear you will lose me and that you will miss opportunities to connect with those you care about, like your family, friends and clients. And then when you notice that has happened, you will be so hard on yourself and perhaps you'll turn to more substances to make yourself feel better even though you know you'll end up feeling down and empty.

Addictions are powerful; just the thought of engaging in them can bring momentary comfort because the chemical stimulation provoked by that thought provides distraction from what is threatening your peace of mind. It is ironic that often the underlying threatening anxious feeling is a result of your frustrated or denied need for nurturance whether from contact with others or your bodyself; yet, when you are engaged in addiction, you are even less available for connection with others or your bodyself. The soothing that you have denied yourself because of a judgment of your need for another or for rest as a "weakness", you now try to get, through the addiction. But then you are even less available to connect with what you really need to be able to let it in and, therefore, be deeply satisfied. Addiction supports the anxious upset of Let's Go! when what you really need for optimal self-soothing is the organismic bodyself-supported shift to Let Go . .

The downside of "up"

Addictions have powerful side effects. In varying degrees most of these are undesirable or less preferable in the long run, to actually facing what is actually troubling you. In the first place, addictions to certain chemicals tend to distort or numb your senses, thereby impeding clear messages from your bodyself. Secondly, you may deplete your energy reserves and be in need of sleep, but you push on with various stimulants and further compromise bodyself balance. Since the various systems of your body are chemically interrelated, you can't affect one without influencing the others. Thirdly, your mood suffers when you tinker with your chemical balance, and on top of that, you have feelings in response to engaging in your addiction. On the one hand, you accomplish your short-term goal of relief so you have a sense of agency. On the other, you may simultaneously feel some shame or a sense of weakness or become critical of yourself. Other people's responses to your behavior can compound this effect. In fact, your addictive behavior may alienate others because of how you change when you engage in your addiction and/or because of how unavailable you are for intimacy during those times. In the face of these troublesome reactions, you may feel even more out of control and engage in addictions again, in an attempt to regain an ever elusive sense of control.

And fourth, the underlying need that is pressing for expression is still unmet, so it motivates the continuation of this "quick fix" behavior. Whether your need is for restorative rest or nurturing contact with another, your addicted state renders your bodyself less available to take in the contact that is needed. And because your addiction works well for the short term, you have less motivation to discover more user-friendly (pardon the pun) ways to soothe yourself. But in fact, because you are likely to deny your need for nurturance, you have even a greater need for nurturing. At the same time, you can't stand the vulnerability of feeling dependent on people and the subtle memory of the overwhelming feelings that turning to others brings up. Truly soothing yourself likely means facing pain and uncomfortable feelings and being able to grieve; for that, you may need the support of another. But you have learned that turning to others has led to hurt and disappointment. Why would it be any different now? Besides, maybe you have convinced yourself you don't really need anyone else.

For example, you may reach for chocolate, instead of the phone, when you begin to feel lonely or sad about the recognition that you have made yourself live in a very small world, out of fear of being rejected or making a mistake. In the throes of the "chocolate-high" heaven, you feel happy, elated, stimulated, expansive and in love with the world. Chocolate is confusing to that needful part of you – it tastes good, you feel better and then it's gone and an empty, anxious feeling pervades without any way to soothe it. Your bodyself sensitivity is altered by the stimulants in the chocolate making optimal soothing less possible.

Afterwards you may experience the crash of realizing that what you really needed is still not available, plus you may have gained weight and now you are over-stimulated and will have trouble falling asleep. If you had been able to allow yourself to cry or to listen to *her* frustration, it might then have occurred to you to call a friend. But then you risk being not heard and that would tap into the pain which the addictive behavior is trying to avoid. Further, indulging addiction usually involves some subtle or not so subtle, negative consequence or punishment. Indulging is like saying to your bodyself, "I don't care if you are tired, hungry or need a hug. I can't stand your neediness, the waiting, the possibility of rejection or feeling of helplessness in the face of your need. Shut up, I'm busy. You are bothering me, get a grip or go away!" Sound eerily familiar? These messages could have easily originally come from an overburdened, critical or hostile caretaker. But the bottom line is that your stance is in control and you are saying in effect to your bodyself, "I don't care how you feel, I am going to do, eat or drink this anyway.

The failure of your caretaker to adequately nurture you just because you were precious to her, could have been interpreted as "I don't care about you!" In order to cope with the resultant feelings of helplessness, shame, anger and fear, you may have responded with a self-protective, "I don't care!" of your own that you said to your need for your caretaker. This protest or "stance" was and is fueled by suppressed rage and terror in the face of your caretaker's unavailability when you reached out for contact. Adding insult to injury is the "I don't care about you" that you now deliver to yourself every time you ignore your bodyself messages and allow yourself to be depleted by your addictions or the behavior dictated by your stance. When you override your bodyself messages with addictive or depleting behavior, you aggress against the vulnerability of your bodyself and its needs for rest, safety, love, respect and nurturing. Your anger at the failure of others to take care of you is turned on yourself by acting out and being critical of yourself. Ironically, all the while you think you are saying a defiant "Yes!" to yourself, you are actually saying "No!" to your deeper needs.

This covert rebellious attitude underlying addiction may be indicative of your difficulty in facing the pain of your caretaker's "No!" to your needs for nurturing contact. You might find yourself saying defiantly, "I'm going to get mine" as you go for the alcohol, cocaine, chocolate cake, new dress, another pair of shoes, or porn site. It may not occur to you that these are ways to both stimulate and numb your bodyself at the same time. Being numb means you are less available for the intimate contact that you fear but for lack of which, you suffer.

Embodying this stance, you are likely to become judgmental of your own and others' neediness. This negative attitude leads to your depriving yourself of nurturing contact in the name of being "strong" and "independent" rather than "weak", "needy" or "self-indulgent". Most stances are a covert expression of this judgment of need for nurturance; they only differentiate themselves in terms of overt behavior in the world. For example, the Codependent Caretaker, the Addict, the Rebel and the Workaholic are all likely to keep others at a distance. The mantra of the rebel is "I don't care" and of the Super-achiever and Workaholic is "Success and/or work are more important than relationships or rest" while the codependent's is "I don't have needs. You need me".

The Rebel: "I'll Get Mine"

The rebellious attitude can be embodied as the "stance" of the "Rebel". The rebel stays up too late at night, getting "his" as he watches TV or surfs the net – and underneath his heart is broken, but he refuses to feel it. His "I'll get mine" attitude keeps him from feeling his closed heart which prevents him from real intimacy. "I'll show you!", "I'll get even", "I don't care!", "I don't have to play by your rules, I'm special" "Where's mine?" are other rebel cries. He might rationalize that this behavior fits the "Living well is the best revenge" motto. However, if "well" means "whole" as it does etymologically, then he will be deprived of wholeness unless he can feel what is hurting him. And staying up late, being tired and out of synch with his body rhythms because he uses chemicals to wake himself up again, only distances further the valuable, but threatening feelings that he is trying so desperately to escape. John Gray* said it with the title of his book "What You Can Feel, You Can Heal!" What Gray didn't say is that you may need the loving support of another to feel what you need to in order to recover your sense of connection with yourself and your needs for nurturing.

On the other hand, if you <u>can't</u> feel it, you can't heal it. But you can attempt to put patches (addictions) on it and imagine that they will hold until the next emotional storm. Talk about a quixotic fix! The rush of the sense of winning and feeling in control is short-lived. The tiredness and the aftereffects of whatever chemicals were used expose the weakness of this stance. In danger of once again feeling out of control, the rebel engages in another round with the same result. Because the support that is needed to feel feelings involves reaching out to another person and people have proved untrustworthy, he has convinced himself he doesn't need the help of another.

Not all stances result in behaviors so obviously self-destructive. In fact, some stance-supporting behaviors have their roots in culturally valued behavior such as the work ethic (workaholism) and taking care of others (codependency). For instance, the codependent caretaker and the workaholic are behavior patterns dictated by stances which often harbor a self-soothing feeling of secret superiority. In fact, those who are less industrious may harbor judgment or suspicion, born of a secret envy. However, the often compulsive behaviors of the workaholic and the codependent result in burn-out and energy depletion due to loss of sensitivity to bodyself messages to rest.

The Workaholic and the Super-achiever

The terms "workaholic" and "super-achiever" can be applied to those who continually "do" and don't allow themselves to "be". Perhaps if the workaholic allowed some time for "being", the feelings and thoughts that drive the incessant activity would be experienced. The workaholic may believe "If I can't be loved for who I am, then maybe I will be loved for how I perform." The bodily tension associated with working so hard helps keep the pain of feeling unlovable or inadequate at bay. Eventually he becomes exhausted, and then the unwanted feelings threaten to come back with a vengeance. If you are wondering if workaholism may play a part in your resistance to self-soothing, read the next few paragraphs, and see if you identify with any of the descriptive statements.

You may deny your need for rest and nurturing because you pride yourself in how much you can do and how hard you work, how skillful you are, how other people are just not good enough to help you, how you are able to do it all alone or maybe deep down, you feel have to do it alone. Perhaps you come from a family where dependency and need for others were discouraged. Taking care of yourself by expressing emotions, asserting yourself and taking time for rest and pleasure may not have been modeled for you. Perhaps you act as though you have unlimited energy and strength in order to compensate for the limitations of your caretakers.

Your self-esteem may be built around your stance of "I can handle it; I don't need anyone; I am self-sufficient" or "I don't need what others need" so you can do without the usual rest that people require for a sense of well-being and health. You may find comfort in feeling superior to others in this way and subtly brag about how little sleep you get or need. You may even judge your impulses (and those of others as well) to reach out for support as evidence of being weak or unnecessarily dependent and feel ashamed. You may find friends who have similar attitudes and so you do not depend on each other for much, lest others disappoint you again. Being exposed to disappointment, failure and despair is what you fear, so you do not allow yourself to get too close to others or to an awareness of your deeper needs. You are not sure you could come through those dark feelings; you fear becoming depressed and stuck.

So you distract yourself from your vulnerability and sensing your bodyself by working and accomplishing and getting recognition and praise for all you do so well. You periodically break down with various physical problems that force you to take time off but do not obviously belie your stance of being strong and self-sufficient. Paradoxically, then you <u>have</u> to indulge your suppressed need for others to attend to you and to take time off to rest. You weather your burn-out stoically. Your driven nature goes for the distraction, the instant rush and reward of doing yet another task instead being drawn to the subtle pleasure of resting into the sweetness of savoring the finished task. You prefer the distracting rush of Let's Go! control over the subtly pervading sweetness of Let Go. . You are likely to embrace the known (control) and shun the unknown (surrender). In order to find balance between Let's Go! doing and Let Go . . being, those feared underlying feelings have to be recognized, integrated and soothed.

The experience of "enough" . . .

You are likely to be drawn to stimulants such as caffeine or chocolate, because they allow you to override the natural feelings of fatigue that result from the driven quality of your life. Like most addictions, caffeine chases unwanted feelings away, at least for the time being. But eventually there is a price to pay for ignoring the subtle cues and warnings *she* tries to give you. Your bodyself signals "Enough!" when you feel little aches or notice your attention flagging. So why do you then grab a coffee or an Advil and keep going instead of taking a break? Is it possible that your caretaker modeled this behavior for you – was her bodyself's "enough" not honored until the project was finished? If so, feeling out what your bodyself really needed was not encouraged because your caretaker was likely not in touch with herself. And because you wanted her approval, you tried to emulate her. Now your task becomes learning to say to yourself, "This is good enough for now – I need a break!" Dear Reader, stay with us, Goldilocks has something to offer you.

Deprivation-indulgence cycle

Depriving yourself of the bodyself pleasure of Let Go . . by working too hard or giving too much can trigger the "deprivation-indulgence" cycle. When you cannot access your bodyself voice for what you need for soothing by asking, "What is the matter?" then you

become more vulnerable to turning to an addiction or numbing out. For shifting to Let Go .
. even in a less than optimal way, is necessary for survival. The plea, "What about me?" now
resounds in the once deaf ear, you turned to your need for connection to be loved for who
you are. Feeling deprived, you can "go crazy" with indulgent compensation and make up
for lost time and lost pleasure. Then you feel guilty and deprive yourself again. This cycle
can occur with eating, sex, drinking alcohol and caffeine and other behaviors which can
keep your threatening feelings and needs temporarily at bay. Bottom line, if you don't give
yourself a break to find out what your bodyself needs for self-soothing in an optimal way,
you are likely turn to your preferred addiction. If you develop your capacity to self-soothe by
listening to your bodyself voice, you can avoid the deprivation-indulgence cycle because you
can feel when it is telling you whatever you are doing is "just right" and therefore, "enough".
I like to call this the "Goldilocks moment". This is the treat I promised you at the beginning
of the chapter when I asked you to hang in there with me.

The Goldilocks Moment of "Just Right!"

The Goldilocks moment is the experience of something being "just right" and savoring
it as you shift to the soothing of Let Go . . and perhaps even fall asleep! "Just right" is when
you feel complete and for the moment, at least, all seems right in the world and you can "rest
into" or savor your experience. Who doesn't remember the story of Goldilocks and the three
bears? Goldilocks, after trying out papa bear's and mama bear's porridge (too cold and too
hot, respectively) found baby bear's porridge "just right" and ate it all up. Now sated, she
grows sleepy and finds papa bear's bed too hard and, you guessed it, mama bear's bed too
soft. But baby bear's bed is "just right", and she promptly falls asleep! Goldilocks didn't stop
trying things out until she felt "just right". When she discovered the just right conditions,
she surrendered her efforting to the feeling of satisfaction and finally slumbered.

A similar theme appears in the beginning of Carlos Castaneda's third book, "Journey to
Ixtlan"*. Under the tutelage of Don Juan, Carlos Castaneda took this exploration of finding
what was "just right" much further. Carlos' task was to find *his* spot on the floor of the hut they
shared. In his case there were nearly an infinite number of places to try out, waaaaay more
than the three possibilities available to Goldilocks. After many hours of crawling around on
the floor, he finally found "his place" and "awakened". What he actually discovered was the
experience of being totally in the moment – the bodyself moment when he felt "just right",
connected, complete and present.

Finding just the right spot to be in or just the right conditions for "lying" or "taking in
food" brings a release from tension, thought and effort and a sense of completion with the
blessed shift to Let Go . . When you find the right lying, you can surrender to resting and/
or falling asleep, just as Goldilocks did or you are "awakened" as Carlos experienced. While
Goldilocks surrendered to sleep, Carlos awakened; but they both experienced the shift to Let
Go . . presence. In any case, there is a sense that "all is right in the world" because you feel
"right" – "right" in the Buddhist Zen sense of complete or whole - being fully in the moment.

But in order for Goldilocks moments to occur, you need to be able to listen to your
bodyself messages and follow through on them. When you are engaged in addictions, you
are by design less likely to clearly feel and respond to what your bodyself is trying to tell you.
You may counter that your addiction has given you plenty of "all is right with the world"
feelings, which have lasted longer than the Goldilocks kind. Our answer is that by definition,

a true Goldilocks moment arises simply by paying attention to what you are sensing in the moment without the "aid" of any bodymind-altering substances or behaviors like gambling or sex. And sure, that moment doesn't last, but then there are no negative side-effects for these blissful, contented moments of well-being as there are with addictions. And if you stay in touch with your bodyself messages and follow through on them, you can have one Goldilocks moment after another! And the more you listen and follow through, the more you will hear! Goldilocks moments spiral upwards and expand outwards, whereas moments spent in addiction lead to a spiral downwards and constrict inwards.

Goldilocks moments never deplete your bodyself energy, while addictions often do because they enable you to ignore the bodyself signs of excess like fatigue and pain. In fact, Goldilocks moments renew your energy, because to have them, you take the breaks you need by following through on what your bodyself is trying to tell you. Earlier chapters showed how listening to your emotional voice and sensing can help you take the kind of breaks you need at any given moment. For instance, when you are rushing around and feeling at a loss about what to do next, lie down, even on the floor. Then you have more of a chance of sensing what is needed and getting it Goldilocks "just right!" with yourself and shift to Let Go . . Create the Let Go . . space, *she* will come!

Addictions to alcohol, sugar and caffeine can compromise your state of health, whereas Goldilocks moments only enhance your health because not only do you take the breaks and get the sleep you need, but also you eat in accordance with what you sense your bodyself needs at the moment. Goldilocks moments arise when you eat just the right amount of food, and just the right kinds, and at the pace that is totally "sense – able". You will have an opportunity to try this out for yourself by following the suggestions in the next chapter. Some addictions, like caffeine, sugar and alcohol interfere directly with appetite, and so the message of "enough" is difficult to sense. Addictive behaviors like working too much or gambling, for instance, sometimes lead to not eating for long periods of time, followed by overeating or eating junk food.

Goldilocks* wouldn't even think of getting in the way of your working through your unresolved trauma, grief and childhood issues, because she wants to share more moments with you. She knows that when you are able to work through your "unfinished psychological business" and shift more readily to Let Go you will spend more time enjoying moments with her. The greater your capacity for bodyself experience and shifting to Let Go . . the more grounded you become which, in turn, facilitates the challenging work on tough issues. Then you are more able to take in, little by little, the supportive, compassionate presence of your therapist, so that you become more compassionate toward yourself and more accepting of the once threatening feelings and needs you tried to avoid through addictions and other dissociative behaviors. On the other hand, addictions support your stance and make it more difficult to work through unresolved trauma, grieving and childhood issues, because they <u>interfere with</u> rather than support your being able to go through the emotional recovery cycle.

And speaking of working on tough issues, Goldilocks won't stand in the way of your getting close to another person. In fact, you are likely to be your most available, loveable, playful, attractive self when you are in the grips of a Goldilocks moment! Whereas when you are under the "influence" of an addiction, you are likely to be somewhat disconnected from your bodyself since the reason most people indulge in addictions is to get away from some unwanted feeling whether it is fatigue or depression or loneliness. Maybe you have noticed the dissociated state that "takes over" during engagement in an addiction to food, alcohol, drugs, gambling, internet, sex and how less available you feel to another. Working in therapy on the issue of your need for another, for reaching out and for being loved and responded to, requires you to touch some very vulnerable feelings which can be easily overridden by addictive behavior. Therefore, many therapists do not work with clients until their addictive behavior is under control whether through a 12 Step Program or some other approach. The feelings that inevitably come up in therapy can be too destabilizing if the client is not working on becoming more grounded in his/her bodyself.

If you are intrigued by the suggestion that Goldilocks moments could become a "positive addiction" and increase your capacity to overcome your resistance to meeting your resistance to optimal self-soothing, I think you can benefit from the next chapter. It will guide you towards having more Goldilocks moments in your daily activities, especially during meal time and exercise. In addition, I share my own experience with how caffeine influences my connection with my bodyself and, therefore, my ability to be present in relationship with others, including my clients.

Going Deeper:

For a week, get to know your "inner addict" by keeping track of whatever activity you notice you engage in that serves to help you "get through" the day and which you suspect might be making it more difficult for you to receive your bodyself messages. This is not about trying to change your behavior but only about becoming more aware of what you do. For instance, you may want to write down everything you eat or spend or what stimulants (such as caffeine) and depressants (like alcohol) you use. Paying close attention, without judgment is the opposite of denial. Perhaps you will experience that the act of observing an event brings about change! But remember, change is not the goal here, awareness is. It is helpful to keep track of the activity itself, how much, what time of day and what were the surrounding events: an argument, fatigue, stress, body chemistry influences such as hormonal, exercise, illness, etc. Don't make this a burden, but rather, an exploration. You may experience "keeping track" as soothing or containing or being in control. Awareness works in mysterious ways.

9

GOING FOR THE GOLDILOCKS GOLD!

"Drink from my cup and you'll wake up."

Now is your chance to experiment with going for the "Goldilocks Gold" which can help you meet your resistance to meeting your resistance to listening to me! In this chapter you will be invited to experiment with several different ways to experience Goldilocks moments in the course of such everyday activities as eating, resting and exercising. Then, you will be enjoined to experiment with the effects of your "addictive" behavior on your availability to experience Goldilocks moments. This latter endeavor is not about asking you to be a "saint". I, too, enjoy my indulgences from time to time, but because I have been experimenting like this for many years, I can now take advantage of having a real <u>choice</u> about whether to indulge or not. Having reaped many rewards from staying with my bodyself voice by listening to and supporting my more vulnerable feelings, I am more motivated to listen the next time. I would like to help make that choice more available to you, too! And *she* is tickled pink at that prospect because *she* knows how much more pleasure you can experience and how pleased with yourself you will be as you approach optimal self-soothing.

Gathering Gold in your Repository of Let Go . . Positivity

The more Goldilocks moments you experience, the more you are likely to seek and that builds confidence that you can create the conditions for them to occur. The pleasure, comfort and satisfaction of these Let Go . . moments bring a deep sense of well-being and embodied agency. With time you may value these golden moments you give yourself as if you were depositing gold for safe-keeping. Even though these moments, like any other moments disappear, the sense of self-efficacy - "I was able to help myself" - stays with you and can nurture you and increase your sense of self-worth. Discovering that this Let Go . . positivity can accumulate in your bodyself repository is both empowering and soothing. You can make "withdrawals" whenever you want to just by slowing down and remembering the last time you allowed yourself to shift to Let Go . . and savor that feeling throughout your whole bodyself. In fact every time you meet *her* more gold is deposited because your repository of positivity is embodied in your bodyself.

Goldilocks moments have a cumulative effect on your bodyself experience. When you are able to have one Goldilocks moment after the other and can savor your experience of Let Go . . you experience that awesome sense of "All is well" or "It is happening the only way it could" or "the way it's meant to be." When you remember that you have had this satisfying experience even though you are not having it now, you can anticipate it happening again, even if just for a fleeting moment. This repository of Let Go . . positivity can become your "resource"* when you need to take a bodyself break or when you encounter some interpersonal challenges or tough emotional issues in therapy. A "resource" is an image or memory which evokes positive feelings like safety, well-being, calm, pride, joy, which can be tapped into when needed whether for everyday soothing or during trauma work. This resource of positivity can be experienced as deep joy, a certain sweetness, well-being or love that originates in your bodyself and provides a sense of something "larger than yourself" that you can rest into. It is "all small stuff" when you can rest into your positivity repository of Goldilocks moments! And hopefully you will invite this Goldilocks experience for its own sake, not just to balance Let's Go! with Let Go . .

Goldilocks moments are an <u>antidote</u> to addiction and to messages from your critic because they can help you meet your resistance to meeting your resistance. For example, the other day, I almost dropped a perfectly ripened peach on the floor but I caught it in the nick of time. Fortunately I was under the influence of Goldilocks and said aloud, "Good save!" I was so pleased hearing this comment, for had my critic been in charge at that moment I could have suffered self-reproach. In another incident, I found myself softly saying aloud, "That was going to happen, wasn't it!" Those words came from a gentle sense of foreknowing the larger picture. When Goldilocks is at hand the world seems more like a welcoming place. But the world hasn't changed, I have! The repository of positivity allows me to look through "golden lenses" for the moment, reflecting a momentary shift in neural functioning. Goldilocks moments may be accompanied by an increase in "de-stressing" body chemicals associated with feelings of well-being as opposed to the "distressing" chemicals which are secreted during stress or when the stance is triggered. So, when I am fully in my bodyself and out of my stance trance, Goldilocks and I can do our dance!

Capacity of your positivity repository

Of course there is a catch to acquiring this cache! And that is the question of the capacity of your repository. How many Goldilocks moments you can access depends on how available you are to feelings which could make you feel vulnerable, like joy, love, pleasure, pride, sexual, sensual and sometimes even sadness, fear, shame or anger. In fact this dilemma could be called a "Catch 22" because in order to be open to Goldilocks moments, you have to be able to slow down and let yourself feel any feeling which might come up. And in order to do that you need to feel securely grounded in your bodyself as well as in a sense of well-being in the first place; otherwise the feelings that come up as you are slowing down could be too threatening and then you shut down your bodyself awareness. So the answer to this conundrum is to go slowly, taking in a little at a time, breathing and resting into the experience of Let Go . . pleasure.

This is similar to the "Catch 22" dilemma facing you as you consult a therapist: in order to take in the attuned presence of the other it helps to have good bodyself support otherwise something about this experience may be so threatening that you shut down. On the other hand, being able to take in the attuned presence of another helps build bodyself support. Again, this is accomplished a little at a time. Fortunately, some of the work that is needed to increase your positivity repository capacity can be done on your own by working with the three listening practices.

"Taking in"

The capacity of your positivity repository for Goldilocks moments has a lot to do with how attuned your caretakers were to your needs to be seen and loved. Recall the description of "ideal parenting" in a previous chapter. If they could really express their love and appreciation for who you were so that you felt it, you would have a very good chance of being able to do that for yourself as an adult. If you were encouraged as a child, you are likely able to encourage yourself (and others) as an adult. If you were "seen" for who you were, you are more likely now to acknowledge and appreciate yourself. A good indicator of the capacity of your positivity repository is how well you can take in genuine compliments. Can you let them warm you without deflecting them? Or do you have to turn the attention away from you or make a self-deprecating or sarcastic remark?

If your caretaker deeply enjoyed being with you, you are likely to be able to savor the pleasure of contact as an adult. Once again, the influence of caretaker modeling and nurturing on your ability to nurture yourself by taking in positive experiences is an essential contributor to being able to soothe yourself in an optimal way and shift to Let Go . . Taking in nurturing can be experienced while taking in the air when breathing, sensing how the air touches your skin, taking in food as well as the loving presence of another. Even if your caretaker lacked adequate nurturing skills, it's not too late as an adult to go for the Goldilocks gold! In the next chapter you can read about how increasing my capacity for bodyself positivity helped me take in the presence of an attuned other in the course of integrating childhood trauma as well as grieving a present-day loss of love.

Because the experience of Goldilocks moments requires your availability to whatever feelings might come up as you slow down, any unresolved situations from the recent or distant past can compromise your ability to be present for what could deeply satisfy in the moment. Unresolved or nonintegrated traumas or losses are not "over" in the sense of bodyself experiencing – the feelings associated with these events could be triggered by a present-day situation and elicit your stance. The bodyself tension invoked by your stance can make it very challenging for you to Let Go . . into a Goldilocks moment because when it's not "over", it is risky to be open enough to sense when it is "just right"!

And even when it's "over" in the sense of your having worked through the feelings from unresolved past situations, you can still be vulnerable to turning away from a chance to experience a Goldilocks moment. Besides, in my experience, it is never completely over, just mostly over. I discovered that even as I was grieving a recent loss which evoked a somatic memory of childhood loss, I could not count on myself to always choose taking a time-out to rest into Goldilocks moments over a bite of chocolate! Sometimes I am feeling just too vulnerable or too close to tears and just not willing to allow them. When the despair and anger of "I don't care" was triggered and was too close the surface, my addiction impulse strikes. The very openness that could have led to a Goldilocks moment becomes threatening because I might again feel the pain and sadness of the recent loss. Unpredictable territory, this journeying into Goldilocks land! And so another "Catch 22" is revealed: Goldilocks moments only happen when you are available to what you are sensing in the moment. Other times, the emergent sense of opening triggers addictive behavior in order to quash that feeling of vulnerability and happiness. Your bodyself "remembers" how your happiness was dashed in the past, perhaps by a caretaker and then sensing imminent danger, your attention turns to getting a "high" you can control.

However, the more you indulge your addiction the less available you will be to experience Goldilocks moments. On the other hand, the more Goldilocks moments you experience, the less you need to turn to your addictions for self-soothing. Sensing feelings without using a substance can feel more threatening because you are more likely to feel them acutely. Utilizing the listening practices outlined in this book will help you increase your bodyself capacity to ground your emotional experience. To increase your capacity for Goldilocks moments, pay attention to your bodyself experience when you notice you have a choice between indulging an addiction or using the moment to ask yourself "What am I feeling right now?" As you develop your capacity for Let Go . . positivity, you will be more grounded in your bodyself as well as build an essential resource for deep emotional healing which can enable you to balance Let's Go! stress with Let Go . . ease.

From Break to Breakfast: Increasing your Positivity Repository Capacity

If your caretakers lacked the skills to adequately connect with you as a child or worse, if their abandoning or abusive behavior became your greatest source of anxiety, you were put in double jeopardy. Not only did you have to deal with a great deal of anxiety on your own but also your ability to learn optimal ways of self-soothing was hindered. While your nervous system is hard-wired for rest, repair and soothing you have to experience this shift many times in your caretaker's embrace in order to be able to initiate it yourself. Children who aren't adequately nurtured often attempt to self-soothe by eating more food, especially "junk" food which is high in fat and sugar and innately pleasurable to the brain. Unfortunately this less than optimal means of self-soothing often continues into adulthood and leads to obesity, poor health, ravaging "critic" attacks, and sleeping problems such as apnea.

What I'd like to share with you is how taking in food can be truly self-soothing which implies no self-destructive side-effects. For starters, your experience of taking in food can be enhanced when you are calm and to that end taking breaks, whether for rest or exercise is recommended. "Sneak up" on your resistance by experiencing pleasure in daily activities! The goal: a sense of well-being and increased Goldilocks repository capacity for optimal self-soothing.

Give yourself a break!

The Goldilocks principle requires being true to your senses and feeling what you need right now. If you rest when you need to, you have more energy for your next "doing". In the chapters on Sensing and Listening to Your Emotional Voice you can find examples of different kinds of breaks and cues for break-taking. And here is another one: as I was writing the previous sentence, I realized I had been typing with my eyes closed! Taking this hint from my bodyself, I left my chair for the couch and felt just how I needed to lie. As I "came to lying" I dropped down into deep resting, barely conscious of my surround. As I awakened I heard myself nosily breathing. Then I dropped down again. Each time I resurfaced I was simultaneously aware of a sensation or movement in my body which was accompanied by an image. I'm not sure what it was that brought me to consciousness each time – the movement/ sensation or the attendant images. Perhaps the image and sensation came together as is often experienced upon awakening from a dream. Gradually I revisited the pleasure of resting and being "carried" as I took in what surrounded me – the air and what was under me – and found the most satisfying way to lie each time I resurfaced.

As I lay there, I realized I had not given myself over to this kind of resting in a long time. Not since before moving my residence – at least three months of moving and putting things away, acquiring new things and storing others. All the while, I was teaching students and seeing clients. Then I realized I had not once during this time, napped as long as I needed to. As I lay there, it occurred to me that I might be getting sick – what else would call me to a 40-minute nap? I hoped by giving myself this rest I could prevent succumbing to illness. I experimented with small movements which yielded lengthening and softening - reacquainting myself with what it is like to inhabit a supple, receptive, well-rested body. Refreshed by my nap and inspired by the wisdom of sensing what my body needed and following it, I returned anew to writing. Thank you, once again, dear *her*, for pointing the way. And thank you, dear me, for following through so Goldilocks moments ensued, leaving me renewed.

Gourmet Goldilocks' recipe for "comfort" food

Goldilocks moments are not only conducive to getting the most thoroughgoing rest but also to being maximally nurtured by the food you eat. And, when you are rested and at ease, you can better sense what and how you are eating. Starting with the selection and preparation of food and ending with the assimilation of nutrients and elimination of wastes, all three listening practices can be very helpful in guiding this process and maximizing the benefit, ease and enjoyment of taking in food while increasing your Goldilocks stash in the Let Go repository of positivity! You can discover how almost anything you eat can become a true "comfort" food – it is all about <u>how</u> you take it in. Eating can still be a source of comfort but with even more pleasure and none of the guilt! Using the three listening practices you can discover how eating can become an "addition" to your life's pleasure rather than an "addiction" that takes away from your sense of well-being.

As promised, you don't have to try to change or deprive yourself, but only to notice, focus and follow through and see what unfolds. Paying attention to your experience is the opposite of the addictive patterns of behavior whose purpose is to block awareness of uncomfortable feelings. The Paradoxical Theory of Change comes to bear when you bring awareness back to your activity without the intention to change yourself. You then have a chance to become more in touch with what is true for you and perhaps then you will become more "you" and that, in itself, can be soothing in a Goldilocks kind of way!

You probably have already noticed that true hunger and thoughts about food are not necessarily connected. That is, if you habitually use food to soothe yourself when you are upset, you may think about eating when you are not actually hungry. Addressing your emotional voice can help you sort out whether your apparent longing is a case of actual physiological hunger or the result of an emotional need. For instance, one afternoon, many years ago I found myself driving around anxiously looking for parking near my favorite ice creamery. As I drove I noticed how anxious I was becoming. Suddenly I found myself asking myself, "What's the matter, honey?" This voice was so heartfelt and compelling, I am not sure to this day whether or not I actually said those words aloud. What I do remember is that this question was so evocative and penetrating that I felt touched and connected to. The resultant relief I felt was so strong that I no longer had any interest in ice cream and I drove away! What I had needed to "take in" to be truly soothed was my own compassionate attention to my bodyself need, not the fickle kiss of chocolate bliss!

Nine months later, on another occasion of emotionally driven eating, I focused on my bodyself experience and felt the presence of sadness as I brought a forkful of cake to my lips. As the tears formed and fell, the desire for the bite of cake evaporated - the fork halting in midair. At that moment the activities of taking in and letting go felt completely incompatible. My emotional hunger was sated by my falling tears as I curled up on the sofa and wept.

These latter two discoveries were made in the course of healing a dessert addiction, which I'd indulged over a period of about ten years. Toward the end of this time, my involvement in body-oriented psychotherapy led to the discovery and expression of long-held emotions and enabled me to begin to release these feelings rather than stuff them and myself!

Once you have taken the time to discover what kind of nurturing you really need, you can use "sensing" to select what foods you eat and in what amounts. When you go to the kitchen or search a menu, take a few moments and imagine what that food would be like once it is inside you. How would it sit in you? When you see and smell the food, notice how your bodyself responds. Eating something that really doesn't attract you is not likely to satisfy either. You may be driven to keep eating things until something really does meet your sensory need for satisfaction. In addition, taking your time with your selection of what to eat is likely to result in more creative and novel combinations of food. If you give *her* a chance *she* will surprise and delight you! This same approach as you shop for foods can be the source of great culinary inspiration. An additional delightful benefit of taking your time in the preparation of your meal is that you are then more likely to artfully arrange the food on your plate. The greater the appeal, the greater the satisfaction and increase in Let Go . . energy in your Goldilocks repository.

"Savor flavor" and build your meal around appealing flavors like mint leaves on yogurt and fruit or cayenne pepper on your egg. A medley of flavors, bright and soothing, sweet and tangy, can satisfy your sensory hunger. When savored can lead to eating less and more enjoyment of what you do take in.

When you slow down and mindfully sense what you need, not only will you feel more satisfied with your meal but you will likely find you are eating somewhat less. Sensing and listening to your emotional voice can help you choose just the right amounts for your momentary hunger. For example, one morning as I poured cereal into my bowl, I noticed that it was my fingers that were sensing the right amount of cereal. Their feedback was guiding me without my even realizing it until that moment when I was really paying attention to the tactile sensations from the pressure of the cereal moving from the box to the bowl. When I looked at the amount of cereal in the bowl, then it was my stomach sensing whether it was too much. "Too much" was sensed as a slight tension in my abdomen, like a mini-stomachache. My job then was to follow through and empty some of the contents or eat it all and suffer an "overfull" feeling and possible sleepiness later.

My bodyself had a memory of how a particular amount felt the last time I ate it. Even though I may not have been conscious of making that assessment, my bodyself knows when the amount is too much. When the uniquely pleasurable taste of whatever it is I am eating disappears, that is my bodyself signal of "enough" and it is time to stop. The digestive system has to work harder when it is overloaded. Then I will have less energy for other activities, even for thinking because as I eat, blood flow increases to visceral muscles which move my food along and decreases to skeletal muscles which move my bones. Physiology dictates that blood flow is either concentrated in the skeletal muscles for Let's Go! action or in the visceral muscles for Let Go . . resting.

And speaking of physiology, a resting, de-stressed bodymind condition is most conducive to the intake, breakdown and assimilation of food. During the resting state the stomach and approximately twenty-five feet of intestines are optimally active in moving along what is taken in. At the same time, more digestive enzymes and fluid are made available to mix with food to create nutritive substances for the body's hundred trillion cells to assimilate. When you eat just the right amount and kinds of food, you feel satisfied and you may even experience a subtle burst of sweet energy. That is, if you can tolerate being present for this subtle pleasure. After a "just right" meal, you, like Goldilocks, may look for the "just right" place to rest and drift off for "a few". For, resting at this point is what your Goldilocks nature guides you to do.

Mastication meditation – choose 20 chews!

Having selected and prepared your meal, you sit down to eat. Experiment with sensing during one meal a day without distraction. That is eschew the newspaper, the TV, conversations, etc. Just eat, sense, breathe, feel your feet on the floor and chew. Chewing each mouthful twenty times will slow you down and bring you into the present. Chewing not only mechanically breaks down your food but also liquefies and mixes it with enzymes that chemically break it down. This breakdown in your mouth makes the nutrients more accessible to continued processing in the stomach and intestines.

You may discover that some foods hardly stay chewable through thirty chews. No matter, stay with it. You can make some fascinating discoveries during your mastication meditation. Do you notice that you prefer to chew on only one side? Favoring one side could have consequences for jaw tension as well as tooth wear and tear. As with any kind of meditation, I find that I have to bring my attention again and again, back to chewing. Closing my eyes during chewing, slows me down, fends off distractions and settles me into sensing what is happening in my mouth.

She implores: *Don't make this a mindless exercise!* Reclaim the spirit of experimentation and discovery. Notice how hard it is to stay with it and don't admonish yourself for not being able to. When you become a tyrant to yourself - too demanding or compulsive about chewing - you have left the realm of Let Go. Twenty chews can be an experiment or an exercise – you "chews"! Do you chew just to get the job done (Let's Go!) or do you savor your meal as you chew (Let Go . .), appreciating your body's finely tuned process of distilling the essence of your food into nutrients? Taking care feeding *her*, you will feel the sweetness that comes when you get it "just right" – a true Goldilocks delight!

For example, one afternoon, I caught myself, again and again, trying to get a glance at the newspaper while I was "supposed" to be mindfully eating my lunch. Finally I moved the newspaper away and resolutely focused on the taste and texture of what I was chewing. Then, when I glanced down at my plate of food, the colors, shapes and textures of the vegetables, "jumped out" at me. As I marveled at the intricate and pleasing patterns of nature, I recognized this was *she*, urging me to savor the experience of taking care of myself. This "eye candy" was a reward for feeding *her* mindfully. A golden Goldilocks moment, indeed!

It is your connection with what you are doing that can build positivity in your Goldilocks repository*. It might help to invoke the nurturing attitude of a mother bird, skillfully preparing food for her fledglings. Or imagine a human mother looking lovingly and tenderly at her baby while nursing – this sense of soothing, intimate contact can be yours each time you eat, if you allow it. Bonding and intimacy can first be experienced with taking in nourishment. You "take in" the nourishment of the milk as well as the nurture of mutual gazing with your caretaker. As an adult you can use your mealtime to renew your connection with your bodyself when you slow down, focus and take time for sensing. Ultimately, you are likely to benefit from improved digestion and less gas and pain. In addition, your body can better access the nutrients available in what you eat because of more efficient breakdown. You are likely to eat less and yet feel more satisfied and know when it is Goldilocks just right! Pay attention to how you tr-eat yourself when you eat and savor bodyself soothing!

Discovering "enough" – the Goldilocks "just right"!

Even more surprising was the discovery that when I ate more slowly, I noticed that at a distinctly different point in time, I eventually lost desire for each of the three categories of food on my plate whether it was fat, protein or carbohydrate. The digestive system actually sends the brain feedback when its quota for each of these food types is satisfied. But to notice this subtle and sensitive signal of substance satiety, I had to slow down and pay attention. I was astonished the first time I experienced it. You are wired for it; you have only to notice it. Take time to find your Goldilocks moment with each of these foodstuffs. Then you may notice when the "taste good" flavor disappears. The biochemical signals from your digestive system to the satiety center in your brain gives you the bodyself sense of "just right" and then "enough". Eating like this can become a pleasurable habit. Then when you once again rush through a meal, your bodyself may feel as though you swallowed it whole! When I eat hurriedly and unconsciously, I notice that afterwards, my stomach aches and my esophagus sometimes feel as if pieces of food were still pressing against its walls.

Feeling out what your best food choice for the moment is, as well for your life, takes repeated mindful experimentation. You will discover which foods and food combinations make you feel sleepy and which heighten your energy. Some people need protein, especially animal protein, at every meal while others seem to have plenty of energy on a vegan diet. Furthermore, what works best for you will also depend on your activities, the time of day, your state of health, how much sleep you have had, your emotional state and your genetic make-up.

What is important is to find the way of eating that works best for you. For example, after two years of not eating meat I had become hypoglycemic and anemic. The "white" proteins of tofu, diary and eggs did not satisfy. I was hungry, tired and irritable much of the time. One afternoon I found myself not only thinking about a hamburger patty but also seeing a compelling image of one in my mind's eye. Deciding this must indeed a message from the "inner food god" I went to the health food store and bought some "natural" beef. I made a patty with chopped vegetables and ground beef – a kind of vegetable burger. Not even halfway through it, I experienced a subtle energy rush. At the same time, I felt more solid, enlivened, and alert. I know that I could not possibly have digested enough protein or assimilated enough iron to give rise to this sensation of increased energy. This undeniable effect I experienced must have been a product of memory and learning embedded in my nervous system from eating meat during the first twenty years of my life. The energy rush was my bodyself talking to me – telling me I got it "just right" – this was what was needed and voila! - another Goldilocks moment was born!

This is not to say, that you should blindly follow what you crave. Food "gold" is not all that "jitters"! A case in point is my experience as I was waiting in line at my favorite bakery many years ago. Standing in front of the display case I found myself staring at the familiar object of my mission - chocolate raspberry truffle bars! After about ten seconds I began to feel an energy rush only somewhat less than the actual sensations I usually experienced upon partaking of this particular delight. Like Pavlov's dog, my brain was anticipating the reward of the expected repast. This anticipation did not produce salivation, but rather, exhilaration and not a "truffling" matter at that! My experience was not unlike what a crack addict experiences when he, deprived of crack for a few days, sees a crack pipe. The difference is only one of degree and consequence. The anticipatory feelings include a body memory of the "high" experienced with the substance.

This phenomenon helps explain why substances such as chocolate (not to mention, crack!) are so addicting. That is, when feelings of well-being are greatly enhanced by a substance, no matter how temporarily, your brain clamors for more. Just the mere memory of these compelling substances produces both a physiological and psychological effect, as "negative" feelings seem to disappear. This bodymind phenomenon is not unlike the placebo effect – the pleasurable arousal experienced is based on expectation rooted in previous experience, not on having just ingested the substance. Both caffeine and sugar are frequently used as agents of mood change and my raspberry chocolate truffle bars contained both!

However, as with any addiction, there is always a price to pay down the road for attempting to avoid feelings. For instance, you may not want to stop eating even when you could be comfortably sated. The drive to avoid the "bad" feelings that threaten to make you feel out of control is stronger than the motive to avoid the uncomfortable feeling of overeating that you can control. You substitute one "bad" feeling for another, preferring to feel for the moment "in control" of the threatening feeling rather than out of control - even at the cost of a stomachache. At that moment the inevitable stomachache seems a small price to pay for avoiding the emotional pain of despair, loneliness and helplessness. But, as with all impulses that drive addictions, you eventually feel out of control anyway, only now you have the pain of a stomachache to distract you from the threatening feeling!

Conundrum of "enough" revisited

For, with any addictive substance, the sense of control is an illusion. Addicts are 'owned' by their addictions and when "under the influence" are therefore, out of control (or struggle with control). "Enough" is an illusive concept for most addicts. As one alcoholic/addict half jokingly summed up his difficulty with "enough": "I almost get enough and then I pass out!" There is no functional middle ground between "not enough" or "too much". The self-regulatory mechanism has gone awry and/or is obliterated by the addictive substance. Addictive substances like caffeine, alcohol and sugar, not too mention "hard drugs" disturb blood sugar levels and bio-rhythms such as the sleep-wake cycle, which in turn influence mood, energy, alertness and focus. Another alcoholic described his experience with sensing "enough" in this way: "There are two points – one when I know that is "enough" and the next when I am drunk. I can't seem to stop at the first, and when I am at the second, it is too late." Whether assessing food or booze, for the addict, the Goldilocks "just right" point, if it is sensed at all, is too ephemeral to embrace.

For sensing "just right" means you need to slow down and tune into your bodyself experience. And that would make you available to feeling whatever distress may be lurking in the shadows. Only if you have sufficient ground in your bodyself experience, so you can emotionally self-regulate and reach out to others, are you likely to tolerate the experience of helplessness without turning to some addictive or dissociative behavior. Addictive behavior is fueled by a sense of urgency as in "I can't wait" and "I can't get enough!" Addicts often have an anxious sense that there is not enough food, sex, love, wine and this anxiety drives the addictive behavior. And often the need "underneath" the anxiety is a psychological need such as for contact with another but that need is too frightening to be expressed and even if it is, the needed contact can't be adequately taken in. While addictions do change how you feel temporarily, you don't learn how to regulate your emotions by truly nurturing yourself which could lead to an organismic shift to Let Go . . Learning to tune into your bodyself and feel your feelings can give you a sense of balance, empowerment and control that you can depend on. Then no hidden negative threatens you when you are feeling vulnerable as it would in a weakened, addicted condition. However as long as you are engaged in addictions, you are running from how you actually feel, and so the savoring and flow of Goldilocks "just right" moments are out of reach.

Goldilocks Meets Starbucks . . .

As you become more bodyself sensitive, you may discover, as did I, that caffeine (after the initial blast) makes you less sensitive to your own emotions and to those of others. Caffeine can evoke a "serious" Let's Go! mode complete with lots of thoughts, which can border on obsessive and can be intensified by fear, anxiety, anger, shame, etc. I noticed that using caffeine before a psychotherapy session could make it more difficult for me to stay with the subtle messages of my bodyself in response to sitting with a client. Caffeine use compromises an important source of information about my reactions to what the client evokes in me, which may have to do with my own issues. Rather than sense the immediate interpersonal bodymind situation, I was more likely to be "in my head" and interpret and then talk too much. My bodyself is less available for the attuned contact that arises from openness and vulnerability. To use a musical analogy, my capacity to resonate with the subtle over- and undertones of my clients' feelings may be limited. My receptive "bandwidth" is narrowed. In addition to not noticing or responding to subtle cues, I may miss the "larger picture" - the theme of the concert - by being over-focused on a single note or refrain. When I am not "caffeinated", something subtle is more likely to occur to me that may have eluded me in a more constricted caffeinated state, whether I am alone or with another.

Moreover, I noticed that sometimes when I was feeling vulnerable, I wanted caffeine. I would partake of caffeine (or chocolate, which contains caffeine as well as other stimulants) when what I really needed was to cry or feel my loneliness and/or make contact with another person. Once stimulated by the caffeine, I would either feel "fine"* or be more outgoing and talkative while at the same time, be less able to take in and be nourished by what attention I was given. To open and feel nurtured by contact, I found I needed to take the risk of feeling the vulnerability of my bodyself heart.

Caffeine makes it more difficult for me to feel through any given feeling thus hindering completing my emotional recovery cycle and shifting to Let Go . . You may remember the emotional recovery cycle involves cycling through feelings of anger, fear, grief and returning to love, calm and rest. Caffeine can truncate the experiencing through of feelings, not the least of which are sexual. Being stimulated by caffeine may limit the intensity and duration of an orgasm, as well as make it more difficult to achieve. In addition, the Let Go . . afterglow is diminished. Caffeine makes it challenging to feel when stimulation is bodyself "just right!" and to allow unfolding, for the sweetness of Let Go . . is squelched by caffeinated intensity.

Further, "just being" with feelings, whatever they might be can be more challenging when caffeine is in the mix. Instead, my experience is that they become muted or they momentarily "take over". And it is the embracing of feelings that allows them to change so the shift to Let Go . . occurs.

For instance, it is difficult enough when anger is felt, to sense the more vulnerable feeling "beneath" the anger. In caffeine-enhanced Let's Go! it can be even more difficult to access the fear, shame or grief that often gives rise to an anger reaction. Anger can make you feel "Let's Go!" powerful, in contrast to the other more vulnerable Let Go . . feelings like sorrow or shame. Anger also tends to narrow the focus so whatever might be irritating or intimidating can be conquered, dismantled, destroyed or otherwise subdued. When awareness of the underlying vulnerable feelings is blocked by a caffeinated state of mind, it is more difficult to cycle through the relevant emotions and return to restful Let Go . . You may stay stuck in less vulnerable states of anger, indignation, judgment or arousal, all the while your body needs to calm down and is prevented from doing so. Because your awareness is constricted by the caffeinated Let's Go! you may lose sight of the "larger picture". Then, it is more difficult to rest into something larger than yourself such as your bodyself experience of breathing, your "safe place", a prayer or mantra and eventually calm down.

Once aroused, anger is fueled by provocative thoughts and that tendency can be heightened on caffeine since both adrenaline and caffeine are central nervous system stimulants and are associated with increased muscle tension, irritability, blood sugar and vigilance. Anger, by design, triggers energy for immediate action and the accompanying adrenalin dissipates within 20 minutes when the threat is no longer perceived. In contrast, caffeine takes 20 minutes to maximize its effect and maintains arousal over many hours. This bodyself arousal can be perceived as anger or fear or anxiety. And in its wake, I may look for a reason to feel angry or afraid even if there is no actual threat. Because the bodyself feedback mechanism is temporarily impaired, letting go of anger can be hindered by caffeinated arousal. In contrast, the unadulterated feeling-through of anger could feel orgasmic when I can go through the emotional recovery cycle, which can end with peaceful or loving feelings and a shift to Let Go . . A case in point, some couples playfully wrestle before sex because the physical engagement heightens blood flow, arousal and subsequent pleasure much in the same way exercise does. Now how's that for some Goldilocks moments to remember?

Often what follows the hyper-arousal of caffeine is hyper-exhaustion. At that point, I am very unlikely to even want to access my feelings. All I can think of is getting rid of the fatigue either by more caffeine or sleep. And sleep only comes when I can stop my caffeinated thoughts. And worse, caffeine makes going back to sleep, once awakened, more difficult because it inhibits the brain chemical which helps us stay asleep. And then the stimulating effect of caffeine makes it nearly impossible to turn off my thoughts, which keep me awake. Perhaps you have noticed how caffeine can act as an anti-depressant in the morning but by nightfall you feel depleted and even, depressed.

Similarly, caffeine can make me feel more focused in the morning but more distractible and disorganized later in the day when I become aware of the uncompleted actions I initiated earlier but now, I just don't have the energy and focus to finish. What I notice consistently about my bodyself perception when I am "on" caffeine is that I feel less able to take in and respond to what is around me, especially four or five hours after caffeine intake. That loss is most reliably sensed when I attempt to experience the three-dimensionality of the moon at the end of the day. On caffeine I can't sense the subtle perceptual shift of the moon from two dimensions to three and so I miss the thrill of that potential Goldilocks moment. On top of that "I don't even care!" On the other hand, when I haven't had caffeine, I find myself more "in tune" with my bodyself and others and more available to the subtlety and beauty of what is around me, not to mention the moon.

Another result of constricted awareness due to caffeine is a compromised ability to self-soothe by getting in touch with my bodyself. I feel at the mercy of my longing and loneliness once it is triggered and worse, I am less able to take in the warmth of loving contact. Caffeine can temporarily take away depression and replaces it with elation or alertness followed by anxiety or exhaustion. However anxiety fueled by caffeine is not pretty! I can tell myself, "It is just the drugs, give it time and it will wear off" but in the meantime there are no Goldilocks moments to be had. How many times do I have to rediscover that while caffeine takes away depression, it doesn't restoreth my soul? My "cup" only runs over with satisfying human contact or with *her*. That early rush of caffeine feels satisfying but then I find I am no longer taking nurturance from *her*, I am looking around to fulfill the anxious longing feeling with something "over there". I can no longer hear *her* wisdom, *"Drink from my cup and you'll wake up!"*

On caffeine, I often find I am less hungry but at the same time, more attracted to sweets. My body senses that sweets will quickly replace the blood sugar stores lost during stimulation by caffeine. At other times, I seem to feel hungrier and when I eat I have a harder time feeling when it is "enough"! Sometimes, the "caffeinated me" can't tell whether I am hungry or anxious. As a result, my diet becomes less balanced and digestion is hindered by the Let's Go! activation of caffeine. And, I reach for gum more often. Of course I am less able to nap because my body is tenser and my thoughts are more active. Even worse, the whole cycle is likely to repeat itself the next day because I go to bed too late the night before. Upon awakening I am not truly rested - still spent and a little anxious about what needs attention. After a few days of this, I am less able to sense what my bodyself needs. Pacing myself is more difficult because I have been out of practice tuning in and listening to myself. By this time, *her* messages have become faint and therefore more easily disregarded, if they are perceived at all. The result is Goldilocks moments are fewer and farther between!

What is then needed is to renew my commitment to myself, to trust *her* and encourage myself. If I am feeling too distressed, it helps to call someone. When I do, the rewards come slowly but surely. I begin to feel the steadiness, ease and eventually the joy of reconnecting with *her*. Perhaps you will discover as I did, that you will be more likely to get it bodyself "just right" and shift to Let Go . . when you avoid stimulants as well as other addictive substances. While I have focused on caffeine as an addictive substance, many of these observations can be applied to other addictive substances and activities. If you pay attention to how you feel before and after you engage in an addictive behavior and attempt to abstain for a week or two, you can find out for yourself!

For example, at the end of a day without caffeine, I found myself acknowledging with satisfaction that I remembered to look in the back seat for the water bottles. Had I had caffeine that day, I would likely have bounded up the stairs to my abode with a sense of urgency after a long day's work, hungry, tired and obsessing about whatever. Instead I walked up the stairs carrying the bottles and all my stuff with a congratulatory smile on my face. I realized too that on caffeine, I might miss significant moments with others. For instance, when I start to feel some closeness with a friend, I might let the impulse go instead of acknowledging it. Or perhaps with a client, when I am not caffeinated, something just right may occur to me to say that would not if I were "going faster" and more in my head. Of course, I will never know the answer to that question for sure, but I enjoyed the reflection and the satisfied feeling I had walking up the stairs at my own speed! And speaking of speed, my energy at night is gentler and actually more available to me to bring the day to a fitting close when I haven't used caffeine during the day.

Eventually by paying attention to how you feel before you indulge your addiction, you are likely to become increasingly able to ride out the impulse to engage your addiction and not give in. When you are able to identify the bodyself need behind the impulse to indulge and meet it, you may experience as I have, a sweet feeling of peace, ease and openheartedness toward yourself and the world. This subtle burst of Let Go . . energy surprises and pleases me every time I make it past the urge for caffeine and just breathe or take a break and feel whatever is needed. Sometimes, to keep from sabotaging myself before a lecture I would stay in my office just little longer writing notes so I wouldn't have time to get that chocolate dessert. Then my lecture flowed because I was more connected to my bodyself interest in the material, not to mention to the students. Goldilocks moments can occur even in lecturing; the audience feels them as well because my open heart allows the audience to resonate with me.

Trick or treat?

My heart opens when I have taken care of myself and have not shut *her* up with caffeine. To use an apt analogy, I have picked up the baby and held it; I have stayed with *her* even when I felt like running away. Now when I find myself thinking about dessert, I look for the source of discomfort - perhaps I am tired, lonely or sick of working so much. I find myself rationalizing that I deserve a treat ("Where's mine?"). Then I remind myself how such a "treat" has shut *her* down in the past, rendering me less sensitive and responsive. This kind of treat is more like a "trick". I will no longer have the connection with myself that I feel in this moment of awareness and so I will have nothing to rest into, to carry me. I will have no one to come home to. What I need then is to embrace myself or perhaps, someone else. I need a connection, not caffeine so I don't feel I have to do it all alone. Lying down and connecting to the pull of gravity could help. Or perhaps some music or singing or dancing. The bottom line is finding another way to connect and soothe myself by giving myself a good feeling, a release, some laughs or affection.

I know the so-called "quick fix" of caffeine can put me into Let's Go! overdrive and then I will have to pay for it. The attraction of caffeine is not only that the fix is quick but also that I don't have to make myself vulnerable to get it. The pleasure fix from getting a hug or lying down could be just as quick. But asking for and opening to a hug exposes my vulnerability and the chance for disappointment. And, lying down and feeling what is needed in me might lead to experiencing the fatigue, emptiness, and loneliness that seems like it will never end. Asking "What is the matter?" could bring tears. If I want to come through the urge for caffeine, I need to be able to give to those tears and go through the emotional recovery cycle to Let Go . .

Sometimes I eat chocolate despite my sensing that tears are underneath my desire for chocolate. While a cry may then come, it is short-lived. But afterwards, instead of soothed, I am still speeded up, a little cut off and later, exhausted. What appears to be an emotional release does not result in recovering my heart because I have lost the sensitive connection with my bodyself. On the other hand, when I have caffeine in service of sleep deprivation or a headache, I am way less likely to experience negative repercussions such as not being in touch with bodyself feelings. For in such cases, the caffeine is in service of my <u>bodyself</u> <u>need</u> for relief and so it supports my aliveness and concentration. Again it is not the substance that is the problem for me – it is the use to which it is put. When I need to break loose and have fun as opposed to escape emergent emotions, the use of caffeine or alcohol gives me no discomforting backlash.

Double whammy of a caffeinated critic

When my lecture is fueled by caffeine, it is less likely to flow or connect because I am neither open nor responsive to myself or to others. In the middle of a sentence, my critic might even terrorize me with the thought, "You don't know what you are talking about and they know it!" In response to this thought, I freeze for a moment and don't know what to say next. I look out at all those faces and imagine that some of them know more than I do or that they are thinking about how inadequate I am. Then my critic tells me my freezing is evidence that they are right, I really don't know what I am talking about. In those panicked moments, I have lost my heart for myself and imagine they have no heart for me either. A horrible feeling of loneliness, isolation, fear and shame momentarily overwhelms me. And caffeine heightens this effect. This is a good example of how addiction and the critic work together, against bodyself support and Goldilocks moments.

And yet at other times, using caffeine seems to make me wittier, more humorous, outrageous and bold – such is the temptation and the thrill of caffeine. That said, the downside to caffeinated spontaneity is that I am more likely to "blurt" – to say things I later regret. To add injury to insult, the resultant thrashing I give myself is fueled not only by caffeine itself but also by my guilt for using caffeine in the first place. I rediscover that caffeine tends to make me less sensitive to the larger interpersonal context as well as to my bodyself. On the other hand, the numbness to my bodyself that caffeine can bring is a blessing when I have a headache for it takes away the real pain with no negative emotional or energetic side-effects.

The "shadow" of addiction

For example, I will never forget the shocked look on my partner's face or my own surprise when I, having consumed an uncustomary Coca-Cola, spontaneously responded to a comment he made. It was late afternoon when we sat down on the floor to eat pizza and watch TV. When I turned off the light, he protested, "It's too dark to see what I am eating!" Uncharacteristically blunt and unthinking, I responded coolly, "You'll get used to it!" My retort might have been more amusing if it hadn't reminded me (not to mention, him) of something my harsh and controlling father might have said. To be sure there were no Goldilocks moments for either of us that evening! After that experience, my partner became wary whenever I had caffeine because my "dark side" would be more likely to express itself.

You, too probably have had the experience of someone else's dark side "under the influence" or perhaps you experienced your own. When a more angry or abusive part of the person emerges under the influence of an addiction I call this phenomenon the "shadow of addiction". The "shadow" can result from the effects of nonintegrated trauma or inadequate caretaker nurturing on the development of the self and is discussed in Appendix F: Healing the Shadow of Addiction. The shadow maintains the resistance to meeting the resistance of taking care of the bodyself often by resisting being compassionate toward the self and others as well. Therefore when working with the shadow, the compassion of an attuned other is likely to be pivotal. In my case, that comment came from the angry part of me that created my stance of "I won't let you get to me!" As a child I felt I had to be very accommodating and vigilant around one of my caretakers lest I would be abandoned or punished; as a result I was angry about having to be so careful. For, who doesn't want to be loved for who one is?

Blood sugar "madness"

On the other hand, irritability can be due to low blood sugar levels. Perhaps you have experienced increased irritability on caffeine or when you have gone too long without eating and your blood sugar is low. Many people experience a personality change when their blood sugar levels are manipulated whether by use of alcohol, caffeine, sugar or fatigue. Mood and blood sugar levels are inextricably related. As a consequence, whatever makes blood sugar levels go up and down can also make moods go up and down. In fact, the symptoms of the condition of chronically low blood sugar called "hypoglycemia" read like symptoms of certain anxiety and depressive disorders. Hypoglycemia results from the pancreas secreting too much insulin in response to rapidly increasing blood sugar levels. As a result, blood sugar drops precipitously and hunger, weakness, shakiness, agitation and irritability results. A diet to address this dynamic includes small amounts of protein throughout the day and excludes refined carbohydrates and other foods with a high glycemic index like fruit juice and of course caffeine and alcohol. By optimizing your blood sugar levels you will experience fewer mood swings and more Goldilocks moments! Now, how sweet is that?

The brain needs a constant supply of glucose for oxidation to maintain its optimal functioning and alertness. Your bodyself does not like extremes and you ultimately have to pay for subjecting yourself to them. I discovered that having sugar before lecturing meant I would feel less centered and be more vulnerable to distracting thoughts and intrusive feelings. Sleep deprivation produces similar effects. My lecture does not flow as it usually does and I feel less connected to my audience. And, it is harder to recover my balance either by remembering what it was I was going to say when I get distracted or by soothing myself when I feel irritated by someone's interruption. When sugar is accompanied by caffeine as it is in chocolate, these effects are exacerbated. And while I may seem to myself more clever on caffeine, this benefit hardly compensates for the difficulty winding down and falling asleep afterwards.

Thus, addictions to caffeine, alcohol and sugar can deprive you of rich sources of Goldilocks moments, potentially available in the everyday activities of eating, resting, and going through the emotional recovery cycle. Let Go . . energy. As already noted, caffeine can truncate the experience of emotional and sexual release, can make it difficult to feel the subtleties of satisfaction when you have eaten "just right", not to mention being able to eat "just right" in the first place, and can deprive you of the sweet Let Go . . energy of napping. In short, because you are likely to become depleted, addictions deprive you of those "just right" moments for your repository of positivity. What you are likely looking for when you turn to an addictive substance is a feeling of well-being and the sense you have enough energy or that you can just relax.

Wired, tired and mired . . . and uninspired

Caffeine as well as other addictive chemicals can give you the illusion, albeit temporary, that you can overcome feelings of inadequacy or weakness associated with being tired, lonely or depressed. The price you pay for trying to make those vulnerable feelings disappear, whether with chemicals or acting out, is that you end up wired, tired and mired. The irony is that now your focus becomes dealing with emotional fallout from the addiction which invokes the same feelings you were trying to avoid in the first place: shame, inadequacy, fear, disgust, grief, regret, loneliness or fatigue. Your only actual gain was a momentary sense of control over them.

A former client of mine, a cocaine addict who was abused as a child, told me she used cocaine to get "in touch" with her feelings and then write about them. It was way too threatening to her sense of self to sit with me and share the pain of her remembrance of what happened to her. She could tell me the story but not feel the feelings. For that she needed to numb herself with cocaine and experience the paradoxical sense of "getting in touch" with feelings while simultaneously numbing herself. Chances are you have noticed how some people seem more emotional when using alcohol or some other drug, even caffeine. But the use of substances in this way does not increase bodyself connection in the long run.

And in fact, the natural de-stressing <u>bodyself</u> chemicals are often less available after continuous drug use of any kind. It is if the drug, caffeine and alcohol included, provides a sense of control or containment so that you can say and feel what comes to mind – just as the presence of a trusted other might if you were open to it. Ideally this trusted other would be saying by his attuned presence, "I love you, I hear you, you can go through this, I am here for you." Perhaps some drugs increase the flow of de-stressing or "well-being" chemicals that are similar to those triggered by the presence of a trusted friend, that is, if you <u>could</u> be open with him. However with addictive substances, no vulnerability is required and no one's presence is <u>taken in</u> so integration of feelings is not likely to occur as is possible when you can go through the emotional recovery cycle with the support of another and of your bodyself experience. The likely end result is simply a severe depletion of your positivity repository.

An example of engaging in addictive behavior around the issue of loneliness, vulnerability and fear of reaching out comes from my experience after a session with my therapist. The trigger for engaging in an addiction can be <u>both</u> <u>having</u> intimate contact or <u>holding</u> <u>back</u> from intimate contact, for both experiences can touch the unhealed emotional memory of not having access to what was needed in childhood. I found myself going for chocolate's bittersweet rush after a session in which I denied myself taking in the sweetness of contact with my therapist. The pain of childhood betrayal was still so compelling even after many years' work. I know I have to take the chance of letting something different happen – of letting myself be met, but in order to discover that, I have to open myself to the contact offered. But taking in chocolate brings up less anxiety because I know how it will affect me, momentarily and later. I know that the sweetness will be followed by bitterness, that the rush will be followed by deadness. With chocolate, I control the course of events, no disappointments or rejection possible. I don't take chocolate's let-down personally!

You might counter that relationship can also bring sweetness followed by bitterness, so what is the difference? The difference is that in a relationship, the timing of the bitterness may be controlled by the other. What I was trying to escape was the helplessness arising from a sense of loss of control. With chocolate, while it may lead to anxious feelings, I have a sense of control. Besides there is always more chocolate to be had. Whereas the other may not come back or forgive or allow a repair when things go bad. The dessert does not bite back and desert me. But in the end, I desert myself. When I trounce *her* yearning with chocolate, I make the subtle sweetness disappear. I trade the subtle sweetness of *her* ephemeral presence for the intense rush of the chocolate that I can control. I don't dare leave the future of my feelings to fate (read "caretakers") I grab chocolate and make myself feel good. I can't stand the uncertainty of <u>waiting</u> to see how it turns out. The repair I needed long ago was never made. So now the arousal connected with waiting for reconnection builds and builds and becomes intolerable and then bring the once overwhelming discomfort to a literally bittersweet end, for the moment at least. What is truly needed is enough bodyself support to feel through the threatening feelings.

To nap or to "cap"?

I want to encourage you to empower yourself by experimenting with other ways of soothing yourself that have no unwanted side effects and that do not compound your uncomfortable feelings. To wit, you might as well get support to stay with the discomfort because you are going to have to feel through it to truly recover - it is just a matter of time and degree. If you engage your addiction you will be even less able to feel through your feelings and therefore increase the likelihood of using again. Instead, get support to feel through what you need to so that you can truly soothe yourself. Ask yourself, "What feeling might I be trying to avoid by this behavior?" So rather than grab a "cap" (cappuccino) or a "coke" or press on when you feel tired, take a break and drop down into gentle Let Go . . energy. Cry when you feel overburdened or sad or lean on someone's shoulder. Ease up instead of getting mad, using caffeine or working harder. Rather than stretch yourself further and play the price for it later, lie down and let your bodyself stretch you and shift to Let Go . . Or go for a walk and renew yourself. Try it as an experiment and see for yourself!

If you stop using caffeine you are likely to experience increased vulnerability for a while. All the feelings you had been managing through caffeine will come to consciousness. Most troublesome is likely to be accepting the tiredness you feel when you can no longer tap into caffeine's boost. It may be difficult to accept that you have limits as an energy being. Prioritize tasks and allocate time for self-renewal. Your best bet for dealing with the fatigue that accompanies caffeine withdrawal is more "eyes closed" time followed by exercise.

Much has already been said about taking care of yourself with adequate sleep and well-placed breaks. No drug gives the kind of calm alertness that can compare with the sweet renewal after a well-placed nap or for that matter, a good cry. It's as if my "windshield" has just been cleaned - my outlook becomes brighter and clearer. During napping and sleeping your brain chemicals renew themselves so, down the road, there is no price to pay for recharging as there always is with stimulants. Once I have had enough sleep, exercise is the best antidote for caffeine withdrawal symptoms because exercise regulates the very sources of energy that caffeine disrupts.

Goldilocks Rocks: An Antidote for Caffeine Withdrawal and Sugar Indulgence

Regular exercise helps regulate sleep-wake cycle (biorhythms), eating habits, and emotions. You are more likely to feel sleepy at night if you have exercised early enough in the day. In any case, you feel more alert and yet calm after exercise. In these ways, exercise helps build readiness to Let Go . . In the meantime, regular aerobic exercise conditions your cardiovascular system, increases your vitality and your energy for Let's Go! activity. As a result of regular mindful exercise, you can experience the paradox that you have to spend energy to get energy.

Many people find that they eat healthier when they exercise regularly. Exercise regulates your appetite, blood sugar levels and facilitates bowel movement regularity. Because of its regulating effect on blood sugar levels, it is useful in dealing with some of the symptoms of diabetes and hypoglycemia. For example, years ago, after an ice cream binge*, I discovered that if I had a strong half hour swim followed by a hamburger, my blood sugar levels would even out and I would feel stable again. Granted it was difficult to exercise after bingeing, but the resultant feeling of stabilization was worth the sluggish performance. Both the protein and the exercise contributed to this stabilization. The exercise helped stabilize my energy level after my pancreas had been over-stimulated by the sudden spike in blood sugar. The protein in the hamburger caused a slow rise in blood sugar, which was followed by a slow drop as the pancreas more discretely released its insulin.

Exercise can aid in emotional self-regulation and going through the emotional recovery cycle with no unwanted side-effects as there are with addictive substances and activities. For one thing, biochemicals like the endorphins and adrenalin are released which can promote a feeling of well-being. For another, you may be able to let off emotional steam when you are working out. You can cry or shout – let it all hang out! If you are in a particularly aggressive mood, you can imagine the face of the person you are angry with on the ground each time you take a step. Exercise can also give you a break from your work routine or a troubling circumstance. Engaging in movement enables you to review what is happening from another perspective and perhaps even gain some insight or sense of the larger picture and shift to Let Go . . Exercise has been shown to combat depression, given that the depressed person can get motivated enough to do it! Exercising to music not only elevates your mood but also makes it easier to move with coordination, fluidity and speed. Playing your favorite heart-touching music can bring up just the feelings you need to express to renew your contact with yourself and the world. Emote with motion: let yourself be moved inside and out! Seize the Goldilocks moment as a fulcrum for change – it could be golden!

Bottom line, your exercise routine should be engaging enough that you take some pleasure in it. For example, I long ago learned six step aerobic exercises from a Jane Fonda videotape. Now I do each of these "steps" for a half hour workout, three times a week to whatever music moves me at the moment – from classical to pop - from Esteban to Bach. Even Flamenco and Marimba music had a turn! As a result not only are my movements inspired by the music I choose, but also, my mind! Bodymindful movement like bodymindful eating insures that I will have a Goldilocks good time – I will feel satisfied and stop when it is "just right". I find when I distract myself with TV or a phone call while exercising I am more likely to end up with a neck ache. Being more mindful of my movement also means more freedom in my creative mind. Distraction puts my neck and my creative mind on hold. Then I miss out on feeling how my lifting my knees can lift my spirits and makes *her* happy.

If you pay close attention to what you are sensing you may discover a new way to move that will delight you for many Goldilocks moments to come. For instance, one morning on the empty beach, I tried running with my eyes closed! What exhilaration that was! I started with short distances at first, counting my steps and then pushed a little further. Amazing how tuned in you become when your eyes are closed. Running backwards also asks for more attention to what each step feels like. And then alternating, forwards, backwards, eyes open or closed; the variations are endless if you listen for what would delight *her*! Walking on your heels, walking tip-toed, walking like a duck, walking pigeon toed, arms flailing, arms pumping, one golden Goldilocks moment at a time!

Be sure to remember the Goldilocks principle to get the "just right" amount in the "just right" way. Mindless or excessive exercise can lead to compromised immune functioning, injury, depletion of important body chemicals, and loss of motivation to exercise and exhaustion. If your stance dictates that you push yourself no matter what the cost and deprives you of compassion for yourself, you could be very vulnerable to over-doing it and not paying attention to what your bodyself is trying to tell you. Go for the Genuine Gold of the bodyself, not the Fool's Gold of the stance! As you learn to get it "just right" exercise can increase your stamina, mental acuity, mood, metabolism, improve your sleep, your love-making, and overall enjoyment of your bodyself experience which in turn increases capacity of your repository of positivity. Then you will have more bodyself support to work through unresolved issues which interfere with optimal self-soothing.

Goldilocks Moments with another Person

More challenging, but highly rewarding are the Goldilocks moments you can have with another person when compared to the moments you experience on your own. The presence of another is likely to bring up your fears, longings and resentments and trigger your stance, sometimes without your being aware of it happening. As was discussed in the first few chapters, the listening practices of sensing, and meditating can bring you quite a distance in gaining greater awareness of your bodyself experience. I could sense and meditate and have Goldilocks moments by myself but when I was with another, my stance was likely triggered which lessened my connection with my bodyself truth. Since mindfulness practices usually involve minimal contact with others, you may not get enough experience navigating the waves of conflict in a contactful way to weather the inevitable interpersonal storms.

If you have unresolved relational issues from the past, developing your capacity to hear unfailingly what your emotional voice is trying to tell you when you are engaged in an interpersonal situation is likely to require the assistance of a compassionate, attuned other. Even the seemingly simple act of taking in a compliment or an 'I love you" is not so easy when your need to be seen and loved for who you are, was not adequately met in childhood. And staying in touch with your bodyself in the presence of anger, whether yours or the other's can be even more of challenge.

Golden Goldilocks moments can arise from simple human contact – a nod, a smile, a "Hello", an embrace, the touch of a hand, looking into each other's eyes. Primal Goldilocks moments occur between the caretaker and the infant shortly after birth when the infant can sense the gold of the caretaker's heart and the infant's heart reflects back that golden light. Over time, with repeated experiences of heartfelt connection, that "gold" is locked in. That fortunate child can now reflect that gold and choose people to love who reflect that golden light in return. What follows are several examples of taking in the "gold" in two very different interpersonal situations, each of which demonstrates the importance of increasing the capacity for Goldilocks positivity in your repository.

Nap, "cap" or lap?

Next time you fantasize about the delights of a "cap" ask yourself, "What am I feeling or wanting to avoid feeling right now"? Maybe you actually need a nap or a break because you are tired, unmotivated, sad or you need to let *her* give you more information about something you are trying to figure out. In my experience the deep Let Go . . soothing that comes from a nap far exceeds what is available from a "cap" and there are no unwanted side-effects. A nap gives a clean green energy boost! And sometimes a wonderful insight occurs during the reverie that would be unlikely to have happened with a blast of "caf"! Or maybe you are feeling a little depressed, sad, or lonely and you need contact with another; someone you don't even know can help restore your balance and shift to Let Go . . Perhaps you would best be served by finding a "lap", even if it's your own!

Recently I had an experience which brought this home to me with delightful clarity. I was on my way to my favorite coffee house to have a last blast of "caf" before I took some time off to work on my book. I figured a few days would be enough time to recover my decaffeinated balance. As I walked up to the counter where one waits for the barista, I was feeling the struggle in myself – to "cap" or not to "cap"! I could have napped, I had enough time, but I was not a bit tired. Some other impulse was bringing me to this house of caffeination. What it was became clear in the course of interacting with the barista, a woman with whom I had had several encounters over the preceding month. The first had not been very pleasant but as I encountered her by chance in the neighborhood a few times more, we warmed up to each other. I had let go of my initial resistance.

When she met me at the counter, I noticed her dark blue beret and her welcoming countenance. Indicating her beret, I said with a smile, "That is a happy cap!" She looked at me questioningly, so I, in a delicate mood and fearing a misunderstanding, changed my tact and said, "Your cap looks great on you and it makes me happy!" Slightly blushing, she replied in a shy and endearing way that it was her favorite cap. She smiled broadly and then looked a little self-conscious as I added, "that color is good with your eyes". I felt her pleasure and that gave me pleasure – I am not sure what was greater, hers or mine or whether I was just resonating with hers or perhaps I was just enjoying what I was seeing and expressing what made me happy.

And then in that moment of pleasure, I realized I had just received what I had <u>really</u> needed in the first place – a warm connected feeling with another person! It really took me by surprise! It occurred to me to just thank her and leave without the "cap". I had already received what I really needed by taking in the contact with her – not the rush of a "cap" but the sweetness of a "lap"! "Lap" in this sense refers to my feeling the happiness and warmth of connection with another person and I lapped it up. No artificial stimulation needed – just daring to share my pleasure of what I saw with another person and being met by her pleasure of being seen. I took the risk of being myself and reaching out to another. Being met, I felt even more pleasure and no longer felt the need to artificially stimulate myself so I wouldn't feel the vulnerability of feeling so alone. It was a REAL "contact high"! But whether you choose lap or nap, feeling your vulnerability is what facilitates the shift to Let Go . . Caffeine stimulates your Let's Go! way of being and creates more distance from your more vulnerable bodyself messages.

Going Deeper:

So if you truly want to meet your resistance to meeting your resistance to taking care of yourself, you can ask yourself what could I be afraid of feeling right now? Is there some vulnerability that lurks in the shadows of my awareness that I need more support to embrace? Is the way I identify myself to myself being challenged right now by the situation I am in and the feelings that are starting to come up? Is my sense of being able to do it, to face it, to handle it, all by myself being compromised right now? Am I on the verge on burning out and feeling helplessness, rage, terror or despair or perhaps afraid of feeling overwhelmed by those feelings? What price do I fear I would pay to ask for help now? Who would I be to myself and others if I admitted I needed help?

Even if you can't answer these questions at the moment, ask yourself anyway. Just asking expresses concern for yourself and makes you more present to your process of dealing with your feelings. *S/he* will be glad you are making the effort! You may, like I, need the support of an attuned other to help you discover the source of your conflicted feelings and work through what is needed so that you can live more fully connected to your bodyself experience. Increasing the capacity of your Goldilocks repository by trying out these experiments in strengthening your bodyself connection will help you be able to take in the attuned presence of another.

Goldilocks in knead

Another way to increase your capacity for Goldilocks positivity is letting another get it "just right" with you! For example, one recent evening near the end of a massage, I noticed that my neck muscles were so grateful that someone was pressing and stroking them in just the right way to meet their holding. I was able to let go of my head into my massage therapist's hands. It was as if someone had come to take this burden from me. As I felt my need to give to him, I rested into his hands. I spoke aloud the bodyself awareness of this efforting in my neck and said, "I have done so much for so long, so alone . . . and so well." Through my tears I cried, "I want to share my life with someone and not be so alone". I realized that there was a point in my last relationship where the treasured sense of "we" was lost and I was, once again, alone. As I wept with this recognition, my head settled more fully into his hands. I felt a warmth opening in my abdomen and then my toes spontaneously reached for more space. I felt as if I was being carried by the experience of giving to what was alive and moving through me. No more effort to hold up, back, in or together. I just rested into the sensations of my massage therapist's holding my head and the rest of me.

I was finally able to give my weight to another like I could give my weight to gravity – despite the greater risk of a surrendering to a person. He could drop me or take advantage of me. But none of these things happened as I sunk deeper into the experience of giving my weight and letting go of holding. I had the sense that whatever came up could move through me, I didn't need to resist or tighten. I rode the wave of "going with" and optimism. I consciously surrendered to the contact.

I was able to choose the right massage therapist for the right amount of time and ask for what I wanted. Then I was able to speak out the words that matched my experience and my therapist was open to receiving them from me. We could then both enjoy the shared experience of giving and receiving. The deep release I experienced would not have happened without him or without my trying to communicate to him what was happening in me. His attuned presence birthed the multi-layered letting go of Goldilocks moments unfolding.

That experience highlights the profound significance touch in the context of massage has had for me throughout my life. My mother told me that she took great delight in bathing and powdering me as her first-born. She was my first connection and even though childhood trauma interrupted our connection early-on, her love and her caring touch gave me a strong bodyself foundation. At the age of 28, I experienced my first neck and head massage which dramatically altered my bodyself perception and led to momentary cessation of thinking. Eight years later, after a 10 day seminar with Charlotte Selver, I gave myself to the experience of a massage so deeply that I experienced golden-lighted Goldilocks moments for hours afterward. And now, with my dear massage therapist and friend, Matthew Hamel, I continue to have golden moments of connection with my bodyself and also with him. He is not only a gifted massage therapist but a highly intuitive and deeply caring social worker with a heart of gold.

Goldilocks on the couch

Allowing my massage therapist to get it "just right" is one thing, experiencing these moments with a psychotherapist, not to mention, a partner is another, especially with a history of trust betrayed. The ultimate challenge for me is to have Goldilocks moments in a deep relationship with a man, which implies being able to live fully in my bodyself and not give into my stance. The listening practices of sensing and meditating brought me many Goldilocks moments over the years as did the early years of writing this book as I lived a relatively monastic lifestyle. After six years of writing I was ready to find someone with whom I could spend the rest of my life. I knew my listening practices would be put to the challenge. The ensuing experience of being in a year's relationship with a man who couldn't return my love made me go deeper into my own therapy work which was supported by my listening practices. It is clear now that had I been further along in my healing, I would have likely not chosen this person in the first place.

Fortunately I had a strong relationship with my therapist, which was built on many interpersonal Goldilocks moments, some of which resulted from coming through challenging places together. Meeting and coming apart, again and again, created the bond that was needed to face the ultimate pain of childhood – the betrayal of my love and trust in my caretakers. My own work with myself over the years with the listening practices that I have described here gave me a solid foundation in my bodyself which supported the sometimes perilous territory that we had to tread toward my bodyself recovery. Therapy is ultimately relationship repair work, both in the sense of working on the past relationship rifts in childhood but also on the present, ever- evolving one between the client and the therapist. We learn from each other how the relationship is strengthened through the courage that honesty requires and we dare to feel through whatever arises.

The story of my own process in therapy, working through childhood trauma and the effects of inadequate caretaker connection is offered in the next chapter on recovering my bodyself voice. You will discover how a therapeutic bond is created and strengthened as well as how integral to healing the capacity for Goldilocks moments is.

Goldilocks revisited

Returning to the Goldilocks analogy, you may remember that when Goldilocks wakes up, she is terrified by the shocked and angry presence of the three bears so she runs away. However, in one version of the fairytale, she then returns to the house in the forest, seeking out the baby bear to make amends. She apologizes to the baby bear for breaking his chair, for eating all his porridge and sleeping in his bed. The baby bear forgives her and turns into a teddy bear and they live "happily ever after". In other words, her inquisitive, innocent yet intrusive behavior led to a shock from which she recovers by making friends with the baby bear, one she hurt. Goldilocks and the baby bear made a "repair" – her contriteness was accepted and the baby bear forgave her. Then the baby bear turned into a teddy bear – a soothing object. But first she had to own her "naughty" behavior or her dark side. She had to bear baring herself to the bear and feel vulnerable in her wanting forgiveness and a connection with the baby bear (her bodyself, perhaps?). She accomplishes all this, without the intervention of a therapist, imagine! Learning to live fully is not all sweetness and light, not even for Goldilocks!

It's over!

Like Goldilocks and me, what you may need to deeply experience is that "it's over" in order to fully connect with your bodyself voice. The "it" is the pain and the overwhelming feelings of unresolved trauma and caretaker misattunement. When it's over on a very deep level, you no longer <u>have</u> to struggle against those feelings; while they may arise, they now can be allowed, felt, and accepted. You have a real choice about being aware of them so you no longer have to engage in addiction, dissociation, distraction, thinking or "doing" to try to keep them at bay. True solace is now available. Whether through psychotherapeutic work with an attuned other or through a strong meditation practice, you can become grounded in your bodyself experience when you receive adequate support for your feelings and increase the Goldilocks moments in your positivity repository.

As you can read in the next chapter, this experience of attunement, connection and feeling through, repeated over and over again, can strengthen your bodyself ground. Supported by the repository of positivity this ground is where you can return whenever you become triggered or upset. As you become more resilient you can do as Rumi exhorts: "Welcome and attend them all!" ("all" refers to emotions*). Until then you are likely to feel as if you are trapped in a cycle that often results in your feeling angry, mistrustful, or lonely. But what you fear has <u>already</u> happened; you were betrayed, abandoned, ignored intruded upon and/or violated. Yet your emotional brain expects that will continue to happen because it has no sense of time – the threat seems always nigh. You are likely to continually anticipate the past until those feelings are finally resolved by going through and integrating them with the support of an attuned other. Finally those feelings have a <u>past</u> because the events that gave rise to them can now be placed in the proper perspective. Then it's finally over. Well, more or less!

It is a very personal journey through pain to the empowerment of being able to face and feel through whatever presents itself. As you become more receptive to the messages of your emotional voice, your meditation is likely to deepen and you will be more able to surrender more fully to what your bodyself messages indicate is needed. Processing the feelings that trigger acting out can strengthen your connection to your bodyself and deepen your ability to self-soothe, allowing you give up addictive behaviors. Released from your addictions you will be free to experience through your feelings and embody a flow of Goldilocks moments.

In sum, having more Goldilocks moments can result from attending faithfully to your bodyself messages by sensing and responding to what is needed at any given moment. You will then be guided to eat just the right amounts of the right foods, to rest when you are tired, to acknowledge or express feelings that are stirring in you rather than repress them. As you work through your unresolved issues, emotions associated with what has happened are integrated. Owning your feelings makes their energy available to you and frees the energy that was used in tightening against them. When your repository of positivity is well-supplied with Goldilocks moments, you have more bodyself support to go through the emotional recovery cycle and enhance Let Go . . energy. Otherwise unwanted emotions are likely to trigger Let Go . . energy depleting behaviors of your stance like obsessing or addictions like care-taking or workaholism. Fortified by your positivity repository, you can feel your need for another and your desire to share your love. You can allow someone else to get it "just right" because you are less afraid of losing yourself. You are drawn to those who can really meet you and love you just as you are. You are free to find out what is "just right" for you and give it to yourself. Applying the listening practices to the five e's of Let Go . . energy (eating, eyes closed, engagement with others, exercise, emotion) you are more likely to engage in joyous expressions of aliveness, dancing, singing, running, just getting out into the air, seeing the sky or embracing a friend which makes even more Let Go . . energy available to your positivity repository. Then you will have less <u>need</u> for artificial sources of energy like caffeine which like all addictions are ultimately Let Go . . energy-depleters and the increased capacity for positivity will support you if you choose to work on unresolved childhood issues that interfere with optimal self-soothing.

Some Ways to Increase the Capacity of your Positivity Repository:

Eating, Exercising and Resting Bodymindfully
Sensing, Meditating
Listening to Your Emotional Voice
Completing Actions
Abandoning Addictions
"Taking in" Compliments
Making Relationship "Repairs"
Reaching out to Another
Massage
Noticing Nature around You, Smelling the Roses!
Savoring Savoring

Some Suggestions for Going Deeper:

Observation of eating and interaction with addictive behaviors

As suggested in an earlier section, pay attention to how you take in nourishment from food, optimizing sensing the whole process by slowing down before you start. Try this for a week and note what you become aware of. Then try going a week without using caffeine or alcohol or indulging in one of your addictive behaviors and see if your experience of taking in nourishment from food changes in any way. Does your sense of appetite change when you are practicing your addiction? Do you make different choices in what to eat? Just keep track, without trying to change anything. If changes come by themselves, take note of them. Try to be gentle with yourself. One of the most memorable discoveries I ever experienced around food occurred several weeks after I had stopped adding salt to my diet (no chips, etc). At first everything tasted bland but after awhile I began to taste the natural saltiness of certain foods, for instance, celery and egg yolks. Even better, everything I ate had a "brighter" unique taste!

Nap, lap or "cap"?

Write about that moment of choice when it comes. What are the arguments for and against? For more questions refer back to the Nap or "Cap"? section of this chapter. Keep track of how you felt before and after that moment of choice. Please don't give yourself a hard time. Judgment is not the point – increased awareness, understanding and compassion is. Collect these moments in a small journal. You may see the pattern.

Tapping Goldilocks' treasures

For one day, keep track of every time you experience a Goldilocks moment. Potential sources of Goldilocks moments are accessed when you sense you got it "just right" while you were preparing a meal, eating, resting, sitting, lying, exercising, being with a friend, noticing what is around you, completing a task, etc. Just ask yourself, what is needed and listen for the bodyself answer. In this way you are discovering how to increase the positivity in your Goldilocks repository. In other words, you are creating a bodyself resource that will help you not only get through the day, through difficult and challenging situations but also will add to your pleasure in everyday living.

Ode to Goldilocks:

My love for you is a treasure,
    Always, just for now.
Your love for me is my pleasure,
    Always, just for now.
Our love for each other's beyond measure,
Always, just for now!

Goldilocks' Poem:

Drink from my cup and you'll wake up:
    And take delight in
        Seagull's flight
        Soaring's height
        Stars so bright
        New moon's sight.

Give up the fight
The shift's so slight
Like dawn's first light
After mystery's night.

Our spirits' might,
Our love requite.
Get it "just right"
Tuck me in tonight!

Goldilocks' Rule:

Do unto <u>yourself</u> as you would have others do unto you!
And someday you may greet everything you meet with loving-kindness.

PART III

RECOVERING THE BODYSELF VOICE

10

RECLAIMING MY BODYSELF VOICE THROUGH RELATIONAL SOMATIC PSYCHOTHERAPY

"A 'heartwork' miracle."

Experiencing how your critic and addictions work together to maintain your stance and, on the other hand, how the listening practices increase your repository of positivity, strengthens your bodyself ground so you can develop an additional resource in facing your resistance. This resource arises from taking in the experience of a compassionate, attuned other as you gradually allow yourself to be seen in your deepest bodyself <u>truth</u>, exactly as you are in the moment. As you experience being seen, cared for and accepted for who you are, you have the possibility of developing compassion and acceptance of yourself which is the ground for optimal self-soothing. If you experienced less than satisfactory caretaking as a child, not to mention nonintegrated trauma, you are likely to experience resistance in the form of anxiety as you try to slow down and listen to your bodyself. This anxiety may be associated with the torment of worrying, self-criticism, self-doubt, indecision and/or hyper-vigilance and stems from residual emotions of unresolved interpersonal situations or trauma. In any case, when bodyself messages threaten your sense of self you may benefit from work with a relational somatic therapist so that you can feel <u>through</u> whatever feelings come up and ultimately find comfort in your bodyself experience.

Not everyone who has trouble with optimal self-soothing has unresolved trauma or unrepaired interpersonal situations to deal with but even so, may still benefit from psychotherapy. There are many types of therapy for anxiety (Cognitive Behavioral Therapy, Gestalt, Voice Dialogue, etc.) as well as approaches to dealing with trauma (somatic experiencing, EMDR, etc.). But what they all have in common is also recognized as the key factor in successful treatment and that is the relationship that forms between the client and the therapist. I was drawn to relational somatic therapy because I had a strong background in bodymindfulness practices and a very positive experience with my previous therapist, Stephan Tobin, Ph.D. who as a Self Psychologist was relationship-focused. I had experienced significant interruptions in my connection to my childhood caretakers and I knew that trauma, especially when it occurs in childhood and is unintegrated, changes the way the brain/body processes experience. Since repeated, unrepaired connection with childhood caretakers is associated with a disturbed bodyself relationship and consequently, impaired self-soothing, it seemed that a relational <u>somatic</u> approach to trauma therapy was most likely to get to the core of my emotional self-regulation issues. When I heard Dr. Robert Hilton lecture on the relational somatic approach, I sensed that working with him could take me to the depth I needed to regain the connection to my bodyself voice that had been compromised a very long time ago. Not everyone who has experienced trauma or difficulties with self-soothing will be best served by this approach but it was the right choice for me.

I knew that my sensitive connection to my bodyself was often challenged when I was relating to a person who was important to me. I wanted to work with a therapist who not only was adept at working with the client-therapist relationship in an attuned way, but also strongly grounded in his own bodyself experience so I could get help with staying grounded in mine while relating to another. In short, someone who knew this territory from the "bodyself" inside out! As a deeply <u>sensed</u> experience, optimal self-soothing requires compassionate listening to what the bodyself is trying to say and I well knew I was sometimes "self-compassion" challenged. As will be elaborated in the next chapter, I experienced a traumatic, prolonged separation from my mother's presence when I was just 2 ½ years old, which resulted in my no longer being available to her attempts to deeply soothe me. My Sophie's choice of saying "No!" to my need for her stayed in place for nearly three score years. My therapist's supportive, grounded presence helped me to express and integrate the terror, rage and despair that had been buried but nonetheless continued to influence the way I responded to others and to my bodyself needs for another, not to mention how I treated myself. Thereby I regained the bodyself awareness of my need for another as well as the primal longing for my mother which I had quashed. Taking in the experience of being heard by another over many years deepened my connection to my bodyself. As a result I could listen compassionately to what my bodyself voice was trying to tell me and unexpectedly, I became more compassionate toward my mother.

Gradually I was able to experience my "Yes!" to my bodyself need for another and then to fully own my self-assertive "No!" so that I could protect myself from being too vulnerable with someone who didn't really see or care enough about me. To own my "No!" as a self-assertive, protective declaration I had to be able to risk losing the caring of the important other, in this case, my therapist. And even more challenging was feeling how deeply committed I was to my contracted "No!" to my need for another. This too, our relationship was able to weather, which certainly counts for something, given that this "No!" sometimes affected my being able to trust him enough to take in his caring presence. Because my narcissistic caretaker could not tolerate even a subtle sign of protest from me, I had had to make another Sophie's choice which had a hold on me until only very recently. Gradually I am losing the need for the contracted "No!" of my stance, which, while it protected me as a child by giving me some sense of control, kept me from being truly myself with others and from consistently feeling compassion for my bodyself needs for contact and soothing. Over time I felt safe enough to take the risk of saying a self-affirming "No!" to my therapist so I now firmly possess a "No!" that is a bodyself-affirming declaration rather than a bodyself-denying constriction. This "No!" does not lead to isolation, self-criticism, self-denial or unsatisfying relationship choices.

In contrast, the "No!" that I had said to my need for the other was a bodyself-limiting "No!" that denied or limited the expression of some important feeling or bodyself need in order to avoid feeling the despair of the caretakers' limitation in not being able to see me. But no matter how strongly I denied my need for them, no matter how hard I tried to <u>squeeze</u> that needy part of me out of existence, my need for my caretakers was still there because it is an organismic bodyself need. No matter how much I judge it and try to convince myself I am strong and "can do it myself", underneath that contracted "No!" is a pleading, needful child that will "do anything" to get whatever <u>attention</u> it can from the caretaker and not be abandoned. And the "doing anything" included making a Sophie's choice, giving up an essential part of itself and holding against the resultant rage, terror and shame that kept the contracted "No!" in place.

The contracted "No!" to my bodyself's deep need to be loved for who I am, also made it difficult to say a self-affirming "No!" to those who were not really available to love me. In an attempt to get their love, I tried to mold myself into what I perceived they wanted me to be. I was likely to create a fantasy or image of the other which obscured their limitations and focused on the positive, however inadequate it was. This idealization helped me deal with the scary feelings connected to the others' negligent and unkind behavior by going "into my head" with a positive fantasy of the other or obsessively thinking about what I did wrong rather than experience the threatening feelings and needs in my bodyself. If I wasn't feeling loved the way I loved them and the way I <u>hoped</u> they could love me, I thought it was my fault or my limitation. Thinking that there was something I could do to change them was fantasizing omnipotence to deal with utter impotence*. This was yet another way the contracted "No!" was limiting to me. Maintaining a fantasy which obscured their inadequacies and my powerlessness helped me ignore the untenable reality that what I needed was not available. I simply could not bear to see there was nothing I could do to make them respond to me the way I so desperately needed.

And finally, this contracted "No!" could limit me in opening to someone who really <u>could</u> love me for who I am. For, as I would begin to experience the possibility of that love, the unresolved pain, anger, sadness, shame, helplessness or despair of not feeling loved in this way as a child was likely to surface, leading to shutting down or rejecting the other in an effort to avoid the old threatening feelings. On the other hand, what if this other's "love" was self-serving as a narcissist's love often is? How could I protect myself if I didn't have access to my self-assertive "No"! in the wake of the Sophie's choice I made long ago. Talk about fodder for anxiety which could keep me up at night!

No wonder listening to my bodyself voice was so challenging, for it spoke the truth that no one, not even I, wanted to hear. No wonder we sometimes need <u>someone</u> else to hear our truth before we can fully embrace it. No wonder penetrating resistance to listening to the bodyself voice is so challenging – for contrary to the stance many of us maintain, we really can't do it all by ourselves. Primal forces for survival are at work here but with the help of an attuned presence, you can enlist the primal force of connection and compassion to slowly melt your resistance to embracing your bodyself messages and tuck yourself in. Becoming able to really see and accept the limitations of those I love as well as to embrace my need for another and my self-assertive, bodyself-affirming "No!" required years of work; some of the key points in the unfolding of the therapeutic process will be cited in what follows and in Chapter 12.**

So dear Reader, if you suspect you have some unresolved issues from childhood or even present-day concerns that are contributing to your difficulty in slowing down and listening to your bodyself voice, this chapter could point the way to your becoming optimally self-soothing through relational somatic psychotherapy. In preparation for this journey toward compassionate self-soothing, you would do well to build your repository of positivity by utilizing the listening practices, managing your addictions and garnering the support of a "posse of positivity" – your friends, family and a finally a therapist. Doing deep work in therapy brings up strong feelings which you may have been trying to avoid by denial, dissociation and addictive behaviors, and so you are likely to feel more agitation at first. If you have a chemical addiction it is recommended that you be "sober" for at least a year before you tackle these issues. On the other hand, not everyone who is challenged by optimal self-soothing needs therapy; some people have found what they need in bodymindfulness practice. What unfolds in this chapter is the path that has worked for me.

Freeing the Bodyself Voice from the Contracted "No!"

How to present to you, dear Reader, this delicate but vital process of regaining your connection to your bodyself voice through relational somatic psychotherapy so you can heed this trustworthy inner guide to a full expression of your life force as well as self-soothing? Let's start with where you are likely to be now, that is, wanting to be kinder and more soothing to yourself rather than compromise your well-being in the ways you already have. You may have some concerns about the prospect of psychotherapy as part of the path toward optimal self-soothing. I invite you to consider some of the key phases of my therapy to better access my bodyself voice; perhaps you will feel heartened and intrigued by how psychotherapy might assist you in coming home to your bodyself experience.

When I began my work in relational somatic therapy I did not understand what I do now about the importance, not to mention the existence of my deep reluctance to admit my need for another. Perhaps that will also turn out to be true for you though it needn't be in order for you to learn something vital to your goal of optimal self-soothing as you read this chapter. It was only toward the end of my therapy that I realized how key to my ultimate well-being, would be the work on loosening the bodyself constriction of the "No!" I said to my need for my caretaker. My commitment to this "No!" compromised my being able to love another fully and to take in the love of another, not to mention, fully embracing my bodyself. Therefore I'm orienting this account of recovery of my bodyself voice through relational somatic therapy around the concept of freeing the bodyself voice from the constriction* of the "No!" for optimal self-soothing. Such <u>constriction</u> limits full bodyself expression through the formation of a need-defying stance which becomes fixed (or "characterlogical") and usually requires intervention of psychotherapy to undo. Whereas, <u>contraction</u> and expansion are phases of natural organismic self-regulation and release and flow.

The process I am describing unfolds uniquely for each person, yet these phases or steps are likely to be essential to the gradual accessing of the bodyself voice, when inadequate caretaker nurturing and/or unresolved trauma is an issue. These phases or steps that I will delineate occur in a fairly predictable order because they build on one another, yet during the course of therapy various phases are revisited again and again as the bodyself ground and the client-therapist relationship strengthens and becomes ever more reliable. To give you a sense of the development of the work, here are some touchstones:

1. Taking in being seen by the attuned, compassionate other.
2. The self-affirming "No!" is respected and embodied.
3. Sensing the need for the other and the attendant emotions.
4. The commitment to the contracted "No!" is fully experienced.
5. The spontaneous gesture of the bodyself toward
   the other is freed and acknowledged.

She summarizes this process with just five words: *Yes!, No!, Yes!, No!, Yes!*
I marvel at *her* ability to be succinct and make things memorable. My "Yes!" couldn't have full bodyself expression until my "No!" could be fully honored and embodied. And for that, I needed the witnessing, attuned presence of another fully embodied person. Now my "Yes!" is free to express my exuberance, love, and life energy fully when I so choose and now I do have a <u>real</u> choice, not a Sophie's choice.

Phases of Undoing the Contraction around the "No!"

Yes! Taking in

"Taking in" refers to the <u>bodyself</u> <u>experiencing</u> of another's seeing me feel whatever I am feeling, not just <u>noticing</u> that the other sees me. This experience of being seen becomes part of my bodyself as an embodied experience of mutual presence. Taking in means I have a bodyself "felt-sense" that the other also doesn't just notice that I am feeling something but actually senses and accepts me feeling what I am feeling. This mode of perception I call "see-feeling", that is, not only do his eyes see me, I sense he may also sometimes <u>feel</u> in his bodyself what I am feeling in mine. His attuned presence helped me notice when and how I was constricting my muscles thereby facilitated my experiencing both pain and pleasure instead of splitting off. Being seen and responded to by him, I could experience through what I needed. Gradually I came to embody a visceral experience of his steadying attuned presence with visual, auditory, tactile and kinesthetic dimensions: his eyes, voice, hands and heart. And over time, this resilient, resonant connection became embodied as a calm bodyself center which increased the capacity of my repository of Let Go . . positivity so I could more easily soothe myself. And not only do I take in being seen, I am likely to have a bodyself reaction to being seen in this deep way and that reaction could include shame, joy, fear, anger or something else. It is also important to share my reaction and experience the other's subsequent reaction to me. Then I have the opportunity to take in the experience of being seen no matter what I am feeling and embody that feeling in a bodyself-contained way.

For this process to work well the therapist needs to be "embodied" in the sense of being able to "live his aliveness" that is, to be able to embrace all of his feelings so that he can resonate with yours. If he hasn't done enough of his own work, he may be so uncomfortable with your terror, shame, rage, longing, sadness, despair or helplessness that he may "abandon" you by "going into his head" as he judges, interprets or simply doesn't respond to your possibly threatening feelings. This could feel like a repeat of your childhood experience with your caretakers and even become retraumatizing over the long haul. From my therapist's demeanor I got the message that no feeling was too terrible not to be experienced together. By the warmth in his eyes I sensed that he really cared about me, that he was moved by me and that he was comfortable with vulnerable and intimate feelings. I also saw in his eyes that he could go with me to the depths of my pain and that he would not falter in his support for what I needed to feel through. I sensed he had experienced similarly painful feelings so it was easier for me to go where my bodyself led.

His being able to go with me into a feeling that I had held so closely and even hidden from myself eventually helped me integrate that feeling. By integration I mean his resonant presence allowed me to contain, ground and thereby embody that feeling so that it became less frightening and more manageable as part of my bodyself experience. I came to possess my emotions and experiences rather than be possessed by them. To deepen this experience of being seen, he might ask me to let him see my fear, anger, or longing and then ask where I felt it in my body. Answering these questions by referring to my sensed bodyself experience, requires me to possess them more fully. I sense he really wants to know my pain. That sense is what I needed as a child when my emotional pain went unacknowledged by my caretakers. I can believe his assurance that it would hurt him to hurt or scare me. When I saw that he saw me in my feelings, the pain of my childhood experience of not being seen was challenged as well.

While this process may sound intricate, this kind of interaction organically unfolds between the infant and the caretaker every day, for the potential to sense and embody our interaction experiences with others is inborn. To accurately interpret and appropriately respond to others is essential to our survival first in our family and then in the world at large. If you want to be more in touch with your bodyself and to be able to listen to its messages, you have the opportunity in relational somatic therapy to become more conscious of what you do feel and embody it. Ultimately, deeply taking in the experience of being seen can be soothing for it implies that your existence, your feelings, your very being is important to the other and taking in <u>that</u> awareness can help you take <u>your</u> <u>bodyself</u> <u>voice</u> more seriously and eventually treat yourself with compassion.

Reciprocity occurs between strengthening your bodyself awareness with the listening practices and embodying the experience of being seen by the other. These experiences reinforce each other and they both increase the capacity of your repository of positivity which supports taking in experiences with the therapist and listening to your bodyself. Over time, the therapist's embodied presence provides an energetic field which supports sensing your way through emotions that once were threatening and coming back to being grounded in your relationship to the therapist and with your bodyself. The embodied experience of my therapist's attuned presence receiving me calmed my bodyself heart, allowing me to be more receptive to my emotions when I was alone. So each time a feeling came up in the course of the therapy hour, I had an opportunity to experience a "mini" emotional recovery cycle – I started off with a Let's Go! emotion and as I experienced it through, grounded in my bodyself and in the presence of the attuned other, I could shift to Let Go . . calm and well-being. I call this sense of calm well-being, the "calm heart center" of my bodyself.

No! The self-affirming "No!" is seen and honored

A critical step in taking my bodyself voice seriously was to experience how my therapist received my "No!" when I was unhappy with something he said or when I felt interrupted in my bodyself experiencing. It took quite a bit of courage and time to say something to him, but it was worth it! My fear of losing this person who was becoming so important to me sometimes kept me from saying what was on my heart. My experience with my caretakers was that my "No!" was not well-received so I soon learned to try to accommodate their needs and not voice mine rather than risk feeling the shame of not being heard. Over time enough trust with my therapist was built so I could dare to voice my displeasure and then take in the experience of his listening to what upset me about what he said. That in itself was soothing to take in – he really did care how I felt and wanted to hear about it and that I didn't need to please him all the time to keep him interested in listening to me.

In fact, saying what I really felt, felt "bodyself good" in an empowered way. When my "No!" was expressed and honored I experienced that my separateness and my differences with him did not bring abandonment or rejection. This self-affirming "No!" differentiates me from the other, thereby making true contact possible as two separate beings. Rather than contraction, this "No!" leads to bodyself <u>expansion</u> and contributes to making my "Yes!" to the pleasurable resonance of our relationship a bodyself strengthening experience. Then this "Yes!" could be a heartfelt bodyself expression of expansion not a self-compromising "Yes!" of accommodation in an attempt to keep the relationship intact. Now I don't have to give up myself by making a Sophie's choice: I have a real choice between "Yes!" or "No!" as I feel it. The experience of saying "No!" and having it respected opened the door to owning

159

my anger in the presence of this attuned other instead of withdrawing from him or turning the anger back on myself or projecting it onto the other. And as I was to discover, owning my expansive "No!" to my therapist brought me closer to dealing with my contracted "No!" - the "No!" I said to my need for another in childhood. But first I had to dip my toes into the rippling waters of my self-assertive "No!" so I could venture further into the turbulent waves of expressing the contracted "No!"

Yes! Sensing the Need for the "Other" and Attendant Emotions

Taking in the experience of being seen and valued for who I am brought up the painful feelings of having been missed too often as a child. Too many times when I was upset, no one came to repair the relationship breach so I could take the experience of soothing deep into my bodyself. No wonder I had difficulty listening to my emotional voice as an adult, not to mention being challenged by opening to my need for another. If you experienced inadequate caretaker nurturance or unresolved trauma, you may be challenged in similar ways. Taking in the attuned presence of another can trigger visual or narrative memories or even "body"* memories of when someone wasn't there for you when you needed support to feel through threatening feelings. Now experiencing a warm, resonating presence that seems to be sensing what you are feeling may trigger sadness, anger, fear, grief or even shame. Shame is likely to be experienced when we reach out to another and the other is not available for whatever reason. And often when we make up a reason, it reflects poorly on ourselves or the other and we might not be moved to check out its veracity. In any case, if a contracted "No!" has formed in your bodyself as a result of a Sophie's choice you made long ago, it is likely to be triggered in the context of work with your therapist when you experience the therapist's presence as inviting. On the one hand this presence can feel welcome and on the other, it can feel unsafe; perhaps if you were to let the other in would you end up being abandoned or engulfed and thus lose your bodyself connection. Ironically the very presence that could truly address the interrupted connection with your bodyself expression now seems to threaten the loss of bodyself connection.

No! The Commitment to the Contracted "No!" Is Fully Felt and Expressed

In the context of embodying satisfying contact, I was able to own my need to reach out to another person and gradually feel less anxious about it. As I felt this need in my bodyself, he might then ask me to imagine my caretaker and pay attention to what happens in my breathing and all through me. I sensed the bodyself constriction of my "No!" begin to form as well as the emotional experience of closing off. This contraction was palpable as tension in my forehead between my eyes, in my neck and sometimes in my throat. Then he would ask me to let him see how that is for me. Now we are both witnessing that contraction and the accompanying fear, pain and the sense of not being seen. I was literally "facing" this pain as I let him see my face baring this pain. As I could deeply take in his seeing me in this pain, my attachment to needing my childhood caretaker to see my pain gradually dissipated. Coming to accept the limitations of my caretakers in this way diminishes my attraction to others limited in a similar way.

Other times he asks me to first feel our resonance in my bodyself and then to imagine my caretaker and report what my bodyself experience of my caretaker is. For instance, I might declare, "S/he is not there!" or "S/he doesn't see me!" I no longer have to deny that reality nor the feelings connected to it because his presence helps anchor me in my bodyself aliveness and my positivity repository has been fortified by the listening practices. I am no longer forced to make a "Sophie's choice" to save my sense of self. Taking in his resonant presence helps me stay with my bodyself voice, so I can experience through all of my feelings and needs instead of becoming overwhelmed and feel contained and soothed. I can finally come to accept my caretakers' limitations and that it was not <u>my</u> fault that they couldn't be protective and/or loving in the way I needed them to be. My bodyself shifts the Let's Go! contraction to Let Go . . expansion.

The process of experiencing fully my commitment to my "No!" was the most challenging of all the phases because it was held so deeply as my stance and expressed in bodyself tension as well as in my beliefs about myself and others. To express it fully felt like I was taking the enormous risk of losing the person who was most important to me as well as my familiar stance self-identification. It was a paradoxical dilemma because on one level I had maintained that I didn't need the other but the ferocity of that conviction belied the intense helplessness I felt in the face of the need for another. Holding onto this "No!" kept me from taking in the deep caring from another which could make me feel vulnerable because I didn't have control over the other yet I sensed I deeply needed him. Holding onto this "No!" made me feel important in the sense of having power to resist, i.e. – "I won't let you get to me!" I feared losing myself if I gave into my need for the other. It had not been my experience with my narcissistic caretaker that we could <u>both</u> be important. I had to diminish my bodyself expression to meet his need to feel important. The subjugation of my need to be loved for who I was and of the awareness that I was not, but still needed this person for my survival, engendered terror and rage which also had to be suppressed. Before I could go deeper with my contracted "No!" I had to feel safe enough to express my self-affirming "No!" to my therapist.

Until the contraction around the "No!" can be fully owned and expressed, the "Yes!" to contact also cannot be fully embodied. At first I couldn't be truly open nor could I express my self-assertive "No!" freely. The contracted "No!" kept my vulnerability and risk-taking in check. The rage and the terror held in place by the contracted "No!" needed to be felt through in the presence of an attuned other because I needed a soothing connection to come back to after intense emotions were expressed and tension was released. Otherwise there would be just retraumatization by the recycling of traumatic feelings like rage, terror, hysterical crying and/or perhaps even, darkest despair. To fully experience my commitment to my contracted "No!" and to express it, I needed the support of a well-established relationship with a therapist who had not only become important to me but whom I could trust to stay with me when I took that risk.

In my experience, the greater the risk, the greater the reward; however time was necessary for repeated experiences of "taking in" and of relationship repair to build enough trust to take this ultimate risk which could open my heart to truly taking in connection with another. It was only when I could finally take the risk of compromising my connection with my therapist that I could really know he was there with because he wanted to be, not because I had to do something to keep him there. I must emphasize that this was a deep bodyself experience; it was not just hearing the words that he said. In fact I had heard his verbal assurances several times in the previous years; while they sounded good, I could not take them in on the level that I experienced when I finally dared to "go to the mat" owning the strength of my commitment to my contracted "No!" and then moving through it. And that opening led to my now certain knowing that my mother must have also felt that way about me but I had been tragically cut off from letting her love touch me after the traumatic abandonment.

When I could trust the relationship with my therapist and my bodyself enough to express the ancient terror and rage which was held in place by the contracted "No!" and then really take in that experience, my need to have my caretakers see my suffering and pain was given up. I was finally seen where and how I needed to be seen and it no longer mattered that it wasn't by my caretakers. Though I didn't realize it at the time, taking in that experience signaled that the contracted "No!" of my stance no longer had a death grip on me. In order to give up needing my caretakers to be different and denying my need for them, I had to have something that was even more desirable than them to come back to. Likewise, in order to give up the self-holding and the attendant fantasy that the important "other" would come around "if only" I had just done this or that, the relationship with my therapist had to have enough value. Then I could risk giving up my stance which had kept me "safe". Accessible only fifty minutes a week, that relationship still had to give me enough resonant connection to make it worth giving up my old way of protecting myself, which kept me from a true deep connection with my need for another, including my therapist.

The experience of being met in my most scary, helpless, needful, angry places was in stark contrast to what I had encountered in childhood. Repeated many times over, this experience became deeply embodied and was stored as a "different" and positive "outcome" in my bodyself. Intense emotions and need for another could be met with compassion and presence. A new neural pathway* was being laid down in my emotional brain which could help me come through emotional upset to a calm connected place rather than dissociate, become anxious, or distract myself with some kind of doing. Instead of being rebuked or left alone because I expressed how I felt, I was met by a warm and sensitive presence. Because my traumatic feelings had been consistently met with compassionate understanding, I could accept and finally deeply grieve the limitations of my caretakers to connect with me as well as have more compassion for myself. I gradually gave up judging the part of me that needed the attention of my caretakers and thereby put me in jeopardy of feeling betrayed or not seen. Instead, I came to have compassion for that need because my therapist unfailingly stayed receptive toward my need for him even when I couldn't admit that need (when I was angry or not trusting of him). Thus the new neural pathway not only served me in relationship to others but also to myself and this new pathway is what makes optimal self-soothing possible. No longer in the grips of my contracted "No!" to my need for another, I could be more vulnerable (say "Yes!") to those who really were capable of seeing me and I was more able to see, thereby soothe and accept myself!

Yes! The "Yes!" of Expansion is Possible as the Contracted "No!" is Fully Owned.

"It" was finally "over" when I fully experienced and expressed the contraction of the "No!" and I could own all of my emotions and move through them, grounded in my bodyself. Now I can ride the waves of upset rather than be thrashed because the trauma of the lost connection with my bodyself is over! *She* and I share our bodyself home. I can go through my emotional recovery cycle and rest into my calm heart center with reliability and when I need to reach out to someone, I do. In fact I take in the contact with friends more than ever before, deeply touched by their tender tones and loving looks.

I can experience whole-heartedly my "Yes!" to contact with another and with my bodyself. Each of my emotions can lead to bodyself expansion, because they are now in service of self-affirmation, not self-denial as they sometimes were when I was in the grip of my stance. Being held in the grip of bodyself constriction as a result of fear of losing connection with the other and myself, made my "Yes!" and "No!" defensively half-hearted. Now when I feel shame or fear, I can soothe myself or reach out rather than contract in despair. And my anger can be expansive because I can use my "No!" and my anger if necessary, to set boundaries and/or to protect myself for this "No!" does not come from the constricted stance place of saying "No!" to my need to another. Instead, saying "No!" and expressing anger frees me to take care of my bodyself needs rather than deny them. This expansive "No!" frees me to say a whole-hearted "Yes!" to another because I <u>can</u> say "No!" and express my differences. This "Yes!" is an expansive bodyself "Yes!" rather than a contracted bodyself "Yes!" in service of codependency or accommodation or maintaining a fantasy of the other or oneself. Behind the self-compromising "Yes!" which is held hostage by the contracted "No!" is the fear of losing the love of the other or one's own identity. Freedom to express a whole-hearted "Yes!" and "No!" is what I want to possess as I grow to love someone. Then when I do experience love from another I know it's more likely for me as I am, not for who I think I have to pretend to be. Having taken the risk of "forever" losing my connection with my therapist gifted me with the discovery that he is there because he wants to be, not because I have to do something to keep him there. I experienced that I "mattered" just as I am.

And when my Let's Go! anger is followed by tears, the expansive state of Let Go . . is further supported. No longer in the grip of my contracted "No!" my tears no longer flow from the inconsolable terror and despair of childhood but rather they arise from sadness, from missing someone, or from grieving a loss. These tears release tension, they are not maintained by tension. These are Let Go . . tears that bring me back to my heart because deeply grieving the loss of love is finally possible when I am not possessed by the contracted "No!" When I sense tension or pain, I am more likely to consciously surrender to my tears and Let Go . .

For example, while I was writing this section, I sensed the tension in my neck increasing as I typed and finally I let myself stop and kneeled on the floor to massage my neck. I found myself crying the words, "Don't keep reminding me of my mistakes!" I had been focusing on the "dumb" things I have said that hurt somebody where no repair was possible as well as the people I haven't heard from, who couldn't be there for me the way I would have liked. My tears melted the tension and helped me give up focusing my attention to what was painful. By giving into the bodyself message that my neck was getting tense, I opened to hearing the underlying message of being kinder to myself from *her*. With newfound compassion I recognize when I am hurting myself and STOP! and take a Let Go . . break and let myself off the hook. *She* pleads, *"Take a break so you can break open!*

The "Yes!" freed from the strictures of the bodyself contraction of the "No!" brings the spontaneous organismic desire to reach out to another – a small movement of a finger, a glance or a spontaneous utterance. This inborn "spontaneous gesture*" of the bodyself toward contact signals the release from self-holding and comes from the heart's desire rather than from the panic, desperation or overwhelming need for another underlying the contracted "No!" My eyes are open, no longer veiled by idealization so I can see clearly who is there and also whether my love has a possibility of being returned. I can say "Yes!" to a specific person, not just <u>any</u> person out of desperation to be seen. This "Yes!" is an open hand, not a grasping hand. Reaching out is self-affirming when it comes from the expansive "heart" place rather than the contracted, blinded place of the stance. Bodyself expansion means I can reach out, take in, give and feel love and compassion for myself, others, and even for my caretakers. I can forgive them because I can see their limitations and as I do, I can begin to forgive myself. In fact, forgiving myself has been more of a challenge than forgiving them. Self-forgiveness is a continual practice - I don't want to live or die with regret nor with the bodyself tension of my contracted "No!" Grieving and forgiving seem to go hand in hand as the contracted "No!" melts in the warmth of human contact and leads to the expansion of Let Go . .

Since working through the constriction around the "No!" to my need for my mother and experiencing my anger being received by my therapist, I have opened to the love she and I shared in my earliest days. I am grateful for the loving body memory to come back to because some are not so fortunate in having a core bodyself experience of bonding with a caretaker. I also experienced regret for not being as good to her as I could have been now because I had been resentful about the way she responded to a number of events in my childhood. However I also know she wouldn't want me to be hard on myself for she knew all too well what that was like. Now that I can let her off the hook, I am learning to let myself off the hook. Now that my contracted "No!" is easing I miss her in a very sweet way and I can bask in the love we shared. Her love has become a resource for me as well as something I can share with others: her smile, her gentleness, her sweetness, her light are accessible and reflected in me.

How the Emotional Recovery Cycle Eases the Contracted "No!" to Access *Her*

Working through the bodyself contraction of my "No!" required taking in the attuned presence of my therapist so I could go through the emotional recovery cycle*, no matter what feeling or need came up in my present or past life, including my interactions with my therapist. My increasing capacity to go through the emotional recovery cycle, first with my therapist and then on my own was <u>essential</u> to the recovery of my bodyself voice. That is, shifting from the emotional arousal of Let's Go! to the soothing calm of Let Go . . and not bypassing feeling through an emotion or expressing a need by acting out or getting stuck in hysteria or frozen in dissociation. When something occurred in our relationship that I was not happy with, I was able to feel through every feeling and come back to my heart for myself and for him. Neither had I compromised myself in anyway, nor had the external situation changed. I felt whole and happy as I embraced the moments we had together. I had the bodyself support to reach out and to say "Yes!", "No!" and express my anger and my love. In other words, the contracted "No!" of my stance no longer limited access to *her*, my bodyself voice. Being able to go through the emotional recovery cycle, again and again supports working through the contraction of the "No!" and reciprocally, working through the bodyself contraction around the "No!" facilitates the emotional recovery cycle so that integration of once threatening feelings and past traumatic experiences can take place. Embodying the emotional recovery cycle makes possible owning every feeling and need as well as, feeling deeply for others.

She wants you to know about the potential rewards of taking the risk of embodying your own emotional recovery cycle because going through this cycle means spending more time with your "*her*". I too, want so much for you, dear Reader, to get the maximum out of this book so you can make life-changing discoveries which can lead to living your bodyself life more fully. Your own emotional recovery cycle will likely differ in detail from mine but not in function. How you experience your feelings of fear, anger, shame, grief and longing and in what order may differ. The places where you get stuck in feeling-through will likely depend on your childhood experiences. But when you can feel through these feelings, you can come back to resting, feeling whole and vital again. Eventually you may be less fearful of what you might feel or need because of growing confidence that you can feel through anything and you can ask for help when needed. You may be less likely to become depressed, shut down or panicked because you are having a particular feeling. Your communication with others is likely to improve as well as your ability to truly soothe yourself.

As a result of this process, emotions can become helpful bodyself signals rather than threats to your well-being. When you notice you are feeling angry, you can ask yourself, "What need is not getting met right now?" You will be less likely to shut down in shame when you feel your need for another or when you feel fear, anger, sad or powerless. If you were treated as though you and your needs were not important, feeling powerless as an adult may trigger the traumatic feelings of helplessness you felt as a child. When you have felt through, with an attuned presence, your shame, rage and despair about your needs not being met, you are likely to be more able to accept your feelings of helplessness. You may discover that when you are feeling powerless there <u>are</u> actions you can take to support yourself even if you can't change the situation because you <u>can</u> change your attitude. When you can accept the helpless, overwhelmed feeling, you can take a break or ask for support from others. Then you are likely to be less prone to rage or other forms of acting out or denial such as indulging in an addiction. As you acknowledge your feelings and accept them, they often dissipate. In other words, you learn to <u>consciously</u> <u>surrender</u>* to the sense of powerlessness by resting into your bodyself experience. And as you do, a new sense of well-being arises. With practice you can shift more easily from the Let's Go! of distress to the Let Go . . of de-stress. In short you are able to listen to *her* voice and take good care of yourself.

When *she* needs you to be tender and vulnerable, you are able to oblige. You are less likely to be controlled by your fear of the vulnerability of needing another. You know you can protect yourself by setting boundaries (your "No!") and expressing your anger. You will be less likely to be at the mercy of your critic or fear being overpowered by your sadistic side because you can protect your vulnerable self in other ways. The battle between love and power has already been decided in your heart because of your experience with the attuned other and the resultant new neural pathway. Because the frightened child of the past has been soothed, the need for a merciless critic or for a rageful part for protection becomes anachronistic. Embodying the stabilizing presence of an attuned other is the basis for bodyself containment of emotions. In other words, "taking in" and embodying the experience of truly mattering to someone important to you, can render you less likely to deny your need for another or engage in stance behaviors to try to get love. You are <u>already</u> loved and you carry that sense deep in your bodyself repository of positivity. You can let your need for the other to be seen; you don't have to hide or manipulate to get your needs for contact met. You can see others more clearly because you <u>accept</u> rather than <u>project</u> your feelings. That is, you are less likely to transfer unresolved feelings toward childhood caretakers onto others.

At the same time you will be less likely to shrink from, but rather, embrace the feeling reality of your situation as a child. You will be less likely to be naïve about your caretaker's limitations and behavior – naïve in the sense of failing to see the destructive side of the other. Feeling through your reactions to both sides of your caretaker allows you to be more clear-eyed in your choices for life partners and friends. When you work through the pain of your childhood disappointments and traumas, you no longer seek a mate to repair the past. You no longer are driven to try to heal your loved one nor do you seek a healing from them. Your choice can be guided by common interests and emotional compatibility rather than by blind passion that is often the result of a "traumatic attachment".** You are less likely to be <u>seduced</u> by your attraction to those who have harmful characteristics similar to your caretakers because you can accept the reality of your caretaker's limitations and have lived through your feeling reactions to them. When you have grieved what was lost and could never be, you can embrace new possibilities for yourself.

You will be more likely to choose an emotionally available person because <u>you</u> have become more available and therefore can bear to see whether the other is truly available to you or not. Your perception of the other is not clouded by the terror of your needy child or the rage of the protective monster or critic inside you. You want a person to love, not to control. When you have learned to listen with your heart to yourself and to the other, you have less need for control. You can truly enjoy your relationships. You don't have to protect yourself by denial because you know you have a right to say "No!" to others as well as "Yes!" to your needs. You don't have to avoid any feeling or need. Because you had the reparative experience of being seen, met and not used or abandoned, you can allow your need for contact to be seen. You have empathy for the other and can reach out to him. The "No!" you may have said to your own nurturing need is no longer held in your bodyself, so you are free to express your need for connection and your love. Going through your emotional recovery cycle and soothing yourself means you can return to the heart of your bodyself, to *her*.

For instance, well into my therapy, I went through what could be called a "mini-emotional recovery cycle", simply through eye contact. As I was opening to the presence of my therapist, a feeling of fear came up and I saw a fleeting image of my abuser's face. Then my therapist's face replaced the abuser's, accompanied by a feeling of connection and ease. The alternating occurred spontaneously, each face appeared for a few seconds. The feelings I experienced with the appearance of each of the faces were appropriate to my dominant experience of each of these two men. It is impossible to say which came first - the feeling or the face. Because of all the previous work we had done together, I was no longer afraid to feel my fear or my longing. I had no need to shrink from any perception. Then the whole cycle repeated itself again and again until I simply just rested into our contact.

I could clearly feel the "then"– the feelings and faces of the past and the "now" of the present. I felt through the old feelings of terror and let them fade away. It was as if my mind was checking out who this person was – was he the "same" or "different." When the alternating stopped, it was as if the new perception had replaced the old image. These were indeed, truly different people and different feelings applied. I could now see clearly with my heart because my eyes and my heart were open. I could finally allow myself to deeply rest into contact with my therapist. I had embodied his presence as a safe one and could rest into that perception. Weeks later I experienced a similar sense of alternation, but this time it was either his face or nothing at all. I speculated that this may have been connected with healing the shock of realizing my mother was not coming. It was as if my mind finally replaced the "nothingness" with his presence. Perhaps the first experience was healing the trauma of intrusion and the second, the trauma of abandonment – in each case, the frightening perception gradually disappeared and was replaced by a sense of the mutual presence in the "now".

The calm heart center

In Conrad Stroud's** words, I found the place "which translates the heart":

"For antelope, two invisible boundaries exist –
  If you cross the first, they will flee,
  If you chance upon the second, they will attack.
  The question is, how to approach without touching either,
  To find the posture which translates the heart."

This "posture which translates the heart" I refer to as the "calm heart center", a neutral ground from which to relate. This neutral ground is not an expression of detachment, but an alive, involved, resonating presence. It does not imply a sense of being "above it all" as if emotions were something inferior or dangerous. Here, my eyes are open and I see what is there. I am neither contracted not dissociated. This alive presence means I am open, not emotionally shut down or spaced out as some spiritual practices might foster. This neutral place arises from the fertile ground of being seen in all my feelings and needs, rendering unnecessary the escalation into terror and rage. Here is where I can listen to *her* and experience through what is necessary to come back to my bodyself – no longer deaf to *her* needs and feelings. From this calm heart center I can hear my heart for myself and for others because I have deeply embodied the experience of another's heart for me.

As I move from bodyself constriction to bodyself expansion, I gain bodyself connection and expression and have nothing to lose but tension, pain, anxiety and depression. As I come to enjoy more and more the experience of expansion, expressing my feelings and respecting my bodyself needs, I find I am more able to accept change as it comes. I find myself more willing to consciously surrender to what is happening at the moment. And that means being open to explore the unknown, the next moment, for instance! For, I already know who I am. To quote Hazrat Inayat Kahn*, "God breaks the heart again and again and again until it stays open." That can work as long as you can find God or the other each time and/or have a calm heart center to rest-into, which allows to you grieve and forgive.

Advice to self after a recent melt-down:

Just sit down and type, just let yourself cry and see what happens. Trust *her* and all the work you have put into accessing your deep truth - that deep truth will emerge and guide you if you open to it. Your bodyself center has enough gravity to keep you grounded so your energy field can exist everywhere at once, and all the while you are Letting Go and consciously surrendering to the unknown with a big smile on your bodyself face! You don't have to <u>know</u>, you only have to trust in letting go into the energetic love field that surrounds you and always has. You only have only to turn toward it and open to it and now you are free to do just that. Whenever you notice that you are self-holding in Let's Go! bodyself contraction, give yourself to being "held" in Let Go . . expansion. When you are so distracted and tense, you don't even notice you are holding out against this field of potential. You lose sight of the larger picture. There is nothing to lose but tension and a whole world of opening to connection to gain.

So dear Reader, if you would like to understand more about the process of going from bodyself constriction to bodyself expansion through relational somatic psychotherapy, you may gain some insight and maybe even inspiration by reading the next three chapters. Once you can access your bodyself voice more easily, you'll find yourself moving more fluidly from Let's Go! contraction to Let Go . . expansion as needed. I do not want to convey the impression that bodyself "contraction" is bad or wrong; contraction and expansion of the bodyself are organic phases of an innate organismic cycle and both are necessary for healthy psycho-physiological functioning. The type of contraction that is limiting and can be ultimately harmful to organismic regulation is the contraction which results from unresolved trauma or unrepaired interpersonal encounters and prevents the shift to Let Go . . to restore balanced functioning. An example is the constriction around the "No!" that is said to the need for another. While it was originally a creative survival mechanism to cope with caretaker limitations, this bodyself contraction becomes fixed and limits the full embodiment of your aliveness and choices.

If you are interested in knowing more about how <u>early</u> <u>experiences</u> of <u>separation</u> of a child from its caretaker can affect an individual's bodyself connection and how that bodyself connection can gradually be restored turn to the next chapter and read the sections on "Working with a Body Memory of Abandonment" and the early memory associated with it. If you suspect you may have been separated from your caretaker early on, whether through a hospitalization, an adoption or foster home you may get an inkling of how that could have compromised your ability to self-soothe as an adult and how consultation with a therapist could help. Also included in that discussion is how my posse of positivity - my close friends and colleagues - assisted in the recovery of my bodyself voice.

If your interests lie with getting more of a flavor of how some of the <u>phases</u> of <u>relational</u> <u>somatic</u> <u>therapy</u> play out, Chapter 12 contains examples of each phase as it unfolded in my own work and in work with others. These anecdotes flesh out the process with dialogue and details – the blood, sweat and tears – as *she* likes to call it, and they may draw you in and make the process of recovery of your bodyself voice come more alive. Whatever you choose to follow up on, I hope you find your way to a more intimate connection with your bodyself voice so you too can develop a greater capacity for healthy self-soothing and enjoyment of your life.

WRESTING MY BODYSELF VOICE FROM THE GRIP OF CHILDHOOD ABANDONMENT TRAUMA

"We so deeply need each other."

She insisted on including this account of my work on the abandonment trauma and on an early memory of a subsequent event because *she* knows firsthand how easily *her* voice can be discounted. *She* was concerned that perhaps, you, dear Reader, might have something similar in your past that you may yet not have even a suspicion of, but which might be interfering with your ability to hear your bodyself voice and self-soothe. As a result of this work, I was finally able to reconnect with my love for my mother after being estranged from her for most of my life as well as regain a connection with my bodyself that greatly increased my capacity for self-soothing and for reaching out to another. I finally found what I had lost: the bodyself experience of our shared love, as well as, compassion for the little one who needed her mother so desperately. With the help of my posse of positivity* - my colleagues in a process group and my therapist - I had enough support to experience and to integrate the nearly devastating feelings and needs resulting from this trauma rather than withdraw into shame and despair or dissociation. Perhaps reading this account will spark something in you that you had previously discounted as unimportant or it no longer mattered because it happened so long ago. Maybe it would help to consider this journey of recovering access to your bodyself voice as a mystery to be solved and you are the detective as well as the one who hired the detective to help. In the very least, you may feel some resonance with what unfolds for me and that resonance could be your bodyself voice signaling you.

Working with a Body Memory of Abandonment

The trauma

You might be wondering what I mean by a "body" memory. Most of our memories we identify as a "memory" because we see a visual representation of an experience even though it probably had kinesthetic, tactile, olfactory, auditory and emotional components as well. A body memory is often only sensed emotionally and perhaps kinesthetically without a visual picture to go with it. Lacking a picture, it is harder to identify or take a body memory seriously. Body memories, especially those resulting from trauma often hearken back to early childhood, sometimes before we have words. The body memory I will address was verified by both my caretakers on separate occasions so I have no reason to doubt these events took place. What my caretakers couldn't tell me was how I felt inside nor could I tell them at the time and that was the crux of the trauma as you will learn.

About five years into my work with my first long-term therapist, Stephan Tobin, Ph.D., I "uncovered" this body memory while addressing the issue of my "on purpose" lateness for our appointments. This was my first awareness of the fall-out from being "left" in the hospital. While I never could recall my experience in the hospital as a visual memory, I had an undeniable sense of the feelings connected to the excruciating experience of waiting in the nursery for my mom to come when I described what it was like to wait for my therapist in his waiting room. As I spoke I became more and more emotional, almost panicked. My feelings became even more intense as I told him the story my parents told me of my hospitalization as a young child during which they were not allowed to see me. Over the course of four or five sessions I was able to feel the truth in my body of what that experience must have been for me, waiting for my mother to come for me, day after day after day. It is so poignant how buried childhood experiences can play out in our adult life. Waiting could have been a time to Let Go . . but not for me. It made me tense and anxious, especially if I was waiting for someone I really wanted to see. I had not made that connection until that day though I had known about that hospital stay for much of my life.

In any case, the trauma and pain of abandonment is experienced whether the abandonment was intentional or not. What matters for future self-soothing capacity is whether and how the consequences of the abandonment are addressed. Does the caretaker want to see what has happened to the child, can she sense the withdrawal and fear? Or does she want everything to be all right because she can't face her own painful abandonment experiences. Does she cajole a smile out of her darling and then not think about the possible impact of the separation? If so, she unwittingly coaxes the child to take care of her feelings, instead of attending to those of the child.

The case in point is my experience of being hospitalized for severe bronchitis for a week when I was about 2 ½ years old. I was in line for a tracheotomy with five other babies because antibiotics were not readily available in the mid 1940's. To make matters much worse parents were not allowed to visit because that would only "upset" the children and make more work for the staff (or perhaps stir up the staff's repressed feelings of primal abandonment!) Better to leave the children to steep in their depressive and dissociative states, they are much quieter that way. When my mother came to get me, she saw that I had lost weight, had dark circles under my eyes and had to be toilet trained all over again. I had truly regressed and was experiencing "infantile depression" a condition that was not diagnosed in those days, let alone treated. It was only in the 1950's that documentation of such cases* was made and even then another 20 years had to pass before American and British hospitals allowed parents to visit their children.

Recounting this incident my mother said that I was "happy to come home." Can you imagine? "Happy to come home!" There was no way I could tell her about the terrible fright and despair not to mention loneliness and anger I experienced while she was gone. I could not tell her of the agonizing pain I suffered when the simmering water in a steamer streamed down my arm, leaving third degree burns. By the time she came to get me, our bond was severely damaged. I had given up on her. Forty years later when I worked with this "body" memory in therapy, I sensed that I turned my head away from her as she came towards me. Perhaps I was trying not to cry or show my anger or feel my frustrated longing for her. Having had to deal with the overwhelming terror of abandonment and being burned, my bodyself had simply shut down and could not receive her once comforting presence. In one fell swoop I lost my soothing connection to my mother and my developing connection with the core of my bodyself was compromised. My physical condition notwithstanding, all my mother remembers seeing was that I was "happy to come home". It seemed that was all that mattered to her? In my mind's eye, even now, when I look at her with longing and need, I see her face tilted upward, smiling, and totally oblivious to my pain and despair. That was how she dealt with the pain of her childhood and beyond.

In response to this perceived abandonment, I felt deep shame and eventually, anger. She could not see my need. It is inherently humiliating to not be seen by someone I loved and so desperately needed. I concluded there must be something wrong with me. This thought was more bearable than there was something wrong with her. For then there truly would be no hope. Better to blame myself than my caretaker. At least maybe then I might some control. I felt so bad and needy but she didn't see it. I dared not reach out lest I feel numbing shame again. After all I am a "big girl." She always said that I was so precocious and smart.

And yet I felt like a baby – a baby that needed to be held for a long time, till it's <u>ready</u> to be put down. But how could I tell her? I'm sure I couldn't even bear to feel that need for very long. Besides by then she had another needy infant to take care of. He usurped her because he was now the baby. No wonder I resented him. I couldn't hate her because I needed her. I sensed her fragility and her sensitivity to criticism. Better to be the big girl who pretends not to need her mother. Pretending in this way continues the maternal family tradition, for my mother had to be her mother's best friend and give up her needs to be taken care of. No wonder my earliest recollection is lying on the icy ground and as it began to snow, fantasizing I would not be found until someone tripped over me as the snow melted in the spring. This fantasy poignantly portrayed how deeply unseen I had felt in my need to be taken care of.

My brain (for surely I did not consciously design this defense) responded to my overwhelming sense of despair by making it seem that I was OK. In actuality, this was a dissociation response to a traumatic situation. In any case my mother could not see my depression and need. Besides, <u>her</u> need was for me to be OK. That is what made her happy. Then she would smile at me and oh, how I needed that smile! My needs and feelings were so well hidden that I fooled myself. Fooling myself and fooling her was better than feeling humiliated by showing my neediness and not being seen or accepted. Feeling my need for her would awaken all the pain, terror, loneliness and longing that I managed by being split off from my bodyself.

The unintentional, unspoken message I got from this experience was that my need for my mother was shameful and that I should be a "big girl" and not a baby. This unarticulated message was carried as tension in my bodyself, especially in my neck, forehead, between my eyes and in my jaw as well as in my preoccupation with whether others who were important to me were mad at me or wanted me. The criticalness I often felt toward my mother was my suppressed resentment toward her for "abandoning" me. This experience was the seed of my "I don't need you!" stance later in life and the installation of my emotional "default setting" which "filled in" the lack of response from someone with "I'm not wanted" or "S/he is angry with me." With therapy I came to understand that this latter response was a projection of my own overwhelming anger and fear.

To regain my connection with her and my bodyself, I would have had to express the fear and anger I felt at being left alone, not to mention being burned and then the grief and despair of her not returning in time. I would have had to cry and cry and kick and struggle against her body while she remained present and held me securely but tenderly in her arms*. I would have needed her to talk to me in a soothing voice and not shrink away from my distraught being. Perhaps then my pain and terror would have dissipated and we would have reconnected; she would have regained her full value as a comforting resource and I, my bodyself connection. Alas, dealing with childhood trauma was itself in its infancy so none of this reconnection occurred. I had to wait 45 years before I even had an inkling of the power

171

of this experience to not only cut me off from my bodyself longing for connection, but also to make me wary of trusting my mother to be there for me, let alone to trust another's love. No wonder my earliest memory is of not feeling wanted and not being able to tell anyone.

A posttraumatic manifestation of this experience was my aversion to waiting for someone who was emotionally important to me such as a friend or therapist. I would rather be a few minutes late and incur their annoyance than experience my anxiety about waiting. Better to make them wait and retain a sense of control. Unknowingly I must have been afraid I might touch the pain of waiting for my mother to show up - that terrible pain of helplessness, loneliness and feeling unwanted. Better to make them feel unwanted by having to wait for me.

The work

The work I did on various aspects of this trauma over the years laid a foundation for integration of the once overwhelming feelings because I was able to let in soothing on a deep bodyself level. During my work in my Master's Group (a group of eight women therapists who have been meeting together for 10 years in a "process" group) I experienced a stunning "working through" of being "left" in the hospital. It had followed a session with my therapist wherein I was so angry at the young needy part of me whose longing for her mother I tried to deny for many years. I held her longing responsible for getting me into a relationship with a man who really couldn't fall in love with me. I just hated her and wanted to wipe her out because that feeling of longing and waiting in pain was just intolerable. I started my work in group by expressing how much I hated this needy part all the while feeling guilty because I knew I shouldn't act that way toward such a vulnerable part of me. The hate was my attempt to push away the painful longing and desperation.

When I started crying, Pat, the group therapist and I were sitting next to each other on the couch, my legs over her lap. My chin and jaw were shaking with the sobbing. Then she said "let out the scream". Her timing was perfect. And what a scream it was! Not a hysterical scream, but a very strong embodied scream. There is a difference; I had had enough bodywork to how feel this single scream connected me right into the center of the pain and the acute sense of loss and terror I had felt. But at the same time I was grounded in my bodyself, experiencing being held by Pat and by the witnessing presence of my dear colleagues with whom we had shared so much.

From that point on Pat just let me follow what my body wanted to do next, rather than try to direct my work. That was perfect. The scream had helped me open to feeling my body and her body and to give into my impulse to be held and comforted. I wanted to hold Pat tightly and I asked her to hold me tightly as well and to not let me go. Squeezing her tightly helped release the tension I was feeling and allowed me then to feel myself and her more clearly. I followed my impulses, one by one as they revealed themselves. I felt my breathing shift from fast and short to hardly breathing at all to slow and long. All the while I was acutely aware of her soft body which I was holding at the same time she was holding me. With my head on her chest, I followed my bodyself impulse to reach up and touch her cheek, just taking in the pleasure of the contact. I was feeling both of our bodies, not merging but distinct, first mine then hers, back and forth as the focus of my awareness.

This went on for about 15 minutes until I felt satisfied. I stayed in my bodyself the entire time and finally embodied my need to reach out to my mother. I later said I felt like I was being freed from the hospital and taken into my mother's arms. I felt my love and my need for contact with her, which I had denied at a very deep level for most of my life in an effort to protect myself from the devastating feelings of waiting and waiting for her to come. I only wish my mother were still alive so I could let her feel my love for her and say how sad I felt that I didn't have access to feeling all this love until now. I know she would have just smiled and then said to me, "I love you, too, sweetheart!" In any case, since then I have been feeling more love for my mother than ever before, she comes to me often in my mind's eye and I feel so appreciative of her. And I love feeling this way, especially after being estranged for so many years.

And *she* is now saying, *Yea! You finally freed me for good! Aren't you glad you didn't kill me off!* *She* is laughing, *she* doesn't take it personally because *she* knows how terrified I was of feeling the darkness wherein no one comes. When I later told my therapist about this experience, he was pleased and said, "That scream <u>was</u> it, not about it." By "it" he meant that I was able to stay with my breath grounded in my bodyself and live through the feelings instead of getting caught in the terror and rage of the original wounding. In Winnicott's terms, I was "living my death"*. When it happened to me as a child, I felt like I would rather die than feel that pain. But I couldn't die and neither could I live in that pain so I shut myself off from my bodyself and from my mother. This was <u>my</u> <u>brain</u> reacting to trauma, not her doing. My mother never wanted this to happen. We were both victims of circumstance. No blame. Just reconnection. After 65 years.

As an adult I was prone to experiencing anxiety when I felt helpless about a situation with a loved one or a psychotherapy client. Sometimes I became so preoccupied, I would experience difficulty falling asleep. I used meditation in an attempt to soothe my anxiety but I could not allow myself to touch the underlying despair. The only times I would come close to experiencing the despair of this early abandonment was upon the breakup of a romantic relationship. Until I found a therapist who could really be with me, I could not truly live through the anxiety and despair and come out whole on the other side. I needed someone who was not afraid of going deeply into his own feelings of fear, anger, sadness and most importantly, his longing for connection. For connection is what you can return to when you are eventually able to live through all the feelings resulting from abandonment. Then you can come back fully into connecting to your bodyself and then perhaps with another. Otherwise you will always be holding something back, sometimes by choosing someone to love who also cannot be there fully. Or as Gibran so beautifully put it, "You will laugh but not all of your laughter and you will cry but not all of your tears."** It was only after many years of therapy that I began to touch this despair, agony, anger and finally, my need for my mother. As I was able to increasingly live through these feelings and experience the love my mother and I had for each other, I could wholeheartedly care for her in her last days.

I know my mother didn't want me to feel abandoned but there was nothing she could do. She couldn't buck the hospital rules. She couldn't break down the door to the hospital nursery. Yet many years passed before I let go of my anger at her for being so impotent (unfortunately this was only the first of many situations she couldn't protect me from). Why she didn't notice that I was so upset inside – that I couldn't relax into her arms like I had before? My very first words, to my mother's sheer delight had been a sentence, "Go'sleep!" They no longer soothed. While the outer signs of depression gradually disappeared, the inner withdrawal from the deep thorough-going comfort her body had heretofore offered me was intractable. At a deep level lay buried feelings of helplessness, rage, terror and despair. These feelings formed a kind of an emotional backdrop which I carried unknowingly into adulthood. They were stirred by a multitude of <u>perceived</u> abandonments and betrayals, which fed my fears that indeed I was not wanted and no one would come to get me. I came to believe I had to fend for myself and that I could do it on my own. These thoughts became beliefs and shaped the story I told myself about what had happened to me and what I could expect in the future. With those expectations came a predictable holding pattern of tension in my jaw, neck, and chest, the bodyself-holding of my stance.

Waiting for contact: the "watcher"

My emotional brain could not tolerate the intensity of that early experience and walled it off. In fact that experience seems to have given birth to a mute "watcher" who resided in the back of my skull, directly behind my eyes. I can still remember how I felt as I tried to articulate to my therapist my sudden awareness of it in a session over twenty years ago. The watcher was a secret even to myself up until that moment. It never spoke but it was utterly convinced of how threatening the world was. It watched wordlessly: vigilant, sad and afraid but unshakably watchful. No one could get to it. And no one even knew about it. The watcher was my "default" setting, my silent background awareness. I took a chance telling him about this watcher. It felt like a real accomplishment and a bit of a risk, but I felt good that I could be so bold and share what I really was thinking – where I really lived. My therapist seemed a little taken aback at the time but interested nonetheless.

And then more recently I had the distinct sensation of my current therapist's being able to actually "see" and connect with the watcher's eyes. It was as though his seeing could penetrate all the way to the back of the inside of my skull behind my eyes from where the vigilant one watched. I welcomed being so deeply seen by him. I had been in the midst of feeling some kind of tortured feeling and it seemed he could see exactly where it was and feel how it felt. That is all it ever needed and wanted, that is, to be found. The years of work with him had made me more trusting of him and myself so I could allow being so deeply seen. A simple but powerful, and palpable experience of being seen.

Earliest Visual Memory, a Vestige of Abandonment Trauma

My earliest visual memory crystallized my perception, born of trauma, that no one cared how I felt. This experience occurred during the winter after the hospitalization when I was about 3 1/2. I was lying on an icy pathway in the courtyard of the brownstone where we lived in New Jersey. I didn't know where my mother was, I must have wandered off while she was busy with my little brother and my feelings had likely been hurt. I felt very sad, very alone and sorry for myself. As I was lying on my stomach with my head turned to the side, I saw snowflakes begin to fall. For a moment I was "caught" by the sight of the softly falling flakes. Then I went back to feeling sorry for myself and had the fantasy that no one would come and I would freeze and the snow would cover me up. The fantasy continued: one day someone would trip over me and discover the little girl (me), frozen, mostly hidden by the snow. I was determined to wait as the snow continued to fall but no one came. Deeply disappointed and a little angry, I eventually got up, brushed myself off and slowly walked back. I felt resolute in my conviction that no one knew or cared how bad I felt. Most likely I couldn't bear to take the chance to tell anyone lest I feel again the shame of not being wanted. I have no memory of telling my mother about it.

Work on earliest visual memory

A few months after working with the body memory of the hospitalization, I worked with my therapist on this visual memory connected to the hospital. This time I experienced my mother's love for me, thereby reclaiming more of my bodyself. Letting love in is often even more of a challenge than feeling one's love for another because "taking in" means giving up the control you feel when you say "No!" to the need for another. The previous work on the hospitalization cleared the way to address my early memory of lying on the icy path. And the latter work turned out to be pivotal in my penetrating the reality that a former lover was no longer available to me, which in turn freed me to grieve. I was very present as I described in detail what I recalled of my memory of lying on my stomach on the icy sidewalk and feeling very sad, lonely and a little angry. My head was turned to the left side and I remembered seeing snowflakes softly falling. For a moment, I realized my attention had been caught by a snowflake and in that moment I was no longer sad or angry, I was just "there". At that moment in the session, it occurred to me for the very first time, that had my mother come to me right then, I could have let her pick me up and hold me and that I would have cried and let her take me home. As I told my therapist this imagining, I began crying and crying and then I was aware from inside of me, that my cheeks were very hot and wet with tears. As I put my hands to my cheeks I felt the moist heat under my hands and I sensed I was <u>here</u> and not there on the ground. As I continued to feel myself so alive under my hands, my whole bodyself was connected to this experience; less of my energy and attention was taken with the memory of lying on the icy path and the fantasy of dying and being covered with snow.

It was as if I was assimilating the energy of the fantasy of dying and the vision of lying there; I was gradually becoming embodied in the here and now, as cliché as that may sound. In all my years of therapy I had never experienced anything like that. Then I sensed I was way into my head, with explanations so I put my hands to sides of my head and came back again to the specter of this fantasy gradually fading before my eyes as I felt more and more, my living presence. It (the "me" on the sidewalk) became me as I fantasized my mother coming to me and picking me up and holding me. I visualized the falling snow melt around our warm embrace and form a stream which flowed down the path. The imagery of melting frozenness turning into a stream, flowing down a path could be a metaphor for my giving into a deep connection with my bodyself and an opening to letting love in. My wish for us all is that we can be supported in our aliveness by our deep bodyself experience and by our openness to experiencing loving connection rather than withholding out of fear of losing ourselves to the helplessness or rage of unresolved trauma and loss.

It seemed that all my previous work had culminated in this event. And even though my therapist had hardly spoken during this time, I sensed that his presence supported the energetic field for this unfolding. Ten years of work together, little openings here and there: the experience of no judgment, his listening to me when I needed more space, his caring for me, his taking my pain seriously and unflinchingly, his hearing my disappointment and anger when he didn't get where I was coming from (which took me almost two years to reveal). All this laid a foundation for the creation of an energetic field to support taking the image of this little one "into my body" because I no longer resented her for wanting her mother. That long-held resentment had rendered me vulnerable to panicked feelings of helplessness, fear and loss. I no longer resented my mother for not coming. I was finally able to <u>truly</u> grieve that fact that she didn't come because now I could stay in touch with my bodyself as I felt the presence of my therapist. I was OK and could take in the beauty of the snowflake and live for another day.

The desire to crush the needy one

Just to think, in a session only a few months prior to this, I experienced wanting to literally crush this vulnerable part of me for it was because of its longing that I was still fantasizing about a man who really couldn't really love me. And up until recently I had added insult to injury by obsessing about what I could have done so that he would love me. Such an effort can result in a near terminal, but for sure, a hopeless case of the "if onlies"! But fantasizing like this serves the illusion of having some control: if it is my fault, I can do something and not face the fact that he is limited in what he can give me. This obsessing about "what I did I do that kept him from loving me" was an attempt to manage the anxiety I felt in his absence and that anxiety was fall-out from not being able to accept the overwhelming feelings of panic and terror because mother never came, that I was alone, not only in the hospital but also on the sidewalk. I would have rather died or fantasized about dying than feel that pain. I could not bear the <u>feeling</u> of her absence. I would rather wait forever in fantasy rather than think she was not coming, let alone accept it. I would rather try to kill that needy baby than feel that pain. The afternoon after I imagined crushing it, I felt relieved. It was several days before I started fantasizing about the man again. While I didn't feel a sense of well-being during that time the pain and longing were gone. My "Sophie's choice" had been to kill off the "needy baby" rather die myself. But there would be no future for loving again. There had to be another option - I just couldn't find it then.

Contact with another could make the anxiety go away but only for a short time. Besides, when caught in the grip of the cycling between the terrified, needy part and the rager part of me, there is no substitute acceptable for the desired other. The dynamic of this wounded place does not accept "reasonable facsimiles". Nothing "reasonable" about any "facsimile"! The impulse to crush the needy baby comes from the enraged part of me which does not want to accept that the loved one is not available. In the original scenario with my mother, acceptance of her limitations when I was still a child was unthinkable because I couldn't go through the pain and grief of knowing there was no hope. There was no one else to go for connection. But now as an adult who has a therapist to walk with me through these feelings I have a chance to come out the other side: bodyself, heart and soul intact. When I grieve my loss with my eyes wide open, I am able to choose someone who <u>can</u> love me.

The desperate needy part will do anything to try to keep the loved one. But when that desperate part is in control the angry part is just under the surface. When things don't go its way, the "rager" comes out, angry that the needy one has to be so careful and say or do the right things to keep the loved one around. It is a closed system and one that often gives rise to <u>obsessing</u> as a way to manage the underlying anxiety due to the unavailability of the loved one. Short term relief is likely to come from shutting down through the numbing of addictions or disengaging through distractions. The alternative discussed here is doing deep work on the original wounding to support the underlying feelings by going through the emotional recovery cycle and returning to a calm heart center which leads to an increased capacity for optimal self-soothing. Two close cousins of obsessing - worrying and over-thinking - also thwart self-soothing attempts to listen to your bodyself voice. In any case, in the absence of therapy to support the underlying feelings, grieving the loss fully and letting love in deeply is unlikely. It is a dance to the death, yet no one actually dies. And no one gets relief, no shift to Let Go . . The alternative is a "heart-work" miracle which gradually unfolded as you can read in what follows and what has already been revealed in the previous three chapters.

The Present of Presence

Apparently, I had to connect with the little girl in the snow, experience the reality of the snowflake moment with my therapist, imagine my mom coming to get me, so I could "pick her up" and take her into me where she could finally give up her anger and truly grieve and Let Go . . Without my therapist's presence and all the work I had done, I wouldn't have been <u>able</u> or even <u>wanted</u> to let go of being mad and sad that my mom never came to get me and didn't even notice I was gone. In my therapist's containing presence I could finally enjoy every moment of the snowflake – and let that become a <u>resource*</u> to shift out of the trance of the story I had been telling myself since childhood. <u>Seeing</u> the snowflake with my <u>whole</u> <u>bodyself</u>, taking in its soft brilliance, brought me into my bodyself when I was a child and for a moment I didn't need my mother to come and find me. I was already found! Now his abiding presence allowed me to live through the once foreboding feelings of being left alone and in pain in the hospital and then once again on the icy path. I was able to cry and come into my bodyself with the realization that my mom was not coming – she was not there - but I was OK, I was quite alive. In taking in the wonder of the snowflake, I could now allow myself to be bodyself alive in that moment as well as imagine that if she had come then, I would have been able to soften into her body and Let Go . . And then I received the present of softening all through as if she were actually there.

My therapist's presence was fundamental in creating the supportive energetic field to go through the experience but I was guided by what my bodyself wanted in each moment. He was very respectful of those impulses and let me take the lead in the work. I didn't do it alone, but I did do it! From my separateness I gradually came into contact with him at the pace and with the movement dictated by my bodyself. I felt great joy just sitting and looking at him, a joy that was mirrored in his eyes. This experience confirms for me what Rumi said, "Keep knocking and the joy inside will eventually open a window and look out to see who's there"**. This resonant contact with him is stored as an abiding nurturing, loving presence – a mutuality which embodies compassion and the "loving kindness" of Buddhism, which can be drawn on for the rest of my life because it has increased the <u>capacity</u> of my repository of positivity.

A snowflake moment

As I look back on this work, it seems that the "moment" of change - the fulcrum for change – occurred when I was able to look at the snowflake and take in its beauty. That moment brought me out of the hold of the trance of the story I was telling myself about the little girl who was not wanted. In that moment, I could see what was "bodyself real" and not a fantasy, that is, the snowflake, and it caught me off "guard" literally. I was no longer guarding myself by engaging the stance trance of my story. Years ago, my hypnosis teacher defined trance as when your "body is responding to an image in your mind". I had been in the grip of a trance when I was lying on the icy ground, telling myself my sad story. The thoughts that made up this story were accompanied by a muscular holding pattern – tension in my forehead, neck, chest, and stomach. But in that moment of contemplation of the snowflake, remembered from nearly 65 years before, I was released from the trance of "I am not wanted". At the same time I was released from the tensing and holding against Let Go . . in the supportive presence of my therapist wrought through years of shared tears. I was no longer angry, despairing or afraid and spontaneously imagined my mother coming

177

and my opening to her embrace and her love. It was true psychological alchemy – the "gold" that comes from years of taking the risk of facing the frightening darkness (lead) inside me and building trust in my bodyself and in another's caring for me.

In sum, the trusted presence of my therapist allowed me to be present with my experience of the snowflake and come out of the grips of the trauma trance and sense the love my mother and I actually shared. The holding pattern connected with my stance released and I came back into my bodyself. My longing to feel connected to was met by taking in my connection to my bodyself and to my therapist. Feeling so fully present I could days later have the sobering realization that my former lover was indeed not available to me, and neither panic nor despair was triggered.

"I want to be in your colors!"

A further experience of integration of my bodyself need for my mother occurred in a subsequent Master's group when I was able to let one of my "posse" see my anxious pain. I accept her embrace rather than go off by myself and cry tears tinged with the anger that no one saw my pain (a belief from my stance). I could feel very clearly the intense anxiety about being "left alone" that I had most of my life. As I shared the intensity of my feeling, I looked over at one of my dear colleagues and was caught by the compassionate look in her eyes. I was "taken" by the sight of her and without thinking, the words, "I want to be in your colors" came straight from my heart. She was wearing a light blue dress with a light apple green long-sleeved wrap – she was all pastels and softness. I said, "Yes!" when she asked if I wanted her to sit next to me. I let her hold me as she wrapped her colors around me.

The voice that had come out of me was the clear voice of a child and was the expression of a "<u>spontaneous</u> <u>gesture</u>" of the bodyself. I was so open to receiving at that moment and what I needed was so freely given. I had reached the bottom of despair but instead of contracting in pain, shame, rage or fear, I was open and asked for contact. I was no longer trapped in the stance trance of "I have to do it myself" or "I won't let you get to me" or "I can bear it!" The tone of my own voice touched even me! It was not a whine, just a simple reaching out from my heart. What a blessing to be able, finally, after all the trauma and compensating for it, to allow *her* to express *her* need and then receive the love that is there for me.

As she held me and I cried, my awareness shifted from the contraction of crying to activated breathing until my breathing deepened and slowed and I felt my toes uncurling, my legs relaxing, my arms and hands softening. As my bodyself awakened more and more, I could take in the comfort of my colleague's body. As another colleague commented, the entry point was my being fully in my "wound" in the sense of consciously surrendering to the ground of my bodyself support, which enabled me to take in her containing presence more deeply and thorough-going than I had been able to ever before.

This powerful half-hour's experience has been with me ever since. Sometimes I can call on it when I start to feel anxious or sad about having no one to come home to. As a matter of fact, a few mornings later as I began my walk on the sandy beach, I thought of my experience with my colleague and the group and said aloud, "I want to be in your colors". I began to sing this phrase, over and over, as images from that afternoon in my colleague's arms flashed before me. I felt happy and energized. I noticed that a melody just came to me; I didn't have to think about it. Another "spontaneous gesture" of sorts. Then as I got closer to the shore I suddenly saw my beloved little birds scampering along the water's edge. I delighted in their rounded shape and quick movement. Some of them crossed my path, ahead of me and then they were on both sides of me. I hoped they wouldn't be disturbed by my presence and fly away. Then I changed my tune and sang to them, "let me walk with you, little birds, walk with me". They did - a little group on each side of me, stepping so quickly but unafraid. I was totally charmed. They are my company and my delight. I zigzag across the sand as I sing, my own happiness, I bring!

"I want to be in my colors!"

To illustrate how deeply embodied an experience of contact with others can be, I relate the following incident which occurred during a subsequent walk on the beach. When I had expressed "I want to be in your colors" to the group member and took in her embrace, I surrendered to my need for another and came over to my bodyself side. A week later during another walk I found myself singing to myself "I want to be in <u>my</u> colors"! Taking in deeply from another strengthened my ability to feel my bodyself rootedness. "Softly blue and green" are my bodyself colors of opening to the need for another. Being open to wanting to be in her colors increased my capacity and desire to be in <u>my</u> colors. To fully possess my bodyself colors, I had to own my anger. <u>Denying</u> my anger about not being loved kept my <u>obsessing</u> in place and took me away from being supported by my bodyself experience. Asserting my needs and expressing my truth <u>is</u> embracing my "true" colors and maximizes the presence and support of my bodyself experience. I want to be seen in my colors for each color anchors me in my bodyself reality. How paradoxical it is that anger, often referred to as a "negative" emotion, contributes to building the capacity of the positivity repository! But I do know that the more I possess my own bodyself colors, the more I can resonate with the colors of others. As the capacity of my positivity repository increases, the more likely I am to "walk on the sunny" bodyself "side of the street!" Sensing bird song, soft lips, and musical rifts are all signs that I'm on the bodyself side of the street. These bodyself gifts sure give me a lift.

There is nothing to lose but a fantasy and every bodyself color to gain! The next chapter can take you deeper into the relational somatic therapy journey from Let's Go! constriction (the unbearable darkness of being) to the Let Go . . expansion (the bearable lightness of being). However if you are even more curious about how to make your home on the bodyself side of the street as you give up Let's Go! doing, thinking and fantasizing which hinders the Let Go . . shift, skip to Chapter 13.

12

LOST AND FOUND: MY BODYSELF VOICE

"The truth will set you free but first it will piss you off" and hurt like hell!*

Preamble and Overview of Chapter:

Hearing this quote for the first time, many years ago, I laughed but I had yet to discover how deeply true it was. Fortunately I found the courage and support from my therapist and friends to experience and work through the truth of this statement. I discovered that in order to hear *her* voice so I could become optimally self-soothing, I first needed to be heard and seen in the deep recesses of my "emotional brain" by an attuned other. This repeated experience gradually freed me to hear *her* no matter what had been triggered. Because my fear had been so great, the protection around my childhood wounds had literally "inter-feared" with my receiving *her* messages. Fear of my own anger and that of others, fear of reaching out to another and not getting the response I longed for, and finally, fear of seeing the truth of the limitations of my caretakers.

As I took in the support of attuned, loving others my bodyself presence grew and the "mute watcher", now seen and heard, no longer served a purpose. The compassionate presence of the other supported the release of the muscular contraction of my "No!" to my need for connection with my childhood caretaker as the long-suppressed words came forth. The repeated experience of expressing my fear, anger and disappointment with him while maintaining contact, freed me to fully embody my experience. We are both "important" and neither of us is diminished by my anger. In fact I discovered that such "aggressive*" energy can enrich my life by supporting the setting of boundaries and achieving goals rather than isolating or diminishing me. Now when *she* is angry I can listen to *her* and give voice to *her needs.* And in the wake of these discoveries I found the freedom of being more spontaneous and present in relationships, more self-soothing and at the same time more capable of embracing the unknown.

Finally I can say, "I know who I am" and that brings a sense of presence, energy, and well-being. I know who I am because I have taken in the repeated experience of being seen and valued no matter what I felt and how I challenged the attuned other. In fact, experiencing that my challenges to our well-established relationship were met by his steadfast presence allowed me to embody a calm heart center, which can weather all manner of interpersonal storms and self-soothe. As I remind myself that "I know who I am" and call upon other bodyself affirming experiences such as taking in another's caring presence, I reinforce the new neural pathway (discussed in the next section) of "All is Well". Each time I follow through in this way weakens the old "All is Hell" neural pathway, the aftermath of unresolved relationship issues from childhood. While the listening practices gave me bodyself presence and the "spiritual awakenings" gave me a glimpse of "grace", it was the working through of the unresolved childhood issues which freed me to live a deeply embodied <u>relational</u> life. My confidence in being able to hear *her* voice no matter <u>what</u> is happening grows every day as I choose to turn toward *her* and listen for what *she* has to tell me. I find myself acknowledging *her* and encouraging myself and together we celebrate our revitalizing connection and tuck ourselves in.

That process took years to unfold because of the intense, habitual "bodyself holding" resulting from my lifelong attempt to cope with feelings in the wake of unresolved childhood experiences. And it was worth every challenging moment of struggle, breakthrough, and heartfelt connection. If you are frustrated by your efforts to soothe yourself in a truly nurturing way, I hope you will find something that will hearten you in my story as it unfolds in the next section.

Of course the details of your story will differ from mine; nonetheless the anxiety that interferes with optimal self-soothing is likely to have common ground in unresolved trauma and inadequate caretaker nurturing or modeling. This deep-rooted anxiety can be triggered by present-day events such as a loss or threat of a loss of love, life, livelihood or feeling trapped by a work or relationship situation which gives rise to a sense of loss of control. If you have difficulty with compassion for yourself, reaching out to others, and/or with experiencing emotions which come with the aforementioned situations, you are likely to attempt to self-soothe in less than optimal ways and be challenged when listening to your bodyself voice. On the other hand, when you have enough bodyself support to feel through your emotions and come back to a calm, centered place, you will be more likely to be able to shift to the Let Go . . sense of well-being even when the triggering situation is not yet resolved. What follows is the unfolding of the work with my relational somatic therapist which in turn was supported by the listening practices.

One More Time with Feeling . . .

YES! Taking In Being Seen by the Attuned, Compassionate Other.

How the bodyself listening practices supported the building of the therapeutic bond became clear from the very beginning of our work. My deepening bodyself experience helped me contain the emotions that came up as I experienced his presence; experiencing his steadying presence helped me feel more connected to my bodyself. This seeming paradox was resolved by taking baby steps. I let in his presence for a few moments and when it was enough, I withdrew. That withdrawal was a gentle "No!" to contact as well as to going deeper into feelings. Sometimes sensing his presence brought up my fear of being seen and being disapproved of. Then I had the chance to notice that I became <u>less</u> bodyself aware as I tensed my muscles and spaced out. With time I was able to tell him of my need to withdraw when I noticed this subtle constriction in my body and breathing. I gradually experienced my own rhythm of contact and withdrawal and what support I needed to stay attuned to my needs and feelings. Because he could honor my contact/withdrawal rhythm, I could discover it for myself. How the therapist reacts to the client's need to withdraw is critical to feeling safe in the therapist's presence. And when I dared to interrupt him, he yielded to my need to speak and so my sense of self was not compromised. I could breathe and open and rest into my bodyself in his presence.

An attuned therapist's availability for contact can help you be more in touch with your bodyself experience. And, the listening practices heighten awareness of grounding through your feet and breathing to support taking in the experience of being heard. Giving up bodyself holding to receive the support of the earth (what is under you) and the air you breathe (what is around you) can help you open to sensing the resonance with another. When you sense you are heard it is important feel what that is like in your bodyself so it can be embodied. Taking in <u>support</u>, whether it is from the earth, your breath or the heart of another asks you to sense what is needed in your bodyself in order to give up the protective holding and allow a shift to Let Go . . As the muscular holding begins to give, Let's Go! anxiety may arise. When you <u>can</u> take in the support needed to feel through the anxiety and give voice to your experience, you may find your bodyself "unwinding" through stretching or yawning or making sounds. As you let in the presence of another, a spontaneous gesture* toward the other may appear. For, *she* revels in the Let Go . . freedom of expression!

The attitude of listening and being listened to are emotionally-containing experiences. The other's witnessing helps me accept and integrate what is real for me at the moment. Being listened to with a non-judgmental attitude allows a connection to be felt between the listener and the person who is heard. "Resonance" may be a more appropriate word than "connection" because it implies that the two resonant participants are attuned and separate rather than "attached". "Resonance" connotes what can be experienced in the moment when two embodied beings embrace the bodyself experience of being in each other's presence. This mutual resonance, sometimes called "mutuality"** can exist as long as clear boundaries are maintained, tested and reaffirmed. As we share our momentary experience, I sense I am heard and accepted whether the other agrees with me or not. No shame, no blame, just witnessing with heart. Listening to the bodyself voice is greatly facilitated by embodying the experience of being heard.

"The wound is where the light enters"***

My heart had been tragically closed to my mother due to an unintentional abandonment trauma since I was about two and a half so I could not rest into my mother's heart. My father wanted my heart for his own. His heart was not only broken but also twisted. Because they had their own unhealed wounds to protect they had no clue about what I needed from them to free my heart from its pain of closure. A closed heart is an aching, shrinking heart that seeks the familiar and the safe. The opening heart is the risk-taking, expanding heart. That heart draws its breath from deep inside.

Imagining my death had been my comfort, being alive without connection was my fear. Then during one therapy session, mid-way through the course of therapy, the "I don't care if I die" protection around my heart was painlessly pierced by resonance with his heartfelt presence like a splinter of <u>light</u>. It was as if a light beam opened a channel to my heart. This very narrow channel was palpable, and seemingly visible. This starling perception felt "real". The tears and years of work in therapy had softened my hardened chest. Resting into this living connection allowed me to feel more deeply into myself. Being touched by another's presence had never been felt so piercingly keen. Until now, I had not experienced someone so steady, so trustworthy, so alive, so present, so open and wholehearted all at the same time.

Through this heartfelt contact with my therapist, I felt an inkling of something worth living for. All at once it seemed my life course was changing. So, this is the "path of the heart" – finding heart and taking heart - the courage to live fully! Entering the pain with a shared heart becomes the path to salve the wound and to live. Crying the tears along the way allows me to open again and again. My feet find the ground as my tears fall. Coming home. Home coming*. Finding a home in my heart through the experience of another's heart opening to me. Once opened, I could more easily find my heart again and rest into it. Just as the child discovers its bodyself through its caretaker's attuned presence, I felt my bodyself more solidly through my therapist's steady presence. Just as the child's heart grows in its capacity for connection as it experiences resonance with an attuned caretaker, I too open to my need to connect deeply with another.

NO! The Self-affirming "No!" of Differentiation is Respected and Embodied

At first, experiencing this resonant connection made me happy. On the heels of this happiness came a variety of other, less welcome, emotions. The pleasure of being met and seen was sometimes immediately followed by sadness, fear, mistrust and even anger or shame. Experiencing heartfelt contact even for a moment can bring up feelings about what has been missing perhaps since childhood. Feelings of sadness, shame or fear connected to childhood loss can quickly truncate the excitement of contact. Perhaps I'll lose what I have now if I'm seen as needy or weak. Or maybe I'll be rejected or my empathy will be used against me as it was in childhood. Sometimes anger arises – anger at myself for letting myself be seen in my need or for allowing the pleasure of contact to be felt. Letting down my guard and becoming soft opens me to the possibility of being humiliated once again. The presence of these seemingly paradoxical needs and feelings gives me a sense of the contracted "No!" that I have carried unawares, in my bodyself for a very long time. This "No!" is not the organismic "No!" of the contact-withdrawal bodyself cycle but the contracted (or constricted) "No!" of the stance.

For instance, during one session, just a few moments after I allowed myself to feel the warmth of connection with my therapist, I found myself saying, "Don't leave me!" And with those words, I had left him. He was still there and available for contact. I had withdrawn out of fear of losing him. The pleasure of the connection led to the fear of losing it, followed by longing and then the fear of being used. My reactions were vestiges of abandonment and intrusion trauma in childhood. After fear, submerged anger might come with the unvoiced warning, "Don't use me!" and with that the challenge of exposing my deepest fears to this person who was so important to me. But over time, I was able to embrace both my "No!" and my "Yes!" rendering me more available for contact whenever I chose rather than suddenly cutting off.

My therapist's availability to his own feelings helped me experience the depth of mine. I discovered at the bottom of my grief was my breath and with that breath, life. As my breath spontaneously grasped at life, my eyes met his. There is life after death, the death grip of holding on, in and out, that is! Gradually it became easier to "die into the moment" of feeling and I welcomed it. As my capacity to contain my bodyself experience grew, I discovered that these feelings supported my essence - they did not obscure it. These feelings were less threatening as I could sense they were an essential source of bodyself resonance with others.

A case in point occurred when I finally was able to express anger to my therapist about his leaving, once again, on vacation. I bitterly complained "I have to do it all by myself again. You said you would help me and now I have to do it myself." Finding the words that fit the anger allowed some angry sounds to come as well. I felt I had to "do it myself" my entire life because of my mother's and father's limitations. The anger I expressed at that moment was from the past, anger triggered by the sensed "betrayal" in the present. But this time the "other" hears my anger - he even invites it. He does not withdraw from my anger-tinged words; he does not retaliate, terrorize, try to silence or shame me. He hears me and my <u>experience</u> of his hearing me brings me <u>more</u> into my bodyself so that my heart can be touched. He asks, "Is this experience now in any way different from then? What do you feel in your body?" After a pause I answer, "I know you are coming back. You have come back before and when you do I feel better." Another long pause ensues. Then a spontaneous bodyself recognition comes that, even now, brings tears to my eyes, I said "I know you didn't <u>want</u> to hurt me!" My cry comes from the open heart of a child. He responds softly, "Thank you."

It is so much easier when the heart of the other can be trusted. What I needed as a child was so simple, yet so unavailable. My paternal caretaker could not give what he had not received as a child. So much could have been forgiven if only he could have opened his heart to me. How long the path has been to trust again! Nonetheless, the eventual feelings of grief and connection are welcome! It is different now. I am different now. I can feel these feelings all the way through and not get lost or stuck along the way. The anger that seemed to be my enemy and sure to get me rejected, hurt or abandoned now can be a doorway to my heart and contact with another. And if <u>you</u> can imagine that, you are on your way to transforming the way you live your emotional life.

To say my self-affirming "No!" and have it respected helped me own my anger connected to my need to be seen and cared about. Both saying "No!" and expressing anger means I am differentiating from the other and declaring my separateness which as a child was likely to mean being cut-off from the other. I was likely to withdraw from contact rather than to express my anger or my difference. As a result I would feel anxious having suppressed my bodyself need for contact. Anger threatened loss of important relationships. The experience of telling my therapist that I needed him to be quiet so I could sense what I was feeling and taking in how he responded to my need laid the groundwork for the next phase as well as for coming out of my contracted "No!"

YES! Sensing the Need for the Other and the Attendant Emotions.

Having been able to <u>feel</u> <u>through</u> my disappointment, fear, hurt and anger had allowed me to come back to my heart for my therapist. What I felt then was that I would miss him when he was on vacation and that I would be all right. I was glad I could feel my connection with him and my bodyself rather than distance myself because of resentment, dissociation, shame of feeling needy or denial of my needs. I felt whole again and able to reach out to this person who was so important to me. I could feel his heartfelt caring because <u>my</u> heart for him was not blocked by held-against emotions. Each feeling was felt as it came up. I allowed him to see my need for him and felt neither fearful of his response nor ashamed. I had expressed my "No!" and my "Yes!" and they were received. Having shared my fear and anger at his leaving, the felt-sense of our mutual caring returned. I felt grateful for our relationship and what it had brought me.

A new neural pathway

Several weeks later when he had returned from vacation I told him about how enthralled I had been watching a Flamenco dancer. Flamenco expresses the shifting moods of passionate aliveness – anguish and exaltation! As I spoke I felt such aliveness come into me and I sensed that he could resonate with what I was talking about. While I noticed the excited stirrings in my bodyself, I did not mention or stay with them but instead moved onto yet another story. He interrupted me and encouraged me to take my time and just feel the resonance of being together which he probably sensed I was rushing past on the way to telling him more things. As pleasurable as those feelings were, I still needed his encouragement to stay with them. Even after all these years, it was still not so easy for me to sit on the metaphorical "lap".

When I saw that my session time was running out, I began to feel anxious. I thought, "Soon I will have to leave this person whose presence mirrors my aliveness so keenly". I felt a sense of mild panic when I found myself wondering how I would manage after leaving him. That I was even having that thought scared me a little since during the several weeks he was gone, I was just fine. I almost kept that fear to myself but remembering how unsatisfying it was to leave a phone message about what I didn't say when we were together, I spoke up. Besides, it would be an even worse feeling, to not have said something when I had the chance. I hate feeling so needy. And what if he thinks I am too much? What if he feels irritated with me? How awful it feels to have limited time: it felt as if the important other was saying "No!" to my need for connection. What I finally did say was that I hoped he knew how <u>important</u> he was to me. He said he did know and that brought tears to my eyes. Thank goodness I stopped my Let's Go! talking and <u>reached</u> <u>out</u> for a connection with him with my words. Gradually I could feel my anxiety lessening. I am OK, I really am OK. I am here, supported by my bodyself.

My continued Let's Go! talking was my Let's Go! way of trying to get more of that feeling of connection but it actually prevented my bodyself from taking in feeling connected. What I wanted was right in front of me but I was not taking it in. To take it in I would have to notice that I was in Let's Go! and then slow down and feel my bodyself in order to shift to Let Go . . Several months passed before I recognized I had chosen the pleasure of being "in control" over the vulnerability of pleasurable contact. And having felt such aliveness and pleasure in his presence, I was afraid it would leave me when I left. In that moment of fear I had forgotten that my bodyself has embodied many years of contact with this person and that the aliveness I feel is mine and it comes with me when I leave him! That <u>thought</u> was the result of the <u>new</u> <u>neural</u> <u>pathway</u> that had already been created and could be traversed if I would remember to think it! As I understood all this, my anxiety slowly dissipated and I realized that what I was feeling was excitement because of the good contact we had. The prospect of taking leave and ending this pleasurable contact may have triggered the memory of previous losses and the associated feelings of fear and anger. Or perhaps the pleasure of the contact itself made me feel vulnerable. The <u>old</u> neural pathway belonging to my stance was starting to light up but as I recognized and named it, it lost its power. I identified what was happening and reminded myself that those feelings belong to the past and this person cares about me and we will see each other next week. Everything really is alright.

Once I feel pleasurable contact the dictates of the stance may start to take over and I fear losing it or myself. The activation of caffeine or chocolate makes it harder to tell whether there is actually something to be afraid of and therefore it is more difficult to soothe myself. I have to say to myself, "This feeling is just the 'drugs', you are OK. You have done this before, that is, imagined that he is upset, that he thinks you are too much, etc. Just because it is time to leave does not mean the connection with him is broken like it felt it was with your caretakers. He does realize how important he is to you and he cares about you and will not abandon you. In fact he will look for you. Come back to yourself and feel your aliveness, breathe and ground yourself, you are alive and whole." When I find my ground and talk to myself like this. I'm making use of the new pathway created by our walking together through many experiences which helped me regain my bodyself in the most harrowing of remembered situations. And as a result I am beginning to be able to actually <u>grieve</u> instead of cycle into hysteria and panic at the prospect of loss which seemed to threaten my very existence and I would be all alone to deal with it. Now I could say, "It is sad to say "Goodbye" for now but I know you know how important you are to me. If you disappear, I will be very sad but I will still have me. While I want to share my aliveness with you, I don't need you to feel alive." That is the new <u>pathway</u> all lighted up.

What a relief that was to find I could actually make a choice and "activate" the new pathway! I did not become trapped in my stance just because I was parting company with what had seemed to be the source of my pleasure. I recognize the source of my pleasure is in my bodyself, unhindered by the grips of the story I once told myself to try to avoid getting hurt in relationship and experiencing terrifying feelings of helplessness. My stance had kept me from making good choices in romantic relationships because I couldn't bear to fully embrace the truth about the availability of the other for loving, once I started to feel a bond. Freed from the stance I see that while my pleasure can be stimulated by the other it is not the possession of other. The new pathway has allowed my eyes to be open because I have experienced my therapist seeing my reality and his presence supporting me in feeling what I couldn't feel by myself without getting overwhelmed. Now I can grieve both the past and current losses and live with open eyes and an open heart, ready to share my aliveness with another. My aliveness depends on my taking good care of my bodyself, not on being connected to a particular person, just as my capacity to love depends on my taking care of my heart, not on whether someone else loves me.

I think we don't have a real choice to give up convictions like "I have to do it alone" or "I am not loveable" until we have identified and worked through those situations in our childhood that resulted in our making those declarations. Those thoughts which make up "the stance" and the attendant muscular holding patterns have been reinforced so many times by our perceived experience that the neural pathways which support those reactions and perceptions are well-worn. To form a new pathway, one which supports the capacity to love with an open heart and with open eyes, early childhood deficits and trauma need to be resolved so that grieving of what was missed or lost can truly take place. This process can be accomplished through relational somatic psychotherapy with a therapist who has done this kind of work, so s/he can be a good guide in blazing a new trail! One of the most damaging aspects of childhood trauma is that there was no one to help process what happened and to contain all the bad feelings. So the child was left to its own devices to deal with many confusing and overwhelming feelings and needs. Often the child created a story to explain what happened and to help him contain all the bad feelings. Its accuracy was less important than whether it gave the child a sense of self and control. So it seems only fitting that one way to form a new neural pathway is to go through these troubling and challenging experiences with a compassionate other who <u>can</u> hear the child's heart which in turn helps integrate feelings and develop a <u>sense</u> of <u>self</u> which is <u>not in service</u> of denying the limitations of its caretakers.

The most difficult part of reclaiming my heart for my bodyself voice has been to deal the feelings of the broken heart of childhood. On the one hand is the pleading frightened child who says, "I will do anything, just don't leave me". On the other is the angry, rageful part which is defiant and wants to take its anger out on someone or turns it in on himself. Both parts are vying for control in the terrifying emotional situation the child finds itself in. As long as your bodyself is held under the sway of your stance, you may be blinded to feeling the truth of what happened because it was just too unbearable. As your feelings are heard in an atmosphere of compassion, the sadness of it all can be felt and true grieving occurs and with that the regaining of your bodyself heart. The new neural pathway which forms allows you to take in love and have compassion for yourself. At the same time the old neural pathway and your stance weakens. Then you can begin to grieve your losses and the caretaker's limitations. You are then more likely to see the limitations of others, not take them personally and so you make better relationship choices. Living in your bodyself allows you to grieve your losses and shift to Let Go . .

You still will have to practice going down the new pathway by making a conscious choice because the other way is so habitual and is reinforced every time it is activated. But the more often you do choose new pathway, the more likely you will find yourself being able to talk encouragingly and lovingly to yourself the way I was able to the day I left my therapist's office. The more you can anticipate the pain of going down the old pathway the more likely you will be to change course. The catch is that to anticipate pain you must be able to feel it! The challenge is that that old pathway was designed to avoid pain and so while that goal is not always reached, it has a strong pull. However, the more support you have to face the pain in your life, the more likely you will be to find better, more bodyself-awareness friendly ways of dealing with painful feelings. The anecdote that follows occurred midway through therapy and illustrates the conflict between the pull of the old pathway and the bodyself desire for the outcome of the new pathway, that is, to be seen by the other as I am rather than as the image I created in response to my caretaker's limitation.

My ambivalence toward contact was seen during one session in the bodyself holding of my face while I reached only with my eyes. My forehead was pinched and furrowed. The holding back in my body was to protect me from being used or abandoned and rendered me unavailable for contact. As I got more in touch with how I was holding myself, I noticed my hands were clasped tightly together – expressing at once, the desire for contact and the refusal to reach to another. My bodyself wanted contact, my wary mind said "No, too dangerous! It's too risky to open." Ambivalence about contact creates muscular tension and thinking. This ambivalence is expressed in the musculature by simultaneous holding in the muscles needed for reaching and for pushing away. That is, the activation of the muscles that would allow me to reach out is simultaneously checked by contraction in the muscles that would counter the reaching. This self-protective, reciprocal activation consumes a lot of muscular energy and often results in tension, fatigue and pain.

As I focused on my facial expression, I recognized I wanted him (and originally my caretaker) to see how much he had scared and hurt me and how angry and sad I was. Subconsciously I had hoped that my caretaker's seeing me like this would soften his heart toward me. My hope held the constriction in place: the hope he would someday see how he made me feel and then feel so sorry. Although now he is dead, the constriction was still there, waiting to be seen, and at the same time, warding off the warmth of another. Until I could take in the experience of my pain being seen by my therapist, my bodyself could not reach out with a spontaneous gesture; I would still be attached to needing my caretaker to see how he hurt me.

It is a tenuous process. I had identified myself so long with my ability to resist - with the holding and wariness in my body. This is the way I knew how to feel safe – by keeping my longing in check, even if it meant being alone. Why take a chance and give it up only to be betrayed again? Do I have enough bodyself support to take a risk? It seems a wonder that anyone ever fully opens again. Especially considering the seemingly perverse pleasure, albeit masochistic, that is felt by withholding or not giving into the desire for another. I was taken aback to recently discover that I had taken satisfaction in being in the presence of someone important to my heart and yet had not taken in the caring I could see in the other's eyes. From the constricted "No!" place of the stance, the power of saying "No!" is more satisfying than softening and taking in the other's caring. Masochistic power had won over the power of letting in love in service of maintaining a sense of control at that moment; power was more important than actually opening to what I so deeply desired.

NO! The Commitment to the Contracted "No!" is Fully Experienced.

The contracted "No!" around which my stance ("I don't need you") was organized, kept me feeling intact but prevented me from truly connecting with another. I could not allow myself to be fully open and receptive to another because as soon as I began to take in, the pain of what had been denied me threatened. My bodyself contracted to defend against the terror of loss. To heal I had to slowly establish a connection with my therapist, first through being seen and valued and then through testing my "No!" with him. In order to venture a little further into the darkness of terror, I needed the experience of my "No!" and then my "Yes!" being received and honored. I found my way in and out, again and again, in his presence - the valuing, supportive presence that was not available enough in my childhood. Gradually a sense of the resonance with his abiding presence was embodied in me, which helped modulate the intensity of my emotions and come back to feeling bodyself centered.

What follows are two examples of ways to experience the bodyself tension maintained by the stance. "Squeezing" refers to the tightening of muscles that children learn to do when emotions threaten to overwhelm. Some traumatic memories can be worked through by expressing the associated feelings in the presence of a compassionate other while the release of other memories, especially those which have no accompanying visual image or words is facilitated by an <u>action</u>. In both of these examples I followed through on what my bodyself wanted to do which resulted in my being able to possess and then release the emotions and the bodily tension which can hold traumatic memories in place.

<u>Squeezing</u> <u>myself</u>: As I tightened every muscle in my body, I "experienced through" my inconsolable anguish, terror, anger and despair in his containing presence. I just didn't want to "be" anymore yet I was terrified of the nothingness that threatened. I would not give in to reaching or wanting anything from anybody. In that moment I defined myself totally through my resistance. In this way, for the first time, I came to <u>feel</u> this contraction around my "No!" thoroughly. As I embraced my resistance to reaching for the other, I felt as if I <u>owned</u> every contracted muscle fiber. Because of his steady attuned presence, I was able to experience my contraction fully, along with all the connected emotions. I gave sound to the holding and voice to the anguish. I saw in his eyes that he could go with me as deep as I needed to go into my suffering to release it. That was an unfamiliar but welcome and pivotal comfort. Then I rested-into his containing presence, giving up the holding as I softened and breathed through tears of release and meeting. To be even able to go through the pain of feeling not seen I first had to sense the possibility of being seen by this other. An outcome different from past outcomes had to be possible or it wouldn't be worth the effort, pain and risk. There had to be something more to come back to. To fully embrace my aliveness, I needed to embrace my pain and for that I needed the embracing, attuned and trusted presence that was needed since childhood.

Squeezing the other: Squeezing the arm of my therapist with my hand allowed my muscles to release the squeezing I had been doing to myself to prevent me from "losing my grip" on myself. Through the safety of contact with this trusted other, I could give up holding myself and the "body" memory of what I had felt many decades past. Allowing the contraction and my emotions to move through me while I maintained eye contact with him, gave me the sense that I could completely communicate to him the intensity of my experience. When I felt satisfied that he received it fully, the squeezing let up and it felt "over". That squeezed-down part of me who suffered so much was no longer an alien part and no longer hidden. I could respond to its needs for connection. Now I find myself more readily giving up the tendency to "squeeze" myself by pushing or being hard on myself, at least when I notice it.

The face of the contracted "No!"

I needed the literal face of my suffering (due to the contraction around my "No!") to be seen through the heart of the attuned other. I needed to see in his eyes he felt how deeply afraid, angry and sad I was. This is what was needed so long ago. Too often my caretakers did not know my pain but instead turned away with deaf ears, blind eyes and worse, with a numb or hardened heart. To deal with the pain of this perceived abandonment I retreated into myself – constricting my muscles and splitting-off into thought. My sense of self became identified with this holding, embodied by my stance. I was now loathe to give it up for fear I would lose myself again through betrayal – betrayal of myself for trusting again and betrayal by the other. Yet I also longed for and needed connection. So I found partners, who like me, seemed to be available but actually were too afraid to really connect deeply.

To become available for contact I needed to first feel the truth and warmth of my therapist's caring for me. Then I needed him to witness my "No!" and the pain and terror behind it. It is as if the holding in my face was saying "I'm not letting go until you see my pain!" Perhaps it wasn't too late for something different to happen - to be seen and accepted, rather than ignored or worse. Maybe then the constriction around my heart and in my face would begin to give. Maybe then I would be able to give up my holding onto myself, just a little at a time and experience the warmth of contact with another. In the gradual unfreezing of my bodyself - the loosening of the self-imposed constriction of the "No!" that had defined me for so long – I just might experience my bodyself's "spontaneous gesture" of reaching toward the other. But that gesture did not come readily for some time.

I'm "not nothing"!

In reaction to the challenging things that happened when I was a child, I had learned to constrict my bodyself awareness until I squeezed down to nearly "nothing". "Nothing" is a constricted entity which has no feelings and doesn't care about anything or anyone and just wishes to die or disappear in an attempt to avoid the pain of not being seen and feeling not wanted and being hurt. If I made myself small and hard and held my breath long enough maybe I would not feel the pain of punishment, not to mention the humiliation. If I could make myself not care that he didn't come back after the punishment to reconcile, maybe I could get rid of my need for the other. While I did give up on someone finding me, try as I might, I could not quite squeeze myself out of existence.

Of course this tactic didn't really protect me from pain, but it did keep me from being seen because I often didn't express my feelings and my need for another. Over the course of years of being seen and heard by my therapist, I could finally go to the depths of those once denied feelings and come back, and eventually, on my own. Sensing his being in the background as a supportive energetic presence allowed me to go through the emotional recovery cycle. Then one day as I was sharing with him a frustrating situation, he responded in such a way that I found myself becoming very quiet. It turned out I was on my way to becoming "nothing" when I witnessed my impulse "to hold my breath until died". I had <u>not</u> been interested in what he had to say at that moment, but I didn't tell him because I feared he'd become angry with me and then I would lose this person who was so important to me. Besides, he was just sharing what he thought I was feeling and how I might express it. Because I felt safe in his presence, I was not only able to observe my impulse but also share it with him. Speaking up was the new neural pathway in action.

In keeping with being nearly "nothing" I almost didn't tell him what I had experienced but then suddenly I realized that this was an important recognition to share. After a few minutes I whispered my truth. It was the truth of the "watcher". I was able to tell him not to tell me what to do but to let me follow my bodyself and find <u>my</u> way. Of course, he listened and backed off and gave me room to sense what my bodyself wanted and to follow through on it. What a triumph that was! So, I am "not nothing". Listen to me! I found a voice for my bodyself need at that moment instead of quietly wishing to die; in my childhood there was no other alternative in dealing with frustration when it came to relating to my caretaker. I had to give in or at least to pretend to and withhold on a deeper level; my only escape was the fantasy of dying. This was an important step: asserting my need to be guided by my bodyself wisdom and asking him to be quiet so I had a chance to listen for what needed to come next. His presence had created an energetic field for listening to my bodyself voice with the expectation of being received; now I had to find the courage to tell him to step back and be a <u>quietly</u> supportive energy field. To be recovered, my bodyself voice needed to be foreground. I wanted him to be curious with me and discover what unfolded but not tell me what to do! We are <u>both</u> important.

In an earlier previous session I had worked with asserting my needs to be loved for who I was and I found myself emphatically declaring, "I'm not nothing!" How freeing that was to state! That night I found myself saying that those words when I was alone and again felt the validation of my selfhood. Out of this good feeling, I spoke to *her* and asked *her* not to desert me and *she* answered with "I won't, don't you desert me!" and then we were connected.

To be "not nothing" frees me to be my "everything". I <u>had</u> to take the risk of asking for the space I needed to express myself and give voice to the "watcher" if need be. I had to discover whether my therapist could once again, hear my displeasure with something he did without defensiveness. He had previously positively impacted me by welcoming my anger when he failed to understand something that was really important to me. But this occasion was different: he was trying to help me understand myself and wanted to facilitate in a particular way that I had found helpful in the past. However our relationship was changing as I grew more rooted in my bodyself and more capable of feeling through my feelings on my own and soothing myself. As I possessed more of my bodyself voice, I needed him in a different way. Something similar happens as a child grows up; the love and caring is mutual and lasting but the role of the parent shifts so that the young adult is more empowered and self-reliant. I discovered that I could confront him, tell him to be quiet and "let me do it" and our connection was not compromised. In fact, I felt stronger and respected because I didn't need to "do something" to keep him interested and caring about me.

Expressing the terror of the caretaker's "No!" to the child

The contracted "No!" in defiance of the need for another was my attempt to avoid the terror of something that had already happened long ago. My terror had to be felt through with support to make it manageable and then the contracted "No!" had to be witnessed and honored, many times over. Then I could finally have deep compassion for myself. I needed the experience of not having to give myself up for the other, to make him happy or to keep him from hurting or turning away from me. To reclaim my need for nurturing and to ultimately be able to soothe myself I had to own my fear and my contracted "No!" in another's presence. After many experiences of being seen in this pain, I was able to let in the heart of another for me. For as humans, we evolved to function in connection with others. To survive, we learn from others what is allowed and what is not. Unfortunately, the lessons from my caretakers did not maximize my chances for a strong sense of self when I encountered certain challenges with those who became very important to me. While some of my attitudes and bodyself patterns helped me creatively survive my original family situation, they ultimately compromised my capacity for optimal self-soothing and intimacy as an adult.

Repressing the terror of the <u>caretaker's</u> "No!" to the child's need for nurturing contact can lead to various kinds of avoidant behavior. In my case, the hierarchy of avoidant behaviors typically went something like this: tensing, thinking, being nice, "understanding" and blaming myself, following my "rules", working hard, depriving myself and finally indulging in chocolate because I was so sick of being "good". In that moment, I just want to <u>feel</u> good, not <u>be</u> good. I don't care if I hurt myself, I just want to take what I could. I had no clue that what I would need to become optimally self-soothing was the support of an attuned other to "experience through" the terror of my caretaker's "No!" to me.

While hidden from your momentary consciousness, the repressed terror at the realization that your caretaker's heart is hardened toward you can still influence your behavior. What you fear has already happened but the terror lives on in the part of your brain that does not know time. When triggered it becomes a purgatory of never-ending terror. Being witnessed in this place <u>anchors</u> this terror in time and space so you begin to experience that it belongs to the <u>past</u>. Whether you experienced the trauma of abandonment or intrusion, you needed someone to come – someone to reach out to who would honor your reaching and give you what you needed all along – a connection. The trauma itself was bad enough, but even worse was that there was no one to help you experience it through and integrate it. So, it remained with all its intensity in your "emotional brain."

To face and feel through your terror in response to the caretaker's "No!" you are likely to need the support of another. If your therapist has had the experience of living through the terror of his own caretaker's "No!" he will be better able to support you through yours. If the therapist is fully embodied in the sense of his not shrinking from any realization or emotion then you are more likely to experience yours, all the way through. He stays connected to his bodyself as he sits with you while you experience what comes up. His eyes, heart, voice and hand are there ready to meet yours when you reach out for contact.

Where you now need to be met is likely to be where you <u>left</u> <u>off</u> in the experience of <u>your</u> bodyself when you were traumatized. When you feel seen, you are more likely to possess your bodyself and your feelings. Just as attuned contact with the caretaker helps the infant inhabit its body, you need the other's embodied presence so you can reconnect to your bodyself. Your emotional brain gets the message that "it's over" as you are repeatedly met and contained the way you needed to be so long ago. You may need to be found in order to find yourself. As he becomes a steadying embodied presence you can gradually feel all the way through your terror and come back to breathing, softening and feeling the earth under you and shift to Let Go . .

The terror of the recognition that my caretaker did not see or care about me had to be felt through. If it remained repressed I could continue to be cold to myself and to others who triggered the memory of my vulnerability. Trying to avoid my own terror, I would end up terrorizing myself through my critic and/or others with my criticism, coldness or silence. We are likely to treat ourselves and sometimes others, the way we were treated. The experience of another, metaphorically or actually holding my hand through this terror is what I needed to break this cycle of terror/denial/attack. I needed to experience the heartfelt presence of another who was not afraid to stay with me through this terror and I needed to <u>see</u> in his eyes that it would hurt him to scare me like this. Then I would know and feel deeply that I was valued – that my well-being was more important than any fleeting emotion on the part of the other. I had needed to experience that my look of terror when my childhood caretaker raged would have stopped him from hurting me and bring immediate remorse. Carrying such an image deep in my psyche, I would have been less likely to attack myself the way I felt attacked. Without such an embodied image I might get sadistic satisfaction in being hard on myself because the pain feels familiar and it relieved tension. At least, for a while. But the tension would continue in the seat of my bodyself and continually press for expression to be acknowledged. I was likely to choose people to love who triggered the pain that needed to be healed. Yet they were the least likely to be able to bridge my needs. Thus continued the frustrating cycle of trying to get my need for a romantic connection met, that is, until more experiences in therapy helped me come more fully into the heart of my bodyself. The therapeutic relationship, not the romantic one, is where these frustrated primal needs for nurturing can be best sorted out. Until I found the support to break this cycle, the repressed terror held hostage my capacity to deeply open to another, not to mention self-soothe.

Rage: the other side of terror

If dealing with terror wasn't enough, there was also rage to face along my path to becoming truly self-soothing. Rage can be seen as the other side of terror. If you, like I were terrorized by your caretaker's abandoning or intrusive behavior, you are likely to have, deep down, an enraged response. This rage results from having felt so humiliated by helplessness and vulnerability at the caretaker's hands. I resented being so fearful, watchful and compliant around others. This response can be especially acute if you perceived your caretaker as intentionally hurting or ignoring you or not being sorry for your being hurt.

If you were sadistically treated, you are likely to have a sadistic part yourself. If you were treated heartlessly, you are likely to have a heartless part. You may be terrified of and therefore judgmental of this aspect of yourself. In addition, you may be critical of your own vulnerability or harshly judge the "weakness" of the other. Another's vulnerability may become a subconscious signal to aggress against them as you were transgressed. Better to be in the position of power when vulnerability threatens. What looks like another's vulnerability is also your own reflected back to you, mirrored in your emotional brain. Sensing vulnerability, the unbearable terror threatens once again and your brain reflexively manages the impending overwhelm. You may feel contemptuous of the one who appears vulnerable. You may attack – yourself or another in a preemptive attempt to try to beat the "perpetrator" to it. Or you may feel foggy, fuzzy or distant – all possibly signs of dissociation. When your brain senses imminent threat, you are likely to do anything to lessen the tension created by the effort to hold back terror.

As you discover you can safely express this mean or raging part of you to the therapist and experience it through, you will likely come to see that it, like the internal critic or the cynic, tries to protect the terrified, vulnerable part of yourself. The raging or sadistic "monster" is the other "side" of the terrified child and often results from unresolved intrusion trauma and fuels the shadow the addiction. Finding the heart of this wrathful part will make it less likely to hurt you or others. This effort usually requires the attuned containing presence of another who has "been there, done that," so you can feel safe to explore, understand and own this aspect of yourself. For, inside this "monster" you will likely find the child's broken heart. Bottom line is that it is likely to need someone else to hear its broken heart before you can embrace it. For as Rumi* says:

> That which haunts us
> Will always find a way out.
> The wound will not heal unless given witness.
> The shadow that follows us
> Is the way in.

The wounded part needs another to listen to it just as the abandoned child or infant needs someone to respond to its needs and overwhelm. When an infant is not heard it escalates its response in rage until it finally gives up in despair, dissociation and exhaustion. In distress an infant's impulse is to cry and flail. The infant flails to survive or it fails to thrive. These responses are designed to bring the caretaker near and for contact. In neglectful or otherwise abusive households, no one comes. No one helps him connect to his body because no "body" is available. As the Mills Brothers aptly sung in their 30's hit tune: "I ain't got no body 'cause nobody cares for me." The child has more adaptation choices than the infant – he could become helpful and compliant, rebellious and aggressive or subdued and withdrawn. But in any case he may likely learn not to ask for help and feel undeserving or unworthy of nurturance and resentful. Besides, asking for help and not getting it could throw him back into intolerable despair or rage.

Rage (and then dissociation) is often triggered by feeling powerless because helplessness is so uncomfortable and even toxic to the organism. The brain fights against the perception of continued helplessness because fear is an intolerable, unlivable state in which to remain. The perception of helplessness and hopelessness is associated with a flood of distress chemicals like cortisol, some of which are associated with depression. The brain tries protects you by disengaging from this perception through dissociation, fantasy, body tension or by urging you into activity. Letting "in" the therapist's presence can put you in contact with the experience of being seen, which was lacking so long ago. The taste of what was missing is likely to invite a flood of feelings – sadness, despair, fear, shame and anger. Feeling all the way through those feelings with an attuned other may eventually allow you to experience your original longing. The attuned presence of the therapist can offer the missing link – the possibility of the connection that can help restore you to your bodyself.

For example, in my work with one trauma client we discovered how much her fear needed to be seen by me so she could feel it through and then be calmed and grounded by our connection. As she connected with me she found her ground in her bodyself. She described the process as coming down from "up there" as pointed to above her head. She had clasped her hands tightly together. I asked her if she would like to hold my hand. She readily took it but held it lightly with her cold fingers. Gradually her hands became warmer, her breathing deepened, her body tension lessened and she felt more connected to her feet and the floor. She described the process as coming down into her body and out of her head. She was already familiar with the ease and pleasurable feelings attendant on just being when she allowed the experience of the bodyself moment to fill her as she walked along the beach. These feelings too, needed to be validated for she at first feared that something bad would happen if she stayed too long in this pleasurable feeling of presence and connection with herself.

We realized that her mother was afraid of her daughter's fear and probably met her daughter's fearful demeanor with her own fear. So she learned to try to hide her fear, lest she feel even more abandoned. The combination of my not being afraid of her fear and offering the support necessary to help her find her ground led to her being able to shift from the highly aroused, tense Let's Go! state to the ease of Let Go . . functioning. Similarly she needed her anger and her need for another to be witnessed by me. She was astounded that I still "liked her" even when she expressed her anger and her need. I was pleased she still liked herself, having revealed those forbidden feelings to me.

This process is working through the trauma. The trauma was originally compounded by the absence of someone to help you integrate what happened. From our very beginning, we humans need another person to help us sense our existence and to "be" in the world. To quote the child psychiatrist, Winnicott*: "Because we are, I am." The successful unfolding of our capacity for emotional self-regulation and communication requires the attuned presence of others so we can navigate the storms of our experience. We so deeply need each other. Ironically, we sometimes resist this notion because we have been so deeply hurt by each other. The successful navigation of breaches in connection, both past and present is the work of therapy, especially when dealing with trauma.

Sensing that the one who hurt you had simultaneously hurt his own heart, could facilitate your recovery from abandonment or intrusion trauma. The caretaker's denial of misdoing or downright blame directed at the child only intensifies the confusion and difficulty of working through trauma. Defenses against feeling weak, helpless or sad for yourself such as self-destructive behavior, addictions or a tyrannical critic become more firmly entrenched, as does the sense of loss and worthlessness. What you are likely to see in the attuned other's eyes is outrage and sadness that you were hurt. But, can you take in that someone could be angry for you on your behalf? Or perhaps the attuned other's anger feels threatening, even though it is not directed at you.

You may even fear your own anger, if you were punished (hurt or abandoned) for expressing anger or if you were abused by another's rages. You may worry that you are like the caretaker when you are angry and so you try to deny your anger. As a result sensing your own anger may make you feel anxious or may worry you that others won't like you. You may repress or deny it and then act out by engaging in some addiction in an attempt to self-soothe. Then when your anger does come up, you get stuck and can't get through it. You may turn it on yourself and engage in self-criticism or obsessive thinking in an attempt to handle the increased arousal and bodily tension. When you can express your anger and be received by someone who does not shrink from your anger, you can begin to own it. You can see that the other is affected by your anger but does not reject you for it. Expressing your anger to a containing presence is likely to lead to your contacting your heart with tears of relief and a sense of deep mutual caring and gratitude. Then you no longer have to go to bed angry - you can move through it and tuck yourself in.

As your contracted "No!" is heard by another you are more likely to own your despair, anger and grief and open again to your heart and aliveness. It is essential to feel how deeply this "No!" is held in your body - in your muscles, your organs, and in the deepest recesses of your psyche. Come to recognize it in your critic, your aches and pains, your sarcasm, your coldness, your addictions, your difficulty playing or loving or experiencing pleasure without paying a price. How long are you going to make yourself pay for the "Sophie's choice" you were forced to make to save yourself so long ago? The listening heart of another could help you feel through that "No!" so you can make a different choice. Owning your "No!" can help you to breathe your "Yes!" and live once again through your open heart. Then eventually you will be more able to listen to your emotional voice and experience the sweetness that is your birthright. Only then will you be able to truly tuck yourself in.

YES! The Spontaneous Gesture of the Bodyself toward the Other is Expressed and Acknowledged.

As I embody my need for a person and my calm heart center I can finally experience feelings of loneliness, longing and even anger without becoming too anxious because I can go through the emotional recovery cycle and shift to Let Go . . I can self-soothe by crying or reaching out to another and come back to feeling content in my bodyself, having listened to my bodyself voice and taken care of *her* needs. The "last" stage of releasing the bodyself constriction of the "No!" is the emergence of the "spontaneous gesture" of reaching for another. It is freed by working through the painful feelings, muscular tension and negative beliefs that hold the "constriction of the "No!" in place. This gesture comes not from desperation but from desire that arises deep within the bodyself – it is an expression of a truly expansive "Yes!" not of an accommodating "Yes!" out of fear of losing the other. This "unfreezing" of the bodyself frees me to take in the sense of mutual resonance and reach out to another as demonstrated by my spontaneous poignant utterance, "I know you didn't want to hurt me!"

From this calm heart center I can hear my heart for myself and for others because I have deeply embodied the experience of another's heart for me. In the following example you can read about the further unfolding of my heart for myself and for my mother as I processed the fall-out from the unintentional abandonment childhood trauma detailed in the previous chapter. After much work and repeated encounters with the tenacious bodyself holding that was put in place more than three score years ago, the grip of my stance trance was finally loosed once and for all. My attempts to protect my heart from being broken again had made it difficult to reliably access my heart for myself and self-soothe. At a deep bodyself level I was committed to my stance of keeping my mother away by holding against my fear of abandonment and holding onto my anger and despair. And paradoxically that commitment kept me trapped by the threat of the terror of abandonment over and over again whether it was triggered by longing for a lost love or an imagined opportunity to be loved. Finally, one day the holding in my bodyself grew so uncomfortable and I had enough bodyself support and trust in my relationship with my therapist that I was able to consciously surrender to my need and love for my mother. I no longer <u>wanted</u> to hold out against my need for her or for another and so I was able to release the last vestiges of the constriction of the "No!" As Hafiz* aptly stated, "God met me full on the lips when I dropped the knife." Later that same day I discovered that not only had my anger disappeared but so did my childhood opting-out fantasy of dying.

In this pivotal session, my therapist was helping me get in touch with the wounded part of me that is so fearful of being rejected and tries to ward off rejection by being clever, witty or accommodating. Once my longing had triggered obsessing, it was very challenging to find neutral ground from which to be myself in relation to a man in whom I was interested. My therapist encouraged me to connect with a memory of when I was so fearful and then to take in his presence as a resonance with another human so I wouldn't feel so terrified and alone. Strangely, I found myself taking issue with him about whether or not I already had a calm heart center as a result of our previous work. It seemed he wanted me to take him in so I would feel OK. I felt a flash of shame and then anger. Thankfully when I told him that, he said he was interested in hearing about that anger. Now <u>that</u> got my attention – this person who is so important to me and with whom I am angry actually wants to hear what my anger is about! "What is the struggle that makes it difficult for you to take in my presence?" he asks. Then he continued, "What I wanted was for you to come back to being with us and feel the resonance that can give rise to the feeling of "I'm OK!"

As I write this now I realize that my anger with him was reminiscent of what I, at 2 ½ years old, likely felt with my mother when she came to pick me up at the hospital after having not seen her for an entire week while I was recuperating from life-threatening bronchitis. She wanted me to be OK but I was not nor was I ready to let her, the "abandoning caretaker", help me be OK. What I needed was for her to see how much I had suffered and to feel my pain of feeling abandoned and during that time, being badly scalded by the simmering water of an old-fashioned vaporizer. I had needed to squeeze her and say how "it hurt like this and it hurt like that" and not have her shrink from my terror and pain. I needed to tell her how terrified I had been in that strange place with no familiar faces and how angry and then how despairing I became, so much that I wanted to die to escape those overwhelming feelings. I needed her to hear my anger so I could stop holding against it and cry it out; then perhaps I could have surrendered to her embrace. I needed to express my desire for her to hold me and never let me go, not matter what. I needed to feel my body's desire to reach for her and to hold onto her tightly so I could break through the dissociation and tension which kept me prisoner in an attempt to protect me from feeling overwhelmed. Nearly sixty-five years would pass before I could do that**. In a similar way, now I needed my therapist to be with me, even though I was angry with him and I had contradicted myself. No matter what I said, I wanted to be heard and taken seriously; I felt like an impossible, demanding child. That feeling and desire was a vestige of having to deal with an impossible situation as a child.

Sobbing, I cried between breaths, "While you were explaining to me what you wanted me to do, I couldn't feel you or me anymore. I was just hearing your words. I got really scared. I had thought everything was OK but then everything I thought I had was gone." Knowingly, he tells me to stay with my breathing. As I sense my bodyself I notice that my arms and shoulders are tense and held against my sides. An image of my mother suddenly appears in my mind's eye: she looks anxious and her arms are held against her sides. As I say, "I feel like I'm my mom", I feel my own arms against my sides and sense the growing tension in my shoulders, jaw and neck. All at once I feel deep compassion for her and for me. Through my sobs I find the words, "I just want to say to her, 'I'm here, I'm here!'" I continued, "I just wanted her so much, I wanted to feel her. But I couldn't show her how much I wanted her. I kept her away." The contradiction of that predicament became frozen in my bodyself as my stance (my contracted "No!" to my need for her) for nearly the rest of my life.

In that moment I sensed the muscular holding, like armor, was keeping me from letting in the presence of my mother and my therapist. Tightening my muscles had kept my anger in check and in place as well as stifled the feeling of longing for connection – my stance trance in action. Sitting across from my therapist I experienced this tension loosening as I gave in to what my bodyself asked of me to relieve this archaic holding. I expressed every bodyself impulse - allowing movement, muscular relaxation, breathing and emotion. As I sensed my bodily tension I looked at him steadily and sensed his receptive, resonant presence, deeply knowing he would stay with me no matter what I felt because he had numerous times before. Through my tears, words gradually came as I reached toward him with my arms and hands. To both my mother and to him I said, "I don't want to lose you." "I want to stay on this side, the side of everything is alright and I want it to stay alright." He replies that he is committed to working it out with me. I sensed that all our previous work was coming to fruition in this moment and that I finally had enough bodyself support to let my stance trance dissolve without resistance, just by sensing what was needed in my bodyself and taking in his presence fully. I was consciously surrendering to my desire to feel my need for connection, both to my mother and with him. It was finally a <u>conscious</u> choice I <u>could</u> make. My attachment to the painful but protective holding of the contracted "No!" was no longer as appealing as allowing my bodyself to be present for taking in contact with another. The pull of the new neural pathway was getting stronger than the old one.

Later that day I realized that on the side of "everything is alright" is the "All is Well" of "I want to live". The "I don't want to be here" of my stance trance was what the "All is Hell" overwhelmed mind of my childhood had formulated to try to handle the despair of that early trauma. I had crossed over, once and for all. This declaration was life-affirming, not life-defying. I am not sure I can find the words to communicate how that profound shift has played out each day since that session. Since then I have been struck by how much more easy it is to come back home to my bodyself and the "All is Well" of Let Go . . even when I begin to obsess about "something is wrong" in a relationship. When I sense the beginning of the dark thoughts of "All is Hell" at the edges of my awareness I can rest into my calm heart center and from this vantage point I can consider what is going on and what might be getting triggered. After all, <u>I</u> know who I am! I know the terrain so well now that I can sort out what <u>is</u> happening from what <u>appears</u> to be going on and I can help myself to shift to Let Go . . I "right" myself in the Zen sense of right meaning whole or complete. Maybe I lie down and sense, or talk to myself or call a friend and in the end, I can tuck myself into the "All is Well" moment.

Now that my calm heart center has firmly coalesced, it is so much easier to observe the way my mind works and to come back to sensing, not so much as something I <u>should</u> do but something that makes sense to do because actually NOTHING <u>is</u> wrong. Thinking, whether obsessive or not, does not serve me at that moment but sensing brings me into the Let Go . . moment, anchored by my calm heart center. I realized as I was writing this paragraph that when I find myself preoccupied with thinking about a new man on the horizon my longing has been triggered*, I don't feel OK. The draw to keep checking my messages comes from a need for contact with another in order to feel OK because in that moment, I don't feel OK by myself. With that recognition, I checked in with my bodyself and found I felt alive and well – I am already OK, no man in sight and I am bodyself OK! While I have had many moments of feeling OK when I was alone in the past, I had not yet possessed a deeply held calm heart center; my "OK-ness" could be shattered as soon as someone who was important to me <u>seemed</u> not to care about me anymore. The operative word in the previous sentence is "seemed" for most often what I perceived in those challenging interpersonal situations was actually an interpretation of what I saw or heard and my interpretation was often distorted by the lens of my stance trance. It turned out I was usually wrong about how the person felt about me in that when I checked it out everything between us really was OK at least from the other's perspective. Then I would have to look at myself and what I may be withholding or imagining. Having embodied a calm heart center makes it much easier to press the "Pause" button and remember that <u>I</u> know who I am!

This break-through session was the culmination of my work on childhood trauma which is inseparable from the work on my relationship with my therapist, all of which was supported by the listening practices. For instance, through the work with "squeezing" mentioned earlier in this chapter, I experienced how my bodyself constricted in a protective effort to maintain my sense of self. In the above-mentioned session I was able to <u>choose</u> to release that self-squeezing and embrace my desire for connection while I <u>maintained</u> my sense of self! I had less need to self-hold against the pain and fear of past relationship trauma. I could let my bodyself release its holding in his presence because I sensed he was there with me because he wanted to be with me. I was less fearful of letting in his presence because he accepted my feelings and needs fully and didn't need me to change in order to care about me. The crucial difference between this occasion and all the prior ones over the years was that my sense of self had become more identified with <u>embracing</u> rather than <u>holding</u> <u>against</u> my need for connection.

The "Ad-Vantage" of the Calm Heart Center vs. the "Disad-Vantage" of the Stance

The biggest challenge in accessing my bodyself voice in the presence of my therapist had been the fear of giving up something vital to my sense of self when I took in his presence. In order to deeply embody the sense of connection with him that crystallized my calm heart center, I had to assert my needs, express my fear, disappointment and/or anger when he did something that I didn't like. In the last year of therapy I often felt annoyed when he theorized or interpreted, when what I needed was his silence so I could feel what was coming up in my bodyself experience and share it with him. Because of previous experience with my narcissistic caretaker, I was sometimes suspicious of my therapist's gratification when we did connect. My concern became that his wanting me to take him in was for his personal gratification rather than in service of my need to embody a calm heart center so I could become more self-soothing.

In short, was this for me or for him? Over the course of therapy I had realized that one of my caretakers had been toxically self-serving in his relationship with me even though he professed to love me. Having repeatedly asserted myself with my therapist and having the experience of not only being heard by him in a non-defensive way but also witnessing him changing his behavior so I would not feel thwarted in my effort to sense and articulate my experience, I felt a strong sense of my bodyself in his presence. He adjusted the way he responded to me because he cared about me, our relationship and my fully coming into my bodyself in the context of our relationship. I am grateful that he could hang in there with me. Gradually I found I could stand up for myself and protect myself by saying how I felt and so I no longer feared losing myself when I took in his presence. As a result I was finally able, in that pivotal session to make the <u>choice</u> of giving up the bodyself holding of my stance and experience a calm heart center. This calm heart center is mine, all mine!

Over the next few months I noticed that the fallout from the stance invoked by early trauma had dissipated: the fantasy of dying as an answer to disappointment in loving, the fear of losing another if I do something the other doesn't seem to like, the mute watcher, my judgment of another's neediness, my turning toward caffeine – were all fading. The calm heart center is the place from which I can now observe what is happening in my bodyself and in my life. Now that my calm heart center is roundly my possession, I am no longer <u>possessed</u> by my stance even though it may get triggered. I have the bodyself support to sort out what I am feeling, what it is connected to and go through the emotional recovery cycle and come back to the "All is Well" of Let Go . . Instead of being controlled by a need to avoid threatening feelings, I am led by my desire to follow *her* urging. I can ask myself the question: "How do I want to live?" and have a real choice. I can consciously <u>choose</u> to nurture myself by turning toward myself and listening to *her* or toward another for a heart connection because from my calm heart center, I no longer fear the once overwhelming feelings and can see my behavioral patterns and where they lead. I don't <u>want</u> to keep holding out, I want something <u>more</u> for myself. Before I fully embodied a calm heart center, my need to avoid threatening stance-sustaining feelings, eviscerated conscious choice.

She Who Laughs, at Last!

Toward the end of my therapy, I noticed that when I was alone, I not only laughed out loud more often but also in a new way. It resounded from a deep place in me - it felt so real and embodied. If I didn't know it was I who was laughing, I would have looked around for "the adult" in the room. It was a "mature woman's" laughter – not a giggle or a guffaw, but a laugh of deep appreciation and recognition, a "welcoming of experience" laugh, an "it's all small stuff " laugh which also acknowledged that it often doesn't feel like "small stuff". I relished the sound of it - this laughter of contentment with the fullness of the moment. It struck me that daring to express my anger with my therapist had freed me to be more spontaneous when I was alone. Ironically, when allowed easy expression, anger which is often labeled "a negative" emotion can bring greater spontaneity of being and even, joy. In retrospect, more laughter seems an obvious consequence of becoming freer, nonetheless, it was a delightful surprise. Embodied aliveness means experiencing more pleasure along with the pain and taking more risk while enjoying more confidence in being.

She Who Plays, Is Amazed!

The awareness of another gift unfolded in a session near the end of my therapy as I was taking in the experience of just being with my bodyself in the mutuality of our presence. During the session I had taken chances by saying what I needed to say to him about what I didn't like; then I experienced his response to me, all the while grounded in my bodyself awareness. After a minute or so of silently sitting and seeing each other, it seemed as if his face was momentarily obscured by an image which now defies description. What I can say is that in attempting to articulate this perception to him, I had a deep experience of feeling very playful and spontaneous and simultaneously feeling quite separate from him. And with that separateness, I was absolutely free to say or do anything that might occur to me. I had never felt so present and free in my bodyself in the presence of another - no tension, no fear, no anticipation. There were no thoughts other than those, which attempted to put my perception into words to share with him. As I looked at him I experienced shifting colors and shapes in the context of ease and shared de-light!

A few days later when I once again, tried to find words to share this experience with a dear friend, I felt it even more deeply. It was as if I were trying to describe a dream image so I could reconnect with the feelings that produced the image, which is a way to restore a bodyself connection that I have described elsewhere in this book. Although the image occurred while I was awake, the result was the same as when working with dreams. Sharing this intimate experience with my dear old friend allowed me to embody it more fully. Then I felt very sad that I had spent most of my life constrained by so much bodyself holding and fear around those who were important to me. On the other hand, I felt joyous that I had experienced those moments of being completely unguarded, not anticipating the reaction of the other nor experiencing bodyself holding. I acknowledged tearfully, that at least I have experienced the freedom of fully being who I am in the presence of another before I died. I will not die not knowing who I am. It was a "Peter Paul" moment - "indescribably delicious!" I can't wait for another bite and neither can *she!*

Everything Changed

Fear of my own anger had distanced me from my bodyself reality and distorted my perception of myself and others. In an earlier session, several months prior I had discovered that when I came out of the fog of obsessive "what-did-I-do-wrong", I felt "sane" and angry at the same time. But I had to go through the cycle of obsessive thinking and then feeling present and angry, one more time before I said something about this experience to my therapist. In a subsequent session my experience of the impact of my denial of my anger deepened as I tearfully declared with amazement and sudden clarity, "There was never anything wrong with me!" It's as if I had gone "mad" because I had not been allowed to express anger! I had learned early-on to leave out the part about expressing anger because it put me in such peril. I had no confidence that my anger would be received. If only I could have said, "I am angry with you" and then be heard and accepted, then I could have possessed my bodyself reality. Because that did not happen, I was compelled to make a gross reinterpretation of what was happening in me and around me during my childhood. In the service of self-survival that way of processing anger became habitual and operated mostly out of consciousness.

The "insanity" of obsessive thinking and distorted perception arose from having to hold back my awareness of my anger. Until that morning, I hadn't realized that fact so keenly or so thorough-goingly. Sitting with him in the energetic field we created allowed me to feel the pervasive impact of having denied an essential part of my bodyself expression. Anger <u>does</u> have meaning and ironically, it often arises when we are denied the connection we need. Based on how I was treated in childhood when I was angry, I had concluded that the anger I was feeling was the "wrong thing" so I tried to quash it. It seemed "nobody" wanted me to be angry. Suddenly, it was crystal clear how my interpretation of my experience and the subsequent suppression of my anger distorted my perception of myself and my interactions with others. I sensed the articulation of this discovery had "<u>completely</u> <u>changed</u> <u>everything</u>" (my words); it was truly a sea (see!) change.

Then my therapist commented that I was feeling self-compassion and that gave me pause. My sense was that I was feeling neutral or acceptance, not self-compassion. This neutral ground felt like the opposite of suffering, paranoia and masochistic impulses, but not like "self-compassion". To stay true to my experience, I searched for my own words and enunciated them. Then he acknowledged my need to find my own voice for my experience. I, in turn, acknowledged how his mere presence assisted in sharpening my experience as I attempted to articulate it to him. I expressed gratitude that he was still there, despite my struggle for the space to say what I needed to say so I wouldn't become imprisoned in a self-imposed, fear-based paradigm of self-blame and resentment. I said, "Even when I tell you to be quiet, I am not afraid of losing you. I know you will accept my anger so I don't have to keep it to myself and be tense and in my head. It is in the struggle with you that I define myself rather than lose myself. But first you had to become a trustworthy object so I could then struggle to individuate from you. How you have become even more trustworthy is by my testing you and discovering you are here with me because you want to be here with me. I don't have to change myself to keep you here." Now this discovery seems so fundamental: in order to completely possess my bodyself and sense what was really happening (becoming sane), I had to own my anger.

And to thoroughly own my anger I needed my therapist to stay with me and not get defensive while I expressed anger with him. It was not enough to have him witness my anger toward my caretakers. To fully embody the new neural pathway to my calm heart center, I needed the bodyself experience of his hearing my anger and my disappointment with him and his not pulling away from me. In fact he encouraged me to speak my "heart" even though it was not loving at that moment; the deep bond between us supported the risk of expressing my anger. There was nothing to lose but the strength of the old pathway of my stance served my denial of the need to be loved for who I am; and there was everything to be gained – every bodyself moment of taking in the pleasure of contact with another who truly sees and cares for me as I am. When the moment of truth comes and I have a choice to make between taking in the connection with another (and/or listening to *her*) and protecting myself by not letting the other in (and/or shutting *her* down), I now have a much better chance of choosing the new neural pathway, which leads to the embodiment of full aliveness. The valence of the pull toward self-protection through isolation, withholding feelings and needs has been weakened and my ability to be assertive and say what I need is strengthened.

With my therapist I came to experience having a real choice but with my caretakers the only choice was a Sophie's choice. To possess a real choice, it was essential to repeatedly experience how deeply committed to my "No!" I was and live through the expression of that commitment with my therapist, experiencing a different outcome than I had with my caretakers. This time I would not be left holding against my need for connection and against my anger with the other and with myself, cut off with no recourse. Expressing my anger does not result in losing him or myself. He is still there because he respects my "No!" and he wants to be with me. And, I can take in that experience because I am less afraid to feel my desire for connection. Making the choice of taking in caring and being assertive when needed, will allow me to make a better choice of whom I want to get close to. I don't expect that everyone I meet will be able to accept me as I am, but now as I do, I can see more clearly who is out there rather than blind myself to their limitations and give up a part of me up as I did have for most of my life. My calm heart center allows me to embrace what I really want and grieve what I have lost which creates openness to something new. Now my protection is my self-assertion rather than self-denial. Rather than bodyself-numbing options for self-soothing, I can choose optimal self-soothing "soul-lutions"! Because I have more Goldilocks moments in my repository of positivity, I can sit with my bodyself experience for longer periods of time in quiet and notice what comes up. In fact, sitting with my bodyself experience is becoming a comfort and you can imagine how *she* loves that!

"You Are Still Here"

In the session the following week, I find myself silently looking at my therapist for some time. I "see-feel" he is still there even though I have expressed anger/disappointment with him in past sessions. Suddenly my mind senses the shock of the breach with my caretaker and everything stops with the realization that I am cut-off from that most important person as well as my bodyself. For an instant, I sense panic and freeze, yet I am fully present to this experience. Then my attention comes back to sitting with my therapist in the alive quiet and I experience that he is still here. I finally say it, "you are still here". More quiet seeing. I continue to take in that he is still there. Even though we have had fallings-out, he is still there because he <u>wants</u> to be there. I don't have to adapt to <u>his</u> needs to keep him there or to stop any threatening feelings from coming up. I am consciously surrendering to the bodyself reality that he is still here and I am still here. As I continue to marvel and savor this reality, the pathway to my calm heart center is strengthened and I experience the "All is Well" of Let Go . .

The Precious "Soulution" of the Muzzle Puzzle: A True "Breakthrough"

Not having a sense of the larger picture makes it very challenging to solve a jigsaw puzzle. Similarly, not having a sense of the "larger picture" from a calm heart center to which I could return no matter what feeling came up, made it nearly impossible to express my anger and frustration when it seemed my therapist did not "get" me (i.e., make room for my articulating my experience). My caretakers could not stay present with me when I became frightened or angry so they could not help me feel through those feelings so I could come back to a peaceful sense of containment and contact. Instead they became angry or frightened and distanced themselves from me. The result was that I was afraid to express anger with those who truly mattered to me for fear of losing them and with that, my sense of self. I learned to muzzle my anger and along with that my assertiveness and my voice. The price I paid for this strategy was distancing from the other and/or turning the anger on myself.

While I was familiar with this dynamic in myself, it wasn't until my therapy was nearly over that I had a deep bodyself experience of it. I'm glad I didn't end therapy before this bodyself realization fully blossomed. This realization occurred when I, once again, expressed how frustrated I felt when my therapist asserted his experience of me instead of allowing me the space to discover it myself. As I began to report the bodyself experience of pressure in my chest and head, I felt as if my blood pressure was increasing. Describing these symptoms, I stated I was feeling a little nauseous. He said, "If you can, stay with that, that is the fight coming up and it is very important!" My caretaker would have never said that to me, never ever. If he sensed I was getting angry I would have been crushed on the spot. But here was a man encouraging my bodyself expression of anger and assuring me he would stay there with me, ready to receive whatever I had to say. I didn't say any more but I did take in the experience of his being there with me as I felt the bodyself tension between the impulse to express my anger/disappointment and my self-protective holding. It remains an unforgettable "somatic relational" experience because it demonstrated to me he wasn't afraid of my anger – in fact he was encouraging me to stay with it as it was coming up even before I had clearly sensed what emotion was emerging. Anger had become so treacherous to experience. This experience of acknowledging the bodyself signs of nascent anger was a true "breakthrough"!

Over the next few weeks, the gifts of his and my staying with this experience of emergent anger came to fruition. During this time he again assured me that he was there because he <u>wanted</u> to be there, not because I behaved in some particular way. It became increasingly clear that I didn't have to think about how to keep him interested and caring for me: I wouldn't lose him because he was there out of his <u>own</u> interest and caring. Because he honored the truth of my anger, it was easier for me to express it rather than turning it on myself or distancing from him. Previously I would have been likely to choke back my anger and then become anxious by filling the unknown with fears of the "previously known". As I learned to pay attention to my process, I noticed the moment of my backing down when I anticipated what I thought he wanted me to say or feel. I more clearly sensed <u>how</u> I lost track of my experience, of what I wanted to say, not to mention the impulse that had not yet clearly formed. Sometimes I told myself that what he wanted to say was more important to <u>him</u> than my expressed need to let my words come from the sensing of my bodyself. Then assuming this was true I would feel angry. At first I didn't check out any of these thoughts with him. For, I had learned the hard way that to "keep the peace" with my father, I needed to hold my "piece" (of mind)!

But now, as I expressed emotions, thoughts and even suspicions and took what felt like a supreme risk, which could have led to annihilation, the result was just the opposite. I didn't alienate the other and I gained a deeper connection to myself. I found more compassion for myself and freedom to say what I needed to say. Sometimes I still sense the old caution, but the experience of what good can come from taking the risk to share my bodyself truth is also there – a reminder that I now have nothing to lose and everything to gain. This experience is what my therapist called appreciating "the preciousness of my soul". Our relationship bore this precious fruit because we were committed to the process of sharing the bodyself moment of truth in relationship.

As I reflect on this experience, the image of the lotus flower comes to mind: its beauty and brilliance takes nourishment not only from the sun but also from its roots in the dark murky depths. Like the lotus, to unfold in the light I must stay rooted in my depths.

"Honeymoons"

I sense it is all coming together. I can sense the moment when I need time to feel what needs to come next and I ask my therapist to give me that space. I can sense and express what that shut-down feels like in me and all the feelings and thoughts that come with it: the tightness in my chest, the anger, the projection of my anger onto him, the fear he won't like me if I don't sit in rapt attention and hang on every word, the fear he won't care about me if I express an objection to what he does and hurt his feelings. He welcomes this opportunity to understand what happens in me and between us. The "honeymoon" is over and real relating is in progress. This, I am told, is the last stage of therapy!

At the same time and not coincidentally I'm sure, I am experiencing an increased capacity to self-soothe. A powerful moonlike image has emerged from the bodyself experience of sensing my depths; it embodies a sense of fullness, comfort, containment and light. Its appearance as a visual image changes with my bodyself experience, it varies in form and coloring, shape and size and even, texture. Sometimes just seeing it is containing, other times, I imagine resting into it as it forms to my body like a soft comforter, and another time, like a cloud. It becomes whatever my bodyself sense needs it to be. Sometimes, I can shift my attention to it when I find myself tempted to long for an unavailable person. This image is a more powerful source of comfort than the old fantasy which now just evokes anxiety. The comforter cradles me, the cloud carries me. Now I can truly rest into something larger than myself that seems to emanate from my bodyself. I rest into my own "lap". This possibility seems always to be there and I can test its availability in any moment. I sense <u>this</u> honeymoon will last as long as I do!

I discovered the power of this image recently when I laid my head down and rested into it one afternoon when I needed to come back to my bodyself. The original image morphed into a big pillow/comforter which cradled my whole body and allowed me to shift into Let Go . . expansive energy. For a few minutes it became my mother and I let myself cry for her comfort. I remembered lying with her in the last days of her life and listening to the words and sounds which came gurgling up from her depths. More tears came when I remembered how she looked just after she died. I felt so sorry for the worry I caused her, some of it on purpose. I know she deeply loved me, but she just couldn't protect me when I needed it so badly and other time she couldn't reach me because I had shut down. I felt my bonds of self-protectiveness soften and melt into Let Go . . giving up the Let's Go! posture of the past many weeks. I felt deeply connected to her and to my bodyself and grateful I could surrender to this moment. The compassion I feel for her and for myself is unfettered as it rises in me. Forgiveness flows for her and me. I recognize this is the ultimate gift of all the work I have done and of all the people I have loved and who love me. This image embodies compassion. This is indeed quite a honeymoon. And it doesn't have to end as long as I continue to take good care of *her.*

In the end, meeting the resistance to listening to my bodyself voice has been all about "repair of relationship": repair of my relationship with my bodyself by working through caretaker relationship issues in the context of forming and repairing the relationship with my therapist. Discovering how we as two people continually find ourselves in relationship with each other in the present is the work - and that is all and it is everything. Had my caretakers "good enough" nurturing themselves, I wouldn't have needed to do all this work and you wouldn't have had a chance to benefit from my story. This "heart-work" miracle can be available to you, if you can build the bodyself support necessary to take the risk of opening to your bodyself voice.

"Just Be with Me . . ."

Those words, "Just be with me" came quietly from such a deep and simple place. I felt as if I could have sat across from him for hours, taking in the shared wordless presence of simply being together. No fears or suspicions, images or concerns arose. I sensed, from time to time, where I was bodyself holding and allowed more ease. My forehead, between my eyes, my jaw then my neck, shoulders, back, all giving up tensing. My toes wiggled making sure they were all there. Then my feet and legs were finding where they felt more supported. All the while I took in our mutual presence as if my bodyself was creating space to take in as much as possible of this experience.

I was rediscovering the experience of letting go of the habitual constriction of the "No!" which kept love out in an attempt to keep me safe from betrayal, despair, and helplessness. This is how I kept another away from me. Not once did it occur to me to say to him, "Don't leave me!" as I had years before when I started to take in his presence and feel how important he was to me. And today I knew he would be gone for a month. I just rested into the experience of being quietly together and was glad there was plenty of time to do just that. No words were necessary and besides they would only distract. Nothing could be better than this way of connecting. This is what I need. At the same time I was deeply connected with my bodyself voice, finally. We (*she* and I) were both at home and in the presence of another who was very important to us. This was my goal for my therapy – to be able to be totally me grounded in my bodyself experience with someone who mattered so much to me and not have to give up one "nano-byte" of my presence.

In sum, the listening practices supported my efforts self-soothe by listening to my bodyself voice as long as I was not concerned about interpersonal conflict or loss. To become optimally self-soothing in the face of interpersonal conflict, I needed to experience the committed presence of an attuned other staying with me as I connected to my bodyself truth and expressed it to him. Once I was in the grips of my stance, I could not save myself. My perception of the present moment was too clouded by the trauma of the past. I needed someone to stay present with me in my struggle so I could say what I felt even though I feared it could alienate the other who was so important to me. I needed someone who had trust in the process and wouldn't get hurt and withdraw; someone who knew the truth of my heart even when I couldn't say it. I needed someone who was committed to staying with me for whatever time it would take for me to clearly sense and own the bodyself container I had built for myself to keep myself safe. This container was wrought from the ambivalent bind of my historical struggle to maintain a sense of myself in the face of my need for the one whom I couldn't trust not to use me. I needed repeated experiences to sense exactly how the container was held in place by patterns of muscle tension, thoughts, and feelings which reinforced its walls. I needed to explore every nook and cranny so I could more readily sense how it was triggered. I didn't want to be drawn back into its lonely confinement. Eventually I will be able to reliably catch the bodyself moment when I begin to retreat and instead say what I need so I can open again. I needed time to embody the experience of expressing my truth to the other and not losing him. My therapist's steadfast presence helped me differentiate the feelings resulting from past trauma from the truth of what I was experiencing with him in the present. This has been no small task. But the more I can hear *her* voice, I have choice.

Dear Reader, one way to conceptualize this process of becoming more responsive to your bodyself voice is by invoking the concept of the "the new neural pathway". Embodying the experience of a compassionate listening other can help you go through those once overwhelming feelings by creating a new neural pathway so you can listen to yourself. This neural pathway lays down the foundation for a "calm heart center" and provides an alternative to your "stance trance" when threatening feelings and needs are triggered. The new pathway, traveled again and again helps you stay with your bodyself because you have the experience of returning to a calm heart center. Using the listening practices and/ or reaching out to another can reinforce this new pathway. The old pathway of the stance was created to survive the "All is Hell" moments in childhood when you may have had no choice but to deny your most basic need to be loved for who you are. The old pathway likely limited your access to your anger, sadness or fear as a way to deal with the limitations of your caretakers as your body contracted around the "No!" you may have said to your need for your caretaker. Perhaps you learned to cope with your need for another through fantasy or denial or isolation or pessimism.

The old pathway impacts your ability to access optimal self-soothing by constricting your bodyself awareness. As a consequence you were left with trying to deal with threatening feelings by obsessive thinking, acting out, addiction, dissociation, bodily pain, depression, fatigue and anxiety. The new neural pathway to the calm heart center leads to a much different outcome in your perception of the bodyself moment and in your response to what is actually going on in the moment. You are no longer reacting out of your wound and the unrepaired relationships of the past. You are likely to have a sense you can go through any feeling that comes up because you have support in your bodyself and you can reach out for contact with another. You can be finally free to be you and live on the "bodyself side of the street". The more you practice listening to your bodyself and following through, you'll find that you have a <u>real</u> choice to consciously surrender to your bodyself needs. Instead of being stuck in your stance you can learn to dance with your bodyself and with others. And speaking of dancing, the next chapter reveals the delightful rewards of walking on the bodyself side of the street, reinforcing the new neural pathway with every step.

Checking in with Yourself:

Do you sense your need for another? How do you feel about this need? Where do you feel this need in your bodyself?

Do you recognize a "No!" to your need for another in your judgments of yourself and others, or in your pessimism or sarcasm, or in your avoidance of feelings or difficulty with compassion for yourself and others?

How do you feel about expressing your anger when it comes up?

13

LIVING ON THE BODYSELF (*HER*) SIDE OF THE STREET

"Soothed by shapes of shells and trees and the sound of leaves shaking."

What is revealed in this chapter could spark your motivation to embrace working with the unresolved issues behind your resistance to listening to your bodyself voice so you can live on the bodyself side of the street instead of remaining a mere visitor. The stable ground of the calm heart center wrought from exercising the new neural pathway eases the shift from the "roaring" of Let's Go! bodyself constriction to the "soaring" of Let Go . . bodyself expansion. Bodyself expansion creates the capacity not only for self-soothing through relaxation but also for pleasure and play, laughter and grace, and exploring unknown space. The power and utility of the interweave of the listening practices and the posse of positivity to support freeing the bodyself voice is demonstrated in the following anecdotes drawn from my work on present-day and childhood loss. These mini "process-memoirs" may inspire you to create some of your own.

Gritty roaring to sweet soaring is never boring nor leaves you snoring. Just don't treat my messages by ignoring! There's so much more for exploring, I'm imploring you to see it through, you'll be glad if you do. You don't know yet how happy you'll be, when your "heart work" sets you free!

A Wakeup Call to the Bodyself Side of the Street . . .

She is urging me to share with you a recent turning point in our relationship because *she* wants you to know what "strong medicine" was needed to wake me up to *her* call to listen to *her*! Despite all that I had learned from our experiences together, I had another challenging moment that resulted in giving in to my stance-dictated way of numbing out instead of tuning in to *her*! I share the following incident with you not to discourage, but to encourage you to keep experimenting because "waking up" is a process – it has its peaks and valleys but the low place is never as low as where you started. But when I've lost *her*, it sometimes feels that way.

Four days of no caffeine and taking good care of my bodyself had gifted me with a sense of well-being as I entered my work week once again. I had worked on my book for three days with limited success and I was trying to be gentle with myself. I had so wanted to be finished. By noon, I was starting to feel a bit "cranky" and then defiant as I detected some neck tension. Therewith, my rebellious part found justification for a macchiato: "Today is my last chance for I have to be caffeine-free for the next week to do my best work on the book!" I sensed some "I don't care" anger. So strong was the urge to not feel whatever underlay my defiant attitude, I questioned my rationale only momentarily. I didn't give myself time to listen to my feelings or for *her* protests and warnings. The caffeine was surprisingly mind-jolting and bodyself numbing – my sense of relative well-being was jarred by an "electric" charge that constricted my field of awareness. The contrast between my former sense of well-being (with only miniscule sparks of agitation) and the now pervasive jittery unpleasantness was stark.

With diminished bodyself awareness, it was difficult to rest into my calm heart center with my clients that afternoon. My focus seemed easily distracted and worse was how upset I was with myself as I drove home. How would I be able to forgive myself?

I tried saying aloud to *her*, "I'm sorry, I tried to silence what you were trying to tell me." I should have reached out to someone but it was late. How would I ever get my Let Go . . state of mind back? I even had trouble reconnecting with what I had been formulating over the weekend for my book. I felt compromised the next day during my sessions with clients. Once again I told *her* I was sorry that I had shut *her* down but experienced little relief. I needed to do more, but what? On the way home that night, as I was leaving a voice mail message for my trusted friend, I felt a strong longing for the compassion that I knew would come from my therapist if I talked to him about this. It was hard to let myself off the hook since I did the deed on purpose and with a sense of aggression. I had wanted to be "high"! I knew that meant losing *her* as well as my sense of "All is Well" but I didn't anticipate I would feel so badly once the caffeine hit. In the wake of identifying my desire to talk to him, I surprised myself and suddenly cried, "I want my mommy!" I realized then that I didn't need to talk to him; what was needed for relief was simply to deeply feel my distress and <u>voice</u> <u>aloud</u> my need for comfort with whole-hearted emotion.

This cry was more evidence that I had truly opened to my need for my mother's nurturing (for soothing as a child and now as an adult for self-soothing) having embodied the compassionate presence of my therapist during the work on the abandonment trauma. In the remainder of this chapter, you can discover how this new neural pathway was further reinforced by the listening practices and supported by reaching out to my "posse of positivity"*. Now all I needed to do was to contact and express my need and cry out. I didn't even need to talk to anyone although leaving a voice mail message to a very dear friend comes close! I felt restored to my bodyself by reaching out to my trusted friend because I can expect to be heard and was able to express my need for someone to help me make the pain of self-torture stop.

But this time that "someone" turned out to be <u>me</u> by unashamedly giving voice to *her* need. My vengeful attitude toward myself melted in my tears as I cried out for what I needed. I sensed a smidge of shame when I said I wanted to hear the compassionate voice of my therapist. I just couldn't seem to forgive myself by simply saying, "I forgive you". My plea had to come out of actually <u>feeling</u> the pain of hurting myself and seeing the image of someone who reliably has had compassion for me. I was sure that my therapist would have compassion for me even when I could not. (In fact, I think he would have compassion for me that I couldn't have compassion for myself!). Punishment in my family was not followed by compassion or repair so perhaps that is why when I do something knowingly against my vulnerable bodyself, I have trouble letting myself off the hook.

I used the memory of my therapist's having heart for me to open and feel my need for my mother's soothing. The new neural pathway had been activated. In that moment I was no longer attached to my bodyself contraction around my "No!" to my caretaker even though I did feel a flash of discomfort with the reflection, "You sound like a baby, crying for your mother!" But mostly I was just happy that I finally felt some relief. Then I felt so sorry I had been ruthless with *her* instead of patiently and compassionately listening to *her* complaints; *she* was sick of our working so hard on the book and not having connection with others, not to mention, fun! (Days later *she* complained to me that I was "too strict" and then my therapist commented with a smile that my indulgence in my caffeine caper was just being human!) I had wanted to be gentle with myself but instead I opted for the caffeine-high road instead of the time-out slow road, which would have meant lying down and listening to *her* so I could find out what we really needed. This strong medicine questioned the truth of "The best part of waking up is Folgers in my cup!" What about waking up to the bodyself moment and tucking myself into it? Perhaps I would have found out that *she* wanted to break out of our bodymindfulness fest by acknowledging that we did our best, and now it was time for some *serious* jest as I made another important discovery on my quest for thorough-going rest! *Balance is what we need if we are going to succeed in living with grace with a smile on our face, all in its rightful time and place!*

I had been "naturally high" from the expanded state which arises from the discipline of the quiet focused work of writing, napping and not "capping". Ironically, the caffeine high had brought me down! Now I see that what I needed was some fun, not an ersatz expansion experience. But there I was, back at work with clients. I had forgotten how meditation students party after a week's intensive practice. The monastic-like discipline of my writing period dictated no distractions like TV or conversations and, as such, involved a subtle deprivation even though my creativity benefited from such focus and the bodymindful way I eat and rest during this time. Lesson learned: Being mild needs balance with wild. Let it be in the mix or you'll end up in quite a fix, while *she* has fun, playing subtle tricks!

On the other hand, this experience was just what I needed to renew my commitment to *her* and to making my home on the bodyself side of the street. I do prefer the high of Let Go . . soaring to the high of Let's Go! roaring, at least most of the time. While I am not suggesting that caffeine is "bad", caffeine does tend to perpetuate the Let's Go! call to action and makes the shift to Let Go . . more challenging. Caffeine makes it harder to hear the bodyself voice and therefore, to access the larger picture that only shifting to Let Go . . can provide. That larger picture could have been more soothing than a caffeine blast if I could have gotten a Let Go . . bodyself moment's glimpse of it. But in that Let's Go! moment, a cap was the lap! Finally, like a child who comes back "home" to its mother's arms after exploring, I needed to come back to my Let Go . . home after my Let's Go! adventures and take comfort in my bodyself embrace. Thank goodness, my "mother" can hear me now and I can hear *her* hearing me, so I can tuck myself in to the bodyself moment!

Embodiment: From Bodyself Constriction to Bodyself Expansion

"Embodiment" implies "living your aliveness"* by being available to embrace your total bodyself experience, including your emotions, sensations, intuition and needs and find expression, completion and satisfaction. The movement from the bodyself contraction of Let's Go! to the bodyself expansion of Let Go . . is more possible when you have embodied a calm heart center, which allows you to feel through the bodyself constriction of the once threatening feelings and needs by completing the emotional recovery cycle. Now you can live the life of your bodyself guided by sensations, needs, emotions and impulses to movement. Loosed from the contraction of your "No!" to your need for another, your awareness can expand into your bodyself as tension, thoughts and fantasy give way to sensation, emotion and movement. The natural rhythm of bodyself contraction and expansion can restore balance to your organismic self-regulation**.

Expansion is more than the absence of contraction. Expansion is embracing your aliveness and is no small challenge, but is so worth the effort and focus. Experience bodyself truth in feeling, thinking, words and movement. Because you can depend on going through your emotional recovery cycle, you are able to listen to your emotional voice and ask for help from others when needed. You are able to connect with others and both receive and give soothing. You own your "Yes!" and your "No!" and allow others theirs. You can be continually coming out of your contracted "No!" and expanding into your bodyself. You know when to hold and when to fold and sometimes you may even need to be bold! You embrace your pleasure and your pain, your laughter and your tears. Because you have less resistance to hearing what *she* has to say to you, you can notice, focus and follow through. Therefore, you can more easily shift from the contraction of Let's Go! to the expansion of Let Go . . giving you greater access to pleasure and self-soothing.

Embodying the Excitement and Energy of Contact

Embodying your excitement requires <u>more</u> than just being released from the tension of holding back feelings and needs. In the same way you learned to experience through the emotions of anger, fear and grief, you come to experience and contain the excitement of joy, love, enthusiasm, play, pride and sex. When excitement is not supported, it can be perceived as anxiety*. Support comes from the steadying influence of your breath, the earth and embodied contact with another. Experiencing the attuned other's delight in meeting your eyes and feeling your excitement met by the excitement of the other are fundamental to embodying the pleasurable energy of contact. These containment experiences can give you the sense that you, your needs, and emotions are not too much for the other. In fact, the other really enjoys and encourages your experiencing these positive emotions. As you take in the experience of being met and contained by the attuned other, you can experience your bodyself excitement fully. Containment of the excitation of emotion and the expansion of Let Go . . are the <u>opposite</u> of the constriction of Let's Go!

The capacity for emotional containment is what allows you to experience the expansiveness of Let Go . . energy which builds your positivity repository and in turn allows for more expansive states. When I feel loving, happy, joyous, generous, creative or moved by beauty, music or tenderness, I am in a state of expansion. Expansion happens when I rest into something larger than myself – for instance, my breath, an attuned other, God or the earth. Then my awareness extends beyond myself into connection with what is around me – whether it is another, the sunset, the movement of water, the sounds of birds or a group of people. This increased awareness is grounded in my bodyself and centered in my heart and allows me to feel deeply connected to the world. This groundedness allows me to tolerate and support the excitement and pleasure of expansion and free to explore the unknown. To become thoroughly grounded, I need to give up bodyself constriction, especially the holding against threatening feelings like helplessness, for constriction is the opposite of expansion and containment. Then I have no problem with the awareness of the seeming paradoxes that continually arise in the expansive Let Go . . state such as feeling both distinct from and connected to others. Let Go . . expansion is the antidote to Let's Go! constriction.

Repeatedly taking in another's attuned heart for me allows me to embrace my feelings and sensations as they move through me like the ripples on a lake until the calm of Let Go . . returns. The embodied sense of a heart connection with another allows me to soothe myself

210

and to "soar" because I can go through my emotional recovery cycle and reach out to another when needed. Soothing and soaring result from surrendering Let's Go! constriction to Let Go . . expansion.

"Soaring" refers to the experience of expanding with various positive or "good" feelings like love, pride, well-being, joy, laughter, creative impulses, sexual excitement, delight and play. The relationship repair process frees these "good" feelings, which can be thwarted through trauma due to sexual abuse, narcissistic parenting, neglect, emotional and sexual abuse. Soaring increases my repository of positivity of Let Go . . energy which fuels my sense of well-being so I can live through my bodyself, not in spite of my bodyself. By listening and trusting my bodyself, I can get it "just right "and find my own way. Then I am better able to balance the human "doing" of Let's Go! with the human "being" of Let Go . .

If you learned early-on to diminish your excitement to adapt to your caretaker's limitations, reparative experiences with a therapist can be critical. Perhaps you experienced that expressing your needs and feelings, angered or overwhelmed your caretaker and led to abandoning or intrusive caretaker behavior. Lacking the experience of being joined in the expansion of excitement, you may now try to make yourself less than you are in order to keep the desired other from abandoning you. For instance, consider the effects of repeatedly hearing admonishments like "Wipe that smile off your face" or "You are too big for your britches!" Taking in support for your excitement from your therapist increases your capacity for creative and spontaneous expression in movement and sound, for joy, laughter, intimacy and sexuality. Such experiences increase the capacity of your positivity repository and optimize self-soothing. Some examples have already been cited and others are found near the end of this chapter.

If you experienced "preemptive caretaker energy" which overwhelmed your bodyself capacity to "take-in" and your need for withdrawal was not respected, you may have had an abusive, intrusive and/or narcissistic caretaker. You may discover you want to stay distant from the needy, vulnerable part of you because it was *she* who needed the intrusive caretaker. *Her* need for attention led to your getting hurt. *She* couldn't see that the other didn't care about *her* because that would have been intolerable. *She* wanted contact and caring and what *she* got was his overwhelming need for control. And to make matters worse you likely blamed yourself for the pain and hurt that followed. And now it is difficult to trust your urges to reach out to someone for comfort or to approach someone to whom you are attracted. Something terrible might happen. Something that seems like it could never be resolved because it <u>never has been</u>. Work on unresolved abuse trauma could help you discern that you are not "bad", but rather, the other was bad or did bad things to you. Experiencing that you are worthy of being cared for and connected to in appropriate ways can help you be able to listen to your bodyself voice and take better care of yourself. In addition, reconnecting with *her* needs will eventually help you become intimate with someone appropriate for you because you will be more likely to desire and embrace the energetic pleasure of contact.

As the presence of an attuned other facilitates your giving up the contraction around your "No!" to your caretakers, you are likely to experience a gradual "unfreezing" of your bodyself. As this self-holding loosens, you may begin to experience the ebb and flow of a subtle energy. On the one hand, this subtle Let Go . . energy may be welcome, on the other, you may feel wary. "What does this mean? What could it lead to? Is this energy somehow sexual? How good are you allowed to feel? When does this feeling become dangerous?"

Count on your critic to be at the ready to reprimand you or scare you or make you question yourself. It is only trying to save you from further harm, yet there is no longer any real danger. It doesn't understand that what you are experiencing are just "feelings." You may need to work on these issues in therapy in order to integrate past experiences and repossess your sensuality as well as your sexuality.

The challenge becomes tolerating the subtle sweet energy of longing, aliveness and connection. You feel it as you are met by the eyes of the other, you feel it in your bodyself, like a subtle tingly vibration. This energy is how the bodyself responds to mutual heartfelt resonance. Can you allow this fine feeling all through you – such a delicate feeling and perhaps so unfamiliar? It is one thing to feel this fine energy when you are alone and quite another in someone's presence. You may question, "Will this openness, this delicate edge I feel, be trampled or used by the other to make his way into me, to subdue me or to trick me or could it just be shared and enjoyed? Hopefully your therapist can help you sort this out as it can be confusing and challenging to talk about, especially if your caretaker was intrusive and/or narcissistic.

A primal example of this resonance can be had by feeling back to when you last communicated with a baby. Recall the baby's pleasurable cooing as it responds to your response to it. The attuned sounds moving back and forth like an alternating current create a delightful resonance between you. This resonance is the fulfillment of nature's design for contact between humans.* Both the baby and the caretaker make efforts toward contact. The baby cries and reaches and the caretaker keeps trying to figure out what is needed and reaches back in return. The baby senses that it matters to the caretaker through the caretaker's <u>repeated</u> <u>efforts</u>. When the caretaker gets it just right, the baby lets go of its tensing and distress and rests into the experience of being met. This calm abiding sweetness and sense that all is right with the world is the baby's neurological birthright. It is the embodiment of the Goldilocks principle of getting it "just right!" This experience lays the groundwork for the repository of positivity from which the sweet subtle energy arises and fills your being and allows your heart to be felt by others. Mutual heartfelt contact can be embodied as a sense of worthiness and well-being and be returned to, again and again, just as you return to contact with an attuned other. While meditation strengthens your core, sensing refines your sensitivity and opens you to feel the subtle energy; listening to your emotional voice allows you to live fully in relationship to yourself and another. As a result, you can embrace *her* subtle sweetness as it comes toward you.

Embodying the Need for Another

Embodying your need for another implies that you, as an adult, can identify this need as a bodyself experience. As an example of how the "felt" experience of this need can unfold, I share my experience of the "unfreezing" of my bodyself. It unfolded in the wake of finally feeling safe enough to allow my therapist to see my need for him. He asked me to let him see my bodyself need for him by allowing it to come through my eyes. Because I felt enough bodyself support in his presence, I gradually came to carry this experience of safe contact with him in my heart. "Heartened" by this experience, I could more deeply feel my need for others and more readily reach out to them. I was empowered both by my ability to say "No! and my being more able to see the other clearly for who s/he was. The experience of my heart being connected to by another heart not only allowed me to feel my need for another, but it also helped me tolerate the anxiety that accompanied becoming more aware of that need.

For as I gradually awakened out of my tightly held "calm", anxiety took me by surprise! I hardly recognized the symptoms, so unfamiliar it was. For so long I had distracted myself with thoughts or "meditated" my anxiety away. Now, if I pay close attention, I can often sense the feeling <u>beneath</u> the anxiety – be it sad, anger, fear, shame or longing. Now that I have embodied a calm heart center, I can feel it through on my own or call someone and share. At first I was not comfortable, in fact, I felt "unnerved" by sensing my need for another. I felt too vulnerable because "others" had not proven themselves to be dependable enough, at least the really important ones. And the more I clearly sensed my bodyself, the more I felt my need for another. Yet over time I became more comfortable with that need because I could better handle the feelings that arose from the desire for contact as well as the contact itself. And I became better at asking for the contact I desired, instead of withdrawing into a constricted bodyself place. Nowadays I can be both more soothed and stimulated by another's presence. At the same time I have strengthened my "positivity" resources which can dissipate anxiety when I bring myself "over to my bodyself side of the street".

Another consequence of the gradual "unfreezing" of my bodyself was the tearful but joyous announcement, "I need a person!" Because I had allowed my therapist to see my longing and did not experience being used by him, I was able to have more bodyself presence. This resonant contact with the other became a containable bodily experience and allowed me to feel more of my bodyself. However at first, with every increase in experienced closeness, came a backlash of fear and doubt that also had to be felt through and supported. Nonetheless, the more of my bodyself I felt, the more I was open to contact with others and the better able I was to contain the attendant emotions.

That a shift had occurred was evident when I left a voice mail message for my friend, at the end of which I found myself crying the words "I need a person!" What a fundamental recognition - I need a person to talk to, not just a machine. Sure I could sense or meditate or cry by myself (though that always seemed so lonely!). For so long I had denied feeling my deep need for another. My caretakers were either ineffective or invasive so it had been useless to reach out to them. My adaptation was to decide to not reach out at all. "I don't need them. I don't even need God. I can do this myself - with my rational brain, <u>I</u> can figure things out." I didn't even notice thereby I had abandoned my bodyself and compromised my ability to deeply connect with myself and others.

"I need a person!" What a revelation! Those words were said without judgment. They were precious to hear. It was *her* voice: *I need a person! I needed a person to find me. I needed a person to help me. I needed a person to tell me I was not bad.* The person I <u>had</u> needed so long ago couldn't see my need nor help me. Rather than continue to feel my helplessness I stopped feeling my longing for someone to help me. I tried to resign my bodyself to this was how it would be: Better not to feel than to long for something that is not going to happen. That way I didn't have to experience the dreaded helplessness as often. It was better to tell myself I really didn't need anyone rather than to admit how useless mom was and how harmful dad was.

"I need a person!" I could finally <u>feel</u> my bodyself need for a person and give <u>voice</u> to my longing for a person to come. And even better, by opening to that yearning, I connected more deeply to my bodyself. I could finally tolerate this desire because I had enough experience of fulfilling, connected contact with the attuned other. Even as I write this, tears come. It is *she* that cries, *"I need a person!"* And I hear *her* and feel sad and grateful all at once that *she* can speak through me so clearly and I am so happy to hear *her*. If your caretakers did not hear you, you may have concluded that your feelings and needs didn't matter, or even worse that <u>you</u> didn't matter. But *she* needs you and *she* needs you to respond to *her* needs for another. When you can hear *her*, you can truly tuck yourself in. At first, you may have difficulty giving importance to the complaints and cries coming from inside you. You will be likely to judge them. Take your time and get support - you are worth listening to. You need a person and you need your bodyself.

Working through a trauma to the point of expressing the feelings that needed to be expressed and grieving what was lost often ends with a spontaneous, organismic movement toward connection with another that arises from <u>deep</u> within the bodyself as it awakens to its desire for contact. I experienced this impulse toward expansion sometimes as a small gesture of reaching, like a finger moving or tingling feeling in my chest and arms or a glance toward the other or even a declaration of affection or need for another. It had been held in check by the contraction around the "No!" that was held in place by my stance. My words, "I need a person" were a result of having acknowledged my bodyself "Yes!" to taking in the presence of my therapist. Taking in the support of my therapist into my bodyself, allowed me to embrace the once intolerable truth that no one was there for me when I so desperately needed someone to help me contain the feelings of helplessness.

My bodyself is no longer in the grips of the "need-for-another-denying" stance so I am free to reach out and express my desire for contact. As I grieve my losses, current and past, I am less likely to contract against my need for another. I can more often recognize when I am longing for contact with another and can either connect with someone or let myself cry, rather than become anxious, obsess, use caffeine, go numb and lose my bodyself connection. I simply feel my loneliness and don't fear crying by myself because it is "too lonely" as I once felt. I can optimally self-soothe and tuck myself in!

Embodiment is Living on the "Bodyself" Side of the Street

In an attempt to deal with the anxiety of opening to my need for a person, I would sometimes think obsessively about frustrating situations with others or tune out my bodyself messages by using caffeine. With the support of my posse – my therapist, friends and colleagues - I had the repeated experience of coming through the threatening feelings to what I, at first called, the "other side". The phrase, "other side" referred to the feeling of aliveness and groundedness I experienced in my bodyself as I surrendered to the Let Go . . soothing and calm of contact. So in this initial stage of accepting my need for another, my goal was to move through troubling feelings to the "<u>other</u> side", the place where I usually was <u>not</u>.

Using the listening practices of sensing and meditating redirected the focus of my awareness away from obsessive thoughts so I could identify myself with my bodyself experience. Resting into the sensations of my bodyself and listening for the faraway sounds brought me over to what I came to call "<u>this</u> side" - the side I was now becoming identified with more and more of the time. "This side" is what the "other side" formerly referred to when I was less able to return to my bodyself experience. An even more palpable sense of "this side" occurred when my massage therapist and dear friend, "backed" me through his touch and his words. As he stood behind me and massaged my back, I felt very alive, strong and rooted in my bodyself. What had disappeared for the time being was the pull to go over to the "other side" to try to get what I longed for because it was now clearly a <u>fantasized</u> "other side". My bodyself did not live on this "other side".

As I was able to repeatedly take in the experience of my posse supporting me in my truth, I experienced "<u>my</u> side". What was once "this side" when affirmed by others became solidly identified as "my side". By backing me and witnessing my truth, they validated my experience and helped me stay on "my side". When I am on "my side" I experience my bodyself truth fully and am most open to the world around me. I know who I am. I sensed I would not lose them, even when I stayed on "my side". They saw me, did not judge me and their hearts were open to me. This awareness is a gift of my opening to my need for another and is a prerequisite for true contact with another – that is, inhabiting my bodyself and not giving myself up. When I am on my side, I sense the aliveness and the warmth of my bodyself.

When I am on my side I feel less anxiety and am less upset by interpersonal glitches such as not taking it on when my friend is grumpy. It is her issue, not mine – her limitation, not mine. I can stay with myself and not get needy or anxious and eventually she comes back to being "herself" again. After decades of friendship I am finally not taking her mood personally. I can rest into a sense of comfort that my intuition is often accurate. On the other hand, being more grounded in my bodyself, my work with clients gets better because I can allow myself to become curious with them about what their experience is, rather than my having to "know" where it is they are going or what it all means.

The more often I am on my side, my bodyself side, the more "positive signs" I see in terms of the "larger picture". The more positive signs I see the more gold for my repository which, in turn, supports my staying on my side. I can better "hold my own hand" when I am on my side and overcome frustration more quickly, not to mention, experience less frustration overall. For instance, I can wait with myself and see what unfolds when I am corresponding with a potential "Match". When I am on my side, I can remember that "love comes towards you" and that I don't have to do all the work. The limitations of the other are more readily seen so they don't make me so anxious that I start to fantasize or obsess. I don't have to make up for the limitations of the other when I can stay on my side. Moreover there is greater opportunity to enjoy life and to self-soothe when I am on my side, my bodyself side!

Coming out of the constricted "No!" and into the expansion of embodiment of my need for another gave me access to the bodyself side of the street. Here I can feel all my feelings and my need for others. When I need to withdraw from contact, I am able to, in accordance with my organismic contact/withdrawal rhythm, because I stay in contact with my bodyself. When I "relax" I am still connected to the aliveness of my bodyself rather than going numb or "flabby". I can more easily penetrate my resistance to listening to my bodyself voice and soothe myself in optimal ways. Living on the bodyself side of the street, I am in touch with the "larger picture", so I can sense "all is well" in the background, even if I am experiencing pain or problems. I know the sky is blue beyond the clouds. The sudden presence of birdsong or the moon or the smile of a stranger can bring me back to my bodyself reality. I know when to back off of Let's Go! and see what unfolds as I shift to Let Go . . *She* will help me, *she* will show me, just encourage *her*, acknowledge *her* and love *her* and rest into Let Go . .

Embodiment or living on the bodyself side of the street requires lots of practice, <u>lifelong</u> practice in fact. The contraction around the "No!" protected the vulnerable part of me with a strongly held pattern of resistance to my bodyself feelings and needs. To give it up requires my turning again and again to listening to my bodyself voice and increasing my repository of positivity. No self-respecting monk would say s/he doesn't need to meditate any more because s/

he has finally arrived and practice made her/him perfect! That is why "practice" is another word for meditation. But not to worry, to paraphrase Suzuki Roshi*: "Progress in meditation is like getting wet in a fog – it takes a long time to get wet and you never dry out!" So too as you continue to invest in your listening practices you are likely to find yourself opening to your bodyself voice as well as responding to the other with compassion. Your bodyself presence allows you to be more receptive to the love of others as well as to experience your love for others and yourself.

The bodyself side of the street is paved with Goldilocks moments which are likely to occur when I get it "just right" in the five "e" activities of eating, exercising, engaging with others, emotional regulation, eyes resting. Engaging the listening practices in each of these activities is KEY to the ease experienced as I move away from Let's Go! constriction to Let Go . . expansion. It's my choice. Just how good can I allow myself to feel; how many moments can I enjoy. *Five "e's – e" street leads the way to the bodyself side of the street!* Gradually I find my way from the Let's Go! stressing of constriction to the Let Go . . ease of expansion.

Tucking myself in that first evening and discovering *her* was my first step toward living on the bodyself side of the street. That first step I took on my own but as I opened more I discovered how to walk with others on the bodyself side of the street. In fact I enlisted a whole "posse" - that story is fleshed out in the next section.

Practicing the New "Pathway" with Open Eyes and an Open Heart

An unanticipated opportunity to practice the new pathway arose a few years ago when I ended an important romantic relationship. Experiencing the loss of love is one of the greatest challenges that humans have and we all have occasion to grieve losses at various points in our lives. My struggle with accepting that it was over led to the deepest and most challenging work in therapy I had ever done. In order to grieve the loss of that relationship I had to revisit and integrate feelings connected to my compromised relationships with both of my childhood caretakers. The good news is that this painful loss led to my making significant discoveries about reclaiming my bodyself voice. If we don't find ways to integrate deep loss, we can pay the price in anxiety, depression and addiction. How well we are able to grieve mirrors how well we are able to embrace each of our feelings and self-soothe, which in turn ultimately enables us to live in concert with our bodyself and each other. In short, how fully we grieve mirrors how fully we can then embrace our humanness and aliveness. And in the process, you may discover how to mine the "gold" of previous losses to become more self-soothing.

My Posse of Positivity at My Bodyself Side

It takes a "posse" to heal a wounded heart, at least in my case. My posse of positivity is made up of my dear friends and family members whose response to my sadness, confusion and distress was so heartfelt that I could feel connected to, take that in and be soothed. While the resonant connection with my therapist had laid the groundwork for taking in on a deep level, I only had access to him once a week. The contact that sustained me on a day-to-day basis was the heartfelt connection I experienced with my posse, one person at a time. This contact helped me come over to my bodyself side of the street when the listening practices were not enough.

As I opened to the love of others, I could reach out to them with less fear of whether I would be met or used/abandoned. Taking in the compassionate look or the loving tonal inflection of my friend's voice, I could feel what my bodyself organismically wanted rather than turn away. When I got "stuck" in my old pattern of bodyself contraction (my stance), I could allow myself to reach out and be touched by another's heart for me and then open to expressing the pain that had become trapped inside me. When I shared my agonizing doubts about whether or not I had made a mistake by breaking up, I took notice of what was really helpful about how my friends responded. When they expressed their sadness that I was being hard on myself by blaming myself for his not loving me, I saw in their faces that they deeply cared about me. Taking in this connection with them eased my bodyself holding around the painful truth that he was not able to love me.

Once reconnected with my bodyself I could feel my sadness and begin to grieve, no longer clinging to the double-edged comfort of the fantasy. As long as I clung to the fantasy wrought from the contracted No! that there was something I could have done or still do to make him love me (which implied he wasn't limited, just unconvinced!), I could avoid feeling completely powerless in my quest to be loved. With the support of my posse and my bodyself, I could embrace both sides of the truth of our relationship: we had a good time together but we were not on the same page with what we ultimately wanted. I made a conscious effort to "store" the empathetic facial expressions and the sounds of my friend's voices in my repository of positivity. Later I could call on those feeling images in order to sense my truth when the pull of the fiction I had created to avoid the pain of my truth had become particularly compelling.

Punishing myself for doing something right for myself

For example, a memorable assessment by an articulate and astute old friend and colleague admonished, "You are punishing yourself for doing something right for yourself!" She meant I was doing the right thing for myself by breaking up with him and she didn't want me to punish myself for it by thinking it was a mistake. How could I ever forget that statement! Each time a friend or colleague would validate my perception of what was missing in that relationship as well as how that made me feel, I felt deeply touched and cried, "I so want that to be true". "I so value your perception, you know me and love me, I hope you are right." I needed so much help and support in holding my truth in my consciousness. As I was going off to sleep I would consciously recall the concerned and compassionate visages of my friends and feel encompassed by the feeling of their love for me.

Over many months' time I took in this "posse of support" which helped embrace the truth. This witnessing of my truth was what was needed but was missing during critical childhood events which therefore became traumatic. Only the silent "watcher" had been privy to how my bodyself responded to those painful, alienating events. Because I was able to share the watcher's truth with my therapist, I began to integrate its perceptions into my bodyself experience, rather than deny its reality through dissociation or fantasy. Because I can listen to and acknowledge its perceptions, it doesn't need to make me hold my breath and wish to die. I more often notice that I could be reading into the reactions of those who are important to me and I share my perception with them. I ask questions rather than assume I know what was meant, especially when I catch myself thinking something negative. Most of the time, I find I am wrong and that I have been reading some kind of "indictment" of myself into the other's gesture or words – a vestige of childhood trauma and lack of relational repair.

Emboldened by the love and support of my posse and the discovery that I am often wrong about what I fear the other is thinking about me, I have greater access to my bodyself experience and can embrace my bodyself truth. During one process group I had the experience

217

of my posse witnessing my truth, seeing "through my eyes", and literally backing me up by standing behind me in a contactful way. This was taken in somatically as though my posse was literally at my side, helping me embody my truth. Then I was not overwhelmed by pain and fear so I could feel through my feelings in their loving presence as it resonated throughout my bodyself. In a very palpable way, I needed backing up and witnessing to embody my truth to resist the pull of the "other side" which I, as a traumatized child had created to survive. The "other side" in contrast to "my bodyself side" was my <u>fantasy</u> of the other's being capable of loving me and it was my fault that I wasn't loved. When I felt my need for the other, I would try harder to do just the "right" thing to get the love I wanted. In an attempt to deny my impotence and the other's limitation, I both idealized him and imagined I was powerful enough to change him – the impotence-omnipotence delusion*.

In allowing my friends to connect with me and support me in my difficult truth, I was <u>simultaneously</u> recovering from the "blindedness" that I created to survive childhood trauma and the loss of my relationship. The loving support from my friends and therapists which I took into my repository of positivity helped ground me in the deeper truth – my caretakers were catastrophically limited in being able to see the pain their actions and inaction created for me. They could not come to my rescue; they could not see or respond to my terror, shame and helplessness and soothe me. This blindedness was paradoxical in that the "watcher" saw the truth but because it was so unbearable another part of me had to deny this truth and create a fantasy. Only when I was finally free enough from bodyself constriction to feel my need for another and was able to act by reaching out, did I have the opportunity to take in what I had needed all along - a human connection for my longing, so I could be soothed and see with my own <u>open eyes</u> and <u>heart</u>. Taking in the loving support I needed to accept the reality that this man did not love me diminished my need to fantasize that there was something I could do to get his love.

When my bodyself truth was met by one of my posse, I experienced the kind of bodyself connection I needed both long ago as well as in the present moment so that I could accept what I was feeling and move through it. But coming into my bodyself through contact with another can be a double-edged sword. The pleasure of that bodyself resonance can open my longing for contact with another. Experiencing that longing can bring up the image of the last person with whom I tried to satisfy that longing. Then I am confronted with a choice: to grieve the loss of that person and come back to my bodyself or to try to avoid the pain of loss by imagining that there is still a chance with that person. The posse of positivity opened up another possibility: I did get "another chance", at least at being able to deeply self-soothe. I just had to wait nearly six decades to find a resonant embodied presence which I could take in as a body memory deep into my bodyself core. Now it is possible to tuck myself into the comfort of knowing I am "easy to love".

Using Listening Practices to Come Back to the Bodyself Side of the Street

Intoning T.S. Elliot: Nothing is Preferable to Something

For several weeks I invoked a few lines of T.S. Elliot's poem, "East Coker"** as a mantra of sorts:

"I said to my soul be still and wait without hope
For hope would be hope for the wrong thing; wait without love
For love would be love of the wrong thing: there is yet faith

But the faith and the love and the hope are all in the waiting.
Wait without thought, for you are not ready for thought:
So the darkness shall be the light, and the stillness the dancing."

Saying it as a prayer before I went to sleep at night kept my mind from reaching out away from my bodyself with thoughts of my former boyfriend. Embracing the darkness as the light while I held off the longing for lost love, brought me back to my bodyself. Intoning it out loud as I walked the beach in the morning kept me from starting the day with misguided fantasies about him. As often as I could remember to, I listened for the sounds of the birds. I discovered that as I withdrew from my thoughts and came into my experience of my bodyself, whether I was lying in bed or walking, I felt more solid, embodied, unified and alive. I was not "over-extended" into the air, into the space between "us". I was residing in my bodyself, my energy was all on "my side", inside me and not projected toward the fantasized object of my desire. This palpable bodyself experience was intriguing, startling and wonderfully gratifying. In those moments, I had no sense of loss only a sense of gaining my bodyself's presence.

On several subsequent evenings when the fierce winds came, I imagined them violently wresting away my obsessive thoughts. During these weeks I became more active in shifting focus from what I was doing or thinking at the moment to what was going on around me, especially the sounds of nature, birdsong, wind chimes, the scent of the air and the fragrance of flowers, and the sight of the moon. I practiced shifting focus from Let's Go! to Let Go . . not preferring one over the other – just taking the opportunity to shift as often as I remembered to.

I noticed I was more easily shifting my attention to the outside world and then back to my bodyself sensations while bypassing obsessive thinking. Sometimes I could wait without hope, love and thought. For moments at a time I could let "the darkness be the light and the stillness the dancing". I could be with the emptiness for a while as I lay in bed and drew my attention away from thoughts to the comfort of my bodyself sensations.

"Filling In"

Then one night I felt a sense of what I have come to call "filling in". When I withdrew my thoughts from their relentless cycling, I had a sense of filling in, of becoming more embodied – there is more of me <u>inside</u> me and less outside of me, projected into longing for him, needing a fantasy to feel filled. I was filling up with my experience of "just being". This experience is hard to describe but unmistakably palpable. I had come over to what I call my "bodyself side".

This coming into being, more in my body and less in my head arises from opening to sensations <u>in</u> my bodyself and also from opening to the sounds <u>around</u> me. I locate myself in the center of all this sensation. The sounds coming in inform me of my existence and connect me to the larger world and that is a Let Go . . experience as is the sense of "filling in" from the inside. Giving up thoughts which accompany the tension of my stance and are an attempt to deal with the fear of losing love and with the emptiness where no one is coming, brings a sense of being present in my body. I can feel how I am sitting, moving, breathing and how my stomach feels. As I lay in bed one recent morning my experience of "filling in" came from sensing bodyself constriction and following through as I allowed tiny movements in my

219

neck and toes. Lying became more satisfying and thorough-going as I made some wave-like movements in my spine and pelvis, sensing my breathing as the movement continued and enjoying the satisfaction responding to what my bodyself wanted in the moment. Another chance to dwell on the bodyself side of the street!

Amazing – The (Almost) Unbearable Lightness of Being

In the context of discussing needing to be seen for who I am, I related to my therapist a recent experience of being caught by the sight of silvery light glancing off the tips of palm tree leaves high in the afternoon's sky. I had stood there taking it in for a minute or two in amazement. I expressed to my therapist, "It is amazing!" He asked me to try on saying "I am amazing" in the Gestalt tradition of turning "it" to "I" to help own what might be disowned. I was surprised at how difficult it was for me to say, "I am amazing!" I had to cry a little before I could even begin to get the words out because my throat was so tight. Even then I couldn't even say the whole sentence without crying. It is so much easier to see someone else as amazing and so difficult to own for myself. Like the experience of letting love in brings with it the pain of having lost it, so does the experience of owning one's own light bring with it the pain of having lost it. Owning my light was amazing. We sat together for a few minutes as I took in the experience of possessing my light and of being "amazing". Then he suggested that I remember these moments and call on them when I need to remember who I am.

And several evenings later, I got my chance! While I was showering, I caught myself starting to think about the old boyfriend and then a new man I had just met instead of focusing on just being with *her* as I had promised myself I would do. I remembered the moments at the end of my last session when I focused on looking at my therapist and how I felt when I had recognized that the light I see is my own light. He reflects my light but he is not my light. He sees my light and does not try to take it away from me by acting as if it belongs to him. He also does not try to snuff out my light. Instead he rejoices in my light, and the fact that I am steadily owning my bodyself light – the light of my soul, if you will. For what I have been calling *her* might also be called "soul". I shied away from doing so because "soul" has so many cultural associations and I wanted a term which was relatively free from connotations, thus "bodyself". But long ago "psyche" meant "soul" which incorporated the body. Body and soul were once conceived of as inseparable*. While I like the term "bodyself" because it seems more palpable, when I connect with my bodyself fully I am likely to sense a "spiritual aspect". This "embodied spirituality"* readily lends itself to an experience of grace or as *she* prefers "sweet surrender".

So that night in the shower, as I called to mind the memory of my therapist "seeing" me, I had the palpable experience of suddenly coming back to my bodyself side, meaning that I felt I was looking out of my eyes rather than searching "over there" for a response, for a mirroring of my longing. Just prior to those moments when I was thinking of the two men, I had once again, been projecting that what I wanted was outside of me so I had lost my bodyself perspective. When I looked at my therapist in my mind's eye, I <u>immediately</u> shifted into my bodyself moment, grounded and centered, solid and relieved. What a profound difference: Let's Go! obsessing had shifted to Let Go . . presence and *she* and I were one and thence this poem did come:

I know my place, it's with amazing Grace!

I now know *her* name, the fit is plain
She and I are one and the same.
And if I call *her* name
She'll come back again.
Giving up Mind's Let's Go! race
I receive *her* sure embrace
As we sit face to face
Knowing my place for the first time.
It's Grace I embrace, no man can replace
The solace I feel, when I become real.

An Invitation to Grace: Consciously Surrendering to Not-knowing . . .

The challenge: I say to myself, "You have to be fully in this moment to really be fully in the next moment! You really don't know the future and something more wonderful than you can imagine right now might happen and you need to BE THERE for it. So start practicing! You have the ego conceit that you know what would have been best but really you don't know." Then I find myself wishing that I could stay with that clarity but I know that is impossible. Besides, the effort to stay with a special moment would contradict my vow to be "fully in the present moment!"

The sunset beckoned as I continued writing. *She* kept calling my attention to it. And I kept responding with an attitude that could be expressed as "Let's keep working, you have seen sunsets before. There will be another one." I wish now I had said that out loud, dear Reader. I think I would have laughed at myself as I am now doing, and then gone down to the beach to take in the colorful specter. It amazes me that even after all those glorious moments I have had following up on what *she* has pointed to, I once again, continued working instead of letting myself be taken by *her* suggestion and experience something that amazed me. In other words, had I consciously surrendered to *her* at that moment and gone down to the beach, I may have experienced the kind of "sweet" surrender that I call "Grace". Grace just happens, it involves no effort on my part. But if I consciously surrender to my bodyself messages by following through I increase the chances of a visitation from Grace.

The next morning, remembering my experience of not heeding *her* urging at the sight of the beckoning beauty of sunset hues, I decided to listen to what *she* wanted to do for exercise. The choice was either to stay at home and do step aerobics or to go for a walk on the beach and see what unfolds. I was grateful I remembered to ask *her* instead of trying to work out the relative merits of each choice in my head. I just went out and I was so glad I did. In the brightness of the morning air, I gave into singing out my lament and to voicing *her* encouragement. Before I left I meditated and then turned to Nepo's Book of Awakening for the day's reading. He had chosen the following verse from Rilke* which hit the "sweet spot" in my soul because it spoke to me about what is needed to be fully bodyself present:

I am too alone in the world
And not alone enough
To make every moment holy.

As my feet met the cool sand, I intoned "Let me be alone enough to hear *you*". I was speaking to *her* as I went. I came back to my bodyself as I asked for *her* guidance. I came back from looking "out there" for connection to just feeling where I was in the moment. I let myself cry as I addressed myself, sometimes singing the words like a three year-old when she is not aware others are listening. I once again had to let myself go into the depth of the pain of being alone in my longing for another. There seemed to be no way to avoid having to go into this pain and letting the tears come. (Even as I write this, I give into the pain as more tears well up from my depths, affirming this very truth.) I suddenly heard birdsong. It had been silent up until now. Were there no birds up until now or was I just not hearing them? Many iterations of this stanza followed, with the final one being, "Be alone enough to hear me" which I sang and chanted all the way home. That was *her* desire being expressed. It occurred to me that perhaps I could even hear *her* when I was with someone else. That means I need have only one focus to stay with and that is my bodyself experience, no matter what and that could be enough to "make every moment holy" and shift to Let Go . .

My way seems to be, at least for the time being, that to fully feel my aliveness, including my sexuality and longing, I will also have to give to the tears of not having that need met right now. Then I can be joined by my bodyself in the moment. I don't like the way the alternatives feel. That is, I don't like feeling "half alive" due to denying my need for connection and then using caffeine to make me feel livelier, albeit momentarily. And, I don't like how I feel when I am fantasizing about a past love, for "I can't get no satisfaction". When my bodyself longing evokes a fantasy and it continues unsatisfied, it feels like an obsession. Better to feel the longing and express whatever feelings come up like sadness, fear, anger or shame and then grieve and come back to bodyself solace. This is the choice of consciously surrendering to my momentary bodyself experience, going through the emotional recovery cycle and shifting to the "All is well" of Let Go . . To riff on the Paradoxical Theory of Change: "When one becomes present in one's bodyself, change can occur, for being present is itself, change."

Living through "It's Over!" by Awakening to Signs that Life Can Begin Anew . . .

I discover I am once again available to what surrounds me and lives in me. Alighting from my car that evening I see the quarter moon partly hidden by a cloudy sky and then a solitary Venus, shining brightly near the horizon. Arrested by this sight, I stood by my car and watched as the dimmed luminescence of the moon slowly gave way to a dazzling glow as the clouds moved across its body. I realized I had not let myself be caught by the night sky in a while, my spirit having been clouded by my preoccupation with the pain of not being met in my loving. I took this sudden lunar beholding as a sign of the loosening of the hold my obsessing had on my bodyself. Now my bodyself had enough spaciousness to take in what I saw. Encouraged, I climbed the stairs to my abode and settled in for the evening's preparation for a three-day writing period.

Sitting in meditation on my bed, I asked for *her* help in staying with my bodyself over the next few days and I promised to check in with *her*. Before I fell asleep under the open window, a gentle cool breeze caressed my face – another sign of the aliveness that is available to me if I allow it. (Thanks to *her*!) The next morning when I found myself starting to think about the man again and imagining what I was missing, I interrupted those thoughts and gently guided the focus of my attention to being easy and kind to myself, as if I were taking an upset child into my arms. "We don't need to go there, it does not help us. Let me be here with you." And then the thinking about him disappeared.

Minutes later as I walked toward the beach, another sign: I noticed new bird songs amongst the familiar ones. What a delightful surprise – it truly was the dawning of a new day! The coolness of the air and the turbulence of the clouds were almost eerily uncommon for July. It was as if my familiar world had rearranged itself overnight and while a bit startling, it was most welcome. The movement, heft and temperature of the air and the variance of the light evoked in me a sense of being unexpectedly in a new place and time that was somehow excitingly reminiscent of another, now unidentifiable time and place. It beckoned me to lose and find myself anew in giving to the experience of just being in it. Eagerly, I accepted the invitation.

Yet, walking on the beach I found myself thinking of him. I softly said to myself "It's over!" and waited to feel what happened inside me. Nothing happened. Again, I listened to my words, "it's over" and waited for a response in my body, perhaps a tensing or a protest. What was it that I sensed? A vague disappointment? Some slight sadness? Once again, I said it, "It's over". I expected the familiar fear, the dreaded despair and desperation to follow. It didn't come. Rather, a sobering sense of reality was in its place. I reminded myself that I lived through the reality of "No more chances!" and "It's over!" two days before with my therapist and I could live it now. In fact, it is the only place I can truly be fully alive. This is not a platitude; this is the truth of my existence in this moment.

When I called on the image of my therapist's caring visage to reorient me, I could sense that even if "It's over!" with this man, I am not "over". I can go on being alive and live in my heart because I can still feel me and can open to connecting with another. Up until now, I felt as if I would rather die than feel the pain of "There are no more chances" and "It's over!" Since I was a child, imagining dying had given me a sense of control (a sense of potency that there was something I could do so I would still matter to them) and that had seemed the only way to end this torturous pain.

I reminded myself that imagining my therapist's caring face was not for the purpose of replacing my lost love with the caring connection I experience with him. But rather, the embodied sense of connection with my therapist is like a bridge which allows me to stay in my bodyself and experience the emotional pain that I have contracted against for so long. Once experienced, with the support of the embodied image of his caring for me, the bodily holding can release and my breathing can fill the open spaces with aliveness and presence. I discover my very own breathing is my true "one more chance" as I shift to Let Go . . !

Finally it dawns on me that what is worse than not having the love of this man is holding my bodyself hostage in the attempt to get it, even if all the attempts are but fantasies of what I could have done or said. I had taken in and embodied enough support from those who do love me to accept the reality of the other's limitations, rather than blaming myself for not being loved by this one person. The pain of not accepting that reality had finally become greater than the anxious pain of holding onto my fantasy of what I could have done had I another chance. Every fantasized attempt was fueled by the emotional energy of longing, fear of "not getting", anger of entitlement and self-blame and despair of "never having" and required muscular contraction to keep those feelings from becoming overwhelming.

Habits of mind die a slow death and so once again, the thought of him pierced my consciousness as I continued along the beach. This time when I reached into my arsenal of obsession-repelling maneuvers, I grasped my favorite stanza from T.S. Eliot's poem, "East

Coker" that begins with "I said to my soul 'Be still' and wait without hope, for hope would be hope for the wrong thing . . ." and ends with "So the darkness shall be the light and the stillness, the dancing". Then I opened myself to experiencing the cool, yielding sand under my feet and with purposeful delight stepped into the moldering sand castles left by yesterday's child.

As I ran along the shore with my eyes closed, I stepped up my pace when I sensed the permeable but palpable wall of warning projected by my mind. I was determined to run through it, no matter what happened next. I knew from past experience of eyes-closed running that this wall is just my mind's begging caution and there is no real danger – it was only my bodyself's expectation of it. It was so exhilarating; I tried it again, extending my self-imposed limits! Finally accepting the limitations of the other had freed me to extend mine! Who needs "hope" when you can experience fully in the moment? Who needs hope when you can find dancing in the stillness and "de" light in the darkness? The gift of "It's over!" is the end of trauma, turbulence, torture, and waiting for repair . . .

The most challenging part for me and perhaps for you will be to gradually accept that the longed-for other can't come through for us and that our primary and most challenging work consists of gradually "letting in" the presence of another who is really there for us. As you open more in this way, you will connect more deeply with your bodyself and give up the bodily tension connected with maintaining your stance, as well as the self-blame, vigilance, and waiting for repair attitude and then surrender to the comfort of Let Go . . Then you are likely to be more able to resist the tyranny of "just one more chance" and accept the limitations of others. You will be more likely to let yourself "off the hook" and soothe yourself whether you are upset, wanting to fall asleep, stay asleep or go back to sleep.

Working through unresolved loss or trauma can help you eventually become grounded in your bodyself as well as in your relationship with your guide so you can penetrate the pain held in your body rather than just re-experience the emotional excitation of the recycled feelings connected to the trauma. In this way, a deep release of that holding occurs and frees you to be able to experience the whole range of feelings of your being, especially those carried near your heart. You can then be "awakened" or brought back to reality by the smile of a stranger, the song of a bird, the gesture of a loved one, the scent of air; the moment's pleasure becomes available to you because you are now available to it. Your bodyself is no longer in a state of heightened alert and you are less likely to fortify yourself with various addictive behaviors and substances. You can choose to live in the moment or to numb yourself with obsessive thoughts or worse. You can choose to identify with your pain in order to feel alive albeit in a constricted bodyself state or to truly live, full bore in the moment. You will be more likely to accept life as it is and deal with uncertainty, because you are less afraid of feeling out of control and helpless. You can develop a loving attitude toward yourself because of your closer connection to your bodyself; you become more tender, forgiving, encouraging and acknowledging so you can afford to experiment, be spontaneous, curious and playful. And while your childhood may not have been so "happy," you can now experience the aliveness of your bodyself with all the wisdom of your adulthood to back you up.

Going Deeper:

What is the reality that you don't want to face in a particular challenging interpersonal situation? What does it really mean if you don't have another chance? What do you have to accept about yourself or the "other" to interrupt the pain/self-blame cycle?

Here are some suggestions to consider:
As painful as it is, this cycle may have seemed preferable to the alternative – being alive without the connection that is so desired. To free yourself you may have to accept that the other is limited and can't give you what you want. Eventually when you really posses yourself, you can see who the other is, complete with limitations.

What triggers the cycle? Perhaps a longing, a disappointment, abandonment, or a loss of self that you can't bear because the feelings connected to it seem too overwhelming. Consider what past traumas, and losses from childhood or adulthood might not yet be resolved. Consider what you witnessed as a child that might have been terrifying or bewildering or worse. Consider how punishments or separations from your parents were handled. Each of those events has the potential of leaving you to your own devices (which were often woefully inadequate) to figure out how to handle the emotions connected with those situations so that you wouldn't feel repeatedly overwhelmed and helpless.

Listening for Sounds of Life Stirring

My therapist had said there would be "days like this", despite all the progress I had made. I knew I had to get myself out of this place. I tried slowing myself down when I got home and didn't ask for more work from myself. I settled into several phone conversations, taking in the loving tones I sensed in the other's voice and allowing that to nurture me. As I rested into my bed, I tried to be attentive to what made my bodyself more comfortable and ask for *her* help as I meditated before I slipped into sleep. Not happy or content, but no longer despairing. Little consolation, but consolation nonetheless. I am glad he had helped me prepare for this. Those dark thoughts and the bodyself holding that had resulted from my adaptive stance were encoded in my brain and could be triggered by disappointed longing. It was up to me to call upon my listening practices to release myself from the grip of the vortex of obsessing and get to the bodyself side of the street for soothing.

The next morning while still in bed, I see the waning moon through my window. I keep looking at it even though my Let's Go! impulse has had enough of that and tries to pull me away. A bird flies across the moon's face and then a cloud drifts by and disappears. Two more birds and in between, the quiet moon becomes more clearly spherical. It is *she* that keeps me there, *she* wants to come back and I have asked *her* to help me. Beheld by the unmindful eye, the moon appears flat rather than spherical. In the same way, life can feel "flat" – emotionally flat when I am not really present for it. Some unfamiliar birdsongs pierce the morning quiet. I miss the mockingbird's song of springtime. I am somewhat settled by all of this and sit down to meditate and listen through the open window for sounds of life stirring.

Twenty minutes later, I enliven my step aerobic work-out by choosing my new CD – the sounds of the Masanga Marimba Ensemble which I first heard in the Farmer's Market the Sunday before. Toward the end of the work-out, I found myself noticing what turned out to be the "tail-end" of the obsessing despairing thoughts as though I were looking down on them from "above". I watched those thought remnants run their course and then disintegrate – no longer part of a whole story but rather just random fragments – it's over! The whole picture had become what I was experiencing in the moment as I moved up and down on the stepper, listening to the infectious joyful sounds – "I am here" – fully present and no longer in my "head". I am still alone - nothing has changed except the inner context from which I perceive my reality. And that is everything.

When I got home that night I recapped my experiences of the day in the following way:

> Starting the day with moon sighting:
> I could not turn away,
> for something in me just wanted to stay!
> *She* wants to see the "spherical," it's like a miracle,
> when it pops out, 'tis delight without a doubt!
> Pure joy and ecstasy, no more dark fantasy.
> Loneliness all gone, joining the whole day long:
> finding opportunity to connect in reality -
> with a person here and a bird's flight there,
> a gentle stroking of *her* soft hair.
> Then I'm all here and can feel myself dear.
> It's up to me to open my eyes and see,
> what's all around and underground:
> I was lost and am finally found.
> Eating slowly, feeding becomes holy, a way to connect with
> my one and only.
> Each tender act, keeps me intact and
> in touch with loving and right on track.
> I feel the shift – it's like a soul "lift" -
> to the bodyself side, where well-being abides.

I have lived through the despair once more. And now I know there will be many more times I will have to rise to this challenge. I don't want to give you, dear Reader false hopes – that you can "cure" yourself, once and for all, of dark thoughts and despair. But you <u>can</u> give yourself more air and room to breathe as long as you have these tricks up your sleeve! It's hard work, but being no shirk, if you'll stay with it, you'll surely benefit! Benefits galore, your "*her*", you'll adore, and with time, you'll "score", soar, and more!

As I drove home that night it became clear to me that my sadness and despair had three sources and that it was important to distinguish which were operating and treat each separately to better communicate with others and to be able to soothe myself. First, there was the plain old loneliness of coming home to an empty place and wishing for a friendly face. Feeding into that sadness is the possibility that I would not find someone that would be a good mate for me and that I will spend the rest of my life without a partner. Second, my sadness could arise from the normal grieving process, having lost the presence of a man with whom I had deeply bonded and was central in my life and fantasy for several years. The third source was the sadness and despair arising from longing for someone who was not available which tapped into the pain of childhood losses. That last source of pain is the one which, in my experience can best be addressed by work with a therapist because treating it requires the presence of an attentive, attuned other who acquires a strong enough emotional valence to give the support needed to come through to the "other side" – out of the trauma vortex of obsessive thought and bodyself numbness and into bodyself aliveness – the bodyself side of the street.

In sum, living on the bodyself side of the street means that you can reliably access your bodyself messages so you can shift from Let's Go! arousal to Let Go . . calmness when needed. Anxiety, thoughts, fantasies and bodily tension which accompanied your stance yield much more readily to your efforts to invoke the listening practices and to reach out to others. So, you don't have to rely on addiction or other forms of acting out to soothe yourself. You can know your habitual bodyself holding so well that your perception of yourself and others is less likely to be distorted by those past experiences, fantasies and beliefs you created to survive those losses. You know you no longer need them because you know that what you feared had already happened. You just needed help to get through the unresolved feelings so you could be free to live in the bodyself present. When you live on the bodyself side of the street, the sensory experience of the present moment is available to you so you can embrace the larger picture and receive a taste of grace. You can drift off to sleep with a smile on your inner bodyself face. And *she* knows no one can ever take *her* place.

Checking in with Yourself:

Ask *her* what do you need from me?
For example, when I asked *her* this question *she* answered:
> *Kindness*
> *Slow down*
> *See me*
> *Be tender*
> *Leave little notes for thee.*

So after all is said, you make your bed and rest your head before you feel like lead and think you're dead. Take what you've learned and reap what you've earned and *she'll* no longer feel spurned but instead *she'll* yearn for your next embrace as you shift from your amazing race to *our* amazing grace. Spending more time on the bodyself side of the street will make it easier to decompress at the end of the day. When you can go through your own emotional recovery cycle and rest into your calm heart center you can more easily enter the deep Let Go . . of sleep. The next two chapters walk you through creating your own best decompression routine, which *she* says in no way has to be a "routine" routine, you just have to set aside the time to experiment!

PART IV

DECOMPRESSING AND AWAKENING

14

CREATING A DECOMPRESSION PERIOD

*"To say 'No!' to something is often very positive!"**

Preparation for sleeping is an excellent time to practice sensing, meditating and listening to your emotional voice. In order to decompress from the day's activities you will need to slow down and listen to what is needed in you. When you find yourself resisting slowing down, you can ask, "What is the matter?" With practice, you will feel the answer and be more able to notice, focus and follow through. In this chapter, a number of psychobiological and biochemical factors critical to slowing down will be considered, followed by suggestions for creating a decompression routine that will facilitate your shifting from Let's Go! to Let Go . .

Learning to soothe yourself involves much more than just deciding to "relax". Carrying out the decision to slow down and get in touch can be even more challenging than to diet or exercise. Slowing down allows emotions and sensations to be felt more clearly and they may make you anxious. Maybe you will feel something that you don't want to or don't know how to handle. Despite your best intentions to take care of yourself by giving yourself time to wind down at the end of the day you may find yourself turning on the TV or going online or just staying up too late. Just one more call, one more email, one more task, one more program or one more computer game! If you find yourself still pulled to work or "play" you are having trouble leaving the Let's Go! behind. But distracting yourself every night insures you will continue to do so and end up being tired the next day. By learning how to tune in to yourself you could get real relief and have more energy rather than less.

The more you take time to listen the more you will hear. You will become aware of ever more subtle messages from this non-verbal part of you - urges, inklings, images, intuitions and flashes as well as sensations and emotions. These messages are invitations to awaken to more of you. You cannot force the appearance of these communications. You can however create an atmosphere that encourages their reception. Slowing down and setting aside time to listen is absolutely necessary to become more available to hear. Dare to momentarily give up your usual mode of thinking, analyzing, planning and doing and start asking open-ended questions which can only be answered by your experience. Questions such as, "What is needed? What is it? What is the matter?" Ask the question and wait for the response.

Some sources of resistance to slowing down and listening have been discussed in previous chapters in the hopes that you will gain some insight into why it may be difficult for you to soothe yourself and what might help you do that. For example, you may not feel deserving of taking time for yourself or you may fear being overwhelmed by what you become aware of as you begin to slow down. But, the fact remains that you will need to slow down in order to successfully soothe yourself and have a really good night's sleep. Listening to yourself is the best way to find out just what you need, and to listen, you need to slow down. Shifting to Let Go . . takes time.

Why Time is Needed to Shift to Let Go . .

It is a biological fact that slowing down from the activities of the day takes time. That may seem unfair since getting aroused takes only seconds, especially if something threatening scares or angers you. Time is required to dissipate the arousing neuro-chemicals of the action oriented Let's Go! mode. Adrenalin is released into your bloodstream during the "fight or flight" response to stress. Research shows that about twenty minutes are required for adrenalin to disappear out of the bloodstream, even when the arousing stimulus is no longer a threat. The fight or flight symptoms of increased blood pressure, muscle tone, alertness, heart and respiration rate, and <u>decreased</u> activity in the digestive and immune systems are a result of the activation of the sympathetic nervous system (SNS). In opposition to this response is the "rest and repair" function of the parasympathetic branch (PNS) of your autonomic nervous system that slows the heart and respiration rate, reduces blood pressure and muscle tone while it <u>increases</u> the activity of digestive and immune system. (Mnemonic device: <u>S</u>tress: <u>S</u>NS, <u>P</u>eace: <u>P</u>NS).

The "flight or fight" response is an extreme case of "Let's Go!" on the arousal continuum. The Let's Go! state is self-perpetuating and is maintained by your thoughts about yourself and the situation you are in. Humans are capable of maintaining Let's Go! for weeks at a time, although at great cost to mind and body. A case in point is the well-substantiated research on the perpetual "I'm Gonna Get Um" attitude of the chronically hostile person and the resultant deterioration of the brain and cardiovascular system which can lead to premature demise.

Your physiology is more attuned to the demands of a time long gone when your survival depended on staying aroused and alert for long periods of time in order to keep the saber-toothed tigers away. If you didn't stay alert you just "weren't"! While the flight or fight state is automatically triggered when you perceive a threat, the antidotal rest and repair function has to be voluntarily invoked. Stressing chemicals continue to be circulated in your body even if you realize you were mistaken about the perceived threat. You have to convince yourself, the danger is over, in an attempt to soothe yourself because the presence of these chemicals make you feel like the danger is still present. The switch from "fight or flight" to "rest and repair" function is triggered by your <u>assessment</u> of the situation.

<u>Time</u> is needed for cognitive reframing. The shift is not automatic. While you are hardwired for the "rest and repair" phase of this stress-destressing cycle, you must learn how to initiate the shift to Let Go . . If you received adequate caretaker nurturing and felt loved for who you are, you are more likely to access the soothing effects of the rest and repair function of the nervous system by using the listening practices to hear your bodyself voice. For, the calming function of the nervous system is potentiated by the repeated experience of being soothed in our caretaker's arms so that it comes "online"*. Embodying the experience of "good enough" soothing from our childhood caretakers makes optimal self-soothing as adults more likely – readily shifting from the "Let's Go!" action mode to the "Let Go . ." calming mode.

Dropping from sheer exhaustion is no guarantee that you will wake up soothed and rested or that the repair job is complete. When you awaken, your anxious, tortured or obsessive thoughts can bring back the Let's Go! state, even without an external stimulus. To shift to Let Go . . you have to figure out whether the danger is gone, and then tell yourself you can rest now. That was easier to do when you only had wild animals or marauding tribes to worry about. You either got eaten or you escaped - there were not so many possibilities on the survival continuum as there are today. Since you wouldn't have had so long a life span, you didn't have to worry about the cumulative effects of prolonged arousal. And in contrast to today's stressful situations, then there was often an action you could take to deal with the threat or the encounter frequently ended in death.

The kinds of threats you now experience (whether real or imaginary) are not dealt with so readily and therefore are harder to recover from. Maybe you've put your family's savings at risk, maybe you fear being laid-off, maybe you feel trapped in a destructive personal or professional relationship, or perhaps you or a loved one have a life-threatening illness. You may be stressing yourself with catastrophic thoughts about a situation and/or with negative messages about yourself. Some of these negative thoughts are likely remnants of unresolved trauma and inadequate caretaker nurturing. With unresolved trauma, danger is not over on a bodyself level. You may find you just can't stop yourself from worrying. With each worrisome thought, your stress chemicals and tension increase and you become more vigilant. Stress chemicals induce inflammatory responses which over time can lead to chronic disease and cancer. There is no resolution and no peace or nothing to rest into. You may not be able to ask for help or admit you need it, especially if you experienced inadequate caretaker nurturing. If you start to relax or fall asleep, you have to pass through a state where you are less guarded. Then feelings and images appear which arise from your underlying sense of powerlessness or despair. These bodyself messages are trying to tell you something is wrong so you can resolve the situation and bring it to completion. But you may be too frightened of feeling overwhelmed to listen. You are literally living a bodyself nightmare.

The challenge of dealing with the end of a stressful day can be formidable. The stress is not over, but you have to find a way to shift to Let Go . . so you will have the energy to cope with another, perhaps, stressful day. This task can seem daunting. Yet bringing an end to the flight or fight state is essential for your emotional and physical health. So *she* and I invite you to learn to Let Go . .

Importance of Taming Your Biochemical Environment

Whether or not you are feeling sleepy or your body is ready for sleep at a particular time depends on a whole host of events that can influence your inner biological environment. Avoiding stimulating activities before bedtime like violent TV shows, arguments or exercise and stimulating substances such as sugar and caffeine contribute to a sleep-friendly biochemical environment. A consistent bedtime and wake up time and dimming the lights an hour before bedtime will also facilitate sleep onset. While sensitivity to these factors vary widely in individuals, it is important to be aware of what could help you prepare for sleep by reducing your body's Let's Go! arousal. How you can make use of your own biochemistry to ease your shift to Let Go . . will be detailed in the last section of this chapter and in the next chapter on decompression activities.

And even when you get all your biochemical ducks in a row, you may still have trouble getting to bed on time. Perhaps you just don't want to stop and accept that is all you can do today. Maybe you feel defeated when your time is up and you have to rest? Perhaps you aren't giving yourself enough of an incentive for taking care of yourself by stopping Let's Go! activity on time. Experiment with imagining how good you will feel in the morning when you are rested. In fact, if you do stop Let's Go! activity, you won't even have to <u>wait</u>

until morning to feel good. If you manage to stop when you have promised yourself, some of that rewarding sweetness may begin to pervade your awareness right away. Additional rewards can come as you go about your decompression activities in the form of delightful impulses you can sense, which you wouldn't have been aware of, had you not taken the time to slow down.

The bottom line is that once you have some experience with receiving *her* Let Go . . gifts, you are more likely to trust that it can happen again. Just give yourself and *her* a chance. When decompression time comes, pretend you are a Zen monk and the bell for meditation practice just rang. You make ready to go to the meditation hall – what could be more important than practice in just being present? Maybe you <u>are</u> trying to do too much. Just ask *her*! *She* is the keeper of your energy and as such *she* knows how much energy you have. *She* can help you renew your energy if you just listen to *her*. And *she* knows what you need to shift to Let Go . . Keep listening. You will find integration and balance, the more you allow *her* to be with you. If you would like to know more about the benefits of balancing Let's Go! with Let Go . . for your creativity, decision-making and general well-being, refer to Appendix A: Balancing Let's Go! with Let Go . .

How Decompression Unfolds

The experience of decompression unfolds as you experiment with various possibilities and make your discoveries. You move from the compressed, aroused workaday state of Let's Go! to the expansive, winding down state of Let Go . . Decompression is about <u>completion</u> – completing the stress-destressing cycle – completing the day, completing tasks, making notes on what can be completed tomorrow, completing conversations in your head, completing lists, etc. In order to have full energy for tomorrow you need to let yourself empty tonight. Remember, just as each muscle cell needs to rest completely, before it can contract again, you, too, can maximize your strength and energy when you rest deeply. The strength of a muscle depends on the number of individual muscle fibers that are available to contract. If the muscle is tense, then some fibers are already contracted, thus reducing the number of available fibers and your strength. The more you can surrender to Let Go . . and deeply rest, the more vitality you will experience the next day. As you create the conditions to allow completion in various ways, you can shift to Let Go . . and experience *her* subtle sweet energy.

Let Go . . is a total bodymind experience, which can be differentiated from Let's Go! – in terms of tension, thoughts, breath, and perspective. Let Go . . is associated with less tension and obsessive thinking, more flow and a positive, easy, receptive attitude. Let's Go! is felt in your body as increased tension in muscles, more thinking and a narrowed, sometimes, crisis-oriented perspective. If you focus on any one of these variables with the intent to allow change, you may notice that eventually, you will experience a shift to Let Go . . For instance, considering the variable of "perspective", when you notice you are feeling anxious and forecasting doom, you might try to encourage yourself or remember when you last had the feeling that things just worked out and you were OK. It seemed so real then, didn't it? Consider the possibility that you actually may not know what the best option is at the moment and you only <u>think</u> you know what is best. When you cling to your take on the situation, you suffer, not allowing for the possibility that something better is ahead. Spiritual wisdom advocates looking for the silver lining, the opportunity in the crisis, to find the "pony" in the situation, God's plan or you could ask yourself "What is it that I need to learn now?" Remind yourself that the clouds are temporary and the "blue sky" is infinite and always there.

Sometimes you can catch yourself before you go too far into the doldrums or panic. If, however, you have already gotten really upset or depressed, you are likely to have to feel the feelings all the way through to come back to balance. In my own experience, the times when I gave myself fully to my despair and felt and expressed it completely, I broke through to a profound sense of contact with life. The utter surrender to the pain of despair led to being permeated by a gentle connected flow and spontaneous movement. As I followed each impulse and let it through, I experienced the unfolding of creativity and being exactly in the moment. Just trying to "rise above" the feelings will likely leave you feeling detached and spaced out and not able to really connect with others or to do creative work. Or perhaps there are underlying deep feelings about which you haven't a clue. Deeply connecting to "what is" real in the moment requires all of you and attempting to rise above often results in shielding yourself from some disturbing part of yourself. You could write in your journal or reach out to someone in order to really connect with your feelings and feel them through so you can in order to decompress and shift to Let Go . .

For example, for several nights in a row I was having trouble falling asleep, even though I practiced many of the techniques offered in this book. I just felt anxious and my thoughts were consumed by a preoccupation with whether I was making the right decision about a new place to live. I could not let myself off the hook for deciding on the place I did. I was tormenting myself. By the time I saw my therapist, I felt anxious and hopeless about everything, so great was the force of the underlying anxiety. Fortunately he saw that the root of the angst was that I had not embraced the grief over leaving my lovely abode of the previous ten years. This grief was compounded by the fact that I was being forced out because of major renovation by the owner. Not only was there the loss of my home to grieve but also the interruption of my work on this book.

To cope with the feelings that were aroused by the notice to vacate, I had flown into the action-oriented Let's Go! mode. I had completely avoided my need to grieve my loss. I cried deeply in his presence and then again at lunch with a friend – the loss of my home and all the memories both happy and sad, that were held in the cozy place I had created. As the crying subsided, I was astounded to find that I was no longer <u>questioning</u> my decision. I may not have chosen the best possible new place to live, but it was the best I could do at that time. The important feeling was that I now felt present and easier with the whole situation. It would be OK. The energy that was bound in holding back the grief which fueled my obsessing was now free to fuel my creativity to make the new place mine. I didn't even want to go near entertaining the other possibilities that had previously made me question my decision. I just wanted to continue going toward the peaceful, alive, present feeling that was now pervading my bodyself. As I rested into being and shared my grief with an attuned other, my calm center returned. In this way, my grief could be borne and became known to myself. And I experienced being "born again" so I could dig into my new life in my new digs!

Diving deep into a "well" of grief

My therapist had wisely said there was no practical decision, no choice right enough that could obviate the <u>need</u> for grieving this loss. The anxiety that I was feeling was due to the pressed down feelings of grief. On one of those pre-mourning mornings I had meditated and had felt a very compelling "in-the-flow" feeling. As I connected to my readings in Rumi and Zen Mind, Beginner's Mind, my notes for my book just flowed out of me. However, when I later sat down to write, I could not access an inner place from which to write. I felt stuck and had

234

no clue what was wrong. I was just anxious and I could not penetrate that anxiety by myself. I needed the support of an attuned other who could resonate with me so I could give up holding against feeling this painful place. I was lost in a sea of anxiety – tormented by a sense of failing myself. I reached out to a friend to find my mooring in mourning. Then, having dived deep into the pain, hopelessness and sadness, I surfaced in calm water, gently soothed by the warm waves of restored connection. The balm of this discovery soothed for several days. And as a bonus, as I allowed myself to rest, I was visited by creative fantasies about my new living space. This was a profound experience of the decompressing power of grieving.

Another example of unfolding decompression is the following: One evening, a week later in anticipation of writing one last time before preparing to move, I started to feel anxious. As I was preparing for bed, I realized I was agitating myself in a similar way as before, telling myself I failed to make the right decisions quickly enough. Remembering the lesson learned earlier in the week, I figured I must have been pressing down some feelings with my constant critical evaluation of my decisions and myself. So I asked "What is the matter?" *She* pointed out that the two things I had said "No!" to, were things *she* was excited about and that I judged too impractical or expensive. I felt sad about stifling *her*. I promised that *she* will have more say in the next decisions and that I appreciated *her* ideas, *her* enthusiasm and vision.

Then I <u>looked</u> <u>for</u> what else might be fueling the anxious thoughts I was having. I remembered that earlier in the evening I was realizing how much there was to be done in preparation for the moving – all the sorting and decision-making. Going through ten years of living, recorded in photos and mementos, files and folders, clippings and clothes. I had been feeling it was all too much, how would I ever get it all done in the few weeks I had? Oh, so that is the anxiety - the move again! The energy behind my nagging and gnawing on myself had to do with, once again, the specter of leaving and feeling overwhelmed with so much to do. I needed some way to deal with that anxiety some way or I would never be able to write! I listened to some phone messages from my friend and left her some in return. Just hearing her voice made me feel more human and more compassionate with myself.

As I was preparing for bed I realized I had better reach out to *her*, for *she* may have been afraid of once again, getting pushed aside. I needed *her*. I acknowledged what a good job we had done with the client billing that night. Yes, I admitted that it took nearly three hours, but we caught several errors that could have resulted in a lot of lost time later. I realized I caught things I might not have, had I pushed myself and gotten tense and anxious. I had made a conscious effort all day not to lose *her* input by resting when I felt tension increasing. I was able to be present much of the time as I painstakingly worked on the details of billing and insurance forms. I periodically checked in with my jaw, lips, feet and pelvic floor. Was there holding? Did I need to get up and move? I really was able to return to being open and easy as I tidied up loose ends and balanced the checkbook. This time I did not need to weep about moving, I just needed to be more <u>understanding</u> and <u>encouraging</u> of myself. Having restored my connection with *her*, I was soothed and fell asleep easily.

Not so great expectations!

I had recognized how unrealistic my expectations were of myself – and especially when it came to desk tasks. I had hoped that I would get a lot more done than I had. There is always way more than I can possibly do to keep up with all the paper and duties that living entails. Why beat myself up? *She* goes away when I do that and then I miss *her* unanticipated gifts.

For instance, on the morning of that same day, *she* had given me an incredible vision. I had been touched by an article on George Harrison's life. On reading that his band was called "Wings", I suddenly saw a large white-feathered wing as a sculpture on a deep red wall. The wing sheltered a resting place. The colors of the image were rich and vibrant as I cried out my grief – a kind of collective grief that seemed to need to find its way through me. I wept at the deprivation I felt for not letting *her* create. All the years of doctoral work and then writing this book denied *her* the pleasure of creating in color. Instead I had chosen "words". Deep grief for lost moments. I mourn to be born again. Even now I can't say what those tears were all about but I was grateful to be so moved and to have this wondrous sight revealed. I wanted to materialize it in my new digs. Riches were revealed through the paroxysm of tears. Grieving was becoming a grounding place for me. The next morning I opened serendipitously to the following quote from "The Illustrated Rumi": "Plant grief seeds and picturing"*!

Shifting to Let Go . . requires that you are able to notice, focus and follow through on your bodyself messages. If you are not tired, rushed or stressed, it is easier to hear *her* and to trust *her*. Since you make the ultimate bedtime decisions, *she* is dependent on you for taking care of *her*. And since *she* regulates your energy, you are dependent on a good working relationship with *her*. If you ignore *her*, you will pay the price in terms of pain, depression and numbness. When you can emotionally self-regulate by going through your emotional recovery cycle, you will be less likely to ignore *her*. You can feel through your feelings and readily shift to Let Go . . In Let Go . . you may not be particularly interested in contact with others, but you will be more receptive to *her*.

She notices when you are following your "rules", making efforts to please *her* and reach *her* and that makes *her* happy. *She* can feel your seeking *her* out, making your way to *her*, for *her*. *Her* recognition of that is the ease you begin to feel. *She* brings sweet satisfaction. *She* waits for you to find *her*. When you follow up on what you know works, what really feels good, more de-stressing chemicals are released. You need these chemicals to restore balance from the pressure you endure all day. *She* is relieved you are listening and gives you de-stressing chemicals as the feeling of sweetness returns.

For instance, one evening, I noticed I was having trouble falling asleep. I realized with a start, I am thinking and thinking and not giving myself a sensory trace to follow. Why, after so many years, doesn't this shift just automatically happen? It appears it will always be an active effort. I have to make a conscious effort to turn my attention to sensations and let them lead me into Let Go . . slumber land. I must keep my promise to *her* to faithfully attend to *her* needs before I can ease off to sleep. "Just lying there" is never enough for any kind of passionate relationship!

Decompression time is about creating space for flow to happen, you can't force the shift to Let Go. . You have to be steadfast in holding the space and act on *her* cues <u>immediately</u> as if you were in Let's Go! So, <u>act</u> when you feel the urge or tug from *her*. Just do it with blind faith and feel what unfolds. To keep decompression unfolding, follow *her*, allow your lips to soften, stretch, finish tasks and conversations and let the cycles end. Let *her* show you what is needed. Encourage, appreciate and console yourself before you go to sleep. If you practice listening to *her* throughout the day, you will find this kind of support easier to access at night when you are tired. The more you listen to *her*, the more you can experience shifting to Let Go . . so the more balance you will feel. You are likely to have more energy and better ideas. You may not do as many things, but what you do do will give you more satisfaction.

Let Go . . does not mean you have to go slow or be quiet while you are in it. You could be quite active and still be informed by *her*. Action and awareness permeate both Let Go . . and Let's Go! - what differs is the quality of focus and goal. You are constantly potentially aware of *her* messages, you just have to turn toward *her*, inviting or recognizing *her*. What *she* offers is access to a vital part of your organismic functioning. I hope you stay with this work long enough to experience the paradox of the Let Go . . mode. Namely that it is a fragile ephemeral state, yet a source of great strength, energy, creativity, soothing and resilience.

Catching the Let Go . . Wave

Catching the decompression wave is responding to the thought, "I should turn off the TV", as soon as it happens. Midway in my decompression routine I sometimes turn on the TV while I do my back strengthening exercises. However, I have found that when I am able to do my exercises without the TV, thoughts come to me that might not occur otherwise. For example, one evening as I turned on the TV, I found myself rationalizing, "TV is OK, you are not writing yet. Watching TV is a treat, go ahead." But then I thought "You will be writing tomorrow and you had some ideas this morning that put you back on track." Upon remembering that fact, I felt encouraged, yet I turned the TV on anyway. Then half way through exercising, I turned the TV off. In the quiet, some fragments of a therapy session with a client came to mind. I was so glad to have captured these pieces so I could reflect on them. Giving myself more time to listen for *her*, strengthens the bodyself aspect of my functioning and better prepares me to soothe myself to sleep. But you don't have to take my word for it, find out for yourself. Soon you too will be surfing the decompression waves.

Once you catch one wave, the next one is easier. You begin to notice more subtle cues to wave movement. When you want to wind down at the end of the day, a good place to begin is to notice what your bodyself is telling you right then. Perhaps you feel the pressure of having to urinate. You may have been delaying following these sensations all day because you could and because there was always something more important to do. Now is your chance to heed this call to release and initiate the Let Go . . flow (no pun intended!). With lessened bodily tension, you are likely to notice another need, like the lights are too bright or your neck is tense or your clothes feel irritating or you are thirsty. Follow whatever is most pressing, take it to completion and then feel what happens next. Before you know it you will be deep into decompressing from the day's stresses. The more relief you give yourself, the more sensitive you will become to what you need next. You will feel a subtle increase in a sweet kind of energy. Other tasks will automatically feel less pressing as you give into comforting your inner creature. More and more of you will become present and your options increase as a result of *her* good ideas and delightful surprises! *She* simply senses more than you do. But because *she* is mute *she* needs you to pay attention to *her*. Then *she* can show you something very meaningful, something you wouldn't have otherwise known and are likely to be grateful to have experienced.

It is amazing to me how often I distract myself while I engage in various self-care activities. The temptation is so strong to turn on the TV or read while I eat, exercise, floss, brush my teeth or go to the toilet. These are all activities that involve intimate contact with my body and could be invitations to deepening awareness of my bodyself as well as a chance to shift to Let Go . . mode. These times are *her* times, *her* chance to talk to me, to remind of important things, to help me chill out, to get new ideas or to notice how I am feeling. Yet I find I am pulled to hurriedly turn on the TV to distract myself while I floss my teeth instead of being present for the few minutes it takes to thoroughly floss.

Another example is an experience I had one afternoon that proved to me that I use the TV to distract* myself from really being with whatever needs to be attended to in myself. I had left a message for my therapist to call me because I needed to talk to him about something upsetting. In the interim I turned the TV on to work out. His call interrupted my workout. An eight-minute talk with him helped me find a deeper connection to myself so when I went back to working out, I no longer wanted the TV on. I turned it off and was content with just being with my bodyself experience.

Shifting to Let Go . . is like catching an ocean wave for a ride. For example, one morning as I read the newspaper the thought occurred that it was time to start working on my book. I didn't want to sacrifice my precious, fresh morning energy by reading the energy-sucking newspaper stories of doom and gloom. I stopped reading mid-sentence. Gotcha! I felt a spark of excitement. Energy can come just by interrupting the action of the moment. It is like catching a wave in body surfing. You need to pay attention, position yourself, paddle like hell (Let's Go!) to get into the right spot, and then allow the wave to carry you (Let Go . .). While riding you need to <u>continue</u> to pay attention so you can stay with the wave and not lose it or get plowed under.

Ahhh! The exhilaration of getting it "just right." Let Go . . energy is awakening energy – a gentle rush. Staying with it requires paying attention, acting at just the right moment and then resting into it. What a rewarding meditation it is to ride these waves with *her*. Each day, every evening, wave after wave comes toward you – will you be there to catch that wave? Will you pay attention – will you make the subtle effort needed to join with *her* and let *her* direction carry you?

On the other hand if you continue to push yourself when you really need to go to sleep or take a break, when you persist with Let's Go! energy when you need to shift to Let Go . . you will find that things get worse and worse for you. In the wave riding metaphor, if you become over ambitious or don't stay attuned, you get thrashed by the turbulent white water. Just as flow builds when you follow *her*, confusion, fatigue and trouble increase when you go against what *she* needs. You will find you drop things, pull out the wrong electrical cord, put things in the wrong place, stub your toe, smash your finger, run your stockings, get a headache and make all kinds of painful and costly mistakes. You really need *her* input, especially at the end of the day. When you are tense or tired, you are especially challenged because it is even harder to tap into *her* wisdom. But the rewards are even greater for self-soothing.

What makes the difference and allows the shift is not the specific message to which I respond but my <u>willingness</u> to respond to *her*. As Suzuki Roshi** says, "Quality of mind is the activity itself!" Sensing and responding to muscle tension is one challenge but feeling through emotions against which you might be constricting is quite another. When you are able to embrace each of your feelings, you are likely to have the bodyself grounding to notice, focus and follow through in any situation. Such bodyself grounding arises from the experience that there is nothing you can't face because you've had enough support in the past to go through it all. Then you can respond to *her* messages and shift to Let Go . .

Establishing a Decompression Period

To start with, set aside an hour for decompression activities before you go to bed. Experiment with how much time you allow for the decompression routine and when it begins. Actually, to be maximally effective and soothing, this decompression routine needs to be treated as a work in progress and not a set of rules to be rigidly followed. Unless, of course you find rigidly following rules, soothing! I get the best results when I set a cut-off time beyond which I promise I will not do any more work. That time needs to be fairly consistent from night to night, because I do not fall asleep easily if the bedtime (the time that I actually lay down to sleep) varies more than a half an hour. This observation is backed up by research and shows that most people have some difficulty falling asleep if bedtime is twenty minutes earlier than the previous night.

On the other hand, unexpected demands are made on your time from friends, family, work or illness. The need for flexibility should be anticipated so changes are less distressing. Tolerating change is also part of becoming more self-soothing. How much liberty you can take with changes in this time period will depend on how consistent you are with maintaining contact with that deeper part of yourself, which is coming to trust that you are really going to follow through and take care of your bodyself. When I have more trouble falling asleep and don't feel so well when I wake up, I know I have been ignoring *her* for too long. *She* is slower to respond to me when I don't honor *her* messages with regularity. Other warnings that I have not been listening to *her* enough are increased head or neck aches.

Sleep onset is determined by a host of biochemical factors related to events such as previous morning wake-up time, duration and timing of daytime naps, tension, stressful thoughts and feelings, residual caffeine effects, amount of light present in environment, time lapse since exercise or bathing, food intake and other pre-sleep activities. So when you set aside this time for decompression, you need to have already taken care of potentially stressful activities, like discussions about finances or conflicts at work, watching the news or putting your children to bed!

Fundamentally a biochemical process, sleep onset is facilitated by increased melatonin secretion into the blood. Melatonin secretion is inhibited by the presence of light, so dim the lights on the onset of the decompression period. Besides with less light, you need to rely on your other senses which are less triggering of thinking. Carrying out decompression activities in candlelight can be particularly soothing. With regular practice at a particular time, you may find that your eyes will tell you when decompression period is about to begin. You may notice that the light seems too bright and you'll be likely to find yourself getting up to turn down the lights or light the candles. Even the act of lighting of the candles <u>itself</u> may have a soothing effect, because of the association with the decompression period. Because you have established new habits, your nervous system will give you the cues. Your job is to notice them and follow through.

While turning down lights or lighting a candle is not the only way to signal the beginning of decompression period, it is an essential one. Other sensory cues are also helpful and can anchor the beginning of the decompression period as the time to take care of yourself and begin the shift to Let Go. . Enlisting other senses such as smell (incense, scented candle, aromatic tea) taste (fruit, juice, tea), sound (music), touch (soft loose clothing and foot coverings) can deepen the response of your bodyself to the decompression activities. Deepening your response on a physiological level means more of your sensory cortex is involved in your bodyself response. In fact with continued practice, your body will anticipate its beginning and you may notice you feel anxious or a little cranky when something threatens to distract you from beginning to decompress. On the other hand when you let yourself slow down as you get these cues to decompress, you will go more quickly and deeply into that Let Go. . "good night". That sweet, soothing feeling you experience is *her* way of saying "Thank you for listening to me". Bottom line, the purpose of all of these sensory cues is to remind you that you are now shifting gears and giving yourself to a slower pace and a more sensory oriented consciousness.

Treat decompression time as a sacred time for yourself. How much time are you willing to give to nurture your connection to yourself? If you don't give yourself this time, your bodyself will not let you sleep. To shift to Let Go . . you have to find out what it is you need, moment-to-moment. Decompression time gives you a chance to attune to your needs and fulfill them. On the one hand, your decompression period functions as a temple in which you faithfully minister to your bodyself. On the other, it functions as a laboratory where you can observe how you divert yourself from tuning in or from following through on messages from your bodyself about what you need to slow down. Whether decompression is conceived of as sanctuary or laboratory, guidelines for decompression are essential. However, if you are too strict you will lose heart and not follow through. Likewise, if you are too lax you won't make the discoveries you need to make, to shift to Let Go . . Besides, not setting aside decompression time means you are likely to miss out on the experience of satisfaction of completing or solving some troublesome matter, coming up with a creative idea, remembering something important, a good cry, getting some encouragement, not to mention a good night's sleep! You have a lot to lose and everything to gain by trying. Again and again. The next chapter will lead you through a series of decompression activities from which you can choose what works best for you to self-soothe.

15

DECOMPRESSION ACTIVITIES

"There are so many ways to open . . ."

Decompression activities can be divided into two main categories: <u>organizing</u> and <u>soothing</u>. While both kinds of activities have both soothing and organizing effects, activities called "organizing" are the ones that tend to be more analytical and cognitive which assist you in completing the day and getting ready for the new one. These should be attempted before you move onto the more soothing activities that take you closer to sleep and can be accomplished in minimal lighting. With practice you will be surprised by how many tasks you can accomplish with ease, in less than usual light. Much experimentation is needed to arrive at what really works for you, and of course each evening will present new challenges and new discoveries! All the more reason to work on getting more attuned to *her* needs because *she* can be a big help to you. *She* can make you feel so pleased with yourself! You may feel all the more soothingly satisfied for it!

Preparation for Decompression

On the way home from work (or after supper), think about how you would like to end your day. Ask *her* what would *she* like? Pay attention to any sensations or images that come up. What feels unfinished? What nags at you? What would give you a sense of satisfaction and readiness for the new day? Consider what soothing activities would be pleasing to you. Stay for a few minutes in your car before you come into the house to just allow yourself to really be with your arrival. Taking time before you leave your car will help settle you and lay some groundwork for what comes next. You may discover that what is needed might change five minutes after you walk in the door, but you can still enjoy the momentary satisfaction of the kind attention you have given to yourself, by imagining what kind of homecoming activities would be soothing and satisfying.

Take this occasion to acknowledge your need for *her* help and allow reconnection if you have lost *her*. For instance, I put a soft rubber ball between my back and the back of the car seat to address my back tension while I drive home at night. I sense my connection through my feet to the floor of the car as I drive home. I try not to be on my cell phone on the last leg of my journey so I can allow my bodyself to truly arrive. There are so many ways to prepare for coming home to yourself. You could ask yourself, "What do I need for myself so I can really be with myself and/or my loved ones tonight?"

Other activities that influence your readiness to fall asleep, either by enhancing or inhibiting your de-stressing chemicals include exercise, bathing, food, caffeine and alcohol intake, and stimulating distractions such as TV and the Internet. After a cursory consideration of the above factors, the Organizing and Soothing Activities will be treated in detail.

Lighting: To maximize the amount of sleep onset inducing melatonin, dim the lighting as soon as you can. Installing dimmer switches in the bed and bathroom will allow you to make adjustments as needed throughout the decompression period. Adjusting the brightness and contrast on your TV and computer monitor allows you to read your email with a minimum of stimulation from light. Research shows that the flickering light from the TV and computer stimulates the brain toward wakefulness. If you must read before you go to bed, use minimal lighting – recent research claims that low lighting does not damage the eyes. If you are living with someone who needs more illumination at night than you do, you could try wearing dark glasses. Have fun! Choose some glasses that delight you. If your partner reads before bed, you may get a head start by using "eye pillows". Gentle pressure on the eyeballs (with the eyes closed, of course!) stimulates the parasympathetic nervous system and helps you shift to Let Go . . Combined with the reduction of light stimulation, this latter effect explains why eye pillows are so rest-inducing.

Exercise: Exercise during the day can help you feel sleepy at bedtime. However exercise performed too close to bedtime could delay your descent into dreamland. No less than 3 to 5 hours before bedtime is recommended because various stress hormones such as adrenalin are released during exercise and promote alertness. Experiment with the amount, type and timing of exercise to discover what works best for you.

Temperature: Seventy degrees or less is recommended because cool air encourages a shift to drowsiness.

Bathing: Taking a warm bath or shower before bedtime can have sleep inducing effects for some people while for others, heat stimulates and keeps them awake. These people will need some time to cool down before they can fall asleep. Research shows that most people need about an hour after a hot shower before they begin to feel sleepy. A drop in body temperature is a biological cue to falling asleep. However the effect of learning has a very powerful influence on this biological variable. For instance, for years I took two showers a day – one in the morning, to wake up and one at night, to prepare myself for sleeping. The nighttime shower I took just before I meditated and went to bed. Sometimes I would imagine the "remains of the day" being washed away as I showered. Showering in the dark became a cue to winding down. However, my morning shower was awakening and got me ready for the day. The common denominator was that showering became a way of getting in touch with my bodyself, and was, therefore, a great way to begin *and* end each day. In short, the shower became part of my sensing, meditating and listening to my emotional voice practices.

Food: Finding just the right bedtime snack takes trial and error. Research shows that eating just the right amount of carbohydrates near bedtime can be sleep inducing. The effects of carbohydrate intake on individuals do vary so this finding should be taken with a grain of salt (oops, better not, salt can be stimulating!) Carbohydrates like grapefruit, melon and berries and other low calorie foods can be helpful for sleep. Toast is a tricky treat because it can become high in calories and fat very quickly, depending on what you put on it. Snacks high in sugar can be initially stimulating and delay sleep onset. Some people find warm milk with a bit of honey and/or vanilla or mashed banana is a soothing bedtime snack. Protein tends to be more stimulating at bedtime and needs to be avoided when maximum sleepiness is desired. While milk has a fair amount of protein, it contains calcium and tryptophan in addition to carbohydrates and all three of the latter substances have been linked to easing the onset of sleep. Just experiment to find what works for you.

242

Caffeine: Caffeine whether in chocolate, coffee, green, white or black tea, mate, kola nut, Gota Kola, guarana, Red Bull, Excedrin, Dr. Pepper, or other colas will interfere with sleep onset and/or soundness of sleep. Caffeine disrupts your most fundamental biorhythm (sleep-wakefulness) which is why it's useful in helping people adjust to new time zones. However on a daily basis, caffeine intake can interfere with falling asleep or staying asleep. While it takes only twenty minutes for caffeine to exert its maximum effect, twelve hours are required until its effect on your body disappears. Like other sleep onset factors these effects vary widely with the individual. Some habitual coffee drinkers can drink an after dinner espresso and fall asleep easily a few hours later. Your body attempts to restore equilibrium in response to whatever you give it. For instance, the blood pressure of non-coffee drinkers increases much more dramatically with a single cup of coffee than does the blood pressure of coffee drinkers.

Drinks and Herbal preparations: The health food store has many preparations that can help you feel calmer and more ready to sleep. Teas and capsules that contain Valerian, passionflower, skullcap, poppy, hops or chamomile have a soothing effect on your bodyself. Be sure to consult your doctor before taking any herbs or even melatonin on a regular basis.

Before you get started on completing your organizing activities, take fifteen minutes to "chill". Use a special "tuck yourself in" cup and while you are savoring your treat, you can read something special or listen to music. When was the last time you read by candlelight? The scent of lavender is said to be soothing whether delivered as a spray through an atomizer, a burning candle or a scented lotion. On the other hand, a "nightcap" containing alcohol is likely to only be temporarily soothing. Alcohol consumption before bedtime is notorious for causing "rebound wakefulness" several hours later.

Organizing Activities

As soon as possible take care of all the tasks that need normal lighting such as cleaning contact lenses. Since your "toilet" involves contact with your body, performing these activities early on enables the embodiment of your homecoming as soon as possible. Changing into more comfortable clothing is an important bodymind signal as well. Giving your feet a change of pace is also a vital step toward decompression. Why not a little foot massage when you take off your shoes? Maybe you would like to lay out your clothes for tomorrow.

Situations that could be stressful are also a priority. Pick up your messages (whether voice, e- or snail mail) and decide which ones you will answer tonight. Take stock: are there any nagging situations you need to attend to so that you can let go of ruminating about them? For bothersome situations you might sketch out a tentative plan of attack. You may find some relief from an upsetting situation if you call a friend or leave a message or write in your journal. Writing in a journal gives feelings a place to be so you can Let Go.. If necessary, you can then consider with whom you could consult the next day to help you handle the situation. Tell yourself that you have done as much as you can now and you don't need to think about it anymore. Of course, you will start to, but when you catch yourself, tell yourself, in the way you might intone a mantra, that you have a plan and you can make an even better plan in the morning when you are rested. Besides, things could change for the better between now and when you have to deal with the situation. Now you need to rest so you will have more energy tomorrow. When you are feeling really stressed out, you may not be receptive enough to *her* messages so your solution won't be as good. So get some sleep and tell yourself that *she* will be there in the morning to help you.

243

You have dealt with your messages, let go of unfinished situations for the day and started making a plan for tomorrow. Add anything that occurs to you now about what you have to do or whom you need to call. Keep that list handy so you can add to it as you go further into decompression period. More will occur to you as you wind down. Even better solutions will evolve. Whatever is unfinished will present itself again. When it does, act on it, so you can continue to shift to Let Go. . unless of course acting on it, means staying up half the night! "Act on it" in this case, means write it down or feel it through, so you can catch the Let Go . . wave and let decompression continue to unfold.

This decision is tricky because you don't want to stay up too late, yet certain things need to be completed so that tomorrow goes more smoothly and you can sleep better. The decompression period gives you a time limit – what will fit inside that? Doing more than that will leave you with less energy for coping the next day. Let *her* help you sort out what really is needed - in your relationships, your job and your body. You just have to give *her* the space and time to speak – in *her* own "words" of course.

Speaking of "words", leave some notepaper by your bedside to jot down anything that comes to you when you are already in bed so you don't have to try to remember it later. Eventually you will trust that it will still be there on the pad in the morning! As a matter of fact, you'll sometimes find that a solution to a troubling problem may spontaneously emerge as you drift off to sleep or upon awakening. Since you will have had a good night's sleep, you'll have the energy and freshness to implement your insight. You are likely to receive some insight into your dilemma simply by allowing whatever words come to you to be written. Many people find that writing in the morning leaves them settled and refreshed much like meditation does. A third reason to have a pad by your bed is in case you have a dream you want to remember. If you also have a lighted pen, you can write in the dark without waking anyone, including yourself!

It can be helpful to write about a problem in more detail just minutes before you go to sleep. Whether it is some interpersonal or a creative dilemma, writing your thoughts and feelings before you go to sleep can prepare your bodymind to give you a solution in a dream. The contribution of dreams to self-knowledge has been recognized by many as evidenced by the following quotes "It is in our dreams, in our idleness that the truth sometimes floats to the top."* and "An uninterpreted dream is like an unopened letter" (to yourself from yourself)**. You may find you awaken with a dream that contains clues to a solution, a different approach or deeper understanding of your issue. This technique is called "dream incubation"*** in many books on dreams. When you prepare yourself in this way, you are giving *her* a chance to help you. *Her* voice, the voice of your bodyself can be heard through your dream images. In any case, leave more time for your decompression routine, if you want to write about a problem.

Gaining insight and expressing feelings connected to an interpersonal conflict can be facilitated by writing a "love letter". This technique, meticulously detailed by John Gray (of "Mars and Venus" fame) is especially useful for couples and can be found in his book "What You Can Feel, You Can Heal"****. By following the protocol of the love letter – writing about what you are angry about, then afraid of, guilty, and then sad about – you can move through your emotional recovery cycle and come back to "love" or to the neutral point or open heart. Warning: this could take an hour or more and may stir up many feelings. In a similar vein, Robert and Virginia Hilton developed a bodyself-oriented method for deepening intimacy called the "intimacy cycle".*****

Preparation of Sleeping Space

Your last organizing activity may be turning down your bed covers, setting your alarm clock or placing a soothing-smelling something at your bedside. Preparing your sleeping space may itself become a very soothing activity. First, it becomes a cue that you are nearing the time when you lower the lights another notch and meditate and/or stretch – taking your Let Go . . to a deeper level. As soon as you place your pillows the way you really like them to be, you may already feel the sweet sleepiness beginning. Secondly, the attitude with which you prepare your sleeping place can deepen the sense of being soothed. Give your full attention to this preparation by turning the TV off and the lights way down and leave your cell phone in another room. Maybe you will need to invest in an alarm clock! Take time to sense what is wanted tonight. If you treat yourself like a special guest, you are likely to discover how *she*, in turn, thanks you.

Leaving a glass of water by the bed to quench a middle of the night dry mouth is an act of kindness that will be gratefully received later on. One friend of mine finds it comforting to let a small tea light candle (in a fireproof container) burn itself out as he drifts off to sleep. Experiment to find out what is soothing to you. Attending to these needs faithfully will likely result in your waking up in a sweeter frame of mind – perhaps with the feeling that you are loved and special.

Cultivating a "Tuck Yourself In" Attitude

The attitude with which you approach these decompression activities is at least as important as the activities themselves. As you anticipate decompression, notice your attitude. Are you feeling resentful of having to wind down now? Can you give yourself credit for the work you did today, even if it didn't go as well as you would have liked? Do you approach yourself with tender consideration or with a sense of dutifulness or even disinterest as you prepare your sleeping space, undress or bathe? Do you throw yourself in bed or do you lay yourself down tenderly?

If you find that you are more likely to treat yourself in a perfunctory or begrudging manner rather than sensitively and considerately, you may get some clues as to why if you consider what bedtime was like for you as a child. How you treat yourself at bedtime may be a reflection of the attitude of your caretaker to towards your needs for soothing and protection. The way these needs were once addressed is likely reflected in your attitude toward your needs as an adult. It is not too late to change them, but it helps to know what they are and where they came from. To discover more about your self-care attitude, you can try making use of the suggestions in this section, and in particular, by consulting your "emotional voice." If you suspect childhood bedtime trauma such as abuse, punishment, bedwetting or other potential sources of abandonment feelings, you may benefit from therapy. In any case, your feelings, positive or negative, about going to bed or sleep may have roots in your childhood experience.

Going to sleep is a complex, vital activity for caretaker and child. The child leaves the arms and voice, the containment of the caretaker and enters the realm of aloneness and quiet, not to mention, darkness. Abandonment is an innate human fear. Attuned caretaking can make the transition from light to dark less scary. The infant or child must feel safe and cared for enough to allow the Let Go shift. Even if these conditions are not met, the child's body will eventually be overcome by exhaustion and sleep will prevail. But the child will likely sleep fitfully and awaken cranky and unsettled, searching for contact. Attuned caretaking can make the difference between a desperate sleep and a sweet sleep. Your caretaker teaches you how to go to sleep. Little ones need to be held, cuddled, talked to tenderly and listened to respectfully to ease the transition from wakefulness to sleep. In order to allow the shift, they need to be able to give themselves over to something "larger than themselves", whether it is the warmth of the caretaker's arms, a rocking motion, the sound of another's heart beating or a soothing voice.

In a very real sense, allowing yourself to fall asleep is letting go into the unknown – the darkness, the "unconscious". You trust that your bodyself will take care of you while you sleep – you will continue to breathe, digest and that you can return to consciousness. As a point of fact, your body does recuperate better when you are sleeping than at any other time. For sleep is accompanied by the secretion of the greatest amounts of immune factor, interleukin 2, and the growth hormone during the twenty-four hour cycle. The term "falling asleep" aptly says it – you give up your sense of self to sleep. You can probably call to mind a time when, as you were "falling" asleep and you had a brief image of actually falling down or losing control in some way. That image is a picture evoked by the sensation of your muscles letting go of control at that moment. In order to "fall safely", it helps to have had the experience of falling into something larger than yourself. The ease with which you fall asleep now may have much to do with having had the experience of falling (resting) into an attuned caretaker as you drifted off to sleep.

Your adult longing to feel connected to something larger than yourself may be a longing for the state of consciousness that you may have enjoyed as a child when you rested in your caretaker's arms, basking in the bliss of giving up the vigilance of the Let's Go! mode. Children who experienced sufficiently attuned caretaking have, within themselves, a calm center into which they can rest even as adults. They also are likely to have the capacity to turn to an appropriate other when their self-soothing fails.

What makes bedtime difficult for children has much in common with what makes it troublesome for adults. The concern a child expresses that he will miss something by going to bed is similar to the adult's wanting more engagement either with people or activity. In addition, both children and adults have periods when they fear being awakened by scary dreams and experiencing the vulnerable state in which they awaken and when no one is available to comfort them. No matter the age of the individual, nightmares often represent unintegrated emotional states that threaten to overwhelm self-soothing resources. Adequate caretaker attunement can lead to soothing of the child's fears by confronting the "monster". Is there much of a difference in the child's need to have a story read to her/him as s/he falls asleep when compared to the adult's need to read him/herself to sleep? Probably the main difference lies in who turns off the light! Remembering what worked for you as a child may give you clues to how to soothe yourself to sleep now. If you were one of the fortunate children who had pleasant bedtime rituals and you now have trouble falling asleep, you may find some comfort (and maybe some fun) in recreating some elements of your childhood bedtime ritual. Go on, give it a try! And even if bedtime was not a pleasant time for you, you may still get an idea of what is now needed to address those deficits. Bedtime does not have to mean deprivation, pain, terror or loneliness.

For instance, if you were sent to bed unaccompanied, you had to work out your own way of tucking yourself in, perhaps through fantasy or reading. Recall any childhood fantasies you created to put yourself to sleep. The underlying themes of these fantasies often address the need to feel safe, loved or special. Maybe you longed for a caretaker to tuck you in, after listening to your tales of the good and bad things that happened to you that day. Remembering this, you might arrange to have a brief talk with someone as part of your bedtime ritual. Alternatively, you might write in your journal about what was particularly gratifying and/or troublesome that day. If bedtime was a stressful time for you as a child, remembering exactly how it was stressful and taking steps now to deal with unresolved feelings could ultimately ease your transition to sleep. In this way, you are taking your troubled feelings seriously, being a good parent to yourself and making sure that, at least now, you can get what you need.

The soothing activities presented here all share an element of letting go into a sense of something larger than yourself because they encourage that state of mind where the division between the self and the world is blurred. This neurophysiologically identifiable state is common to what are generally referred to as a "spiritual" experience. In fact, your first "spiritual" experience may have been in the arms of your childhood caretaker! The essence of this kind of experience is that your sense of your small self is lost through merging with something larger.

Whether you are listening to sound, or saying a prayer or attending to sensations in your body or breathing, you are making use of your ability to focus on some aspect of your sensory world to surrender a sense of connection with something larger than yourself. To shift to Let Go . . try <u>resting into</u> something, even it is just a fantasy of something or an idea like "emptiness" or "God's love". Ultimately it is your experience, not the thing itself into which you rest and "disappear". In some sense, focusing in this way is listening with a longing to join – to become whole, complete. ("Healing" and "whole" have the same root and the root of the word "religion" means "to reconnect"). In one sense, your heart opens to the larger heart whether it is the heart of your caretaker, friend, lover, stranger, or God. By "God" I mean whatever you conceive of as the source of your strength or inspiration: God, Higher Power, Inner Self, Life Force, Heart, It, the Organism, the Eternal, or your True Nature. It is always there to call upon, if you remember to open to it. In this sense of joining, you become "larger" than you were.

So too, in a very concrete, embodied sense, when you decompress, <u>you</u> become larger - your breathing expands, your muscles lengthen. At the same time, you let go of what you don't need in that moment: concerns, worries, judgments and "have-tos". Although you are likely unaware of it, such inner dialogue or negative self-talk is accompanied by mini-contractions in your muscles, especially in the neck, face, head, and shoulders. Tips on how to relieve some of this tension through self-massage, sensing and stretching these areas will be given in the next section.

Soothing Activities

"Organizing activities" and the completion of tasks are inherently soothing because they can give a sense of order and that someone (in this case, you!) cares about how your day went and how tomorrow will be. "Soothing activities" are those that not only reduce your level of arousal but also help you shift to more bodyself-oriented processing so you can hear your bodymind voice more clearly. Sensing, meditating and listening to your emotional voice are soothing activities that are ideal for decompressing. Bathing and eating are potentially soothing, if they are done early enough in the decompression period and are discussed further in the following chapter on Awakening. Remember, turn down the lights when you begin the soothing activities of your decompression period.

Sensing experiments are considered first because sensing is the fundamental practice from which the others flow. Sensing brings you more closely in touch with the sensations of breathing and of where you are compressing your bodyself. As you practice sensing in lying or sitting as a preparation for meditation, you will eventually feel the "Goldilocks moment " – the moment when you get it "just right" and can shift to Let Go . . In sensing, Let Go . . <u>is</u> the experience of ease. Sensing prepares you to sit in meditation more comfortably and to focus on breathing with more clarity. In the course of meditating, various concerns, uncompleted tasks and conversations will emerge. Meditating sometimes allows you to experience completion of unfinished situations and the consequent shift to Let Go . . In meditating, Let Go . . is the experience of subtle energy. While meditating, your emotional voice may speak up about various worries, woes and joys. You can better listen to this voice when you are grounded in your bodily experience (sensing) and more focused (meditation). If you have embodied adequate caretaker attunement or reparative emotional experiences as an adult, you may be better able to go through your emotional recovery cycle and experience the sweetness of Let Go . .

Sensing: The Let Go . . Energy of Ease

Many people just kind of throw themselves into bed. Now, ask yourself, would you throw your baby into bed? Why then you would you treat yourself any less tenderly? Is your organism not precious to you? Are you not precious to yourself? You may try to fall asleep in some habitual position without really assessing whether or not you are lying comfortably or cramped and constricted. For instance, when I have the presence of mind to notice how I am lying after flinging myself down, I find my head is often a little too far back. That position compresses the back of my neck, a familiar tension left over from the stress of the day. I may notice my jaw is clenched, and my legs are too close together. Sometimes I notice a general sense of holding in, back, and together as if there were some toxic contact that threatened so I must make myself small. Perhaps it is unsafe to take the space that is needed for comfortable lying.

This constricted state may simply be a result of continuing to embody the tensions of the day - the worries, conflicts, disappointments and fears. The tension in your body mirrors your existential situation – you may feel boxed in and trapped. Even after having written about your concerns, you may carry some residue to bed. On the other hand, this constricted bodyself holding pattern may be a reaction to unresolved trauma and as such may be habitual and unconscious; in that case, you may need help to resolve it. Or perhaps you are just unfamiliar with sensing your bodyself and with noticing the need for more space. Or maybe, you notice but do not follow through with giving yourself what you need. In any case, the following experiments can help you sense the space you need so you can get a refreshing, good night's sleep. With practice, you can have greater bodyself awareness so that you can spontaneously notice yourself in a cramped, constricted position even when you are not lying. And you may be more likely to follow through by allowing more room for your living.

Sensing invites you to feel what your organism needs at the moment and follow through with the desired changes. The suggestions offered below are to be treated as if they were experiments, not exercises. The attitude of experimentation* is one of trying something out and noticing what is felt. Whereas, an exercise is often tackled as something to be <u>mindlessly</u> repeated instead of <u>mindfully</u> experienced. Focus your attention in your bodyself and allow what is needed. The resultant movement may not be visible to someone else but only felt as space, opening inside you. Notice if you are starting to make an exercise out of lying. Does this "doing" mirror how you have been in the world today? "Give it up!" as Charlotte would say. If a change is really needed, paying close attention is likely to bring about the needed organismic changes. You do not have to try to make yourself different or better, just pay attention.

"Coming to lying" is a phrase coined by Charlotte Selver to indicate that lying is an organismic process. This phrase acknowledges that it takes time to sense out what is needed so that there is enough room for breathing and circulation. In lying you are invited to give your weight into what supports you. You begin to notice where you feel constricted due to your muscular holding, your clothing or inadequate support under you. You let your attention travel from your toes to your head, sensing the changes that are needed to come more fully to lying. It takes time to sense how lying wants to be right now. Eventually you may feel the Goldilocks moment when your lying feels "just right" or complete.

What follows are ways to enliven your lying and simultaneously to come to more resting. As you sample from these suggestions, you can discover what meets you and your own experimentation will evolve from there. In addition to the fundamental sensing practice of "coming to lying", other interesting experiments are offered that can help you become more aware of sensations as you prepare for sleeping. Remember, slowing down and feeling sensations is what eases you into the soothing of Let Go . .

Coming to lying

Lie on the floor or bed on your back, with your feet unhindered by the covers. (You may want to prerecord the following so that you can just listen in the darkness). Take time to feel how you are lying now. Do you recognize this position or posture as familiar? Do you notice any discomfort or constriction, especially in the area of your joints? Where do you notice you are pressing into the mattress and where are you resting? Gradually give your weight into the mattress and allow yourself to be supported. Perhaps you can sense the pull of gravity on you through the mattress. Allow your weight to yield to this pull. Let your awareness travel from your head along your neck and spine through your pelvis, hips and legs, and finally into your feet. Notice where you feel breathing. Just notice, without trying to change anything.

Notice how your legs feel as you are lying. Reach a little with your heel, lengthening your leg and how that influences you elsewhere. Then give up the reaching and allow your leg to come to rest where it wants to. How does the foot come to rest now, into the mattress? Do you notice any changes from before you reached with your heel? Try the same reaching experiment with the other leg. Any influence in breathing? Notice how your two feet and legs feel now as you are lying.

Can you feel the air on the bottoms of your feet? Do you feel the spaces in between your toes? Gradually spread your toes apart, just a little, without straining. Allow a little more space, a little more room between them. Notice how this first foot feels, now that you've allowed your toes to experiment with the space they would like. Try it out with the other foot, spreading your toes gently. Notice how that foot feels as you give up the effort of spreading and allow your toes to take the space they need right now.

Gently raise your knee toward the ceiling, allowing the back of your knee to come a little way from the mattress. Then give up the effort and let your leg rest into the mattress. Notice how your leg settles into the mattress. Try out the same movement with the other knee.

Gently tilt your pelvis so that your lower back comes closer to the mattress. What happens in breathing as you allow this small movement? Gradually give up the effort of movement and allow your pelvis, back and legs to rest more into the mattress.

Notice how your shoulders and upper back feel right now as you are lying. Reach gently with one of your elbows toward the foot of your bed. Give up the reaching, and allow any changes that are needed in lying. Try out the reaching movement with your other elbow. Do you notice any influence in breathing?

Notice the sensations in your hands and the sense of space between your fingers. Spread your fingers and allow your hands to widen. This movement may travel like a stretch into your wrists and beyond. Just be true to the sense of need for more space in you, as you pay attention to the sensations of these small movements.

If a yawn wants to come, let it. Give it all the space it wants. As you inhale, let your mouth open as wide as it wants. Free all those squelched yawns of yesterday! As the inhalation expands, let it move in you. As you take in air, let it go as far back into your head as it wants to. Let it pull your chin down or back or up. Maybe your neck responds with movement as the yawn climaxes. Is there a particular place from which this yawn seems to come? Trust that the yawn knows where it wants to go and will bring oxygen to needful areas. Trust that the parts of you that respond in your yawning are those areas which need movement, more space and oxygen or to be rid of carbon dioxide.

Yawning can be a space-making, energizing process that allows your body to attend to its needs. With a yawn, there is a contraction of the diaphragm muscle and then a relaxation. The jaw muscles have to give up their clenching to allow the yawn to reach its apex. Notice what you feel in your body, after a round of yawning. Watch infants and animals yawn and stretch for inspiration!

When you notice an urge to stretch in your shoulder or hip, allow the inhalation to come, mouth open, as if it was originating from this place in your shoulder or hip. With the next breath, feel the urge to stretch and allow the stretch and the breath to come from the same place. You might imagine you are breathing into that place.

Notice how your head is lying, how it meets the bed. Is there any sense of constriction in your neck or in the back of your head? Gradually bring your chin toward your chest, lengthening the back of your neck. Gradually give this movement up and allow your head and neck to find the space they need. What do you notice in breathing? Is there some movement that you could allow that would help create more space for circulation through your neck and head?

If you notice tension in the back of your neck, you may want to experiment with tennis balls in a sock. Put two tennis balls in a sock and tie the end. Place the sock under your neck and find just the right place to meet your holding. Breathe. Or you could use a vibrator. Or you could curl your fingers and place them where your skull meets your neck as you are

250

lying. The weight of your head on your fingers creates tension-relieving pressure. Notice your breathing as you rest into your finger tips or tennis balls. Allow those muscles to soften so that circulation can move between your head and the rest of you.

Spacious head

Using the heels or the fingertips of both hands make small circles moving the scalp over your skull bones. Focus on your temples and behind and above your ears. Knead your ears between your fingers and gently pull on them. Can you feel that inside your ear? Using the fingers of one hand, stroke firmly from the bridge of your nose, up into your forehead and then over to one eyebrow and then the other. Smooth and widen your forehead, wiping away all cares and concerns of the day.

Turn your attention to your mouth and jaw area. Notice whether you feel some constriction or clenching. Gently, but firmly, press into your jaw muscles with your fingertips. Let your jaw muscles soften and allow your jaw to sink as if its own weight was pulling it down. Allow the inside of your mouth to soften. Feel how your tongue lies. Let your tongue rest and give up any suction (on the insides of your mouth) you might become aware of. Explore the front sides of your teeth with your tongue, as if you were wiping away any residue of food from them. Take a minute and notice how your mouth feels now. How much space is inside your mouth? Experiment with taking inventory of your teeth with your tongue, unless it tickles too much!

Place the heels of your hands just under the edge of your jawbone on each side, extending your fingers up toward your ears. Allow your hands to take the shape of your jaw. Let your fingers and hands soften, allowing your cheeks to fill your hands with their softness.

Notice where the breath comes into your head; follow it inside your head. Feel the area between your two eyes as the breath moves through it. Notice the temperature of the air as it moves into your nose. Feel the breath travel down into your neck and chest. If you find yourself thinking too much, allow your lips to part slightly, still breathing through your nose. Rest into the movements of breathing. Place your palms over your eyes with the heels of your hands resting on your cheekbones and your fingers reaching up to your forehead. Allow the warmth and darkness provided by your hands to comfort your eyes. Let your eyes find a resting place inside your head, giving up all efforts to see.

If you want to go to sleep now, sense your way into your favorite sleeping position and do the "rest into it" meditation. On the other hand you may want to use this experiment to prepare for meditation before you go to sleep.

Pelvis curling

Experimenting with "curling" your pelvis will help you get in touch with your neck, spine, pelvis and pelvic floor as well as breathing. If you first awaken your neck and the rest of your spine with the Child Pose experiment you are likely to feel more clearly what unfolds in your bodyself with this experiment.

Lie on your back with your knees bent, the soles of your feet resting on the bed or floor. Experiment with moving your two feet closer together or further apart to discover where they best support your legs for the moment. Massaging your feet beforehand will help you

251

sense the support of what's under you. Enlivening your feet in this way "grounds" your energy so it literally has some place to land. Or you can massage your feet while you are lying by putting one foot on your knee and reaching down with both hands. Grasp your foot with both your hands and work the bottom of your foot with your thumbs. Treat each toe individually by holding the toe back with one hand and stroking the underside of that toe with the finger of your other hand. Then you are likely to sense each toe's existence. What is happening in breathing as you stroke?

Notice how you are contacting what's under you through your back, neck and head. Allow your weight through you into the mattress or floor as you sense breathing. Gradually tilt your pelvis so your lower back comes closer to the mattress. Allow the deeper muscles to do this movement so you don't have to use your abdominal muscles. At first it may feel as if you are gently pushing against the floor with your feet to create this tilt. If so, this pushing is not necessary. There are deep core muscles beneath your intestines that can create this movement. Let this movement be small. No need to lift your pelvis away from the floor. Just as gradually give up this effort and allow your pelvis to come to resting on the floor. What happens in breathing as you make this movement? Is there any influence along your spine, neck and head?

Do you sense anything of your sit bones and the soft pelvic floor between them? As you continue to curl and uncurl your pelvis notice breathing and at the same time, the condition of your pelvic floor. Experiment with tightening your "pelvic diaphragm" and then allowing it to soften. If you are not sure how to sense your pelvic floor, tighten the muscle you would use to interrupt the flow of urine. This subtle but important muscle called the "pubo-coccygeal" muscle lies in the center of your pelvic floor and connects your sitting bones. Sometimes called the "pelvic diaphragm", it does not cause respiration like the diaphragm in the chest does but it can respond to breathing. To strengthen and increase awareness of this vital muscle, tighten pelvic floor to the slow count of ten and soften to the count of five. Repeat this ten times. Be sure you can feel the softening and release in between contractions. If you begin to feel uncomfortable practicing this movement, you may be experiencing some emotion in reaction to the sensations being stirred up. You could be feeling fear, anger, shame or sexual or any combination of these. Take a closer look at what is coming up for you by listening to your bodyself voice could increase your capacity for self-soothing.

If you notice you are distracted by your thoughts, let your lips part slightly. Easing tension in the jaw can help quiet the mind. Jaw, neck and eye tension are stimulated by thinking. You might also try bringing your hands to cover your eyes, palms resting on your cheekbones, fingers on your forehead. Or place an eye-pillow over your eyes. This light weight stimulates the calming function of the nervous system. Scented with a soothing fragrance such as lavender, this pillow can be even more conducive to shifting to Let Go . . Alternatively, let the heels of your hands rest on your jawbone so your fingers bring soothing awareness to your cheeks and jaw.

Continue with gentle curling and uncurling the pelvis as long as it interests you. Take your time to let each movement complete itself. You may notice a need for more lengthening in your neck. Pay attention to changes in breathing or sensation. This movement can be very helpful for easing tension and lengthening the lower back as well as increasing awareness of the pelvic floor. You may notice how your neck, jaw and lower back tension are connected – easing one area facilitates letting go in another. As you gently rock your pelvis, you may eventually rock yourself to sleep. Now how is that for tucking yourself in!

As you are lying, notice how breathing feels. How much space does breathing want? Without trying to alter breathing to be some preconceived way, notice how it is right now. Allow any changes in lying so that breathing can have its way in you. Your need for circulation, here or there, changes with each moment. The inner space you need for living changes momentarily with the requirements of your external and internal situation.

This sensing experiment, which is also an excellent preparation for meditation, will help you release tension in your neck, jaw and pelvis as you move more into your bodyself experience and out of your busy thought-filled head. As such, it can be helpful in fostering that drifting off feeling when you first lie down or to help you fall back asleep if you wake up during the night.

Abdominal massage

Whether performed in the morning or evening, an abdominal massage is helpful to keep your intestines functioning properly – moving things along, shall we say? Stretching the visceral muscles, like those in your intestines causes them to reflexively contract thus moving along whatever is in the intestines. Lie on your back with your knees bent and your feet about a foot apart, "standing" on the floor or bed. Gently press into your abdomen with the fingertips of one or both hands. Notice what you feel in response to this touch. At first just press into your abdomen, breathe and then let your hands come away. Are there any aftereffects such as changes in sensation or subtle movements? Then once again, sink into your abdominal depths with your fingertips and then move your fingertips back and forth a few inches. Feel for rope-like cords and dense areas. You may be able to tell when you have found your colon because of the internal sensations your deep stroking evokes. Take your hands away and notice what you feel now.

In general, the colon begins in the lower right hand corner of your abdomen and continues up the right side to about the height of your navel. Then it turns and stretches across your middle to your left side, where it bends once again and descends along the left side toward your back and down into the lower pelvis and into the rectum. You can massage along this pathway starting on the left side with pressing and gently rocking. Work slowly back up the colon to where it crosses your middle to the right side and then follow it back to where it begins. You are likely to experience some movement of gas under your fingertips during this time or immediately afterwards. The next morning you may find that your bowels are moved more easily. In any case, this kind attention is gratefully received by your bodyself. Just try it! Take note of any images that arise.

Waving "Goodbye" to tension and stress

Lie on your back and become aware of your whole length, from your toes to the top of your head. You can begin with a small circular movement in your ankles and feet, both feet at the same time, if that appeals to you. Let this movement increase so that you feel a stretch in your calves. Spread your toes, allowing them to become involved in the movement as you feel it. Let the movement travel up your legs into your pelvis.

As your knees get into it, allow your legs to move as they like, taking up as much space as they want to. Let your wrists and hands pick up the movement, rotating your hands and spreading your fingers apart, as it feels good to do so. Allow the movement to spread into

253

your elbows and shoulders, neck and head. Let your whole spine come into undulating movement. Perhaps like a snake shedding its skin. Or, a beleaguered person who sheds the cares and fuss of the day for a renewed sense of aliveness. Or a belly dancer that is too tired to stand up but still has some movement left in her. Or a hardworking individual who feels compressed and trapped by the requirements of his/her life and seeks the freedom and flow of movement. Or some primordial being whose essential nature is movement.

Let the movement grow as big or as small as it likes. The wave can move up or down your body. It can die out or bring your whole body into movement. Begin it in your belly or in your pelvis. Thrashing around is permitted, even recommended as long as it comes by itself. Don't forget breathing! You may try opening your mouth so your breath is more audible. Let some sound come out with your breath. Continue until you are satisfied. Lie quietly afterward and allow yourself to feel the space you call your "self". Take all the space you need, take all the space you dare! Pay attention to your contact with what lies below you and above you - what is touching you now?

As you breathe in and out, notice how moment-to-moment, the space you occupy increases and decreases with the size of the space around you. Your shape and the shape of what surrounds you changes with each breath. At the same time, you exchange molecules with the surrounding air. Your essential life processes involve rhythm and exchange - the intense and immediate intimacy of living and of breathing. Rest into this sense of contact and accommodation with what surrounds you. What you need for the night's sleep is at hand (and afoot!) and freely available as you make yourself available to it by sensing and giving into it. Allow your tension to move out with your exhalation.

This wave motion can also be experienced when you lie on your side or stomach. Or, lying on your back you can "wave" from side to side. You can start anywhere with the "wave" and allow it to travel to another area of yourself or to include all of you at once. Play with it. Each time you try it, experiment and find out what invites your total attention. The movement that involves you completely will be most satisfying and release the most tension. Your involvement in that movement can bring you into the present moment and you may experience an energy shift. What was once a tight holding place perhaps accompanied by pain, will become more fluid and eased. You may experience a delightful kind of awakening energy or you may feel a quiet aliveness. When you feel out exactly what is needed in your movement – stretching, yawning or breathing, you will feel more present and peaceful because you are in contact with your bodyself and entered the moment. A sad commentary on the everyday mind-set is the fact that the experience of being present is often referred to as an "altered state!"

Contacting what is needed in yourself, whether it is a movement, a yawn, a glass of milk or a good cry, brings you into the present and makes it more likely you will be able to satisfy this need. Once satisfied, you may experience a truly deep resting state. When you focus on the small detail of a need and embrace it, your focus will broaden as you shift to Let Go . . If you are not present to your need state, you can't satisfy yourself and the tension of that need lingers so you remain contracted and "smaller". Sometimes all that is needed for a sense of relief is for you to focus precisely on your need and embrace it. As you feel through the need for change and allow it, you are likely to come to a new lying and then another; before you know it, you are fast asleep.

"Hang twenty" wave

The expression "Hang Twenty" is a play on the surfer's term "Hang Ten" which refers to the ten toes on the edge of the surfboard. Hang Twenty refers to the contact of the ten toes and fingers on the bed or floor! The "on all fours" position is very conducive to releasing spine tension. It is best done on the bed because the bed can support you as you allow the wave movement to carry you into new positions. A good place to start the movement is in the pelvis, tilting forward and backward. Let a wave pulse develop and travel up to your shoulders and into your neck and back down to your hips. You can also move side to side, swaying left to right along your spine. The wave can move in any direction. Initiate the first pulse and then the movement can continue. Try not to make an exercise out of it as in "Ten times to the right, ten times to the left", but allow the wave to find its own form. Explore the space with your waving body in all three dimensions, front to back, side-to-side, top to bottom. This undulating movement is a welcome change from the more linear movement characteristic of most daily activities and *she* loves it!

Rag doll ball

It's hard to think about anything when your arms and legs are rolling about on your bed. Rolling each limb like it is attached to a rag doll instead of to a stressed-out, tense human being is a quick way to get some relief from bodymind tension. Add your head and trunk to that rag doll action and you'll forget about those worries in no time. Sometimes it's fun to let out some sound as you shake yourself loose from those pesky, daily bodymind concerns.

Make a guided tour of your contact points

Contact points are where you contact the world. Visit each place and remember how it has helped you today. Thank it and let it rest.

Ankles and feet: for allowing you the sense of ground to take a stand and to take steps, especially those "baby" steps toward something difficult

Arms and hands: for reaching out to others to give and receive support

Trunk and spine, sit-bones and breathing: for supporting your actions and life force energy, giving you "guts" and "backbone"

Jaw and lips: for taking in nourishment, expressing feelings and desire

Eyes: for contacting – receiving and reaching
Heart: for resonating - giving and receiving love

Alternatively, pick one area as a sensory focus during decompression activities: lips, brows, feet, neck, abdomen, legs, pelvic floor or hands. As soon as you get home from work, you could take some time to heighten the sensations in this area (massage, sensing experiment or exercise). In the shower, you could attend especially to this area and afterward, massage lotion into it. You could bring your attention back to this area as a kind of meditation until you drift off to sleep. In fact you are likely to increase your ability to shift to Let Go . . when you cultivate your awareness of this one area for the next 24-hour period.

Eye pillows

Tension around your eyes is often so habitual, you have no sense of it until it beings to melt. Thinking and eye tension, not to mention, tension in the neck are intimately connected. The experience of these relationships can be had by following the guidelines for coming to lying and sitting or you can read my own experiential accounts of them. To increase the sensations you feel around and in your eyes, try using a weighted eye pillow. They come in many varieties - various sizes, weights, colors, textures and scents. They can be put in the refrigerator for cooling to give you a refreshing new perspective. The darkness fosters melatonin release and the gentle pressure on the eyeball facilitates the shift to Let Go . . Eye pillows can also be used for naps or for falling back asleep when you wake up in the night.

Feet first!

Coming fully into your feet will help you get out of your busy head. Before you get in bed, wash your feet. Use a small brush or foot scrub to stimulate and soften the skin of your feet. For an additional sensory treat, try lying on your back and apply lotion on both feet simultaneously with your opposite hands! That is, massaging your left foot with your right hand and vice versa, heightens sensitivity to what you are doing and keeps you on the bodyself side of the street. Then, using the fingers of your left hand, slide between each set of toes on the right foot and vice versa. Go slowly, one at a time, using a different finger for each space. Taking your time will increase sensitivity in your hands as well as your feet. Then bend back each toe, one at a time, toward the top of your foot. As you hold the toe back with one hand, use the forefinger of your other hand to stroke from the toe tip down the underside of your toe to the ball of your foot. Notice how your toes and foot feel now. Do they feel longer, more connected, more open or more sensitive? As you are lying explore the kinds of movement your toes, heels and ankles like to make.

Smallest movement

If you need a nearly effortless bodyself focus to help you drift off to sleep, try making the smallest possible muscle contraction you can - a contraction so small that someone else would not be able to see it. I like to initiate this contraction in my trunk, either in my abdomen or lower back. Since this movement is so small it takes very little energy and the focus it requires helps you stay with your bodyself experience and brings your attention away from your Let's Go! mind waves.

Rest into it – creating sensory em<u>bed</u>dedness

"Rest into it" experiments can help you fall asleep more readily whether you are just going off to sleep or when you have awakened in the "middle of the night". You have already created a restful place for sleeping and you have decompressed with exercises such as stretching and writing. You may have just finished working with lying and taking the space you need. You may find that while you are feeling more restful, your mind is still too busy and needs something soothing to focus on. These "rest into it" suggestions can take you one step closer to resting into a deep and rejuvenating sleep. And, even if you don't fall asleep, you will feel rested.

These "rest into it" experiments can give you a feeling of being contained or received by something larger than yourself. They can create in you a sense of settling into, being supported and nurtured, and perhaps listened to, as you go off to sleep. These practices may give you a feeling of protection so you can trust yourself to the tug of sleepiness without fear of harm as you give up your normal watchfulness. The sense is like when a child is soothed by its caretaker so it can gradually yield to sleep. You are now the caretaker and the one who needs caretaking. You prepare the environment – the soft or crisp sheets, the soft or firm mattress, the light or heavy blankets, just the right amount of air and temperature. You may spray a soothing scent in the air. You can charge the luminous plastic stars, which are stuck to your ceiling and create your own sleeping universe. You place a peaceful painting, poster or sculpture by your bedside. Before you close your eyes, take in this inviting environment you have created.

Resting into <u>lying</u>: As you lie in bed, allow your weight to be supported by the bed. Allow any changes that are needed so you can come more fully into contact with what you touch. Notice the feel of the sheets and your nightclothes against your skin. Is there a sense of the weight or softness of the covers? What do you need to feel even more "snuggled" in? Covers higher around your shoulders? More space to be? Are your feet free or pressed?

Some people find comfort in "hugging" a pillow or laying an arm and/or a leg over a body pillow as they fall to sleep. Feel your weight sink into the pillow and notice how its softness accommodates you. You may also enjoy the feel of a pillow behind you, whether or not you have one in front of you. Your ultimate pillow arrangement may look like a fort. No matter! Your appreciation of your relationship with your pillows can grow as you experiment.

You may find a sense of containment in putting something soft, silky or smooth over the top of your head, your eyes and/or around your ears, leaving only space for breathing. Notice how your head and neck are lying and whether more support is needed. You may need to allow a small shift so you can give your weight into the pillow, as your neck muscles lengthen and your head sinks. Can you sense the air on your skin or a scent in the air? Rest into the sense of lying in bed, caressed or cradled by the sensations of comfort all around you.

Resting into <u>breathing</u>: Let yourself expand into the bed and the pillows with each breath. Can you feel the movements of breathing against the bed and the bedclothes? Tune into those sensations and the rhythm of your breathing. Can you feel the air going into your nose or mouth? Can you feel the air on the back of your throat? The movement in your chest? And abdomen? Maybe your head moves ever so slightly with each breath? Let your attention rest on one place where you most notice breathing. When thinking penetrates your sensing, gently bring your attention back to the sensations of breathing.

Resting into the sense of <u>being</u> <u>taken</u> <u>care</u> <u>of</u> <u>by</u> <u>your</u> <u>organism</u>: You may become aware of the sense of exchanging air with what surrounds you. You may find comfort in the recognition that there is plenty of oxygen to breathe and at the same time, the air around you dutifully absorbs what you don't need. You may be soothed by the thought that your organism, your physiology, will take care of your breathing needs all through the night, without your having to do anything. In fact, your organism, by design, will repair and restore itself as you sleep.

Resting into the "surround": The sense of exchanging air with your environment may also comfort you in another way. As you inhale, you expand into the space around you. That surround space becomes smaller as it accommodates your need for space. As you exhale, the surround fills up the space created by the compression of your abdomen. The surround faithfully maintains contact with you and allows you the space you need, never coercing or never abandoning you. The experience of contactful breathing is available whenever you want it. Rest into the intimacy of breathing as you drift off.

Resting into images: You may have a special peaceful place that you can create in your mind. Once you are deeply relaxed, imagine this place and pay particular attention to the sensations attendant on being in this place. What do you see? What do you touch, smell and hear? Imagine yourself resting into this peaceful place as you go off to sleep. If you don't have such a restful place, you may find one by listening to a guided visualization tape made for this purpose. Being able to connect with this peaceful place requires practice and not trying too hard. You can also use an image from a memory of the steadying, heartfelt presence of another. Rest into the eyes of the other, taking in the feelings of being seen in your distress and being taken seriously and cared for.

Resting into sounds: You may find that listening to a tape through headphones or using a sound generating machine is helpful in taking you over the crest of wakefulness into sleep. Sophisticated devices are available for this purpose and are available through holistic health catalogues and websites. Certain sounds are helpful in masking potentially disturbing sounds, such as those made by unruly neighbors! Comforting sounds like soothing music can help quiet your mind. Sounds of nature like a stream flowing over rocks or ocean waves, create a kind of white noise that I have found particularly effective in blocking out random background sounds. Several meditation-enhancing devices have been created which range from fountains to tiny balls that fall over chimes making a random pinging sound. Using a mantra is another way to rest into a "sound" – a self-generated sound.

In sum, sensing prepares you to rest into something larger than yourself by heightening your sense of your bodyself. As you notice, focus and follow through on what your bodyself needs at the moment, you can give yourself more to resting into your bed, breathing, prayer, etc. When you feel out exactly what you need and give it to yourself, you can experience an easing of tension and an increase in your inner space. When you get it just right, you may experience the Goldilocks principle and feel a sense of completion and shift to Let Go . . And just as sensing can lead to an energetic experience of completion, so too, can meditation.

Meditation: Experiencing the Let Go . . Subtle Energy of Completion

Through releasing muscle tension and increasing awareness of breathing, the activity of sensing expands your sense of inner space and leads to a sensory sense of completion. Meditation, on the other hand, affords the space for a more cognitive sense of completion. When you meditate at the end of your day, various unfinished situations, tasks, conversations, and events will often come to mind. You are likely to remember things you'd forgotten in the course of your busy day, so keep some note paper handy. Give those thoughts a place to be so they do not have to continue to recycle. Meditation not only affords the occasion for completion but also, for beginnings. Creative ideas are also likely to come to you during this time.

I've noticed that a pleasurable feeling of satisfaction arises upon completion of a task. It is as if I am completed in some way, not just the task. I feel less scattered and more peaceful. This feeling is as if some other part of me is thanking me for giving attention to what it has had to hold onto, keep up in the air, while I was distracted doing other things. The tension of incompletion is released and I come more to resting. So whether it is a completion of a task or internal conversations, the expression of an emotion, the remembering of something forgotten, give it time to unfold. It is waiting for you to slow down and take time to listen and acknowledge its presence.

Completion of tasks

Focus on each activity as you do it and bring it to completion. The completion of each task will build the subtle Let Go . . energy and give you a sense of peaceful union with your bodyself. For example, you are engaged in brushing your teeth and you suddenly remember you need to set out your vitamins for the next day, try to resist the impulse to leave the bathroom. Instead, focus on your breath, exhale and feel your feet on the floor – one at a time. Breathe and focus. Don't fragment your bodyself experience by interrupting yourself. Take the first task to an end and savor the sense of completion by noticing how clean your teeth feel. Perhaps you would like to take this cleaning a step further by using the gum stimulator? Finishing the cleaning and savoring the feeling will deepen your Let Go . . sensing.

You might be wondering now how to reconcile the advice in the preceding paragraph with the admonishment in the previous chapter to follow your spontaneous impulses and "Do it now!" in order to ride the Let Go . . wave and keep the Let Go . . shift unfolding. Which option you choose depends on your goal and your assessment of the situation. In the decompression period you want to maximize the sense of slowing down to increase the momentum of Let Go . . While it is true that completion of tasks increases Let Go . . positivity, there are only so many tasks you can complete in any decompression period. If you find that notion unsettling, you may need to consider other, more slowing-down kinds of self-soothing besides the number of tasks you can complete in a given period! Shades of the familiar Let's Go! vs. Let Go . . challenge.

A good guideline is to try not to interrupt yourself when you are already in a task and bring that task to completion before starting another. Leaving tasks incomplete can lead to a scattered, anxious feeling that may result in more forgetting and mistakes. Each unfinished task that snags your attention, triggers a bodyself impulse to the movements that are needed to complete the act. When you don't carry out the act, you have to repress the movement toward completion and that takes energy. Enjoy the subtle energy of satisfaction with task completion and then embrace the next task. If you fear you'll forget what occurred to you, write it down. Or in the previous example, you could put the vitamin bottle out on the table as a reminder and continue brushing your teeth. If you find you just <u>have</u> to move about, tune into the sensations in your feet as you walk and stay with your bodyself experience.

Completion of efforting Let's Go! by resting into Let Go . .

Meditating before sleeping is an ideal time to practice "resting into". "Resting into" in the context of <u>sensing</u> invites you to rest into sensations, such as resting into the sensations of breathing or lying. "Resting into" in the context of <u>meditation</u> involves more of a sense of resting into an intention such as to be mindful, to surrender or to focus on a mantra or affirmation. "Resting into" embodies the sense of being listened to, whether you feel listened to by yourself,

259

God or the "universe". Just the sense of being listened to can be stress-relieving. When you sense you are being listened to, you have the possibility of "turning over" or surrendering your concerns to a larger "something", at least for the time being. As you sit, imagine giving over yourself, your fate or your concerns to something "greater than yourself". Perhaps you'll invoke a sense of opening yourself to guidance in order to feel which way to go now. In this effort, silently focusing on the phrase "Thy will be done" can be helpful. Sometimes I ask *her* to guide me and this intention makes me more available to my bodyself messages as I go off to sleep.

Sensing before meditating can greatly facilitate your ability to sit more comfortably and to notice your breathing. If you sit cross-legged, experiment with which leg you fold under first. I notice a distinct difference in the balance of weight in my sitting bones when the right leg is folded first. No right or wrong here - just experiment to feel out what allows you to feel more supported and present. Freeing the holding in your neck, shoulders and head will allow you to come to more quiet as you sit.

Allowing your head to sink toward your chest and then gradually return to "the vertical" is a sensing meditation that prepares you for sitting meditation. As you do, your neck muscles lengthen, your breathing responds and you may feel changes all through you. As you give yourself to these sensations, your thoughts become quieter and your breathing comes more easily. Notice any tension in your jaw, lips or forehead and allow those areas to soften. Sometimes you will feel an impulse that brings your head back to the "vertical" seemingly effortlessly. Other times you may feel a need to allow your head to come back up, so follow through with it. As you give to the needs for change all through you, you come to more quiet and readiness to focus on breathing.

As you sit, allow the unfolding of your thoughts, feelings and images – let them play out as if you were watching a movie. Meanwhile continually and gently return your attention to breathing. Remember, key to meditating is in the gentle attitude with which you guide your attention back to your breath and now you are preparing yourself for resting. Perhaps it would be helpful to treat your mental activity like a filmstrip that will eventually run out, only to start up again the next morning. But for now, it's time to just let it run its course as you prepare for a long, peaceful, sound sleep. You listen respectfully with kind attention, accepting whatever comes up and thereby, letting go. As situations and thoughts complete themselves you will experience a settling and a sense of peaceful energy. There is only one thing to do now and that is to return your attention to your predetermined focus.

You may find that your focus is enhanced if you silently repeat to yourself a word with each exhalation, like "Peace" or "One". Or perhaps you prefer a "double header" mantra like a word or phrase with your in-breath as well as with your out-breath. For example, with inhalation, intone the phrase "Let Go" and with the exhalation, "Let God". You can rest into the rhythm of breathing by focusing on the kinesthetic sensations attendant on breathing. Or you can rest into the tactile and temperature sensations of breathing as you notice where you feel the breath moving in and out of you. Whatever helps you return to your focus in a gentle way can be of value.

Such listening and acceptance can bring a sense of resolution and quiescence. I make this pre-bedtime meditation time less formal so I don't set a timer. Instead of sitting on my meditation cushion or in a chair, I sit on my bed. When I feel more peaceful, I can more easily slip between the sheets and fall asleep.

Completion of emotional situations

As you meditate you may also experience emotions connected with various unfinished situations. How easily you can "experience through" these emotions so that the situation can come to completion, may have much to do with how comfortable you can be with feeling powerless to change a situation. Meditation as it is offered here is not about dampening yourself or becoming detached from your emotional nature. Meditation can give you the possibility of allowing your emotions to move through you, just as you allow your thoughts to pass through you. However, as frequently noted in this discourse that is far more easily said than done. Many people have some difficulty with feeling emotions, especially those associated with helplessness. When threatened by an unwanted emotion you may notice a tendency to detach, deny or do something to distance the experience.

The energy of the unwanted emotion(s) accumulates and threatens to overwhelm, the more the experience of the emotion is resisted. Resistance could mean increased muscle tension, obsessive thinking, anxiety, depression, acting out, dissociation or turning on the TV. You may even try to meditate in order to detach from unpleasant emotions. At those times you may seem a little spacey to others. Sometimes this kind of "detachment" results from a "closed heart"– a heart that has closed in response to the pain of having to live with other closed hearts. Sadly, a closed heart can influence another's heart in the same direction. Happily, an open heart can support the opening of another's heart. In order to not use meditation to push away your emotions, you are likely to have to feel your heart to its very bottom. A very good way to start doing that is to listen to your emotional voice.

Listening to Your Emotional Voice: Let Go . . Sweetness

The following expresses my sense of how *she* would say what *she* wants. *How important am I to you anyway? How respectfully could you treat me? Would you lay me tenderly in bed? Would you notice me as you put lotion on your body? Would you massage your neck and feet so we can really rest and let go of the day's cares? Would you really pay attention to me while you feed me? Would you chew our food so we don't get a tummy ache? Will you fill your head with anxious thoughts and scare me just before we go to bed? Will you listen to me for a while before we go to sleep so I can finish telling you about what I felt today?*

If you take the time, I can remind you of things you've forgotten in the rush of getting home from work. You seem so anxious to open the mail and pick up your messages that you often don't realize that I need to just <u>be</u> for a few minutes. You act like you are hungry for stimulation and yet you have been stimulated all day! Why don't you take time to listen to me first? I could help you feel more soothed sooner in the evening if you listened to me. Give me a chance. I can save you time and energy. You know how I can help you prioritize. I have a good sense of what you really need to slow down when you get home. I'm dying to help you come home to me. And I will disappear if you keep ignoring me. What a waste, what a loss that would be!

Sometimes you act like you are too tired to take time to listen to me. Yet, you are still in a hurry. But even if you are tired, you can discover a renewed and softer energy when you listen to me and do what I want you to do. You rediscover that every time you do it, so why don't you keep doing it? The more you listen to me, the more I will talk to you. We could have a much more comfortable, satisfying and vibrant life. And you would have more energy and sleep better. We would do just the right amount of things and have fun too.

Sensing slows you down and eases tension so your inner space opens. Meditating helps you become more focused so you can hear what your emotional voice has to say. Now the question becomes whether you can support the feelings that come up as you listen for *her*? If you have had adequate childhood attunement or sufficient reparative work as an adult you will be better able to tolerate the frustration, angst and despair of not being able to control what is happening to you or around you. Even so, feelings of powerlessness or helplessness can be so noxious that you likely try to avoid them in any number of ways. Typical avoidance activities include the various addictions, dissociation, thinking, analyzing, overworking and net or channel surfing.

Learning to listen to *her* helps you penetrate your resistance to decompression activities that slow you down and prepare you for a good night's sleep. When you notice you are avoiding taking care of yourself in accordance with your decompression routine, ask *her* "What is the matter?" Alternatively, you could ask yourself, "What might I be feeling or avoiding if I wasn't watching TV?" You may be reluctant to turn off the TV or computer when you know it is time for you to make preparations for bed. Listen carefully for *her* attempts to let you know what is up. *She* may be withholding because you have not been in touch with her lately. Perhaps you've been engaged in Let's Go! for days, so you are out of practice shifting to Let Go . . and therefore woefully, out of balance. Ask again. Then attune to your experience in terms of images, sensations, urges, movements, gestures, facial expressions and sounds. Stay with it! *She* will answer eventually.

Your emotional voice expresses how you are feeling in the moment, be it tired, sad, happy, anxious or sleepy. Just ask! *She* has an opinion about any number of sensual things such as the taste of the food, the feel of the material against your skin, the temperature of the room, the position you are sitting in, how bright the lights are, the view out of the window, the sound of music and the antics on TV. *She* has strong likes and dislikes. *She* expresses *herself* simply as in "I like that! Yuck! Feels good! Tastes good! That hurts! Mmmmmm! Ouch! It's soft!" *She* also senses your needs such as for taking a nap, having fun, talking to someone, eating some protein or getting a hug.

If you have trouble imagining or sensing what I am suggesting, take a few minutes and try the following experiments. You are likely to have the best results if you have taken time to sense into your bodyself and are in a space free from distraction.

(1) Close your eyes and notice how it feels to be sitting or lying. If you notice any discomfort or even comfort, find some words or sounds to express that feeling. At first you may notice only sensations as you would in a sensing experiment. Or you might hear yourself thinking in words as this sense is forming in your mind (or as you feel for a sense of *her*). Next speak these words or make these sounds out loud. Having expressed the discomfort (or the comfort), sense what you would like now. Then allow some words to emerge to express that desire. Do you hear an emotional tone? How do you <u>feel</u> about this emotional tone?

(2) Imagine that you are about to go to bed. What would please you to see, smell, feel or hear upon entering your bedroom? How could you make it more appealing for yourself to snuggle into your bed? What image comes up? What are the words? "I want a ---" or "I wish ---" Do you notice an emotional tone in your words or feel any sensations in your body as you speak?

If you notice you feel critical of the emotional tone in your voice or of the discovery that you have certain needs and complaints, reading the chapters on meeting your resistance could give you clues as to what is behind this, less than charitable attitude. Your emotional voice is the key to understanding and dealing with your resistance to going to bed and to taking care of yourself. The catch is that, for the same reasons you have trouble taking care of yourself, you will also find it difficult to hear what your bodyself needs to communicate. The tension, thinking and preoccupation that accompany the sometimes stressful, busyness of Let's Go! can block out the more subtle sensations, urges, emotions, intuitions and images. However, as you begin to slow down sensations and emotions are more likely to be experienced.

How open you are to hearing how you feel will also vary from hour to hour, activity to activity. If you are very stressed or tired, you may find it difficult to tune into what that part of you needs or wants to tell you. More than any other time of day, your decompression period offers ideal opportunities to discover how to contact your emotional voice. Bathing or showering, getting a snack and sliding into bed all provide occasion for rich sensual experience to which you are likely to have an emotional response. As you get into bed, sense the sheets and the softness of the pillows and let some sounds come out to express how it feels. You might find yourself saying "This feels good" or "We like this!" or simply, "Soft!" or "Cool!" or "Hmmmm!" The purpose of encouraging you to express yourself this way is to help you feel that it is possible to feel more connected to your bodyself. The selection and savoring of a bedtime snack can give rise to numerous responses which can lead to your feeling more alive and in touch with *her* as you shift more and more into Let Go . .

Bathing or showering is a great time to elicit your emotional voice. One of the first times I contacted my emotional voice was when I got out of the shower into the cool air. The words "I'm freezing!" came. Feeling playful, I took it further and let myself express my reaction like a child would. Recall how children, fresh out of the bathtub, dance around, shoulders held high, arms waving, shaking and saying excitedly, "I'm freezing!" I felt a burst of happy energy just trying it out! No wonder they do that instead of stoically waiting through the whole drying process, not uttering a word, and silently shivering to themselves as self-respecting adults would do. What fun is that? Adults have learned not to be silly, not to be "so sensitive", dramatic or expressive. That is part of the problem. Another part is that adults often come to ignore the sensory aspect of bodyself experience.

The point of this experiment is not to become a child, of course, but to get more in touch with your bodyself so you can lighten up and shift to Let Go . . It is an attempt to make your sensory and emotional experience more salient and available to you so you can become less tense, stressed and preoccupied. Then you are better able to soothe yourself and get more rest.

So, getting in touch with *her* is about <u>expressing</u>, not <u>compressing</u> your bodyself. When you elicit *her* comments by asking, "What is the matter?" be prepared for complaints! If the idea of complaining is repugnant to you, it may be because of the same reasons you don't attend to your nurturance needs. Unexpressed complaints often underlie not going to bed on time. Perhaps you are not giving yourself enough time to just be or to have fun. All work and no play. *She* hates that kind of regimen. It nearly kills *her*. You will find yourself engaging in self-destructive activities if you do not give *her, her* due. You may end up with a headache, feel exhausted or suddenly indulge in candy or beer. You may have to be driven to extremes before you break down and get *her* message. *She* might then say, "This is too hard!" or "You are not listening to me" or "You are scaring me!" Why not cut to the chase and simply ask *her* "What is the matter?" and wait for *her* answer?

Ask, "What is the matter?": *She* speaks through complaints.

Let *her* answer in movement, sound, spontaneous writing, cries, images, and sensations. Ask the question and then wait for an answer. It will come in different ways. You may have to ask several times. *She* is there. *She* needs encouragement. Sometimes you will not be able to hear *her* until things get pretty bad. Then you may find yourself crying or feeling angry. If you suspect you are angry underneath, try stomping around. For example, showering is a good time to connect with *her*. The running water creates a sense of containment, privacy and dampens *her* sometimes boisterous sounds. You can do anything you want, you can even spit water at an imaginary someone. You can jiggle, yell, shake, stomp or cry. *She* is the guardian of the emotional recovery cycle that brings you back to Let Go . . If you need more support to feel what *she* is trying to tell you, call someone. When *she* feels heard, you can fall asleep more easily.

She can also give you clues as to "What is the matter?" in relationships. Getting in touch with *her* is the key to going through the emotional recovery cycle rather than staying stuck in an impasse. It is through *her* heart that you connect with others. If you close yourself to *her*, you will lose access to your heart and then you cannot accept the love that is in your life. When you ask *her*, "What is the matter?" *she* has a chance to share what is on *her* heart. *She* needs to show it to you so you can hear it, accept it and openheartedly share your feelings with the other person. You need *her* to feel love for yourself as well as to feel love for others and to receive their love. Then your sleep can be all the more sweet.

Sound your feelings: *She* speaks through sound and words not heard!

When you notice you are feeling a little down or cranky as you enter your decompression time, let some sound out that meets that feeling. It may be a growling or a grunting sound, a noisy or a soft sound, a cry or whining sound or perhaps some jibber jabber - it really doesn't matter! What counts is that you meet your feeling with a sound that moves your energy along. You may find a movement or a gesture or a facial expression that goes with that sound. By embodying the feeling through sound and movement, you can move right through that feeling and shift to Let Go . . If you are feeling bound up and burdened by tasks or people, try jerking your elbows back, one at a time with your exhalation. It might feel apropos to say, "Off!", "No!" or "Off my back!" at the same time. Or you may feel like stomping around, expressing those same sentiments. The point is to get your energy moving, to become unstuck, embrace and then move through whatever is blocking you right now so you can recover your aliveness before you fall off to sleep. Then you can awaken to the new day with more of your energy. Give *her* a chance and let *her* dance for *she* loves to sound and bound and giggle and wiggle.

Talk out loud: *She* may even make you laugh!

Speaking out loud is an excellent way to open communication with *her*, not to mention amuse yourself! For instance, voice your feelings about what is on TV or how you feel about the announcer telling you to stay tuned. You are having reactions anyway, so try externalizing them. You can talk to *her*, acknowledge her, thank *her* and encourage *her*.

Allow *her* to complain or to express *her* delight. Just open the communication – making it audible will help you move out of compulsive thinking and doing and into a more immediate experience of your moment. You may even have fun! What a way to end the day! You may find you experience more energy and a sweet sense of satisfaction. Talk to yourself in the interests of awakening and strengthening your bodyself voice which holds the key to your being able to shift to Let Go . .

Instead of saying, "Oh, I am having trouble right now" try "Oh, we (you) are having trouble!" Or, "We (you) don't like this show, this feeling, that person!" Or, "We (you) like this, this feels good!" Gradually you may notice your voice is more alive and you are feeling more playful and/or compassionate!

Consider becoming a "good enough" parent who is interested in the well-being of its child. However, in this case, the well-being you are interested in is your own. In the same manner a "good enough" parent attunes to its child, getting support to listen to your emotional voice will allow you to experience through fear, anger and grief as well as joy, love and pride. A good enough caretaker encourages play, expression and exploration as well as discipline and boundaries. As you discover how you need to be supported, you can come into balance and be better prepared for a new day. No matter whether you need more play or more discipline, *her* input can be of enormous value in strengthening your decompression routine.

Acknowledgment and encouragement: *She* responds with a sweet feeling of satisfaction

At last! And I am last __again__! You still look for me last! Like I am your last resort. I could be a real "resort" for you, if you let me be your first resort! If you tune into me and do what I guide you to do, you can feel as if you were on a mini-vacation. I can free you, if you ask me what I need! I am a direct line to your life force, delight, and passion even if I am angry, sad, or afraid. If you will contact me, I can bring you back to life! To give me life, you have to go after me and give me space to breathe and to inform your movements and sounds. You will sense me in waves of energy as you dance or even as you rest into bed.

Granted you discovered me last, after sensing and meditating didn't soothe you deeply enough. But, those practices did eventually lead to finding me. That's how you came to sense and massage yourself on that first "tucking-yourself-in" night. You didn't even know I existed until the morning after you tucked me in! To show you how happy I was, that morning I gave you the sweetest feeling I could. I was trying to insure that the next night, you would try to tuck me in again. On the whole, you have pretty faithful to me. But still why write about me last when you know that I am key to your well-being?

OK, I get it, you are writing about me last because that is logical. I would rather believe that you are saving the best for last, like dessert! Desserts are sweet and so am I. OK, I am not always sweet. In fact sometimes I get very angry or scared or sad. That is when you have trouble connecting with me. That is when your caretakers deserted you. And not the good kind of "dessert"! They left you in those scary out of control places where you felt overwhelmed by feelings. So you did to me what they did to you. I am so glad you found a therapist to talk to. He was not afraid of our feelings. In fact he liked being with feelings and he felt along with us and so we didn't feel so alone. Now that you can be with me so your upsets don't last as long and are not as intense as they used to be. All I ever wanted was to be taken seriously. And now you are doing that, most of the time anyway. I'm so happy you are telling others how they can be with their "me."

I love it when you when you tell me, "We did good!" or when you reassure me with "It's going to be OK!" I can tell you really mean it. That's why you feel so good after you say those things – I hear you and feel happy! That good feeling you feel is my "Thank you." I release de-stressing chemicals whenever you praise or reassure me. That old saying is true, "What goes around, comes around" – you thank me, I thank you. I'm the gold in the Goldilocks principle.

As you can hear, *she* expresses *her* gratitude as a sweet feeling. *She* likes to play on words and has a sense of humor. If you can connect with *her* before you go to sleep, you may have a happier feeling as you drift off and as you wake up.

Dance: *She* speaks through movement

At the beginning of decompression find some great music and let yourself be moved. Let the energy of your feelings literally move you through one feeling and then the next. Dancing is a good way to move through your emotional recovery cycle. As constriction gives way to expression, you are energized, happier and freer.

I know how to move you, just give me the time and space and I will show you. But you have to trust me. I thought you were going to burst the other night when you were feeling so bad, so constricted, so unseen, so alone and so frustrated. You felt so anxious because you were not really feeling me, you were pushing me down. Finally, you let yourself follow what I kept nudging you to do: you got up and let that amazing music that was playing take you into movement. You surrendered to me and let me move you. You burst into movement instead of exploding or getting tighter or more anxious. Why do you wait so long to let me take you? It is like my way is the last thing you consider. Why don't you get up and go when I flash you images of the ocean or the beautiful sky? You always put work first. That is why we end up watching TV so late. We have to have some fun – but according to you, only after we finish our work. But then we are just too tired to do anything fun. Besides, when you are tired you can barely hear me.

And, when you are too busy or too serious, you dismiss me like you did earlier that day when you played that thrilling music. I know you felt my urging you to dance – the music was so beautiful, it almost hurt to stay still. But you ignored me and when you got off the phone, you went back to work. Then as your frustration mounted (that was my doing!) you finally gave in. Only then could I fill you with the feelings of a ballerina and make you move your feet so fast, you could scarcely believe it was you. Finally you were free – light on your feet – lost to work and found to me. You let yourself be moved by the passion in the music that connected and resonated with your own pent-up passion. You see, you really do get tired of just sitting there and working. It is admirable, but only to a point, that you can hold yourself to the task the way you do. After that, you cause yourself undue constriction. You push further, resisting my pleas and then you feel depressed and unmotivated. Let me motivate you. You have to let me break you! That is what you are trying to tell the readers and yet in that attempt you hold yourself so tightly to the task that you stop doing what you are trying to promote with your writing! Well, I guess this is how you became an expert on resistance!

You know that if you let me speak through you, you will have better ideas and more energy. But tuning into me means slowing down and giving me space. When you are too anxious you are afraid to slow down. So you get tense and retreat into action and thinking. Then you make premature decisions that sometimes are costly in terms in time, money and emotional fallout. And all because you won't just sit with me or reach out to someone who will reach back to you. Then you get desperate and finally allow me to burst through. If you didn't hold yourself back from me, you wouldn't feel so desperate. And you are getting better. You are letting me talk to you more and you are talking to me.

Ask "what would be good or fun to do now?": *She* speaks through images, urges, intuitions, inklings and that "funny feeling".

She rarely uses words. The words I give to *her* come from the feelings that arise when I turn toward *her* and ask "What is the matter?" or "What would you like right now?" What I call "*her*" is really a "felt sense". *She* is a direct line to the language of bodyself in all of its manifestations. However, often *her* voice has a decidedly emotional tone because *she* really knows and feels what *she* likes and wants.

For example, in preparation for your decompression snack, you might ask yourself, "What would you look forward to, what would be fun to eat?" Fun might mean savoring something special to eat: some fresh mango, passion fruit yogurt or pomegranate ice cream. It may mean be being warmed by a favorite tea in a lovely cup as you leisurely read a set aside newspaper or magazine article. Something special, reserved just for you. It may mean slipping into your cozy kimono and accommodating slippers. What would feel good now? *She* knows, but will you listen and follow through?

Another consideration is whether you can wait for "dessert" – or do you need dessert first? Most of the time, I like to change clothes and take out my contacts before I treat myself to an evening snack and a looked-forward-to "read." But other times, the Let's Go! momentum doesn't give way to the need for bodyself connection and so *she* and I remain estranged.

What is needed at that very moment is <u>acknowledging</u> *her* need for relief and allowing a deep breath. "We did well today and now we get to have some fun, some rest, some time just for us!" That acknowledgement, in itself, brings relief and makes the time it takes to get ready to have this "dessert" break more tolerable. Acknowledgement is sweet. If only the contact lenses could be spirited out of my eyes, rinsed and disinfected. If only I had an invisible valet who could neatly hang up my work clothes and give me a little shoulder massage before I sit down to my evening's repast. Why not leave the tea bag, cup and the article, out on the table in the morning? Then it will be waiting for you when you get home, perhaps with your slippers. You might do that for a loved one, so how about yourself? How can you make your return home more welcoming, more fun, more delightful, and more soothing? If you follow through, you are likely to have the sense that somebody loves you!

If you literally find yourself fixated on what is for dessert, you might try checking in with *her*. Maybe you have not been nice enough to yourself lately and now are trying to feel sweet by eating sweet, instead of connecting with *her* and feeling what *she* really wants. When you get it just right, you are likely to experience a sense of sweet satisfaction.

You may need more discipline or you may need more play in your life. Tuning into *her* can help you with both. *She* likes to have some structure in *her* life because that structure helps with getting important things done. With those things accomplished or a plan to accomplish them, the feelings of helplessness are less threatening. So, set up a routine for yourself and then allow some flexibility. Sometimes the best thing is to first watch some TV and/or have some popcorn or a peach. Then get ready for the next day. If you tune into *her*, you will be more likely to get it right each night. Then you will feel easier, more settled and taken care of as you go off to sleep.

267

Stop criticizing yourself and check in with *her: She* speaks through cries in the night and feelings of dread and fright

The first time you really let me talk to you was in the shower one night, when I cried out that you were scaring me. You were scaring me with thoughts of what might happen and who was mad at you and so on. I just hated it. It was the last thing I needed to hear before bed. You were on your way to upsetting me so much that I would never have let you fall asleep. Thank goodness you listened to my reaction and felt sorry for what you were doing to me. I so needed for you to listen to me and then to stop terrorizing me. That is what you needed from your father but he just kept scaring you and then ignored you. You made a big impression on me when you let yourself feel my pain. I will never forget that! And now you are getting better and better about stopping yourself when you begin to be mean to yourself.

When you catch yourself being critical of yourself – "Stop!" Try to feel what you are feeling in response to the criticism. Give voice to your bodyself feelings. *She* needs to be heard. You may not have been able to speak up to the criticisms of your caretaker. At least *she* has a chance with you now. When you listen you might hear something like this: *Stop criticizing me. You make me feel so bad. I didn't do anything wrong. I try so hard. You don't give me any credit for that. I am not trying to do bad things. I am not bad. I am just being here waiting for you to notice, love and play with me. Stop scaring me. This is awful. It hurts me. I don't want to live when you do that. I just want to cry and hide and get away from you. But I need you, too. Please help me. Stop hurting me!*

You may find those words said in an angry or plaintive tone which gets you to really listen and be more compassionate. On the other hand, *she* may cry and then you are crying and through your tears, you reconnect to yourself again. Crying deepens the release by easing muscle tension and permitting fuller breathing. The release of pain-modulating endorphins soothes and can make you sleepy. Then it is even more likely that you can stop beating yourself up.

Customizing Your Decompression Period

1. Select a decompression time period.
2. Choose some signals to yourself that it has started.
3. Slow down, breathe and ask yourself "What would you like to do in this period?"
4. Complete organizing activities that need light. As you do, sense how you
    are sitting, standing, moving - breathe and ease.
    Clean contacts, teeth, etc.
    Write plans for next day, acknowledge accomplishments.
    Answer e -, voice, snail mail
    Plan for tomorrow: make a "To Do" list.
    Who do you need to call for consultation?
    Write about troubling issues in detail to give them a place to be
    until tomorrow - write "love" letters.
    Tidy up.
5. Prepare a treat for yourself: Drink, eat, read and savor!
6. Prepare your sleeping space:
    Bed, water, notepad, set clock, scents, lighting, temperature.
7. Bring tasks to completion and savor the satisfaction.
8. Notice, focus and follow through on sensations, emotions,
    images and that "funny feeling" so you can finish, find and feel
    what is needed and keep decompression unfolding.

9. Express, don't compress: dance and sound, breath and ground
   Talk out loud:
   Give voice to sensations and tension.
   Encourage yourself and acknowledge *her*.
   Talk back to TV.
   Interrupt criticism or worry and ask "What is the matter?"
   Ask what would you like to do, what would be fun/feel good?
10. Bathe or wash feet and face.
11. Trouble-shooting resistance by listening to your emotional voice:
    Listen for complaints.
    Ask what feeling might I be avoiding by distracting myself now?
    Allow tears, laughter, tantrums.
    Invite *her* back.
12. Go for the "Goldilocks" moment: Choose sensing
    activities: Lying, Pelvic curl, two-lip sensing, etc.
13. Meditate:
    Select a focus: sensory, mantra, breathing, Contact Points.
    Notepad nearby
    Dream incubation
    Thank *her*, it, God, yourself.
    Affirmations
14. Rest-into something "larger" than yourself, your bodyself, breath, God.

Decompression Principles for a Shift to Let Go . .

SLOW DOWN, BREATHE AND FEEL YOUR FEET ON THE GROUND.
NOTICE, FOCUS AND FOLLOW THROUGH.
SAVOR COMPLETION OF TASKS, ONE BY ONE.
EXPRESS, DON'T COMPRESS.
WHEN IN DOUBT, ASK, "WHAT IS THE MATTER?"
GO FOR THE "GOLDILOCKS" MOMENT.
REST INTO IT.

Tucking Yourself Back In

When you find you have awakened "in the middle of the night", say two or three AM, you must be careful not to further stimulate yourself so you can get back to sleep. The resultant wakefulness is fertile ground for nagging ruminations that go on for hours when your daytime defenses are no longer operative. Do not turn on the light for it can cue your biological clock that the sun has come up and it really is time to get moving. It is also very important not to look at the clock because your reaction to whatever time is indicated could increase your wakefulness and worry. If you have gotten up to go to the bathroom, don't let your mind go to scary places and terrorize yourself. This is a time when you are very vulnerable to worry and fears, so treat yourself tenderly in order to go back to sleep. In addition to vulnerability to emotional pain, sensitivity to physical pain increases in the wee hours of the morning and can trigger your awakening.

Try using your favorite simple sensory focus experiment such as allowing your lips or jaw to soften or your facial muscles to ease. Notice the softness and ease of your mouth and how gently your lips come together. Allow your eyes to soften into their resting places, taking the space they need. Sometimes it is helpful to gently touch the two corners of one eye with two fingers of one hand (forming a V) as you drift off to sleep. You make want to focus on feeling the space between your toes as you allow a slight spreading of your toes. Or perhaps you can attend to breathing, noticing the sensations of your breath in your nose or the movement in your abdomen. With each exhalation you could say "rest" or "peace". A simple focus is best for "resting-into" because effort making leads to wakefulness.

Refer to the Sensory Embeddedness section of this chapter for suggestions for "resting into". If you need stronger "back to sleep sensory medicine" because your head is already way too busy, try lying on your back, knees bent, with your feet flat and about a foot apart. Let your focus rest into the sensations in your feet and legs as you drift off. Alternatively, you could massage your feet. Grounding through your feet and legs, as mentioned previously helps quiet your thoughts.

You many find some relief by writing your concerns on paper and putting them into a box and close the lid for the rest of the night. Tomorrow is soon enough to attend to them and when you do, you will be more rested. If you find certain sounds soothing, then turn on your sound machine. Perhaps you have a peaceful or safe place that you like to travel to in your head. Or you could imagine the face of a trusted person or a spiritual image or icon and rest into it. Or keep some herbal drops by your bedside (as long as they are not contraindicated for you). You could take yourself through the progressive relaxation exercise of tensing and relaxing each part of your body, starting at your toes. You are likely to fall asleep before you even get to your knees! Alternatively or simultaneously, you could say to yourself something soothing like "You don't have anything to do now except rest. Rest is the best preparation for tomorrow. Even if you don't actually sleep, resting will help you."

If you expect you may be awakened in the night because that has been a pattern, it may help to know that it normally takes several weeks to decondition your nervous system. So when you do wake up you can soothe yourself by saying, "I am in the process of deconditioning my brain and eventually it will recognize that nothing is to be gained by waking up at this time. All is well and now we can go back to sleep." You can also give yourself some suggestions during your bedtime meditation about what you can do in the event you wake up. You can tell yourself that it is OK, if you do wake up and that you will easily drift back to sleep. Ask for *her* help or God's help or appeal to your organism to take care of you.

If you are consistently awakened by scary dreams or nightmares, you may want to consult professional help. Treat the nightmare as a vital communication from her, your psyche or your organism that needs to be addressed. You may be experiencing intense helplessness or powerlessness in some situation in your life and need more support than is available to you right now. Working with a therapist could lead to your feeling through and integrating your feelings of helplessness as well as dealing with the underlying problem which is causing those feelings so that you can get a good night's sleep.

16

WAKING YOURSELF UP

*"Each day is a little life"**

Awakening in the morning can be likened to being reborn. You have a chance each morning to feel renewed, refreshed, and recreated for a "little" life. Just as there is a period of labor before birth, giving time to waking up is excellent preparation for your delivery into the new day. Give yourself extra time in the morning for this process by setting your wakeup time fifteen minutes earlier. Experiment with what amount of time best meets your morning needs. Lying in bed in the morning in semi-wakeful quiet can ease your transition from the Let Go . . of sleeping to the nascent Let's Go! of wakeful activity. In fact, you may already prolong this delightful Let Go . . state by hitting your snooze button a few times. That behavior may be evidence that you need this pleasurable experience of Let Go . . deep resting and gradual awakening devoid of the demands of Let's Go! That said, now you can stop feeling guilty about that snooze button workout and indulge your morning's pleasure.

Dream-Catching

To invoke another metaphor, completion of the long night's journey into day is like the "Hero's Journey" on a small scale. What treasures or troubles have you brought back from your travel into darkness? Did you fly or did you cry? Or did you barely get by? What inspiration comes as you catch a hold of the remnants of sensations, emotions and images from your night's journey. Do you have a sense of any dream fragments? If so, write them down as soon as you remember them. Keep a special "dream catcher" notebook by your bed for your "dream mail"! With practice you will be able to write with your eyes closed so as to minimally disturb your recall from this fleeting state. Later you can work with these images. Try not to move or talk until you have reclaimed the dream experience. Remember, an uninterpreted dream is like an unopened letter to yourself.

Consider these fragments as messages from your bodyself – "pictures" of feelings that need to be felt through and integrated. You may have received an answer, in image form, to a question or dilemma on which you concentrated before going to sleep. A creative solution may be ready at your "dream-tips" if you just sink back into resting for a few minutes to catch the edge of your "dream net". These dream-catching techniques are offered <u>before</u> the following sensing experiments to underscore how important it is to <u>first</u> look for these bodyself messages upon awakening, even before your eyes open. So take time to drift and dream, letting inspiration arise and jotting it down.

You can receive clues about where you are stuck by looking at your dreams and identifying with the dream images. Treat the dream images as metaphors or narratives of emotional situations you find yourself in. For example, one morning I was feeling stuck, a little angry and unhappy. I felt as if I had I squashed myself. In the shower I asked myself, "What is the matter?" I saw an image of the worn-out, fungus covered, stubby toothbrush I had seen in a

271

dream earlier that morning. I recognized that this worn-out toothbrush was an apt metaphor for what I was doing to myself the past week. I was pushing myself by working hard and taking care of too many people.

On top of that, I had turned down two friends who offered support because I was engaged in writing. I had said "No!" to connection in order to write about balance. Now how ironic was that?! As I focused on the image of the toothbrush, I went into the contraction. This is what I am doing to myself: squeezing, using myself up, criticizing myself, imagining that people are mad at me, or will reject me. I realized then that I had been subtly beating myself up all day, the day before. No wonder that my brain gave me the image of a worn-out toothbrush to portray my existence: the toothbrush functions dutifully and repetitively with little thanks or joy – it just wears out and is unceremoniously thrown away when it is used up. Connecting with the toothbrush image allowed me to feel how worn-out, used up and neglected I felt. I cried and felt my anger – I took responsibility for what I had been doing to myself. I then had a chance to free myself. In fact, I was freeing myself as I connected with the stuffed-down energy – it was already flowing. Working with the listening practices and with my unresolved issues has allowed me to access and contain the feelings which evoke the dream images so I can recover and express my bodyself impulses.

A Sound Awakening

And yet a third metaphor: Consider your daily cycle of activity being like the earth's annual cycle of four seasons – "summer" corresponding to the active Let's Go! period of the day, and "fall" the slowing down decompression period of the evening. Then sleeping is likened to the season of "winter" and awakening to "spring" of morning. The somnolence of your sleepscape is pierced by the early morning noises of life awakening all around you. As you lie in bed, leave your eyelids closed. Take time to become aware of your sensory environment so you can awaken fully before leaving the bed. Feel the texture of your bedclothes against your skin, notice how the temperature of the sheets changes as your foot moves an inch or two.

Listen for the sounds inside and outside your room. Can you hear any birds chirping? Allow the bird sounds to create a larger universe in which to awaken. You may sense that your boundaries include all of the space that is circumscribed by the sounds, even when it comes from outside your abode. Can you allow this sense of quiet expansion of yourself into this world? A bird's song has become my "wake up call" to come back to myself in the morning. Hearing the bird makes me notice when I am already losing myself in thought. The bird's call penetrates the web of thought, I am already weaving and into which I am quickly disappearing. Now I have a choice and gratefully attune to what I can in the outside world. The bird's call gives me a choice about how to begin my day.

Waking up to the sound of a chime alarm can ease your entry into the day. The one I chose was the "Zen Timepiece*" which chimes once at the appointed time and then at successively shorter intervals after that. This way I have a progressive series of wakeup calls, all sonorously intoned as their gradually increasing frequency signals increasing urgency.

The following sections contain more suggestions for awakening to your bodyself experience and easing your entry into the day. Let sound and sensation be your guide to awakening. Give yourself time to feel life move through you into your toes, your fingertips and your nose! As you awaken, notice your expression, your posture, and your attitude as it is expressed throughout your whole bodyself. I find it helpful to lie on my back as soon as I awaken because it is more difficult (though, unfortunately, not impossible!) for me to fall back asleep in this position. Besides, this position has become a kind of "entering the day" signal to me, like the dimming of the lights marks the beginning of the decompression period. I take the prone position for naps as well, because then I tend to doze rather than sleep, with the resultant lesser likelihood of interference with my readiness to fall asleep at night.

The importance of acknowledging the moment of awakening with a change in position is underscored by the following example. One morning, when my chime alarm sounded, I didn't change my position nor did I take a sip of water, as is my habit when I first awake and sense the inevitable dryness in my mouth. I stayed in this sleeping posture, thinking and thinking. I did not drop down into sensing. I noticed my arms were pressed too close to my sides and my elbows stiff and achy. Still I did nothing to help myself. Could I be waiting for someone to help me? To drop down out of thought, I would have to follow through on what I sensed and stay with it. Eventually, I conceded I would continue in this discomfort until I took action. Finally I turned over on my back, put a pillow under my knees and began to sense. A stretch and a yawn came and then a sound. The lovely soft feeling began to grow as I felt a fluid connection all through me. What is key to a true "awakening" is my willingness to bow to my bodyself needs.

So, if your mouth is dry, take a sip from the glass of water by your bedside. Speaking of watering, if you need to go to the bathroom, get up and go as soon as you feel it. That "full bladder" sensation won't lessen, the longer you wait. You will only think more and become tenser. Once you get back in bed, you can continue your gradual awakening and surrender to the sweetness of your bodyself's gratefulness.

Sleep Mask Sensing

As you lie in bed notice how your head is lying. Is there tension in your neck or jaw? With your eyes still closed, allow your head to move so that the back of your neck elongates and your head is fully supported in this position by your pillow. Allow your head to sink into what supports it. As you turn your attention to your face, do you sense your "sleep mask?" Your sleep mask is the face you wear as you sleep and reflects habitual holding patterns. You may have noticed that the older you get, the more creased your face looks when you first awaken. Some of these creases come from frowning, grimacing or grinding your teeth as you live your tension during sleep.

Becoming sensitive to the holding pattern of your "sleep mask" will serve you throughout the day. During meditation, working at the computer, driving, exercising, reading (like right now!) or washing dishes, sense what is happening in your face and lips. Notice, focus and follow through on any holding you sense in the area around your mouth. Allow ease through your jaw area by letting your jawbone give to the pull of gravity by "sinking" a little. Are your lips pressed together? Is there a sense of not letting anything in or out? What do you sense of the inside of your mouth? How is your tongue lying? What is the condition of the inside of your cheeks? Notice if you are slightly sucking on the sides of your mouth. Can you give that up? How does the experience of your overall condition change? Sleep mask sensing is yet another way come into the moment with ease and presence and increase your capacity to shift to Let Go . .

Notice the sensations around your eyes. Are your eyes squinting or your eyelids squeezed together? Allow the area around your eyes to soften. Let your eyes find their resting place, giving up any efforts to see. I have noticed a direct correlation between holding around my eyes and obsessive morning thinking. It is much too early to start thinking like that! I need awareness of my bodyself to support and ground mental activity. Sensing my eyes during these times, I notice they feel crossed as if they were focused on the center of my forehead. If my eyelids were open and my eyes still in that position, I surely could not navigate. Gradually I feel what is needed to allow my eyes the space to rest. My attention moves to breathing, to birdsongs and to the budding sensations of lying in my bed.

Baby's "Awakening"

As you continue to lie, give to your need for space wherever you sense constriction and habitual holding. What do you sense in your torso? Are your legs akimbo? Is there a sense of compression in your neck? Are your toes crumpled or crunched by the covers? Give your toes a little more room - perhaps by gently spreading them. Are your heels pressing against the mattress? As you sense breathing, you may notice a yawn and a spontaneous stretch developing.

Explore what space is needed by your arms and legs. How do your legs want to lie? Gradually you begin to move out of your "sleeping pose" which reflects your habitual tension and defense pattern, even in sleep. As in the waking state, your protection takes the form of bodily contraction that is reinforced by your thoughts. But now is the time for awakening, another chance at opening to life and bodyself expansion.

To this point is the following reflection: As I lay in bed one morning, I noticed how my lips were pressing together and remembered to let them soften. At the same time I wondered, what is it that wants to stay constricted and small? If I stay tense and small perhaps I won't be hurt or feel afraid. To open exposes me to face the fear again of what happened when I did not watch myself. My expansive feelings led to getting hurt again and again. My caretaker was likely to pounce on me when I was playful and punish me when I was noisy. Expressive and spontaneous, I became a target whereas small and still, I felt more safe.

Charlotte Selver called this gradual morning sensing while still lying in bed the "Baby's Awakening." The next time you get a chance to watch a baby wake up, observe how it goes with the baby. It may be your best teacher. Next best is watching a cat or dog return from slumber. Until then what follows are some further suggestions for feeling into your gradual awakening. Some of these suggestions involve pure sensing, while others, massage and still others are more like "exercises". Discover what meets your needs on a given morning. Let something evolve anew each morning. Approach each day with a beginner's mind – full of possibilities.

Reaching and Breathing: Experiment or Exercise?

You can approach "Reaching and breathing" as an experiment or an exercise. Experiments differ from exercises in four essential ways. First, in an experiment, you will have a sense of allowing something to unfold rather than doing or performing it. You notice your bodyself responding to gravity with breathing and the easing of muscle tension – paying attention rather than doing something to make the release happen. You Let Go . . rather than Let's Go! Secondly, an experiment cannot fail whereas an exercise can. Third, in an experiment, you sense your overall condition before you focus on the sensation or movement and then again, afterwards. Whereas, an exercise is done for its own sake and in fact may be <u>mindlessly</u> repeated (encouraging Let's Go!) rather than <u>mindfully</u> sensed (fostering Let Go . .). This observation leads to the fourth quality of experiments – namely that in an experiment you will be noticing what <u>influence</u> <u>this</u> <u>movement</u> has on your breathing as well as the rest of you. In an exercise, <u>you</u> are likely to be asked to influence your breathing in some way.

This difference in the relationship of breathing to exercises and experiments is crucial. In an experiment, you do not breathe in any prescribed way but instead, you allow your breathing to respond however it "wants" to, whereas in an exercise you are often asked to breathe in accordance with certain principles. For example, you might be asked to inhale with the stretch and to exhale as you allow yourself to sink into the bed. Of course, you could make an experiment out of the aforementioned exercise by doing one round of breathing in the prescribed way and then sense your experience before and after, noticing any resulting influences. In any case, both exercises and experiments can lead to a shift to Let Go . . However, an experiment embodies Let Go . . as you are doing it. You spend a longer time focusing on sensations and you strengthen your capacity to shift to Let Go . . And that is exactly what you need during decompression as well as in your waking up regimen, not to mention during a potentially stressful day.

Consider what happens on a muscular level when you are doing a movement as an exercise, in contrast to an experiment. For instance, in the sensing experiment "coming to hanging", you gradually allow yourself be pulled by gravity from standing to "hanging" as your upper torso and head come closer to the floor. To give to gravity, you have to let go of muscle tension – contracting your muscles will not help you with this experiment. You can sense the erector spinae muscles in your back lengthening as they give up their habitual holding. Then you are encouraged to rest into and savor what happens next. Eventually, you will come back up to standing with the same sense of movement unfolding rather than "doing" it.

Experiments tend to be done with more awareness and often more slowly than exercises. Therefore experiments strengthen <u>awareness</u> rather than <u>muscles</u>. If you do this movement as an exercise in "bending over", you are likely to contract your abdominal muscles to pull yourself forward. The experiment of hanging engages the capacity of the bodyself to release tension and come more into balance. No analysis or coaching or imagery or exercise is needed. As long as you can give yourself to it, surrendering to Let Go . . brings about organismic balance.

If you want to try "Reaching and Breathing" as an exercise rather than an experiment, then the protocol below can serve as a guide. My choice of the word "reaching" rather than "stretching" is intentional because it invites a connection with the expression of a psychologically-oriented organismic need. Consider that your diaphragm is the same type of muscle as that which moves your arms and legs and supports your spine. When you inhale your diaphragm contracts. Exhalation is usually produced by the relaxation of your diaphragm. Your muscles are more available for giving up tensing as you exhale. So, when you stretch your leg, inhale at the same time. As you inhale, focus on the lengthening feeling in your muscles and on the sensation of expansion in your trunk. As you exhale allow yourself to settle into the bed, while your bodyself senses how it wants to lie in this moment. Allow another breath cycle – inhalation and lengthening followed by exhalation and settling - before you begin a stretch in another area.

On the other hand, you may feel the urge to experiment with breathing and stretching in a more spontaneous and intuitive way. Begin by noticing where more space is wanted in you and then reach with some part of you that is connected to that constricted area. As you reach and after you give up the reaching, feel what happens in breathing and in the rest of you. The essence of an experiment is that you sense your condition before and after you do something whether it is a movement, massage or just focusing your attention on something. Then notice what continues in you in the wake of what you initiated. Let it unfold! The outline that follows is merely a guide to get you started. You are likely to feel most enlivened when you sense you are being led by your sensations as in Baby's Awakening. No one needs to teach the baby how to wake up. The baby just yields to what its organism wants.

A warning!

If you make a Let's Go! exercise out of breathing and stretching you are likely to "over" stretch your muscles with a resulting muscle cramp. Your muscles are especially vulnerable in the morning when they are not yet warmed up. A cramp would be a rude awakening, indeed! Screaming and writhing in pain is not exactly a Let Go . . kind of wake-up call! Slow down and sense, sink and savor. The extension movement of stretching can feel like the gentle expansion of taking a breath. Allow this gentle expansion of inhalation to spread through your body as it brings oxygen and blood to your cells. As you exhale, your breath takes away what you don't need. After the stretching is completed and you are just lying, take time to sense how you feel all through you. For variation, try stretching and breathing while you are lying on your side.

You can start anywhere with reaching and breathing or you can be very systematic. Here are some guidelines and also a pattern to follow, if you are so "reclined"! Start with your legs, one at a time, reaching with your heel toward the end of the bed. Breathe into your heel, following your awareness down into your leg. Inhale as you reach. Then as you exhale let the stretch go and rest into the delicious feeling of sinking and space.

Tilt your pelvis so that your back comes closer to the bed as you exhale and give up this effort with your inhalation. Then allow another breath cycle.

With the next inhalation, allow your abdomen to expand fully and as you exhale, push the air out until your abdomen is somewhat contracted. Then allow two more breath cycles to occur without any special movement.

Reach with your hand or elbow as you inhale and as you exhale, give up the reaching. Allow at least one breath cycle to finish before going on. Notice what you are sensing as you lie. If at any point yawning and/or spontaneous urges to stretch occur, follow them.

As you inhale, notice how your head moves. Does your chin come closer to your chest or does it move away? As you breathe, experiment with the movement and discover what feels more natural to you. Perhaps you can allow extension in your neck and spaciousness in your head as you breathe.

Pelvic Floor Awareness

The purpose of this exercise is to heighten your awareness of the condition of your pelvic floor - contracted or at ease. Lying in bed in the morning and evening is a good time to practice sensing, as well as, strengthening this muscle because you are quiet and can feel it clearly. Placing a pillow behind your head and neck can give you the proper support. In the morning, it is an ideal first exercise since it requires a minimum of body movement and is pleasurable to do. As a matter of fact, a well-toned pubo-coccygeal muscle (PCG) heightens the sensations of sexual orgasm in men and women, not to mention, aids in bladder control. One effective way to engage this muscle is to contract it maximally for ten long seconds and then rest for five seconds.

Repeat the exercise ten times. Be sure to really feel the softening and release in between the contractions to maximize the strengthening of the muscle. The tightening and then the softening of this muscle is a subtly pleasurable way to practice the shift from Let's Go! (PCG contraction) to Let Go. . (PCG relaxation). This exercise can serve as a reminder to savor the Let Go . . satisfaction when a task is completed. You can practice this movement anytime you are sitting, lying or standing. How about, right now?!

As you go about your day, whether standing or sitting notice the sensations in your pelvic floor. With practice, you will be able to feel whether it is well-toned and soft or constricted, flabby and lacking in tonus. Allow softness when you notice constriction. At the same time notice the condition in your jaw and lips. Let your jawbone sink a little, if you find it clenched. If you find your lips pressed together, allow them to soften. Often you will find your lips unnecessarily pressed together as if not letting anything in or out. Can you allow softness around your mouth? Does the experience of your overall condition change? What happens in the floor of your pelvis? Allow your eyes to soften, finding their resting place and giving up efforts to see. Can you still feel your feet? Breathing? Is there any sense of the movements of breathing in the floor of your pelvis?

Child Pose

The "child pose", so-named in Yoga practice, incorporates the theme of being reborn in the morning and can keep you in bed just a little longer! This is a convenient position in which to massage your neck as well as to heighten awareness of your back and sit bones. Bring yourself to kneeling on the bed by curling over your legs with your knees bent. Put a pillow under your belly if you can't bend over easily. Support your upper body weight with your elbows. Cradle your head with one or both hands so your head can rest in your hands. Allow your spine to lengthen as your pelvis sinks and tilts backward so that your lower back curve fills out. Notice how breathing responds. Using your fingers or loosely curled fists, tap or slap your back all the way down to your sitting bones with a staccato movement while your head rests on the floor or bed or pillow. Can you feel what influence this tapping has had? Is there any response in breathing? Maybe you sense the weight of your pelvis pulling down as your back opens, yielding a little more space between your vertebrae. Allow breathing to open your back. Does your neck lengthen as your head rests on the bed? Allow yourself to settle into breathing. To "treat" your feet, rest your lower body weight on your toes so they are pressed back, stretching the undersides of your toes and opening the sole of your foot. Then tap and slap your feet.

Notice how your lips come together and allow them to soften where they meet. Gently grasp and squeeze your neck muscles with one hand, using the fingers to press into one side of your neck and the heel of your hand to hold the other side. Repeat the same movement with the other hand as you allow your head to hang. Release your grip and rest, noticing any signs of giving in your neck and head. Using the heels of your hands, massage your scalp, both sides at the same time. Pay particular attention to the area above your ears and around your temples. Rest your forehead on the heel of one hand. Slowly slide the heel of your hand up your forehead, between your eyes, allowing the weight of your head to give the pressure. Nestle your cheekbones into the heels of your hands and allow the resultant pressure to ease the tension in your jaw. Tap your head and neck.

Reach out with your arms in front of you with your head still touching the bed. Stretch your arms, one at a time as far in front of you as they want to go. Notice your breathing. Then soften into the stretch. Reach behind you and tap your sitting bones and as much of your back as you can reach. Notice any aftereffects of the tapping. Then bring your pelvis into the air by slowly unbending your knees. Tap the back of your upper leg from your knee to your sit bone. Repeat on the other side. With your elbows supporting the weight of your head, gently push your head toward your chest using your fingers and then let it spring back. Notice the ease with which your head responds. If you want to come up to standing, take your time and come up in the way recommended in the "Hanging" experiment.

"Hang Ten" Wave: Standing

While standing, notice the sounds in the house (clocks ticking) and outside (birds singing). Close your eyes and feel your feet in contact with what is under them. Let your arms be wherever they are comfortable as you gradually and gently make small circles in the air with your pelvis. Let your weight shift from one leg to the other as your hips move in a gentle circle as if you were following the movement of a hula-hoop. Let the movement get larger and smaller and take you with it.

You could also explore the waving movement from front to back as if you were a handsaw and were being bent to make sound. Initiate a bend and then let the movement travel. The gift of wave movement is that it uses muscles in ways not required by your work (unless you are a professional belly dancer!) and therefore requires your full attention. Because the movement itself is sensual and soothing, it therefore releases hidden tension and is renewing. Soon after discovering this waving movement one morning, *she* urged me to try it out while washing the dishes!

A third direction to explore the wave movement is up and down. This is most easily initiated by raising one shoulder and rotating it in circles. Let the other shoulder join in alternately or together and then let that movement travel in whatever way it wants to. You may find your whole torso being pulled into a wave motion that spreads down to your hips, knees and ankles. Standing and gently turning form side-to-side, letting arms follow and head turn with the movement. Allow your eyes to have a relaxed focus.

Playing Footsies with Tootsies

Or should this be called "Playing Tootsies with Footsies"? I loved discovering this playful deep way to massage one foot and lower leg with the foot and ankle bone of my other foot!

Wait until you try it, before you judge it! It may turn out to be one of your all-time favorite ways to wake up your feet and legs in the morning while still lying in bed. Just rub one foot and leg with the other foot, using your heel, the sides of your foot, ankle bone and toes. Those different shaped "tools" can get into some great places and go pretty deep without your getting tired as you might, if you were using your hands to get the same depth.

Grand Opening: Top of the Morning to You!

One of my favorite ways to awaken to my bodyself in the morning approximates the sequence that follows. You may notice elements of the preceding experiments and exercises incorporated here and there.

While still lying in bed with your eyes closed, turn over on your back. (If you are aware of dream fragments, write them down before you turn over.) Listen for the sounds outside your room ("A Sound Awakening".) Notice your overall condition and where you feel aliveness or constriction in you. If you need more space for lying, take it as soon you notice your need for it. Notice in particular how your legs and arms are lying. Bring your elbows away from your sides so your armpits have more space for the movements of breathing. Spread your toes a little apart and notice how this small movement affects you. Any change in breathing? Try the same movement with your fingers. Sense the area of your mouth and allow softness and space where needed. Run your finger just under the inside of your lips. Sense your "sleep mask." Turn your attention to the area around your eyes and allow ease and space as needed. Notice breathing and rest into its rhythm.

Sometimes you may want to start with the subtlest movements as you lay so peacefully nestled in your bed. The pelvic floor exercises, the "Smallest Movement", the "Wave" may be the best place to begin on these occasions. Otherwise, you can proceed with more active stretching as follows:

Bring your knee toward your chest and with the fingers of both hands, pull your toes toward your knee, stretching the backs of your toes and your Achilles tendon. Breathe. Grasp the sides of your foot with the fingers of each hand and slide very firmly along the sides of the sole of your foot, from the ball of your foot to your heel. Continue to slide fingers up the back of your calf, with moderate to strong pressure. Then using both fists, stroke as deeply as is comfortable into the back of your thigh from knee to top of leg, sensing the lengthening of your leg as you go. Let this leg come to standing, knee bent, on the bed. Repeat on the other leg.

Pull both knees to your chest, hold them and notice breathing. Allow your pelvic floor and your jaw to soften. Allow your inner space to expand in your awareness. Bring your feet back down to contact with the bed, your legs standing. Feel out how far apart your feet need to be to support your legs in standing.

Notice how your head is lying and where there may be constriction in your neck. With both hands, one on top of the other, grasp your neck. Massage your neck muscles by pressing the heel of your hand into one side of your neck, while the fingers of that same hand press into the other side. Move your head, side to side, as you grasp your neck to give more pressure exactly where it is "kneaded"! Alternatively, grasp your neck between the forefingers and thumbs of each hand, one hand on top of the other. This way of holding your neck makes it possible to exert more pointed pressure. A third way to get into the deep holding at the base of your skull is to press with your thumbs into the base of your skull as you lie with your head supported by the bed and your fingers. As you breathe feel the subtle softening of your musculature and your awareness gradually expanding through your bodyself. Let your head come to resting on the bed.

Using the heels of your hands, massage your scalp especially around and above your ears and into your temples. Slowly move your scalp over your skull bones. Press the heels of your hands under your cheek ridge and back toward your jaw. Allow the muscles underneath your hands to soften. Allow your arms to rest. Then using the heel of your hand, slide from the bridge of your nose up into the middle of your forehead, wiping away any thought residue from the early morning's rumination. Allow spaciousness to occupy your brow and forehead area. Place your palms over your eyes and notice breathing. Do you feel any openings anywhere else in you as you faithfully attend to yourself in this way?

With your feet standing so that your legs feel well supported, do the pelvic floor awareness exercises. Continue to check in with how your feet feel in contact with what is under you. If you discover you are pressing against the bed (or floor), give up the pressing and allow your legs to simply stand. If you would like to stimulate your intestines or your awareness of your breathing, you could massage your abdomen. Now that your awareness of your jaw, neck, abdomen and pelvic floor is heightened, you are likely to make some interesting discoveries by sensing the pelvic tilt movements. Placing your hands on your chest with your elbows out to the sides will allow you more room to sense your breathing and your heart. You may discover a need for more space in the area of your sides and armpits and then you can respond to this need in whatever way feels appropriate.

You can either allow your breath to respond naturally to the movement or you can breathe in accordance with some principle or belief about how breathing "should" be. The nature of your experience changes when you breathe in a certain way and you are more likely to "perform" the movements as an exercise rather than discover, moment to moment, how the movements feel. For example, according to the Bioenergetics and Reichian* theory of the orgastic reflex, you should inhale as you rock your pelvis away from you and exhale as you flatten your lower back against the bed. But in the end, as long as you are feeling what you are doing and sensing breathing, you will awaken to more aliveness in your pelvic region. As you do, notice the condition of your neck and jaw and continue to allow the area around your mouth to soften. Allow your inner space to expand in your awareness.

A further awakening of your pelvic region is invited by the Bioenergetic "Butterfly" legs exercise. As you inhale allow your legs to fall to either side and as you inhale, slowly bring them back up to standing. If you call to mind how a butterfly looks as it suns its wings while perched on a leaf, you'll realize why it's called the "butterfly legs" exercise. You may notice some trembling or vibration in your legs as you bring them from the splayed position back to standing.

Then turn over and move into the "Child Pose" experiment. The child pose can be done on the bed or floor. The advantage of being on the floor is that you can come out of it by slowly coming up to standing. If you decide to get out of bed, give your feet some more enlivening attention first.

Put Your Best Foot Forward!

Before you get out of bed, stroke the back of each toe from toe tip into ball of foot, gently pulling the toe back towards the top of the foot with your other hand. Continue the stroke down the metatarsal from the ball of the foot to the heel. Exhale with each stroke to help you keep a sensory focus. Notice how your foot feels compared to the other one. For a fresh experience, walk around on your tiptoes. Alternatively, if you have a tendency to pronate, pull up on the inside of your arches when you walk around while you brush your teeth or make your bed. The goal is to bring your awareness down into your feet so that you are more bodyself aware. You have a whole day ahead of you, or rather, afoot!

Get off to a Rolling Good Start!

One area at a time, roll, side to side, your legs, hips, chest, arms and head. Add some rollick to your roll and bounce your torso on your bed! As you get into it, you'll find these movements can be quite invigorating without leading to a Let's Go! kind of excitation. You will also find it difficult to think too much when you are rolling about on the bed. For more "un-thinking" techniques, see the next section entitled "Stop-Gab" techniques. To make this exercise more like an experiment, notice how you are lying before and after rolling each body part. Allow the changes necessary for feeling more bodyself-connected.

Having a Ball!

Lie on your back on a large physical therapy ball and allow your arms to hang to the sides. Allow your chest to open with breathing. Rest into your lying and stretching. As you breathe, imagine your breath going into your heart and as you exhale, the breath carrying what you don't need out into the environment.

Morning "Hangover"

While sitting in bed, put pillows on your lap and let yourself hang over your pillows. Breathe and allow lengthening in your back. Feel the gentle stretch and breathe into it, not forcing only softening. Alternatively, turn onto your stomach and allow your head and neck to hang over the side of the bed. Breathe. Allow your neck to elongate as you pull your chin in toward you. With your elbows braced against the side of the bed, massage your head and scalp. This movement can also be done in sitting by just leaning over with your elbows on your knees. Caution: these stretches should not be done if you have symptoms of a pinched nerve or a disc problem.

White Rabbit Wake up: I'm Late, I'm Late, I'm Late!

If you are in a big hurry, take a few minutes while you are still in bed and spread your fingers and toes, rotate your wrists and ankles, allow some movement in your neck, jaw, spine and pelvis to free yourself from your sleeping mask and pose. Feel how breathing responds to your bodyself awakening.

So Many Ways to Open . . .

As you lie in bed, notice where you feel some constriction or discomfort. As you focus in on this area, try one of the following suggestions for increasing awareness. As you follow through, breathe and notice if there are any effects anywhere else in you. There are so many ways to open:

(1) Stretch or lengthen this place upon inhalation and then allow the softening and sinking into the bed. Sense your increasing aliveness.

(2) Shorten or contract the area – for example, raise your shoulders even more and exhale with release.

(3) Vibrate, wiggle, or initiate a wave in this place.

(4) Make the smallest movement possible in this area, so small that someone else couldn't see it, but you can feel it. Let that movement become bigger. Let that movement spread and involve more of you.

(5) Bring your hands to this place and breathe. Can you allow just the weight of your hands? Alternatively, place a stone on this area and allow the weight of the stone through you.

(6) Talk to this place and let it talk to you (give it a voice).

(7) Find a sound that meets this place and intone it.

(8) Return your focus to this area during the rest of the day as a kind of body mantra to bring you back to yourself.

Teeth Brushing

Brushing your teeth in the morning can be used as an occasion to awaken and refresh your mouth and tongue. As you brush your teeth, feel the coolness of the water. Where else would you like to feel this coolness? Eyes, wrists, mouth? What will it be today? Try brushing your teeth with your opposite hand, if you want to have the experience of "beginner's hand!" When I first tried it, I felt as if someone else was brushing my teeth. In any case, slowing this habitual movement will bring you more into your senses, the language of your bodyself and into Let Go . .

Meditation

Start the day the way you ended it - by listening to bodyself messages instead of electronic ones. Your voice/e-mail and text messages are likely to get you into Let's Go! mode while sensing, meditating and listening to *her* will ground you in your bodyself and make it easier to resist the pull of Let's Go! Remember you are discovering how to extend your time in Let Go . . so you will have more balance in your life. So, after sensing, take some time to meditate and tune into *her*. Open to being more sensitive to messages from this deeper, more hidden aspect of yourself. Ask *her* to show you what is needed. Remember how *she* has communicated in the past. Promise to look for *her* signs. If you have not been paying much attention to *her* lately and feel remiss, express that and deepen your resolve to reconnect with *her*. *She* <u>will</u> hear you.

Before meditating, run cool water on your wrists and hands or rub your wrists and forearms up to your elbows to awaken sensation. Allow your head to sink toward your chest and notice what influence this movement has on you. Allow whatever changes need to be made now as well as when your head returns to the vertical. As you give to that "sinking" feeling, energy from habitually held musculature is freed and your thoughts become quieter. Let each day begin with the "little death" of conscious surrender – the disappearance of ego as you give yourself to breathing and the stillness of morning. Perhaps then, you can begin this day with the "beginner's mind" of your bodyself!

As you sit, listen to the morning sounds around you and feel the life inside you. Sense your muscles contracting and softening. Where is there tenderness, pressure, and breathing? Sense the air coming in and out of your nose. Follow it deep into you. Allow your breath to create the space for your aliveness. As you notice breathing, can you sense your arms and fingers at the same time? Do you feel the air touching your hands and the spaces between your fingers?

Reentry into the world is maximized by grounding yourself through awareness of your contact points: your eyes and eyelids, lips and jaw, sit bones and floor of pelvis, hands and feet. This sensing meditation can be experienced while you are sitting, lying or standing. As you feel more grounded, you will notice an increased sense of presence throughout your bodyself. Other sensory meditations include Two-lip sensing and Unmasking the Face. How your lips gently come together reflects the attitude needed to hear *her* – attentive and at ease. When you finish meditating, you may be more open to taking in some inspirational reading. After your reading, you may enjoy coming up to standing the way you would from the child pose – that is, vertebra by vertebra.

Soul Food

Keep an inspirational book by your bedside, meditation or breakfast area. Opening it randomly and reading what you have serendipitously found can be very uplifting and uncannily appropriate. *She* just seems to know exactly the right reading for me on a given morning. Discovering for yourself how apropos *her* selections can encourage you to seek *her* out. Books I have found inspirational are "Zen Mind, Beginner's Mind" by Shunryu Suzuki, "The Illuminated Rumi" by Coleman Barks and Michael Green or "Tonight the Subject is Love"* by Hafiz. Or you might prefer to consult a book that has a particular message for each day such as Mark Nepo's "Book of Awakening" or Melody Beattie's "The Language of Letting Go"**. Whether you prefer the methodical or spontaneous approach, inspirational soul food is a great way to start to your day. The more you give yourself over to your bodyself wisdom, the more you can see how what <u>is</u> happening is the only thing that could happen and you can feel at peace with it. Feeling more connected to *her* and more trusting of your bodyself for guidance can, in turn, deepen your trust in how things do work out.

"Morning Pages"

Instead of meditating you may want to try writing "morning pages" when you first wake up, as suggested by Julia Cameron*** in "The Artist's Way". Just write three pages of whatever comes to mind, without censorship or criticism. The idea is to just let yourself be with your flow – a kind of clearing yourself for the day. You may be surprised how freeing and refreshing it is to write "stream of consciousness" and how good you feel afterward.

Stop "Gab" Techniques for Emergencies

At least until after breakfast, try to stay with the sensations of Let Go .. rather than be drawn into the whirlwind of Let's Go! thoughts. There will be time enough later to indulge in them. Here are some thought-stopping (Stop "gab") techniques for instant diversion from what "nags" as you awaken:

(1) Just shake your head "No!" when you catch yourself engaging in obsessing, criticizing or engaging in otherwise runaway, unwanted thinking.

(2) "STOP!" or "NO!" spoken loudly can help by interrupting thoughts. Such pronouncements can be followed by foot stomping or mock punching or jerking your elbows back, one at a time. However, if you continue with this technique for long, you may find yourself entering the Let's Go! mode. Rather than physical activity, the "No!" or "Stop!" can be followed up by pleadings such as "I need to rest", "I'm sick of your scaring me with those thoughts, be gentle with me" or the less emotional "This thinking is so boring, let's do something fun". You might say, "You are hurting me with those thoughts, I want you to hold me" and then put your arms around yourself or stroke yourself. This technique seems to be especially satisfying in the shower or tub, where the sounds you make are contained in your personal space.

(3) In the shower, sound OM! Experiment with different tones. Feel them resonate throughout your body. Hear them resound off the shower walls. Fill the stall with sound. AAUUOOMM! Experiment with other simple sounds like peace or yes. Whatever fits. Let it rip. As long as you focus on letting that sound come out from deep inside you, your roaming thoughts will not have room to root.

(4) Remember how some grown-ups may have acted silly by making noises or by letting the muscles around their mouth go slack. Let your jaw muscles and your lips relax and blow air out as if you were blowing bubbles in the water. As you allow your lips to vibrate noisily, shake your head back and forth for added effect. This is most convincing and fun when you are standing under the shower, wetting your hair as well as everything else!

(5) Mock the voices inside your head by making up your own tones and jibber-jabber language. Answer back. This fun, creative exercise can give you a paradoxical sense of control and perspective. With time it will be more difficult to take those voices so seriously.

(6) Sing "Zippity do dah!"

(7) Make up your own lyrics to a familiar tune.

Live Your <u>Own</u> Life Each Morning

One morning upon awakening, I found myself thinking of my friend's alcoholic son. When I caught myself I marveled at how codependent that was - obsessing about <u>someone else's</u> alcoholic! An old 12 Step joke came to mind, namely, "When a codependent dies, some else's life flashes before their eyes." Then, I found my focus shifted to the alcoholic that was in my life and what he might be doing. Desperately I tried to get back into my own life in the moment, to feel my sensations, be with the morning, this morning. Just me in my bed, beginning the day, feeling the day begin in me. Connecting to the birdsongs I could hear. I made the smallest movement I could make in my lower back. I located myself, right here and now. Presence is the present I can gift myself.

The Serenity Prayer

If you find yourself obsessing about a situation upon awakening that you feel helpless about, you may get some solace from the serenity prayer. One colleague of mine finds it extremely helpful to get on her knees and pray for guidance when she finds her mind obsessing. She uses the form of the serenity prayer and at various points she adds specific content she is concerned about:

Grant me the serenity to accept the things I cannot change: my father's narcissism, my daughter's alcoholism, etc

The courage to change the things I can: my attitude, my work habits, and my self-care routine, reaching out to others

And the wisdom to know the difference.

The Dew of Little Things . . .

Take guidance from another inspiring recognition of Kahlil Gibran: "For it is in the dew of little things the heart finds its morning and is refreshed."* You might find it helpful to tune into some aspect of nature in the morning such as watching the dawn, listening for birdsong, walking on the dewy grass or in your garden or tending to your houseplants or herbs. Some mornings I replenish my bird feeder and watch the wild birds displace each other at the feeding tray.

Slip on your cozy robe and fuzzy slippers to receive yourself in the morning. These may be the same things you wore during your decompression period. This soft clothing can help cue in an attitude of ease, restfulness and taking care of yourself. Wear other clothing when cleaning the house. You may want to experiment with waking up ten minutes early just to sit in a comfortable chair or in bed and just "be" for a while. Be with the beginning of the day, with your first breaths, yawns and stretches as you gradually reconnect with yourself and your world.

Bathing

Bathing provides many opportunities to connect with your bodyself. You can be touched all over with water, washcloth, soap, towel and lotion. In the shower you can stretch as well as massage your neck and back, facilitated by the flow of water wherever you need it. You can make sounds to express the tension and pleasure you feel as you get in touch with your emotional voice. My intuitive self loves the steamy privacy of the shower, for many a creative idea is birthed there.

As you wash your hair, massage along your hairline and into the sides of your head above your ears where an important jaw muscle attaches. Releasing any leftover tension from the night or morning interactions or news will give you a "head" start on the day. Notice the shape and size of your head as you gently massage the shampoo into your hair. You may be surprised at how narrow or how wide your head feels. Notice how you hold your head while you are washing your feet and legs. Let your head hang, releasing the muscles in the back of your neck. You may need to hold your nose with one hand to let your head go fully. Come back to the sensations in your feet throughout your time in the shower.

If you choose not to shower or fill the tub to bathe, you might try refreshing contact points such as your hands, feet and head. These areas are direct conduits to your bodyself because there are more sensory nerve endings in the skin of those body parts than in the skin of all the rest of your body. For each occasion, select your washing implement with care - a wash mitt or a soft brush. Experiment with body washes, scrubs or just plain water. Take time to appreciate each of these areas of yourself as you touch, stroke or rub them. When you towel dry your hair, press deeply with your fingers or the heels of your hands through the towel into your scalp to give a deep massage to your skull. In early morning, wash in the dark or by candlelight. You may enjoy choosing different lotions for different areas: a tingly peppermint lotion for the feet, a thicker moisturizing lotion for the hands, and a soothing splash for your face. Pay attention to how each part of you wants to be touched and appreciated. Discover your habitual order of drying your body parts and change it to bring yourself into the Let Go . . moment.

"I Don't Want to Wake Up!"

When you have trouble waking up in the morning, get up anyway and go in another room and turn on the light or open the shades. It is very important not to go back to sleep because you may not be able to fall asleep early enough the following night. Your wake-up time is determined by the time you go to sleep the previous night. Whether you need 6 or 9 hours of sleep to feel rested, your brain will wake you about the same time you woke up the morning before. To change your wake up time, you may have to endure a few days of feeling tired. You could always take a short (half-hour) nap before 4 PM, however, without disturbing the length of your nighttime sleep or the hour at which you begin to feel sleepy.

As long as you are up, try writing about how hard it is to wake up. Dialogue with the part of you that wants to go back to sleep rather than let it have its way. Invite that part to complain and then listen as compassionately as possible. Let your *"her"* speak. Maybe you have not been listening to *her* lately - *she* may need more tenderness, fun, touch, nurturance and contact in order to give you *her* gifts. Listening to *her* makes *her* comfortable and *she* likes to be comfortable. Instead of just reacting and acting out, do what you can to mediate the conflict and to hear *her* side. If you ignore your needs, again and again, there will be backlash. You will find yourself in a cycle of indulgence (reward, entitlement) and deprivation (punishment) - the politics of bodyself "disregulation".

Waking up Routine

Experiment with a morning waking-up routine. One that works for me is writing dreams, sensing, brushing teeth, meditating, reading Nepo, bathing, and checking messages while preparing breakfast and then getting the newspaper. Gradually, I expose myself to the outside world. Experiment with the order in which you do various parts of your getting-ready routine. For example, shower before breakfast rather than after. Choose a sensory focus for the day - lips, breath, feet, neck, pelvic floor - and come back to it as you go about your morning routine. This focus will slow you down and help you come back to Let Go . . In the process of establishing the habit of taking time for yourself in the morning, you will encounter resistance. And by now, you know what to do when you meet resistance. Yes, ask *her,* what is the matter? You will find your mornings are sweeter and your day goes more smoothly when you start the day on the bodyself side of the street. Besides, you'll get the sense of continuity of coming home to your bodyself, from the decompression period, all through the night into the morning: this is your bodyself voice recovery time.

17

AN INVITATION TO BODYMINDFULNESS: FINDING YOUR OWN WAY

"Pacing is everything."

Finding you own way is ultimately about learning to listen to your bodyself so that you can live more fully. There is no one perfect way*; even listening to your bodyself is not perfect, nor is finding your own way. But better, as one Zen master said, to "see with your own crooked eye" than to blindly follow someone else and never know yourself. Even if you try to follow the way of a teacher or guru, you have to trust yourself and your own sense of what is heard. And, you listen to yourself for guidance through meditation or prayer. In the end, the strength of my practice and the openness of my heart is really I you have. Of course, I have the love and support of others, but how supportive that turns out to be depends on my availability to "take in" from others.

Listening to your bodyself voice is about reconnecting with a deep, sometimes hidden source of wisdom. Reconnecting involves first noticing, then focusing and following through on what you hear. Listening in this way is the practice of consciously surrendering to the source of your life energy. To hear this voice clearly, a daily listening practice and healing unresolved trauma and loss can be pivotal. You are likely to be challenged listening to your bodyself if you cannot feel through all of your feelings and come back to a calm heart center. As you have read, unresolved trauma can keep you from becoming somatically grounded, going through the emotional recovery cycle and embodying a calm heart center. Therefore, you may have difficulty self-soothing, taking good care of yourself, savoring and taking in caring from other people, not to mention seeing the larger Let Go . . picture.

Taking in the experience of being seen can build bodyself support to accept your own and the other's limitations, to express your fear, anger and to accept your powerlessness so you can ultimately grieve the loss behind the fantasy you created to protect yourself from the pain of the past. No longer in danger of being stuck in Let's Go! "All is Hell" you can shift to Let Go . . "All is Well" because you have worked through trauma and other unresolved issues. Because now you possess a boundary setting, self-affirming "No!" which can free you to say a whole-hearted "Yes!" to life and love, you can forgive yourself and others. You more often experience the part of your brain that creates a sense of the larger picture – that place where the "paradoxes of presence" are no longer befuddling but can be experienced as truths. Such paradoxes are "less is more", "more is less", "in asking is the answer", "the only hope is in giving up hope", "'staying with' brings change". This latter is the promise of the paradoxical theory of change. In short, grounded in your bodyself, you can experience deep presence and connection with life all around you, that is, "embodied spirituality".

While doing trauma resolution work can help you better take care of yourself, fall asleep at night and improve your relationships, it is still not enough if your goal is to live in close connection with your bodyself and experience a deep sense of well-being. Trauma work just helps get the "boulders" of stance and "stuckness" out of your way. No matter what breakthroughs you have experienced in therapy or in meditation, no matter what exalted or blissful enlightenment experiences you have had, you still have the laundry to do, the wood to chop and the water to carry.* A daily focusing practice can help you balance the Let's Go! of your everyday busy self with the Let Go . . of taking care of your bodyself. Doing the "footwork" of a daily practice helps you stay in the spirit of acceptance that life is just what it is and what is happening now is the only thing that <u>could</u> happen, no matter how <u>you</u> <u>feel</u> about it. As a result of your daily practice and an open heart, you can have many more Goldilocks moments of reconnection, delight, and grace that reinforce listening to your bodyself.

Each of the listening practices offered in this book makes a contribution to living in connection with your bodyself. Since each of them involves staying with a sensory focus, your Let Go . . energy can build and you are likely to become more present. Going on a meditation, prayer, yoga or sensory awareness retreat could jump-start your bringing a daily focusing practice into your life. The more somatically oriented the retreat is, the more full-bodied presence you can experience. Some "spiritual" practices are actually more "head" oriented and encourage rising above the lowly realm of so-called "body" (as separate from soul) experience. I recommend a practice that embraces the full somatic experience so you can come to fully inhabit your bodyself – your sensations, emotions and movement. Then you will be better prepared for "full catastrophe"* living, which includes deeply connecting with others.

In any case, keeping a focus transforms your experience whether you are focused on a sensation, emotion, image or thought. Energy builds as you focus, and when you stop you may sense a subtle energy. Various meditation practices take advantage of this phenomenon to build energy to "break through" into other "levels" of awareness. On a retreat you are likely to experience profound states of peace and well-being because you have a single focus and the pull of Let's Go! activities is purposely weakened. As an aid to your focusing attention on your immediate experience, retreats often control the amount and type of food, contact and activities you engage in. You are likely to be eating vegetarian style, avoiding stimulants, alcohol and sugar and not talking, let alone having sex! While walking is permitted, strenuous working out is "verboten". Following these guidelines, you have the opportunity to become completely focused on your immediate experience of being alive. Doesn't sound like fun? You may be surprised. If you find your curiosity has been aroused, there is likely something here for you. Remember, the root of the word "curious" is the same as the root for the word "cure". Your curiosity could be a clue that some part of you is trying to help or "cure" you by discovering more of your bodyself.

The Power of "Staying With"

I experienced this power of "staying with" in a variety of weekend and weeklong meditation retreats in the seventies. In these sessions we had only to follow the rules for meditation practice and the schedule for breaks, interviews, eating and sleeping. Distractions were kept to a minimum, no talking, no reading, no TV, no working out, no sex, no sugar, no meat, no caffeine, no alcohol, etc. The entire time was spent staying focused on a simple practice – breathing or the question "Who am I!" I was struck by the intense Let Go . . energy that accumulated as the days went by. Very focused, yet gentle. On one occasion, the startling, but welcome outcome was a pervasive strong feeling of my being guided which brought an enormous sense of gratefulness and relief. This sense of being guided, seemed retroactive as if it had been with me all my life but now, at that moment, it was finally palpable. During another retreat, poetry sprang to mind in response to whatever I looked upon. When I grew tired of writing, I contented myself with being absorbed in the utter brilliance and aliveness of whatever I looked at. There was no need to do anything, just being with it was enough. This, whatever it is, is always potentially there, waiting for me to open to it*. If I make Let Go . . efforts to come closer to it and then it can find me. "Staying with" can give rise to the experience of subtle Let Go . . energy of "All is Well".

If you don't have time, money or the heart to go on a retreat, try a twenty-four hour period of silence at home. A food fast or a talking "fast" can precipitate discoveries about yourself, a sense of calm and at the same time heightened clarity and energy. When you set aside this time, refrain from distractions such as TV, computer games, Internet, etc. Instead, dance, walk, make music, clean house, make a meals, or just quietly be with others. Perhaps you will want to journal, "stream of consciousness" style. Schedule this period so that when you come off the "fast", you can pay attention to what it is like to enter the speaking world. Take time to reenter your everyday, busy mind world, where you usually don't just feel, you <u>do</u> something. Did you notice a shift in your sense of presence during the fast? And afterwards? Sometimes you won't notice anything special until you break the silence, then you may detect a shift in your experience of being. Perhaps you may feel enlivened like you do after a "just right" workout or meditation. Can you savor the feeling of being able to communicate again? What about it pleases you or on the other hand, disappoints you? Does the occasion of speaking feel precious now or does it feel like it "brings you down?" Do you speak with the urgency that a person who is coming off a fast feels when beginning to eat again?

Just as with depriving yourself of food, not speaking can lead to a calm focused state of Let Go . . energy and an increased sensitivity. However, the temporary deprivation of food or speaking can give rise to pressure to make up for lost time. When the fast is over, you are likely to find you have to hold yourself back to keep from talking or eating too much. (No wonder such deprivation is called a "fast", because "fast" is the pace at which one feels driven to make up for lost time!) After the fast, eating and talking again can seem to take away from the rarefied energy that was building when you were withholding words or food. While fasts can be valuable doors to self-knowledge, they are not such viable ways to live out your days. A case in point was a recent article in "The Yoga Journal" about how abstaining from sex builds energy. But who wants to practice abstinence as a life style? There must be another way to enjoy bodyself contact other than depriving yourself of something essential to your overall, everyday well-being. What is needed is a way of connecting with yourself that is livable and relational and brings with it the sweetness of deep connection with *her* and others.

Similarly, when you deprive yourself of calories you can lose weight, but how are you going to manage when deprivation takes over as you go off the diet? Or, consider the diets that leave out one category of food, fat, protein or carbohydrate. At first, you easily lose weight on such a diet, but then a craving develops for the missing food and you are likely to feel driven to eat it, lots of it, and quickly, to restore your usual balance (homeostasis). Then you feel even more out of control as your bodyself reacts to the deprivation you imposed on it, in hopes of increased health and well-being. Depriving yourself (which is paradoxically, a kind of excess) is much easier than finding balance. This cycle of deprivation and indulgence can keep you out of touch with what you feel and need to come more into bodyself balance. If, however you practice daily using your focused attention to stay with your experience and notice how change unfolds, you are likely to discover a greater sense of balance and less need for your <u>old</u> ways of trying to control yourself.

A distinct sense of well-being, gentle energy and ease can result from staying with a focus for a prolonged time. Maybe that is why some people find such comfort in solitary activities such as reading, studying, writing or practicing an art, trade or craft. It is as if your brain likes to be called to the task of focusing and thanks you by rewarding you with this deeply satisfying feeling. In addition, if you stay in touch with your bodyself as you do what you do, you are likely to feel less tense when you stop focusing. After holding yourself to a task, even if it is meditating, you are likely to need a break. What you do with your mind in that break is important so you don't lose the momentum of focusing and contact with your bodyself. The appropriate break allows the consolidation of your Let Go . . energy, as if you were recharging the repository of positivity, your Let Go . . energy reserve.

If you become too demanding of yourself while focusing, you are likely to lose touch with your body. While "dropping off mind and body" may be desirable during meditation practice, you still have to meet the challenge of living in the everyday world and showing up for relationships. In fact, some meditation masters were renowned for having trouble balancing their austere practice with the everyday life of teaching and contact with Western students. If you have unresolved trauma, you run the risk of dissociating in service of trying to "enter the now" by focusing. Psychotherapy could help you resolve that issue by helping you build ground in your bodyself experience. Then you could be less likely to fall into the "trauma trap" of engaging in some sort of addictive, adapted or dissociated behavior to keep from being overwhelmed by the helpless feelings surrounding the unintegrated trauma.

Bodyself focusing can transform your experience. Learning to stay with a focus can help heal the fragmentation of helplessness as the pieces of yourself come together in a peaceful, integrated bodyself experience. So when faced with helplessness, stop your Let's Go! efforts and get support to feel your feelings all the way through by crying, meditating, writing and/or calling a friend. Staying with feelings of helplessness is the acid test of being able to Let Go . . When you can support yourself and your awareness of *her* by increasing your positivity repository, you can more easily move through difficult situations with optimal energy, a sense of well-being, discovery, and connectedness.

Of course, you can always choose to be a little disconnected and "rise above" the threatening feelings. However, the resultant dampening of your emotional life will cost you in terms of the depth of joy, love, and contact you can have with others. Attempting to "cling to bliss" and not relate to the world in a grounded way is a choice some make, just as some therapy clients become "attached" to their pain and do not heal deeply. Which way do you choose – clinging to pain or to bliss or on the other hand, taking the middle road by resolving trauma, feeling through your emotions by connecting to your bodyself and reaching out to another so you can live a fully embodied life? "The Alchemy of Opening" poem below, written about my experience, points to this possibility:

Wishing with eyes closed tightly,
wishing with all my "might-ly,"
that what was true, was an illusion,
which only added to my confusion.

They couldn't see me in my suffering and pain,
and as it happened again and again,
my wound became a place where I solely reigned,

unseeing and clinging to my distorted view
no chance to survive and see the unbearable truth.

Until I could dare to share the horror and despair
'cause I found a strong heart who deeply cared
     to help free me from my self-made lair
     and partake of a far more nourishing fare.
His unflinching seeing allowed my eyes to reclaim
the truth I'd seen, which had led to self-blame.

My heart opened to loving, beyond compare
'cause for the moment, I no longer feared the pain of despair.
Then breathing more freely the bounteous air,
    my eyes opened, accepting what I couldn't before,
    my heart opened to more and yet more!

Now opened to my heart's desire,
And ready to melt in love's blessed fire:
she and I, tenderly shaped anew,
together, we make a most tasty stew.

Change can feel achingly slow even with the occasional breakthroughs. However, I notice that the "Here we go again!" times are fewer, less intense and of less duration, in short, resilience abides. Just as I can't actually <u>see</u> the growth of the grass, the opening of a flower or the movement of the earth as it happens, I still have confidence that growth and movement is occurring. Likewise you may not be able to sense your actual growth until something happens and you notice you are responding in a new way (the new neural pathway* in action!). That new response could be attributed to your newly strengthened bodyself foundation which allows you to go through the emotional recovery cycle and return to your calm heart center, reach out to others and have more Goldilocks moments - all of which build the repository of positivity and makes the shift to Let Go . . more accessible for self-soothing. Then using the listening practices and asking *her* questions, yields cues that can be noticed, focused on and then followed through, for optimal self-soothing.

In sum, <u>staying</u> <u>with</u> your bodyself experience, whether it be the contraction around pain, helplessness or other threatening emotions or the expansion of feeling connected with your bodyself, others or nature, can bring you into the realm of Let Go . . As Let Go . . energy builds in the positivity repository, you more easily find your way back, again and again.

Developing Your Own Bodymindfulness** Practice

Finding your balance point, moment to moment is the central issue in finding your way. What is "enough" and when is it "just right"? When the unresolved trauma issues are "over," you are likely to be more aware of the subtle cues of "enough" and "just right" because you can bear to be fully in touch with your bodyself. Two elements are essential in developing a daily practice that will enliven your bodyself connection and give you more Let Go . . soothing energy. The first is that your practice must help you develop a somatic <u>focus</u> and the second is setting aside <u>time</u> to <u>practice</u>.

All three listening practices, sensing, meditating and listening to your emotional voice make necessary contributions to finding your bodyself way. For each of them supports staying with or consciously surrendering to your somatic experience as you notice, focus and follow through on what you sense. Yet, each of them alone is incomplete. Since they all help strengthen somatic focus, practicing one will enrich the practice of the other. For instance, sensing your bodyself can bring up emotions and feeling through your emotions can connect you more deeply to your bodyself experience. Further, each of these can be soothing, but in different ways.

Sensing allows you to deeply rest by noticing and following up on what is needed. In meditation you consciously surrender everything – thoughts, feelings, sensations and desires and return to your focus, rather than letting your mind have its way at every moment. This gentle corralling, if done with the right attitude is, in the end, soothing. You can feel peaceful even after lassoing your focus again and again. Gradually you settle deeply into your experience. Listening to your emotional voice allows you explore your resistance to taking care of yourself so you can let yourself rest, renew and deeply enjoy your living.

When experimenting with your bodymindfulness practice, start with sensing, for it opens the door to bodyself contact. Through sensing, you literally gain a sense of ground and support available to your bodyself. Sensing asks the question, "What is wanted now?" For starters:

> Feel what is under you while standing, sitting, lying.
> Give your weight into it.
> Notice what is happening in breathing.
> Take all the space you need. Soften. Expand. Ease.
> Feet! Pelvic floor! Armpits! Lips!
> Feel what touches you.
> Slow down.
> Listen.

Meditation will strengthen your focus and empower you to stay with yourself. A sensory focus will strengthen your connection to your bodyself. Meditation asks the question, "What is it?" Through meditation you embody:

> An attitude of acceptance of what is by gently returning to your focus, again and again.
> "Staying with" until you are "being with".
> Giving up what is extra.

Listening to your emotional voice will help you deal with your resistance to feeling what comes up as you sense or meditate and asks the question, "What is the matter?" Listening to your emotional voice can lead to the following:

> Opening your heart to yourself and others.
> Reaching out and taking in.
> Making sound and moving as you feel what is alive in you.
> Talking out loud to yourself with encouragement and appreciation. Dancing, singing, laughing and loving.
> Sourcing of grace and compassion.

Sweet surrender

Turn your avoidance into a "void dance" of sweet surrender! While the practice of each of these ways of listening brings the ease of Let Go . . energy into your life, listening to your emotional voice can bring the greatest sweetness. For me, it is as if I were in love all through *my* bodyself. I find that connecting to *her* by following up on what *she* wants can bring me great joy and connectedness with what is around me. *She* exists to reconnect me with what I have lost, time after time. The refrain of Cyndi Lauper's song* "Time after Time" beautifully expresses the mutuality of the relationship between *her* and me.

At least, this is the way it is on a good day! *She* is always within my reach, but not necessarily within my grasp. So I reach for *her* with open hands and wait. This deeply touching relationship has the elements of an attuned caretaker-child relationship as well as the lover and the Beloved, both in a corporeal and a Divine sense. But isn't that the whole point? That the Divine can be and is lived through us in our relationship to ourselves and each other? That our body is the seat of our soul so when we love with our full-throttled heart, we express this love in tones resonant with sacred poetry? This sense of abidingness is how the love of God for humankind is talked about among Christians and touches on the concept of "constancy" that Suzuki Roshi** refers to as "the unchanging ability to accept things as they are". Or as Rumi*** remarked, "For sixty years I have been forgetful, but not once has this flowing toward me stopped or slowed". It is what we all deeply long for and fortunate, indeed, is the child who experiences attunement and constancy in early in life.

Repeated attuned experiences with my therapist allowed me to have more choice about how I protected my heart. Trauma resolution and relationship repair can not only help you reclaim your heart and your bodyself, but also can make it more possible to connect with others who have an open heart for you. Imagine a connection with another person who you don't have a need to control; you can just trust that this person deeply cares for you and will return again and again, no matter what. If you can imagine this, you are already on your way!

The sweetness to be gained when you can surrender to a bodymindfulness practice is a little like the feeling you would have near the end of a few weeks' all expense-paid vacation. "Coming to lying" is surrendering to what you sense. Meditating is a kind of conscious surrender where you keep a focus and surrender all else. Forgiveness is surrendering to the love in your heart, for "The heart is always the heart of a child"****. Surrendering to *her* urgings can bring sweetness into your life. Love songs can have a new relevance to you, the way they may have when you last fell in love. For example, sing to yourself the refrain from the old familiar love song, "I'll Be Seeing You"***** and when you come to the word "you", maybe it will fit for you to sense your bodyself.

The sweetness with *her* is seductively satisfying, but after a time you may feel your loneliness for another and hopefully find someone with an open heart for you. For me, the pleasure of human contact and contact with *her* are different shades of subtle sweetness. Both kinds of contact are vital to well-being. Then, whether alone or with someone else, you can experience "sweet surrender".

When you feel lost, let *her* find you. Here's how: take one bodyself moment and just notice one thing, focus on it, and follow through on what you sense and you can come into the bodyself moment of truth. Just turn off the TV when it first occurs to you, give yourself praise or let your eye be caught by the colorful patina on the pipe under the sink! Then the happiness of bodyself connection can be yours once again. Following through on that one moment's awareness can lead to the next bodyself moment, which can take you deeper into a sense of connection with what is inside and all around you. As you allow the completion of that moment's action and acknowledge whatever comes up next, you may experience "flow" – that sense of effortless unfolding as in catching a wave, which takes you along for a wonderful ride. When you fall out of the Let Go wave and find yourself in a breathless "Let's Go!" rush, take a break and let your breath come back into your awareness, settling into your bodyself experience as you watch the larger Let Go . . picture emerge. That's the shift from amazing race to amazing grace!

Speaking of the larger Let Go . . picture, when I hear my Now and Zen clock chime the hour, I "Stop!" and let the reverberating sound surround me and bring me back to my bodyself home. The question I ask myself then is more important and more enduring than the question, "WHAT am I doing right now?" Instead I ask, "HOW am I doing it?" Bodymindfully or not? Am I with *her* or not? Then I can shift, acknowledge, savor, or respond to whatever is asked for in the moment. Sweet surrender strikes again.

Here are some opportunities I often take to "Stop!" what I am doing and then notice, focus and follow through and Let Go . .

Sudden sighting of a bird, the moon, a smiling face
Neck tightening or toes constricted
Impulse to indulge addiction
Hunched over, stuffing face, no longer tasting
Morsels still in teeth
Cap, nap or lap?
Attention flagging
That funny feeling . . .
Crooked towel (I ask how will I feel when I see it again?)
Feeling of "just right" or "enough"
Something catches my eye . . .

The Challenge of Balance: Taking Time for Your Practice

You practice listening to your bodyself in order to shift from the stressing Let's Go! to de-stressing Let Go . . Practice is called "practice" because it is important to practice as often as possible so that it becomes inextricably woven into your life – like a faithful, loving spouse. And even then more practice is needed! I can never get too much practice! When you are old you, like I, can still practice. Practice is both a noun and a verb. You practice your practice. You may want to find your own word for your practice. What word do you want to use for what you do to calm yourself down at the end of the day or for getting a good start on the new one? Words such as "ritual" or "routine" may have associations that wouldn't work for you.

In any case, it is important to create times for practice. Start with taking time before bedtime for decompression and then set your alarm for ten minutes earlier to give yourself time for a more bodymindful awakening. Over time and with practice, a bodyself sense of continuity can develop from the beginning of the decompression period to getting out of bed in the morning. Choose one mealtime a day to sense your food as it becomes part of you.

Take short breaks during the day, even five minutes, one minute, thirty seconds to sense how you are sitting, standing or breathing. On the way home in the car, listen for *her*. Attuned listening is what is needed to find your way to balance, many times, every day. You may gradually discover that you can find yourself, each time you lose yourself.

Gradually you create regularity in your listening practice. Your bodyself counts on you to remember to slow down and listen at the accustomed times. The discipline you create must neither be too lax nor too strict. If it is the former, it will not work and if the latter, you may become discouraged*. It is important to me not to turn what can bring delightful discoveries and a sense of flow into some kind of rigid practice. As I have already shared, when I am too demanding of myself for too long a period, I experience the backlash of indulgence**. In this regard, it may be important to notice if and how your internal critic is advising you as you go about your bodymindfulness practice.

In other words, you can make progress in your practice as you find out what is "just right" or "enough". One thing is for sure, my bodyself likes regularity. When I am consistently attentive to the way I treat myself, I am "treated" in return! A sweet synergy arises between me and my bodyself. And remember, it takes twenty minutes to slow down, once stress hormones have been activated and three weeks for a habit to become yours. Be patient. Change takes time. Be gracious. Your attitude toward yourself, toward your efforts, toward *her* is the medium <u>and</u> the message. Don't leave *her* behind - slow down, hold *her* hand, let *her* hold <u>your</u> hand and breathe through it together. As Charlotte exhorted: "Take your time! Sometimes very little makes a great difference."*** And for good measure, Rumi indicates: ". . . how one gives birth to oneself slowly."****

The time you spend slowing down and tuning into your bodyself will pay off in increased vitality, ease and well-being. Pace yourself. In mindful Let Go . . you may not get as much done in a day, but you will feel a whole lot better than you did when you spent so much time in mindless Let's Go! If you are not attending to what you are doing in a mindful way, you are training your mind in Let's Go! Why not go for balance? What kind of a mind or a life do you want to have, anyway? You do have a choice. And, there will always be more to do. Always.

"Oldilocks" moments

Besides, the older you get, the more there is to do with less energy to access. So, start now with building your capacity to focus and stay with yourself so you can fully enjoy the time you have left. As a matter of fact, one of the best memory strengthening exercises is to completely focus on what you are doing and then try to recall it the details of what you just did. For instance, when you shut off the gas valve, focus on the sensations in your fingers and hand. Then you will be less likely to question yourself later as to whether you actually did turn off the gas, because you'll have a somatic memory to anchor the sense of completion of the task. The implication here is that bodymindfulness practice can strengthen your short-term memory. What I have described as ways to build your repository of positivity (the five E's of ease: exercise, diet, sleep, social contact, savoring the moment) are also among the primary recommendations for enhancing memory in the Memory Bible*****. Since aging heightens the power of stressful emotions to impair memory, successfully navigating your emotional recovery cycle becomes even more important as you age. Indeed, being able to accept the frustration of helplessness at not being able to do or to remember what you once could, plays a big role in aging gracefully. What is often needed is taking a few minutes to slow down, feel feelings through and shift to Let Go. . Then the memory is more likely to come. And more importantly, you have the chance of accepting aging, full of grace!

An example of the empowerment of being able to feel through feelings of helplessness, which can come with aging, occurred some five years before my mother died. She was just beginning to show signs of what came to be diagnosed as Alzheimer's. This particularly poignant incident of consciously surrendering to helplessness points to how both of us needed to find some way to deal with those feelings. My mother needed help in dealing with her increasingly angry outbursts directed at her caregiver and family members. To be able to accept her helplessness, she needed me to understand her anger at her caregiver. She could "give" me her anger, because I didn't argue or retaliate, but instead I heard how angry, humiliated, and helpless she felt. She needed to accept that she was losing her ability to understand and retain certain kinds of information, not to mention to manage her life. My supporting her anger and humiliation allowed her to grieve that her childhood caretakers had not taken good enough care of her, and now she was no longer able to do it herself. She would have to find some way to accept she needed others to take care of her.

As she cried and allowed herself to rest into my arms, she gave up her struggle. Then we talked about how she could remind herself that the caregiver was there to help her, not hinder her. I suggested she put her two hands together and bow when she felt herself getting angry with him. If that wasn't enough to remind her that she needed to back down, then she should go off by herself until she could speak from a calmer place. When I checked back with her a week later, she said, they were doing a lot better. Whenever she felt herself starting to get angry, she would bow and then they would both smile. It was "over." She said that bowing helped her listen better. "When I am at the end of my rope, I put my hands together and listen with my heart." I was amazed at the words she chose to express her sense of the shift. I am sure I did not use the words "listen" or "heart" to describe what bowing meant to me. I had only said "When you feel angry, bow and remember that your caregiver is here to help you and not out to get you." Two weeks after this incident she said she felt like she was "opening to the world" when she put her hands together in this way.

My mother, who was 86 at the time, was unusual for her generation, in that she had many years of therapy, some forty years prior. In her late thirties, following the birth of her sixth child, she suffered from excessive bleeding and a hysterectomy threatened. At the time she took her religion very seriously and experienced a significant lifting of fear and pain, as well as, the cessation of bleeding when she received a blessing by the church fathers. I suspect that because of her previous experiences with psychotherapy and her faith, she was now, with my support, able to surrender to her feelings of helplessness and come through. She could then utilize the nonverbal cue of bowing to communicate when she needed to slow down, to feel what she was feeling, and let it go. Putting her hands together brought bodyself containment, so she was able to give up her struggle against helplessness and feel calm again. This was embodied spirituality and conscious surrender in action. She did not repress or suppress these uncomfortable feelings, nor did she feed them. Grounded in her bodyself she consciously surrendered to the helplessness and came back to a peaceful feeling of connection with herself and the other. She said she felt empowered because she could stop herself from yelling and screaming, which had never been her way in the first place. She said, "Now I recognize this is all a part of aging".

297

In addition, aging seems to bring with it the perception that time is going faster. Slowing down and noticing what you are sensing will put you more in the moment and can thereby alter your time perception. Perhaps one reason time seems to go faster when you are older is the same reason that a movie seen for the second time seems to go faster – you anticipate what happens next. Slowing down and coming into the moment may help you anticipate less. You can be "here" to enjoy this moment rather than "not here" in anticipation of the next.

Speaking of honoring the moment, I have found the practice of "bowing", which is an ordinary part of life in a Zen Monastery, to be very helpful. I put my hands together and bow at the beginning and ending of every meal. In the monastery, bowing can occur to signal the beginning and ending of every activity such as work, meditating, entering or leaving a room, or greeting or taking leave of another. Why not bowing before climbing into bed and after arising in the morning! Or bowing in response to the bird that alights on your window pane or to your cat, the sun, the moon! A deep bow or a shallow bow, a fast bow or a slow bow. The practice of bowing offers an opportunity to pause and experience the transit between one activity and another, an ending and a beginning. Experiment with honoring your bodyself participation in the moment!

As you age and continue your bodymindfulness practice, you are likely to become more sensitive to your bodyself needs, emotions, and the effect of substances like caffeine. You are also more likely to be in touch with the larger picture and therefore, less reactive and take comfort in your relationships. When you are more open to your experience and *her* messages, you are likely to have more choices. *She* can expand your conscious mind so you will experience more flow in your day-to-day life. So when you catch yourself running around, bumping into things, tensing your jaw, shoulders, neck or back, dropping things, making messes, gulping food, tripping, forgetting things, <u>slow</u> down and focus. Breathe, feel your feet on the ground and let out a sound. Recognize where you are and what you are doing. Talk to yourself, encourage, appreciate, instead of chastise. Turn toward *her, she* can help you age gracefully. *She* knows what feels right. Together, you can make a sweet difference in the rest of your life. Let Oldilocks be your attentive caretaker in your Golden years. For, as the Zen Master Suzuki Roshi responded to the question of why do zazen (meditate): "So you can enjoy your old age."* Another paradox of presence: embracing the moment becomes ground for entering the unknown. In this way, bodymindfulness is essential to thriving in old age and enjoying "golden years" of Goldilocks moments. And lastly, practice in consciously surrendering to the unknown can serve you in your final bodyself moments.

Staying With "Staying With"

All of this preparation is so that you can <u>be</u> in each moment, as it unfolds. Staying with is the ability to notice, focus and follow through on your bodyself experience. You meet what is there in the moment – listen for it and join it. Then you can become more self-regulating in many respects: you eat when you are hungry, rest when you are tired and acknowledge how you feel as you feel it. Joining with your bodyself allows completion in the moment with the resultant satisfaction, release and sense of expansive Let Go . . energy. Then you are truly ready for the next moment's feelings, action, contemplation or rest. "Staying with" yields increased sensitivity, resiliency, energy and ease. You can feel when it is "enough" and get it "just right" so you have Goldilocks moments, one after the other!

The more Goldilocks moments you experience, the greater the capacity of your positivity repository, which supports your staying going through the emotional recovery cycle and coming back to Let Go . . reaching out and taking in, your compassion for yourself and others, taking responsibility for your actions, exploring the unknown and experiencing grace – in short, soothing, savoring and soaring! The creative strategies you had to employ to survive your childhood but which cost you precious life energy, gradually yield to the clarity and grounding that comes with "staying with" – in short, the constriction of Let's Go! holding yields to the expansion of Let Go . . surrender.

For example, when I can actually feel all the way through what is coming up, I can come back to the moment and what I was doing. For example, one evening when I noticed I was starting to think obsessively while putting lotion on my body, I came back to just being with how applying lotion felt. Since what I was thinking about no longer carried much emotional weight, I easily could turn away from it. And at that moment of return, it was as if a film, created by my thoughts, had dissolved. What I experienced was brighter and clearer as I continued to rub the lotion into my skin. I felt more at ease and present. At that moment it all seemed so simple – to stay with, I have only to gently turn my attention back to what I am doing.

Months before, even if I had noticed I was no longer with what I was doing, the emotions connected to the obsessed about situation would have been daunting. Now that I can more easily accept what I am feeling, the obsessing is easier to turn away from, and I can return to what I am doing. You too, can be soothed by embracing the moment when you have the freedom of feeling through anything that might come up. Your bodyself welcomes your attention with ease and gratitude.

Stay with your meal until it is over. And just when <u>is</u> the meal over? When the food has disappeared from the plate inside your body? When you feel sated, no matter how much food is left on your plate? When the dishes are washed? When the particles of food are no longer in your mouth or between your teeth? When do you feel finished and ready for the next activity? <u>Sensing</u> <u>completion</u> is a living, interactive bodyself process.

Developing the discipline to stay with what you set out to do, to follow your guidelines can bring you the reward of deeply satisfying Let Go . . energy. In my experience, the greatest <u>resistance</u> seems to come just before the greatest <u>breakthrough</u>. Staying with the impulse to engage an addiction but not giving into it, has given rise to a deeply sweet feeling of well-being. What is the source of that sweetness when you manage to avoid indulging your addiction? Could it be bodyself relief that the cycles of addiction/depletion and indulgence/ denial are truncated? Could it be the sense of empowerment that you have been able to stay with your feelings? Could it be *her* gratefulness that you did not shut *her* down again by numbing your bodyself awareness?

This sweet sense of well-being embraces all of those sources. The empowerment of being able to manage my feelings and being true to myself yields a pleasure that is unparalleled and unattainable by any other means. *She* wants to celebrate and wants acknowledgement so when I hear *her* and follow through, I feel even better. Build your capacity to embrace and enjoy the moment. With enough of these experiences, you are likely to find that the pleasure of addictive substances pales in comparison with the overall benefits of staying with yourself and feeling through what is needed.

Staying with meditating until the bell rings rather than deciding yourself when it is time to stop, gives you the chance to notice how you struggle in the passing of time. When you become impatient or discouraged, you may be tempted to get up. Perhaps you will discover that something is building even though you can't feel it. Maybe you aren't even "supposed" to feel it, for if you did you would likely try to grasp it and then it would disappear. When I stay put in the face of temptation to get up, in that moment I <u>gain</u> in <u>strength</u> of staying with myself. My core is strengthened. I deepen my ability to accept what is. Acceptance is like being held in the caretaker's arms and being soothed – there is no feeling that is too terrible not to get through and then to rest. Keep rocking the baby. Eventually it is soothed and falls sleep, resting into something larger than itself. Gradually a calm center is embodied and optimal self-soothing becomes possible. The larger Let Go . . perspective emerges and "All is Well", just as it is.

Staying with writing or some other project allows the information to be worked with, as well as, a feeling of accomplishment just because you put in the time. No matter that the work didn't flow, you were there. The goal is staying with it. That is "right" effort, in the sense of "complete". That is enough. Then you can rest.

Staying with your exercise for the prescribed time. If you sense resistance, find some music you really like and let the rhythm of the music inform your movements. Let the emotion that rises in you come into your motion as you find your own way in the movement moment.

Staying with the impulse to turn off the TV or computer means you won't miss the inspiration that was in process in your bodyself, but which needed empty space, to unfold.

Staying with hanging until you are standing again. Staying with lying until you rest deeply. Staying with your heart until you are able to open again.

Finding Your Own Way

Finding your own way is allowing yourself to be guided by your bodyself messages and consciously surrendering to the expansive energy of Let Go . . soothing, savoring, and soaring. You make the Let Go . . effort of "staying with" until you find yourself "just being". "Just being" is when you have surrendered your habitual ways of holding yourself in your muscles, your attitudes and your thoughts. In Charlotte's words: "You do not have to create yourself, you are already created."* Gradually you give up what is extra and your true self emerges.

For example, many years ago during a swimming workout I discovered the transformative power of staying with the sensations of moving through the water. I focused on how the water felt between my toes as I kicked, and I let the tension in my feet and legs dissolve. I allowed my arms to fall through the air and splash into the water. It was as if I was "lounging" in the water instead of my usual effortful thrashing which eventually left me breathless when I reached the other side. Then the most amazing thing happened! I swam and swam, one lap after the other, many more than ever before and I never ran out of breath. I only stopped (after 30 minutes) because I had no more time to swim. Focusing on the sensations of moving through water and following through on releasing the sensed tension, freed energy once bound in efforting, yielding boundless energy.

When you find your own way, moment to moment, you go <u>with</u> the changes. The meal preparation, the showering, the dressing, the morning meditation, the bowing, the sitting is never the same, from one time to the next. You need not be confined by a single way. As you listen to your bodyself voice, moment to moment, you can let yourself be guided by what you hear. You can feel enlivened by finding your own way, moment to moment because Let Go . . energy is freed as you go about your daily activities. You follow your curiosity. You are less likely to fear what comes up as you listen. You have many options when you can feel through the pain of helplessness – you could join with it, you could cry, you could call someone, you could meditate and let its message unfold. You can deeply embrace being alone or being with another, because you are grounded in your bodyself and can feel through whatever comes up in the contact and connect more fully.

For instance, as I was stretching my hip, I brought my focus to the exact point of constriction and then felt something giving, very subtly, in a new way. As I sensed my way into the tiny opening, it became more dimensional. A little more give, a little more alive. Then my lips softened, signaling a Goldilocks "just right" moment in stretching. Just as Tolstoy observed: "True life is lived when small changes occur."* Each day, each moment offers the possibility of something new. I have never been here before, I have never before been quite this "me". And as Suzuki Roshi said, "You cannot stop your life, you know. You are always changing into something else. Always, Incessantly."**

The listening practices can help you access the riches, joys, depth and sweetness of your bodyself. Following your own rules and cues, you can find *her*. Guided by your bodyself messages, your heart can open again. You can experience the depths of despair and heights of delight. You can be surprised as you surrender to the mystery of your bodysoul – soulbody. You can dance wildly, work intently, love wholeheartedly, cry deeply and rejoice. Joy again – "re – joice" as you reconnect – *she* is there. You can sense *her* and *she* will sense your abiding presence, just as an infant senses the attuned caretaker's presence. You give *her* your attention and *she* returns your favor. You are touchable and touching, you are available for contact, moment to bodyself moment. Then you experience the unmistakable sweetness of tucking yourself into the Goldilocks moment.

Finding Your Way to Connect with *Her* and Tuck Yourself In . . .

Press the "Pause" Button or "Stop!"
Notice, Focus and Follow Through . . .
Sense, Meditate and Listen to Your Emotional Voice
Let *Her* Guide You
Acknowledge *Her* and Encourage Yourself Aloud: "I did it" "You did it!
Savor Completion of Tasks and Events: "We did it!"
Fortify Your Repository of Positivity with Goldilocks Moments
Eschew a "Cap" for a Nap or a "Lap"
Let Yourself "Rest Into" and Be Guided by "Something Larger" than Yourself
Gather a Posse of Positivity
Reach Out and Repair Relationships
Embrace the Constriction of "All is Hell" and Open to Expansion of "All is Well"
Increase Your Capacity for Aliveness by Meeting Discomfort with Support
Sense, Sing, Shake, or Dance Away Obsessive Thinking
Create a Bodyself Mantra of Your Own
Stay with and Consciously Surrender
Bow

ACKNOWLEDGMENTS

I am especially grateful to Len Felder, Ph.D, for his heartfelt encouragement and valuing of what I wanted to share, as well as for his generous editorial comments. Much appreciation also goes to Bill Littlewood for his painstaking, page-by-page, editing of the entire manuscript the first time around, for his unflinching commentary and reactions, and for his sensing the heart of the book, namely *her*, despite the fact he didn't fancy the descriptor, "sweet"!

I deeply appreciate my teacher, Charlotte Selver and my mentor and therapist, Robert Hilton, Ph.D. for sharing their wisdom with me. By going to their depths to discover their personal truths, they were able to make the fruits of their personal exploration available to me, as well as, impart a practice so I could make my own discoveries. Thus, my own journey was supported and deepened and in turn, I offer this practice to others. I am grateful to Stephan Tobin, Ph.D who made it safe enough for me to work with a male therapist and who helped me discover the "watcher" inside. This work continued with Bob and supported my heart in opening again. During a critical juncture in my personal work, Scott Baum, Ph.D.'s unwavering presence helped me secure more ground in my being. The subtle, yet powerful and acutely focused work with Gestalt therapist, Todd Burley, Ph.D. was pivotal in finally finishing therapy!

Thorough-going gratitude to my dear friends and family, who each in their own way, have believed in me and supported my efforts over the past 15 years: Jan, Liv, Barbara, Ahmos, Matthew, Judy, Margaret and Janet. Special thanks go to my friends, Jan, Connie, Carol, Lee and Victoria who gave me valuable critical feedback, which supported the heart of this effort. Heartfelt acknowledgment goes to colleagues who are also part of my "posse of positivity": the women in my Master's process group and my peer consultation group with whom I have met for more than ten years. Much appreciation for input on the cover design from Liv, Phil, Gary, Jeb, Pat, Sharon, Marni, and cousin Pat, and to my sister, Sherry, for helping proof the final draft. And to Mordechai, my computer "tech", who saved me and my manuscript many times over the course of fifteen years!

My clients' and students' enthusiasm for the listening practices heartened me and invigorated my belief in the need to share this work.

I acknowledge *her* for responding to me when I listened for *her* and for being unfailingly heartfelt and creative in *her* response. *I acknowledge Ginger for listening for me again and again!*

And finally, I feel ever deepening gratitude for my mother's spirited perseverance in her quest for her truth as well as for her love, delight and enthusiasm for my efforts to follow what was meaningful to me. We share a deeply held valuing of the human spirit.

COPYRIGHT ACKNOWLEDGMENTS

APPENDIX A

The Yin and Yang of Balancing Let's Go! with Let Go . .

While it is tempting for discussion's sake to make clear delineations between the two modes, Let's Go! and Let Go . . as well as between the concept of "I" and *"she"*, in reality these functions are interdependent. The same can be said for the concepts of SNS- and PNS-dominated activity as well as left hemisphere (LH) and right hemisphere (RH) processing. In each case, each individual of the pair, considered separately has a specific definable, observable function, often seeming to be the opposite of the other. However, in vivo, the pairs are active simultaneously and do not operate in isolation. It is the relative *balance* or proportion of their functioning that makes an observable difference in behavior. For instance, when you desire to shift to Let Go . . from Let's Go!, you must act immediately and swiftly when you discover that you have just received a message from your bodyself (*her*). If you delay, you stay committed to Let's Go! Paradoxical as it may seem, you need to take Let's Go! action to shift to Let Go . .

The yin yang symbol aptly depicts how these paired facets of your functioning facilitate each other. Each contains the seed of the other – neither is completely black or white. Reality is relational. Human reality is especially relational. This truth is reflected in nature in many ways - in the movement of waves, the ebb and flow of the tide, the filling and emptying of the lungs or the bouncing of a ball. "What goes up must come down." You bounce the ball and it falls down. You apply force to the ball and gravity does the rest. You exercise Let's Go! on the ball and then Let Go . . takes over while you wait. Already the coming down is in the going up. Gravity is still pulling as the ball rises. One phase is dependent on the other - like the proverbial chicken and the egg. Each contains the other and neither exists without the other – always the flow of becoming, the beginning without inclination to end*. Each completes the other, complements the other, and in the case of *her* and me, we also <u>compliment</u> each other! The practice of meditation seems to enhance the awareness of such "paradoxes of presence".

For example, creative activity most easily lends itself to demonstrating how the two modes work together. The model for creative activity delineates several relatively distinct phases: (1) immersion, (2) incubation and (3) action. In the mode model offered here, those phases would translate into (1) Let's Go! 2) Let Go . . (3) Let's Go! action modulated by Let Go . . sensibilities. There are times when Let's Go! is experienced exclusively and other times when you are deeply resting that Let's Go! is nowhere near. But most of the time, the two modes complement each other, just as the functioning of the right and left cerebral hemispheres is interdependent and "on" all the time. The relative portion of influence they may have, may vary widely at a given moment in time, in a given person and during a particular activity.

For instance, when I write, I know *she* is there when I think a humorous thought or fashion a delightful phrase. *She* is the emotional voice that sparks the humor, and sounds the alliteration. *She* loves to create – to expand rather than expound! But *she* needs me to <u>yield</u> to *her* impulse for expression. We have to work together – each in our own way, discovering how we join and contribute to each other. We come to appreciate our differences, like a successfully married couple. Two heads (hemispheres) *are* better than one. Two noted neurophysiologists, the husband and wife team, Antonio and Hanna Damasio offer their research findings to demonstrate that the contributions of both hemispheres are necessary for the best decisions.

Sometimes, one hemisphere or the other dominates to the detriment of the other. If you are like most people, your bodyself voice is much weaker than your more analytical, logical voice. These "voices" can be associated with the right cerebral hemisphere (RH) and the left hemisphere (LH), respectively – RH facilitating the domain of what I call "*her*" – intuition, sensation and emotion-oriented bodyself functioning and LH supporting the more analytical, linear, logical processing associated with rational thinking. The executive functions of LH could be associated with the controller or ego or "I". But in the end, I am *she* and *she* is I. The terms "*she*" and "I" just speak to different aspects interactive functioning.

In reality they both process information and inform decisions simultaneously. The question is how much do you pay attention to what your bodyself is saying? Do you hear it, and when you do, do you discount or judge it? The relative loading of one side or the other varies from person to person and from one state to another. In Let's Go! state you are likely to experience LH dominant functioning. On the other hand, in Let Go . . the RH processing is more likely to dominate. Slowing down and paying attention to sensations facilitates Let Go . . and RH activity. Practicing the self-soothing experiments and techniques in this book will help you tip the scale toward Let Go . . to achieve greater balance between these two types of functioning.

The shift from "flight or fight" to "rest and repair" or from Let's Go! to Let Go . . is, in part, mediated by a shift from the sympathetic nervous system (SNS) to parasympathetic nervous system (PNS) dominated activity. As you shift to Let Go . . you are likely to notice a concomitant shift from LH dominant activity which is often characterized by analytical, linear thinking to RH dominant activity which is sometimes referred to as the intuitive, emotional brain.

While it is tempting to associate Let Go . . with RH, PNS and "rest and repair" and Let's Go! with LH, SNS, and "fight or flight", the association should be only loosely taken. For that matter, the terms "Let Go . ." "Let's Go!", "RH" and "LH" are oversimplifications of complex processes and oversimplification can lead to false conclusions. However, it is useful to treat these associations as suggestive of possibilities to enrich your understanding of your functioning. Each mode has characteristic physiological and psychological attributes – each mode is a discernible bodyself experience with an accompanying perspective.

For example, when you won't listen to your bodyself (*her*) – when you try to push down your feelings, you begin to feel anxious, you have anxious thoughts, you tense your muscles and may have other body symptoms like stomachaches or heart palpitations. In an attempt to avoid feeling overwhelmed by emotion you "go into your head." What is needed is to find a way to let *her* speak so you can hear *her* feelings. Ask, "What is the matter?" or encourage yourself. All *she* needs is to be heard and to feel like you care and then *she* can help you feel calm. Then you are likely to sense is that "All is well" so you can Let Go . . Your anxiety will disappear and your muscles relax and your breathing becomes easier. With practice and support you will be able to listen to yourself and allow yourself the time you need to prepare yourself for a deep sound sleep.

To get the best perspective on any situation you need the integration of both aspects of your functioning, for each only grasps only a little more than half of what is to be perceived. When I write, I need *her* to help me stay loose and flexible so I can feel the larger picture while another part of me can figure out how the elements fit logically together. If I get too stressed by worrying about time or someone's reaction or become too self-critical or tense, I lose the perspective I need to find the best fit. I need the logic of LH, the drive of Let's Go! as well as the intuition and sense of RH and the ease of Let Go . . While the LH calculates, the RH just knows and doesn't need to know why it knows. I have to take *her* word for it and to be able to do that requires a lot of experience with letting *her* lead me. In Let Go . . it is "the readiness of the mind is wisdom"* (S.Suzuki). In Let's Go! wisdom is knowledge. Both are essential.

In Let Go . . you are more likely to feel positively about the present moment and to project that into the future. Like when the baby cries and the caretaker comforts, the baby feels content. When you have a calm center through adequate childhood attunement, allowing yourself to grieve can restore you to your bodyself. Through grieving you can regain your aliveness. For grieving requires a deep bodymind "letting go". As you feel through the pain of disappointment and loss, you are comforted by deep contact with yourself and the de-stressing chemicals that are released in the process. For example, emotional tears contain natural pain modulating endorphins while tearing in response to a chemical stimulus does not. Your bodyself tries to take care of you through grieving so you can rest and shift to Let Go . . Give it a chance. Just when your world seems diminished, it will open to you, nurtured by your tears. The Vietnamese Buddhist teacher, Thich Nhat Hahn expresses this discovery with these words: "The tears I cried yesterday have become rain." (Greeting card).

To Let Go . . you connect with your bodyself or another. With support for your being, you can discover the next step. You begin to sense that everything will be all right (or is all right). Whether your support comes from another or from your calm heart center, it allows you to better face the uncertainty of what will happen next. What felt like a <u>crisis</u> in Let's Go! mode can now become an <u>opportunity</u> in Let Go . . Then the glass appears half full, everything seems to be working out or "happens for a reason" because you have easy acceptance in this mode. In Let's Go! the perspective is more task oriented - your organism is energized to perform, remove obstacles, carry out plans and analyze results. The Let's Go! focus is narrow and can be crisis-oriented, whereas in Let Go . . the focus is broad and oriented toward seeing a situation as an opportunity for growth and discovery.

In a very real sense, learning to Let Go . . is like becoming a "good enough" parent to yourself. You keep trying to find out what your bodyself needs at the moment. You give yourself a break when you are tired, you listen and then encourage yourself when you are down. Encouraging, acknowledging and thanking yourself (*her*) will help you shift to the sweetness of Let Go . . These activities have a similar positive effect as do affirmations, "good parent" messages* and various Twelve Step mottos. But these efforts are only deeply meaningful and lasting if underlying pain or trauma is addressed. Otherwise, you remain detached from your deeper emotions and from *her*. As you become familiar with your patterns and you take the necessary steps to support yourself, you will be able to prevent yourself from falling deeper into confusion, anxiety and depression. When you notice you are anxious, you can find out what is behind that by asking *her*, "What's the matter?" Then you take care of those feelings by staying with your bodyself experience. The once defended against emotions can become vehicles for grounding yourself. If you need contact with another, you can reach for it.

You don't have to do what *she* wants all the time. *She* just needs to be heard and loved. *She* can bear disappointment as long as *she* does not lose you, as long as you listen to *her*. Your acknowledging *her* is felt by *her* as an attempt to connect. Research indicates that being a "good enough" parent means you are attuned thirty percent of the time. The remaining seventy percent of the time you spend repairing the misattunements! Connecting with *her* is how you return to a calm center and shift to Let Go . . When the baby connects to the attuned caretaker, it gives up its tension and arousal – the distressed Let's Go! shifts to de-stressed Let Go . . Research on premature infants shows that shoulder tension dissipates when the crying infant can grasp the caretaker's finger. This response is present at birth; contact brings the bodyself experience that "All is well." Despair and panic vanish because the baby is soothed by the de-stressing chemicals of contact and is able to stay in its body rather than be overwhelmed by distressing chemicals. When its Let's Go! efforts of flailing and crying bring contact, the deep peace of Let Go . . follows and the stress/de-stressing cycle is complete.

Connecting with a friend, reading a story or seeing a film or photograph can also help you find *her*. As long as the contact touches you or moves you, it can lead to your connecting with *her*. While you can hear *her* in both Let's Go! and Let Go . . it is easier to find *her* when you slow down.

C. Barks, *The Illustrated Rumi* 85.
A. Damasio and H. Damasio as cited in A. Damasio, *The Feeling of What Happens*, (New York: Harcourt, Brace and Company, 1999).
S. Suzuki, *Zen Mind, Beginner's Mind* 113.
J. Rosenberg, "Good Parent Messages" Hand-out in training of the Institute of Body Psychotherapy, 1991.

APPENDIX B

Contact Point Awareness

As you sit, notice the support of what is under you. As you more clearly feel your contact with the earth beneath you through your feet and/or sit bones, you may have the experience of allowing your weight through you into the ground. In terms of grounding, <u>sit</u> <u>bones</u> are to the <u>pelvis</u> in <u>sitting</u> as <u>feet</u> are to whole <u>body</u> in <u>standing</u>. When you are sitting, whether cross-legged or in a chair, some of your weight goes through your feet into the ground.

Once you feel solid contact with what is under you, you can use this contact to extend upward and outward into space, to rise and expand with breathing. Breathing pulls you upward and outward, while gravity pulls down. There is a dynamic tension between breath and earth that moves through you. Breathing helps you meet the pull of gravity.

The sensations of this dynamic tension can be experienced as you come to more quiet. Free yourself to feel the expansion of breathing and the pull of gravity. Resting into giving to these forces can feel comforting. Gravity keeps you connected to the earth and breathing allows you to expand and reach. As you are sitting, allow your elbows to come a little away from your sides so there is more room for air to your armpits and more room for breathing in your chest. Notice your breathing – how wide is it? How deep does it go? Trace the flow of air inside you – all the way up – all the way down – all the way in – all the way out. Rest into the movements of breathing.

To feel your sit bones more clearly, you can bend over your knees and tap your sit bones. Or, while sitting, place hands under your sit bones. Shift your weight from one sit bone to the other as you gently rock side to side. Allow your weight through your sitting bones into the support under you. Once you sense your sit bones clearly you are more likely to feel the floor of your pelvis. What is its condition? Can you allow it to soften? The pelvic floor is sometimes called the pelvic diaphragm. It is said to respond to the movements of breathing. How about that for a focus for your breath meditation!

Sense how your lips meet. Do they press together or are they gently resting on each other? If you sense tension in your lips allow them to soften along with your jaw. Feel the pull of gravity on your jaw and allow more room for the insides of your mouth. Let yourself down into the ground and at the same time, be responsive to the rising and expanding movement of breathing.

Notice how your eyelids come together. Are they pressed together or gently resting? Let your attention go to the area above your eyes. You may feel as if your eyebrows are being pulled up as you sense your forehead. Can you allow more ease in this region? Allow your eyes to open softly, letting in some light, but without trying to see anything in front of you. Is it possible to allow your eyes to open without raising your eyebrows? Eyelids softly opened help you stay more present and awake. However, some people prefer to leave their eyes closed during meditation because concentration seems better. Try it both ways and notice how your experience changes.

As you sit you will become aware of changes in sitting that want to be made. Allow them. Shift your attention from your sit bones and floor of your pelvis up to your lips and then to your eyes and forehead. As you feel breathing, notice if it wants more room in your ribcage, especially in your sides and armpits. Let your hands rest on your thighs. Allow your elbows to come a little more away from your sides and then gradually find the place where there is a sense of freedom in your chest and arms. Bring your shoulder blades down so they lay flat against your back by pulling down with your elbows toward the floor. Then give up that effort. If you would like a little more refreshment in your sides, slap the area around your armpits. Allow the back of your head rise, elongating the back of your neck.

Notice how breathing allows you to expand out and up as gravity pulls down. You are sinking and rising, all at the same time. This balanced dynamic tension runs through you, supporting your life. Rest into the rhythm of breathing and the support of the life forces within you. As you inhale, you take in what was outside and you become a little larger. As you exhale, you give up what was inside and you become a little smaller – your contour and the contour of the world changes with each breath – expanding and contracting.

During breath meditation, bring your awareness back to how it feels to be sitting. What changes do you need to make to allow a more supported sitting? What changes need to be allowed so there is less constriction here and there? Allow your attention to shift back and forth between sitting and breathing. At some point, sitting, breathing and your bodyself may feel like one experience.

If you sit on the floor, it may be helpful to sit against a wall so that the base of your pelvis is supported. Some prefer to lean against the wall as well. Others find the appropriate support for sitting by putting a cushion under the sit bones, raising the pelvis higher than the knees and feet. Experiment with what works best for you. Well-supported by your sit bones, your spine will more easily find the vertical. Are you available to sense and follow through on impulses toward change? Even though your feet are not likely to be flat on the floor, notice what you are feeling through your feet.

APPENDIX C

Adequate Caretaker Nurturing: The need for connection, repair and self-assertion

Attunement: Need for Connection - The mutual "Yes!"

How you come to be able to experience and tolerate emotion, be it happy or sad, afraid or mad, depends on the dynamics of your experiences with your caretaker. Your interactions with your caretaker determine whether and how you are able to tolerate the bodily excitation of frustration, fear, anger, disappointment, loneliness, love, longing and sexuality. You are not born with the ability to self-regulate your emotional and need states. You learn how to tolerate having emotions and how to recover from them in the context of sensitive attuned human interaction.

Your first need was for nurturing through food and contact. The two needs are fundamentally intertwined. Infants cannot survive without human contact and food. The need for attunement exists at the moment of birth, fostering the mutual stimulation between the mother and infant through touch and later with smiles and coos. The responsibility of the caretaker is to provide sensitive attunement, which stimulates the infant to become more responsive to and aware of the environment and its body. The light in the mother's eye is mirrored in the baby's – they are mutually de-"lighted." This is the primal experience of "Yes!" in your body – it is experienced as connection, love and that certain "sweetness". De-stressing chemicals flow through the mother and infant as the infant rests into the contact and experiences "all is well". The infant comes to experience its bodyself through the exchanges of loving looks, sounds and touches. In this way, it increases its capacity for feelings of pleasure, connection, pride and love for itself and others. Lacking the somatic experience of affirmation of pleasurable connection in childhood, the adult may experience anxiety or confusion in the face of the "good feelings" of intimacy, sex, pride and self-esteem.

When your caretaker notices your upset and sensitively goes about trying to find out what your need is, you are likely to have the bodily experience that need states do not go on and on, unfulfilled. Your brain gets the message that the disturbance is quelled and a quiet, yet alert, relaxed Let Go . . state is restored. Your cries are heard, your tummy is filled and you are gently rocked to sleep. You understand on a bodily level that disturbance is met with attunement and relief. After repeated experiences of a need arising and its being met, the infant's brain begins to anticipate the need being fulfilled. Being in a need state becomes gradually somewhat more tolerable. The infant can wait a little longer. (On the other hand, when the infant's needs are not met consistently, the very emergence of a need state signals anticipatory distress – the distress that help will not come. To make matters worse, when distress has been allowed to escalate for too long, too many times, the infant has great difficulty taking in the nurturing when it finally is available.

The infant not only needs to be connected to and stimulated by the caretaker but also needs reverie, rest and withdrawal from interaction. This need for withdrawal must also be seen and respected by the caretaker. The caretaker must be able to take care of her own needs for stimulation to not infringe upon the infant's need for withdrawal. Otherwise, the infant experiences disregulation of its organismic state. The infant needs to rest but instead is coaxed into responding. Ultimately, it becomes overstimulated, cranky, and finally despondent and may even dissociate. When such disregulation occurs, the caretaker's responsibility is once again, to help restore balance to the infant. In this way, the infant comes to experience its own rhythm of contact and withdrawal or engagement (Yes!) and separation (No!) through the attuned caretaker responses. In this way, the infant gradually embodies the experience of shifting back and forth between Let's Go! excitement and Let Go . . reverie. Ultimately, through connecting to its bodyself experience, the infant differentiates itself from the caretaker.

In sum, the mutual "Yes!" is the result of the mutual efforts of the baby and its mother. The baby cries and coos, and reaches for the mother - the mother smiles and soothes, and reaches for the baby. The baby's job is to draw the mother near and keep signaling until the mother gets it "just right!" (The mutual "Yes!" experience of getting it "just right" as a result of continued mutual efforts is the template for what I call the "Goldilocks moment"). At that moment, the efforts cease, the tension dissolves, the baby can rest into the mother and shift to Let Go . . The mother's job is to help the infant "inhabit its body" through repeated attuned experiences of greeting and quelling of disturbance due to an emergent need or the repair of misattunement. The repeated experience of attuned caretaker interactions is embodied as a calm heart center in the infant and a sense that "All is well."

Need for Repair after Misattunement - The caretaker's "No!"

As the infant becomes a toddler he begins to explore the environment and encounter situations where the responsible caretaker must say "No!" The censuring tone induces shame and perhaps fear or hurt. The toddler's bodyself contracts - his head lowers, his muscles and breathing constrict. He may even cry. As he gets older he may react with anger and a "No!" of its own. His sense of attunement with the caretaker is interrupted. Now the caretaker's job is to repair the breach. The repair needs to happen soon, so that the child can reconnect to the caretaker and thence to himself. As the child experiences relief from the bodyself tension of misattunement – his muscles relax, he breathes easily and he shifts to Let Go . . He finds out that censure does not mean ultimate loss of the caretaker and thereby himself as well. Through appropriate caretaker behavior, he has the bodily experience that saying, "I'm sorry" and forgiveness are ways to repair breaches and shift to Let Go . .

When the caretaker punishes the child, a similar breach in connection occurs, accompanied by a cascade of emotional and attendant bodily reactions. The caretaker's responsibility is to bridge the gap and be available for listening to how the child feels and to assure him that he is still loved even though his behavior was not.

Need for Separation and Self-assertion - the child's "No!"

Successful attunement to the child's needs includes affirming the child's need for self-assertion and separation. As a child, your "No!" needed to be respected into order for you to develop a strong sense of self. The caretaker's job is to respect your boundaries and love you even when you are angry. Your caretaker's respect for your "No!" allows you to define yourself and paves the way for your setting appropriate boundaries as you mature.

The toddler's "No!" expresses a need for self-assertion and that needs to be respected by the caretaker. Respect does not mean the caretaker must agree with the child's "No!" but it does mean that the "No!" must be honored as the child's position. If the caretaker has problems with having differences, confrontation or separation from the child because she equates the child's need for self-definition with her own emotional abandonment then she is likely to override or punish the youngster's "No!". Losing her support, the child is threatened with a loss of self just as he was attempting to define himself. When the caretaker cannot tolerate the child's "No!", the child begins to fear the consequences of taking this developmentally necessary stand of separation. He is now in a real bind – he has to choose between himself and his need to be taken care of and loved (the Sophie's choice). This bind is intensified with repeated misattunement, punishment, abuse and trauma.

Self-assertion includes being able to ask for what you want. If you were shamed for asking for what you wanted, you may have trouble hearing the answer when you ask your emotional voice, "What is the matter?" For that matter, you may even have difficulty asking the question. Consider this sad(istic) but true story - Child: "I want an ice cream cone!" Caretaker: "You can't have it!" Child: "Why not?" Caretaker: "Because you asked for it!" This child will likely come to feel anxiety and fear of disapproval when it asserts itself or expresses itself emotionally. Or perhaps you witnessed your caretaker depriving herself. Simply through her example, her verbal expressions of self-denial or very subtle bodyself messages such as body posture or sighs you may come to feel guilty when you try to take care of yourself. Perhaps you saw how burdened your caretaker was and you tried to take care of her by not asking for what you wanted. Or maybe someone shamed you when you were chose the biggest or the last piece of cake.

Fearing the caretaker's shaming or anger can silence your expressing your needs or even feeling like you have a right to have them. Your body responds to your silencing its voice with muscular tension and busyness in your head. You may develop a relentless critical voice that echoes the voice of your caretaker. Even if what this internal critic is saying does not sound like what your parent would think or say, you are likely to feel as if you are in the presence of your need-denying parent when you hear it. This critical voice serves to keep your feelings and behavior in check to prevent you from further harm. You might say its admonitions are designed to function preemptively. It strikes before the other (someone else) does. Further discussion of the critic's functioning in relation to your being able to listen and soothe yourself continues in the critic-caretaker section of Chapter 8.

Taking care of yourself through self-assertion also includes being able to identify and express your anger. However you may have had the experience that your anger was dangerous. Dangerous might have meant that your caretaker either withdrew and fell apart in response to your angry reproaches or retaliated by annihilating you. So to save yourself you try to tuck away your anger as well as your fear and unmet needs. Now just try to get a good night's sleep! No wonder you have trouble listening to your emotional voice, not to mention falling or staying asleep.

So now as an adult when you ask your emotional voice "What's up?" and you are actually angry, you may instead feel numb or anxious or suddenly remember the stashed-way cookies or ice cream. If you were made to fear anger, whether your own or another's, you will likely have difficulty listening to *her* complaints and therefore understanding how you feel. In fact you may even imagine that others are mad at you when actually *you* are angry with them. Your efforts to try and not upset others may make you mad on some level, that you feel you have to be so careful. How confusing it becomes when you have to hide from yourself! *She* wants to be found but it has to be by the right person. *She* learned early on that *her* anger put *her* at risk of loss of caretaker approval. You have work to do to gain *her* confidence but *she* will eventually be glad to tell *her* secrets to you.

Successful repair of misattunement, whether it stems from the child's or the caretaker's "No!" enables the child's being able to connect with others and to set good boundaries. He will be able to honor his and another's needs, experience emotion, ask for help, stand up for himself and truly self-soothe. He will have compassion and respect for others and himself. And, he is not likely to need to read this book!

When attunement consistently fails and no repair is made, then the disturbing need state and accompanying emotion itself becomes a signal that more disturbance will follow. No help will come. Your brain may then respond to the sensing of a need as if it was an impending crisis and you become more anxious and hyper-vigilant. Ultimately in effort to avoid overload, your brain may shut down the excessive excitation and you may experience dissociation or even depression. Your body may still be tense and your need unmet but at least you no longer feel the emotional and physical pain of impending overwhelm and helplessness. As an adult you may find yourself engaging in one or more of your addictions. You dare not hear your own cry. For, the experience of helplessness and vulnerability is still stored, untempered, in your emotional brain as a potentially fearsome and toxic state. Consequently, you are less likely to avoid situations which draw you nearer to re-experiencing this painful sense of powerlessness – such as slowing down and asking yourself, "What is the matter?"

APPENDIX D

The Purgatory of Waiting in the Shadow for Repair

Unrepaired childhood trauma or caretaker breaches can color your perception of day-to-day interpersonal encounters. When you lose the connection with the beloved parent, you lose your bodyself which is why an unrepaired caretaker breach can be so annihilating and traumatic. The child needs "good enough" contact with caretaker in order to develop an integrated experience of its bodyself. When the caretaker does not repair the breach, you are left in "anxiety hell" – afraid, angry and perhaps so ashamed, you can't ask for help. The resultant terror and rage become deeply embedded in the synaptic connections through which emotional messages are routed. Helplessness thrives in the face of these overwhelming emotions and can lead to dissociation or other forms of avoidance. You may recognize some of the symptoms of "Waiting for Repair" listed below:

1. You may imagine others are mad at you, especially when you are mad at them.
2. You may expect the relationship is over every time
someone is angry with you or vice versa.
3. You may try to make up for feeling angry, mean or intrusive.
4. You may obsess about whether you have hurt someone.
5. You may bend over backward to make a repair yourself because
you can't stand how helpless uncertainty makes you feel.
6. You may be careful about hurting others and end up annoying them
or hurting them anyway because you have become so codependent
and resentful you don't have enough energy for your own life.
7. You may let others "off the hook" too soon because you can't stand
to feel "on the hook" yourself and then you resent them.
8. You may have difficulty concentrating and falling asleep.
9. At the other end of the spectrum, you may habitually act out on others,
strike before you are stricken, be unforgiving, cynical and hostile.
10. Alternatively, you may have given up in despair and
become apathetic or profoundly depressed.
11. Or worse, you may be detached, remote or even sociopathic, not feeling much of
anything for others and taking advantage of every opportunity for personal gain.

Once the repair process begins and the traumatic feelings are integrated, changes occur in your emotional brain. You become less obsessed with controlling good or bad feelings. Once you have embodied a calm heart center as a result of the repeated experience of being responded to by an attuned other, you will be more likely to:

Self-soothe, knowing on a deep level you are OK.
Express deep feelings of anger, fear, shame, grief and let love in.
Set appropriate interpersonal boundaries, knowing you don't have to sacrifice yourself to be loved.
Confront another and appropriately express anger.

Express love and joy in living and connecting with others.
Embody your aliveness as you fully resonate with the world.
Have many Goldilocks moments.

A breach with yourself is the unkindest cut of all, but it can heal, one Goldilocks moment at a time.

APPENDIX E

Using a Guide to Explore the Growing Edge of Bodyself Awareness

Your bodyself voice itself is a good guide to sensing your need to rest, to eat well, to exercise and to minimize stress, stimulants and depressants. But even then, you may need a guide to help you stay with your experience long enough to hear your bodyself's response to a question like "What is needed right now?" A guide can be helpful in each of the listening practices so that you can hang out on the edge of developing awareness. Just as a regenerating neuron tip grows toward a minute energy field, so too, the energy field created between you and your guide will support and give direction to your exploration and subsequent growth. In sensing, the leader asks questions to help you stay present in the experiment and explore the edge of bodyself holding when you ask "What does it want"? A guide can encourage you to stay with the discomfort of feeling that edge of tension – to wait in it and be curious about what unfolds – perhaps a shift in perception and a new freedom of movement.

Similarly, in working out, a coach can help you expand your capacity to exercise without injuring yourself. The coach's experience can help you discern what pain is simply "pushing the edge" pain which stimulates muscle growth and what pain is actually damaging your body. Someone who has "been there and done that" knows the warning signs and can help you differentiate between a condition, which leads to bodily injury and that which precedes the breakthrough to a "second wind". Likewise, a sensitive massage therapist can help you distinguish between "hurts good" and "hurts bad" – "good" pain results from riding the "melting edge" of tension as the holding gives way to release, whereas "bad" pain can signal damage to underlying tissues due to over-stimulation. Staying with the sensations of touch and tension helps relieve the constriction and promotes the shift to Let Go . .

In meditation a teacher can help you develop your capacity to stay with the focus so that you don't space out or dissociate when an unwanted feeling or thought comes up. Unresolved trauma can surface in the course of meditating and result in panic attacks or dissociation, and a sense of being retraumatized through being flooded by memories and/or associated emotion. A bodyself injury could also result from sitting too long in one position in an attempt to "sit through the pain". On the other hand, the sense of urgency that sometimes comes up while meditating – a sudden urge to get up which could be accompanied by thoughts like "the timer must be broken" or "the building is on fire" – is another kind of phenomenon and continuing to sit through that sense of urgency often brings an opening and a sense of well-being and deepens your ability to stay with yourself. A strong meditation practice - developing the capacity to stay with an object of focus (breath, mantra, etc) does not have to include bodily injury or dissociation.

But most important to increasing your capacity to listen to bodyself messages is developing a compassionate attitude toward your "emotional voice". Paying attention to sensations and heeding their messages is one thing but receiving without judgment what your emotional voice is trying to tell you can be quite another challenge. The concept of an energetic field which supports neuronal regrowth after injury is also an apt metaphor for the way repair of an impaired connection to our emotional voice occurs. With time and continued contact between a psychotherapist and a client a growth-enhancing energetic field is created. The experience of the compassionate presence of the therapist as conveyed through his eyes, his countenance, and his voice, facilitates your contacting your own vulnerability - your fear, shame, sadness, anger, hopelessness and longing. It's almost as if this other's heartfelt presence acts as an energy field, which makes it safer to feel what was secretly felt but not expressed. Further, the therapist acts a guide who can help you distinguish between emotional expression which is retraumatizing and that which is healing.

This energetic field forms a ground, which supports your ability to go deeper into what you are feeling without judgment of what your bodyself voice is expressing. His thorough-going presence encourages your once-held back feelings as if saying, "There is no feeling too awful to experience together. I will be here with you through whatever you are feeling. I will not shrink from anything you feel, you will not have to feel it alone." For the first time, you may be able to feel through feelings that got frozen in time because no one was there to listen to you. When you look at him you do not see unfeeling, vacant eyes, nor a cold or angry countenance. Instead, you experience a living presence, which may embolden you to feel as much as you can integrate at the moment because you sense that you are seen and your feelings are understandable and justifiable. As you are seen with compassion, you may come to feel compassion for yourself. And gradually your stance can loosen its grip on you. As you are being responded to in a different way, you gradually become able to respond to yourself in a different way. You may come to tell yourself a different story about your life or perhaps, you will need no story at all.

APPENDIX F

Healing the Shadow of Addiction

At the bottom of abandonment and intrusion trauma lies terror – the unbearable terror of helplessness. The very people who were supposed to protect you did not and/or could not. They may not have even seen your plight and even if they did, they were helpless to rescue or even comfort you. In response to feeling this terror you tightened your muscles and tried to block it from awareness. You may engage in dissociative or addictive behavior to keep yourself from feeling overwhelmed and squeezed by the tentacles of terror. Better to numb yourself to the psychic awareness of helplessness and the stressful chemicals of terror.

The "shadow of addiction" arises from the nonintegrated experience of intolerable helplessness. The shadow reflects disowned feelings and impulses resulting from trauma or inadequate caretaker nurturing and can be acted out on other people or on oneself. For instance, you might terrorize yourself as you once felt terrorized or you might terrorize someone else. You may have an excessive concern with whether you are liked, as a result of being raised by a pathologically narcissistic caretaker or a rageholic. Caretakers such as these are unlikely to be able to deliver you, the soothing you need because they themselves are a source of terror and upset for you. Therefore, you are more likely to attempt to self-soothe through practicing an addiction whether it involves a chemical substance such as alcohol, food, or an activity such as gambling or workaholism. Bottom line, you can count on your addiction - you don't have to wait or make yourself vulnerable to another person. It seems under your control and there is often no momentary risk. Your pain is now and long-term risk seems to pale in comparison with the urgency of the threatening feelings.

Many an alcoholic protests that the boisterous, obstreperous or otherwise obnoxious person who comes out when he drinks is not himself. "That wasn't me", "that's not like me", "I don't know what got into me" is the common cry. This "other" who lives inside him is sometimes referred to as his "shadow" or "dark side". This "feeling and behavioral complex" may not be owned in a normal waking state. This "disowned self" operates similarly to a dream image or nightmare of a monster or other undesirable character. Dream images can be understood as "pictures" of feelings that bear the energetic imprint of past experiences. When you are traumatized by past experiences, your feeling reaction to the perpetrator's action is stored in your emotional brain. Your first reaction may have been fear and then shame because of your helplessness. The impotence and shame, in turn, likely triggers your own rage. In addition, you may have rage because no one came to help you. Perhaps another witnessed your trauma and turned a deaf ear to it. You may hold against this rage because it threatens your integrity to be so angry with, perhaps, the one person who did not directly harm you. And this unacceptable rage fuels the monster you dream of and also your acting out.

Your emotional brain also bears the imprint of the frightening, sadistic or abandoning behavior of the perpetrator. In altered states (alcohol-induced or sleep), this "shadow" side can be reenacted through a frightening dream or by your acting out on others or yourself. Consider the number of homicides and suicides occur in connection with intoxication.

The shadow is part of you even if is it denied to your conscious mind. As long as it is not integrated, there is the potential for you to dream of it or act it out in an altered or dissociated state. Acting out such undesirable or destructive impulses is often followed by shame and denial.

You may be especially likely to disown the capacity for this kind of behavior, if you were deeply hurt by it when you were growing up. You may have come to judge it harshly. When you drink too much alcohol or use stimulants, this disowned part of you, released from normal inhibitions, is freed to act. If is as if this "other' person comes out, someone quite different from what others have come to expect from you. A mild example mentioned earlier is my uncharacteristically cold and callous comment to my friend, "You'll get used to it!" Similarly, as you fall asleep, your conscious defenses dissolve and an image produced by the frightening feelings returns in the shape of a "monster", a killer or an intruder. No wonder you have trouble falling asleep or going back to sleep, once awakened! With proper support of an attuned other, working with the dream image by "playing" the part of the monster can reconnect you with the feelings of your early experience. Then you have the possibility of expressing and integrating your terror as well as your aggressive impulses that arise to try to protect you.

The pain, terror and horror you may have experienced at the hands of a perpetrator must be owned and experienced through in order for you to heal. Otherwise those "monstrous" feelings will continue to replay in your worst dreams and drive your addiction or other forms of acting out. The parts of you that bear witness to the stored traumatic experiences can be integrated with the support of an attuned other. It's almost as if through trauma, some of your life energy got locked away in your emotional brain. As you are able to integrate these experiences and feelings, you can reclaim the lost energy of emotion and the energy used in holding back your feelings. As you accept the powerlessness you experienced as a child, you will be better able to accept the powerlessness you face now. In other words, the present day powerlessness that everyone faces will no longer trigger the unbearable, "unlivable" anguish of childhood trauma or inadequate caretaker nurturing. Then you will begin to more fully live, one moment at a time.

The shadow of addiction is evidence that the trauma is not "over" yet. You are looking at the world through trauma-colored glasses. You project your disowned parts, dream of them, and act them out in dissociated states. You are not comfortable with who you are, so you are not fully present. In order to embrace the shadow - the disowned feelings and parts of yourself - you will likely need the support of an attuned other. Anchored in your experience of being alive (gravity and breath) and in contact with another (his eyes, hands, voice and heart), you have possibility of experiencing and gradually moving through the complex feelings that accompany trauma and inadequate nurturing in childhood. Feelings such as terror, rage, grief, and especially, unending longing, threaten the loss of self due to the perceived betrayal by those you loved. When you have repeatedly experienced moving through these feelings with another, you are more likely to be able to do it on your own, grounded in your experience of being present to your breathing and what is under you. When it is "over", the presence of an emotion, distress, or even a sense of helplessness, will be less likely to signal that soothing will never come.

The experience of attunement, connection and feeling through various emotions, repeated over and over again, strengthens your bodyself by increasing the capacity of your repository of positivity to which you can return, whenever you become triggered or upset. As you become more resilient and then you are able to do as Rumi exhorts: ". . . A joy, a depression, a meanness, some momentary awareness that comes as an unexpected visitor. Welcome and attend them all, even if they are a crowd of sorrows . . ."* Until then you may feel as if you are trapped in a cycle that results in your feeling angry, mistrustful and lonely. But what you fear has <u>already</u> happened: you were betrayed, abandoned, intruded upon and violated. Yet, your emotional brain continues to expect that will continue to happen because it has no sense of time; the threat seems always nigh. You are condemned to anticipate the past until those feelings are resolved by re-experiencing them in titrated amounts, so that you can integrate them. Then those feelings can have a <u>past</u> because they have been experienced through and integrated, and the events that gave rise to them are placed in the proper perspective. Then it is finally "over" and the shadow gradually fades.

See C. Barks, *The Illustrated Rumi* 77.

APPENDIX G

Step-wise Summary of Process of Embodying the Experience of the Therapist's Presence

(1) Connection and "Yes!"

You feel the presence of the other as interested and available to you. You feel connected to and valued, seen and heard. You come to understand that he senses your preciousness and that it would hurt him to hurt you. You feel reached to and gradually come to reaching back. You feel all this in your body, little by little. You may grieve that you missed this kind of connection and affirmation of self as a child.

(2) Separation and "No!"

You discover that your "No!" is respected, valued and even encouraged and not judged punished or ignored. You discover there is no feeling that can't be understood and accepted by this "other".

(3) The Contracted "No!"

You notice when and how you are not available for contact – you might feel mistrustful, frightened, ashamed or angry. As you feel your contracted "No!" in your bodyself, you discover that your anger covers up

(4) The Terror behind the Contracted "No!"

The terror behind the contraction is the terror of the caretaker's "No!" (his/her limitation) to your need for nurturing. Experiencing another's embodied, containing presence enables you to experience your emotions all the way through as you release your body holding. You feel the struggle in your mind and bodyself between your contracted "No! I don't need you!" and your need for the other. This time the other is available to you, so you come to experience a different outcome to this old conflict. Undoing "Sophie's choice" you come through the terror and rage to

(5) Opening to Longing and Connection and the "Yes!"

You become familiar with "experiencing through" fear, shame, rage, grief and love and with spontaneous movement in your body as it attempts to free itself of the holding. You find movement, sound and words to free your contracted "No" from your body. You can express anger (your "No!") with the other and come through it to a heart connection with yourself and the other. You can allow the other to see your need for connection and express spontaneous gestures of reaching. You can separate what was "then" from "now". You can find words for what you feel so you can set boundaries and no longer have to "self-hold".

(6) Your Embodied Presence

This experience, repeated again and again, allows you to stay present in your bodyself and incorporate the calm heart center that is now more available to you even when you are not in the therapist's presence. You can go through your emotional recovery cycle without the presence of the other.

You will likely travel this road as many times as you have feelings and each time, you find your way back to your heart. You heart opens gradually, to yourself and to others. You are able to say "No" and "Yes" in your own best interests. You experience your separateness and enjoy connecting. You can experience through terror, rage, shame, grief, need and love. Eventually there are no strangers on this road and every encounter has something to offer you. Every feeling leads you back to your heart where you embrace yourself with the internalized presence of the other. This experience becomes the ground for becoming optimally self-soothing.

APPENDIX H

Embodied Spirituality and Presence

"Embodied spirituality" refers to the unity of body and soul and is another way to describe living through or in resonance with your bodyself. Soul and body, like mind and body, were not always considered separate entities in Western civilization. In fact, the word "soul" comes from the Greek "psyche" which meant breath, life and soul. Similarly in other spiritual traditions the word for life energy or essence is the same as the word for breath, for example in Hindi "prana" means breath and life force. The living body and the soul were not separate concepts in Aristotle's mind. He used the metaphor of a waxen shape to describe how soul and body were inseparable. Or as Rumi* put it, "body flows out of spirit and spirit flows out of body".

However, the analytical machinations of the minds of Socrates and Plato separated out the soul from the body and relegated the body to a lesser domain. In fact, Plato refers to the purity of the soul, "untainted by the body." (Because of his agreement with the Pope he did not discuss matters of the soul.) Unfortunately this bias has persisted throughout the history of Western philosophical thought up until recent times. The final blow to fractionation of bodymindspirit was dealt by Descartes, who doubted the validity of emotions and sensations of the body, when he declared, "I think, therefore I am". That statement implied he considered the mind to reign supreme over the body's senses. This point of view has recently been convincingly and thoughtfully challenged by authors like A. Damasio** in his book, "Descartes' Error".

This divorce led to the conceit of the mind over the body, as the mind was considered superior in the task of knowing and analyzing, functions, which were considered the basis of intelligence. What could the body know that was valuable and reliable? After all, the body bore suffering. The mind could split off from the body and escape awareness of suffering, at least for a time. The arrogance and conceit of the mind in service of the ego is so delusional that escape from suffering seems possible. Panicked at the specter of helplessness, the mind splits off and rises above. But when the bodyself is grounded in a calm heart center, it knows the way out is "through". The bodyself becomes the vessel for the journey. If you listen to your bodyself, you are likely to get the support you need so you can ride the wave of suffering. Embrace and join with suffering, submerge to the depths and emerge with treasure*. Not by denying but embracing your bodyself will you be able to come fully into aliveness. For your soul and body are one, inextricably related and dependent on each other.

The triumvirate of body, soul and mind freed up experimentation and lead to many scientific discoveries. However, the relegation of intuition, emotion, the heart and the "feminine" to a lesser role, paved the way for further exploitation of the earth and its inhabitants. Compassion, humanity and the connectedness of all beings were less valued than progress, discovery and domination. Mind and machine over emotion and nature, a profound sense of disconnectedness on many levels pervaded Western civilization. The analytical functioning of the mind is a valuable tool for dealing with certain aspects of reality and for developing theories but should not be mistaken for "knowing" itself. The intellect, like theory is a fine slave, but a poor master. While understanding is analytical, knowing is experiential. The bodyself "knows" and experiences, the analytical part of the mind "understands" and explains. Mystery and paradox are the domain of the bodyself and the Let Go . . mode. The bodyself experiences mystery and paradox that the mind cannot comprehend. My use of the term "bodyself" connotes the concept of embodied soul or the unity of body and soul. I could have just as easily used the term "bodysoul" to suggest the same reality.

The traumatic separation of body, soul and mind has been waiting for repair throughout centuries of Western thought. The proclivity toward the duality of the analytical mind (black or white), reinforced by the moralistic judgment of the "church" (right or wrong) and reified in language, kept the soul split from the body. Disembodied spirituality refers to spirituality ungrounded in the body. Emotions are suspect and self-denial (read bodyself-denial) is lauded. The denied or disowned aspects of bodyself then become the shadow (as in shadow of addiction. The human being is left to understand himself in terms of good and bad, and see the world in those terms as well. The pain of separation from bodyself leads to great suffering because the "heart" connection is missing, that is a sense of connection with the compassion of a forgiving and generous heart. This suffering is mirrored in the suffering of the individual who lives with unhealed trauma. In both cases, the attempt is often made by the mind to try to rise above the suffering rather than embrace it.

Healing trauma is then "bodysoul" healing. Recently the word "mindbody" or bodymind" was coined in an attempt to repair the mind-body rift. But the problem of what is the soul remained unaddressed! Is the soul reflected in the term mindbody? Soul is still considered by many as something separate from mind and body, or even from "mindbody". Yet my experience of being present belies that notion. When I am present, I feel unified, connected and aware. Presence comes through being connected to my bodyself. If my heart isn't "open", if I am closed to taking in love, I am not quite present. Perhaps it is this heart aspect that some refer to as "soul". But what would a body be without a heart, or for that matter, a heart without a body? But now I am appealing to reason and this matter cannot be satisfactorily resolved through reason but rather through experience. Besides, when I am present, I am not bothered any longer by this question. I am just grateful to be.

Presence cannot be commandeered, only invited through various listening practices. You can only force your body to do so much because in the end, it wins. In other words, "If you don't take care of your body, how will you live?"* When you are too neglectful of what your bodyself needs, you suffer an unnecessary suffering and perhaps even an early death. Why add avoidable suffering to the suffering that is not under your control? How ironic! In an attempt to avoid the suffering inherent in your vulnerability and powerlessness, you create more suffering for yourself.

Various spiritual traditions teach embracing suffering as a path to being reborn into a greater connection with the world, with God or the Divine. This expanded sense of being in the world opens you to more compassionate connection with others. Conscious surrendering allows deep acceptance of suffering. For example, according to S. Suzuki***, even after Buddha attained enlightenment he still experienced suffering. "But his view of life was not shaky . . . it was stable. He watched himself and others with the same eyes that he watched stones or plants . . . He had a very scientific understanding." His view of life was steady because he lived through what I call, the "calm heart center".

325

In a similar way, embodied spirituality asks you work through your pain so you are no longer given to hating yourself or rejecting your needs. While you may regularly engage in body-oriented activities such as Yoga, Tai Chi and exercise, you may still be disconnected from your bodyself in an attempt to avoid emotions. Similarly, meditation can help you more deeply connect with yourself but it does not necessarily open your heart. By opening your heart I mean, being able to give and receive love and feel compassion for others in an embodied, grounded way. Although you may attain some measure of calm, your sense of presence may be shattered when you relate to another. You may find that you retreat in the face of the vulnerability you feel in the presence of another. If you carry unhealed trauma, you may need to embody another's heart for you in order to heal your "soulbody". Then you will have a calm heart center to rest into in order to have deep contact with yourself and another so you can give and receive love, set boundaries, soothe, be soothed and to soar. Presence without heart is still not a truly embodied presence but rather a "soulless spirituality". How about that for a paradoxical term!

The attempt to escape suffering rather than embrace it, leads to all manner of addiction. The addictions and stances (adapted selves) that form to avoid unhealed helplessness keep you isolated and unfulfilled. A connection with the heart of another can help you accept your suffering and live through the terrifying feelings of helplessness by embodying a calm heart center. Owning all your feelings allows you to fully connect with your bodyself and your heart – for yourself and for others. Embracing suffering can develop your capacity for compassion and passion – for both the agony and the ecstasy. Passionate embodied living includes being able to tolerate the suffering of helplessness.

Similarly, if you feel your longing deeply, you may begin to feel the answer to your longing within your longing. To quote the Sufi master, Rumi****, "This longing you express is the return message. The grief you cry out from draws you toward union. Your pure sadness that wants help is the secret cup. Listen to the moan of a dog for its master. That whining is the connection. There are love-dogs no one knows the names of. Give your life to be one of them." And from the Buddhist tradition the enlightenment of Dogen-zenji***** (106-017), the Zen Buddhist patriarch, is said to have flowered from his observation of the evanescence of life as he watched the incense smoke waft above the dead body of his mother when he was yet a boy of thirteen. Deeply embracing the longing for his parent led to a profound deepening of his experience of being. The path to deeply experiencing the essence of being "connected" goes straight through the heart. I encourage you (take heart!) to follow that path known to many of the great spiritual traditions to find your way to greater connection with the life all around and in you. When you find the support you need to feel through what you have been holding against, your life can open up in profound ways. *She* will be so happy you have decided to make your home in *her*.

A few words of caution: The trauma of profound loss can catapult one into a dissociated, out-of-body state that can feel like a profound, pervasive sense of peace. It may even be experienced as literally "rising above" the pain, panic and despair that would ordinarily accompany such loss. While Dogen-zenji (who undoubtedly was already an experienced meditator when his mother died) attained enlightenment in response to this tragic loss, it is important to find out for yourself, whether the trauma you think you have come through unscathed, has actually compromised your ability to open to loving again and to be able to reach out to another.

* See C. Barks, *The Illustrated Rumi*, 28.
** See A. Damasio, *Descartes' Error* (New York: Avon, 1994).
*** See S. Suzuki, *Zen Mind, Beginner's Mind*, 101.
**** See *C. Barks, The Illustrated Rumi*, 78.
***** See *S. Suzuki, Zen Mind, Beginner's Mind*, 107.

APPENDIX I

Ode to Homecoming

She needs a place to live in me
where we can be happy and free.
Listening closely to my heart
surely gives a very fine start.

Taking time, slowing to hear *her*
gives a sense I'm drawing near *her.*
Give up thinking, notice sensing
brings me into the moment where *she's* "commencing".

She welcomes me home as I turn toward *her*
I welcome *her* home, I surely missed *her.*
My nod gives *her* a place to be,
right where *she's* been waiting for me.

And then when we meet, it's so very sweet
from the top of my head to the soles of my feet.
"Sweet"* describes *my* feeling of meeting with *her:*
joyous, precious, and tender, she'll surely concur.

Notice what's unfinished, and what's incomplete
take action to address it, gives a feeling so sweet.
Crying instead of grabbing a treat,
gives us another chance to meet.
My neck needs more room to breathe,
my bladder needs a chance to relieve.
Sensing my feet in contact with the floor,
and please, oh please, shut the open cabinet door.
Ah, sweet feeling of certain relief,
of completion, letting down, and perhaps even grief.

Pick up the bright apple that catches the eye
take time for the moon and the stars in the sky.
Stop to gaze, let the brightness pass through:
eventually the moon will land inside you!

Feeling the warm sun dance on my back
brings me home to my bodyself, right on track.
Lie on the ground and give to the pull:
breathing responds and my heart is full.

The music resounds in my bodyself so deep
it moves me, through me, the rhythm I keep.

Savoring taste takes its course:
attuned to bodyself,
no eating like a horse.

A Goldilocks moment! My bodyself smiles
all is "just right", my senses beguiled:
Let's Go! shifts to Let Go . .
I give up the old fight,
I tuck myself in and say "good night!"

For the moment is the moment -
a fulcrum for change:
when I pay attention and don't let my thoughts range,
staying focused and present, and efforting no more,
I find out what my bodyself has in store.

Change happens effortlessly if only I stay
with the moment's experience, I pray.

The bodyself moment is blessed with magic;
pay attention and sense, to miss it 'tis tragic.
Yet always *she* gives one more chance
she is generous, gracious and so loves the dance!

When I'm feeling stuck and don't know what's wrong
I call a friend who'll sing me a song:
a song of caring and friendship, s/he hears my cry,
tension leaves as my bodyself sighs,
Thanks for getting help, that was wise!
Now *she* has reason to trust where *she* didn't before.
"Before" was the time when I didn't even know
How scared and lonely I was, I so feared to show.

Once my bodyself was found, I needed to explore
how I lost trust in opening my heart's door.
Experiencing the warmth and the intensity too
of another who had suffered and then had come through,
did pierce my anxious armoring, my heart felt he's true.
And 'cause this other was there for me, my bodyself grew.

As my bodyself grew, my heart expanded,
I could reach out to another and take in what was handed.
What was handed was loving presence, which became part of me.
This gift I was given, keeps on giving to me
and to others, as so I may choose -
since I came home to my bodyself, I have nothing to lose.

The gift of loving presence, now grounded in myself
means no longer must I put my grief, on the backroom shelf:
I can weep and cry, deeply giving to my tears.
For the loss of this or that, I no longer have to fear
that I'll lose my bodyself, overwhelmed by despair
and the seeming certain knowledge that no one cares.
The alchemy of grieving opens my heart to receiving
another's love and my bodyself connection, a true heart convection.

Now giving my weight through my legs to the floor
The "release" breath comes though the opened door
of my heart, as I feel my connection to you,
Dear bodyself, it's much more cozy with you!

*Again that word "sweet", sweet's hard to beat,
Heart to beat, it's sweet, I say, again I repeat:
"Sweet's very neat, no word competes,
'Sweet's' not to be tweaked."

NOTES AND SOURCES

Introduction

Page vx *In this book the use of italics is reserved for indicating a reference to *her* and when *she* is speaking.

Page xvi *For the meaning of Let's Go! and Let Go . . see the discussion which begins on Page 24.

Page xvi *See Jon Kabat-Zinn, *Full Catastrophe Living* (New York: Delta, 1990). Kabat-Zinn is the founder of the Mindfulness - Based Stress Reduction Program at University of Massachusetts Medical School and the Center for Mindfulness in Medicine, Health Care and Society.

Chapter 1: Tucking Myself In

Page 3 *What I mean by "sweetness" may be close to what Mark Nepo refers to as a feeling of "satisfaction somewhere between peace and joy" in his book of daily readings, *The Book of Awakening: Having the Life You Want by Being Present to the Life You Have* (San Francisco: Conari Press, 2000), 5. "Sweet" is "gratifying" or "pleasurable" in the *Merriam-Webster Colligate Dictionary*, 10th ed. (Massachusetts: Merriam-Webster, 1995).

Page 3 **See Note for Page xv.

Page 4 *Bodyself (*her*) refers to experiencing your aliveness through your sensations, emotions, and intuition.

Page 6 *Monhegan Island is where Charlotte Selver, my sensing teacher gave her classes.

Page 6 ** "We are the pain and what cures the pain". Rumi in Coleman Barks, illus. Michael Green, *The Illuminated Rumi* (New York: Broadway Books, 1997), 111.

Page 6 ***Charlotte Selver referred to what we sensed as "it" or the "organism". It really doesn't matter what you call it as long as your curiosity is aroused and you want come into closer connection with this subtly-felt part of yourself, which I call "bodyself".

Page 7 *The "Let's Go!" attitude as in "Get up and go!" is developed conceptually in Chapter 3.

Chapter 2: Discovering *Her*

Page 9 *I finally understood what Fritz Perls, one of the founders of Gestalt psychotherapy had tried to communicate to me in a session some months earlier when he placed his hand on mine and asked me, "What do you feel here?" I had gone to great lengths to tell him about what was troubling me so I was completely mystified at his asking me such a question. Eventually I realized that he was trying to tell me that I was out of touch with my bodyself and was not present to my emotions and sensations as I was telling my "story" to him. What a wake-up call!

Page 9 **See William C. Littlewood ed. *Waking Up: The Work of Charlotte Selver* (New York: Sensory Awareness Foundation, 2004); See Charles V.W. Brooks, *Sensory Awareness: The Rediscovery of Experiencing* (New York: Viking Press, 1974). Also Charlotte Selver and Charles Brooks, edited by Richard Lowe and Stephan Laing-Gilliatt, *Reclaiming Vitality and Presence: Sensory Awareness as a Practice for Life,* (New York: 2007).

Page 9 ***Charlotte did not like to use the word "body" because she felt it separated the person from the experience of the living organism. When a student used the word "body" as in "my body felt this or that" she would sometimes ask another student to get up and walk across the room. Then she would ask the class, "What just happened? Did Susie or Susie's body walk?" I use the word "bodyself" here to denote the experience of the living organism through sensations, emotions and intuition.

Page 10 *She led classes up until just months before she died at 102 in 2004!

Page 10 **It seems that Charlotte did not include "humans" as a third aliveness-sustaining cosmic force in the sense that earth and breath were.

Page 11 *Claudio Naranjo, *The One Quest* (New York: Ballantine, 1972).

Page 11 **Zen Mind, Beginner's Mind* is the title of Suzuki Roshi's book of lectures from which the following quote is taken: "In the beginner's mind, there are many possibilities, in the expert's, there are few". The beginner has fewer expectations, having had no previous experience. See Shunryu Suzuki, *Zen Mind, Beginner's Mind* (New York: Weatherhill, 1970), 21.

Page 11 ***Such inspired and down-to earth meditation guides as Pema Chodron, John Kabat-Zinn, and Stephan Levine were yet not well-known.

Page 13 *Perhaps you will recognize that the left side of the body corresponds to the right hemisphere of the brain, which processes primarily emotional rather than analytical content. To use my full intelligence, I needed to balance efficiency, schedule, logic, control and analysis with intuition, sensing, emotional responses and playfulness. See research in Antonio R. Damasio, *Descartes Error: Emotion, Reason and the Human Brain* (New York: Avon Books, 1994).

Page13 **"Just right" as it is used here refers to "Right" in the Zen sense of whole" or "complete".

Page 16 *"Felt sense" is a term coined by Eugene Gendlin. See Eugene Gendlin, *Focusing* (New York: Everest House, 1978).

Chapter 3 From Let's Go! to Let Go . .

Page 20* Rumi See Barks, *The Illuminated Rumi*, 45.

Page 20** Arnold Beisser, "Paradoxical Theory of Change" in Fagan and Shephard eds., *Gestalt Therapy Now* (New York: Gestalt Journal Press, 1970).

Page 24 *"Flow" is a term coined by Mihaly Csikszentmihalyi in *Finding Flow* (New York: Basic Books, 1997).

Page 24 **"See-feel" is a term I created as a massage teacher to connote my experience of perceiving another with my whole bodyself awareness. I not only notice the shape, size, color, smell, and movement of the other, but also I sense where there appears to be tension or ease, pain or excitement in the other.

Page 26 *"Conscious surrender" involves the same three steps: noticing, focusing and following through.

Page 27 *See Timothy Gallwey, *The Inner Game of Tennis* (New York: Random House, 1971); See also Michael Murphy, *Golf in the Kingdom*, (New York: Penguin, 1972); See also George Leonard, *The Ultimate Athlete* (New York: Viking Press, 1975).

Page 28 *Contact/withdrawal cycle See M.P. Korb, J.Gorrell, V. Van De Riet, *Gestalt Therapy: Practice and Theory* (New York: Pergamon Press, 1989).

Page 28 **The emotional recovery cycle (ERC), formulated by Robert Hilton who called it, the"personal recovery cycle" is the process of shifting from the emotional arousal of Let's Go! to the soothing calm of Let Go . . by feeling through each emotion and is discussed in Chapter 10.

Page 29 *Fritz Perls theorized that contact with the interrupted organismic need is needed to complete the cycle. See F.S. Perls, *Ego, Hunger and Aggression: The Beginning of Gestalt Therapy* (New York: Vintage/Random House, 1969).

Page 29 **The bodyself cycle concept has some similarity to the concept of Organismic Self-regulation as taught by the Gestalt Institute of Los Angeles in their training program in Santa Monica, CA. However, my formulation of "noticing, focusing and following through" came from direct observation of my own experience of bodyself sensing, especially during the initial ten year period of writing this book. I encourage the Reader to discover how your own process unfolds, as Charlotte advocated, "Find out for yourself!"

Chapter 4: Sensing

Page 32 *Injunction of Charlotte Selver on multiple occasions in class.

Page 33 *See Edmund Jacobsen, *Progressive Relaxation* (Chicago: Chicago Press,1938): Valerie Hunt, Professor of Kinesiology, UCLA, 1976 lecture.

Page 33 **For example, when the Yogi, Jack Schwarz, focused on the thought "this is not my body" he didn't feel the pain of the torture he endured at the hands of the Nazis. See Kenneth Pelletier, *Mind as Healer, Mind as Slayer,* (New York: Delta Books, 1977); See Jack Schwarz, *Voluntary Controls* (New York: Dutton, 1978).

Page 33 ***See Barks, *The Illuminated Rumi*, 45.

Page 37 *As you turn toward the subtler and slower paced sensory world, you turn away from what meditation teachers call your "monkey" mind which is incessantly active.

Chapter 5: Meditation

Page 49 *Charlotte Selver as quoted in *Every Moment is a Moment: A Journal with Words of Charlotte Selver,* (New York: Sensory Awareness Foundation, 2004).

Page 50 *Elsa Gindler, the teacher of Charlotte Selver.

Page 50 **Thich Nhat Hanh refers to breathing as the mindbody interface.

Page 51 *Laura Perls, another student of Elsa Gindler is the other founder of Gestalt Therapy (with her husband, Frederick).

Page 52 *Robert Hilton, Ph.D. definition of "embodiment" in a therapy session.

Page 54 *The Now and Zen Timepiece is specifically designed with meditation in mind so that you can be brought out of meditation by the sound of a Tibetan Bowl Chime being struck in a similar manner as it is in a meditation hall. See Now-Zen.com.

Page 55 *"agita" is a general feeling of being upset.

Page 56 *Suggested by Babette Rothschild, author of numerous books on healing trauma through relational somatic therapy such as *The Body Remembers: the Psychophysiology of Trauma and Trauma Treatment* (New York: Norton, 2000).

Page 58 *Virginia Wolfe quoted on a greeting card published by World's Greatest Minds in London, 1994.

Page 58 **Footnote: A psychologist named B. Zeigarnik reported a related observation half a century ago that came to be called "the Zeigarnik effect". Through experimentation she found that when an act was not completed a certain tension remained. In her experiment, the missing object stood out among an array of other, not relevant objects. The experience of spotting the missing item and thus completing the task was one of elation and relief - as in "Eureka, I found it!" See B. Zeigarnik "On Finished and Unfinished Tasks. In W.D. Ellis ed. *A Source Book of Gestalt Psychology* (New York: Humanities Press, 1967).

Page 64 *See Nepo, *The Book of Awakening*.

Chapter 6: Listening to Your Emotional Voice

Page 67 *See Note for Page 124 for a distinction between the emotional voice and the bodyself voice as well as other members of the "Tuck Yourself In" cast of characters!

Page 73 *"Match.comer" denotes a potential candidate for a date through the Internet dating site, Match.com

Page 75 *"Amazing Grace" by John Newton, 1779.

Page 76 *See Suzuki, *Zen Mind, Beginner's Mind*, 110. This quote refers to "nyu nan shin" – a soft or flexible mind.

Page 76 **Barks, *The Illuminated Rumi*, 50.

Page 76 ***See note for page 129.

Page 76 **** Suzuki, *Zen Mind, Beginner's Mind*, 97.

Page 79 *"re-mind" means *she* gives me back the part of my mind that I have lost.

Page 85 *Suzuki, *Zen Mind, Beginner's Mind*, 82.

Chapter 7: Meeting Resistance to Listening to Your Bodyself Voice

Page 91 *See Chapter 11 for an accounting of my abandonment trauma work.

Page 93 *"A trance occurs when your body is reacting to an image in your mind" – in this case, a past childhood trauma. See Robert S. Stone, *Clinical Hypnotherapy* (Los Angeles: Self-published Manual, 1992).

Page 94 * See Peter Levine, *Waking the Tiger* (Berkeley: Atlantic Books, 1997).

Page 94 ** See Patty Wipfler's *Listening to Children: Tantrums and Indignation* (Palo Alto: Hand in Hand, 2006). See handinhandparenting.org.

Page 95 *Robert Hilton cites Lorrain Granit for this statistic on Page 213 in M. Sieck, Ph.D. (ed), *Relational Somatic Psychotherapy: Collected Essays of Robert Hilton, Ph.D.* (USA: Santa Barbara Graduate Institute, 2007).

Page 96 *See Appendix C: Adequate Caretaking: Need for Connection, Repair and Self-Assertion

Page 97 *See Hal and Sidra Stone, *Embracing Ourselves* (Novato, CA: New World Library, 1998).

Page 98 *Personality Disorders are serious dysfunctional behavior constellations. See J. Morrison, *DMS-IV Made Easy: A Clinician's Guide to Diagnosis* (New York: Guilford Press, 1995).

Page 98 **See Appendix D: The Purgatory of Waiting in the Shadow for Repair

Page 99 *See Melody Beattie, *Codependent No More* (San Francisco: Harper and Row, 1987).

Page 100 *See Robert Hilton, *Relational Somatic Psychotherapy*.

Page 101 *In the eponymous film "Sophie's Choice", Sophie had to make the impossible, horrendous choice of which of her two beloved children to give up to be sent to the gas chamber.

Page 101 **The concept of the body's contracted "No!" comes from Wilhelm Reich and was elaborated by his student, Alexander Lowen, the founder of Bioenergetics Therapy. I chose to stay with his use of the word "contracted" rather than "constricted" however, "constricted" seems the more appropriate term because it implies that this "contraction"in the bodyself, while protective, has a numbing or interruptive effect on organismic self-regulation in terms of movement and emotional expression. "Contraction", on the other hand, is part of the organismic self-regulating cycle of contraction and expansion. Constriction of the bodyself reduces functionality and responsiveness of the organism because it implies a prolonged contraction even after the danger has passed. It can result from shock and trauma and may even give rise to scar tissue in muscles as well as reduce blood supply and mobility. See Alexander Lowen, *Betrayal of the Body* (Toronto: Macmillan, 1967). In fact, Reich and Lowen described certain "character types" by delineating patterns of defensive attitudinal/physical posturing called "character armor". "Stance" as used in this book has similar implications.

Page 102 *Some aspects of the adaptive selves are similar to the "disowned selves" of Voice Dialogue Therapy created by Hal and Sidra Stone in that all of these "selves" are creative attempts to adapt to an environment, which didn't support the fullness of your human "being". Engaging in dialogue with the various "voices" of the disowned selves can help ground the person in an integrated sense of being, which embraces all realms of human experience, including the bodyself. See footnote on page 97 The Inner Critic is one example of a disowned self and is discussed in Chapter 8.

Page 103 *See Appendix E: Using A Guide to Explore the Growing Edge of Bodyself Awareness.

Page 106 *New neural pathway is discussed in Chapter 10 and the concept is developed and discussed in Daniel J. Siegel's *The Mindful Brain: Reflection and Attunement in the Cultivation of Well-Being* (New York: Norton, 9007).

Chapter 8: Meeting Your Resistance to Meeting Your Resistance to Your Bodyself Voice

Page 111 *See Hal and Sidra Stone, *Embracing Your Inner Critic* (San Francisco: Harper and Row, 1993).

Page 121 *See John Gray, *What You Can Feel, You Can Heal* (MN: Heart, 1984).

Page 123 *See Carlos Casteneda, *Journey to Ixtlan* (New York: Simon & Schuster, 1972).

Page 124 *"Goldilocks" is just a playful term to refer to those golden moments of "just rightness" that are bodyself experiences. To clarify the cast of "Tuck Yourself In" characters I offer the following: I refer to the "voice" of my bodyself as "her" which includes the messages I receive from sensations, emotions, intuition, inklings, "funny feelings" and even "body memories" and may be similar to what A. Damasio calls "somatic markers" (See *The Feeling of What Happens: Body and Emotion in the Making of Consciousness* (New York: Harcourt, 1999). When I use "she" or "her" I am referring to the whole array of bodyself intelligence. This voice is sensed and can be listened for but does not speak in words, per se. The term "emotional voice" refers just to emotional messages, one source of bodyself intelligence. When I speak of the "watcher" I use the pronoun "it" because it is more like a dissociated entity, which I gradually became aware of in the course of therapy. None of these "voices" represent the "inner child", a concept I do not address. While sometimes my emotional voice sounds young, emotions are also part of my bodyself experience of being an adult. You may decide to use other terms or make no distinctions at all. Whatever helps you feel more bodyself-connected is what I would like for you to discover. I resist pinning down exactly what the bodyself voice is, once and for all, because I want to follow my curiosity and be open to discovering how I can connect more deeply with my aliveness. For, as S. Suzuki put it, our practice is to study how "this body becomes a sage." *Zen Mind, Beginner's Mind*, 56. "Grace", "the guest", "the friend" are all terms that some spiritual traditions use to refer to the expanded state of awareness associated with the presence of God or the state of Enlightenment. In my experience, when I have closely followed the promptings of my bodyself voice, I have been led to experiences that could be called a state of Grace. My sense of the wordless omnipresence of *her* is in some ways like the "friend" or the "guest" that Sufi teachings refer to or "unio mystica" which is "a lived thing, not a theological concept" as described by Barks in *The Illuminated Rumi*, 53.

Chapter 9: *Go for the Goldilocks Gold!*

Page 126 *A "resource" is an image or memory which evokes positive feelings like safety, well-being, calm, pride, joy, which can be tapped into when needed whether for everyday soothing or during trauma work.
Page 132 *"The quality of mind is the activity itself." See Suzuki, *Zen Mind, Beginner's Mind*, 106.
Page 135 *"fine" as in "stance fine" which is actually not so fine.
Page 143 *Thirty years ago during the course of three years of somatically focused, Reichian emotional release work, the ice cream binges stopped.
Page 148 *See Barks, *The Illustrated Rumi*, 77.

Chapter 10: Reclaiming My Bodyself Voice through Relational Somatic Psychotherapy

Page 156 *Gestalt therapist, Robert Resnick, Ph.D. expressed this relationship between impotence and omnipotence in a training workshop in 2012.
Page 156 **See Appendix G: Stepwise Summary of the Process of Embodying the Therapist's Presence and compare to steps outlined in Appendix C: Adequate Caretaker Nurturing: Connection, Repair, Self-assertion. The term "Emotional Self-regulation" refers to the ability to calm down when upset as well as to contain excitement, which is acquired through consistent attunement of the caretaker to the infant or/and the therapist to the client.
Page 157 *"Constriction around the 'No!'" rather than "contraction around the 'No!'" seems the more appropriate choice to describe the bodyself limitation of the adaptive stance because contraction is a phase of healthy organismic regulation whereas constriction is not and can even become pathological. However, A. Lowen, the founder of Bioenergetics used the term "contraction around the 'No!'" and he isn't on the planet any longer to defend his choice! Most Bioenergetic therapists are familiar with this term.
Page 160 *A body memory is a bodily memory without a visual image, which results from events, usually traumatic, from early childhood.

Page 162 *The "new neural pathway" concept will be elaborated in Chapter 12.

Page 163 * See D.W. Winnicott in *Selected Letters of D.W. Winnicott* (London: Karnac Books, 1987).

Page 164 *The phrase "Personal Recovery Cycle" was coined by Dr. Robert Hilton who first described the recovery of the equilibrium of the bodyself in this way. I chose to call it "The Emotional Recovery Cycle" but it refers to the same process that Dr. Hilton has described and is the foundation for emotional self-regulation.)

Page 165 *Consciously surrendering is like saying the Serenity Prayer with bodyself support, i.e. embodying the Serenity Prayer! It says: "God grant me the courage to accept the things I cannot change, to change the things I can and the wisdom to know the difference."

Page 165 **Traumatic attachment refers to becoming attached (falling in love and feeling emotionally dependent) to someone who triggers the feelings and behavior, which originated in traumatic interactions with your caretaker.

Page 166 *I found this poem by Conrad Stroud many years ago in a clipping I had saved but I have not been able to find a record of where it was originally published.

Page 167 *Hazrat Inayat Khan as quoted in Nepo, *Book of Awakening*, 419.

Chapter 11: Wresting My Bodyself Voice Away from the Grip of Childhood Abandonment Trauma

Page 169 *Posse of positivity is further elaborated on Page 216.

Page 170 *See Derek Routledge, "James Robertson's Vision and Moving Pictures" which appeared in the One Man's Vision Column in an unknown publication, 23-24. See letters in response to Robertson's work shown on the BBC and in *The Observer* which were published as "A Parent's Eye View" (London: Gollancz, 1962).

Page 171 *See Patty Wipfler, *Listening to Children: Healing Children's Fears*, (Palo Alto, CA: Hand in Hand, 2006).

Page 173 *See Jan Abram, *The Language of Winnicott* (London: Karnac, 1996).

Page 173 **See Kahlil Gibran, *The Prophet* (New York: Alfred A. Knopf, 1968)12.

Page 177 *"Resource" is defined in Notes and Resources for Page 126.

Page 177 **See Note for Page 20.

Chapter 12: Lost and Found: My Bodyself Voice

Page 180 *The words between the quotation marks are attributed to Gloria Steinem, the last four were added by a dear, knowing friend.

Page 180 **For Alexander Lowen, the founder of Bioenergetics, aggression and assertion come from the same energetic source. See *Bioenergetics* (USA: Penguin, 1976).

Page 182 *"spontaneous gesture" See Abram, *The Language of Winnicott*.

Page 182 **See Martin Buber, *I and Thou* (New York: Charles Scribner's Sons, 1970).

Page 182 ***Rumi quoted in Goodreads.com.

Page 183 *See Appendix I for "Ode to Homecoming".

Page 193 *Rumi quoted in Goodreads.com.

Page 194 *See Abram, *The Language of Winnicott*.

Page 196 *See Introduction to Daniel Ladinsky's, *The Subject Tonight is Love: 60 Wild and Sweet Poems of Hafiz* (South Carolina: Pumpkin House Press, 1996).

Page 196 **See Chapter 11 for account of my work on abandonment trauma.

Chapter 13: Living on the Bodyself *(Her)* Side of the Street

Page 208 *See Notes for Page 169.

Page 209 *"Living your aliveness" is Robert Hilton's definition of embodiment.

Page 209 **Organismic Self-Regulation is process by which organism, human or otherwise is able to get its needs met and restore homeostasis. A pivotal concept in Gestalt Therapy Theory.

Page 210 *F. Perls defined "anxiety" as "unsupported excitement" as quoted by Liv Estrup, MA, faculty, Gestalt Associates Training in Los Angeles, 2012.

Page 212 *SeeThomas Lewis, Fari Amini, Richard Lannon, *A General Theory of Love*, (New York: Random House, 2001). See also J. Abram, *The Language of Winnicott*.

Page 216 *Suzuki, *Zen Mind, Beginner's Mind*, 46.

Page 218 *See Resnick in Notes for Page 156.

Page 218 **Excerpt from "East Coker" Part III *Four Quartets,* copyright 1940 by T.S. Eliot and renewed 1968 by Esme Valerie Eliot, reprinted by permission of Houghton, Mifflin Harcourt Publishing Company. All rights reserved. (Page 28).

Page 220 *See Appendix F for more on embodied spirituality and soul/body.

Page 221 *Excerpt from M.R. Rilke's "I am too alone" in *Selected Poems of R.M. Rilke* (New York: Harper and Row, 1981), 25.

Chapter 14: Creating a Decompression Period

Page 230 *Selver as quoted in *Every Moment is a Moment*.

Page 231 *"online" is an apt term used by Somatic Experiencing practitioners to refer to the engagement of the parasympathetic nervous system to calm the bodyself, providing a neurological foundation for optimal self-soothing.

Page 236 *Barks, *The Illuminated Rumi*, 50.

Page 238 *I am told the Tibetans use the same word for "entertainment" as they do for "wasting time."

Page 238 **See Note for Page 132.

Chapter 15: Decompression Activities

Page 244 *Virginia Wolfe quoted on a greeting card published by World's Greatest Minds in London, 1994.

Page 244 **This quote is attributed to Karl Jung however the Talmud may be the original source of the quote, "An uninterpreted dream is like an unopened letter from God".

Page 244 ***Dream Incubation: See Montague Ullman and Nan Zimmerman, *Working with Dreams: Self-Understanding, Problem-Solving, and Enriched Creativity Through Dream Appreciation* (Los Angeles: Tarcher, 1979).

Page 244 ****See John Gray's *What You Can Feel You Can Heal: A Guide for Enriching Relationship* (Mill Valley, CA: Heart, 1984).

Page 244 *****Robert and Virginia Hilton's Intimacy Cycle lecture, Costa Mesa, CA, 2009.

Page 249 *See Page 275 for a detailed discussion of experiment vs. exercise.

Chapter 16: Waking Yourself Up

Page 272 *Len Schneider, Ph.D. my late friend and mentor is the source of this statement: "Each day is a little life".

Page 273 *This time-piece is made by Now and Zen. Contact Now/Zen.com

Page 281 *"Orgasm Reflex" See *Wilhelm Reich: Selected Writings* (New York: Farrar, Straus and Giroux, 1951).

Page 284 *See Daniel Ladinsky's translations of the poetry of Hafiz, *Tonight the Subject is Love* (South Carolina: Pumpkin House Press, 1996). "I dropped the knife" is referred to in the introduction to this volume.

Page 284 **Melody Beattie, *The Language of Letting Go* (MN: Hazeldon, 1990).

Page 284 ***See Julia Cameron, *The Artist's Way* (New York: Penguin, 1992).

Page 286 *Kahlil Gibran quoted on a greeting card.

Chapter 17: An Invitation: Finding Your Own Way

Page 289 *"Moment after moment we have to find our own way. Some idea of perfection, or some perfect way which is set up by someone else, is not the true way for us." Suzuki, *Zen Mind, Beginner's Mind*, 111.

Page 290 *See Jack Kornfield, *After the Ecstasy, the Laundry* (New York: Bantam Books, 2000) and also Rick Fields, *Chop Wood, Carry Water* (New York: Tarcher, 1984) which address the integration of the experience of enlightenment into everyday living.

Page 291 *See Barks, *The Illustrated Rumi,* 107.

Page 293 *"new neural pathway" is used here as a metaphor to suggest the possibility of altered neural functioning, which allows for new responses to familiar, sometimes "triggering" situations. More research is needed to validate the hypothesis, advanced by Daniel Siegel, of the formation of new neural pathways which account for these kinds of changes in behavior.

Page 293 **"Bodymindfulness" connotes listening to the bodyself messages as a path to mindfulness which is defined by John Kabat-Zinn as paying attention "on purpose" to the experience of the present moment without judgment.

Page 294 *Cindi Lauper and Rob Hyman, "Time After Time" 1983.

Page 294 **"'nin' is our way of continuous practice" from Suzuki, *Zen Mind, Beginner's Mind,* 6.

Page 294 ***See footnote for Page 291

Page 294 ****"I'll Be Seeing You" lyrics by Irving Kahal, 1938.

Page 296 *See Suzuki, *Zen Mind, Beginner's Mind,* 58.

Page 296 **See Pages 207-208.

Page 296 ***See Selver, *Every Moment is a Moment.*

Page 296 ****See Barks, *The Illuminated Rumi,* 49.

Page 296*****See Gary Small, *The Memory Bible: Ten Commandments for Keeping Your Brain Young* (New York: Hyperion, 2003).

Page 298 *A quote from a letter sent out to potential donors to raise money for a retirement community of Zen practitioners to a fund organized by the San Francisco Zen Center, CA.

Page 300 *A quote from a class she led in 1975 on Monhegan Island.

Page 301 *This quote is attributed to Leo Tolstoy (which I found on a greeting card) but Tolstoy did not write these words. Rather his words were "True life begins where the tiny bit begins - where what seems to us minute and infinitely small alterations take place." Quotesnack.com.

Page 302 **Suzuki, *Zen Mind, Beginner's Mind.*

INDEX

adaptive self 100, 102
addiction 117-124
  focusing attention on impulse 63-65, 142
  giving up cigarettes 36-38
  Goldilocks moment 134
  shadow of, 112,130 Appendix F
anger work 112, 200-201; rage 192-193
attitude, tuck yourself in 245, 296

bathing 242, 262, 286
Beisser, Arnold 20
blood sugar 140, 142, 143
"body" memory 160, 169; "bodyself" memory 94
bodyself cycle 28-30
bodyself side of the street 214
breaks 55, 79-82, 129-130, 142, 145, 163

caffeine 135-139, 141, and critic 139
calm heart center 167, 195 - 199
calming breath technique 51
completion 58-60
  completion-interruption 28-29, 58
  interruption 191
conscious surrender 26, 29, 65, 165, 292
contact-withdrawal rhythm 28, 114-115, 181-183
contraction of the "No!" 156-158, 182
  commitment to the contracted "No!" 188
contraction vs. constriction 80, 157, 167
critic-caretaker cycle 109
critical voice 102 (footnote), 108-111, 115, 116, 139
curiosity 31, 63

"dying" into the moment 37, 61, 63, 183
dreams 62, 83, 84, 244, 272, 273

ease, five e's of 149, 216, 296
eating, mindful 34, 78, 130-134
effort, quality of 65, 66, 296
Elliot, T.S. East Coker 218, 223
embodiment 209-214; embodied therapist 158
embodied spirituality, 26, 49, 220 Appendix H
emotional recovery cycle 28, 111, 130, 164-165, 209

natural cycle in child 96
emotional voice example 113
"enough" 34, 122, 123, 131-133
exercise, mindful 142
exercise vs experiment 38, 275
expansion 209
experiment guidelines 46-48

"felt sense" 16, 158, 267
"flabbiness" 10, 215
fulcrum for change 58, 114, 143
"funny" feeling 85

Gestalt psychotherapy, founders 51, 52
Goldilocks 124 (footnote)
Goldilocks moment 123, 133-135
grace 180, 220, 221
        "amazing graces" 75
grieving 94, 163, 216, 234

her xv, 3, 7, 69, 85, 261-268
headache premonition 57
Hilton, Robert 154, 209
        adaptive self 100
        embodiment definition 52, 209
        intimacy cycle 245
        personal recovery cycle: 28 (footnote)

"just right" 13, 40, 68, 74, 77, 123, 139, 144, 212, 238, 279,
        alcoholic 134, 141
        exercise 143-144
        with baby and caretaker 95-96, 212
        in decompression 247
        in lying 249

Let Go . . vs Let's Go! 24, 26-31, 37
        balance 26, 64, Appendix A
Let Go . . wave 237-239
"larger picture" 24, 136, 215
        reach out to another 115
loss of love 216-217
lying, "coming to lying" 39, 249-251, 257

"moment" as the fulcrum for change 20, 26, 58, 114
moon 24, 63, 64, 76, 137, 225
muscle fibers available for contraction 59

"new neural pathway" 105, 162, 180, 184-188, 190, 201, 206, 208, 216

"Oldilocks" moments 297-299
organismic self-regulation 209

paradoxes of presence 26, 289, 296, 299
        paradox of Let Go . . 237
Paradoxical Theory of Change 20-22, 31, 114, 130, 142, 222, 289
        and pain 61-63
        and tension 130
        and work on critical voice 114
Perls, Fritz 20 (footnote), 51, 209
pleasure as a threat 61, 92, 211
posse of positivity 169, 216-217
prayer 12; serenity prayer 165 (footnote), 286

repair of relationship 97-98, Appendix D
repository of positivity 126-127
resonance 187, 272 and bandwidth 135
resource, for trauma work, self-soothing 126, 177
retraumatization 56, Appendix E
"right", in the Zen sense 13, 60, 124, 197

savoring 58, 76; savor flavor 131
"see-feel" 24 (footnote), 158, 202
self-assertion vs. contraction 158
Selver, Charlotte 9, 10, 50, 230
sleep deprivation and mood 141
Sophie's choice and the contracted "No!" 101, 201
soul 220; preciousness of my soul 202, 105
soaring 210, 211
spiritual "by-pass" 49, 67
spontaneous gesture 178, 182, 195, 213, 214
        "I need a person" 213
        reaching out for another 114-115, 212-214
        asking for help 112
squeezing 114, 173, 188-189, 198
        in dream 273
stance 100-101, stance trance 100, 102-104
staying with 53-54, 290, 299-301

"taking in" 29, 127-128, 188
thinking vs. sensing 32, 127
        and muscle tension 252
Tobin, Stephan 154, 169
trance 93
trauma, twin 92
        abuse, intrusion 92
        abandonment 91, 169-181
trauma vortex 94
traumatic attachment 165-166 (footnote)

"unfreezing" the bodyself 211, 213, 195

"watcher" 177, 188, 190, 199, 218
wave, catching the Let Go . . 29, 237-239

RECOMMENDED RESOURCES

Sensory Awareness:

"Tuck Yourself In" CD recording of sensing experiments by Ginger Clark.

Sensory Awareness Foundation: sensoryawareness.org
See this website for tapes and transcripts of Charlotte Selver's classes and for leaders of the work world-wide.
Sensory Awareness: The Rediscovery of Experiencing by Charles V.W. Brooks, (Viking: New York, 1974).

Relational Somatic Psychotherapy:

Southern California Institute for Bioenergetics Association: sciba.org
Relational Somatic Psychotherapy: Collected Essays of Robert Hilton, Ph.D. ed. M. Sieck, Ph.D. (USA: Santa Barbara Graduate Institute, 2007).

Relational Developmental Therapy:

Anne Issacs, MSW, bodynamicsusa.co; email; a-issacs@verizon.net

Gestalt Therapy:

Gestalt Associates Training Los Angeles: gatla.org
Bay Area Gestalt Institute: bagi.org and see site on Facebook
Films by Liv Estrup: "Flying Without Wings" Life with Arnie Beisser, author of the Paradoxical Theory of Change); "What's Behind the Empty Chair? Gestalt Therapy Theory and Methodology", and "The Four-footed Therapist". See livestrup.com

Trauma Therapy:

The Body Remembers: The Psychophysiology of Trauma and Trauma Treatment by Babette Rothschild, MSW, (New York: Norton, 2000). See somatictraumatherapy.com
Somatic Experiencing: traumahealing.com
Eye Movement Desensitization Reprocessing EMDR: EMDR.com

Parent Education:

Bring Out the Best in Your Child and Your Self: Creating a family based on mutual respect by Ilene Val-Essen, Ph.D. (Quality Parenting: Culver City, CA 2010). See qualityparenting.com.
Hand in Hand: Parenting by Connection at handinhandparenting.org

ABOUT THE AUTHOR

Ginger Clark, Ph.D. stepped onto the bodymindfulness path in 1968 when she experienced her first Esalen massage, which literally and figuratively, turned her head around. During the 32 years she taught massage and sensory awareness at the Massage School of Santa Monica, she developed *sensawareness* massage. She became a certified leader of Sensory Awareness under the tutelage of Charlotte Selver in 1979. In the 1970's she practiced meditation with Zen Centers in Los Angeles and in San Francisco. Licensed in California as a Marriage and Family Therapist in 1968, she then completed her doctoral studies in psychology at UCLA in 1983. She created a bodymind course for the Master's Program for Marriage and Family Therapy at Antioch University in Los Angeles and the *Tuck Yourself In* workshop for students, clients and professionals. In 2004 she became a certified relational somatic psychotherapist and is currently in her fifth year with Gestalt Associates Training Los Angeles. Since 1989 she has had a private practice in psychotherapy and bodymindfulness in Venice, California. Living just 80 steps from the beach, she delights in experiencing and photographing the natural and artful surround.

CONTACT INFORMATION

Website: www.tuckyourselfin.com
"Tuck Yourself In" CD is available from this website.

E-Mail: ginger@tuckyourselfin.com
opnyris2@gmail.com

Mail: Ginger Clark, Ph.D.
1107 Abbot Kinney Boulevard
Venice, California 90291

Phone: (310) 281-6059